LEWIS CARROLL'S DIARIES

THE PRIVATE JOURNALS OF

CHARLES LUTWIDGE DODGSON

(LEWIS CARROLL)

COMPLETE INDEX

to the nine surviving volumes

prepared by

EDWARD WAKELING

With a Reconstruction of Two Missing Volumes
Private Journals 1 and 3
1851-1855

The Lewis Carroll Society

2007

First published in 2007

Published by

THE LEWIS CARROLL SOCIETY

Clifford, Herefordshire

British Library Cataloguing in Publication Data
The Private Journals of Charles Lutwidge Dodgson
The Lewis Carroll Society
1. Carroll, Lewis - Biography
2. Authors, English - 19th century
I. Wakeling, Edward
ISBN10: 0 904117 34 0
ISBN13: 978 0 904117 34 9

Printed at the L. & T. Press, Stagsden, Bedfordshire

INTRODUCTORY NOTES

In compiling this complete index to all nine volumes of *Lewis Carroll's Diaries*, I have taken the opportunity of making a number of improvements and of correcting a number of mistakes that occurred in the individual indexes. As far as possible, I have tried to find the birth and death date of each person included in the index, and this information is now added to these entries. The professions of key people are also now included. I have also added details of Charles L. Dodgson's relatives; i.e. aunt, cousin, great-uncle, etc. On occasions, Dodgson used the term "cousin" very loosely – in many instances these are actually distant cousins. I have used sub-headings for key related families, for example the Collingwoods, Lutwidges, Pooles, Smedleys, and Wilcoxes, among others.

Members of one family are listed alphabetically under their surname. The father is usually identified by his title, for example Mr., Dr., Rt. Rev., etc. The mother is identified by her maiden name, but when this is not known, the term Mrs. is used. The rest of the names under the heading are the children. Any other relationship (for example, niece, cousin, etc.) is identified. In some cases, a son from one family becomes the father of another family, or a daughter becomes a mother; as far as possible this is indicated by a cross-reference. If a title is not used under a surname heading, the names listed are siblings only.

Access to census data and other family records have made it possible for me to identify more carefully some people previously only described by their title; for example, "Misses Allen" are now identified as Mary, Charlotte, and Jane Allen. I have combined under one heading members of the Royal Family including Queen Victoria's extended family across Europe. One or two people were mistakenly identified in the *Diaries* and these have been corrected. Therefore, it may be the case that the name in the Index does not always match the name given in some footnotes in the original volumes. A full list of these corrections and changes is given at the end of the Index.. For example, Prof. Katsuko Kasai has revealed that Dodgson's description of "Liddon" refers to *two* people; Henry Parry Liddon and his brother, John. Most references were accepted as being Henry, but it is now clear that John is the more likely candidate, especially when he joined Dodgson for visits to the

London theatre, an activity that Henry did not indulge in. I am grateful to Katsuko for her thorough research in this matter.

I have also expanded some entries by including sub-headings. For example, under the heading "Oxford University" will be found places, events, and activities associated with the University. Some key sub-headings now occur under the section headed "Dodgson, Charles Lutwidge." For example, the "photography" section has been expanded to include a list of photographic sitters and subjects, and a series of related topics such as "Meeting {other key} photographers" and "Photographic expeditions." Anything written by Dodgson will also be found here under the sub-heading "Works" including books, poems, games, circulars, and documents, whether published or not. Published items are recorded in italics.

For place names, I have included the County taken from the *Imperial Gazetteer of England and Wales* (1870) edited by John Marius Wilson. A number of boundary changes have taken place since this gazetteer was compiled, but it is appropriate, I think, to use the county-boundaries that existed in Dodgson's day.

Every entry has been checked before being included in this complete index. Some entries have been deleted as irrelevant, for example a few book references included in footnotes which are now covered by the Short Title list, and additional information given in footnotes not specifically relevant to Dodgson's text. References to places such as "Oxford" and "London" would become too numerous to serve any useful purpose, and these have been deleted. My guiding principle has been that if Dodgson included the name or subject within his text, then an index entry is provided.

Titles of books, plays, and paintings are followed by the name of the author, dramatist or artist in parenthesis, if known. This also applies to sculptures, poems and songs. In addition, operas are identified with the surname of the composer only, and operettas with the names of librettist and composer. I have listed separately all the books that Dodgson mentions and all the plays and other theatrical performances that Dodgson saw. In addition, there is now a complete list of these books and plays, arranged alphabetically, under the heading "Dodgson, Charles Lutwidge."

I have tried to eliminate errors in the construction of this Index, but I am aware that a book of this nature is prone to lapses of my concentration and effectiveness from time to time. So I take this opportunity of apologising for any errors that remain. I am always happy to hear from people who identify errors that have escaped my notice. I am grateful to a number of people who have given me constructive help and support during the process of compiling this index, especially Clare Imholtz, Amirouche Moktefi, Brian Partridge, Mark Richards, Roger Scowen, and Jeffrey Stern.

In the appendix, I have included my reconstruction of two missing volumes of C. L. Dodgson's private journals; numbers 1 and 3 covering the years between 1851 and 1855. These are properly introduced in the appendix, where I have explained my *modus operandi* for the reconstruction.

Edward Wakeling
May 2007

COMPLETE INDEX

Index to *Lewis Carroll's Diaries*, Volumes 1 to 9

Entries in this index are indicated by the volume number printed in bold, followed by the page number, and then the footnote number in italics where appropriate. Dates of birth and death of people are given, if known. There are separate headings for:

Christ Church
Churches
Churches abroad
Collingwood
Dodgson (Family)
Dodgson, Charles Lutwidge
Eastbourne
Guildford
Hotels abroad
Hotels and Inns
Lutwidge
Oxford
Oxford University
Pollock
Poole
Puzzles and Games
Raikes
Royal Family
Shakespeare's Plays
Smedley
Theatres
Weddings
Wilcox.

There are sub-headings under Dodgson, Charles Lutwidge, for:

Books (any title mentioned in the *Diaries*)
Curator of the Common Room
Drawings made by Dodgson of
Holidays
Illnesses
Letters from
Letters to
Mathematics
Photographs taken by Dodgson
Photography

Presentation copies of Dodgson's works
Pseudonyms
Religious matters
Theatre performances seen
Works by Dodgson.

Books, plays, and paintings appear under their title with author, dramatist, and artist in parenthesis. They are identified as "bk" for book, "dr" for drama (play, opera, musical, or pantomime), and "pic" for picture or painting.

Abandoned, The (pic. Clarkson Stanfield), **2:** 75 n.*151*
Abbé Bessan, Moscow, **5:** 332 n.*503*
Abbey Gardens, Reading, Berkshire, **6:** 477
Abbot, Reginald Charles Edward (1842-1919), 3rd Baron Colchester, **4:** 199 n.*203*
Abbot's Hospital, Guildford, Surrey, **9:** 290
Abbs, George Cooper, Rev. (1798-1878), **3:** 111 n.*159*
Abdy:
Albert Channing, Rev. (1829?-1885), **9:** 188 n.*311*
Dora Channing (1872-1950), **9:** 188 n.*311*, 199, 215, 216, 223, 251, 286
Dora née Merriman (1842-1915), **9:** 188 n.*311*, 205
Aberfeldy, Scotland, **6:** 184
Abingdon, Berkshire, **5:** 55, 74, 82, 90; **6:** 438; **7:** 89, 251, 279, 330, 335, 531; **8:** 102, 188, 320, 329; **9:** 61, 181, 193, 199, 223, 224, 239, 264, 279
Abingdon Vicarage, **5:** 55 n.*78*, 56
Acland (of Broad Street, Oxford):
Alfred Dyke (1858-1937), **2:** 111 n.*217*
Francis Edward Dyke (1857-1943), **2:** 111 n.*217*
Henry Dyke (1850-1936), **2:** 111 n.*217*; **3:** 45
Henry Wentworth Dyke, Dr. (1815-1900) – professor of medicine, **2:** 111 n.*217*, 112, 126; **3:** 28, 29 n.*41*, 36, 62 n.*93*, 122 n.*172*, 125, 155, 157 n.*232*; **4:** 35, 38
Herbert Dyke (1855-1877), 111 n.*217*; **3:** 45
Reginald Brodie Dyke (1856-1924), **2:** 111 n.*217*
Sarah Angelina (1849-1930), **2:** 111 n.*217*; **3:** 45; **4:** 33
Sarah née Cotton (1815-1878), **2:** 111 n.*217*, 118, 121; **3:** 33, 155, 156 n.*229*, 157; **4:** 215, 35
Theodore Dyke (1851-1931), **2:** 111 n.*217*; **3:** 45
William Alison Dyke (1847-1924), **2:** 111 n.*217*, 118; **3:** 34, 45
Acland (of Christ Church, Oxford):
Alice Sophia née Cunningham (1849-1935), **7:** 146, 147 n.*276*, 265 n.*479*, 270
Arthur Herbert Dyke, Mr., later Sir (1847-1926) – steward of Christ Church, **7:** 265 n.*479*, 270

Cuthbert Charles Dyke (b. 1875), **7:** 265 n.*479*
Francis Dyke (b. 1874), **7:** 265 n.*479*
Mabel Alice (b. 1891), **7:** 265 n.*479*
Acland, John Barton Arundel (1823-1904) – barrister, **3:** 62
Actors' Benevolent Fund, **7:** 539
Adair, Alexander William, Capt. (1829-1889) – army officer, **6:** 33 n.*43*
Adams (of Lambeth, Surrey):
Ada (b. 1864), **7:** 504 n.*823*, 509, 524
Adelaide "Addie" Blanche (b. 1871) – child actress, **7:** 504 n.*823*, 509, 522, 524
Rosaline "Rose" (b. 1869), **7:** 504 n.*823*, 524
Sarah A., Mrs. (b. 1833), alias Miss Cicely Nott – actress and vocalist, **7:** 504 n.*823*, 509, 524, 530
Adams, Catherine A. née Hume (b. 1803), **3:** 121
Adams, Gemma, **2:** 81 n.*160*
Adams, J., Mr. – actor or performer, **7:** 470 n.*773*
Adams, Miss – friend of Cunnynghames, **8:** 267 n.*451*
Adams, Miss – friend of Husseys, **8:** 510 n.*822*
Adams, Mrs. née Richards, **6:** 235
Adamson, Charles Stennett (1867-1897) – teacher, **9:** 154 n.*267*, 216, 238, 239
Adderley, Charles Leigh (1846-1945), 2nd Baron Norton, **5:** 119 n.*186*
Addison, Carlotta (1849-1914) – actress, **6:** 406 n.*666*; **7:** 514 n.*832*
Addison Hall, London, **9:** 351
"Adelaida" (Beethoven) – song, **4:** 82 n.*34*, 88
Adelphi (dr. Terence), **3:** 140 n.*207*
Adeson, Charles – child actor, **8:** 311, 312 n.*514*
Adey, Emily (b. 1837), **8:** 130 n.*211*
Adkins, Elsie (b. 1877), **9:** 130 n.*227*
Administration of the Lord's Supper, The (pic. John Horsley), **2:** 75 n.*151*
Admiralty, The, London, **8:** 46, 47, 53
Admiralty Platz, St. Petersburg, **5:** 288
Adventures of a Brownie as Told to My Child, The (bk. Dinah Craik), **6:** 255 n.*406*
Adventures of a Love-Letter, The (dr. Charles Mathews), **4:** 270 n.*313*
Adventures of Fritz, The (dr. Andrew Halliday), **7:** 199, 200 n.*374*
Aeneid (bk. Virgil), **1:** 41
Aeschylus (525?-456 BC), **1:** 73; **4:** 16; **5:** 253 n.*417*
After Dark (dr. Dion Boucicault), **7:** 75 n.*120*, 182 n.*338*
Afterglow in Egypt, The (pic. William Holman Hunt), **4:** 245 n.*275*
After the Chase (pic. Thomas Riley), **8:** 410, 411 n.*665*
Agamemnon at Home (dr. Anon), **5:** 253 n.*417*
Agnew, Misses, **7:** 185 n.*345*
Agricultural Show, Ludlow, Shropshire, **7:** 127
Agricultural Show, Shalford, Surrey, **9:** 149

Aids to Reflection (bk. Samuel Coleridge), **1:** 56 n.*20*, 116 n.*140*; **3:** 147 n.*212*
Ailsa Craig Island off Scottish mainland, **7:** 447
Ainger, Alfred, Rev. (1837-1904), **9:** 37 n.*65*
Ainger (of St. Bees, Cumberland):
Eliza Janet née Hodgson (b. 1825), **2:** 94 n.*185*
George Henry, Rev. (1819-1886), **2:** 93, 94 n.*185*
Ainger (of St. Bees, Cumberland):
Elizabeth née Humphries, **2:** 94 n.*185*
William, Rev. (1785-1840), **2:** 94 n.*185*
Airey (of Newcastle-upon-Tyne, Northumberland):
Emily Isabella Jane (b. 1839), **1:** 134 n.*170*
Frances Anne (b. 1838), **1:** 134 n.*170*
Georgina (1845-1929), **1:** 120, 126, 127, 129, 134 n.*170*
Jane Anne, Mrs. (b. 1788), **1:** 120 n.*148*, 127, 129, 134 n.*170*
Mary Augusta (b. 1843), **1:** 120, 126, 127, 129, 134 n.*170*
Robert, Mr. (1788-1861) – pilot master, **1:** 120 n.*148*, 127, 129, 134 n.*170*
Robert Henry Burrell (b. 1841), **1:** 134 n.*170*
Susan Emma (b. 1837), **1:** 134 n.*170*
Airey Force (pic. Henry Witherby), **2:** 103 n.198
Alabama (dr. Augustus Thomas), **9:** 215 n.*343*, 219-221, 226
Alabama, The (dr. Albert Smith), **4:** 281 n.*331*
Aladdin (dr. Edward Blanchard), **6:** 376 n.*615*
Aladdin (dr. Frank Green), **7:** 313 n.*559*
Aladdin and the Wonderful Lamp (dr. Anon), **5:** 311 n.*481*
Aladdin and the Wonderful Lamp (dr. John Morton), **3:** 14 n.*13*
Albani, Marie Louise Emma Cecile née Lajeunesse, Dame (1852-1930) – singer, **7:** 120 n.*225*
Albany, see Princess Helen under Royal Family
Albermarle Street, London, **7:** 118
Albert Hall, London, **6:** 310; **7:** 185
Albrighton, Shropshire, **2:** 12 n.*13*
Albury, Surrey, **6:** 43, 45-47, 82, 162, 170, 308
Albury Park, **6:** 80; **9:** 304
Alder, Constance E. A. (b. 1873), **8:** 348 n.*573*
Aldershot, Hampshire, **6:** 421
Alderson (of Holdenby):
Augustus E. (b. 1864), **6:** 247 n.*392*, 248, 373, 441
Edith "Eda" Cecilia (b. 1868), **6:** 247 n.*392*, 248, 373, 441; **8:** 77 n.*120*
Frederick Cecil, Rev. (1837-1907), **6:** 246, 247 n.*392*, 248, 249, 335, 373, 375, 441; **8:** 76, 77 n.*120*, 143
Katherine Gladys née Guest (1837-1926), **6:** 246, 247 n.*392*, 335, 373, 441; **8:** 76, 77 n.*120*, 143
Margaret Helen "Nellie (1862-1955), **6:** 247 n.*392*, 248, 373, 441; **8:** 77 n.*120*, 78

Montague (b. 1870), **6:** 247 n.*392*, 248, 373, 441

Alderson (of London):

Charles Henry (1831-1913) – inspector of schools, **6:** 373, 374 n.*613*

Edward Hall, Sir (1787-1857) – judge, **6:** 164 n.*254*

Edward Pakenham (1828?-1876), **6:** 164 n.*254*, 246, 247 n.*392*

Georgina Caroline (1827-1899), see Cecil

Louisa H. (b. 1830), **6:** 162, 163 n.*252*, 221, 246, 373, 441; **8:** 77 n.*120*, 110, 461, 467

Alderson (of Paddington, London):

Florence née Alderson (b. 1844), **8:** 77 n.*120*, 116, 189, 222 n.*380*

Henry J., Col. (b. 1835) – army officer, **8:** 77 n.*120*

Ralph E. (b. 1879), **8:** 77 n.*120*, 189

Alderson (of London):

James, Sir (1794-1882) – physician, **6:** 374 n.*613*

Marianne née Berthon, Lady (d. 1877), **6:** 374 n.*613*

Aldgate Station, London, **7:** 453

Aldrich, Henry, Dr. (1647-1710) – dean of Christ Church, **8:** 238 n.*400*

Alec Forbes of Howglen (bk. George MacDonald), **5:** 125 n.*199*

Alexander, Beatrice née Fearon (b. 1862), **6:** 209, 213, 369; **7:** 76 n.*121*, 95, 97, 110, 111, 118, 119, 124, 171, 181, 183, 184, 194, 256, 387; **9:** 157 n.*272*

Alexander:

Evelyn "Evey" Sophia née Dubourg (1861-1917), **6:** 86 n.*129*, 258, 288, 289, 295-297, 314, 315, 316, 397, 398, 404 n.*664*; **7:** 13, 14, 95, 96, 111, 114, 117, 122, 123, 158, 159, 186, 278, 442; **8:** 110, 165 n.*270*, 345, 456; **9:** 55 n.*96*

Robert Gustavus, Capt. (1851-1921) – army officer, **8:** 165 n.*270*

Alexander, George (1858-1918) – actor and manager, **8:** 456, 562 n.*896*, 577; **9:** 23 n.*28*, 56

Alexander, William, Rt. Rev. (1824-1911), **5:** 248 n.*405*, 249 n.*407*; **6:** 458 n.*753*, 459; **8:** 55 n.*82*

Alexander Nevski Monastery, St. Petersburg, **5:** 294, 295, 347, 348

Alexander's Feast (Handel), **3:** 32 n.*47*

Alfred Place, London (Uncle Skeffington Lutwidge), **4:** 85, 86, 96, 103

Alfred the Great (dr. Robert Brough), **4:** 263 n.*308*

Alfreton, Derbyshire, **8:** 146, 148 n.*240*

Alfrick, Worcestershire, **9:** 66, 69

Alfriston, Sussex, **7:** 458

Alhambra Circus, London, **4:** 282, 327

Alice in Fairy-Land (dr. Elliston Family), **7:** 138 n.*253*

Alice in Wonderland (pic. George Leslie), **7:** 179 n.*332*

Alice in Wonderland (dr. Nigel Playfair), **9:** 204 n.*333*

Alice in Wonderland – dramatisation with music, **7:** Sullivan approached 25 n.*28*, London Polytechnic prod. 42, 43 n.*64*, 44; **8:** Mackenzie approached 15, 20, 23, 102, 105, 183 n.*310*, Savile Clarke production

291 n.*487*, 304 n.*504*, first performance 309 n.*512*, 311, 312 n.*514*, 313 n.*515*, 316 n.*520*, 318, 319, 320, 327, 348, 357, 361 n.*589*, 370, 383 n.*629*, revival 408 n.*662*, 412, 420, 421 n.*681*, 428, 430, 433, 439, 440, 442, 443
Alice Ottley School,The, see Worcester High School for Girls
Alison, Archibald, Sir (1792-1867), 1st Bart. – writer, **1:** 27
All Abroad (dr. Owen Hall and James Tanner), **9:** 197 n.*323*
Allen (of Dalton-le-Dale, Durham):
Beatrice (b. 1865), **6:** 208 n.*327*
Mary "May" Anne (1848-1904), see Wilcox
Allen (of Headington, Oxfordshire):
Charlotte (b. 1844), **4:** 216 n.*230*; **5:** 153, 155, 157, 158, 252; **6:** 438; **7:** 89, 161, 543; **8:** 178 n.*292*, 218, 256, 261, 266, 270, 272, 376, 435, 605; **9:** 121 n.*211*, 123, 156
Charlotte L., Mrs. (b. 1814), **4:** 210; **5:** 120 n.*189*; **6:** 438; **7:** 89, 161, 329, 427; **8:** 178 n.*292*, 218, 261, 266, 272
Jane (b. 1846?), **5:** 153, 155, 157, 158, 252; **7:** 304, 305
Mary (b. 1843), **4:** 216 n.*230*; **5:** 54 n.*77*, 153, 251
Thomas, Mr. (1800?-1873) – hospital superintendent, **4:** 210 n.*219*, 215, 216; **5:** 120 n.*189*
Allen (of Eastbourne, later St. Leonards, Sussex):
Edith K. F. (b. 1864), **7:** 459 n.*757*; **8:** 352, 578; **9:** 176, 329
Katharine R., Mrs. (b. 1831), **7:** 459 n.*757*; **8:** 39, 149, 232, 352, 422, 578, 585; **9:** 29, 161, 176, 207, 220, 277, 329
Robert, Rev. (1833-1898), **7:** 133 n.*247*, 282, 284, 300, 352, 455, 459, 460, 479; **8:** 22 n.*19*, 34, 39, 128, 149, 232, 239, 285, 352, 422, 475, 482, 578, 585; **9:** 29 n.*46*, 161, 175, 176, 207, 220, 277, 329, 335, 338, 343, 344
Allen, see Egerton Allen
Allen, Udney John Thomas, Rev. (b. 1824), **8:** 102 n.*168*, 564
All England (cricket team), **2:** 72; **3:** 64
Allingham, Helen née Paterson (1848-1926) – artist, **7:** 533 n.*863*, 537 n.*870*
Allington, Mr., **4:** 343 n.*445*
All in the Wrong (dr. Arthur Murphy), **3:** 79, 80 n.*126*
All Souls College, Oxford, **4:** 209; **6:** 120, 380, 410, 474; **7:** 22; **8:** 603, 621
All the Year Round (ed. Charles Dickens), **4:** 26; **5:** 229
Almond, Hely Hutchinson (1832-1903) – teacher, **1:** 78 n.*75*
Alphabets, **1:** 63
Alton Locke (bk. Charles Kingsley), **2:** 8 n.*5*, 10, 12
Alum Bay, Isle of Wight, **4:** 346, 351, 352
Alvaston, Derbyshire, **2:** 105; **6:** 176
Always Intended (dr. Horace Wigan), **5:** 63 n.*93*
Amber Heart, The (dr. Alfred Calmour), **8:** 406 n.*660*
Ambleside, Westmorland, **2:** 95; **3:** 104, 107, 109, 110, 115, 117, 119, 144,

145
Ambrose (of Ludgate, London):
Louisa G. née Liddon (b. 1836), **6:** 178 n.*274*, 220, 221, 247, 335, 373, 465
Mary L. (b. 1863), **6:** 178 n.*274*, 220, 221, 335, 465 n.*766*
America, **5:** 10, 140, 143; **7:** 112, 122, 293; **8:** 307 n.*509*, 528
America in a Hurry (dr. Harry Furniss), **9:** 252 n.*395*
Americans, **2:** 97
Ample Apology, An (dr. George Roberts), **5:** 64 n.*95*
Amy (b. 1875?) – train companion, **7:** 197, 198 n.*370*
Ancient Mariner, The (bk. Samuel Coleridge), **1:** 56 n.*20*
Ancrum, Sydney Rutherford (b. 1861) – solicitor, **8:** 610 n.*967*
Andersen, Hans Christian (1805-1875) – writer, **8:** 402, 403 n.*656*
Anderson, Archibald (b. 1836), MA Exeter, **2:** 111 n.*215*; **3:** 97, 99
Anderson, Maria "Minnie" Katherine (1846-1889), see Moseley
Anderson, Mary (1859-1940) – actress, **8:** 190 n.*320*
Anderson (of Kensington Gate, London):
Sophie née Gengembre (1823-1903) – artist, **4:** 285 n.*340*, 290 n.*346*, 312 n.*389*, 337 n.*435*; **5:** 25, 60, 61 n.*88*, 67, 71, 89 n.*137*, 98 n.*153*, 126, 137, 143, 158, 217, 218 n.*347*, 221; **6:** 22, 23 n.*23*, 44 n.*62*, 45, 81 n.*119*
Walter, Mr. (d. 1886?) – artist, **4:** 285 n.*340*, 290 n.*346*, 312; **5:** 25, 67, 71, 89, 126, 137, 143, 158, 217, 221; **6:** 44 n.*62*, 45
Andover Family from Cheshire, **5:** 120 n.*189*
Andrews, Kate (b. 1857) – teacher, **8:** 123 n.*197*
Andrews, Septimus, Rev. (1832-1914), **1:** 87, 88 n.*91*, 91; **2:** 126; **3:** 28 n.*39*, 44, 45, 49, 52, 61, 63, 161; **4:** 33, 73 n.*19*, 159, 161, 226, 250, 253, 269, 271, 272, 282, 315, 333, 336 n.*433*; **5:** 37; **7:** 100 n.*187*; **8:** 460 n.*740*; **9:** 197 n.*322*
Angel, Andrea (b. 1877) – teacher, **9:** 292 n.*462*
Angel in the House (bk. Coventry Patmore), **1:** 115 n.*138*
Angerstein (of Weeting Hall, Norfolk):
John Richard Julius (b. 1846), **5:** 209 n.*333*
Julia Augusta (b. 1851), **5:** 209 n.*333*
Anglo-Danish Exhibition, **8:** 402, 403 n.*656*, 406, 410, 411
"Anne Boleyn" (in *Henry VIII*), **2:** 20 n.*36*, 21, 22
Annesley, Arthur, Lord (1843-1927), 11th Viscount Valentia – politician, **9:** 193 n.*318*, 206 n.*336*
Annesley, Nottinghamshire, **2:** 104 n.*200*
"Annie Anderson" (in *Alec Forbes in Howglen*) **5:** 125 n.*199*
Anno 66 (Russian play), **5:** 281
Anno Domini (pic. Edwin Long), **8:** 115 n.*188*; **9:** 58 n.*106*
Ansell, Mary (1867-1950) – actress, **8:** 614 n.*974*
Anson, George William (1848-1920) – actor, **7:** 438 n.*727*
Antechamber at Whitehall (pic. Edward Ward), **5:** 161

Antoinette, Cecilia, real name Reynolds – actress, **5:** 193, 203
A Pas de Fascination (dr. Anon), **5:** 123 n.*195*
Apple Blossoms (pic. John Millais), **5:** 212 n.*340*
Appleford, Berkshire, **5:** 90
Appleton, Berkshire, **3:** 165
Appleton, Charles Edward Cutts Birch, Dr. (1841-1879) – editor of *The Academy*, **6:** 364 n.*599*
Appleton, D., & Company, New York – publishers, **5:** 101 n.*158*, 140 n.*224*
Appleton, Samuel, Dr. (b. 1815) – physician, **6:** 402 n.*659*
April Afternoon at Easby Abbey, An (pic. James Peel), **2:** 75 n.*151*
Aquarium, Brighton, Sussex, **6:** 232, 444
Archbishop of Canterbury (Archibald Tait), **6:** 320
Archbishop of Dublin (Patrick Fitzsimon), **2:** 62
Archbishop of York (William Thomson), **4:** 316 n.*397*
Archdeacon of Berkshire (Edward Berens), **2:** 73
Archer (of Haslemere, Surrey):
Anne "Annie" (b. 1854), **5:** 214 n.*343*
James, Mr. (1822-1904) – artist, **5:** 214 n.*343*, 215, 218, 233
Jane Clark née Lawson (b. 1832), **5:** 214 n.*342*, 218, 233
Margaret "Maggie" (b. 1857), **5:** 214 n.*343, 215*
Archer, Frank (1845-1917) – actor, **7:** 105, 106 n.*197*
Archery Meeting at Oxford, **5:** 90
Arctic Regions, **4:** 28
Arding, Miss (b. 1886?) – child actress, **8:** 405 n.*659*
Ardington, Berkshire, **8:** 124
Area Belle, The (dr. William Brough & Andrew Halliday), **4:** 337 n.*436*
Arga, Madame – singer, **1:** 103
Argles (of Barnack, Cambridgeshire):
Agnes Beatrice Jane "Dolly" (1857-1944), see Thicknesse
Alice (b. 1852?), **6:** 24 n.*26*, 107
Charles Davys (1843-1879), **6:** 24 n.*26*, 106
Edith Margaret (1853-1935), **6:** 24 n.*26*, 25, 26, 107; **8:** 85 n.*136*, 170, 171 n.*285*, 259, 280; **9:** 192 n.*317*
George Marsham, (1841-1920), see below
Margaret Julia née Davys (b. 1816), **6:** 24 n.*26, 97*, 107; **7:** 227, 263 n.*475*
Marsham, Rev. (1814-1892), **6:** 24 n.*26*, 25, 97, 106, 108; **7:** 227
Marsham Frederick (1851-1883), **6:** 24 n.*26*, 25, 107
Mary L. (b. 1846), **6:** 24 n.*26*
Argles (of York):
George Marsham, Rev. (1841-1920), **6:** 24 n.*26*, 109; **7:** 263 n.*475*
Mary Ann née Harrison (b. 1851), **7:** 263 n.*475*
Ariston (mechanical musical instrument), **9:** 160 n.*275*, 178
Aristotle (384-322 BC), **2:** 12 n.*14*
Arlesey, Bedfordshire, **6:** 495

Arlington Street, London, **6:** 225, 286
Armbruster, Carl (1846-1913?) – composer, **9:** 348 n.*557*
Armitstead (of Sandbach, Cheshire):
Henry Sidney (1837-1912), **3:** 65 n.*98*
John Richard (1829-1918), **5:** 24, 25 n.*23*
William George (1833-1907), **3:** 65 n.*98*; **4:** 259 n.*303*
Armitstead, Thomas Bell, Rev. (1840-1916), **3:** 67 n.*102*
Armytage (of Hammersmith, London):
George F., Mr. (b. 1854) – landowner, **8:** 187 n.*315*
Rosamond "Rose" née Ball (b. 1861), **8:** 187 n.*315*, 196, 199, 219, 271, 319, 368
Arnold (of London):
Alice "Blanche" (b. 1878?) – child actress, **7:** 504 n.*823*, 509
Charles, Mr. (1855-1905) – actor, **7:** 504 n.*823*, 509
Arnold (of Oxford):
Arthur (1856-1878), **6:** 145 n.*220*
Ethel Margaret (1866-1930), **6:** 145 n.*220*, 152, 192, 203, 209 n.*328*, 217 n.*338*, 268, 306, 317, 323, 325, 328, 369, 389, 412, 430, 451, 452, 470; **7:** 18 n.*13*, 80, 87, 88, 99, 109 n.*203*, 160, 162, 177, 189, 228, 274, 380, 383, 405, illness 428, 429, 494, 497, visit to London and Guildford 513-516, 522, 524, 534, 536; **8:** 60, acting 68, 69, 93, 100, 168, 169, 218, 272, 273, 278, logic 283, 376, 379, paper on Dodgson 516 n.*832*
Francis "Frank" Sorell (1861-1927) **6:** 145 n.*220*, 306
Julia "Judy" Frances (1862-1908), see Huxley
Julia née Sorell (1826-1888), **6:** 145 n.*220*, 148, 153, 201, 226, 268, 317, 329, 369, 379, 389, 393, 400, 412, 418, 426; **7:** 80 n.*132*, 147, 160, 177, 189, 224, 264, 271, 274, 380, 383, 405, 428, 429, 482; **8:** 379, 380 n.*624*
Lucy Ada (1858-1894), see Selwyn
Mary Augusta (1851-1920), see Humphry Ward
Theodore (b. 1854?), **6:** 145 n.*220*
Thomas, Mr. (1823-1900) – writer, **6:** 144, 145 n.*220*, 148, 153, 192, 201, 369, 381, 418, 486 n.*801*; **7:** 80, 147, 160, 177, 224, 271, 274, 383, 405, 428, 482
William Thomas (1852-1904), **6:** 145 n.*220*
Arnold, Edwin (1832-1904) – poet and writer, **1:** 46
Arnold, Frederick (1833-1891) – writer, **2:** 49 n.*100*, 52, 84 n.*167*
Arnold, Matthew (1822-1888) – poet, **1:** 41; **3:** 35 n.*54*
Arnort (of Kensington, London):
Alice, **6:** 129 n.*200*
Constance, **6:** 129 n.*200*
Florence, **6:** 129 n.*200*
Arrah na Pogue (dr. Dion Boucicault), **5:** 64 n.*95*
Arran, Scotland, **6:** 179 n.*277*, 181, 184; **7:** 447
Art and Love (dr. Augustus Dubourg), **6:** 289

Arthur's Seat, Edinburgh, **3:** 97; **6:** 181
Art Journal, The, **2:** 7 n.*1*
Arundel, Sussex, **8:** 359
Arundel Society, **4:** 31
Ascension, The – sermon, **2:** 67
Ascot (ship), **7:** 166
Ash, H. (fl. 1851-1858) – artist, **2:** 75 n.*151*
Ashcroft, W. E. (d. 1906) – actor, **9:** 310 n.*493*
Ashley, Henry (1831-1890) – actor and singer, **7:** 194 n.*361*
Ashley-Cooper, Anthony (1801-1885), 7th Lord Shaftesbury, **6:** 346; **8:** 133 n.*216*
Ashmolean Club, Oxford, **7:** 225
Ashmolean Museum, Oxford, **3:** 22 n.*28*; **4:** 143; **5:** 163; **6:** 287; **9:** 266 n.*420*
Asia Minor, **1:** 102
Assistant Charity Commissioner, **6:** 380, 381
Association for the Education of Women, **9:** 327 n.*525*
Astill, Mr. – theatre manager, **5:** 109 n.*172*
Astle, Thomas (1735-1803) – palaeographer, **1:** 63 n.*38*
Aston, John Meredith, Rev. (1826-1886), **7:** 236 n.*436*
Athenaeum, The, **5:** 11, 12 n.*2*; **7:** 80, 81 n.*135*, 83
Athens Club, The (dr. Anon), **7:** 194, 195 n.*362*
Atkins (of Blandford, Dorset):
  Alice A., Mrs. (b. 1847) – artist, **7:** 249 n.*456*, 250
  Beatrice Alice (b. 1871), **7:** 249 n.*456*, 250
  William H. (b. 1873), **7:** 249 n.*456*
Atkins (of Rickmansworth, Hertfordshire):
  Emily Mabel (b. 1876), **8:** 290 n.*486*, 291-295, 303
  Gladys M. (b. 1877), **8:** 290 n.*486*, 291-294, 303
Atkins, Robert – actor., **4:** 223 n.*245*
Atkinson, Captain, **4:** 24
Atkinson (of St. Helier, Jersey):
  Edith Gertrude Dickson (b. 1874), **8:** 96, 97 n.*158*, 559
  Edith Mary née Vatcher (1852-1933), **8:** 96, 97 n.*158*, 559
  Dorothy Home (1887-1962), **8:** 97 n.*158*
  Francis G. (b. 1876), **8:** 97 n.*158*
  Francis Home, Rev. (1840-1901), **4:** 87 n.*42*, 88, 89 n.*46*, 90, 92-94, 96, 97; **8:** 96, 97 n.*158*, 99 n.*164*, 450, 559; **9:** 87 n.*157*
  Henry Ernest (b. 1871), **8:** 97 n.*158*, 450, 537, 559
  John Clayton (b. 1877), **8:** 97 n.*158*
Atkinson, Miss – actress, **4:** 160
Atkyns & Burton, Messrs. – photographers, **3:** 170 n.*248*
At the Seaside (dr. Richard Corney Grain), **7:** 131 n.*245*
Attlee, Mr. – churchwarden, **9:** 274 n.*437*
Atwood, Clare, **9:** 316 n.*505*, 324

Atwood, Mr., **6:** 94 n.*147*
Aubrey House, Key Haven, Hampshire, **4:** 348
Aubrey-Moore (of Oxford):
Catharine Maria née Hurt (b. 1841), **9:** 259 n.*409*, 267
Catherine "Kate" Ellen (1883-1953), **9:** 259 n.*409*, 267
Ethel Margaret (1880-1965), **9:** 259 n.*409*, 267
Stephanie Margery (b. 1879), **9:** 259 n.*409*, 267
Auckland Castle, Durham, **3:** 86 n.*134*, 87, 144, 166 n.*240*; **4:** 23
Audran, Edmond (1840-1901) – composer, **7:** 304, 305 n.*549*; **8:** 565 n.*900*; **9:** 164 n.*279*
Audrey, Mrs. née Watt, **4:** 131 n.*106*
"Auld Robin Gray" (Anne Barnard & William Leeves) – song, **5:** 225, 226 n.*359*
Aunt Judy's Magazine (ed. Mrs. Gatty), **4:** 46; **5:** 12 n.*2*, 251 n.*410*, 370 n.*547*, 375; **6:** 134
Aurora Borealis, **4:** 29
Aurora Leigh (bk. Elizabeth Barrett Browning), **3:** 148 n.*213, 149*
Austen (of Chilworth Manor, near Guildford, Surrey):
Alice (b. 1847), **6:** 47 n.*66*
Beatrice (b. 1842), **6:** 47 n.*66*
Caroline (1843-1905), **6:** 47 n.*66*
Elphrida (b. 1848), **6:** 47 n.*66*
Emily (b. 1850), **6:** 47 n.*66*
Maria Elizabeth née Godwin (d. 1904), **6:** 47 n.*66*
Robert Alfred Cloyne, Mr. (1808-1884) – geologist, **6:** 47 n.*66*
Sophia Harriet (b. 1833?), **6:** 47 n.*66*
Victoria Augusta (b. 1840?), **6:** 47 n.*66*
Austen (of Shalford House, near Guildford, Surrey):
Henry Edmund, Sir (1785-1871), **6:** 47 n.*66*
Robert Alfred Cloyne, see above
Austin, Alfred (1835-1913) – poet, **4:** 109; **8:** 467 n.*757*
Austin, Harry – pupil at Richmond School, **1:** 21, 115 n.*139*
Australia, **1:** 56; **5:** 33 n.*38*; **8:** 64-66
Austrian Dungeons in Italy (bk. Teobaldus Orsini), **3:** 9 n.*5*, 145
Author's Daughter, The (bk. Mary Howitt), **2:** 17 n.*30*
Autumn Leaves (pic. John Millais), **2:** 75 n.151; **4:** 252 n.*290*; **5:** 15 n.*6*; **7:** 327 n.*580*
Avent (of Broughton, Oxfordshire):
Alice, Mrs. (b. 1845), **8:** 267 n.*449*
John, Rev. (b. 1837), **8:** 267 n.*449*
Away with Melancholy (dr. John Morton), **1:** 105 n.*118*, 128, 132; **2:** 56 n.*110*, 103, 128; **3:** 7 n.*1*, 45, 85 n.*131*, 146
Awful Rise in Spirits, An (dr. Tom Taylor), **4:** 248 n.*282*
Axtell, Thomas (1826-1901) – craftsman and builder, **7:** 521 n.*846*, 523, 545; **8:** 123 n.*199*, 126, 500

Aytoun, William Edmonstoune (1813-1865) – writer, **2:** 44 n.*89*

Babbage, Charles (1791-1871) – mathematician, **5:** 192 n.*316*
Babel, **2:** 11
Babes in the Wood, The (dr. Anon), **6:** 311 n.*514*
Babington (of Rothley, Leicestershire):
Florence Lucy (b. 1832), **4:** 320, 321 n.*407*
Frances née Sykes (d. 1878), **4:** 320, 321 n.*407*; **5:** 148 n.*238*
"Baby Costello" – performer, **9:** 164 n.*280*
Bach, Anton (b. 1826) – watchmaker, **7:** 532; **8:** 66 n.*106*, 216
Bach, Johann Sebastian (1685-1750) – composer, **6:** 265, 266 n.*427*
Bachelor of the Albany (bk. Marmion Savage), **1:** 90 n.*94*
Backgammon:
Blot, **5:** 378
Co-operative, **9:** 126 n.*221*, 129 n.*226*, 131, 134 n.*235*
Co-operative German, **9:** 185
Thirdie, **9:** 125, 126 n.*221*
Badcock (of Queen Street, Oxford):
Amelia, Mrs. (b. 1836), **9:** 130 n.*227*, 142
Charles, Mr. (b. 1830) – draper, **9:** 130 n.*227*
Elizabeth "Bessie" H. (b. 1877), **9:** 130 n.*227*, 142, 143
Badcock, William (1799-1884) – retailer, **2:** 125
Badcock's Yard, **4:** 194 n.*193*, 216, 261, 321 n.*408*
Baddeley (of Onslow Square, London):
Blanche Adelaide (b. 1859), **4:** 178; **5:** 141 n.*227*, 142; **8:** 58 n.*90*
Grace (b. 1857), **8:** 58 n.*90*, 59, 131, 566, 573, 590, 594, 615
John Fraser Lodington, Lt. Col. (d. 1862?) – army officer, **5:** 141 n.*227*, 142; **7:** 115 n.*212*
Mabel, **7:** 115 n.*212*; **8:** 58 n.*90*, 59, 131
Maud, **8:** 58 n.*90*, 210, 319
Mrs. née Cobourg?, **5:** 141 n.*227*, 142
Welbore St. Clair (b. 1856), **5:** 141 n.*227*, 142
Baddeley, Joseph Jeremiah, Rev. (b. 1844), **8:** 418 n.*677*
Baddeley, Miss, **9:** 156, 157 n.*271*
Baden Powell, George Smyth (1847-1898) – politician, **8:** 63 n.*101*, 65, 326
Badgeley, Major, **9:** 103 n.*187*
Badham (of East Burgholt, Suffolk):
Anna née Hume (1808-1870), **3:** 132 n.*191*; **4:** 314 n.*393*
Charles David, Dr. (1805-1857) – physician, **3:** 132 n.*191*
Charles Hume (1849-1901), **3:** 132 n.*191*; **4:** 314 n.*393*, 324
Minnie (b. 1848), **3:** 132 n.*191*; **4:** 314 n.*393*, 324
Baffin, William (d. 1622) – explorer, **4:** 28
Bagot, Charles Samuel, Sir (1828-1906) – barrister, **8:** 278 n.*467*
Bailey, Alfred (1830-1898) – barrister, **2:** 72 n.*145*
Bailey, Philip James (1816-1902) – poet, **4:** 109

Baillie, Joanna (1762-1851) – poet, **2:** 100
Bainbridge (of Ruswarp, near Whitby, Yorkshire):
Agnes Constance (b. 1850), **2:** 15 n.*25*, 102, 103; **4:** 179
Florence Hilda (b. 1848), **2:** 15 n.*25*, 102, 103 n.*199*; **4:** 36, 179
George Henry (b. 1841), **2:** 15 n.*25*
Henry, Lieut. (1816-1877) – navy officer, **1:** 54 n.*13*; **2:** 15 n.*25*, 85, 88, 102-104; **4:** 36
Laura L. (b. 1854), **4:** 180
Mary Agnes née Harvey (b. 1824), **1:** 54 n.*13*, 94, 95 n.*98*, 96, 100; **2:** 15 n.*25*, 88, 102, 103 n.*199*; **4:** 36
Bainbridge (of Whitby, Yorkshire):
Ann Adelaide Hippolyta née Harvey (1811-1893), see Pickard
George Hobson, Lieut. – navy officer, **2:** 103 n.*199*
George H. S. (b. 1840), **2:** 15 n.*25*
Bainbrigge, Philip Thomas, Rev. (1848-1919), **6:** 261 n.*418*
Baird (of Rawlinson Road, Oxford):
Dorothy "Dolly" Forster (1875-1933), **9:** 121, 122 n.*213*, 135, 138, 141, 145, 146, 158, 178, 212
Emily Jane née Brinton (1830-1910), **9:** 122 n.*213*, 136, 138, 141, 145, 183, 212, 223
John Forster, Mr. (1823-1882) – barrister, **9:** 122 n.*213*, 145
Margaret A. "Daisy" (b. 1877), **9:** 141 n.*243*, 145, 178, 183, 212, 223
Baker (of Winchester, Hampshire):
Agnes C. (b. 1864), **6:** 413 n.*676*
Catherine "Kate" (b. 1861), **6:** 413 n.*676*
Emily (b. 1857), **6:** 413 n.*676*
James, Rev. (1825-1897), **2:** 59 n.*119*, 84; **4:** 83 n.*36*; **6:** 413 n.*676*
James B. (b. 1863), **6:** 413 n.*676*
Mary J. (b. 1860), **6:** 413 n.*676*
Sarah E., Mrs. (b. 1833), **6:** 413 n.*676*
Baker, Alice (b. 1846) – Eastbourne lodging-house keeper (not Bluett), **7:** 463, 464
Baker (of Abingdon, Berkshire):
Alice Margaret Isabel (b. 1871), **7:** 252 n.*460*
Margaret Ann, Mrs. (b. 1844), **7:** 252 n.*460*
Slade Innes, Mr. (b. 1829) – surgeon, **7:** 252 n.*460*
Baker (of Nuneham Courtney, Oxfordshire):
Charles (b. 1833), **4:** 83 n.*36*
Henry (b. 1835), **4:** 83 n.*36*
Montague Bernard (b. 1843), **4:** 83 n.*36*
Baker, Stanley, Rev. (1868-1950), **9:** 285 n.*451*, 300
Baker, Thomas, Rev. (1784-1866), **5:** 41 n.*49*
Baker, William (b. 1833) – upholsterer, **7:** 482, 483 n.*786*, 495
Balaklava (or Balaclava), **1:** 54 n.*14*, 72, 119 n.*145*; **2:** 88
Balfour (of East Lothian, Scotland):

Alice Blanche (1851-1936), **6:** 374 n.*613*, 375
Arthur James (1848-1930) – politician, **6:** 374 n.*613*
Eleanor "Norah" Mildred (1845-1936), **6:** 374 n.*613*
Balfour (of Durham):
Ella Sophia Anna (1854-1935), **4:** 157 n.*145*, 179, 325 n.*412*; **5:** 12 n.*3*
Georgina "Georgie" Mary (1851-1929), **4:** 157 n.*145*, 180, 325 n.*412*; **5:** 12 n.*3*, 19, 191 n.*313*
James Leycester, Mr. (1826-1854) – teacher, **4:** 157 n.*145*
Sophia née Cathcart (1830-1902), **4:** 157 n.*145*, 324; **5:** 12 n.*3*
Balfour (of Croydon, Surrey):
Florence "Birdie" May (b. 1865), see Collie Foster
James Lucas, Mr. (1835-1904) – stockbroker, **6:** 357 n.*590*, 358, 411
Balfour (of Bracknell, Berkshire):
Hilda (b. 1863?), **6:** 89 n.*134*
Linda (b. 1859?), **6:** 89 n.*134*
Mr., **6:** 88, 89 n.*134*, 96, 116
Mrs., **6:** 88, 89 n.*134*, 96, 116
Ball (of Guildford, Surrey):
Helen, Mrs. (b. 1842), **6:** 389 n.*639*; **9:** 345 n.*553*
Joseph, Mr. (b. 1843) – teacher, **6:** 389 n.*639*
Ball, Miss – governess, **8:** 270 n.*456*
Ball, Ralph (b. 1837) – civil servant, **6:** 130; **7:** 518 n.*840*
Ball, Sidney (b. 1857) – tutor, **9:** 199 n.*326*
Ball, Walter William Rouse (1850-1925) - mathematician, **9:** 307 n.*487*
Ballad Concert, St. James' Hall, London, **6:** 26
Ballads of Crewe (bk. Bon Gaultier), **2:** 44 n.*89*
Ballantyne, Mrs., **7:** 497 n.*810*
Balliol College, Oxford, **4:** 151, 346; **7:** 224, 273
Balloch, West Dunbartonshire, **3:** 104
Ballot Bill, **6:** 219 n.*345*, 222
Bally, Capt., **6:** 418
Bally (of Lewisham, Kent):
Ellen "Nellie" G. M. (b. 1875), **8:** 34 n.*42*
Mary R. S., Mrs. (b. 1849), **8:** 34 n.*42*
William, Maj. (b. 1837) – army officer, **8:** 34 n.*42*
Balthasar (of Kensington, London):
Elise M. (b. 1872), **7:** 283 n.*514*, 284, 286, 305; **8:** 24
Fanny A., Mrs. (b. 1839), **7:** 283 n.*514*; **8:** 23 n.*20*, 24
Gustave M. (b. 1874), **7:** 283 n.*514*, 284; **8:** 24
Ida M. (b. 1871), **7:** 283 n.*514*, 284, 286, 305; **8:** 24
Olga M. (b. 1880), **7:** 283 n.*514*, 284; **8:** 24
Oscar M. (b. 1877), **7:** 283 n.*514*, 284; **8:** 24
Otto, Mr. (b. 1841) – lace merchant, **7:** 283 n.*514*; **8:** 23 n.*20*
Stella M. (b. 1875), **7:** 283 n.*514*, 284, 305; **8:** 24
Baltimore, United States of America, **4:** 277

Baltzer, Richard Heinrich (1818-1887) – mathematician, **5:** 125 n.*198*
Baly (of St Christopher Le Stocks, London):
Alice Mary née Richards (b. 1847), **8:** 585 n.*935*, 589; **9:** 48 n.*84*
Dorothea Alice (b. 1879), **8:** 585 n.*935*
Edward Charles Cyril (1871-1948), **8:** 585 n.*935*
Edward Ely, Mr. (b. 1844) – banker, **8:** 585 n.*935*
Ernest Hugh (b. 1876), **8:** 585 n.*935*
Gladys Mary (b. 1884), **8:** 585 n.*935*, 587, 589, 592, 633; **9:** 48 n.*84*, 186 n.*307*, 231 n.*366*
Bamlet, Robert (1772-1863) – farmer, **4:** 22
Bampton Lectures, see Oxford University
Banbury, Kate, Mrs. (b. 1839), **7:** 526 n.*850*
Banbury, Oxfordshire, **5:** 53; **7:** 337; **8:** 609, 610
Banbury Road, Oxford, **9:** 181, 238, 300, 319, 326, 354
Bancroft:
Marie Effie née Wilton (1839-1921) – actress, **4:** 221 n.*242*, 272; **5:** 125, 126 n.*200*, 231; **6:** 397 n.*649*, 443; **7:** 186 n.*348*, 231 n.*425*, 540; **9:** 57 n.*104*
Squire, Sir (1846-1926) – actor, **5:** 125, 126 n.*200*; **7:** 231 n.*425*, 320, 540; **9:** 57 n.*104*
Banfather, Mrs., **7:** 271 n.*490*
Banks, Arthur E. (b. 1858) – agricultural student, **7:** 446 n.*737*
Banks, Miss – singer, **6:** 18
Barber, Charles Burton (1845-1894) – artist, **8:** 204 n.*348*, 212; **9:** 79 n.*146*
Barber (of Upperton, Eastbourne, Sussex):
Charlotte Lucy née Plume (b. 1849), **9:** 175 n.*294*, 176, 177, 185 n.*306*, 207, 208 n.*337*, 278, 329, 342
Edward Coates Massey, Mr. – surgeon, **9:** 175 n.294
Mary "May" Lucy (1877-1962), **9:** 175 n.*294*, 176, 178, 179, 182 n.*303*, 207, 218, 277, 278, 329, 348 n.*558*
Barber, John (1819-1883) – lawyer, **7:** 52 n.*82*, 53-55
Barbiere di Seviglia, Il (Rossini) – opera, **1:** 104 n.*116*
Barclay, Edith, **8:** 193 n.*323*
Barclay (of Sussex Square, Brighton, Sussex):
Ethel Florence (1864-1947), see Southwell
George Alexander Noël (b. 1866), **6:** 205 n.*320*, 309, 377, 414; **7:** 71, 92, 217, 312, 423, 519; **8:** 160, 248 n.*415*
Henry Alexander, Mr. (1833-1888) – teacher, **1:** 43, 54 n.*15*, 67, 68, 132 n.*165*; **3:** 24 n.*31*, 90 n.*139*, 91, 93-97, 144; **6:** 205 n.*320*, 308, 309, 376-378, 388, 414, 443; **7:** 28, 50, 70-72, 91, 128, 153-155, 215, 217, 303, 312, 313, 362, 366, 399, 423-425, 456, 473, 479, 508; **8:** 37 n.*48*, 38, 40, 130, 146, 160, 193, 226, 242, 347
Lucinda C. née Macy (b. 1834), **6:** 377, 378, 414, 444; **7:** 50, 70-72, 74, 91, 128, 153-155, 215, 217, 303, 312, 313, 362, 366, 399, 423-425, 456, 473, 479, 503, 508, 510; **8:** 37 n.*48*, 38, 40, 130, 146, 160, 193, 226,

242, 347, 415, 532; **9:** 84, 85 n.*153*, 169
Barclay, John, Rev. (1817-1886), **2:** 117 n.*224*, 118
Barclay, Mrs. (formerly Joyce), **7:** 211 n.*394*
Barclay Thompson, see Thompson
Bard, The (bk. Thomas Gray), **1:** 34
Bard and His Birthday, The (dr. William Brough), **4:** 322, 323 n.*409*
Barefaced Impostors (dr. John Doe and John Noakes), **4:** 205 n.*214*
Barff, Albert, Rev. (1829-1913), **5:** 135 n.*217*; **7:** 166 n.*313*
Baring, Frederick, Rev. (1806-1868), **4:** 11
Baring, Walter (1844-1915) – diplomat, **4:** 263 n.*308*
Barker (of Spelsbury, Oxfordshire):
Charlotte Olivia "Olive" (b. 1860?), **4:** 181, 304
Edith Mary (1864), **4:** 304
Edward Neale (b. 1854), **4:** 304
Helen Margaret (b. 1862), **4:** 180, 304
Margaret, Mrs. (b. 1830), **4:** 304; **7:** 499 n.*816*, 500
May Heatherington (b. 1857), **4:** 304, 305, 306 n.*375*, 333 n.*427*; **6:** 489; **7:** 499 n.*816*, 500, 515; **9:** 199 n.*326*
Mr. C. (brother), **4:** 304
Rayner C. (b. 1849), **4:** 304
Thomas Childe, Rev. (b. 1827), **4:** 303, 304 n.*371*, 305, 306 n.*375*; **7:** 499 n.*816*
Barker (of Thirkleby, Yorkshire):
Emily Jane (b. 1811), **4:** 238 n.*266*, 271
Jane, Mrs., **4:** 238 n.*266*, 271
Laura, see Mrs. Tom Taylor
Leila Florentina Catherine (b. 1825), **4:** 238 n.*266*, 271
Louisa Ann (1808-1819), **4:** 238 n.*266*, 271
Lucette Elizabeth (b. 1816), **4:** 238 n.*266*, 271
Lucy Perronet (b. 1805), **4:** 238 n.*266*, 271
Octavia Constance (b. 1827), **4:** 238 n.*266*, 271
Rosamund (1814-1853), **4:** 238 n.*266*, 271
Thomas, Rev. (1779-1868), **4:** 238 n.*266*
Barker, Mary Elizabeth née Bozzi-Granville (b. 1849) – elocutionist and reciter, **8:** 480 n.*778*, 530
Barker, Miss – dramatist, **7:** 515, 516 n.*835*
Barker, Mrs. – lodging-house keeper, **1:** 53
Barker Family – met at Eastbourne, **8:** 28 n.*30*
Barkly, Henry, Sir (1815-1898) – civil servant, **8:** 49 n.*72*, 52
Barmby, James, Rev. (b. 1823) – mathematical moderator, **2:** 107 n.*207*, 112, 117, 118
Barmby Moor, Yorkshire, **4:** 129, 130; **5:** 110 n.*173*
Barnack, Lincolnshire, **6:** 25, 106, 108
Barnard (of East Meon, Hampshire):
Anna Maria, Mrs. (b. 1818), **7:** 116 n.*216*

Henry, Mr. (b. 1815) – farmer, **7:** 116 n.*216*
Barnard, Charlotte "Claribel" Arlington (1830-1869) – song-writer, **6:** 26 n.*29*
Barnard, Frederick (1846-1896) – artist, **7:** 538, 539 n.*871*
Barnard, Miss – artist's model, **7:** 106
Barnard Castle, Durham, **2:** 97, 98; **3:** 119
Barnardo, Thomas John, Dr. (1845-1905) – physician, **9:** 109 n.*193*
Barnes – Vanbrugh (of Heavitree, Devon):
Angela Annie (b. 1869) – violinist, **8:** 317 n.*521*, 327, 361, 364, 368, 605, 621, 623 n.*986*, 628; **9:** 28 n.*43*, 29, 59, 92, 156
Edith S. Helen (b. 1868), **8:** 317 n.*521*, 322, 327, 357, 358, 360, 361, 373, 427, 439, 441, 451; **9:** 92, 156, 218
Frances M. E. née Nation (b. 1849), **8:** 317 n.*521*, 327, 328, 358, 361, 364, 373, 374, 406, 419, 420, 424, 429, 440, 441, 450, 451, 472, 503, 531, 581; **9:** 55 n.*97*, 156, 179
Irene (1872-1949) – actress, **8:** 317 n.*521*, 322, 327, 328, 339, 356, 357 n.*583*, 358, 361, 364, 418-420, 427, 429, 439, 441, 451, 556, 574, 575, 614; **9:** 219, 220 n.*349*
Kenneth Ralph (b. 1878), **8:** 317 n.*521*, 322, 327, 361, 373
Reginald Henry, Rev. (1831-1889), **8:** 317 n.*521*, 321, 327, 361, 364, 373, 374, 378, 419, 429, 441, 445, 450, 472, 486
Reginald "Reggie" W. R. (b. 1870), **8:** 317 n.*521*, 322, 327, 358, 361, 451
Violet "Vi" Augusta Mary (1867-1942), see Bourchier
Barnes, Catherine "Katie" (b. 1872), **8:** 147 n.*237*
Barnes, E. C. (fl. 1856-1882) – artist, **5:** 219 n.*350*
Barnes (of Christ Church, Oxford):
Frederick, Rev. Dr. (1771-1859), **3:** 24 n.*32*, 25, 26, 44, 61, 133; **4:** 23
Miss, **3:** 61; **4:** 89 n.*46*
Phillipa C. (b. 1809), **3:** 27, 44
Barnes (related to the Hendersons):
Miss, **7:** 271 n.*489*
Mrs., **7:** 273 n.*496*
Barnett, Morris (1800-1856) – dramatist, **8:** 575 n.*918*
Barons of Halton, **1:** 13
Barr, Elizabeth (b. 1821) – nurse, **8:** 364 n.*595*, 373, 445
Barraud:
Henry (1812-1874) – artist, **2:** 18 n.*31*
William (1810-1850) – artist, **2:** 18 n.*31*
Barrett (of Kensington, London):
Alfred W. (b. 1871), **7:** 533 n.*864*
Caroline E. née Heath (1835-1887) – actress, **7:** 533 n.*864*
Edith Dorothea (b. 1872), **7:** 533 n.*864*
Ellen A. (b. 1868), **7:** 533 n.*864*
Frank A. (b. 1870), **7:** 533 n.*864*
Katherine M. (b. 1869), **7:** 533 n.*864*

Wilson, Mr. (1846-1904) – actor, **7:** 525 n.*849*, 533 n.*864*, 540; **8:** 38 n.*50*, 59, 80, 81 n.*125*, 168, 208, 229 n.*387*, 381, 587
Barrett, George (1850-1894) – actor, **7:** 525 n.*849*, 540; **8:** 52 n.*77*, 80, 81 n.*125*, 168, 208, 381
Barrie, James Matthew (1860-1937) – writer and dramatist, **8:** 614 n.*974*; **9:** 226 n.*357*, 352 n.*564*
Barrington (of Cavendish Square, London):
Bernard Eric Edward, Hon. (1847-1918) – civil servant, **8:** 464 n.*749*
Christina née Graham (1848-1937), **8:** 464 n.*749*, 465
Barrington, Rutland (1853-1922) – actor and writer, **8:** 572 n.*912*
Barrow (of Southlands Park Road, Ryde, Isle of Wight):
Benjamin, Mr. (b. 1815?) – surgeon and Mayor of Ryde, **6:** 417, 418 n.*685*, 421
Mary, Mrs., **6:** 417, 418, 421
Barry, Ada – actress, **8:** 610 n.*966*
Barry (of Acton, Middlesex):
Arthur L. (b. 1870), **6:** 255 n.*405*
Edith Alice (b. 1862), **6:** 255 n.*405*
Flaneisto{?}, Mrs. (b. 1831), **6:** 254, 255 n.*405*
Foster Stable, Rev. (1829-1908), **6:** 254, 255 n.*405*
Mary Louisa (b. 1865), **6:** 255 n.*405*
Barry (of Whitby, Yorkshire):
Emily Eupatoria (b. 1854), **4:** 235 n.*262*; **5:** 178
John, Rev. (1819-1856), **4:** 235 n.*262*
John "Johnnie" Warren (1851-1920), **4:** 235 n.*262*
Letitia Anna née Mercer (1824-1911), **4:** 36, 235 n.*262*; **5:** 150 n.*241*, 178
Louisa Dorothy (b. 1852), **4:** 36, 180, 235 n.*262*; **5:** 178
Robert Mercer (b. 1853), **4:** 235 n.*262*
Thomas Gordon (1855-1856), **4:** 235 n.*262*
Barry (of Edmonton, Middlesex):
Ethel M. (b. 1867), **7:** 95 n.*174*
Horace, Mr. (b. 1829) – stockbroker, **7:** 95 n.*174*
Juliette B., Mrs. (b. 1829), **7:** 95 n.*174*
Barry, Katie – actress, **8:** 417 n.*675*
Barry, Sheil (1842-1897) – actor, **7:** 369, 370 n.*643*; **8:** 135 n.*220*
Barrymore, Maurice (1848-1905) – dramatist, **7:** 369 n.*641*
Bar Sinister, The (bk. Charles Collins), **8:** 15 n.*9*; **9:** 190 n.*314*
Bartlett, Robert Edward, Rev. (b. 1829), **8:** 395 n.*642*
Bartlett, William H. (1858-1932) – artist, **8:** 413 n.*669*
Bashford, Miss, **7:** 438 n.*726*
Basing, Hampshire, **6:** 437, 466
Basingstoke, Hampshire, **6:** 278, 334, 437, 438
Bassenthwaite, Cumberland, **2:** 94; **3:** 116
Bateman:
Ellen Douglas (1844-1936) – actress, **6:** 312 n.*515*

Hezekiah Linthicum, Mr. (1812-1875) – theatre manager, **6:** 301, 312 n.*515*

Isabel (1854-1934) – actress, **6:** 254 n.*403*, 311, 312 n.*515*; **8:** 586 n.*936*

Kate Josephine (1843-1917) – actress, **6:** 221 n.*349*, 311, 312 n.*515*

Sidney Frances née Cowell (1823-1881), **6:** 311, 312 n.*515*, 315

Virginia Frances (1853-1940) – actress, **6:** 312 n.*515*, 315 n.*523*; **8:** 478 n.*774*

Bateman, Jessie (1877-1940) – actress, **9:** 21 n.*24*

Bath, Somerset, **7:** 249, 250

Bath, The (pic. Sophie Anderson), **5:** 217, 218 n.*347*

Battersea Park, London, **6:** 232, 233

"Battle of Waterloo, The" (Lionel Tennyson) – poem, **4:** 61-63

Batty, Misses, **7:** 364 n.*635*

Battye (of Ingerthorpe Grange, near Ripon, Yorkshire):

Margaret née Scholefield, **2:** 57 n.*113*

Richard (1834-1873) – barrister, **2:** 57 n.*113*

William Walker, Mr. (b. 1797) – magistrate, **2:** 57 n.*113*

Baugh (of Portsmouth, Hampshire):

Mrs., **7:** 211 n.*393*

Thomas, Rev. (b. 1828), **7:** 211 n.*393*

Baughan (of James Street, Oxford):

Eliza Ann (b. 1860), **5:** 234 n.*376*

Rebecca, Mrs. (b. 1828) – dressmaker, **5:** 234 n.*376*

Baxter, Charles (1809-1879) – artist, **3:** 51 n.*77*

Baxter, Elizabeth (b. 1828) – printer, **7:** 503 n.*821*; **8:** 16, 21, 163, 166, 248, 307 n.*509*

Baxter, George (1804-1867) – engraver, **2:** 16 n.*27*

Bayard, Thomas Francis (1828-1898) – first American ambassador to Great Britain, **9:** 264 n.*416*

Bayly, Thomas Haynes (1797-1839) – dramatist, **1:** 26; **3:** 171 n.*250*; **8:** 478 n.*774*

Bayman, Mrs, **3:** 73 n.*114*

Bayne:

Mary Anne née Allen (1805-1888), **4:** 128, 207, 210 n.*219*, 269, 284, 287, 309; **5:** 70, 88, 99, 117, 153, 155, 157, 158, 252; **6:** 68, 71, 196, 198, 251, 272, 282, 292, 294, 397, 443, 466, 467; **7:** 41 n.*61*, 78, 93, 105, 112, 123, 140, 180, 182, 186, 187, 189, 193, 212, 220, 256, 277, 278, 304, 317, 348, 353, 354, 398, 429-431, 438, 441, 442, 444, 457, 460, 514, 515, 528, 536; **8:** 127, 140, 165, 219, 271, 319, 435

Thomas, Rev. (1803-1848), **1:** 14, 15, 61 n.*35*

Thomas Vere (1829-1908), **1:** schoolboy friend 14, 15, 43, takes MA 61 n.*35*, 101; **2:** 66 n.*131*, 109 n.*213*, 121; **3:** 72, 126, 127, 134; **4:** 54, 72 n.*16*, 73, 80-82, 128 n.*103*, 134, 135, 152, 194, proctor 206, 210, 259, 273, 295, 305; **5:** 25, 120 n.*189*, 148, 154, 157, 163 n.*268*, 164, 181, 184, 200, 244 n.*396*, 252, nominates Dodgson as pro-proctor 375,

376 n.*557*, 381; **6:** 66, 87, 89, 116 n.*180*, 148, 151, 153, 213-215, 263, buys picture 292 n.*482*, visits The Chestnuts 294, 295, 367, 381, 395, 438, 447, 461, prints *Fame's Penny Trumpet* for Dodgson 477; **7:** 36, 39, 80, 85, 89, resigns as censor 90, theatre trip 123, 187, 189, 193, 223, 256, 264 n.*477*, 270, 276, 279, 317, tests *Lanrick* 336, 348, Eastbourne trip 353, 354, 419, 423, 424, 429, 434, 440, 446, 453, 457, 458, resigns as curator of Common Room 499, 500, 501 n.*818*, 537; **8:** 11 n.*1*, commissions painting of Liddon 201 n.*343*, 245, 257 n.*433*, 260 n.*439*, discusses resignation of Faussett 262 n.*441*, 263, 265, 266 n.*447*, 273 n.*460*, 276 n.*464*, 283 n.*475*, 284 n.*476*, invests in steamships 289 n.*485*, 308 n.*511*, 317, sees *Alice* on stage 319 n.*523*, 380, 40th anniversary of matriculation 400, 429 n.*692*, death of mother 435, 455, 544, 551, 566, 593; **9:** 123, 232, 238-240, 251, 268 n.*424*

Baynes (of Norham Gardens, Oxford):
- Edward Reginald (b. 1890), **8:** 370 n.*608*; **9:** 229 n.*365*
- Robert Edward, Mr. (1849-1921) – lecturer in science, **6:** 307 n.*508*, 323, 328, 329, 410, 431, 436; **7:** 21 n.*19*, 23, 36, 108, 162, 370, 440, 490; **8:** 103 n.*170*, 153, 207, 245, 247, 296, 596; **9:** 229 n.*365*
- Thomasine Anne née Hutton (b. 1851), **8:** 370 n.*608*, 596; **9:** 229 n.*365*, 309, 324 n.*520*

Bayswater, London, **6:** 424, 454

Bazaar, Horticultural Gardens, London, **4:** 317

Bazaar, St. John's College Gardens, Oxford, **4:** 205-210

B.B. (dr. Francis Burnand), **4:** 279 n.*328*

"B.B." (early pseudonym), **1:** 48; **2:** 37, 39 n.*79*

Bea, David – friend of Putney cousins, **2:** 81

Beadon, Eleanor A. (b. 1856), **8:** 267 n.*451*

Beadon, Frederick, Rev. (1778-1879), **7:** 113 n.*209*

Beale, Kitty (b. 1877) – fellow lodger at Eastbourne, **9:** 177 n.*297*, 179, 214

Beale (of Grosvenor Street, London):
- Lionel Smith (1828-1906) – physician, **6:** 258 n.*410*, 288
- Miss, **6:** 258 n.*410*, 288, 349

Beales (or Beale), Miss, **9:** 161 n.*276*, 176, 220, 330, 340

Bean, Alexander Louis Wellington, Rev. (b. 1816), **1:** 56

Bean (of Bitterley, Shropshire):
- Henry Haffey, Mr. (b. 1810), **3:** 169 n.*246*
- Jane née Maister (b. 1808), **3:** 169 n.*246*

Beaton (of Battersea, Surrey):
- Caroline L., Mrs. (b. 1849), **6:** 482 n.*795*
- Ernest (b. 1871), **6:** 483
- Florence Louise "Boofy" (b. 1866), **6:** 482 n.*795*, 483; **9:** 146 n.*252*
- Walter H., Mr. (b. 1842) – timber merchant, **6:** 482 n.*795*

Beaumaris, Anglesey, **1:** 14

Beaumont, Margaret Anne, Lady (1832-1888), **6:** 120

Beaumont, Miss, **7:** 479 n.*780*

Beaumont, Mr. – actor, **8:** 609, 610 n.*966*
Beaumont Street, Oxford, **7:** 109
"Beautiful Star" (Sayles), **4:** 110 n.*79*
Beauty and the Beast (dr. Anon), **6:** 310 n.*513*; **7:** 367; **8:** 314
Beauty and the Beast (pic. Arthur Hughes), **5:** 86 n.*134*
Beauty and the Beast (dr. Eliza Keating), **7:** 95 n.*174*
Beauty and the Beast (dr. James Planché), **5:** 42 n.*52*
Beazley, Samuel (1786-1851) – dramatist, **8:** 334 n.*549*
Bebb (of Oxford):
  Alfred L. (b. 1888), **9:** 253 n.*396*
  Beatrice (b. 1889), **9:** 253 n.*396*
  Catharine (b. 1898), **9:** 253 n.*396*
  Gwyneth (b. 1890), **9:** 253 n.*396*
  Humphrey (b. 1894), **9:** 253 n.*396*
  Llewellyn John Montfort, Rev. (b. 1862) – lecturer, **9:** 253 n.*396*
  Mrs., **9:** 253 n.*396*
Beckenham, Kent, **6:** 254 n.*404*
Becker, Bernhard H. (b. 1833), alias "Hanson Lewis" – journalist, **8:** 150 n.*245*
Becket (dr. Alfred Tennyson), **9:** 78 n.*144*
Beckwith swimming entertainers, Hastings, **8:** 425 n.*686*; **9:** 25 n.*33*, 29, 334
Beddard, James, Dr. (b. 1837) – physician, **8:** 147 n.*238*
Bede, Cuthbert, real name Edward Bradley, Rev. (1827-1889) – writer, **1:** 41-43, 47
Bedford, Paul (1793-1871) – actor, **4:** 337 n.*436*; **5:** 17 n.*11*
Bedford Chapel, London, **7:** 23
Bedingfield, Louisa J. (b. 1843), **8:** 515 n.*831*
Beebe (of Yeovil, Somerset):
  Henry Thomas, Rev. (b. 1834), **7:** 491 n.*801*
  William Newton Percy (b. 1853), **7:** 491 n.*801*
Beerbohm Tree (of Sloane Square, London):
  Herbert, Mr. (1853-1917) – actor and manager, **8:** 584 n.*933*, 615, 616 n.*976*, 628 n.*993*; **9:** 212 n.*339*, 233
  Maud née Holt (1859-1937), **8:** 616 n.*976*, 628 n.*993*; **9:** 212 n.*339*, 233, 316
  Viola (1885-1938), **8:** 628 n.*993*, 634; **9:** 212 n.*339*, 316
Beere, Fanny Mary née Whitehead (1856-1915) – actress, **7:** 468 n.*769*
Beeston, Miss – governess, **7:** 472
Beeston Observatory, near Nottingham, **4:** 56
Beethoven, Ludwig von (1770-1827) – composer, **3:** 32, 134; **6:** 69
"Before Alice – The Boyhood of Lewis Carroll" (Collingwood), **1:** 37
Behind Time (dr. Benjamin Webster), **5:** 137 n.*220*
Behrends Family (of Blackwater Road, Eastbourne, Sussex), **9:** 17 n.*15*
Belasco, David (1859-1931) – dramatist, **5:** 38 n.*46*, 85 n.*133*

Belfast, Ireland, **7:** 447
Bell (of Upperton Road, Eastbourne, Sussex):
Agnes M. née Law (b. 1839), **7:** 68 n.*111*, 69, 70-72, 139, 469, 472
Ernest W. (b. 1877), **7:** 68 n.*111*
Grace (b. 1868), **7:** 68 n.*111*, 69, 72, 74, 75, 218
Helen F. "Nellie" (b. 1874), **7:** 68 n.*111*, 69, 75, 218
Major – army officer in India, **7:** 68 n.*111*, 69, 139, 469, 472
Mary F. (b. 1865), **7:** 68 n.*111*, 218, 472
Maud A. (b. 1869), **7:** 68 n.*111*, 69, 72, 74, 75, 218
Winifred (b. 1875), **7:** 68 n.*111*, 218
Bell (of Portland Place, London):
Charles Frederic Moberly, Mr. (1847-1911) – *Times* journalist, **9:** 96 n.*173*, 99, 118, 140
Clive (1885-1959), **9:** 96 n.*173*, 99 n.*179*, 118, 140, 219
Cynthia (1887-1961), **9:** 96 n.*173*, 99 n.*179*, 118, 140
Enid Hester Chataway Moberly (1881-1967), **9:** 96 n.*173*, 100, 101, 140
Ethel née Chataway (1854-1933), **6:** 421 n.*693*; **9:** 95, 96 n.*173*, 99, 118, 140, 219
Hilda Rotherwick (1879-1898), **9:** 96 n.*173*, 97 n.*176*, 101, 140, 219
Iris Mary (1883-1968), **9:** 96 n.*173*, 99-101, 140
Moberly (1877-1929), **9:** 96 n.*173*
Bell (of Westminster, London):
Elizabeth Sophia née Milner (b. 1828), **7:** 260 n.*470*, 495 n.*806*
George Charles, Rev. (1832-1913) – lecturer, **7:** 260 n.*470*, 495 n.*806*; **8:** 344 n.*568*
George Milner (b. 1872), **7:** 495 n.*806*
Helen Frances (1870-1946), **7:** 260 n.*470*, 495 n.*806*
Olive Dade (b. 1875), **7:** 495 n.*806*
Bell (of Devonshire Place, Eastbourne, Sussex):
Esther E. (b. 1846), **7:** 135 n.*251*
Margaret, Mrs. (b. 1811), **7:** 135 n.*251*
William, Dr. (b. 1805) – physician and homeopath, **7:** 135 n.*251*, 291
Bell, Francis Dillon, Hon. Sir (1822-1898) - agent-general for New Zealand, **8:** 66 n.*104*
Bell, George Charles (1832-1913), **4:** 110 n.*78*, 114, 116-118
Bell (of Camberwell, Surrey):
Mrs., **9:** 101 n.*183*
Percy, Mr. (b. 1848) – actor, **9:** 101 n.*183*
Bella's Birthday (dr. Charles Stephenson), **6:** 253 n.*402*
Belles of the Kitchen, The (dr. Anon), **8:** 285, 286 n.*480*
Belle's Stratagem, The (dr. Hannah Cowley), **7:** 326, 327 n.*579*
Bellet (of Great Malvern, Worcestershire):
George (1835-1886), **1:** 87, 88 n.*91*, 101; **2:** 73 n.*147*, 109 n.*213*; **7:** 268 n.*482*
George, Rev. (b. 1798), **7:** 268 n.*482*

Belletti, Giovanni Battista (1813-1890) – opera singer, **3:** 98 n.*147*
Bellew, H. Kyrle (1855-1911) – actor, **7:** 387 n.*667*
Bellingham, Henry (1852?-1897?) – dramatist, **5:** 117 n.*182*, 145 n.*232*
Bellini, Vincenzo (1801-1835) – composer, **1:** 103 n.*114*; **3:** 101 n.*149*; **4:** 104 n.*69*; **5:** 253 n.*417*
Bell's Life, **3:** 56 n.*85*, 147; **5:** 182, 183 n.*302*
Belmore, George (1828-1875) – actor, **6:** 135 n.*208*
Beloe, Henry John Greswell, Rev. (b. 1857), **8:** 161 n.*261*, 184, 186, 240
Beloved, The or *The Bride* (pic. Dante Rossetti), **5:** 71 n.*107*
Benett, William Charles (1844-1922) – civil servant, **3:** 136 n.*197*
Benham (of Norham Gardens, Oxford):
  Agnes, Mrs. (b. 1870), **9:** 267 n.*422*
  Alfred, Mr. (b. 1869) – hospital porter, **9:** 267 n.*422*
  Philip, **9:** 267 n.*422*
  Ruth, **9:** 267 n.*422*
Benham (of Wigmore Street, London):
  James, Mr. (b. 1820) – ironmonger, **8:** 123 n.*199*, 124, 153, 156
  Walter J. (b. 1851), **8:** 123 n.*199*, 124, 153, 156
Ben Lomond, Scotland, **3:** 104
Benn, Joseph (b. 1836) – land owner, **2:** 92
Benner, Emanuel (1836-1909) – artist, **8:** 366 n.*599*
Bennett, Charles Henry (1829-1867) – illustrator, **1:** 117 n.*142*; **2:** 37 n.*74*, 38 n.*77*, 61 n.*123*, 113 n.*219*; **3:** 30 n.*43*; **5:** 241 n.*390*, 242 n.*394*
Bennett, George John (1800-1879) – actor, **1:** 133 n.*167*
Bennett, John W., Rev. (b. 1844), **8:** 59 n.*93*
Bennett, Mr. – dentist, **7:** 485 n.*789*, 486, 494
Bennett, William James Early, Rev. (1804-1886), **5:** 51 n.*70*
Bennie (of The Rectory, Glenfield, Leicester):
  Elizabeth "Doe" A. (b. 1856), **5:** 20; **6:** 53 n.*77*, 54, 55, 110; **7:** 129; **9:** 216 n.*344*
  James Noble, Rev. (1832-1899), **6:** 53 n.*77*, 55, 110-112; **7:** 70 n.*113*, 128, 296; **9:** 216 n.*344*
  Madeline L., Mrs. (b. 1836), **6:** 54, 55, 110, 112; **7:** 70 n.*113*, 128, 130, 131, 296
  Mary "Minnie" J. (b. 1856), **5:** 20; **6:** 53 n.*77*, 54, 55, 110; **7:** 129; **9:** 216 n.*344*
Benson, Ada (1840-1882) – teacher, **7:** 32 n.*43*
Benson:
  Frank Robert, Mr. (1858-1939) – actor and manager, **8:** 423 n.*684*, 501, 619; **9:** 21 n.*24*, 22, 280
  Gertrude Constance née Featherstonhaugh (1860-1946), **9:** 280
Benson, Lizzie, **6:** 400
Benson, Richard Meux, Rev. (1824-1915), **4:** 33, 76 n.*23*, 163 n.*157*; **7:** 440
Bentley, Edith – nurse, **9:** 32, 33 n.*55*
Béranger, Jean Baptiste Antoine Emile (1814-1883) – artist, **5:** 222 n.*354*

Beresford, Selina Mary Emily (1861-1880), **6:** 29 n.*35*
Beresford Hope (of Beresford Hall, Staffordshire):
Agnes (1849-1917), **6:** 162, 163 n.*252*, 165
Alexander James, Rt. Hon. (1820-1887), **6:** 162, 163 n.*252*, 220; **8:** 76, 77 n.*120*, 78
Bridget (d. 1896), **6:** 162, 163 n.*252*, 165
Catherine (d. 1869), **6:** 163 n.*252*
Charles Thomas (1855-1906), **6:** 163 n.*252*
Etheldreda (b. 1847), **6:** 162, 163 n.*252*, 165
Hugh (1861-1863), **6:** 163 n.*252*
Louisa Mary (d. 1923), **6:** 163 n.*252*
Margaret (1847-1900), **6:** 162, 163 n.*252*, 165
Mary Frances (1855-1944), **6:** 162, 163 n.*252*, 165
Mildred (1846-1896), **6:** 163 n.*252*
Mildred Arabella Charlotte née Cecil, Lady (d. 1881), **6:** 162, 163 n.*252*, 220; **8:** 76, 77 n.*120*
Philip Beresford (1851-1916), **6:** 163 n.*252*
Berger, Nettie – orphan, **8:** 194, 195 n.*328*, 208, 501
Beringer (of Marylebone, London):
Aimée "Amy" née Daniell (1856-1936) – dramatist and writer, **8:** 407 n.*661*, 409, 411, 415, 442, 457
Esmé "Dolly" (b. 1875) – actress, **8:** 400, 401 n.*653*, 407, 411, 427, 429, 457
Mary "May" (b. 1875), **8:** 407 n.*661*, 457
Oscar, Prof. (1844-1922) – composer, **8:** 407 n.*661*
Véra (b. 1879) – actress, **8:** 400, 401 n.*653*, 402 n.*654*, 404, 407, 408, 411, 427, 429, 442, 457
Berkeley (of Lindsay Lodge, Hook, Surrey):
Algernon (b. 1865), **7:** 255 n.*464*
Comyres R., Mr. (b. 1811) – solicitor, **7:** 255 n.*464*
Edith Mary Alice (b. 1874) – grand-daughter, **7:** 255 n.*464*
Mary (b. 1847) – widowed daughter-in-law, **7:** 255 n.*464*
Mary A., Mrs. (b. 1826), **7:** 255 n.*464*
Berkeley, Olly (b. 1880?) – reciter, **8:** 364 n.*596*
Berlin, Germany, **5:** 265
Berners, Charles Hugh (b. 1842), MA Christ Church, **4:** 263 n.*308*
Berry, Mary P. (b. 1821), **6:** 94 n.*147*, 96
Bertram, Dixon (b. 1826) – undergraduate at Christ Church, **4:** 163 n.*156*
Bertrand, Joseph Louis François (1822-1900) – mathematician, **8:** 306 n.*507*
Berwick, Northumberland, **3:** 93, 94
Beryl, Sara – actress, **8:** 230 n.*388*
Besilsleigh, Berkshire, **3:** 165; **7:** 330, 531; **8:** 102, 188, 320, 329; **9:** 61, 181, 183, 185, 193, 199, 223, 224, 239, 264, 279, 302, 307, 313, 314, 323, 328

Besley, Henry – dramatist, **9:** 87 n.*157*
Best, William – dramatist, **5:** 117 n.*182*, 145 n.*232*
Betchworth, Surrey, **9:** 345 n.*552*
Betsy Baker! (dr. John Morton), **4:** 263 n.*308*
Bevan (of Marylebone, London):
  Margaret C. (b. 1845), **7:** 532 n.*861*, 536, 537
  Mrs., **7:** 536
Bevers (of Broad Street, Oxford):
  Edmund Augustine (b. 1850), see below
  Edmund, Mr. (1812-1880) – dentist, **4:** 65 n.*2*
Bevers (of Woodstock Road, Oxford):
  Edmund Augustine, Mr. (b. 1850) – dentist and surgeon, **7:** 243 n.*446*; **9:** 131 n.*229*, 195
  Edmund Cecil (1876-1961), **7:** 243 n.*446*
  Helen J., Mrs. (b. 1853), **7:** 243 n.*446*; **9:** 131 n.*229*
  Maud (b. 1877), **7:** 243 n.*446*; **9:** 131 n.*229*
  Violet (b. 1878), **7:** 243 n.*446*; **9:** 131 n.*229*
Bewell, Rev. – American clergyman, **2:** 73
Bewerley Hall, Yorkshire, **5:** 247 n.*401*
Bexhill, Sussex, **9:** 220, 275
Bexhill Convalescent Home, **8:** 240
Bexley School, **9:** 303
Beyer, Helene – artists' model, **4:** 254 n.*293*
Bible, The, **1:** 63, 123
Bible Society, **4:** 85
Bickersteth (of Hampstead, London):
  Amy (b. 1857), **7:** 262 n.*476*
  Edith (b. 1870), **7:** 262 n.*476*
  Edward Henry, Rev. (1825-1906), **7:** 262 n.*476*
  Effie Maude (b. 1868), **7:** 262 n.*476*
  Elizabeth Sarah (b. 1852), **7:** 262 n.*476*
  Emily Rose (b. 1850?), **7:** 262 n.*476*
  Mary Jane (b. 1859), **7:** 262 n.*476*
  Samuel (1857-1937), see below
Bickersteth (of Aylesbury, Buckinghamshire):
  Edward, Dr. (1814-1892) – archdeacon of Buckingham, **7:** 63 n.*99*
  Martha Mary Anne née Vickers (1799-1881), **7:** 63 n.*99*
Bickersteth, Edward, Rt. Rev. (1814-1892), **5:** 105 n.*163*
Bickersteth (of Ripon, Yorkshire):
  Edward Ernest (1853-1872), **3:** 150 n.*218*; **5:** 62, 106 n.*164*, 126
  Elizabeth née Garde (1815-1894), **3:** 150 n.*218*; **5:** 67, 126, 138
  Florence Elizabeth (1852-1923), **3:** 150 n.*218*; **4:** 179; **5:** 19, 55, 106 n.*164*, 107, 126; **6:** 16
  Henry Cecil (1848-1896), **3:** 150 n.*218*
  John "Johnnie" Joseph (1850-1932), **3:** 150 n.*218*; **5:** 105; **6:** 150 n.*229*

Montague Cyril (1858-1936), **3:** 150 n.*218*; **5:** 106 n.*164*; **9:** 226 n.*358*
Robert, Rt. Rev. (1816-1884), **3:** 150 n.*218*; **5:** 42 n.*54*, 57 n.*82*, 105 n.*163*, 106 n.*164*
Robert "Robin" (1847-1916), **3:** 150 n.*218*; **5:** 57 n.*82*, 67, 105 n.*163*, 106 n.*164*
Bickersteth (of Lancaster Gate, London):
Edward Monier (1882-1976), **7:** 264 n.*476*
Ella Chlora Faithfull née Monier Williams (1859-1954), **4:** 179; **5:** 19, 146 n.*235*, 151 n.*243*, 163 n.*268*, 164 n.*271*, 207; **6:** 342; **7:** 32 n.*42*, 119 n.*223*, 264 n.*476*, 431; **8:** 115, 116 n.*189*
Geoffrey Langdale (1884-1974), **7:** 264 n.*476*
John Burgon (1888-1979), **7:** 264 n.*476*
Kenneth Julian Faithfull (1885-1962), **7:** 264 n.*476*
Samuel, Rev. (1857-1937), **7:** 264 n.*476*, 431 n.*718*
Biddulph, Sarah Wilfreda née Palmer, Lady (d. 1910), **8:** 562 n.*895*, 566, 621, 622
Bigby Family – fellow lodgers at Eastbourne, **7:** 198 n.*371*
Bigg (of Christ Church, Oxford):
Charles, Dr. (1840-1908) – tutor, **4:** 171 n.*166*; **7:** 543 n.*876*; **8:** 85 n.*138*; **9:** 255, 256 n.*404*
Dorothy May (b. 1880), **8:** 85 n.*138*; **9:** 255, 256 n.*404*
Millicent May née Sale (b. 1844), **8:** 85 n.*138*, 336; **9:** 255, 256 n.*404*
Millicent "Millie" C. (b. 1872), **8:** 85 n.*138*, 336, 337, 340, 368; **9:** 255, 256 n.*404*
Bigg, Lionel Oliver, Rev. (b. 1842), **6:** 47 n.*67*
Bignell, Mr. – landlord of York Hotel, Sandown, **6:** 411
Bilbao Bar, off Spain, **7:** 398
Bingen, Germany, **5:** 361, 362
Binsey, near Oxford, **7:** 175, 341
Binsey Church, **6:** 389
Binsted House, Reading, **6:** 115
Birch (of Abbot's Hospital, Guildford, Surrey):
Miss, **6:** 94 n.*147*, 96
William, Mr. (1804-1880), **6:** 94 n.*147*
Birch, Miss – singer, **1:** 53
Birdlip, Gloucestershire, **4:** 186
Birds in Their Little Nests Agree (dr. Charles Rae), **7:** 23 n.*24*
Birkenhead, Cheshire, **7:** 414
Birkett (of Sevenoaks, Kent):
Dorothy E. (b. 1880), **9:** 88 n.*158*, 166
Gertrude (b. 1883), **9:** 88 n.*158*, 166
Birks, Thomas Rawson (1810-1883) – writer, **7:** 351 n.*613*
Birmingham, **3:** 121; **5:** 189; **6:** 279; **7:** 53; **8:** 122, 496, 498
Birthday Picnic, A (pic. Arthur Hughes), **5:** 211 n.*339*
Birthplace of Podgers, The (dr. John Hollingshead), **8:** 574 n.*916*

Bischoff (of Long Ditton, Surrey):
Charles "Charlie" Edward (1873-1914), **6:** 485 n.*799*; **7:** 255
Constance "Connie" Mabel (b. 1875), **6:** 485 n.*799*; **7:** 255
Fanny née Pollock (1850-1878) – first wife, **6:** 485 n.*799*
Flora Homera (b. 1876), **6:** 485 n.*799*; **7:** 255
Frances Mary "May" (b. 1871), **6:** 485 n.*799*; **7:** 255; **9:** 77 n.*142*
Hugh Crompton (1877-1942), **6:** 485 n.*799*; **7:** 255
Menella "Marla" Frances née Dodgson (1848-1917) – second wife, **1:** 106 n.*120*; **2:** 51 n.*102*, 81; **6:** 484, 485 n.*799*; **7:** 176 n.*325*, 255, 289, 314, 415, 527
Percy William (1881-1953), **6:** 485 n.*799*; **7:** 176 n.*325*
Thomas Hume (1886-1951), **6:** 485 n.*799*
Thomas William, Mr. (1845-1928) – solicitor, **6:** 485 n.*799*; **7:** 176 n.*325*, 255
Bishop, Alfred (1848-1928) – actor, **8:** 400, 401 n.*653*
Bishop, Henry Rowley (1786-1855) – composer, **2:** 87 n.*174*; **5:** 225, 226 n.*359*
Bishop, Matilda Ellen (1844-1913) – teacher, **8:** 195 n.*330*, 331, 338, 340, 342; **9:** 236 n.*372*
"Bishop and the Caterpillar, The" (Mary Manners) – poem, **8:** 530 n.*850*
Bishop Auckland, Durham, **3:** 85, 86; **4:** 22
"Bishop Gardiner" (in *Henry VIII*), **2:** 9
Bishop of Bangor, James Colquhoun Campbell (1813-1895), **4:** 198 n.*201*
Bishop of Calcutta, Edward Ralph Johnson (1829-1911), **8:** 560 n.*891*
Bishop of Carlisle, Harvey Goodwin (1818-1891), **8:** 208 n.*357*
Bishop of Central Africa, Charles Alan Smythies (1844-1894), **8:** 517 n.*833*
Bishop of Chester, William Stubbs (1825-1901), **8:** 89 n.*144*, 470 n.*761*, 545, 553 n.*882*
Bishop of Columbo, James Chapman (1799-1879), **2:** 73; **4:** 80 n.*32*
Bishop of Derry, William Alexander (1824-1911), **6:** 458 n.*753*, 459; **8:** 55 n.*82*
Bishop of Durham, Charles Thomas Longley (1794-1868), **2:** 119 n.*228*; **3:** 64 n.*96*; **4:** 22
Bishop of Elphin, Charles Dodgson (1722-1796), **1:** 9; **2:** 62 n.*124*
Bishop of Exeter, Henry Phillpotts (1778-1869), **1:** 46
Bishop of Kildare, **2:** 62
Bishop of Limerick, **2:** 62
Bishop of Lincoln, Edward King (1829-1910), **8:** 542, 543 n.*867*, 550 n.*877*
Bishop of Lincoln, John Jackson (1811-1885), **2:** 69; **4:** 34
Bishop of London, Henry Compton (1632-1713), **1:** 26, 27
Bishop of London, John Jackson (1811-1885), **7:** 173
Bishop of Mississippi, Hugh Miller Thompson (1830-1902), **9:** 315 n.*503*
Bishop of New York, Horatio Potter (1802-1887), **1:** 46
Bishop of Ossory, Charles Dodgson (1722-1796), **1:** 9; **2:** 62, 63
Bishop of Oxford, John Feilder Mackarness (1820-1889), **8:** 253 n.*426*

Bishop of Oxford, Samuel Wilberforce (1805-1873), **1:** 46; **2:** 73; **3:** 37 n.*58*; **4:** 21, 34, 55, 57
Bishop of Oxford, William Stubbs (1825-1901), **8:** 89 n.*144*, 470 n.*761*, 545, 553 n.*882*
Bishop of Ripon, Charles Thomas Longley (1794-1868), **1:** 93 n.*97*; **2:** 8 n.*4*, 9 n.*7*, 10, 56, 86 n.*171*, 101, 102 n.*197*, 119 n.*228*
Bishop of Salisbury, Walter Kerr Hamilton (1808-1869), **4:** 59
Bishop of Southwark, Huyshe Wolcott Yeatman (1845-1922), **9:** 317 n.*506*
Bishop of Victoria, John Shaw Burdon (d. 1907), **8:** 189, 190 n.*319*
Bishop's Palace, Ripon, **1:** 51; **2:** 9 n.*7*, 55, 56 n.*111*, 58
Bishopstone, Sussex, **7:** 458, 470
Black, William (1841-1898) – writer, **7:** 285, 286 n.*518*
Blackett, Selwyn (1854-1935) – stockbroker, **6:** 462 n.*762*
Black Eyed Susan (dr. Francis Burnand), **5:** 233 n.*372*
Black-eyed Susan (dr. Roy Redgrave, adapt. Douglas Jerrold), **9:** 332 n.*531*, 333
Blackfriars Road, London, **5:** 88 n.*135*
Blackgang Chine, Isle of Wight, **6:** 424
Blackheath, Surrey, **7:** 158, 159
Blackmore, Mr. – theatrical agent, **8:** 617 n.*979*
Blackmore, Richard, Rev. (b. 1835), **1:** 87, 88 n.*91*; **2:** 49 n.*100*, 113, 114 n.*220*, 116; **3:** 41, 42 n.*66*, 53 n.*80*
Blackwater, Hampshire, **6:** 91, 94
Blackwell (of Mattingley, Hampshire):
John William, Rev. (b. 1835), **6:** 425 n.*700*
Sybil Agnes (b. 1868), **6:** 425 n.*700*
Blackwood's Magazine, **2:** 52
Blackwood's Theatrical Agency, **9:** 54
Blagrave (possibly of Guildford, Surrey):
Alice (niece of Miss Blagrave), **6:** 92 n.*143*
Miss, **6:** 92 n.*143*
Blair, Miss – friend of the Husseys, **8:** 88 n.*142*, 90, 91
Blakeley, Mrs. – friend of Frederick Holiday, **8:** 212 n.*362*
Blakemore (of Birmingham):
Annie Alice (b. 1858), **7:** 53 n.*83*, 526; **8:** 122, 496; **9:** 68 n.*123*
Arthur Villiers (b. 1866), **7:** 53 n.*83*, 69; **8:** 122, 149 n.*243*, 496
Arthur Villiers, Mr. (1824-1883) – hardware merchant, **7:** 53 n.*83*, 69, 70, 136, 526
Edith Rose "Dolly" (1872-1947), **7:** 52, 53 n.*83*, 54, 55, 56, 58, 61, 63, 69, 70, 74, 129, 130, 133-136, 238, 292, 295; **8:** 122, 123, 132, 134, 137, 496, 498, 566 n.*902*; **9:** 68 n.*123*
Sarah Elizabeth née King (b. 1838), **7:** 53 n.*83*, 55, 58 n.*93*, 61, 63, 64, 69, 70, 129, 133-136, 295, 526; **8:** 122 n.*195*, 124 n.*200*, 134, 137, 496, 498
Blanchard, Edward Leman (1820-1889) – dramatist, **2:** 24 n.*44*;

5: 127 n.*203*
Blanche, see Adams
Blandain (French/Belgium border), **5:** 258
Blandford, Dorset, **7:** 248, 249
Blenheim – ship, **4:** 24
Blenheim Palace, **9:** 109 n.*194*
Bligh (of Cobham Hall, Kent):
Alice Isabella Harriet (1860-1943), **4:** 178, 239 n.*267*, 326 n.*415*
Arthur Frederick Pelham (1865-1924), **4:** 239 n.*267*
Constance Violet Lucy (b. 1869), **4:** 239 n.*267*
Edith Louisa Mary (1853-1904), **4:** 239 n.*267*
Edward Henry Stuart (1851-1900), 7th Earl of Darnley, **4:** 239 n.*267*; **6:** 340 n.*565*
Harriet Mary née Pelham, Lady (d. 1905), **4:** 239 n.*267*
Ivo Francis Walter (1859-1927), **4:** 239 n.*267*, 326 n.*415*
John Stuart, Lord (1827-1896), 6th Earl of Darnley, **4:** 239 n.*267*
Kathleen Susan Emma (1854-1928), **4:** 239 n.*267*
Mary Rose Florence (1868-1896), **4:** 239 n.*267*
Bligh (of Cobham Hall, Kent):
Edward, Lord (1795-1835), 5th Earl of Darnley, **4:** 239 n.*267*, 326 n.*415*
Emma Jane née Parnell, Lady (d. 1884), **4:** 239 n.*267*
John Stuart (1827-1896), see above
Blomfield, Frederick Charles (b. 1865) – pupil of Wilfred Dodgson, **7:** 126 n.*236*
Blondin, Charles (1824-1897) – acrobat, **4:** 88 n.*44*
Blore (of Canterbury, Kent):
George John, Dr. (1835-1916) – teacher, **1:** 87, 88 n.*91,* 91; **2:** 113, 114 n.*220*; **4:** 68 n.*8*; **5:** 54 n.*77*, 55, 153, 155, 251, 252, 375; **6:** 147; **7:** 519; **8:** 270 n.*456*, 273
Mary Margaret "Margie" (b. 1873), **8:** 273
Mary née Allen (b. 1843), **7:** 93 n.*168*; **8:** 270 n.*456*, 272, 273, 305, 315
Blücher (of Elsinore, Denmark):
Emily Alice (1875-1941), **7:** 274 n.*498*
Gustav Bridges Fergus Gebhard Lebrecht (1873-1935), **7:** 274 n.*498*
Leila Constance née Taylor, Countess (b. 1853), **7:** 274 n.*498*
"Blücher's War Song," **2:** 48 n.*96*
Bluebeard (dr. Anon), **5:** 41
Blue-beard (dr. Henry Byron), **5:** 157 n.*255*
Blue Beard (dr. George Colman), **6:** 378 n.*619*
Blue Beard (dr. Louisa MacDonald), **6:** 224, 225 n.*353*
"Blue Beard" (Perrault character in imaginary tale), **3:** 13
Blue lady ghost, **6:** 391 n.*642*
Bluett, see Baker
Blunt (of Hackney, Middlesex):
Alice (b. 1876), **7:** 51 n.*80*

Arthur (b. 1874), **7:** 51 n.*80*
Catherine (b. 1868), **7:** 51 n.*80*
Edith (b. 1879), **7:** 51 n.*80*
Edwin, Mr. (b. 1831) – Admiralty legal clerk, **7:** 51 n.*80*
Elizabeth, Mrs. (b. 1839), **7:** 51 n.*80*
George (b. 1871), **7:** 51 n.*80*
Harry (b. 1869), **7:** 51 n.*80*
Blunt, Arthur, see Cecil
Blunt, Herbert William (b. 1864), MA Christ Church, **8:** 446 n.*715*
Blunt, John Henry (1823-1884) – writer, **5:** 103 n.*160*
Blyth, Arthur Sir (1823-1891) – agent-general for Australia, **8:** 64 n.*102*, 66
Board of Health, London, **4:** 271; **5:** 33
Board of Trade, London, **6:** 41
Boase, Charles William (1828-1895) – lecturer, **7:** 33 n.*44*
Boat Race (Oxford & Cambridge), **2:** 51
Bodda, Frank – singer, **1:** 53
Boddington, Mrs., **7:** 71 n.*116*, 72, 128
Bode (of Warnborough Road, Oxford):
Edith E. (b. 1852), **6:** 85 n.*127*; **7:** 130-132
Hester, Mrs. (b. 1810), **3:** 35 n.*54*
John Ernest, Rev. (1816-1874), **3:** 35 n.*54*, 42, 43; **4:** 38
Bodington, Nathan (1848-1911) – teacher, **7:** 330, 331 n.*588*
Bodleian Library, Oxford, **2:** 39 n.*78*, 62, 118 n.*225*; **4:** 82, 309; **6:** 455; **7:** 104, 346, 347, 520; **8:** 196; **9:** 197
Bodley, George Frederick (1827-1907) – architect, **6:** 340, 341 n.*566*
Boger, Amelia (b. 1841), **7:** 41 n.*61*, 189
Bognor, Sussex, **6:** 227-231, 233, 236
Bois de Boulogne, Paris, **5:** 362
Bolland (of Worcester):
Margaret "Meta" J. M. (b. 1874), **9:** 43 n.*73*
William Ernest, Mr. (b. 1847) – headmaster, **9:** 43 n.*73*
Bolster, John Abraham, Canon, **4:** 34
Bolton Manor, Cumberland, **1:** 11
Bonchurch, Isle of Wight, **6:** 295, 298, 343, 362, 478
Bond, Anne Lydia (1822-1881) – artist and photographic colourist, **6:** 318 n.*527*, 342, 485
Bond, Jessie (1853-1942) – actress and vocalist, **8:** 572 n.*912*
Bond of Brotherhood (bk. Elihu Burritt), **1:** 134 n.*169*
Bond Street, London, **4:** 256, 341
Bond Street Gallery, **8:** 366 n.*599*
Bo'ness, Scotland, **6:** 179 n.*278*, 180, 181
Bon Gaultier, alias Sir Theodore Martin (1816 -1909) – writer, **2:** 44 n.*89*
"Bonnie Prince Charlie" (Anon) – song, **2:** 100
Bontein (of St. James's Palace, London):

Eva Louisa (b. 1861), **6:** 224 n.*352*, 424
James (1821-1884) – gentleman usher to Queen Victoria, **6:** 224 n.*352*, 424
James Shelley (b. 1859), **6:** 224 n.*352*
Katherine Cecilia née Shelley (1840-1902), **6:** 224 n.*352*, 424
Booker, Harry, alias M. H. Egan (1850-1924) – American comedian, **7:** 153 n.*290*
Bookseller, The, **8:** 21
Boole, George (1815-1864) – mathematician, **6:** 463, 464 n.*764*; **8:** 153 n.*250*
Booth, Hiram Crompton – photographer, **1:** 54 n.*15*, 80
Booth (of Northampton):
Mr., **6:** 309 n.*511*
Mrs., **6:** 309 n.*511*
Richard J. (b. 1866) – pupil of Henry Barclay, **6:** 309 n.*511*
Boothby (of the Rotheram area, Yorkshire):
Alice, **6:** 109
Mr., **6:** 109
Bootle's Baby (dr. Hugh Moss), **8:** 405 n.*659*, 469, 485, 569
Boots at the Swan, The (dr. Charles Selby), **3:** 153 n.*223*, 171 n.*250*
Born to Good Luck (dr. Tyrone Power), **4:** 358, 359 n.*468*
Borobridge (or Boroughbridge), Yorkshire, **3:** 170
Borough (of Chetwynd Park, Shropshire):
Charles Gawen (b. 1859), **6:** 387
Elizabeth Charlotte née Roberts-Gawen (1824-1907), **6:** 387
John Charles Burton, Mr. (1810-1894) – magistrate, **6:** 387 n.*633*
John Sidney Burton (b. 1852), **6:** 387 n.*633*
Thomas George (b. 1856), **6:** 387 n.*633*
Borrage Terrace, Ripon, Yorkshire, **2:** 14 n.*23*
Borrell's (or Borell's) Restaurant, Great Morskoi, Russia, **5:** 338, 347
Borrowdale, Cumberland, **2:** 92
Borrowman, Mary (b. 1819) – nurse, **9:** 235 n.*371*
Bosanquet (of Dingestow Court, Monmouth):
Frederick Albert (1837-1923), **4:** 318 n.*403*
Samuel Courthorpe (1832-1925), **1:** 49, 50 n.*2*, 58 n.*24*, 66, 78, 79; **2:** 79; **3:** 36 n.*55*; **4:** 33, 318 n.*403*; **6:** 28 n.*33*, 149, 239
Bosanquet, Robert Holford Macdowall (1841-1912) – lecturer, **7:** 486 n.*791*, 517 n.*837*; **8:** 196 n.*332*
Bostock, Phoebe, see Irwin
Bostock Scholarship, **1:** 97, 98 n.*104*
Boston, Massachusetts, **4:** 145; **8:** 205 n.*351*
Bosworth, Joseph, Rev. Dr. (1798-1876) – professor of Anglo-Saxon, **5:** 208 n.*332*
Botanical Gardens, London, **1:** 102
Botanical Gardens, Oxford, **4:** 200; **8:** 196, 216, 339; **9:** 223

Bothmar, Countess von née Taylor, **8:** 438 n.*703*
Bottle of Smoke, A (dr. Anon), **2:** 80 n.*158*
"Bottom" (in *Midsummer Night's Dream*), **2:** 124
Boucicault (possibly of London):
Agnes Kelly née Robertson, **4:** 159, 160 n.*150*; **5:** 64
Dion, Mr. (1822-1890) – dramatist, **2:** 20 n.*36*, 123 n.*238*; **3:** 106 n.*154*, 120 n.*170*; **4:** 159, 160 n.*150*, 248 n.*282*, 337 n.*436*, 359 n.*468*; **5:** 64 n.*95*, 123 n.*195*; **6:** 86 n.*129*; **7:** 318 n.*567*; **8:** 374 n.*616*
Dionysius "Dot" George (1859-1929) – actor, **7:** 369 n.*642*, 438 n.*727*; **9:** 347, 348 n.*557*
Nina (1867-1950), **6:** 86 n.*129*
Boughton, Mrs. – lodging-house keeper, **4:** 81
Bouguereau, William Adolphe (1825-1905) – artist, **5:** 223 n.*355*; **6:** 73 n.*108*
Boulter Scholarship, **1:** 45
Bourchardt or Bourshaw, Mr., **5:** 123 n.*196*, 127
Bourchier (of Hove, Sussex):
Arthur (1864-1927) – actor and manager, **8:** 68, 69 n.*111*; **9:** 219, 220 n.*349*
Violet "Vi" Augusta Mary (Vanbrugh) née Barnes (1867-1942) – actress, **8:** 317 n.*521*, 322, 327, 333, 360, 373, 374 n.*616*, 418, 419, 424, 451, 473, 586, 587, 620; **9:** 83, 132 n.*231*, 219, 220 n.*349*
Bourke (of Pulborough, Sussex):
George Wingfield, Rev. (1829-1903), **4:** 313 n.*391*
Mary Henrietta née Longley (1837?-1906), **1:** 93; **2:** 10 n.*10*, 55, 104; **3:** 85, 151, 152 n.*220*; **4:** 313 n.*391*; **5:** 179 n.*296*
Walter Longley (1859-1939), **4:** 313 n.*391*, 325 n.*412*
Bourne (of Kenilworth, Warwickshire):
Charlotte Jane (1818-1909) – distant relative, **6:** 355 n.*587*
Lucy Henrietta (1829-1903) – distant relative, **6:** 410
Bournemouth, Hampshire, **4:** 348
Bousfield, Misses, **7:** 155 n.*292*, 235 n.*434*
Bouverie, Edward Pleydell (1818-1889) – politician, **4:** 201 n.*208*
Bowden, James, Rev. (b. 1835), **7:** 436 n.*724*
Bower (of Ripon, Yorkshire):
Abraham, Mr. (1802-1884) – magistrate, **3:** 11 n.*8*
Anne Henrietta Gage (b. 1851), **3:** 11 n.*8*
Caroline Cornelia van Cortlandt (b. 1852), **3:** 11 n.*8*
Cornelia née Morris (1820-1905), **3:** 11 n.*8*
Frederick Orpen (1855-1948), **3:** 11 n.*8*
Herbert Morris (1854-1940), **3:** 11 n.*8*
Sophia Mary Felipse (b. 1848), **3:** 11 n.*8*
Bowers (of Manchester):
George Hull, Rt. Rev. (1794-1872) – dean of Manchester, **6:** 21 n.*23*
Georgina (b. 1836) – *Punch* illustrator, **6:** 21 n.*23*

Bowes, Yorkshire, **2:** 98
Bowlby (of Oldbury, Worcestershire):
Eleanora Frances (b. 1858), **4:** 180
Henry Bond, Rev. (1823-1894), **4:** 35
Mary (b. 1854), **4:** 35, 180
Bowles (of Kensington, London):
Dorothy "Weenie" Jessica (1884-1971), **7:** 159 n.*299*; **8:** 563, 591, 633; **9:** 346 n.*555*, 352
Geoffrey (b. 1879), **7:** 159 n.*299*
George (b. 1877), **7:** 159 n.*299*; **9:** 346 n.*555*
Jessica née Gordon (1852-1887), **7:** 159 n.*299*
Sydney (1880-1963), **7:** 159 n.*299*; **8:** 563, 591, 633; **9:** 346 n.*555*, 352
Thomas Gibson, Mr. (1841-1922) – dramatist and editor of *Vanity Fair*, **4:** 318 n.*401*; **7:** 159 n.*299*, 163 n.*307*, 165, 170-172, 187; **8:** 563 n.*898*, 564, 566, 569 n.*908*; **9:** 346 n.*555*, 347, 352
Bowles, Edward W. – dramatist, **9:** 251 n.*394*
Bowles (of Ryde, Isle of Wight):
Henry O., Col. (b. 1818) – soldier, **6:** 342, 354
Ida A. (b. 1863), **6:** 297 n.*490*, 342
Bowling (of Leeds, Yorkshire):
James Whimall (b. 1860) – musician, **8:** 14 n.*7*
John (b. 1818) – musician, **8:** 14 n.*7*
John Penn (b. 1852) – musician, **8:** 14 n.*7*
Bowling, West Dunbartonshire, **3:** 104
Bowman (of West Ham, Essex):
Charles Andrews, Mr. (b. 1851) – organist and pianist, **8:** 366 n.*599*, 373, 449, 453; **9:** 21 n.*23*
Charles "Charlie" Holmes (1876-1893) – actor, **8:** 366 n.*599*, 439, 454, 531, 619; **9:** 53, 54
Emma "Empsie," "Emsie" or "Emmie" Holmes (1881-1964) – actress, **8:** 366 n.*599*, 369, 403, 412, 425, 439, 460, 477, 531, 546, 566, 569, 594, 617; **9:** 21 n.*23*, 23, 53, 54, 55, 138, 139
Helen Herd née Holmes (b. 1851), **8:** 365, 366 n.*599*, 367, 368, 403, 406, 408, 410, 421, 439, 442, 449, 451, 453, 455, 460, 474, 477, 511, 531, 546, 556, 564, 582, 590, 593, 594, 617, 619, 630; **9:** 21 n.*23*, 23
Helen "Nellie" Holmes (1877-1953) – actress, **8:** 366 n.*599*, 369, 373, 403, 412, 425, 439-442, 451, 455, 474-481, 487, 531, 566, 569, 594, 617, 619; **9:** 21 n.*23*, 55, 139, 251 n.*394*
Isabella "Isa" (1874-1958) – actress, **8:** 316 n.*519*, 365, 366 n.*599*, 367, 368 n.*602*, 369, 373, 402, 403, 406, 408-410, 412, 421-428, 431, 439-442, 444, 446 n.*716*, 449, 451, 453, 455, 457, 474-481, 486, 487, 511, 512, 519, 526 n.*843*, 528-531, 546, 556, 564-568, 582-591, 593, 594, 617, 619, 627, 629, 630; **9:** 21 n.*23*, 32, 89, 138, 139, 197 n.*323*, 198 n.*325*
Margaret "Maggie" Florence Holmes (1879-1947) – actress, **8:** 366 n.*599*,

369, 373, 403, 412, 469, 470, 481, 485, 531, 568, 617-619; **9:** 21 n.*23*, 23, 55, 139, 251 n.*394*
Bowman, Charles Henry, Rev. (b. 1835), **2:** 29 n.*56*
Bowman, William, Sir (1816-1892) – surgeon, **2:** 22 n.*41*
Bowmont, Miss, **8:** 193 n.*323*
Bowser (Bowner or Bowsier), Constance, **8:** 371 n.*610*
Bowyer (of Clapham, Surrey):
Fitzwilliam Wentworth Atkins, Rev. (1839-1889), **8:** 335 n.*552*
Margaret Rosamond Fanny née Cuming (d. 1895), **8:** 335 n.*552*
Boxall, William, Sir (1800-1879) – artist, **6:** 125 n.*193*
Box and Cox (dr. John Morton), **1:** 105 n.*118*, 129; **4:** 225 n.*249*
Box B (dr. Richard Corney Grain), **9:** 88 n.*159*
Boyd (of Guildford, Surrey):
Andrew Kennedy Hutchison, Very Rev. (1825-1899), **9:** 246 n.*389*
Herbert Buchanan (1865-1941), **9:** 246 n.*389*
Boyd, Henry, Dr. (1831-1922) – principal of Hertford College, **7:** 275 n.*499*; **8:** 624, 625 n.*988*; **9:** 38 n.*67*
Boyd, William (1845-1928) – composer, **6:** 132 n.*203*
Boyd-Carpenter, William, Rev. (1841-1918), **7:** 431 n.*718*
Boyes (of Harrow Road, London):
Charlotte Augusta née Cobourg (1828-1901), **4:** 345 n.*449*, 346, 356; **5:** 141 n.*227*; **6:** 260 n.*413*, 272, 351; **7:** 112, 114, 115 n.*212*, 444; **8:** 58 n.*90*, 59, 63, 131, 205, 210, 319, 566, 573, 590, 615; **9:** 57 n.*102*, 141, 220
John Frederick (1811-1879) – teacher, **4:** 345 n.*449*, 346, 356; **5:** 141 n.*227*; **6:** 260 n.*413*, 272, 351; **7:** 112, 114, 115 n.*212*
Boyhood of Raleigh, The (pic. John Millais), **6:** 122 n.*186*
Boyle (of Prince's Gate, Westminster, London):
Agnes Margaret, **3:** 110 n.*158*
Agnes née Walker (b. 1820), **3:** 109, 110 n.*158*
Alexander, Vice-Adm. (1810-1884) – navy officer, **3:** 109, 110 n.*158*
Elizabeth Helen (b. 1847), **3:** 110 n.*158*
Frances Montgomerie, **3:** 110 n.*158*
Henrietta Camelia, **3:** 110 n.*158*
Janet, **3:** 110 n.*158*
Boyle (of Kelburne Castle, Ayrshire):
Alexander (1810-1884), see above
David, Mr. (1772-1853) – chief justice of Scotland, **3:** 110 n.*158*
William (1821-1874), see below
Boyle (of Shewalton, Ayrshire):
Anna Louisa Alexandrina (b. 1854), **3:** 110 n.*158*
Louisa Catherine née Parsons, **3:** 109, 110 n.*158*
William, Col. (1821-1874) – army officer, **3:** 109, 110 n.*158*
Boyne, Lord, see Hamilton Russell
Boynton Wood, see Wood

Boys, Thomas Shotter (1803-1874) – engraver, **2:** 17
Brabant, Frederick Gaspard (b. 1855) – mathematician, **9:** 65 n.*119*
Bracknell, Berkshire, **6:** 96, 116
Bracy, Henry (1848-1917) – actor and singer, **7:** 541 n.*874*
Bradford, George Frank (b. 1852), BA Exeter, **7:** 64 n.*101*, 67, 134
Bradford, Yorkshire, **6:** 168 n.*262*
Brading, Isle of Wight, **6:** 342, 359, 360, 421
Bradley (of Marlborough School, Wiltshire):
  Arthur Granville (1850-1943), **4:** 344
  Emily Tennyson (1862-1946), **6:** 142 n.*215*, 154, 204, 228
  George Granville, Mr. (1821-1903) – teacher, **4:** 344 n.*448*; **6:** 142 n.*215*, 148, 380
  Hugh Vachell (1865-1907), **6:** 142 n.*215*, 154, 204, 228
  Mabel C. (b. 1860), **6:** 142 n.*215*, 154, 204, 205, 228
  Margaret Louisa "Daisy" (b. 1855?), **4:** 344; **6:** 204, 228
  Marion Jane née Philpot (1831-1910), **6:** 142 n.*215*, 148, 154, 188, 204, 380
  Rose Marian (b. 1868), **6:** 142 n.*215*, 154, 228
Bradley, Francis Herbert (1846-1924) – philosopher, **9:** 137 n.*239*
Bradley, William (b. 1867) – servant, **8:** 602, 603 n.*957*
Bradshaw, Robert Wilmot or William (b. 1837), **2:** 42 n.*82*, 113, 114 n.*220*, 116
Bradshaw's Railway Guide, **1:** 19, 82 n.*84*; **6:** 216; **7:** 108
Braemar, Scotland, **7:** 452
Brain, Mary A. (b. 1828) – boarding-house keeper, **8:** 336 n.*554*, 337, 343, 376, 574 n.*917*
Braithwaite (of Epsom, Surrey):
  Adeline "Baby" (b. 1853), **5:** 67 n.*102*
  Alfred (b. 1843), **5:** 67 n.*102*
  Basil (b. 1845), **5:** 67 n.*102*
  Elizabeth "Lizzie" (b. 1850), **5:** 67 n.*102*
  Emily, **6:** 53 n.*73*
  Florence (b. 1852), **5:** 67 n.*102*
  Isaac, Mr. (1810-1890) – stockbroker, **5:** 67 n.*102*, 177; **6:** 52, 53 n.*73*, 54
  John Masterman (1846-1889), **5:** 67 n.*102*
  Louisa (b. 1842), **5:** 67 n.*102*
  Louisa née Masterman (b. 1816), **5:** 67 n.*102*, 177
  Reginald (b. 1847), **5:** 67 n.*102*
  Walter (b. 1848), **5:** 67 n.*102*
Braithwaite, Cumberland, **2:** 94; **3:** 115
Braithwaite Lodge, **3:** 116
Bramah (of Davington Priory, Kent):
  Emma M., Mrs. (b. 1831), **4:** 308
  Joseph West, Rev. (1820-1884), **4:** 308 n.*382*
Bramall (of Hove, Sussex):

Mr., **8:** 235 n.*398*
Mrs., **8:** 235 n.*398*
Bramley, Henry Ramsden, Rev. (1833-1917), **4:** 82 n.*35*; **6:** 67 n.*99*, 390
Bramley, Surrey, **6:** 45, 411; **7:** 128
Bramshott, Liphook, Hampshire, **7:** 527, 544
Bramston, John, Sir (1832-1921) – civil servant, **8:** 45 n.*67*, 46, 49
Bramston, John Trant, Rev. (1843-1931) – teacher, **9:** 51 n.*89*
Brandram, Samuel (1824-1892) – theatrical reciter, **7:** 96 n.*178*, 378, 418 n.*698*
Brandram, Thomas P., Rev. (b. 1841) , **7:** 459 n.*757*
Brandt, Miss, **9:** 227 n.*361*
Brasenose College, Oxford, **4:** 141, 201 n.*207*, 205, 260; **6:** 145, 212; **7:** 309, 519
Bray, Theresa "Tiny," **5:** 20; **6:** 54 n.*79*
Break, break, break (pic. E. C. Barnes), **5:** 219 n.*350*
Bremer (of Tulse Hill, London):
Catherina "Trina" E. (b. 1861), **6:** 129 n.*200*, 130, 196
Elizabeth, Mrs. (b. 1835), **6:** 129 n.*200*, 130, 196, 209
Emilie Florence (b. 1866), **6:** 129 n.*200*, 130, 196
Frederika "Freda" Adeline (b. 1863), **6:** 129 n.*200*, 130, 196
Joachim F. (b. 1830) – shipping insurer, **6:** 129 n.*200*, 196, 209
Breslau, Germany, **5:** 351-354
Brett, Charles (1815-1867) – police sergeant, **5:** 372, 373 n.*553*
Brett, John (1830-1902) – artist, **2:** 75 n.*151*
Brewer, Mary (b. 1827) – teacher, **6:** 93 n.*144*, 96, 99, 258, 285
Briar Rose (pic. Edward Burne-Jones), **8:** 512 n.*825*
Bridgenorth, Shropshire, **7:** 311, 446; **8:** 519
Bridger, Mr. A. (of Leomington, Warwickshire), **7:** 116 n.*216*
Bridgwater (of Banbury Road, Oxford):
Martha, Mrs. – lodging-house keeper, **9:** 318, 319 n.*511*, 321
May (b. 1877), **9:** 319 n.*511*, 321
Winifred (b. 1879), **9:** 319 n.*511*, 321
Bridlington, Yorkshire, **7:** 298 n.*541*
Brigg, Lincolnshire, **4:** 236
Bright (of Headington Hill, Oxford):
Alice Clara Franck (b. 1867), **6:** 380 n.*623*
Emily Gertrude Franck (b. 1868), **6:** 380 n.*623*
Emmeline Theresa née Wickham (d. 1871), **6:** 380 n.*623*
Evelyn Isabel Franck (b. 1869), **6:** 380 n.*623*
James Frank, Dr. (1832-1920) – teacher, **5:** 185 n.*304*; **6:** 380 n.*623*, 450, 451
Margaret Franck (b. 1866), **6:** 380 n.*623*, 450
Bright, Amy – child actress, **9:** 332 n.*530*
Bright, William, Dr. (1824-1901) – professor, **6:** 215 n.*335*; **7:** 164, 440, 495; **8:** 62 n.*99*, 127

Brighton, Sussex, **4:** 184, 230; **6:** 232, 308, 376, 414, 443; **7:** 17, 27, 50, 71, 72, 91, 93, 128, 131, 140, 153, 182, 193, 199, 215, 216, 288, 303, 312, 362, 364, 366, 399, 456, 461, 468, 473, 479, 508, 511; **8:** 33, 37, 40, 130, 146, 159, 160, 193, 226, 235-237, 242, 302, 347, 348, 360, 362, 363, 415, 424, 425, 475, 481, 529, 532, 577, 584, 587; **9:** 22, 24, 25, 82, 84, 86, 87, 169, 170, 173, 216, 344
Brighton Aquarium, **7:** 50, 131, 182, 199, 303, 362, 461, 511; **8:** 146, 226, 424, 426, 529; **9:** 85
Brighton Chain Pier, **7:** 456
Brighton College, **9:** 248
Brighton Electric Railway, see Volks Electric Railway
Brighton Hospital, **9:** 84
Brighton Pavilion, **7:** 131, 473; **8:** 363
Brighton Pier, **9:** 170
Brine (of Chardstock, Dorset):
Catherine "Katie" Gramina (1860-1878), **4:** 180; **5:** 19, 154 n.*249*, 155 n.*250*
Georgina M. E. (b. 1863), **6:** 190
James Gram, Rev. (1819-1901), **5:** 154 n.*249*
Mary Amelia née Pusey (1833-1910), **5:** 154 n.*249*, 155 n.*250*
Brinklow, Warwickshire, **1:** 25
Bristed (of Margate, Kent):
Alice Maud (b. 1865), **6:** 129 n.*200*
Clara H. (b. 1861), **6:** 129 n.*200*
John, Mr. (b. 1828) – chemist, **6:** 129 n.*200*
Bristol, **3:** 54; **4:** 243; **5:** 20; **7:** 446
Bristol Suspension Bridge, **7:** 446
Britannia Tubular Bridge, North Wales, **1:** 14
British and American Artists, **7:** 460, 461
British and Foreign Artists Exhibition, **6:** 73 n.*108*
British Artists (The Society of) Exhibition, London, **4:** 290 n.*346*; **5:** 67 n.*101*, 117, 136, 143, 219; **6:** 22, 79; **7:** 26 n.*31*, 257, 543; **9:** 60
British Association for the Advancement of Science, **4:** 34
British Institution, London, **4:** 285, 290; **5:** 60
British Museum, London, **3:** 28 n.*40*
British Poets with Memoirs and Critical Dissertations (bk. George Gilfillan), **2:** 34 n.*66*
Britomart (pic. George F. Watts), **4:** 334 n.*431*
"Brittany" – Channel Island ferry, **8:** 96
Broadstairs, Kent, **6:** 400
Brock (of Doncaster, Yorkshire):
Alexandra (b. 1866), **6:** 108 n.*169*
Carrie, Mrs. (b. 1846) – second wife, **6:** 108 n.*169*
Eveylen (b. 1854), **6:** 108 n.*169*
Henry Frederick, Rev. (1820-1889), **6:** 108 n.*169*

Sybul (b. 1865), **6:** 108 n.*169*
Brockham Warren, Box Hill, Surrey, **6:** 46
Broderick, George Charles (1831-1903) – politician, **7:** 831 n.*860*
Brodie (of Box Hill, Surrey, and Oxford):
Benjamin Collins, Prof. (1817-1880), **4:** 54, 112 n.*80*, 219; **5:** 77 n.*117*; **6:** 46 n.*64*, 211
Benjamin Vincent Sellon (1862-1938), **4:** 112 n.*80*
Ethel (1856-1926), see Glazebrook
Ida Philothea (1852-1917), **4:** 111, 112 n.*80*, 113, 194, 219, 220; **5:** 77 n.*117*
Lilian "Lily" (1853-1916), see Cardwell
Margaret Ann (b. 1850), **4:** 111, 112 n.*80*, 113, 194, 219; **5:** 77 n.*117*
Mary Isabel (b. 1858), **4:** 112 n.*80*, 194, 219
Philothea Margaret née Thompson (d. 1882), **4:** 110, 112 n.*80*, 194, 219, **5:** 77 n.*117*, 186; **6:** 211
Brodie, Robert (b. 1841) – teacher, **4:** 294 n.*353*
Brodrick, William St. John Fremantle, Sir (1856-1942), 9th Viscount Dunsford – politician, **8:** 250, 251 n.*421*; **9:** 14 n.*8*
Broken Hearts (dr. William S. Gilbert), **7:** 442 n.*732*
Broken Melody, The (dr. Herbert Keen and James Leader), **9:** 277 n.*442*
Bromfield, Henry (b. 1835), BA Christ Church, **5:** 54 n.*75*
Bromley, Nellie (1850-1939) – actress, **3:** 79, 80 n.*126*
Bromley-Davenport, William, Brig.-Gen. (1862-1949) – politician, **8:** 68, 69 n.*111*
Brompton, Middlesex, **1:** 101-103, 107; **2:** 24, 50-1, 83, 123; **3:** 76, 80, 132, 171-173; **4:** 97, 124, 284, 314; **5:** 36; **7:** 122
Brompton Cemetery, **8:** 141 n.*229*
Brontë (of Haworth, Yorkshire):
Charlotte (1816-1855), **3:** 82, 83, 85, 86 n.*133*, 90
Emily Jane (1818-1848), **2:** 74 n.*150*
"Brook; an Idyll, The" (Alfred Tennyson) – poem, **1:** 119 n.*145*, 120
Brook – pupil of Arthur Wilcox, **7:** 63 n.*100*
Brooke, Edward Adveno (1821-1910) – artist, **3:** 22 n.*28*
Brooke (of Manchester Square, London):
Emma Diana née Beaumont (d. 1874), **6:** 242, 234 n.*368*, 236, 264
Evelyn Anna (b. 1867), **6:** 233, 234 n.*368*, 242, 406 n.*667*; **7:** 23, 91
Honor Florence (b. 1862), **6:** 233, 234 n.*368*, 242, 244, 378, 404 n.*664*, 406 n.*667*; **7:** 12, 111 n.*206*
Maude (b. 1865?), **6:** 233, 234 n.*368*, 242, 378
Olive (b. 1869), **6:** 233, 234 n.*368*, 242, 406 n.*667*; **7:** 23, 91
Stopford Augustus, Rev. (1832-1916) – writer, **6:** 233, 234 n.*368*, 236, 242, 244, 263, 264; **7:** 12 n.*6*, 23
Stopford William Wentworth (b. 1859), **7:** 12 n.*6*
Sybil (b. 1870?), **6:** 233, 234 n.*368*, 242
Verone Rosalind (b. 1871), **6:** 234 n.*368*, 242

Brooke, John Towshend, Maj. (1845-1899) – magistrate, **4:** 103 n.*67*
Brooke, William Henry (1772-1860) – artist, **3:** 22 n.*28*
Brookes, Joshua Alfred Rowland, Rev. (b. 1865), **8:** 247, 248 n.*414*, 605
Brookfield, Charles Hallam Elton (1857-1913) – actor, **7:** 319, 320 n.*569*
Brooks (of Holywell, Oxford):
Adelaide "Nona" (b. 1886), **9:** 316 n.*504*, 319
Gwendoline (b. 1888), **9:** 316 n.*504*, 319
Mrs., **9:** 300, 316
Walter Tyrrell, Dr. (1859-1942) – physician, **8:** 549, 550 n.*876*, 551, 600; **9:** 65 n.*119*, 270, 300, 317
Brooks, Charles William Shirley (1816-1874) – Editor of *Punch*, **5:** 241 n.*390*
Brooks, George – scout at Christ Church, **2:** 71 n.*141*, 85
Brooks, Henry Samuel, Rev. (b. 1843), **9:** 33 n.*56*
Brooks, Horace G. (b. 1880), **9:** 229 n.*364*
Brooks, Mrs. – Eastbourne landlady, **7:** 130
Brooks, Phillips, Rev. (1835-1893), **8:** 205 n.*351*
Brother Sam (dr. John Oxenford, Edward Sothern, and John Buckstone), **5:** 88 n.*136*, 92, 93 n.*143*
Brotherton, Alfred H. (1803-1887) – merchant, **8:** 332 n.*545*
Brough (of London):
Fanny Whiteside (1854-1914) – actress, **9:** 139 n.*240*
Robert Barnabas, Mr. (1828-1860) – dramatist, **3:** 12 n.*10*, 79, 80 n.*126*, 153 n.*223*; **4:** 263 n.*308*, 310 n.*386*
Brough, G. – actor, **8:** 59 n.*92*
Brough (of South Lambeth Road, London):
Lionel, Mr. (1837-1909) – actor, **6:** 378 n.*619*; **7:** 532 n.*862*, 540, 542 n.*875*; **8:** 34 n.*41*, 38, 63 n.*100*, 113, 114, 237 n.*399*, 428, 440, 478; **9:** 91 n.*166*
Margaret "Daisy" (1870-1901), **8:** 63 n.*100*, 113, 428; **9:** 91 n.*166*
Margaret Rose née Simpson (1841-1901), **8:** 63 n.*100*, 113
Mary Bessie "Polly" (1863-1934), **8:** 63 n.*100*, 113, 428 n.*691*, 574, 575
Percy (b. 1872), **8:** 63 n.*100*
Brough, Sydney (1867-1911) – actor, **9:** 100, 101 n.*182*
Brough, William (1826-1870) – dramatist, **2:** 52 n.*104*, 56 n.*110*, 109 n.*211*; **4:** 263 n.*308*, 291 n.*348*, 337 n.*436*
Brougham, John (1810-1880) – dramatist, **4:** 182 n.*177*
Broughton, Amy – child actress, **8:** 164 n.*168*
Broughton, Frederick W. (1851-1894) – dramatist, **8:** 286 n.*480*
Brown (of Stockton, Durham):
Ann née Webster (1818-1874), **2:** 59 n.*120*
George, Rev. (1811-1888), **2:** 59 n.*120*
Brown (of Brighton, Sussex):
Brontea, Mrs. (b. 1825), **8:** 529
Henry, Mr. (b. 1819) – clothes dealer, **8:** 528, 530

Brown, Charles Abbott (b. 1838), BA Christ Church, **2:** 114 n.*220*, 115; **6:** 213 n.*331*
Brown (of Selkirk, Scotland):
Donald W. (b. 1853), **6:** 176 n.*271*, 177
George R. (b. 1857) , **6:** 176 n.*271*
Gideon Scott née McKenzie (b. 1820), **6:** 176 n.*271*, 177
Mary Suter (b. 1861), **6:** 176 n.*271*, 177
William, Mr. (b. 1821) – manufacturer, **6:** 176 n.*271*
Brown (of Jarrow, Durham):
Drewett Ormonde (1838-1910), **3:** 9 n.*6*, 90, 91 n.*140*, 119 n.*167*
Isabella née Chaytor (1810-1894), **3:** 9 n.*6*; **5:** 175 n.*290*
Thomas Drewett (1808-1870), **3:** 9 n.*6*, 90, 91 n.*140*; **5:** 175 n.*290*
Brown, Ford Madox (1821-1893) – artist, **5:** 72 n.*109*
Brown, Henry Clerke (b. 1852) – barrister, **7:** 445 n.*735*
Brown, Herbert William (b. 1873) – solicitor, **9:** 258 n.*407*
Brown, Miss – lodging-house keeper, **9:** 236 n.*372*
Brown, Mr. – friend of William Ranken, **1:** 104
Brown, Mr. & Mrs. – relatives of the Smiths of Dinsdale, **2:** 84, 85 n.*169*
Brown, Mr. & Mrs., of East Hill, Wandsworth, **4:** 339
Browne (of Mitchelmersh, Hampshire):
Barrington Gore, Rev. (1847-1914), **9:** 186 n.*307*
Louisa Mary Alice née Sumner, **9:** 186 n.*307*
Miss (b. 1886), **9:** 186 n.*307*
Browne, Bertha Louisa (1863-1963) – teacher, **9:** 155 n.*269*, 179
Browne (of Fareham, Hampshire):
Ellen Rose née Anderson, **9:** 186 n.*307*
Miss (b. 1887), **9:** 186 n.*307*
Thirwall Gore, Rev. (b. 1850), **9:** 186 n.*307*
Browne, George Forrest (1833-1930) – teacher, **3:** 95 n.*145*
Browne, George John (1820-1896), 3rd. Marquess of Sligo, **6:** 373, 374 n.*613*, 376, 391 n.*642*
Browne, Hablot Knight (1815-1882), known as "Phiz" – illustrator, **1:** 113 n.*132*
Browne, Maggie, pseud. of Margaret Andrewes née Hamer - writer, **8:** 579 n.*925*
Browning (of Florence, Italy):
Elizabeth née Barrett (1806-1861) – poet, **3:** 148 n.*213*, 158 n.*234*
Robert, Mr (1812-1889) – poet, **4:** 109, 247 n.*280*
Brownrigg (of Shalford, near Guildford, Surrey):
Constance S. née Huleatt (b. 1863), **9:** 292 n.*459*, 293
H. J. Ernest, Lieut. (b. 1863), **9:** 292 n.*459*, 293
Brucciani, artists' suppliers, London, **7:** 118 n.*221*
Bruce (of Glamorgan, Wales):
Elizabeth "Lily" Fox (1861-1935), **6:** 273 n.*444*
Henry Austin, Rt. Hon. Sir (1815-1895), 1st Baron Aberdare,

7: 497 n.*812*
Isabel Ellen (1861-1934), **7:** 426, 427 n.*712*
Jessie Frances (1849-1940), **6:** 302 n.*499*
Bruce, Lilian – actress, **5:** 69 n.*104*
Bruce, Robert (1274-1329), **3:** 99, 100 n.*148*
Bruce, Robert, Maj. Gen. (1813-1862) – governor to Prince of Wales, **4:** 39, 41-43
Bruce, William, Rev. (b. 1817), **7:** 497 n.*812*
Bruce-Joy, Albert (1842-1924) – sculptor, **6:** 277 n.*456*
Brunel, Isambard Kingdom (1806-1859) – civil engineer, **4:** 32
Bruni, Fedelio (1800-1875) – artist, **5:** 339 n.*509*
Brunton (of Brook Street, London):
Basil (b. 1872), **7:** 463 n.*761*, 464, 469; **8:** 23 n.*20*
Beryl (b. 1872), **7:** 463 n.*761*, 464, 467, 472, 480
Dorothy (b. 1873), **7:** 463 n.*761*, 464, 472, 480
Enid (b. 1874), **7:** 463 n.*761*, 464, 467, 472, 480
Guy (b. 1879), **7:** 463 n.*761*, 464
Janet, Mrs. (b. 1850), **7:** 463 n.*761*, 464, 466, 471, 473; **8:** 23 n.*20*, 27
Muriel (b. 1870), **7:** 463 n.*761*, 464, 472, 480
Olive (b. 1876), **7:** 463 n.*761*, 464, 467, 472, 480
Spencer, Mr. (b. 1846) – stockbroker, **7:** 463 n.*761*, 466, 471, 473; **8:** 23 n.*20*, 27
Brussels, Belgium, **5:** 257-259
Bryant, William Cullen (1794-1878) – poet, **4:** 24
Buchanan, Lilian (b. 1865) – art pupil of Theo Heaphy, **7:** 523
Buchanan, Robert (1842-1901) – dramatist, **8:** 412 n.*667*
Buchantry Hill, near Glenalmond, Scotland **3:** 97
Buchel, Annie, Mrs. (b. 1833) – hotel keeper, **6:** 377 n.*618*
Buckingham, Leicester (1825-1867) – dramatist, **5:** 73 n.*110*
Buckland, George – actor and impresario, **6:** 457 n.*752*; **7:** 44
Buckner, Richard (1812-1883) – artist, **5:** 61 n.*88*; **6:** 22, 23 n.*23*
Buckstone, John Baldwin (1802-1879) – dramatist, **3:** 106 n.*154*; **5:** 17 n.*11*, 32 n.*35*, 47 n.*62*, 52 n.*72*, 88 n.*136*, 137 n.*220*, 139 n.*223*, 220, 221 n.*351*; **7:** 186 n.*348*; **9:** 20 n.*22*
Bué (of Bordeaux, France, and Oxford):
Georges Henri (1843-1929), **3:** 124 n.*177*; **5:** 232 n.*370*
Jules Thomas Théodore, Mr. (b. 1817), **3:** 124 n.*177*; **5:** 36 n.*44*, 250 n.*409*
Bulkeley, Richard Williams-Bulkeley, Lord (1801-1875), 10th Bart., **1:** 14
Bull (of Lathbury, Buckinghamshire):
Caroline Frances Martha (b. 1842), **5:** 245 n.*399*
Cyril John Spier (1845-1888), **5:** 245 n.*399*
Florence S. (b. 1848), **5:** 245 n.*399*
Frances Sophia née Hughes (b. 1809), **5:** 245 n.*399*
Henry, Rev. (1797-1888), **5:** 245 n.*399*; **6:** 370 n.*608*

Henry Edward (1843-1905), **5:** 245 n.*399*
Bull, Henry Dawson Ellis, Rev. (1833-1892), **3:** 49 n.*75*
Bull, John, Dr. (1790-1858) – canon of Christ Church, **1:** 93; **2:** 120 n.*231*, 126; **3:** 42, 43 n.*67*, 58, 157 n.*231*, 161; **4:** 23, 67 n.*6*
Bullar (of Putney, Surrey):
Anna Katharine "Katty" (b. 1847), **2:** 81 n.*159*
Anne Mary (b. 1841), **2:** 81 n.*159*, 82 n.*161*
Edith F. (b. 1844), **2:** 81 n.*159*, 82 n.*161*
Henry, Mr. (b. 1815), **2:** 81 n.*159*
John, Mr. (b. 1807) – barrister, **2:** 81 n.*159*
Rosa née Follett (b. 1818), **2:** 81 n.*159,* 120
Suzanna Rosa F.A. (b. 1839), **2:** 81 n.*159*, 82 n.*161*
Bullingdon Cricket Club, Oxford, **5:** 119 n.*186*
Bullivant (of Beckenham, Kent):
Frederick A. (b. 1862), **7:** 464 n.*762*, 466
Lillian "Lily" (b. 1869), **7:** 464 n.*762*, 465, 466, 480
Mary B., Mrs. (b. 1834), **7:** 464 n.*762*, 465-467
Rosa M. (b. 1863), **7:** 464 n.*762*, 466
William M., Mr. (b. 1829) – manufacturer, **7:** 464 n.*762*, 466
Bulman, Miss, **2:** 87 n.*175*
Bulmer, William, Rev. (b. 1832), **6:** 391 n.*642*
Bumblebee Bogo's Budget (bk. William Synge), **8:** 269 n.*452*, 279 n.*469*, 286
Bundle of Ballads, A (bk. George Lawrence), **4:** 266 n.*310*
Bunsen (of Prussia, and London):
Christian Charles Josias, Chevalier (1791-1860) – diplomat, **2:** 48 n.*96*
Ernest de (1819-1903), **2:** 48 n.*96*
Frances née Waddington (d. 1876), **2:** 48 n.*96*
Burch (of Norham Gardens, Oxford):
Constance Emily née Jeffries (1855-1937), **7:** 364, 365 n.*636*; **9:** 58 n.*105*, 64, 65, 78, 110, 121-123, 142, 146, 194, 201-203, 230-232, 236, 240, 247, 250, 253, 256, 257, 320, 326
George James, Prof. (1852-1914) – professor of physics at University College, Reading, **7:** 365 n.*636*; **9:** 58 n.*105*, 148, 194, 232
Irene Constance (1887-1944), **9:** 57, 58 n.*105*, 64, 65, 71, 78, 121-123, 230, 247, 250, 253, 255, 313
Violet Dorothy (b. 1890), **9:** 78 n.*145*, 247, 253
Burd, Mr. – friend of Skeffington H. Dodgson, **6:** 421 n.*691*
Burdett-Coutts, Angela Georgina (1814-1906) – philanthropist, **4:** 249
Burdon, John Shaw, Rt. Rev. (d. 1907), **8:** 189, 190 n.*319*
Burfield, Henry John, Rev. (1828-1882), **6:** 168 n.*262*
Burford, near Tenbury, Shropshire, **6:** 168
Burges, Ynyr Henry (1834-1908), MA Christ Church, **1:** 63 n.*39*, 87, 88 n.*91*, 89
Burgess, John Bagnold (1830-1897) – artist, **6:** 73 n.*108*

Burghley House, near Stamford, Lincolnshire, **6:** 108
Burgomaster's Wedding, The (dr. Anon), **5:** 313
Burgon, John William, Rev. (1813-1888), **1:** 59 n.*30*; **5:** 206 n.*329*, 228, 302 n.*471*; **6:** 441; **7:** 142, 309
Burke, Ione (b. 1845?) – actress, **5:** 221 n.*351*
Burke, Thomas Henry (1829-1882) – politician, **7:** 425, 426 n.*709*
Burke's *Peerage and Baronetage*, **1:** 10, 13, 14
Burley, Minnie – actress, **8:** 547 n.*871*
Burlington House Gallery, London, **7:** 96, 505; **8:** 381
Burn, Stacey Southerden, Dr. (b. 1852) – physician and photographer, **7:** 255 n.*465*
Burnaby, Miss, **6:** 415; **7:** 57, 58 n.*92*
Burnand, Francis Cowley (1836-1917) – dramatist, **4:** 279 n.*328*, 300 n.*366*, 316 n.*396*; **5:** 73 n.*110*, 93 n.*143*, 157 n.*256*, 233 n.*372*, 240 n.*389*, 241 n.*390*; **7:** 225; **8:** 113 n.*184*, 565 n.*900*; **9:** 164 n.*279*
Burne Jones, Edward Coley (1833-1898) – artist, **1:** 40; **2:** 40 n.*80*; **3:** 26 n.*37*; **7:** 253; **8:** 441 n.*706*, 512 n.*825*, 556
Burnett, Frances Hodgson (1849-1924) – writer, **8:** 401 n.*653*
Burnett (of London):
  Frank (1852-1896), **4:** 355 n.*463*; **5:** 20 n.*13*, 30
  Harriet née Jeaffreson, **4:** 355, 356; **5:** 20 n.*13*, 30, 100
  Mary (b. 1853), **4:** 181, 355 n.*463*, 356; **5:** 19, 20 n.*13*, 30
  Robert French, Mr. (1813-1872) – clerk to solicitor, **4:** 355, 356; **5:** 20 n.*13*, 100
Burnett, James Compton, Dr. (b. 1841) – physician, **8:** 431 n.*694*
Burnett (or Ripon):
  Jane née Chambers (b. 1790), **2:** 55 n.*108*
  William (1791-1858) – verger, **2:** 55 n.*108*; **3:** 7 n.*2*, 147
Burnley (of Kensington, London):
  Charlotte "Lottie" H. (b. 1866), **7:** 56 n.*89*, 57, 58, 75
  Emily A., Mrs. (b. 1832), **7:** 56 n.*89*, 58
  Emily A. C. (b. 1862), **7:** 56 n.*89*, 58, 75
  Joseph H., Mr. (b. 1822) – retired diplomat, **7:** 56 n.*89*
Burns, Robert (1759-1796) – poet, **2:** 100
Burritt, Elihu (1810-1879) – writer, **1:** 134 n.*169*
Burrows (of Godalming, Surrey):
  Anna Louisa née Bovill (d. 1934), **9:** 289 n.*455*
  Hedley Robert (1887-1983), **9:** 289 n.*455*
  Leonard Hedley, Rev. (1857-1940), **9:** 289 n.*455*, 293
  Leonard Righton (1888-1915), **9:** 289 n.*455*
  Mary Geraldine (b. 1892), **9:** 289 n.*455*, 293
Burrows (of Chipping Norton, Oxfordshire):
  Christine "Chrissie" Mary Elizabeth (b. 1872), **7:** 46, 47 n.*72*
  Esther Elizabeth née Bliss (b. 1848), **7:** 46, 47 n.*72*
Burrows (of Witley, Surrey):

Leonard Francis, Rev. (1821-1907), **9:** 289 n.*455*
Leonard Hedley (1857-1940), see above
Mary Mansfield née Vicars (b. 1831), **9:** 289 n.*455*
Burrows (of Norham Gardens, Oxford):
Mary Anna née Gardiner (1817-1916), **9:** 248 n.*390*
Montagu, Commander (1819-1905) – professor of modern history, **5:** 181 n.*300*, 376; **6:** 380, 381 n.*624*; **9:** 247, 248 n.*390*, 346
Burrows, Winfrid Oldfield (1858-1929) – lecturer, **8:** 71 n.*116*, 83, 598
Bürse-Garten, Königsberg, Russia, **5:** 280
Burt, Miss – lodging-house keeper, **8:** 81 n.*127*
Burton, Edward, Dr. (1794-1836) – professor of divinity, **1:** 80 n.*80*, 84, 85; **2:** 117 n.*223*
Burton, Edward Lingen (1836-1865) – undergraduate at Christ Church, **1:** 58 n.*27*, 60, 61, 87, 88 n.*91*
Burton (of Clerkenwell, London):
Florence (b. 1856), **7:** 60 n.*95*, 441; **8:** 47, 48 n.*69*, 121
Harriet, Mrs. (b. 1830), **7:** 60 n.*95*, 64, 127, 141, 179, 441
Mabel Amy (b. 1869), **7:** 60 n.*95*, 61, 64, 74, 127 n.*239*, 141, 179, 193, 441; **8:** 47, 48 n.*69*, 49, 121
Burton, William Shakespeare (1824-1916) – artist, **2:** 75 n.*151*
Burwarton, Shropshire, **6:** 165
Burwarton Hall, **6:** 166
Bury (of New Ferry, Cheshire):
Augusta née David (d. 1884), **9:** 45 n.*80*
Edith (b. 1884), **9:** 45 n.*80*
Edward Alexander, Rev. (1851-1896), **9:** 45 n.*80*
Violet (b. 1882), **9:** 45 n.*80*
Bush, Miss – friend of the Terrys, **5:** 35, 99
Bushell, Ann Eliza (b. 1855) – teacher, **9:** 202 n.*331*, 203
Bushey Art College, Hertfordshire, **8:** 330 n.*544*, 353, 566
Butcher, Emma – pupil at St. Aldates, **2:** 32
Bute, Lord, see Crichton-Stuart
Butler (of Stoke, near Guildford, Surrey):
Ada C., **8:** 372 n.*613*
Edith F. (b. 1873), **8:** 372 n.*613*
Gertrude M. (b. 1867), **8:** 372 n.*613*
Harold B. (b. 1876), **8:** 372 n.*613*
Margaret A. (b. 1879), **8:** 372 n.*613*
Maud M. (b. 1870), **8:** 372 n.*613*
Sarah S. née Parson (b. 1844), **8:** 372 n.*613*
Thomas Mapleson, Dr. (b. 1839) – physician, **8:** 372 n.*613*
Butler (met in Margate):
Ada Chambers, **6:** 129 n.*200*
Daisy, **6:** 129 n.*200*
Sophie, **6:** 129 n.*200*

Butler (of Oxford):
Arthur Gray, Mr. (1831-1909) – teacher, **3:** 58 n.*87*; **6:** 427, 459; **9:** 36 n.*63*, 38 n.*66*, 39, 40, 77 n.*143*
Christina Violet (b. 1884), **9:** 36 n.*63*, 37, 39, 40, 41
Harold Edgeworth (b. 1878), **9:** 36 n.*63*
Harriet Jessie née Edgeworth (1851-1946), **6:** 459; **9:** 36 n.*63*, 37, 39, 40, 41 n.*71*, 53 n.*91*, 135 n.*237*
Olive Harriet (1879-1971), **9:** 36 n.*63*, 37, 39, 40 n.*70*, 41
Ruth Florence (b. 1881), **9:** 36 n.*63*, 37, 39, 40, 41
Butler, Henry Montagu, Rev. (1833-1918) – headmaster of Harrow School, **7:** 221 n.*405*; **9:** 323 n.*516*
Butler, The (dr. Herman Merivale), **8:** 333, 334 n.*549*
Butterfield (of Banbury Road, Oxford):
Dorothy, Mrs. (b. 1865), **9:** 196 n.*321*, 197
Frederick William Louis, Mr. (b. 1874), MA Balliol, **9:** 196 n.*321*, 197
Marie Louise (b. 1889?), **9:** 196 n.*321*, 250
Butterfly's Ball and the Grasshopper's Feast, The, or Harlequin and the Genius of Spring (dr. Edward Blanchard), **2:** 23, 24 n.*44*
Buttermere, Cumberland, **2:** 93, 94
Buxton, Eliza, Mrs. (b. 1830) – lodging-house keeper, **7:** 297 n.*538*, 359
Byers, Miss – actress, **8:** 364, 365 n.*597*
Byrne, Leo (b. 1881) – child actor, **9:** 78 n.*144*
Byron (Newstead Priory, Nottinghamshire):
Anne Isabella née Noel, Lady (d. 1860), **4:** 27
George Gordon Noel (1788-1824), 6th Lord Byron – poet, **1:** 73
Byron, George Frederick William (1855-1917), 9th Baron Byron – undergraduate at Christ Church, **6:** 460 n.*757*
Byron, Henry James (1835-1884) – dramatist, **4:** 270 n.*313*, 309 n.*384*; **5:** 69 n.*104*, 126 n.*200*, 156 n.*253*, 157 n.*255*, 160 n.*264*, 168 n.*277*; **7:** 123 n.*232*, 356 n.*623*, 387; **8:** 113 n.*184*; **9:** 119 n.*206*, 162 n.*277*
Byron's Early Love (pic. Edward Ward), **2:** 75 n.*151*
Bywater, Ingram (1840-1914) – lecturer, **6:** 91 n.*141*

Cadogan (of Cadogan Place, London):
Beatrix Jane née Craven, Lady (1844-1907), **8:** 464 n.*747*
Emily Julia (1871-1909), **8:** 464 n.*747*
George Henry, Lord (1840-1915), 5th Earl Cadogan, **8:** 464 n.*747*
Cadogan Place, London, **6:** 12
Caffirs of South Africa, **5:** 65
Caius College, Cambridge, **8:** 545
Calais, France, **5:** 257, 368
Calcutta, India, **4:** 24
Caldecott, Randolph (1846-1886) – illustrator, **7:** 517 n.*838*
Calder Bridge, Cumberland, **2:** 92, 93
Caldicott, Alfred James (1842-1897) – composer, **9:** 88 n.*159*

Calmady Children, The (pic. Thomas Lawrence), **2:** 17 n.*29*, 69 n.*137*
Calmour, Alfred Cecil (1857-1912) – dramatist, **8:** 406 n.*660*
Calton Hill, Edinburgh, **3:** 97
Calver (of Roker, Durham):
  Edward Killwick, Capt. (1813-1892) – navy officer, **5:** 175 n.*290*
  Jessie née Spence (b. 1816), **5:** 175 n.*290*
Calverley, Charles Stuart (1832-1884) – barrister and poet, **6:** 242 n.*385*, 245
Cambell, Hugh, Dr. (b. 1825) – physician, **6:** 347
Cambridge, **4:** 176, 303
Cambridge Gardens, London, **6:** 114, 195, 352
Cambridge University, **2:** 40 n.*80*; **3:** 58, 60; **7:** 221
Camden Town, London, **4:** 222; **5:** 84
Camera Obscura, Brighton, **7:** 456
Cameron, Beatrice (1868-1940) – actress, **8:** 440 n.*705*, 451
Cameron (of Freshwater, Isle of Wight):
  Charles Hay (b. 1848), **3:** 127 n.*183*; **4:** 345 n.*450*
  Charles Hay, Mr. (1795-1880) – Indian jurist, **3:** 127 n.*183*; **4:** 345 n.*450*, 346, 356
  Eugene Hay (1840-1885), **4:** 345 n.*450*
  Ewen Wrottesley Hay (1843-1888), **4:** 60, 63, 127 n.*100*, 140 n.*119*, 345 n.*450*
  Hardinge Hay (1846-1911), **4:** 345 n.*450*
  Henry Herschel Hay (1852-1911), **3:** 127 n.*183*; **4:** 345 n.*450*
  Julia Hay (1839-1873), **4:** 345 n.*450*
  Julia Margaret née Pattle (1815-1879) – photographer, **3:** 127 n.*183*; **4:** 60, 127 n.*100*, 315 n.*395*, 333, 335 n.*432*, 345, 346, 356; **5:** 117 n.*183*; **6:** 274 n.*446*
Cameron, George Thomas, Rev. (b. 1821), **2:** 36 n.*72*, 40, 41
Cameron, Violet (1863-1919) – actress and singer, **6:** 257 n.*409*; **7:** 232, 532 n.*862*; **8:** 546 n.*870*
Cameron, William Mouat, Rev. (b. 1855), **8:** 547 n.*872*
Cameron Studio, Regent Street, London, **8:** 362 n.*590*, 365, 366, 375
Camille, Mdlle. (b. 1860?) – actress, **5:** 364 n.*539*
Campbell – pupil of Alexander Webster, **2:** 90 n.*181*
Campbell (of Bangor, Carnarvonshire):
  Arthur Bruce Knight (1851-1881), **4:** 198 n.*201*
  Blanche née Bruce-Pryce (d. 1873), **4:** 198 n.*201*
  James Colquhoun, Rt. Rev. (1813-1895) – bishop of Bangor, **4:** 198 n.*201*
  John Archibald (1842-1877), **4:** 198 n.*201*
  Sarah Bruce (1843-1846), **4:** 198 n.*201*
  Sutherland Colquhoun (1846-1847), **4:** 198 n.*201*
  Wilhelmina Mary (b. 1846), **4:** 198 n.*201*
Campbell (of Bruton Street, London):

Cecil Arthur (1869-1932), **6:** 248 n.*393*, 373
Hallyburton George, Lord (1829-1918), 3rd Baron Stratheden and Campbell, **6:** 248 n.*393*, 373
John Beresford (1866-1915), **6:** 248 n.*393*, 373
Louisa Mary née Beresford, Lady (d. 1923), **6:** 248 n.*393*, 373
Mildred Louisa (1867-1951), **6:** 248 n.*393*, 373, 375
Campbell (of Inverneill, Argyllshire):
Isabella Mary Adelaide (1833?-1892), **2:** 15 n.*25*
James Archibald, Capt. (1800-1878) – army officer, **2:** 103 n.*199*
Sophia Amelia Alexandrina née Harvey (d. 1839?), **2:** 103 n.*199*
Campbell, Margaret – friend of the MacDonalds, **4:** 228 n.*253*
Campbell, Mary Maxwell (d. 1886) – song-writer, **2:** 100
Campbell, Miss – friend of the Dubourgs, **7:** 96 n.*177*
Campbell, Mr. – cousin of the Bennies, **7:** 131 n.*244*
Canfield, Francis Ramie "Eugene" (1851-1904) – American comedian, **7:** 153 n.*290*
Canning, Charles John Spencer George, Lord (1852-1915), 3rd Baron Garvagh, **8:** 136 n.*222*, 138, 143
Canongate, Edinburgh, **3:** 97
Cape, Africa, **8:** 37, 46, 47, 49-53, 58, 64, 66, 326
Capes (of Bramshott, Hampshire):
Mary née Leadbeater (1838-1908), **7:** 544 n.*878*; **8:** 43 n.*60*, 53, 62, 90
William Wolfe, Rev. (1834-1914), **5:** 36 n.*44*; **7:** 544 n.*878*; **8:** 90
"Captain Needlegun" in *Living Miniatures*, **5:** 201
Cardew (of Liss, Hampshire):
Ada (or Ann) Margaret (b. 1856), **9:** 298 n.*473*, 299
Christopher Baldock, Capt. (b. 1818) – army officer, **9:** 298 n.*473*
Eliza Jane née Bethell (b. 1828), **9:** 298 n.*473*
Cardew (of Wimbledon, Surrey):
Alexandra "Xie" Rhoda née Kitchin (1864-1925), **6:** 85 n.*128*, 87 n.*130*, 124 n.*191*, 209 n.*328*, 213 n.*331*, 264, 273, 276, 279, 282, 300, 305, 313, 317, 320, 321, 325, 330, 337, 388, 400 n.*657*, 471, 472; **7:** 43 n.*65*, 63, Holiday's portrait 79, 92, 125 n.*234*, 164, 244, 251, 272 n.*492*, 329, plays violin 376; **8:** 392; **9:** marriage 60 n.*112*, 298 n.*473*
Arthur, Mr. (1852-1933) – barrister, **9:** 60 n.*112*, 298 n.*473*
Cardinal Richelieu (pic. Thomas Heaphy), **6:** 71, 72 n.*105*
"Cardinal Wolsey" (in *Henry VIII*), **2:** 19 n.*34*
Cardwell (of Eastbourne, Sussex):
Christine L. (b. 1879), **7:** 365 n.*637*
Hugh Brodie (b. 1877), **7:** 365 n.*637*
Irene M. (b. 1880), **7:** 365 n.*637*
Lilian née Brodie (1853-1916), **4:** 54, 111, 112 n.*80*, 113, 219, 220; **5:** 77 n.*117*; **7:** 365 n.*637*; **8:** 41 n.*57*
Sylvia M. (b. 1876), **7:** 365 n.*637*
William Alexander, Lt. Col. (1848-1916) – army officer, **7:** 365 n.*637*;

8: 41 n.*57*
Cardwell, Edward, Rt. Hon. (1813-1886) – politician, **3:** 43 n.*68*; **6:** 329 n.*544*
Carey, Tupper, Rev. (b. 1834), **2:** 109 n.*213*, 110 n.*213*
Carfax, Oxford, **9:** 310
Carisbrooke Castle, Isle of Wight, **6:** 296, 299, 342, 359, 424, 481, 496
Carlisle (of Bowden, Cheshire):
Alice (b. 1858), **6:** 177 n.*272*
Catherine (b. 1864?), **6:** 177 n.*272*
Douglas (b. 1870), **6:** 177 n.*272*
Ellen, Mrs. (b. 1827), **6:** 177 n.*272*
Helen (b. 1853), **6:** 177 n.*272*
Herbert (b. 1858), **6:** 177 n.*272*
John, Mr. (b. 1813) – magistrate of schools, **6:** 177 n.*272*
John Hildied (b. 1866), **6:** 177 n.*272*
Leonard A. (b. 1868), **6:** 177 n.*272*
Lucy (b. 1859), **6:** 177 n.*272*
Mary E. (b. 1851), **6:** 177 n.*272*
Maud (b. 1863), **6:** 177 n.*272*
Carlo (of Lambeth, Surrey):
Elizabeth "Lizzie" (b. 1876), **8:** 197 n.*334*, 348, 357
Phoebe Ellen (b. 1874) – actress, **7:** 525 n.*849*; **8:** 197 n.*334*, 198, 208, 215, 216, 219, 226-228, 234, 242, 282, 298, 304, 311, 312 n.*514*, 318, 348, 357, 362, 375, 381, 417
Phoebe née Rawlings (b. 1854), **8:** 197 n.*334*, 216, 219, 227, 305, 348
William, Mr. (b. 1841) – packer and factory hand, **8:** 197 n.*334*, 216, 305
Carlton House, Ventnor (Miss Froud's lodging house), **6:** 358
Caroni, Emmanuele (b. 1826) – artist, **5:** 363 n.*538*
Carpenter, A. née Sparkes, **7:** 288 n.*522*
Carr, Henry (b. 1823) – auditor's clerk, **8:** 261 n.*440*
Carr, Henry Martin, Rev. (1835-1868), **5:** 41 n.*49*
Carr, Margaret (b. 1853) – housekeeper, **7:** 398 n.*676*
"Carroll, Lewis" (pseudonym), **2:** 39 n.*79*
"Carroll, Louis" (pseudonym), **2:** 39
Carter, Matilda (b. 1839) – former nurse, **7:** 27 n.*33*
Carter, Mrs. – Guildford lodging-house keeper, **6:** 344, 348
Carter, Mrs. – mother of Mrs. Mary Holman, **7:** 215
Carton, Richard Claude (1857-1928), real name Critchett – dramatist, **8:** 578 n.*921*; **9:** 56 n.*101*, 84 n.*152*
Cary, Offley Henry (b. 1837) – teacher, **4:** 57
Case, Thomas (1844-1925) – lecturer, **8:** 213 n.*364*
Case of Conscience, A (dr. John Oxenford), **3:** 132 n.*190*
Cassell, Miss – governess, **6:** 378
Cassell's Edition of Euclid, **1:** 83
Cassington, Oxfordshire, **9:** 64, 127

Caste (dr. Thomas Robertson), **5:** 231 n.*369*
Castle, Amy (b. 1872) – logic pupil, **8:** 341
Castle, Eliza (b. 1840) – lodging-house keeper, **9:** 300 n.*476*, 301, 306, 321
Castle Eden, Durham, **1:** 98 n.*106*, 123; **3:** 100
Castlet, Cumberland, **2:** 91
Cathedral, The (bk. Isaac Williams), **1:** 98 n.*105*
Cave, Emmeline F. (b. 1846), **6:** 226, 353
Cavendish, Dr. – conjuror, **7:** 199
Cavendish, Frederick Charles, Lord (1836-1882) – politician, **7:** 425, 426 n.*709*
"Cavendish," see Jones
Caversham, Oxfordshire, **6:** 369
Caversham Road, Kentish Town, London (Terrys), **5:** 127, 379
Cayley, Arthur (1821-1895) – mathematician, **4:** 307 n.*378*
Cayley, Charles Bagot (1823-1883) – writer, **4:** 251 n.*288*
Cecil (of Eccleston Square, London):
Algernon (b. 1879), **8:** 76, 77 n.*120*, 226
Blanche Louisa (b. 1872), **6:** 373, 441, 466; **8:** 76, 77 n.*120*, 226
Eustace Brownlow Henry, Lord (1834-1921), **6:** 246, 248, 373, 441, 466; **8:** 76, 77 n.*100*, 78, 110, 113
Evelyn (1865-1941), **6:** 248 n.*393*, 373, 404 n.*664*, 441; **8:** 76, 77 n.*120*, 226 n.*383*
Gertrude Louisa née Scott, Lady (b. 1841), **6:** 373, 376, 404 n.*664*, 441, 466; **8:** 76, 77 n.*120*, 78, 110, 113, 226, 346, 622
Cecil, Arthur, real name Blunt (1843-1896) – actor, **5:** 240 n.*389*; **6:** 259 n.*412*, 304; **7:** 278 n.*505*, 319, 369; **8:** 199 n.*339*; **9:** 57 n.*104*
Cecil (of Hatfield House, Hertfordshire):
Beatrix Maud (1858-1950), see Palmer
Edgar Algernon Robert "Bob" (1864-1958), see below
Edward Herbert "Niggs" (1867-1918), **6:** 118 n.*181*, 398; **8:** 76, 77 n.*120*
Fanny Georgiana Mildred (1866-1867), **6:** 118 n.*181*
Georgina Caroline née Alderson, Lady Salisbury (1827-1899), **6:** 118 n.*181*, 120, 121, 127, 132, 135, 160, 161, 163, 165, 221, 246, 256, 336, 352, 374, 398, 467; **7:** 189, 194, 306; **8:** 76, 77 n.*120*, 110, 333, 461
Gwendolen (1860-1945), **6:** 118 n.*181*, 120, 121 n.*183*, 125 n.*194*, 127, 134, 135, 160-163, 165, 169, 200, 220-222, 224, 225, 240, 248, 286, 336, 380, 398, 441; **7:** 111 n.*206*, 306; **8:** 110, 333, 462, 467
Hugh Richard Heathcote (1869-1956), **6:** 118 n.*181*; **8:** 457 n.*733*
James "Jim" Edward Hubert (1861-1947), see below
Robert Arthur Talbot, Lord (1830-1903), 3rd Marquess of Salisbury, **6:** 118 n.*181*, 120, 125, 127, 163, 164, 221, 222, 246, 248, 352, 380, 442, 460 n.*756*, 467; **7:** 194, 306, 337; **8:** 76, 77 n.*120*, 150 n.*246*, 254, 333, 461; **9:** 309 n.*491*
Rupert Ernest William "Fish" (1863-1936), see below

Cecil (of Grafton Street, London):
Cicely Alice née Gore, Lady (1867-1955), **8:** 462 n.*742*
James "Jim" Edward Hubert (1861-1947), Lord Cranborne, **6:** 118 n.*181*, 120, 121 n.*183*, 125 n.*194*, 127, 134, 135, 162, 169, 200, 225, 250, 286, 441; **8:** 76, 77 n.*120*
Cecil (of Manchester Square, London):
Edgar Algernon Robert "Bob" (1864-1958), Viscount Chelwood, **6:** 118 n.*181*, 200, 398; **8:** 462
Eleanor née Lambton, Lady (1868-1959), **8:** 462 n.*744*
Cecil (of Bishop Hatfield, Hertfordshire):
Florence Mary née Bootle-Wilbraham (1863-1944), **8:** 462 n.*743*
Rupert Ernest William "Fish," Rev. (1863-1936), **6:** 118 n.*181*, 120, 121 n.*183*, 125 n.*194*, 127, 134, 135, 163, 169, 200, 225, 374; **8:** 259 n.*437*, 462
Cecil Alderson, see Alderson
Cecil Ursula, Aged Three Years (pic. Arthur Hughes), **5:** 211 n.*339*
"Celebrities at Home" from *The World*, **8:** 150 n.*245*
Celeste, Celine, Madame (1811-1882) – actress and choreographer, **2:** 123 n.*238*, 128
Celli, Madame, **4:** 225
Cellier, Alfred (1844-1891) – composer, **8:** 367 n.*601*, 631 n.*999*; **9:** 24 n.*32*, 213 n.*340*
Cenci, The (bk. Percy Shelley), **1:** 118 n.*144*
Cephalus and Procris (pic. Joseph Turner), **2:** 65
Chamberlain, Geoffrey Phayre (b. 1859) – barrister, **7:** 148 n.*279*
Chamberlain (of Birmingham):
Joseph (1836-1914) – politician, **8:** 132 n.*216*, 279 n.*468*, 509 n.*819*; **9:** 264 n.*416*
Miss R. (niece), **8:** 496, 497 n.*799*
Chamberlain, Mrs. – fellow lodger at Eastbourne, **7:** 454 n.*750*
Chamberlain, Thomas. Rev. (1810-1892), **4:** 33, 107, 108 n.*75*, 170; **5:** 51 n.*70*; **7:** 440
Chambers, Charles Haddon (1860-1921) – dramatist, **8:** 562 n.*896*; **9:** 23 n.*28*
Chambers (of Crick Road, Oxford):
Colonel, **6:** 29 n.*35*
Maria, Mrs. (b. 1827), **6:** 29 n.*35*, 66, 348; **7:** 110 n.*204*
Rose, **6:** 29 n.*35*, 66, 348; **7:** 110 n.*204*
Chambers, William (b. 1827) – fellow of Worcester, **4:** 276, 277 n.*323*
Chamber's Euclid, **1:** 82, 83
"Champion Skaters," **5:** 379
Champneys, Basil (b. 1843) – architect, **6:** 341
Champs Elysées, Paris, **5:** 362, 365
Chance Acquaintance, A (bk. William Howells), **8:** 15 n.*9*
Chandler, Henry William, Prof. (1828-1889) – professor of moral and

metaphysical philosophy, **5:** 150 n.*241*, 152, 160, 231, 365; **6:** 33, 34 n.*45*, 91, 303, 421, 426, 458; **7:** 178, 421; **8:** 394 n.*640*, 457 n.*735*, 459
Chandler, Joseph (b. 1821) – hotel manager, **7:** 27 n.*33*
Chandler, Mrs., **6:** 198, 421
Channel Islands Parliament, **8:** 99
Chantry Woods, near Guildford, Surrey, **6:** 350
Chapman (of Brading, Isle of Wight):
Edward, Mr. (1839-1906) – botanist and railway director, **6:** 354 n.*585*, 411, 423, 425, 480, 485; **7:** 35 n.*51*; **8:** 469, 470 n.*761*
Elizabeth B., Mrs. (b. 1842), **6:** 354 n.*585*, 411, 412, 425, 480, 485; **7:** 35 n.*51*; **8:** 469, 470 n.*761*
Chappell (of Gloucester Place, London):
Edward, Mr. (b. 1852) – music publisher, **7:** 430 n.*717*
Flora Emma Sarah née Ward (b. 1853), **5:** 161 n.*266*, 168 n.*278*, 169, 170, 229; **6:** 275, **7:** 430 n.*717*
"Charge of the Light Brigade, The" (Alfred Tennyson) – poem, **1:** 72, 119 n.*145*
Charing Cross Station, London, **5:** 255; **6:** 44; **7:** 304, 477, 503; **8:** 316, 321, 333, 345, 366-368, 381, 439, 546, 565, 567; **9:** 44, 53, 131, 138, 139, 146, 156, 172, 202, 203
Charity Begins at Home (dr. B. C. Stephenson, Clement Scott and Alfred Cellier), **8:** 632 n.*1001*
Charlbury, Oxfordshire, **4:** 303; **5:** 380; **9:** 69, 73
Charles, Frederick, real name Solomon – actor, **5:** 202, 222
Charles I (dr. William Wills), **6:** 253, 254 n.*403*, 272, 311; **7:** 185 n.*347*; **9:** 78 n.*144*
Charles Dickens Esq. (pic. Hendrick Scheffer), **2:** 75 n.*151*
Charles Kean, Esq., in the Character of Wolsey (pic. Edgar Papworth), **2:** 75 n.*151*
Charles O'Malley (bk. Charles Lever), **1:** 109 n.*126*
Charlottensburg, Germany, **5:** 270
Charlotte Street, Caledonian Road, London, **2:** 53
Charlton Kings, Gloucestershire, **4:** 185-187
Charrington (of London):
Janet Achurch née Sharp (1864-1916) – actress and manager, **9:** 334 n.*535*
Nora (b. 1890), **9:** 334 n.*535*, 335
Charsley (of Oxford):
Catherine (b. 1819), **3:** 49
Robert Harvey (1826-1907), **3:** 49; **4:** 176 n.*173*; **8:** 21 n.*16*, 217, 221
William Henry (1820-1900), **2:** 120 n.*229*; **3:** 48 n.*74*, 54; **7:** 435 n.*722*, 481, 483, 485, 488
Charsley Hall, Oxford (later Marcon's Hall), **9:** 47
Chart:
Henry Nye (1822-1876) – actor, **8:** 237 n.*399*

Mrs. (d. 1892) – theatre manageress, **8:** 237 n.*399*
Charterhouse School, Godalming, Surrey, **6:** 355; **7:** 252, 268
Chase, Drummond Percy, Dr. (1820-1902) – principal of St. Mary Hall, **4:** 56; **8:** 448 n.*717*
Chataway (of Rotherwick, Hampshire):
Alice (1863-1876), **6:** 421 n.*693*, 422, 470
Annie Gertrude (1866-1951), **6:** 421 n.*693*, 422, 423, 425, 427, 438, 470, 488-490; **7:** 64; **8:** 255 n.*429*; **9:** 94 n.*171*, 95, 140, 219
Bessie Drinkwater (b. 1858), **6:** 421 n.*693*, 423, 438, 488, 489
Charles C. (b. 1870), **6:** 421 n.*693*
Clifton (b. 1869), **6:** 421 n.*693*, 425, 438; **8:** 255 n.*429*
Elizabeth Ann née Drinkwater (1833-1893), **6:** 421 n.*693*, 424, 428, 432, 438, 488, 489; **7:** 73 n.*118*, 74, 160; **8:** 255 n.*429*; **9:** 94 n.*171*
Ethel (1854-1933), see Bell
George H. (b. 1871), **6:** 421 n.*693*
Herbert (b. 1874), **6:** 421 n.*693*; **8:** 255 n.*429*
James, Rev. (1827-1907), **6:** 421 n.*693*, 424, 438; **7:** 160; **8:** 255 n.*429*, 256, 275; **9:** 94 n.*171*, 140, 219
Mary (b. 1861), **6:** 421 n.*693*, 423, 425, 438; **7:** 73 n.*118*, 74; **8:** 255 n.*429*, 256, 275
Norman H. (b. 1872), **6:** 421 n.*693*
Olive Arnold (1875-1933), **6:** 421 n.*693*; **8:** 255 n.*429*; **9:** 94 n.*171*, 219
Thomas Drinkwater (b. 1867), **6:** 421 n.*693*
Chatterton (pic. Henry Wallis), **2:** 75 n.*151*
Chaundy, Mary (b. 1815) – St. Aldates lodging-house keeper, **6:** 394, 488; **7:** 48, 546; **8:** 11 n.*2*, 215
Chaytor (of Clervaux Castle, Croft, Yorkshire):
Harriet (1815-1901), **1:** 81 n.*83*
John Clervaux (1806-1894), **2:** 7 n.*2*: **3:** 9 n.*6*
Lydia Frances née Brown (d. 1889), **2:** 7 n.*2*; **3:** 9 n.*6*
William Richard Carter (1805-1871), Sir, **1:** 81 n.*83*; **3:** 87 n.*136*
Checkmate (dr. Andrew Halliday), **6:** 261 n.*418*
Chedieu, Mons. – French teacher, **7:** 497 n.*812*
Cheeseman (of Eastbourne, Sussex):
Ella E., Mrs. (b. 1855), **7:** 298 n.*540*, 299
Stewart B. (b. 1879), **7:** 298 n.*540*
William, Mr. (b. 1849) – solicitor, **7:** 298 n.*540*, 299
Cheeseman, Florence E. (b. 1871) – logic pupil, **8:** 337 n.*556*, 376
Chelsea, London, **4:** 11; **7:** 494, 524
Chelsea Bridge, London, **3:** 173
Cheltenham, Gloucestershire, **3:** 26; **4:** 177, 185 n.*180*, 187, 191
Cheltenham College, **7:** 543 n.*876*; **8:** 129
Cheltenham Ladies College, **4:** 202 n.*209*, 213, 214 n.*226*, 217, 218 n.*236*
Cheltnam, Charles Smith (b. 1823) – dramatist, **5:** 47 n.*62*
Chepmell, Havilland (1810?-1887) – historian and writer, **1:** 11

Cherry, Apsley, Lieut. (1832-1907) – army officer, **1:** 95 n.*100*
Chertsey, Surrey, **6:** 58, 76
Cherwell (River), Oxford, **3:** 32, 36, 48; **4:** 172; **5:** 77
Chesney, George Tomkyns, Sir (1830-1895) – politician, **9:** 13 n.*6*
Chess Tournament at Redcar, Yorkshire, **5:** 172 n.*286*
Chester, Greville John, Rev. (1830-1892), **7:** 175 n.*324*
Chester Square, London (Mrs. Bayne), **4:** 269
Chestnuts, The, **6:** 44, 46, 48 n.*69*, photographed 57 n.*86*, 58, 85, 137, 193, 294, 363, 386, plans for improvement 388 n.*636*, 390, 397, 410, 456, 465; **7:** 140, 303, 312, 323, 325, 344, 393, 395, 396, 508; **8:** 75, 184, 365, 440, 442, 443, 500, 515, 607, 613; **9:** 45, 192, 234, 277
Chetwynd, Shropshire, **6:** 328, 386
Chevalier, Albert (1861-1923) – actor and singer, **8:** 400, 401 n.*653*, 473; **9:** 83, 84 n.*152*
Chevreul, Michel Eugene (1786-1889) – writer, **1:** 54 n.*12*
Chichester, Sussex, **6:** 227, 228, 231, 235; **7:** 313, 400; **8:** 241
Chichester Deanery, **6:** 235
Chichester Theological College, **6:** 186, 193
Child, Gilbert William, Dr. (1832-1896) – physician, **8:** 378 n.*622*
"Children in Theatres " (meeting in London), **8:** 349 n.*574*
Children in the Wood, The (dr. attrib. Edward Blanchard), **6:** 257 n.*409*, 378
Children in the Wood, The (pic. James Sant), **2:** 75 n.*151*
Children of the King, The (dr. Carl Armbruster and Arthur Rushton), **9:** 347, 348 n.*557*
Children's Pinafore (Gilbert & Sullivan) – operetta, **7:** 316 n.*565*
Children's Tea, The (pic. Helen Allingham), **7:** 533 n.*863*
Children's Theatre, **8:** 288
Childs (of Marylebone, London):
  Marianna. Mrs. (b. 1839), **6:** 129 n.*200*
  Philip A. (b. 1866), **6:** 129 n.*200*
  Ralitha Mildred (b. 1863), **6:** 129 n.*200*
  Robert W., Mr. (b. 1821) – solicitor, **6:** 129 n.*200*
Child's Bible, **6:** 262
Chili Widow, A (dr. Arthur Bourchier and Alfred Sutro), **9:** 219, 220 n.*349*
Chilley, Charles (b. 1857) – singer, **8:** 36 n.*45*
Chinese Music, Paris Exhibition, **5:** 366
Chippendale:
  Mary née Snowden (1832-1888) – actress, **5:** 139 n.*223*
  William Henry (1801-1888) – actor, **4:** 300 n.*366*; **5:** 32 n.*35*, 139 n.*223*
Chipping Norton, Oxfordshire, **7:** 46, 47 n.*72*
Chirgwin, George H. (1855-1922) – actor and singer, **7:** 400 n.*678*
Chislehurst, Kent, **8:** 210
Chitty, Joseph William (1828-1899) – barrister and politician, **7:** 267
Choosing (pic. George F. Watts), **4:** 335 n.*432*
Chopin, Frédéric Francois (1810-1849) – composer, **4:** 48

Chorister, The (pic. Henry Barraud), **2:** 18
Chosen Five, The (pic. Edwin Long), **9:** 58 n.*106*
"Chough and Crow, The" (Joanna Baillie) – song, **2:** 100
Chriemann, Mary Ann (b. 1845) – teacher, **8:** 194 n.*327*, 195, 208; **9:** 96 n.*174*

Christ Church:
Amateur Dramatics, **4:** 88, 263; **6:** 67
Anatomy Museum and School, **2:** 45, 46; **3:** 62; **4:** 36
Anatomy Quad, **7:** 491
Archdeacon, **7:** 145 n.*270*
Architectural changes, **6:** 238 n.*380*, 265, 363, 366, 367, 372
Athletic Sports, **4:** 162
Ball, **5:** 252; **8:** 461 n.*741*
Barge, **8:** 343; **9:** 257, 258
Belfry, **6:** 214 n.*333*, 340, 341 n.*566*
Biographical Record, **7:** 264 n.*477*
"Blenheim Ball" Row, **9:** 109 n.*194*, 110 n.*195*
Boulter Exhibitioners, **3:** 123 n.*175*
"Bread & Butter" Controversy, **5:** 116 n.*181*
Broad Walk, **1:** 66; **3:** 34, 36; **4:** 162, 172-174, 305 n.*374*; **7:** 454; **8:** 196, 216, 339, 409
Buttery Audit, **6:** 305 n.*505*
Canons (Chapter), **1:** 17, 61 n.*34*, 97, 98 n.*104*; **2:** 44 n.*88*, 64 n.*127*, 79 n.*157*, 86 n.*171*, 120 n.*231*; **3:** 19 n.*21*, 23 n.*30*, 42, 52, 70, 134, 165; **4:** 23; **5:** 49, 120, 121, 128; **7:** 276, 306, 419; **8:** 197, 203
Cathedral, **2:** 65, 110, 114 n.*220*; **3:** 23, 177; **4:** 39, 57, 59, 63, 177, 211, 263; **6:** 265, 266 n.*427*, 490; **7:** 85, 108, 115, 225, 346, 537; **8:** 126, 127 n.*207*, 245, 339, 492, 516, 567, 594; **9:** 123, 232, 240, 322
Cathedral West Entrance, **6:** 265, 267 n.*430*
Celibacy abolished for Dons, **7:** 113, 114 n.*210*
Censors, **1:** 61 n.*35*, 66 n.*49*, 71 n.*61*; **2:** 9 n.*7*, 66 n.*131*, 76 n.*152*, 120 n.*231*; **6:** 382; **7:** 90, 338, 339, 373, 384, 484, 511 n.*829*; **8:** 153; **9:** 232, 268, 323
Censor's Dinner, **4:** 149; **5:** 120; **6:** 104, 136, 306, 370, 438; **7:** 89, 149, 228, 310, 384, 501; **8:** 70, 156, 253, 308, 371, 438, 545, 603; **9:** 48, 232, 286, 354
Chapel, **2:** 107, 111; **3:** 23, 28, 48, 59, 158; **9:** 189, 191, 197, 232, 323
Chaplain, **1:** 96 n.*101*; **2:** 118 n.*225*
Chaplain's Quadrangle, **2:** 76 n.*152*; **4:** 63, 64
Chapter House, **7:** 306 n.*550*
Choir Festival, **7:** 277
Choristers' School, **5:** 29
Christ Church Oxford Act (1867), **3:** 19 n.*21*
Christmas treat for servants, **7:** 385, 386, 403

Clerical Students, **7:** 113
Cloisters, **2:** 64 n.*128*
Cloister Staircase, **4:** 63, 64
Collections, **2:** 76, 121 n.*236*; **3:** 125, 167, 177; **4:** 39, 87, 174, 176, 204, 265, 275, 277; **5:** 26, 29, 56, 58, 132, 152, 187 n.*307*, 189, 250; **6:** 266, 330, 382, 452; **7:** 103, 251; **8:** 95, 449
Collector of Rents, **7:** 257, 258 n.*469*
College Servants' Party, **9:** 49
College Servants' Service, **8:** 459, 502, 509, 540, 549, 612, 629; **9:** 38, 40, 105, 247, 302
Committee of Salaries, **7:** 239, 244
Common Room (see also under Dodgson, Curator of the Common Room), **2:** 31, 40, 42 n.*82*, 126; **3:** 16, 17, 19, 20, 21, 28, 31 n.*45*, 35, 37, 40, 46, 66, 68, 86, 122, 144, 180; **4:** 38, 54, 100, 158, 163, 207, 219, 279; **5:** 25, 49, 51, 228, 244; **6:** 303, 331, 410, 476, 492; **7:** 124, 193, 270, 321, 346, 370, 445, 453, 491, 496, 497, 499, 500, 513, 524; **8:** 13, 14, 62, 169, 256, 266, 276, 339, 383, 391, 450, 491, 514, 559, 560; **9:** 185, 193, 239, 286
Common Room Coal-Cellar, **7:** 530 n.*858*
Common Room File Book, **2:** 125 n.*243*; **3:** 27 n.*38*, 164; **4:** 279 n.*327*
Common Room Newspaper Archive, **3:** 42-44
Cook, **9:** 138, 229 n.*364*
Cricket Team, **3:** 64
Curator of the Common Room, **7:** 500, 501 n.*818*
Curatorship of Livings, **7:** 239 n.*441*, 242 n.*444*, 434
Dean, **1:** 48, 61 n.*34*, 62, 63, 70, 79, 97, 98 n.*104*, 101, 135; **2:** 25, 27, 29, 33, 43 n.*86*, 67, 70, 73, 78, 100 n.*193*, 107 n.*206*, 108, 110, 111 n.*217*, 122, 125, 126; **3:** 19 n.*21*, 38, 40, 74, 87 n.*135*, 121, 129, 144, 145, 177; **4:** 23, 39, 40, 59, 63, 78, 79, 103, 137 n.*115*, 138, 149, 152, 192, 200, 266, 268, 269; **5:** 46 n.*61*, 49, 59, 113, 187 n.*307*, 197 n.*320*; **6:** 131, 155, 274, 382, 492 n.*815*; **7:** 227, 244, 306, 320, 338, 371, 373, 377, 378, 382, 387, 440, 489, 490 n.*798*, 497; **8:** 123, 127, 196, 203, 256, 590, 607, 632; **9:** 109 n.*194*, 148, 151, 194, 195, 200, 230, 232, 247, 268, 300, 309, 323, 347
Deanery, **2:** 45, 48, 65, 66, 70, 72, 77, 79, 110, 112, 116 n.*222*, 118-122, 125, 126; **3:** 16, 20, 24, 45, 48, 55, 59, 64, 65, 72-4, 121, 123, 129, 178; **4:** 11, 35, 39, 43, 57, 67, 69, 93, 95, 112-115, 148, 161, 163, 172, 173, 176, 195, 196, 198, 199 n.*202*, 200, 201, 205, 206, 211, 220, 265, 266, 277; **5:** 187, 188, 243; **6:** 149, 187, 190, 326; **7:** 342, 534; **8:** 512; **9:** 34, 224, 308
Dinner Allowance, **7:** 230 n.*423*, 237
Disturbances, **7:** 338
Electoral Board, **7:** 427, 433, 434, 436, 440, 484 n.*788*, 489, 490 n.*798*; **8:** 123
Electors, **4:** 138, 268 n.*311*; **5:** 53

Fell Exhibitioners, **2:** 109 n.*213*; **3:** 123 n.*175*
Gaudy, **2:** 67 n.*132*, 109; **3:** 123; **4:** 87, 305; **6:** 155, 340; **7:** 41, 275, 544; **8:** 461 n.*741*, 517, 632; **9:** 152, 203, 264, 323
Governing Body, **4:** 23; **6:** 155, 363, 372, 447; **7:** 90, 113, 114, 227 n.*419*, 230 n.*423*, 237 n.*438*, 239 n.*441*, 242 n.*444*, 247 n.*452*, 247 n.*453*, 257, 258 n.*469*, 261, 262 n.*473*, 265 n.*479*, 276 n.*503*, 349, 385, 386, 387 n.*666*, 403, 433, 434, 436, 440 n.*730*, 484 n.*788*, 489, 490 n.*798*, 511 n.*829*, 545; **8:** 83 n.*132*, 123, 213 n.*364*, 263, 264 n.*443*, 265 n.*446*, 276 n.*464*, 284 n.*476*, 339, 461 n.*741*; **9:** 110 n.*195*, 148, 268 n.*424*
Hall, **1:** 59 n.*31*, 66, 67, 77, 95; **2:** 25, 27, 36, 76-7, 79, 110; **3:** 17, 48, 122, 123, 134, 176, 177; **4:** 32, 39, 40, 152, 153 n.*139*, 173, 174, 197, 209, 263, 305; **5:** 56, 81, 111, 149; **6:** 492; **7:** 108, 163, 225, 227, 269, 306, 336, 338, 346, 421, 425, 427, 436, 498, 531, 537; **8:** 62, 67, 169, 196, 215, 216, 245, 304, 339, 383, 391, 409, 460, 461, 489, 490, 516, 540, 544, 559, 560; **9:** 49, 109, 148, 190, 191, 193, 198-200, 223, 250, 309, 312
High Table, **2:** 77; **4:** 152, 153 n.*139*; **7:** 321
History of the Reforms, **7:** 419 n.*700*
Junior Common Room, **4:** 63; **8:** 276, 514
Junior Studentships, **5:** 46 n.*61*, 51 n.*71*, 53, 54 n.*75*; **6:** 318, 323, 324, 363; **7:** 20
Kitchen, **7:** 269, 336, 454, 537; **8:** 169, 215, 216, 245, 339, 409; **9:** 223, 232
Latin Chapel, **8:** 459; **9:** 124
Lecturers, **3:** 40; **7:** 440 n.*730*, 489, 490 n.*798*, 496; **8:** 83, 123, 213
Lee's Reader in Anatomy, **4:** 38
Lee's Reader in Chemistry, **4:** 23
Lee's Reader in Physics, **6:** 306, 307
Library, **1:** 61 n.*34*, 63, 70, 72, 76, 78, 79, 85, 89, 93, 100, 101; **2:** 9, 42, 43, 63, 67 n.*132*, 68, 73-4, 76-7, 79, 117; **3:** 26, 31 n.*45*, 124, 177; **4:** 39; **7:** 346; **8:** 607
Library Visitation, **2:** 73, 76, 77; **9:** 151, 200
Livings, **8:** 124, 196, 203
Mathematical Lectureship, **1:** 49, 62 n.*36*, 70, 79, 132
Mathematical Scholarships, **3:** 22, 38; **7:** 276 n.*503*
Mathematical Studentship, **7:** 20
Matriculation, **2:** 71; **3:** 66; **4:** 78, 136, 192, 257, 267; **5:** 81, 111, 233 n.*373*; **6:** 238, 301 n.*496*, 317, 379, 425, 458; **7:** 30, 44 n.*67*, 99, 142, 221, 305, 306, 320, 323-325, 328, 370, 384, 536; **8:** 203, 398, 400
Meadow, **6:** 327; **9:** 232
Meadow Buildings, **4:** 63; **7:** 422
New Common Room, **6:** 187, 277; **7:** 164, 244
Ordinance (1858), **4:** 23, 268
Peckwater Quad, **2:** 106 n.*205*; **3:** 15
Physical Science Fund, **3:** 21 n.*26*

Reader in Mathematics, **6:** 28
Reading Society, **8:** 200 n.*340*
Reform, **5:** 27 n.*27*, 48, 49 n.*65*, 50 n.*67*, 158 n.*260*, 190, 191 n.*312*, 197 n.*320*
Scouts, **9:** 268
Senior Censor, **3:** 16 n.*15*, 134, 135
Senior Masters, **2:** 36, 126
Senior Masters' Estates, **9:** 286 n.*452*, 322 n.*515*
Senior Proctor, **6:** 370
Senior Students, **5:** 200 n.*326*; **6:** 66 n.*97*, 69 n.*100*, 103, 132, 137, 154, 155, 306, 307, 372, 440, 494
Steeple Chase, **6:** 383, 384 n.*630*
Steward, **7:** 265 n.*479*; **9:** 268
Steward's Audit, **6:** 368
Students, **3:** 19 n.*21*, 37, 38, 40, 68, 87 n.*135*, 161; **4:** 20, 23, 54, 55, 59, 63, 149, 150, 268 n.*311*, 294; **7:** 227, 264 n.*477*, 419, 436, 440, 484 n.*788*; **8:** 71
Students' Meeting, **5:** 48, 49 n.*65*, 50 n.*67*, 120 n.*188*, 121, 128, 197 n.*320*, 376
Sub-Dean, **3:** 23 n.*30*, 24 n.*32*, 35, 42, 66, 135, 177; **4:** 39, 40; **5:** 149, 197
Tasting luncheon, **7:** 517 n.*837*
Tom Gate, **2:** 106
Tom Quad, **4:** 63, 64; **9:** 310
Tom Tower, **8:** 376, 378
Treasurer, **8:** 261-264, 265 n.*446*, 284
Tutors, **2:** 25, 66 n.*131*; **3:** 52, 86; **4:** 294
Tutors' Meeting, **5:** 187 n.*307*
Undergraduates, **5:** 191 n.*312*
University Readers, **7:** 436
Westminster Students, **3:** 19 n.*21*
Wine Accounts Ledger, **7:** 503
Wine Committee, **7:** 500

Christian Fathers, **4:** 10
Christianity, **3:** 8; **4:** 10
Christian Missionary Society, **9:** 28, 29 n.*44*
Christie (of Edinburgh):
Annie (b. 1861?), **6:** 185
Mrs., **6:** 184, 185 n.*286*, 351
Christie, Dora (b. 1867), **7:** 52 n.*82*, 54, 74
Christie (of Oxford?):
Edith, **6:** 290
Margaret, **6:** 290
May, **6:** 290; **7:** 432 n.*719*
Christ in the House of his Parents (pic. John Millais), **4:** 78, 79 n.*29*

Christ in the Temple (pic. William Holman Hunt), **4:** 31, 55
Christmas Bookseller, The, **5:** 11, 12 n.*2*
Christmas Cards, **7:** 151 n.*285*
Christmas Carol (bk. Charles Dickens), **7:** 299
Christmas Dramatic Wanderers, Oxford, **9:** 121
Christmas Eve (pic. Walter Anderson), **5:** 217, 218 n.*347*
Christmas Stocking (bk. Elizabeth Wetherell), **1:** 99 n.*108*
"Christmas Waits" Henry Savile Clarke) – song, **8:** 316 n.*519*
Christy Minstrels, **5:** 162 n.*267*; **6:** 97
Chromograph, **7:** 196 n.*366*, 200 n.*375*, 204, 210, 215, 216, 219
Church (of Retford, Nottinghamshire):
  Alfred John, Rev. (1829-1912) – teacher, **7:** 203 n.*379*
  Charlotte J., Mrs. (b. 1844), **7:** 203 n.*379*
  Ernest E. (b. 1869), **7:** 203 n.*379*
  George E. (b. 1873), **7:** 203 n.*379*
  Harold S. (b. 1875), **7:** 203 n.*379*
  Maurice (b. 1867), **7:** 203 n.*379*
  Richard A. (b. 1870), **7:** 203 n.*379*
  Sylvia M. E. (b. 1879), **7:** 203 n.*379*
Church, Helen Beatrice (1858-1900), see Paget
Church, William Selby, Dr. (1837-1928) – Lee's reader in anatomy, **4:** 38
"Church and Stage Guild" (prospectus by Stewart Headlam), **7:** 173
Church Congress, **4:** 100 n.*62*
Church Dictionary, The (bk. Walter Hook), **1:** 60 n.*32*

Churches:
  Abbey Church, Malvern, **4:** 119
  All Saints', Eastbourne, **8:** 418
  All Saints', Windsor, **5:** 84
  All Souls', Eastbourne, **8:** 293, 294
  Beverley Minster, Yorkshire, **4:** 241
  Christ Church, Cheltenham, **4:** 187
  Christ Church, Eastbourne, **7:** 130, 132-137, 198, 202, 212, 282, 300, 455, 456, 459, 461, 466, 470, 472, 473; **8:** 22, 40, 228, 358, 421, 426, 476, 485, 529, 568, 578; **9:** 15, 30, 91, 94, 157, 211, 271, 272, 274, 328, 331, 333-335, 340, 341
  Christ Church, Hull, **1:** 10
  Christ Church Cathedral, Oxford, **2:** 65, 110, 114 n.*220*; **3:** 23, 177; **4:** 39, 57, 59, 63, 177, 211, 263
  Coatham Church, Yorkshire, **5:** 102
  Covent Garden Church, London, **4:** 339
  Easby Abbey, Yorkshire, **3:** 91
  Fountains Abbey, Yorkshire, **1:** 55 n.*19*
  Gloucester Cathedral, **4:** 192
  Iffley Church, **4:** 176

Iron Church, Oxford, **4:** 163
Magdalen College Chapel and Tower, **4:** 55, 81, 82
Osney Chapel, Oxfordshire, **4:** 170
Richmond Friary, Yorkshire, **3:** 91
Ripon Cathedral, **1:** 50; **2:** 13 n.*17*, 55 n.*108*; **3:** 7 n.*2*, 147; **4:** 13
St. Alban's Abbey, Hertfordshire, **6:** 248
St. Aldates, Oxford, **2:** 25, 30 n.*57*, 71 n.*141*
St. Aloysius, Oxford, **7:** 100 n.*187*; **9:** 320
St. Andrew's, Wells Street, London, **4:** 283
St. Anne's, Upperton, **8:** 418, 421, 423, 426, 476
St. Anne's Hill, Chertsey, **6:** 77
St. Barnabas, Oxford, **6:** 474
St. Bridget's, Dublin, **2:** 63
St. Catherine's, Guildford, **7:** 117
St. Clements, London, **5:** 210
St. Ebbe's, Oxford, **1:** 40; **2:** 36 n.*72*
St. Frideswide, Oxford, **7:** 126 n.*237*
St. John's, Drury Lane, London, **6:** 288, 349
St. John's, Whitby, **5:** 178
St. John's Chapel, Cheltenham, **4:** 187
St. Margaret's, Westminster, **4:** 222
St. Martha's, Guildford, **8:** 240, 271
St. Martin's, London, **4:** 338, 343, 359; **5:** 47, 139
St. Martin's, Scarborough, **9:** 226
St. Mary Magdalene, Oxford, **5:** 134, 163, 185; **6:** 475
St. Mary's, Guildford, **6:** 46, 205; **8:** 305, 312, 375, 434, 439, 440, 546, 615; **9:** 50, 290
St. Mary's (University Church), Oxford, **2:** 69; **3:** 33, 35, 167; **4:** 88; **5:** 205, 228, 234; **6:** 212, 305, 462; **7:** 119, 145, 324, 519, 521, 534, 545; **8:** 410; **9:** 72 n.*132*, 153, 199, 252, 257, 278, 285, 297, 300, 315, 346
St. Mary's, Shrewsbury, **7:** 126 n.*237*
St. Mary's, Westminster, **3:** 132
St. Mary's, Whitby, **2:** 101, 102 n.*196*; **5:** 234; **6:** 54
St. Michael's and St. Ninnian's, Whitby, **5:** 178
St. Nicholas, Guildford, **8:** 396
St. Pancras, London, **6:** 495
St. Paul's, London, **6:** 178, 201 n.*313*; **7:** 166
St. Paul's, Oxford, **2:** 25, 117, 118 n.*225*; **4:** 141; **5:** 44 n.*57*, 46, 48, 75 n.*114*, 76, 79, 81, 111; **9:** 236
St. Peter's, Eastbourne, **8:** 22, 529; **9:** 91
St. Peter's, Vere Street, London, **4:** 105, 160, 222, 309, 310, 330
St. Peter's in the East, Oxford, **6:** 147
St. Philip's and St. James' Church, Oxford, **4:** 80 n.*32*; **9:** 238
St. Saviour's, Eastbourne, **7:** 60-62, 67, 129, 134, 136, 139, 200, 212, 461,

462, 466; **8:** 286, 423, 529; **9:** 14
St. Stephen's, Westminster, **4:** 249 n.*285*
St. Werburgh's, Dublin, **2:** 62
Temple Church, London, **9:** 37 n.*65*
Trinity Church, Eastbourne, **7:** 52, 54, 67, 132, 300
Trinity Church, Malvern, **4:** 118
Vere Street Chapel, London, **5:** 210 n.*337*
Westminster Abbey, London, **4:** 270
Worcester Cathedral, **4:** 120

Churches abroad:
Aldstadt Kirche, Königsberg, **5:** 279
Apostle's Church, Cologne, **5:** 263
Armenian Church, Troitsa, **5:** 344
Cathedral Church, Moscow, **5:** 321
Cathedral Church, Nijni Novgorod, **5:** 312
Cathedral Church, St. Petersburg, **5:** 291
Church of the Annunciation, Troitsa, **5:** 344
Church of the Assumption, Moscow, **5:** 335
Dom-Kirche, Berlin, **5:** 274
Dom-Kirche, Danzig, **5:** 275
Dom-Kirche, Königsberg, **5:** 282
English Church, Moscow, **5:** 315, 335
Greek Church, St. Petersburg, **5:** 348
Isaac-Church, St. Petersburg, **5:** 285, 340
Kazan Cathedral, St. Petersburg, **5:** 286
Kreutzkirch, Breslau, **5:** 354
St. Basil's, Moscow, **5:** 303
St. Christopher's, Breslau, **5:** 353
St. Dorothy's, Breslau, **5:** 353
St. Elizabeth's, Breslau, **5:** 353
St. Gereon's, Cologne, **5:** 263
St. Gudule, Brussels, **5:** 259
St. Mary in Capitolio, Cologne, **5:** 263
St. Mary Magdalene's, Breslau, **5:** 353
St. Michael's, Breslau, **5:** 354
St. Nicholas, Berlin, **5:** 268, 269
St. Peter's, Berlin, **5:** 266
St. Peter's, Cologne, **5:** 263
St. Ursula, Cologne, **5:** 263
Troitsa Church, **5:** 344

Churchman, The, **5:** 181 n.*300*, 184 n.*302*
Church of England, **4:** 11, 20
Church of Scotland, **9:** 278

Cinderella (dr. Anon), **5:** 45 n.*58*; **6:** 156, 250, 275
Cinderella (dr. Edward Blanchard), **7:** 155 n.*291*, 156, 159
Cinderella (dr. Frank Green), **7:** 153 n.*290*, 193
Cinderella (dr. Horace Lennard), **9:** 122 n.*214*
Cinderella (dr. Louisa MacDonald), **4:** 324
Cinderella (pic. George Hicks), **7:** 539 n.*872*
Cinderella (pic. John Millais), **7:** 347, 348 n.*609*
"Circulation" – topic for study **7:** 150
Circus:
  Holborn Amphitheatre, **6:** 156
  Hutchinson & Tayleure, **7:** 286
  Myer's, **7:** 173, 174 n.*322*
  Sanger's, **4:** 211 n.*222*; **7:** 135
Civil Service, **5:** 135
Clapham (of Tunbridge, Kent):
  Charles G., Mr. (b. 1839) – stockbroker, **8:** 228 n.*386*
  Frances Eliza, Mrs. (b. 1846), **8:** 228 n.*386*
  Frances Maude (b. 1872), **8:** 228 n.*386*, 230, 242
Clapham, Surrey, **3:** 82; **4:** 342; **7:** 348, 398
Clapham Junction, **6:** 232, 352
Claremont, Esher, Surrey, **9:** 225 n.*356*
Claribel, see Barnard
Clark, Jessie Howard – acrostic on her name, **6:** 407
Clark, William George (1821-1878) – writer, **5:** 172 n.*287*
Clarke, Catherine, Mrs. (b. 1829), **7:** 232 n.*426*
Clarke (of Paddington, London):
  Clara Savile (1869-1898), **8:** 291 n.*487*, 304, 318, 327, 370, 408, 442
  Helen née Dawson (1840?-1898), **8:** 291 n.*487*, 304, 327, 370, 408, 441, 442, 486
  Henry Savile, Mr. (1841-1893) – dramatist and journalist, **8:** 291 n.*487*, 304, 309 n.*512*, 311, 312, 316, 320, 327, 370, 402, 403, 408, 412, 420, 421 n.*681*, 428, 430, 433, 486, 546 n.*870*
  Katherine "Kitty" Dawson (1872-1901), **8:** 291 n.*487*, 304, 313, 318, 327, 370, 408, 442, 486
  Margaret "Maggie" E. (b. 1871), **8:** 291 n.*487*, 304, 313, 318, 327, 370, 408, 442
Clarke, Ella, **9:** 326, 327 n.*524*
Clarke, Evelyn – friend of the Terrys, **5:** 62 n.*91*; **6:** 310
Clarke, John Erskine, Rev. (b. 1828), **8:** 449 n.*719*
Clarke, John S. (1833-1899) – actor, **5:** 17 n.*11*, 32 n.*35*, 126; **6:** 135 n.*208*
Clarke, Katharine L. (b. 1877) – actress, **9:** 166, 167 n.*284*
Clarke, see Langton Clarke
Claudian (dr. Henry Herman and William Wills), **8:** 80, 81 n.*125*, 103 n.*172*, 108
Claudius – steamship, **8:** 258, 259 n.*436*, 293, 521, 540 n.*865*, 541

Claughton, Piers Calverley, Rt. Rev. (1814-1884) – bishop of Colombo, **4:** 80 n.*32*
Clay, Cecil (1847-1920) – dramatist, **8:** 618 n.*980*; **9:** 13 n.*5*
Clay, Frederick (1839-1889) – composer, **5:** 45 n.*58*
Clay, Richard (1790-1878) - printer, **5:** 10, 100, 101 n.*158*, 115 n.*180*; **6:** 140, 188; **8:** 221 n.*378*, 247, 303, 307 n.*509*, 355, 369, 487, 488, 491, 492, 520; **9:** 51, 105, 106 n.*190*, 107, 111, 157, 183, 191, 197, 201, 231
Clayton, John (1845-1888), alias John Alfred Clayton Calthorp – actor, **6:** 315 n.*523*; **7:** 438 n.*727*, 514, 536
Clearsby, Yorkshire, **4:** 154; **5:** 107, 111
Cleaton, John Davies, Dr. (1825-1901) – physician, **8:** 48 n.*71*
Cleave, William Oke (1830-1904) – teacher, **8:** 97 n.*159*
Cleaver, Charles William Euseby, Rev. (b. 1861), **7:** 379 n.*654*, 384
Cleaver, William Henry (b. 1834), MA Christ Church, **3:** 161 n.*236*
Cleeve (of Guildford, Surrey):
  Beatrice C. (b. 1869), **7:** 221 n.*404*
  Frederick J. (b. 1863), **7:** 221 n.*404*
  Janet (b. 1873), **7:** 221 n.*404*
  Maria L. (b. 1867), **7:** 220, 221 n.*404*
  Stewart A., Lt. Col. (b. 1826) – retired army officer, **7:** 220, 221 n.*404*, 229, 230
Cleft Stick, A (dr. John Oxenford), **5:** 117 n.*182*
Clemens, see Twain
Clements, Mrs., **8:** 530 n.*848*
Clementson, Alfred, Rev. (1838-1927), **8:** 267 n.*449*
Clendon, see Collis
Cleobury, Shropshire, **7:** 311, 325, 446; **8:** 261, 262, 268, 501, 519, 545, 557, 597; **9:** 47, 110, 115, 245, 271, 314, 315
Clerical Duty, **4:** 16
Clerical Error, A (dr. Henry Jones), **7:** 540 n.*873*; **8:** 52 n.*77*
Clerical Fellowships, **7:** 38 n.*55*, 39 n.*57*
Clerke (of Christ Church, Oxford):
  Caroline née Ashhurst (b. 1812), **6:** 327
  Charles Carr, Rev. Dr. (1799-1877), **3:** 24 n.*32*, 25, 35, 42, 135, 177; **5:** 29 n.*30*, 130 n.*208*, 149; **6:** 67 n.*99*, 326
Clervaux Castle, near Croft, Yorkshire, **1:** 81 n.*83*; **3:** 90
Cleveland, Lord, see Powlett
Clifton, Edith (b. 1854?) – friend of the Slatters, **5:** 48 n.*64*
Clifton, Fanny – see Stirling
Clifton, Robert Bellamy (1836-1921) – professor of experimental philosophy, **6:** 4, 339; **9:** 113 n.*198*
Clifton Family of Whitby, **5:** 178 n.*295*
Clifton Hampden, Oxfordshire, **4:** 73, 195, 204
Clinical Lectures and Essays (bk. James Paget), **7:** 56 n.*88*
Clisham, Katie (b. 1875) – fellow steamship passenger, **7:** 447, 448 n.*740*

Clitherow, Maude E. (b. 1877) – actress, **7:** 524, 525 n.*849*
Clito (dr. Sydney Grundy and Wilson Barrett), **8:** 274 n.*462*
Clive, Caroline (1801-1873) – novelist, **3:** 82, 83 n.*128*
Cloches de Corneville, Les (Henry Farnie, Robert Reece and Robert Planquette) – operetta, **7:** 369, 370 n.*643*; **8:** 135 n.*220*, 136, 363
Cloran (of Ireland):
  Aileen, **8:** 572 n.*913*, 574, 591, 633
  Gerald, **8:** 572 n.*913*, 574
  Michael, **8:** 572 n.*913*, 574
  Mrs., **8:** 572 n.*913*, 573
Clough, Arthur Hugh (1819-1861) – poet, **1:** 41
Clyde (River), Scotland, **3:** 104
Coape, Henry Coe (fl. 1860) – dramatist, **5:** 210 n.*336*
Coates, Charles, Mr. (1826-1909) – surgeon, **6:** 278 n.*457*
Coates, Emily (b. 1822) – wine merchant, **6:** 402 n.*659*
Coates, James (b. 1840?) – pupil-teacher, **1:** 109 n.*124*, 111, 112
Cobb, Walter William (b. 1856), MA Christ Church, **6:** 453 n.*744*
Cobbe, Frances Power (1822-1904) – social reformer, **6:** 381 n.*626*, 390
Cochin China (dr. Anon), **5:** 311
Cochrane (of Croft, Yorkshire):
  Constance A. (b. 1851), **1:** 131; **4:** 179
  Julia, Mrs. (b. 1817), **1:** 130
  Robert, Mr. (b. 1816), **1:** 130
Cockburn (of Paddington, London):
  Edith Mary (b. 1855), **5:** 170
  Julia Clementine née Sant, **5:** 169 n.*280*
  Julia Sant (b. 1856), **5:** 170
  Ruth (b. 1858), **5:** 170
  William Alexander, Mr. (b. 1821) – civil servant, **5:** 169 n.*280*
Cock Mill Woods, Whitby, Yorkshire, **6:** 54
Cocks (of Guildford, Surrey):
  Frank Robert, Rev. (b. 1858), **8:** 372 n.*612*; **9:** 76 n.*139*
  Mrs., **8:** 372 n.*612*; **9:** 76 n.*139*
Cocks, Robert – publishing company, **6:** 189 n.*294*
Cockton, Henry (1807-1853) – writer, **1:** 57 n.*21*
Cody, William Frederick "Buffalo Bill" (1846-1917) – entertainer, **8:** 368 n.*604*
Coe (of Westminster, London):
  Arthur Ernest (b. 1869), **5:** 205 n.*328*; **6:** 254
  Ellen Blanch née Hanson (b. 1842), **5:** 201, 202, 204, 205 n.*328*, 222; **6:** 170
  Nelly Cordelia (b. 1874), **5:** 205 n.*328*; **6:** 486
  Thomas, Mr. (1822-1886) – actor and manager, **5:** 25, 193 n.*317*, 200-204, 205 n.*328*, 222, 242 n.*393*, 380; **6:** 69, 170, 486
Coghlan, C. F. (1838-1899) – actor, **7:** 514 n.*832*

Cohen, Arthur (1829-1914) – barrister, **1:** 109; **8:** 107 n.*177*, 108 n.*179*, 126
Cole (of Greywell, Isle of Wight):
  Edith Ann Lydia (b. 1863), **6:** 343 n.*569*
  Francis Charles, Rev. (b. 1834), **6:** 343 n.*569*
  Lydia Hannah, Mrs. (b. 1834), **6:** 343 n.*569*; **7:** 46, 47 n.*72*
Cole, George (1810-1883) – artist, **5:** 219 n.*350*; **6:** 22, 23 n.*23*, 79 n.*114*
Cole (of Brighton, Sussex):
  Josephine "Pussy" (b. 1880), **8:** 519 n.*835*, 520, 529, 536
  Mrs., **8:** 519 n.*835*, 529; **9:** 84, 85 n.*153*
  Winifred, **8:** 536
Cole, Lieut. – ventriloquist, **8:** 414, 415 n.*672*
Cole, Miss – friend of the Parnells, **4:** 22, 328 n.*419*
Cole, Misses, **8:** 251 n.*422*; **9:** 187 n.*310*
Cole, William Willoughby (1807-1886), Earl of Enniskillen, **4:** 35
Colebrook Terrace, Bognor, Sussex, **6:** 229
Colegate (of Eastbourne, Sussex):
  Amy E., Mrs. (b. 1839), **7:** 134 n.*249*, 356
  Mary (b. 1852), **7:** 134 n.*249*
  Robert, Mr. (b. 1818) – surgeon, **7:** 134 n.*249*, 356
Coleman, John (1831-1904) – actor and dramatist, **7:** 356 n.*623*; **8:** 476, 477 n.*772*
Coleman, William Stephen (1829-1904) – artist, **7:** 395 n.*673*, 429 n.*716*, 482 n.*784*, 485, 486, 496, 522, 536
Colenso, John William (1814-1883) – mathematician and cleric, **4:** 329 n.*420*
Coleridge, Amy – actress, **9:** 162 n.*277*
Coleridge, Samuel Taylor (1772-1834) – writer and poet, **1:** 56 n.*20*, 73, 116 n.*140*; **3:** 147 n.*212*
Coles (of Eastbourne, Sussex, and Tonbridge, Kent):
  Amy N. (b. 1870), **7:** 208 n.*387*, 209, 213, 215, 218, 284
  Beatrice (b. 1869), **7:** 208 n.*387*, 209, 213, 215, 218, 283, 284
  Elizabeth M. (b. 1860), **7:** 208 n.*387*, 218
  Helena "Nellie" C. V. (b. 1874), **7:** 208 n.*387*, 209, 213, 218
  Henry H. (b. 1862), **7:** 208 n.*387*
  Jessie M. (b. 1867), **7:** 208 n.*387*, 209, 213, 215, 218, 283
  John B. C. (b. 1858), **7:** 208 n.*387*
  John H. C., Mr. (b. 1832) – solicitor, **7:** 208 n.*387*, 209, 218, 297
  Sarah E., Mrs. (b. 1837), **7:** 61 n.*97*, 208 n.*387*, 209, 218
Coles (of Eastbourne, Sussex):
  Campion, **8:** 41 n.*56*
  Miss, **8:** 41 n.*56*
Coles, James (b. 1844) – printer in Broad Street, Oxford, **7:** 279 n.*509*
Coles, Richard Edward, Rev. (b. 1841), **4:** 71 n.*13*, 89, 90, 195, 339; **8:** 214 n.*366*
Colleen Bawn, The (dr. Dion Boucicault), **4:** 109 n.*77*

College Rhymes, **1:** 48; **4:** 37, 48, 65 n.*1*, 71 n.*13*, 89, 108 n.*76*, 121 n.*93*, 122, 136 n.*113*, 142 n.*122*, 144 n.*126*, 146, 148, 149 n.*133*, 169 n.*162*, 173 n.*169*, 177 n.*174*, 321; **8:** 214
Collette, Charles (1843-1924) – actor, **8:** 405 n.*659*
Colley, Richard Henry (1832-1902), MA Christ Church, **1:** 95 n.*99*
Collie Foster (of London):
Florence "Birdie" May née Balfour (b. 1865), **6:** 357 n.*590*, 358, 361, 411, 412, 481; **7:** 18, 19 n.*15*; **8:** 568 n.*904*
John, Mr. (1862-1926) – upholstery manufacturer, **8:** 568 n.*904*
Collier, Florence – friend of the Napiers, **6:** 478, 479
Collier, John (1850-1934) – artist, **7:** 539 n.*872*
Collingwood, Adelaide, Mrs. (b. 1823), **6:** 223, 224 n.*352*

Collingwood:

Collingwood (of Sunderland, Durham):
Amelia "Amy" Thompson (b. 1840), **6:** 207 n.*324*; **9:** 158 n.*274*, 226, 306
Ann Jane née Corbett (1799-1881), **6:** 82, 207 n.*324*; **7:** 335 n.*590*; **9:** 158 n.*274*
Caroline Stuart Wortley (b. 1828) – see Taylor
Charles Edward Stuart (1831-1898) – see below
James Wilkie, Mr. (1799-1864) – merchant, **6:** 207 n.*324*; **9:** 158 n.*274*
Mary Olivia (1842-1894), **7:** 26, 360 n.*628*; **9:** 158 n.*274*
Collingwood (of Southwick, Durham):
Bertram James (1871-1934) – nephew, **6:** birth 193 n.*300*, 225, 246, 262, 363, 410, 482, 484, 485; **7:** 125, 133, first Eastbourne holiday 135, 136, 181, 189, 193, 281, 296, 299, 301, 303, 312, illness 315, 323, 325, 343, 359, 360, 363, 370, 414, 423, 437, 462, 464, taken to concert 465, 468-470, 477, 481, silver watch gift 532, 545; **8:** 82, 101, 102, 148, 159, father declines trip to theatre 161, 162, 183, 236, 238, 290-292, 328, 356, staying with aunt Henrietta at Brighton 481, at Cambridge 545; **9:** at St. Mary's Hospital 193, 196, 227, 345, divisibility rules 350
Charles Edward Stuart, Rev. (1831-1898) – brother-in-law, **6:** 43 n.*59*, 60, 66, 82 n.*122*, 175, 206, 207, 280, 414, 485; **7:** 25, 39, 40, 170, 181, 183, 359, 360, 460; **8:** 161, 235-238, 244, 255, 256, 296, 338, 342, 353, 395, 396, 404, 429, 433, 445, 510, 514, 566, 567, 628; **9:** 14, 22, 102, 179, 225-227, 269, 306 354 n.*567*
Mary Charlotte née Dodgson (1835-1911) – sister, **1:** 13, 27, 50 n.*3*, 51, 54 n.*13*, 111, 117, 121; **2:** 12 n.*15*, 16, 58, 100; **3:** 41 n.*64*, 171; **4:** 28, 31, 43, 47, 60, 98, 233, 274; **5:** 42, 102, 107, 172, 177, 233 n.*373*; **6:** 11 n.*1*, 41, 42, 51, 66, 76, wedding gift 81 n.*119*, marriage 82 n.*122*, 85, 175, 193, 206, 208, 225, 226, 229, 233, 235, 239, 240, 280, 284, 361-363, 410, 414, 477, 481, 484, 485, 496; **7:** 25, 39, 40, 125, 133, 170, 181, 183, 189, 193, 303, 312, 343, 359, 360, 370, 392, 460, 477, 481, 502, 531; **8:** 75, 101, 170, 235-238, 244, 296, 298, 328, 338, 342,

353, 400, 403, 404, 433, 438, 514, 566, 567, 628; **9:** 14, 22, 102, 173, 179, 226, 269, 306, death of husband 354 n.*567*
Stuart Dodgson (1870-1937) – nephew, **1:** references from his biography of Dodgson 13, 18, 20, 27-29, 32, 35, 37, 41, 45, 47, 135; **4:** 12-15, 32, 33, 39, 40, 45, 54, 56; **6:** godson 11 n.*1*, first meeting 206 n.*322*, 208, 225, 229, 246, 262, 363, 410, 482, 484, 485; **7:** 125, 133, 135, 136, 181, 189, 193, 281, 296, 299, 301, 303, 312, 315, 323, 325, 343, 344 n.*603*, 345, 359, 360, 363, 370, 414, 423, 437, 462, 464-466, 468-471, 477, 481; **8:** 82, 83, 101, 102, 113, 148, 159, 161, 162, 183, 236-238, 255, 290-292, 356, 395, matriculation at Christ Church 398-400, 403, 404, 429, 435, 443, 454, 455, 457, 458, 469, 490, 502, 515, 516, 539, 540, 545, 551, 557, 565, gains BA degree 566; **9:** 51 n.*88*, 158, 159, 302, 303, 354 n.*567*

Collins, Charles Allston (1828-1873) – writer, **8:** 15 n.*9*; **9:** 190 n.*314*
Collins, Emma A. (b. 1837) – housekeeper, **8:** 474 n.*769*
Collins, John (1804-1874) – actor, **5:** 17 n.*11*
Collins, Robert Hawthorn, Sir (1841-1908) – royal administrator, **6:** 393 n.*644*, 394, 396; **8:** 465, 466 n.*752*, 468, 514, 596; **9:** 224, 225 n.*354*, 329 n.*528*
Collins, Wilkie (William) (1824-1889) – writer, **6:** 141 n.*212*; **7:** 285 n.*517*
Collins, William Allston (1828-1873) – artist and novelist, **3:** 68 n.*106*, 144
Collis, Hugh G. (b. 1843), alias "Hugh Clendon" & "H. Ponti" – composer, **7:** 510 n.*826*
Collyer, Mrs. – lodging-house keeper, **8:** 615
Collyns, John Martyn (1827-1912), MA Christ Church, **1:** 65 n.*44*, 71; **2:** 31 n.*58*, 32, 67, 68, 89, 91-99; **3:** 17, 18 n.*19*, 21, 119, 135-137, 174; **4:** 15, 100 n.*63*; **9:** 323 n.*517*
Colnaghi, C. P. – dramatist, **8:** 478 n.*774*; **9:** 274 n.*435*
Colnaghi – art dealers:
Dominic Paul (1790-1879), **2:** 22 n.*42*; **3:** 139 n.*206*; **5:** 88, 117 n.*183*
Martin (1821-1908), **2:** 22 n.*42*; **5:** 88, 117 n.*183*
Cologne, Germany, **5:** 262
Cologne Cathedral, **5:** 262
Colomba (dr. Alexander Mackenzie), **8:** 15 n.*8*
Colonial Office, London, **8:** 45-47, 51, 52, 64
"Columbine" (in harlequinade), **2:** 22
Colvin, Sidney, Sir (1845-1927) – Slade professor of fine art, **6:** 294 n.*484*
Colyer-Fergusson (of Sevenoaks, Kent.):
Beatrice Stanley née Müller, Lady (1865-1902), **5:** 254 n.*419*; **6:** 123, 124, 127, 380; **8:** 595 n.*949*
Thomas, Sir (1865-1951), 3rd Bart., **8:** 595 n.*949*
Combe (of University Press Yard, Oxford):
Martha Howell née Bennett (1806-1893), **4:** 169, 176, 225. 278; **5:** 165 n.*272*, 314; **7:** 148, 149 n.*281*, 269, 329, 497, 538; **8:** 56 n.*84*,

97, 633; **9:** 12 n.*1*
Thomas (1797-1872) – director of the Clarendon Press, **3:** 33 n.*51*; **4:** 31, 35, 83 n.*36*, 146, 176, 217, 220, 221, 225, 258, 303, 305, 308, 347; **5:** 15 n.*8*, 76 n.*115*, 100, 165 n.*272*, 314; **6:** 204 n.*318*, 226, 240 n.*383*
Combe, Richard (b. 1859) – subject of portrait by Sant, **5:** 209 n.*334*
Comic Times, The, **1:** 112 n.*130*, 116, 117, 120, 122 n.*151*, 126; **2:** 14 n.*20*, 34, 52 n.*104*; **3:** 53 n.*80*
Commin, J. G. – bookseller, **9:** 275 n.*438*
Commissariat (Crimean War), **1:** 62
Commission, A (dr. Weedon Grossmith), **9:** 303 n.*482*
Commissioners in Lunacy, **6:** 346
Common Pleas, London, **7:** 125
Compendium of Algebra (bk. John Ward), **1:** 81 n.*82*
Compton, Ada Cavendish (1847-1895) – actress, **5:** 139 n.*223*
Compton, Edward (1854-1918) – actor, **8:** 478 n.*774*, 619; **9:** 273 n.*434*, 274, 313
Compton:
Emmeline née Montague (d. 1910) – actress, **4:** 300 n.*366*
Henry, Mr. (1805-1877) – actor (real name Charles Mackenzie), **5:** 32 n.*35*, 139 n.*223*
Compton, Henry, Rt. Rev. (1632-1713) – bishop of London, **1:** 26, 27
Compton, Surrey, **7:** 460
Comrades (dr. Brandon Thomas and B. C. Stephenson), **7:** 513, 514 n.*832*
"Comte de Brissac," **7:** 98, 109 n.*203*, 189, 190 n.*352*, 192 n.*356*
Comyns Carr (of Blandford Square, London):
Alice L. Vansittart née Strettell (b. 1850), **8:** 375 n.*617*, 452
Arthur Strettell (1882-1965), **8:** 375 n.*617*, 452
Dorothy "Dolly" (b. 1878), **8:** 375 n.*617*, 411, 429, 452
Joseph William, Mr. (1849-1916) – dramatist and editor, **7:** 468 n.*769*; **8:** 375 n.*617*, 452
Philip V. (b. 1875), **8:** 375 n.*617*
Conder (of Middleton, Sussex):
Alfred, Rev. Alfred (b. 1834) – teacher, **6:** 231 n.*364*
Eliza M., Mrs. (b. 1839), **6:** 231 n.*364*
Conder (of Wendy, Cambrideshire):
Christiana, Mrs. (b. 1840), **6:** 230 n.*361*, 232, 257; **7:** 251 n.*458*
Cyril (b 1874), **6:** 230 n.*361*
Eric, **6:** 230 n.*361*, 232, 255, 257
John, Rev. (b. 1838), **6:** 230 n.*361*, 232, 257; **7:** 251 n.*458*
John Edward (b. 1867), **6:** 230 n.*361*, 255, 257
Kate Matilda (b. 1863), **6:** 230 n.*361*, 232, 255, 257
Lizzie Mary (b. 1862), **6:** 230 n.*361*, 232, 255, 257; **7:** 251 n.*458*, 252
Nellie, **6:** 230 n.*361*, 255, 257
Sydney (b. 1873), **6:** 230 n.*361*
William Fenn (b. 1872), **6:** 230 n.*361*, 255

Conder (of Guildford, Surrey):
Francis Roubillac, Mr. (1815-1889) – civil engineer, **7:** 75 n.*119*; **8:** 79 n.*123*, 498 n.*801*
René Francis Reignier (b. 1858), **7:** 79 n.*129*
Confessions of Con Cregan (bk. Charles Lever), **1:** 109 n.*126*
Conic Sections (bk. George Salmon), **1:** 63 n.*40*; **4:** 13, 24
Conington, John (1826-1869) – professor of Latin literature, **5:** 28 n.*29*
Coniston Water, Lancashire, **3:** 107, 108, 110, 113, 115, 117, 145
Conjugal Lesson, A (dr. Henry Danvers), **4:** 300 n.*366*
Conolly, Olivia – friend of the Huleatts, **9:** 292 n.*459*
Conroy, John, Sir (1845-1900) – lecturer in chemistry, **9:** 238 n.*375*
Conservative Club, London, **6:** 335
Conservative Fête, Reading, **6:** 474
Constance (dr. Frederick Clay and Thomas Robertson), **5:** 45 n.*58*
Contemporary Review, The, **5:** 12, 12 n.*2*
Convent of St. Thomas, Paris, **5:** 367, 368 n.*545*
Conway, H. B. (or Coulson), Mr. (1850-1909) – actor, **7:** 16 n.*10*, 278 n.*505*, 319, 536
Conybeare (of Itchen Stoke, Hampshire):
Charles Henry (b. 1861), **7:** 379 n.*654*, 380, 382
Charles Ranken, Rev. (1821-1885), **3:** 25 n.*33*; **4:** 89 n.*46*; **6:** 330 n.*545*
Mrs., **3:** 25 n.*33*
Conybeare (living with Arnolds in Oxford):
Ethel Mary "Linda" (b. 1863), **6:** 389, 393, 394, 412, 426, 430, 451, 452
Maud A. (b. 1857), **6:** 389, 394, 426
Conybeare, Frederick Cornwallis (1856-1924) – writer, **7:** 535 n.*867*
Conyngham (of Mount Charles, County Donegal):
Blanche (b. 1856), **5:** 19, 121 n.*190*, 122
George Henry (1825-1882), Earl of Mount Charles, **5:** 121 n.*190*, 122
Cood, Eliza (b. 1839) – housekeeper, **7:** 235 n.*434*
Cooke, Henry Pennant, Rev. (1824-1891), **1:** 67 n.*51*, 71
Cooke, Kathella née Palmer (b. 1850) – teacher, **8:** 38 n.*52*, 39, 295, 297, 300, 322 n.*531*, 499
Cooke, Miss – logic pupil, **9:** 293 n.*463*
Cooke, Thomas Potter (1786-1864) – actor, **3:** 79, 80 n.*126*
Cookson, Christopher, Rev. (1824-1874), **4:** 307 n.*377*
Cookson, Montague Hughes (1832-1913) – Dodgson family solicitor, **1:** 49, 78 n.*75*, 79; **6:** 240 n.*381*; **7:** 324 n.*575*
Cool as a Cucumber (dr. William Jerrold), **4:** 270 n.*313*
Coomans, Pierre Olivier Joseph (1816-1889) – artist, **5:** 223, 224 n.*356*
Coombe, John Henry, Rev. (1811-1887), **4:** 154 n.*141*, 155; **5:** 107 n.*166*
Cooper, Alice Jane (1846-1917) – teacher , **8:** 89 n.*145*, 122, 496; **9:** 68 n.*122*, 263 n.*415*, 306, 315, 318
Cooper, Frank, Rev. (1834-1870), **5:** 134 n.*214*
Cooper, George William (b. 1834) – master baker and Christ Church tenant,

7: 258 n.*469*, 260
Cooper, H.C. – violinist, **3:** 10 n.*7*
Cooper, Isabel – see Hooper
Cooper, Mr. – engraver, **8:** 488 n.*791*, 490
Cooper, Mrs. – sister of Rose Armytage née Ball, **8:** 187 n.*315*, 196, 368
Coote:
Albert "Bertie" (1868-1938) – actor, **6:** 309 n.*512*, 310, 311; **7:** 13, 14 n.*8*, 24, 75-77, 91, 98, 107, 111, 123, 189, 315, 396, 509
Caroline "Carrie," Mrs. (b. 1836), **7:** 15 n.*9*, 16, 24, 76, 98, 106, 107, 112, 114, 118, 119, 123, 141, 201, 315, 509, 510, 512; **8:** 59, 60 n.*94*, 274, 281, 282, 452
Caroline "Carrie" Eva (1870-1907) – actress, **6:** 309 n.*512*; **7:** 13, 14 n.*8*, 16, 24, 44, 75-77, 91, 98, 107, 108, 111, 114, 115, 118, 123, 142, 189, 315, 509, 510; **8:** 274, 281, 452
Charles (1858-1897), **7:** 15 n.*9*, 525 n.*849*
Edwin (b. 1864), **7:** 15 n.*9*, 509
Lizzie (1862-1886) – actress, **6:** 309 n.*512*, 310, 377, 385, 444, 474; **7:** 15 n.*9*, 16, 17, 24, 75-77, 98, 107, 108, 110-112, 115, 118, 122, 123, 141, 189, 201, 233, 315, 509, 510; **8:** 258
Cope, Charles West (1811-1890) – artist, **3:** 78, 79 n.*124*; **5:** 221
Corbet (of Blandford, Dorset):
Evelyn (b. 1877), **7:** 249 n.*456*, 250
Harold (b. 1878), **7:** 249 n.*456*, 250
Hylda (b. 1880), **7:** 249 n.*456*, 250
John William, Rev. (b. 1850), **7:** 249 n.*456*
Octavia, Mrs. (b. 1845), **7:** 248, 249 n.*456*, 250
Corbet, Miss, **6:** 391 n.*642*
Corbet, Rowland (b. 1836) – undergraduate at Oxford, **1:** 87, 88 n.*91*, 91
Corelli, Marie (1855-1924), alias Mary Mackay – writer, **9:** 208 n.*337*
Corfe, Charles William (1814-1883) – composer, **3:** 32 n.*47*, 66 n.*100*, 134
Corneille, Pierre (1606-1684) – dramatist, **7:** 473 n.*776*
Cornhill Magazine, The, **1:** 40
Cornish – pupil of William Ranken, **6:** 476
Cornwall, M. A. (b. 1836) – governess, **6:** 233, 234 n.*368*
Corpus Christi College, **1:** 60; **2:** 110; **3:** 69 n.*107*, 93 n.*144*, 121, 124; **4:** 150; **6:** 242, 303, 440; **7:** 79, 414, 427, 497 n.*811*, 498; **8:** 71; **9:** 33
Correggio, Antonio Allegri (1489?-1534) – artist, **5:** 357 n.*530*
"Corrigenda" – pseudonym of correspondent, **8:** 17 n.*12*
Corry, Montagu William Lowry, Sir (1838-1903), 1st Baron Rowton, **8:** 464 n.*748*, 471
Corsbie, Dorcas – actress, **9:** 166, 167 n.*284*
Corsica – steamship, **7:** 171, 172, 174, 178
Corsican Brothers, The (dr. Dion Boucicault, adapt. Alexandre Dumas), **4:** 248 n.*282*; **7:** 317, 318 n.*567*; **8:** 567 n.*903*
Costello, Ada (b. 1871) – circus performer, **7:** 287 n.*520*

Coster, Rosalie (b. 1865) – friend of the Peets, **6:** 416
Cotton (of Frodsham, Cheshire):
  Arthur Benjamin (b. 1832), **3:** 68 n.*104*
  William Charles (1813-1879), **3:** 68 n.*104*, 76
Cotton, George Edward Lynch (1813-1866) – teacher, **1:** 29
Cotton, Henry, Rev. (1789-1879) – writer, **2:** 62 n.*124*, 63
Coulson, see Conway H. B.
Country Fair, The (dr. Anon), **2:** 47
"Court, The," North Cleobury, Shropshire (home of Wilfred Dodgson), **7:** 311, 446; **8:** 261, 262, 268, 501, 519, 545, 557, 597
Court Circular, **8:** 412
Courthope, William John (1842-1917) – poet, **8:** 249 n.*418*
Courtney, Cordelia Blanche née Place (1864-1907), **8:** 69 n.*112*
Courtney, Leonard Henry Rt. Hon. (1832-1918) – politician, **8:** 166 n.*277*
Cousin Joseph (dr. John Oxenford), **9:** 332 n.*530*
Cousins, The (dr. Lord Newry), **5:** 121 n.*191*
Cousmacker, Lena, **9:** 305 n.*484*
Covent Garden, London, **3:** 12; **4:** 326, 327
Coventry, Warwickshire, **4:** 32
Cowes, Isle of Wight, **6:** 296, 299, 360, 424, 480
Cowie, Helen E. M. (b. 1871), **7:** 300 n.*543*, 301 n.*545*, 305
Cowley, Hannah (1743-1809) – dramatist, **7:** 327 n.*579*
Cowley Hospital, **8:** 215, 256-258, 260, 261, 264, 266, 268, 270 n.*455*, 272, 273, 275
Cowley Military College, **9:** 111, 127, 205
Cowley School, Oxfordshire, **4:** 76 n.*23*, 83, 202, 205, 306
Cowton School, Yorkshire, **1:** 130
Cox, Harry (1840-1882) – actor and singer, **7:** 194 n.*361*, 304, 305 n.*549*
Cox (of Litton Cheney, near Dorchester, Oxfordshire):
  James Septimus, Rev. (1807?-1876?), **5:** 135 n.*218*
  Mrs., **5:** 135
Cox, see Cocks
Cox and Box (dr. Francis Burnand and Arthur Sullivan), **5:** 240 n.*389*; **6:** 197 n.*307*
Coxe (of Oxford):
  Charlotte Esther née Turner (b. 1804), **8:** 332 n.*546*
  Henry Octavius, Rev. (1811-1881), **4:** 134, 135 n.*112*, 296 n.*356*; **6:** 155 n.*238*; **7:** 347 n.*608*, 348
Coxe – fellow lodgers at Whitby:
  Colonel, **6:** 177 n.*273*
  Mrs., **6:** 177 n.*273*
Coxe, Laura C., Mrs. (b. 1858), **8:** 619 n.*981*
Coxe, William, Rev. (1747-1828) – historian and writer, **1:** 24
Coxwell (of South Bank, Great Malvern, Worcestershire):
  Charles Rogers, Mr. (1806-1893) – magistrate, **4:** 119 n.*88*

Mary Elizabeth née Cresswell (d. 1867), **4:** 119 n.*88*
Coyne, Joseph Stirling (1803-1868) – dramatist, **3:** 133 n.*193*
Cracroft, Alice M. (b. 1851), **6:** 224 n.*352*
Cradley Rectory, Herefordshire, **4:** 116
Cradock (of Brasenose College, Oxford):
Edward Hartopp, Rev. (1810-1886) – principal of Brasenose College, **6:** 213 n.*330*
Harriet née Lister (b. 1810), **6:** 212, 213 n.*330*
Craig, Isabella "Isa" (1831-1903) – poet, **5:** 23 n.*19*
Craigie (of Guildford, Surrey):
Archibald (b. 1869), **6:** 84 n.*126*
Dorothea (b. 1865), **6:** 84 n.*126*
Ernest John, Mr. (b. 1826), **6:** 84 n.*126*
Horace W. (b. 1856), **6:** 84 n.*126*
Isabel C. (b. 1857), **6:** 84 n.*126*, 95 n.*148*, 99
Josephine (b. 1854), **6:** 84 n.*126*, 99, 104 n.*163*
Mary Jane, Mrs. (b. 1826), **6:** 84 n.*126*
Reginald, **6:** 84 n.*126*, 101
Craik (of Beckenham, Kent):
Dinah Maria née Mulock (1826-1887) – writer, **1:** 69 n.*55*, 107; **3:** 141, 142 n.*210*; **5:** 24, 61 n.*89*, 89; **6:** 182 n.*284*, 254 n.*404*, 255, 301, 336; **7:** 165, 166 n.*312*, 334, 356; **9:** 190 n.*314*
Dorothy Mulock (b. 1868), **6:** 254 n.*404*, 255, 336; **7:** 165, 166 n.*312*, 356
George Lillie, Mr. (1837-1905) – partner in Macmillan & Co., **5:** 61 n.*89*, 89, 140 n.*224*; **6:** 182 n.*284*, 200, 254 n.*404*, 294, 301; **7:** 93, 165, 166 n.*312*; **8:** 219 n.*373*, 471, 495; **9:** 171 n.*287*, 172
Craik, Georgina Marion (1831-1895) – writer, **6:** 254 n.*404*
Crake, Edward Neville, Rev. (1826-1909), **7:** 461, 462 n.*760*
Cramer & Beale – publishers, **2:** 121
Cranbourne, Berkshire, **4:** 292, 293 n.*351*, 320; **5:** 83, 99
Cranbourne Street, London, **7:** 110
Crane, Mr. – Guildford photographer, **6:** 57 n.*86*
Crane, Walter (1845-1915) – illustrator, **7:** 85 n.*146*, 104 n.*194*, 253, 254 n.*462*
Cranford (bk. Elizabeth Gaskell), **1:** 131 n.*163*; **3:** 169 n.*247*
"Cranford Tea-Party, A" (dr. Beatrice Hatch), **9:** 296 n.*469*
Crase & Company, Wigmore Street, Cavendish Square – retail suppliers, **2:** 125, 126
Craven, Henry Thornton (1818-1905) – dramatist, **1:** 133 n.*168*; **2:** 88 n.*177*; **3:** 85 n.*132*; **5:** 233 n.*372*
Crawford, William (1825-1869) – artist, **5:** 237 n.*383*
Crawshay (of Tynemouth Hall, Northumberland):
Arthur George Dufaud (1851-1917), **1:** 121
Elizabeth née Fife (d. 1889), **1:** 121 n.*149*; **3:** 171 n.*251*
Florence (b. 1850), **1:** 121; **4:** 179

George, Mr. (1821-1896), **1:** 121 n.*149*
Martin (1854-1908), **1:** 121
Cray, Mr. – friend of the Rogers, **4:** 106 n.*74*
"Creation and Criticism" – lecture by John Shairp, **7:** 100
Crenaia (pic. Frederick Leighton), **7:** 188 n.*350*
Crest Books, **4:** 110, 146, 149
Crewe, Cheshire, **7:** 211
Creyke, Freyda – orphan, **8:** 82 n.*130*
Crichton-Stuart, John Patrick (1847-1900), 3rd Marquess of Bute, **4:** 64; **5:** 130 n.*208*; **6:** 38 n.*54*, 59; **8:** 470
Cricket, **2:** 72, 73
Crimean Gun, Ripon, **3:** 170 n.*249*
Crimean War, **1:** 54 n.*14*, 62, 95; **2:** 8 n.*4*, 17 n.*28*, 25 n.*47*, 56 n.*112*, 58, 59 n.*118*, 66 n.*131*, 79 n.*156*, 88
Crinoline (dr. Robert Brough), **3:** 12 n.*10*
Cripps, Alfred (b. 1850) – college servant, **8:** 214 n.*365*, 602
Critchett, George Anderson, Mr. (1845-1925) – surgeon and oculist, **6:** 169, **7:** 236 n.*435*
Crocker, Professor – entertainer, **8:** 364 n.*596*
Croesus – steamship, **8:** 540 n.*865*, 541
Croft National School, Yorkshire, **1:** 108 n.*123*; **2:** 8 n.*2*, 31 n.*61*, 59, 119 n.*227*, 123, 127, 128; **5:** 110
Crofts (of Newlands Lodge, Sevenoaks, Kent):
Beatrice A. (b 1870), **6:** 263 n.*423*, 270, 425 n.*699*
Cecil (b. 1865), **6:** 263 n.*423*, 270
Charles (b. 1862), **6:** 263 n.*423*, 270
Ethel Harriet (1866-1902), **6:** 263 n.*423*, 270
Eva Maria (b. 1868), **6:** 263 n.*423*, 270
Florence (b. 1860), **5:** 90 n.*138*; **6:** 263 n.*423*, 269, 270; **7:** 426 n.*711*, 427
Jane Britton née Dowell (b. 1829), **5:** 90 n.*138*; **6:** 263 n.*423*, 269; **8:** 620 n.*984*
John David McBride, Rev. (1827-1907) – teacher, **5:** 90 n.*138*; **6:** 263 n.*423*, 269; **7:** 426 n.*711*, 427; **8:** 620 n.*984*
Mary "May" Dowell (1859-1941), **4:** 181; **5:** 90 n.*138*; **6:** 263 n.*423*, 269, 270; **7:** 426 n.*711*, 427
Crofts, Mary "Mamie" née Woodhouse, **8:** 153 n.*251*
Croft Terrace, Tenby, Pembrokeshire (Smedleys), **4:** 188 n.*183*, 189
Crompton, Alice (1866-1958), **7:** 19 n.*15*
Cromwell – boy actor, **6:** 310
Cromwell Place, London, **4:** 288
Cronstadt, Russia, **5:** 340-343
Cross – pupil of Alexander Webster, **2:** 89, 90 n.*181*
Crosthwaite, Cumberland, **2:** 90 n.*181*
Crouch, H. – actor, **8:** 569 n.*906*
Crowder, Thomas Mosley, Lt.-Col. (1830-1892) – army officer, **9:** 33,

34 n.*57*
Crowe – related to the Hassalls (formerly of Croft, Yorkshire):
Mr., **8:** 382, 383 n.*628*
Mrs., **8:** 382, 383 n.*628*
Crowe, see Bateman
Crowe, Sidney, Miss – actress, **9:** 273 n.*434*
Crowther, Mr. – champion skater, **7:** 295 n.*534*
Croydon, Surrey, **7:** 155, 370; **8:** 42, 474
Crumb, Harriet (b. 1864) – friend of Mrs. Moberly, **9:** 318 n.*510*, 319
Crust:
Emily, **4:** 179
Mary, **4:** 181
Cruttwell, Miss – cousin of Mrs. Daniel, **8:** 215 n.*367*
Crystal Palace, Sydenham, Kent, **7:** 232
Cuckoo (pic. John Millais), **7:** 278 n.*506*
Cuddesden College, Oxfordshire, **2:** 73 n.*147*; **4:** 66, 302
Cudmore, Emily – actress, **9:** 23 n.*28*
Culham, Oxfordshire, **4:** 194, 195, 204, 278; **5:** 90; **6:** 474
Culver Cliffs, Isle of Wight, **6:** 296, 355
Culverton House, Sandown (Miss Bode's lodging house), **6:** 357, 416
Cumberland (of Maidstone, Kent):
Charles Edward, Col. (1830-1920) – army officer, **8:** 97 n.*159*
Elizabeth Anne née King (d. 1891), **8:** 97 n.*159*
Cummings, Charles L. (b. 1862) – accountant, **8:** 521 n.*836*
Cummings, Mr. – singer, **5:** 225
Cumnor, Berkshire, **3:** 165
Cundall, Messrs. Joseph & Company – photographer, **4:** 31, 229, 247, 251, 332 n.*426*, 341, 356; **5:** 171 n.*283*
Cunnynghame (of Filkins, Oxfordshire):
Clara T., Mrs. (b. 1821), **6:** 461; **8:** 329 n.*541*, 499
Hubert Robert, Rev. (1820-1882), **6:** 150 n.*229*, 461
John "Jack" Macpherson (1849-1931), **6:** 150 n.*229*; **8:** 499 n.*802*
Margaret "Maggie" Symers (1855-1931), **8:** 329 n.*541*, 499
Cup, The (dr. Alfred Tennyson), **7:** 317, 318 n.*567*, 326, 327
Cupid (pic. Arthur Frost), **7:** 107 n.*198*
Curates' Aid Society, **4:** 237
Currey (of Greenwich, Kent):
Florence (b. 1853), **4:** 123 n.*96*
Frederick, Mr. (1819-1881) – barrister, **4:** 123 n.*96*
Frederick Innes (b. 1849), **4:** 123 n.*96*, 324 n.*410*
Georgiana Innes née Pocock (1822-1867), **4:** 123 n.*96*
Hamilton (b. 1857), **4:** 123 n.*96*
Isabel (b. 1855?), **4:** 123 n.*96*
Menella "Minnie" (b. 1850), **4:** 123 n.*96*
Walter Francis (b. 1860), **4:** 123 n.*96*

Currie, Donald, Sir (1825-1909) – politician and shipowner, **8:** 50 n.*74*, 66
Currie, Philip Henry Wodehouse, Sir (1834-1906) – civil servant, **8:** 465 n.*751*
Currie, Theresa "Lisa" Henrietta Charlotte née Wood (b. 1844), **3:** 150 n.*217*; **8:** 14 n.*7*
Curteis, see Curtis
Curtis (of Guildford, Surrey):
Henry George Constable, Rev. (b. 1866), **8:** 547 n.*872*; **9:** 188 n.*311*
Laura M., Mrs. (b. 1863), **9:** 188 n.*311*
"Curse of Kehama, The" (bk. Robert Southey), **1:** 35
Cust, Daniel Mitford, Rev. (1821-1889), **1:** 120 n.*146*; **2:** 101 n.*195*
Cuthbert, George Seignelay (b. 1840), MA Christ Church, **4:** 152 n.*138*
"Cuthwellis, Edgar" (pseudonym), **2:** 39
Cyclorama of Egypt, London, **9:** 58-60, 75
Cyril (376-444) – bishop of Alexandria, **3:** 7 n.*3*, 8, 28
Cyril Bickersteth (pic. James Sant), **5:** 86 n.*134*
Cyrus – steamship, **8:** 293, 540 n.*865*, 541

Dabbs (of Shanklin, Isle of Wight):
George Henry Rocque, Dr. (1845-1913) –physician, **7:** 525, 526 n.*850*; **8:** 576 n.*919*
Nina L. née Giraud (b. 1847) – formerly Mrs. Peet, **6:** 341 n.*567*, 416-418; **7:** 345 n.*605*, 525; **8:** 301 n.*502*
Daddy Hardacre (dr. John Simpson), **3:** 51 n.*78*
Daily News, **4:** 275; **7:** 512 n.*830*; **8:** 107
Daisy Escape (dr. Arthur Pinero), **8:** 614 n.*974*
D'Albuquerque, or D'Alcourt (of London):
Antonio (b. 1880?), **8:** 345 n.*569*
Clara (b. 1875), **8:** 345 n.*569*, 346, 357, 369
Dorothea "Dorothy" (b. 1878), **8:** 311, 312 n.*514*, 316, 345 n.*569*, 346, 348, 362, 369, 439, 517
Francisco Antonio Pedrozo, Mr. – hotel keeper, **8:** 345 n.*569*
Mary Jane née Scott, **8:** 345 n.*569*, 348, 517
Dalby, Francis Higgs, Rev. (1854-1933), **6:** 141 n.*213*
Daldy, Arthur Mantell, Dr. (b. 1870) – physician, **9:** 30 n.*49*
Dale, Godfrey, Rev. (b. 1861), **9:** 314 n.*501*, 321
Dallin (of Norham Gardens, Oxford):
Edith Mary, Mrs. (b. 1851), **8:** 154 n.*253*
Francis T. (b. 1874), **6:** 479
Hetty J. (b. 1873), **6:** 479
Isabel M. {Mabel?} (b. 1872), **6:** 479 n.*792*; **8:** 611 n.*969*
Thomas Francis, Mr. (1841-1880) – lecturer, **8:** 154 n.*253*
Dalmeny, see Primrose
Dalton (of Rochester, Kent):
Charles Browne, Rev. (1810-1893), **9:** 31 n.*52*

Herbert Andrew (1852-1928) – teacher, **6:** 440 n.*722*; **9:** 31 n.*52*
Daly, Arthur R. (b. 1833) – merchant, **7:** 527 n.*853*
Daly, C. – actor, **8:** 419 n.*679*, 425
Dalziel Brothers – engravers (of London):
Edward (1817-1905), **5:** 22; **8:** 182 n.*305*, 183, 187
George (1815-1902), **5:** 22; **8:** 182 n.*305*, 183, 187
John (1822-1869), **5:** 22
Thomas Bolton Gilchrist (1823-1906), **5:** 22; **8:** 182 n.*305*, 183, 187
Dance, Charles (1794-1863) – dramatist, **3:** 12 n.*10*; **4:** 205 n.*214*; **5:** 42 n.*52*
Daniel (of Oxford):
Charles Henry Olive, Mr. (1836-1919) – printer, **7:** 372 n.*647*; **8:** 11 n.*2*, 12, 86, 396 n.*643*; **9:** 47 n.*82*
Emily née Olive (1853-1933), **7:** 372 n.*647*, 377; **8:** 12, 86, 215, 515, 517
Rachel Anne Olive (b. 1881), **7:** 372 n.*647*; **8:** 11, 515, 517
Ruth Olive (b. 1883?), **8:** 515, 517
Daniel, William Eustace, Rev. (1841-1924), **8:** 362 n.*591*
Daniell Family of Daresbury, **1:** 13
Danischeffs, The (dr. Lord Newry), **7:** 536, 537 n.*869*
Dan'l Druce, Blacksmith (dr. William S. Gilbert), **6:** 486 n.*800*
Dann, Isabella (b. 1814), **7:** 316 n.*562*; **8:** 59 n.*91*
Dante Alighieri (1265-1321) – poet, **1:** 84; **3:** 157 n.*232*
Danvers, Henry (fl. 1850-1856) – dramatist, **2:** 82 n.*162*; **4:** 300 n.*366*
Danzig, Prussia, **5:** 275-278
Darbishire, Samuel Dukinfield, Dr. (b. 1847) – physician, **7:** 378 n.*653*
Darcy:
Colonel, **6:** 358
Mrs., **6:** 358
Dare, Eva (1875-1931) – actress, **9:** 87 n.*157*, 154, 157
Darell, Lionel Edward, Sir (1845-1919), 5th Bart., **5:** 178 n.*295*
"Dares" (pseudonym), **2:** 37, 38
Daresbury, Cheshire, **1:** 9, 12-15, 29, 39; **3:** 41 n.*65*; **4:** 26, 27
Daresbury Hall, **1:** 13, 14
Darlington, Durham, **1:** 82, 127, 131; **2:** 59 n.*120*; **4:** 30, 231, 242; **5:** 38
Darlington Polytechnic, **1:** 131, 132
Darnley, Lord, see Bligh
Dartmouth, Devon, **7:** 314
Darvall, Henry (fl. 1848-1889) – artist, **4:** 272 n.*317*, 276, 280, 290, 310, 331 n.*425*; **5:** 86 n.*134*, 144 n.*231*, 219 n.*349*
Darwin, Charles Robert (1809-1882) – scientist, **6:** 244 n.*388*
Darwin (of Newnham Grange, Cambridge):
George Howard, Prof. (1845-1912) – professor of astronomy, **8:** 155 n.*254*
Maud Haskins née De Puy, **8:** 155 n.*254*
Darwinism, **4:** 34, 36

Dasent (of London):
George William Manual (1849-1872), **6:** 209 n.*328*
John Roche (1847-1914) – civil servant, **6:** 370 n.*608*
Dauncey, Mrs., née Anderson, **6:** 490 n.*808*
Davenport (of Buffalo, New York):
Ira Erastus (1839-1911) – magician, **7:** 199 n.*373*
William Henry (1841-1887) – magician, **7:** 199 n.*373*
David Copperfield (bk. Charles Dickens), **1:** 26
David Elginbrod (bk. George MacDonald), **4:** 160 n.*152*
David Garrick (dr. C. P. Colnaghi and Eustace Ponsonby), **8:** 478 n.*774*; **9:** 274 n.*435*, 313
David Garrick (dr. Thomas Robertson), **4:** 300 n.*366*; **5:** 160 n.*264*
Davies, John Llewelyn, Rev. (1826-1916), **8:** 70 n.*113*
Davies (of London?):
Mrs., **6:** 399
Thomas, Mr. (1832-1880) – photographer, **6:** 399, 400 n.*634*
Davies Family of London, **7:** 95 n.*174*
Davis, Alfred – actor, **1:** 133
Davis, Dora – friend of Enid Stevens, **8:** 624 n.*987*, 631, 632, 634
Davis (of Betchworth, Surrey):
George, Mr. (b. 1836) – station-master, **9:** 345 n.*552*
Martha, Mrs. (b. 1847), **9:** 345 n.*552*
Nellie (b. 1885), **9:** 345 n.*552*
Davis, Mary A., Mrs. (b. 1821), **8:** 343 n.*566*
Davys (of Wheathampstead, Hertfordshire):
Alan, **6:** 107 n.*166*, 443
Blanche Helen (b. 1865), **6:** 107 n.*166*, 443
Douglas H. (b. 1862), **6:** 107 n.*166*, 443
George, **6:** 107 n.*166*, 443
Helen le Fleming née Stanley (b. 1828), **6:** 107 n.*166*
Lucy Marianne (b. 1861), **6:** 107 n.*166*, 443
Montague S. (b. 1860), **6:** 107 n.*166*, 443
Owen William, Rev. (1829-1914), **6:** 107 n.*166*, 443
Trevor (b. 1866), **6:** 107 n.*166*, 443
Daw (of Oxford):
Emma – pupil at St. Aldates, **2:** 32
William – pupil at St. Aldates, **2:** 30
Dawes-Watson, Mr. – actor, **8:** 523, 524 n.*841*
Dawson, Anna Maria, Lady (d. 1866), **4:** 272 n.*316*, 296, 297 n.*358*
Dawson, Captain, **9:** 186 n.*307*
Dawson, Lydia – pupil at St. Aldates, **2:** 32
Dawson, Mrs., **6:** 354
Day, Captain of the *Corsica*, **7:** 178
Day, Mary (b. 1825), **9:** 69 n.*126*
Day & Son, Messrs., London – luggage retailer, **5:** 37

Deacon, Mary (b. 1848) – teacher, **8:** 366 n.*600*
Deaf as a Post (dr. John Poole), **4:** 309 n.*384*
Deane, Henry, Rev. (b. 1839), **8:** 166 n.*276*
Deane, Mary J. (b. 1853) – photographer's assistant, **7:** 535 n.*868*, 536
Deane and Company – architects **6:** 340
Dean of Ripon, **3:** 8
Dean of Ripon's Verger (William Burnett), **2:** 55 n.*108*; **3:** 7 n.*2*
Dean of Westminster (Richard C. Trench), **3:** 35 n.*53*
Dean's Yard, Westminster, **4:** 269
Dearest Mama, my Mother-in-Law (dr. Gordon Walter), **9:** 119 n.*205*
Deasy, Timothy, Capt. – Fenian, **5:** 373 n.*553*
"Death of the Prince Consort" (Lionel Tennyson) – poem, **4:** 62, 63
Debenham, Arthur (b. 1846) – photographer at Ryde, Isle of Wight, **6:** 419 n.*688*
De Brisay (of Oxford):
  Henry, Rev. (b. 1832), **9:** 122 n.*213*
  Jane A., Mrs. (b. 1829), **7:** 145 n.*272*
  Miss, **9:** 121, 122 n.*213*
De Bunsen, Victoria née Buxton (b. 1853) – singer, **8:** 590 n.*941*, 591, 593, 595, 615, 618
Deed (of Lee, Kent):
  Alfred, Mr. (b. 1841) – leather manufacturer, **8:** 143 n.*233*
  Elsie (b. 1873), **8:** 143 n.*233*, 149
  Emily, Mrs. (b. 1843), **8:** 143 n.*233*
  Jessie G. (b. 1876), **8:** 143 n.*233*, 149
  Lilian "Lily" M. (b. 1875), **8:** 143 n.*233*, 149
Deedes, Cecil, Rev. (1843-1920), **6:** 475 n.*784*
De la Rue, Messrs., London – photographic dealers, **5:** 137
De Lea:
  Sybell, see Hoghton
  William, Sir (b. 1237) – very distant relative, **1:** 11
Delianov, Ivan Davydovich (1818-1897), **5:** 344, 345 n.*514*
Delicate Ground (dr. Charles Dance), **3:** 12 n.*10*
De Mallet:
  Anna (b. 1841), **4:** 133 n.*110*
  Ernestine, **4:** 133 n.*110*
  Evastra M. I., **4:** 132, 133 n.*110*
  Franck (d. 1848), **4:** 133 n.*110*
  Maria Indiana née Sykes, **4:** 133 n.*110*
  Molesworth, Baron (b. 1808), **4:** 133 n.*110*
De Mallet:
  Anne, **4:** 133 n.*110*
  Francois, Baron (1765-1839), **4:** 133 n.*110*
  Molesworth (b. 1808), see above
De Morgan (of Gower Street, London):

Augustus, Prof. (1806-1871) – mathematician, **3:** 158 n.*234*; **9:** 295
William Frend (1839-1917) – potter and designer of tiles, **7:** 502 n.*820*, 524, 542; **8:** 321 n.*529*
Demosthenes (384-322 BC), **3:** 156 n.*230*
Denman (of Kensington, London):
Arthur (1857-1931), **4:** 319 n.*405*, 327, 328 n.*417*; **5:** 70; **6:** 20
Charlotte Edith (1855-1884), see Draper
Charlotte née Hope (1830-1905), **4:** 319 n.*405*, 326, 327, 337; **5:** 70, 88; **7:** 187, 234, 235, 396; **8:** 216 n.*369*, 412; **9:** 160
Francis Richard Amory (1862-1900), **4:** 319 n.*405*
George, Hon. (1819-1896) – judge, **4:** 319 n.*405*, 326; **5:** 23 n.*18*, 88; **6:** 20 n.*21*, 284 n.*466*; **7:** 112, 113 n.*208*, 235, 396; **8:** 216 n.*369*, 412, 560 n.*892*; **9:** 141 n.*244*, 159, 160
George Lewis (1854-1929), **4:** 319 n.*405*
Grace "Gracie" (1858-1935), see Gambier-Parry
Launcelot Baillie (1861-1935), **4:** 319 n.*405*, 340; **6:** 20
Denman, Richard (1814-1887) – barrister, **7:** 113 n.*208*
Denman, Richard Douglas (1876-1957) – politician, **9:** 141 n.*244*
Dennery, Adolphe (1811-1879) – dramatist, **5:** 38 n.*46*
Denvil, Clara (1849-1867) – actress, **5:** 45 n.*58*, 69
De Quincey, Thomas (1785-1859) – writer, **3:** 130 n.*188*, 145, 148 n.*213*, 149, 156 n.*230*, 164
Derby, **5:** 189
"Derby Gallop" – dance, **6:** 281
Derby odds, **3:** 55, 56 n.*85*
Dermer, Edward Conduitt, Rev. (b. 1843), **9:** 238 n.*376*
Derwentwater, Cumberland, **2:** 94
Desanges (of London):
Beatrice Laura (1864-1922), **6:** 126
Eleanor, Mdme., **5:** 218 n.*348*, 240, 241; **6:** 86, 232, 295, 296, 298
Eleanor Fanny "Nelly" (b. 1858), **5:** 20, 168, 218 n.*348*, 240; **6:** 75, 86
Louis William, Chevalier (1822-1887?) – artist, **5:** 218 n.*348*, 240, 241; **6:** 232, 295, 296, 298, 358
De Sausmarez, Frederick Barlow (b. 1849) – school inspector, **6:** 261 n.*418*
Desmond, Eily – actress, **9:** 277 n.*442*
Desprez, Frank (1852-1916) – dramatist, **7:** 541 n.*874*
Devaux, Alfred – arranged operas for piano solo, **2:** 121 n.*235*
Dever, Alfred (fl. 1859-76) – artist, **5:** 86 n.*134*
De Vere, Aubrey Thomas (1814-1902) – poet, **4:** 125 n.*98*, 126 n.*99*, 140 n.*119*, 244 n.*274*
Devil-May-Care (dr. Henry Besley), **9:** 86, 87 n.*157*
Dewhurst, Miss – actress, **8:** 440 n.*704*
Diamond, Hugh Welch, Dr. (1809-1886) – photographer, **2:** 24 n.*45*
Dibdin, Charles (1745-1814) – composer, **7:** 160
Dibdin, Thomas John (1771-1841) – dramatist, **5:** 168 n.*277*

Dickens, Charles (1812-1870) – writer, **1:** 26, 75, 106, 113 n.*132*; **2:** 12, 13 n.*16*, 37 n.*75*, 52, 82 n.*162*, 98
Dickson, John Frederick, Sir (1835-1891) – civil servant, **7:** 520 n.*843*
Dictionary of Dates (bk. Joseph Haydn), **2:** 36 n.*71*
Dictionary of the Anonymous and Pseudonymous Literature of Great Britain, A (bk. Samuel Halkett & John Laing), **7:** 309, 310 n.*553*
Dictionary of the English Language, A (bk. Joseph Worcester), **5:** 208 n.*332*
Didcot, Berkshire, **5:** 90; **6:** 60; **7:** 320, 335
Difficulties of Belief (bk. Thomas Birks), **7:** 351 n.*613*
Dillon, Charles (1819-1881) – dramatist, **3:** 120 n.*170*
Dindorf, Karl Wilhelm (1802-1883) – Greek professor, **4:** 34
Dinèr Européen, Paris, **5:** 363
Dingley (of London):
  Allen, Mr. (1857-1925) – surgeon, **8:** 583 n.*930*; **9:** 100 n.*181*, 219, 230
  Allen Roy (1892-1978), **9:** 100 n.*181*, 230
  Emma Louisa "Loui" née Waddy, **7:** 48 n.*74*, 49, 50, 74; **8:** 25 n.*25*, 29, 583 n.*930*; **9:** 100 n.*181*, 219, 230
  Eric (b. 1891?), **9:** 100 n.*181*, 219, 230
Dinsdale, Durham, **2:** 84 n.*168*, 85; **3:** 84, 140, 144; **4:** 22; **5:** 105
Diocesan Education Society, **2:** 117
Diocesan Registrar, Oxford, **4:** 55
Diogenes, **1:** 116 n.*141*, 117
Diplomacy (dr. Clement Scott & B. C. Stephenson), **7:** 96 n.*176*; **9:** 57 n.*104*
"Dirge over Dundee" – song, **6:** 104
Disraeli, Benjamin (1804-1881) – politician, **5:** 215 n.*344*; **6:** 12, 13 n.*6*, 65
Diversions of Hollycot (bk. Christian Isobel Johnstone) **1:** 27
Diversions of Purley (bk. John Horne Tooke), **1:** 52 n.*7*, 73 n.*66*
Dix, Mr. – actor, **9:** 166, 167 n.*284*
Dixey, Frederick Augustus, Dr. (1855-1935) – medical tutor, **8:** 446 n.*714*
Dixon (of London):
  Ada née Frost (b. 1874) – artists' model, **8:** 376, 377 n.*620*; **9:** 222 n.*351*
  Charles, Mr. (1872-1934) – artist, **9:** 222 n.*351*
Dixon, Dora "Dolly" Mary (b. 1872), **8:** 122 n.*196*, 123
Dixon, Edward Travers (1862-1935) – mathematician, **8:** 555 n.*884*
Dixon (of Egham, Surrey):
  Emily Phyllis (b. 1864), **6:** 477 n.*789*
  Mrs., **6:** 477 n.*789*
Dixon, John, Rev. (1821-1885), **6:** 110 n.*172*
Dixon, Mr., **7:** 454 n.*752*
Dixon, Mrs. – John A. Stewart's sister-in-law **8:** 163 n.*266*
Dobell, Sydney (1824-1879) – poet, **3:** 141 n.*209*, 175; **4:** 14, 109
Döbler, Ludwig Leopold (1801-1864) - conjurer, **4:** 187 n.*182*
Dobson, Henry Austin (1840-1921) – writer, **7:** 372 n.*647*
Dobson, William Charles Thomas (1817-1898) – artist, **2:** 75 n.*151*;

3: 77 n.*121*; **7:** 429, 538, 539 n.*871*
Doctor, The (pic. Samuel Luke Fildes), **8:** 561 n.*894*
Dodd, Westmorland, **2:** 91

Dodgson (Family):

Dodgson (of Cleobury, Shropshire):
Alice Jane née Donkin (1851-1929) – sister-in-law, **4:** 131 n.*106*, 131 n.*107*, 132 n.*109*, 134, 231 n.*256*, 299; **5:** 110 n.*173*, 149 n.*240*, 180 n.*298*; **6:** 52 n.*74*, 66, 67, 134, 137, 149, 152, 171, marriage 173 n.*270*, 192, 193, 237, 246, 308, 332, 362, 363, 407, 477-479; **7:** 125, 126, 179, 311, 446, 531; **8:** 220, 260, 261, 270, 399, 472, 476, 551; **9:** 245-247, 248 n.*392*, 269, 270, 301, 318, 319, 324
Beatrice Hilda (1882-1949) – niece, **7:** 126 n.*236*, 446, 531; **8:** 472; **9:** 245, 246, enters Oxford High School 250-258, 260, 263, 266, 271, 278, 280, 286, 296-299, 301, 306, 308-310, 315, 318, 319, 321, 323-325, 354
Charles Hassard Wilfred "Willie" (1876-1941) – nephew, **6:** 452 n.*743*, 477, 478; **7:** 125, 126 n.*236*, 181, 311, 446; **8:** 220, 256, 269; **9:** 145, 257, 258
Edith Alice (1872-1942) – niece, **6:** 11 n.*1*, 237 n.*378*, 239, 246, 332, 477-479; **7:** 47, 125, 126 n.*236*, 181, 311, 446; **8:** 220, 450, 453, 455, 505 n.*811*, 506, 507, 515, 516, enters Lady Margaret Hall 537-539, 545, 551, 557; **9:** 192, visit to Eastbourne 273, 274 n.*437*, 283, 284, 314, 315
Frances Menella "Nella" Jane (1877-1963) – niece, **7:** 125, 126 n.*236*, 181, 311, 446; **8:** 328, 501, 503, 557; **9:** 54 n.*93*, 59, 60, 73, 78, 102, 115, 118, theatre trip 122, 139, 140, 145, 150, 192, 202, 203, 235, 245, 284, 285, 291, 305, 306, 352 n.*564*, 354
Gladys Marjorie (1886-1968) – niece, **7:** 126 n.*236*; **8:** 472; **9:** 245, 246, 250-258, 260, 263, 266, 271, 280, 286, 296-299, 301, 306, 308-310, 313, 315, 318, 319, 321, 323-325, 354
Lucy Margaret (1874-1959) – niece, **7:** 125, 126 n.*236*, 181, 311, 446; **8:** 220, 450, 453, 455; **9:** 45 n.*78*, 139, 140, 192, 195, 235, 245, 306
Mary Evangeline "Eva" (1873-1945) – niece, **6:** 308 n.*510*, 332; **7:** 125, 126 n.*236*, 181, 311, 446; **8:** 220, 399, 450, 453, 455, 501, 503, 557; **9:** 45 n.*78*, 78, 139, 140, 179, 205, 250, 291, 294
Reginald "Reggie" Henry Lutwidge (1880-1918) – nephew, **7:** 126 n.*236*, 311, 446, 531; **8:** 472; **9:** 115 n.*199*, 118, 122, 195, 245
Violet Eleanor (1878-1966) – niece, **7:** 126 n.*236*, 311, 446, 531; **8:** 328, 501, 503, 584; **9:** 23 n.29, 24, 26, 54, 59, 60, 73, 78, 102, 115, 118, 122, 139, 140, 145, 150, 192, 202, 203, 218, 235, 245-247, enters Oxford High School 250-254, 256-260, 262-264, 266, 267, 270, 271, 278, 280, 283, 286, 296-301, 306, 308-310, 313-315, 318, 319, 321, 323-325, 327, 354
Wilfred Longley, Mr. (1838-1914), land agent – brother, **1:** 13, 123;

2: matriculation 71, 72, 85, 89, enters Christ Church 106 n.*205*, 109, 121; **3:** 7, 10, 11, 18 n.*20*, 32, 52, 58, 74, 76, 82, 85, 97, 101, 109, 121; **4:** 15, 19, 32, 130, 133, 138 n.*116*, 241 n.*269*; **5:** 15, 47, 59, 63, 65-67, 71, 72, 99, 110 n.*173*, 111, 149, 158, 180 n.*298*, 200, 208, 211, 212, 220-222, 235, 377, 380; **6:** 11 n.*1*, 44, 48, 49, 57, 68, 71, 72, 74, 104, 134, 138, obtains position as Lord Boyne's land agent 144, 149-151, 165, 166, 172, marriage 173 n.*270*, 192, 193, 237, 240, 246, 308, 360, 362, 363, 385, 407, 452, 478; **7:** 28 n.*36*, 47, 55, 125, 127, 181, 311, 324 n.*575*, 325, 444, 446, 532; **8:** 154, 256, 269, 453, 519, 537, 610; **9:** 47, 110, 173, 195, 203, 237, 246, 270, 271, 300, 301, 318

Dodgson (of Alfrick, Worcestershire):

Amy Irene Hume (1884-1980) – niece, **8:** 540 n.*864*; **9:** 66 n.*120*, 69, 218

Isabel Mary née Cooper (1848-1937) – sister-in-law, **7:** marriage 299 n.*541*, visiting Dodgson 546; **8:** 11, 326; **9:** 66 n.*120*, 69, 287

John Hassard (b. & d. 1887) – nephew, **8:** 369 n.*605*

Skeffington Hume, Rev. (1836-1919) – brother, **1:** 13, 27, 115 n.*139*, 123; **2:** matriculation 71, 72, 85, 89-92, enters Christ Church 106 n.*205*,109, 121; **3:** 7, 11, 32, 52, 54, 60, 63, 65, 67 n.*103*, 68, 74, 76, 82, 85, 97, 101, 107, 113, 121, 140, 147, 165, passes Little-Go 166 n.*241*; **4:** 19, 136, 138, 148 n.*132*, 149, gains BA degree 150, 154; **5:** 102, 107, 122 n.*194*, 172; **6:** 46, 48, 49, 58, 74, 76, 77, 131, 132, 170, 227, 229, 232, 238, 360, 362, 363, 411, 421, 437, 438, 464, 465, 474; **7:** 113, 116 n.*216*, 151 n.*284*, 232, 248, serious problem with curacy 249, 250, 294, marriage 299 n.*541*, 375, 376 n.*649*, 546; **8:** 11, 91 n.*148*, 217, 369, 540, 559, 610; **9:** 14, 66, 69, 192 n.*316*, 277, 287 n.*454*

Winifred Mary (1888-1977) – niece, **9:** 66 n.*120*

Zöe Frances (1890-1975) – niece, **9:** 66 n.*120*

Dodgson (of Putney, Surrey):

Amy Menella – cousin, see Pollock

Caroline neé Hume (1809-1875) – aunt, **1:** 12, 67 n.*51*, 106 n.*120*, 126 n.*156*; **2:** 80, 85 n.*170*; **4:** 116; **5:** 65, 158, 211, 226, 227 n.*361*; **6:** 223, 352, 355, 359, 361, 384; **7:** 183

Charlotte Mary (b. 1839) – cousin, **1:** 106 n.*120*, 107; **2:** 23, 24, 50, 51; **3:** 80, 173; **4:** 340; **6:** 19; **7:** 253, 415, 503; **8:** 57, 319, 404, 450; **9:** 120 n.*208*, 150

Francis Hume "Frank" (1834-1917) – cousin, **1:** 67 n.*51,* 71, 106 n.*120*, 107; **2:** seeks commission in army 19 n.*32*, 25 n.*47*, 33, 43, 49-51, 60, 70, 77, 78, 80, 82; **3:** 53 n.*81*, 56, 58, 139; **5:** emigrates to Australia 33 n.*38*

Hassard Hume, Mr. (1803-1884), barrister – uncle, **1:** 10, 12, 16, 67 n.*51*, 106 n.*120*, 107, 109, 126 n.*156*; **2:** 18, 19 n.*32*, 23, 50, 82, 85 n.*170*, 110 n.*214*, 122; **3:** 26 n.*37*, 80, 132 n.*191*, 140, 173; **4:** 30, 86, 128 n.*102*, 198, 284, 323, 326, 339, 340; **5:** 65, 158, 196, 211; **6:** 11 n.*1*, 15, 71, 72, 196, 198, 238, 239, 256, 348, 352, 355, 359, 361, 385, 427; **7:** 51, 62, 125, 183, 224, 253, 335, 415, 503, 527; **8:** 57, 103, 141 n.*229*

James Hume (1845-1912) – cousin, see below
Laura Elizabeth (1853-1882) – cousin, **1:** 106 n.*120*; **5:** 19; **6:** 19; **7:** 253, 255, 335, 401 n.*681*
Louis Henri (1841-1849) – cousin, **1:** 106 n.*120*
Louis Henry "Hal" (b. 1850) – cousin, **1:** 106 n.*120*, 107; **6:** 11 n.*1*; **7:** 253, 415, 503; **8:** 57, 103, 319, 404, 450
Lucy Caroline (1836-1894) – cousin, **1:** 106 n.*120*, 107; **2:** 50, 80; **6:** 19, 361; **7:** 253, 335, 415, 503; **8:** 57, 103, 141 n.*228*, 404, 450; **9:** 120 n.*208*, 150 n.*258*
Menella "Marla" Frances (1848-1917) – cousin, see Bischoff
Percy (1838-1886) – cousin, **1:** 106 n.*120*, 107; **2:** 18, 19 n.*32*, 23, 50, 81, 82; **5:** emigrates to Australia 33 n.*38*
Dodgson (of Croft-on-Tees, Yorkshire, and Guildford, Surrey):
Caroline Hume (1833-1904) – sister, **1:** 13, 127 n.*157*, 129, 130; **2:** 58, 59; **3:** 84; **4:** 109; **5:** 43, 107; **6:** 42, 51, 58, 66, 76, 90, 157, 158, 170, 205, 224, 226, 262, 269, 292, 308, 330, 332, 342, 343, 349, 370, 386, 414, 443, 457, 477, 478, 480-482, 485, 496; **7:** 11, 25, 26, 39, 45, 47, 48, 74, 96, 104, 120, 125, 150, 166, 170, 189, 193, 219, 229, 233, 281, 294, 303, 312, 343, 370, 392, 423, 437, 460, 469-471, 477, 481, 501, 514, 531, 544; **8:** 30, 75, 83, 100, 113, 131, 140, 148, 159, 214, 215, 220, 240, 251, 254, 282, 290, 291, 296, 298, 303, 304, 310, 328, 356, 371, 374, 400, 433, 439, 450, 453, 455, 498, 503, 514, 533, 545, 562, 565-567, 603, 610, 612, 615, 628, 629; **9:** 14, 26, 45, 49, 54, 59, 73, 78, 102, 115, 123, 139, 150, 158, 179, 187, 192, 205, 216, 234, 235, 245, 269, 277, 284, 288, 302, 345
Charles (1800-1868), archdeacon – father, **1:** 10, 12, 15, 16, 21, 22, 26-29, 39, 43-45, 50 n.*1*, 55 n.*18*, 59 n.*31*, 60, 80, 108, letter of advice 121 n.*150*, 127, 129, 130; **2:** 8 n.*2*, 14, 41, 55, 74 n.*149*, 90 n.*181*, 106 n.*205*; **3:** 83, 85, 139, 140 n.*208*, walks with 150-152, 166 n.*241*; **4:** 10, 13, 19, 34; **5:** 38, 43; **6:** death 39 n.*55*; **7:** 62
Edwin Heron (1846-1918) – brother, **1:** 13, 25; **2:** 56, 58 n.*117*; **3:** 11, 140 n.*208*, 148, 171, 172, enters Twyford School 174; **4:** 10, 28, 30-32, 43, visits Oxford from Rugby School 171 n.*165*, 172, 173, 279, 282; **5:** 15, 102, 107, 109, 177, 178; **6:** 41 n.*56*, applies for a Post Office clerkship 48, 49, 58, 72, 74, 85, 104 n.*163*, 122 n.*187*, 130, 135, 169, 172, 176, decides to take Holy Orders 186, 193, 219, 227, 235, 279, 344, 472, 474; **7:** 50, 51, 126, 145 n.*270*, 146, 164 n.*308*, leaves for Zanzibar 166, 228 n.*420*, 229, 233, 243, 244, 277, 294, 298-300, 302, 311, 312, takes up post as priest on Tristan da Cunha 314, 438, 518; **8:** 37, 44, 45, 47, 51, returns from Tristan 163 n.*267*, 172, 183, 184, 200, 220, 240, meets Lord Salisbury before going back to Tristan 254, 255, 298, 324 n.*537*, Dodgson seeks support of Tristan islanders 326, 391 n.*637*, 492 n.*796*, ordered home through ill health 501-503, 506, 507, 514, 533, 537, goes to St. Vincent 539; **9:** 211 n.*338*, returns 234 n.*370*, 235, 245, 266, 267, 269, 302

Elizabeth Lucy (1830-1916) – sister, **1:** 10, 18, 20, 21, 25, 36, 39, 45, 46, 71 n.*62*, 108 n.*122*, 115 n.*139*, 121 n.*149*, 129, 130; **2:** 14, 16, 55, 58 n.*116*, 59, 85, 118, 119 n.*227*; **3:** 10; **4:** 80, 81, 97, 98, 174; **5:** 102, 177; **6:** 42, 51, 84, 85, 175, 186, 193, 206, 225-229, 262, 330, 332, 337, 361, 482-485; **7:** 50, 51, 125, 135, 136, 181, 281, 294, 296, 297, 303, 312, 325, 343, 344, 359, 360, 363, 370, 392, 423, 437, 462, 464, 468, 477, 481, 501, 531, 544; **8:** 75, 82, 101, 113, 148, 159, 163, 183, 236, 238, 240, 256, 268, 270, 275, 290, 291, 336, 353, 354, 356, 368, 498, 503, 562, 566, 567, 603, 610; **9:** 78, 149, 150, 193, 245, 345

Frances "Fanny" Jane (1828-1903) – sister, **1:** 10, 21, 26, 27, 39, 108 n.*122*, 115 n.*139*, 117, 127 n.*157*, 129, 130; **2:** 14, 16, 58 n.*116*, 85; **3:** 10, 84, 168; **4:** 80, 81, 97, 98, 233, 234; **5:** 15, 33 n.*36*, 43, 102, 107, 172; **6:** 41, 42, approves new home at The Chestnuts 46-49, 51, 58, 66, 69, 76, 90, 94, 106, 128, 149-151, 157, 158, 169, 193, 222, 223, 229, 235, 239, 262, 270, 279, 280, 284, 292, 296, 297, 308, 344, 347, 349, 355, 357, 362, 363, 384, 386, 388, 390, 394, 395, 397, 432, 443, 466, 467, 477, 483-485, 496; **7:** 11, 12, 78, 90, 104, 117, 120, 125, first trip to Eastbourne 133, 150, 166, 170, 189, 193, 228, 229, 253, 281, 288, 293, 294 n.*532*, 296, 299, inherits house at Hastings 302, 303 n.*547*, 312, 343, 344, 370, 392, 414, 460, 462, 467-469, 477, 481, 501, 531; **8:** 29, 75, 82, 100, 113, 131, 140, 148, 183, 200, 219, 220, 240, 251, 254, 255, 260, 273, 275, 282, 290, 291, 296, 298, 303, 304, 310, 328, 356, 368, 371, 374, 375, 388 n.*633*, 400, 418, 433, 439, 445, 450, 453, 490, 498, 503, 514, 533, 545, 562, 565-567, 603, 610, 612, 615, 628; **9:** 14, 26, 45, 49, 54, 59, 73, 78, 102, 115, 123, 139, 150, 173, 179, 187, 192, 205, 216, 234, 235, 269, 277, 284, 288, 302, 345

Frances Jane neé Lutwidge (1803-1851) – mother, **1:** 10, 12, 23-25, 28, 39, 60 n.*33*, 102 n.*112*, 102 n.*113*, 109 n.*125*; **2:** 108 n.*209*

Henrietta Harington (1843-1922) – sister, **1:** 13, 100 n.*109*; **2:** 56; **4:** 37, 52, 109, 139, 233; **5:** 107; **6:** 51, 58, 85, 149-151, 157, 158, 171, 175-178, 192, 205, 224, 229, 231, 270, 271, 297-299, 308, 316, 330, 332, 335, 336, 344, 370, 386, 457, 461, 465, 477, 479-482, 485, 496; **7:** 11, 25, 40, 45, 48, 51, 74, 104, 116, 117, 125, 151, 166, 170, 189, 219, 229, 233, 236, 253, 288, 294, 303, 312, 343, 344, 370, 392, 394, 396, 414, 423, 437, 460, 477, 481, 501, 514, 531, 544; **8:** 29, 75, 100, 113, 131, 140, 148, moves to Brighton 159 n.*256*, 160, 193, 200, 220, 235, 251, 254, 289, 310, 344, 348, 360-363, 371, 415, 424, 439, 476, 481, 498, 532, 536, 545, 578, 582, 584, 585, 587, 603; **9:** 22, 25, 49, 82, 101, 115, 159, 170, 173, 187, 207, 216, 235, 273, 288, 332

Louisa "Loui" Fletcher (1840-1930) – sister, **1:** 13, 82 n.*86*, 84, 127 n.*157*, 129, 130; **2:** 16, 100; **3:** 86, 171; **4:** 48, 98; **5:** 42, 102, 172, 177; **6:** 41, 51, 85, 128, 186, 205, 209, 229, 232 n.*365*, 233, 246, 270, 280, 281, 284, 344, 362, 370, 386, 394, 395, 397, 407, 465, 477, 481, 484, 485; **7:** 11, 25, 39, 45, 50, 78, 104, 125, 150, 166, 170, 189, 229, 281, 294, 296, 303, 312, 343, 370, 392, 395, 414, 423, 437, 477, 481,

501, 514, 531, 544; **8:** 30, 75, 81, 83, 101, 113, 131, 140, 149, 159, 162, 183, 200, 273, 282, 298, 303, 304, 310, 328, 344, 353, 371, 372, 374, 400, 432, 433, 439, 450, 453, 472, 474-476, 514, 531-533, 538, 545, 551, 597, 603, 610, 612, 615, 628; **9:** 14, 23, 26, 45, 49, 54, 59, 73, 102, 115, 123, 126, 139, 140, 158, 179, 187, 190 n.*313*, 192, 205, 211, 216, 226, 269, 277, 279 n.*445*, 284, 288, 302

Margaret Anne Ashley (1841-1915) – sister, **1:** 13; **4:** 109, 139, 233; **5:** 102, 107, 172, 175, 177, 178, 378; **6:** 41, 51, 128, 149-151, 157, 158, 170-172, 175, 186, 205, 225, 227, 229, 231, 238, 246, 262, 269, 270, 308, 332, 342, 343, 370, 407, 443, 461, 465, 467, 477, 478, 480, 481, 485, 496; **7:** 11, 25, 26, 39, 45, 50, 51, 74, 77, 90, 96, 117, 120, 125, 135, 136, 151, 166, 170, 171, 181, 219, 220, 229, 232, 288, 294, 296, 303, 312, 343, 359-361, 363, 370, 392, 414, 423, 437, 460, 477, 481, 501, 531, 544; **8:** 29, 30, 75, 81, 83, 101, 131, 149, 159, 162, 170, 183, 193, 220, 236, 238, 240, 251, 254, 260, 282, 296, 298, 303, 304, 310, 328, 344, 356, 400, 433, 439, 450, 453, 472, 476, 498, 503, 514, 533, 538, 562, 584, 585, 607, 612, 628; **9:** 26, 49, 54, 59, 78, 101, 102, 115, 119, 120, 158, 179, 192, 216, 234, 235, 269, 273, 277, 284, 286, 288, 302, 314, 315, 319, 321, 354

Mary Charlotte (1835-1911) – sister, see Collingwood

Skeffington Hume (1836-1919) – brother, see above

Wilfred Longley (1838-1914) – brother, see above

Dodgson:

Charles (1722-1796) – great-grandfather, **1:** 9; **2:** 62 n.*124*, 63

Charles (1769-1803) – grandfather, **1:** 9, 10, 107 n.*121*, 122 n.*152*, 133 n.*166*

Charles Heathfield (1855-1898) – distant relative, **6:** 145 n.*221*

Christopher Charles (1686-1750) – great-great-grandfather, **1:** 9

Elizabeth Anne (1770-1836) – great-aunt, **1:** 9, 12

John (fl. 1500-1520) – antecedent, **2:** 43

Lucy neé Hume (1775-1818), later Marwood – grandmother, **1:** 9, 107 n.*121*, 133 n.*166*

William (fl. 1530-1540) – antecedent , **2:** 43

Dodgson (of Stubb Hall, Whorlton, Durham):

Charlotte (b. 1806) – distant relative, **8:** 532 n.*853*

Decima Anne (b. 1820) – distant relative, **8:** 532 n.*853*

Elizabeth (b. 1809) – distant relative, **8:** 532 n.*853*

Sarah C. (b. 1819) – distant relative, **6:** 142, 143 n.*216*; **7:** 138 n.*254*, 139, 181

Thomas, Mr. (1776-1873) – distant relative, **8:** 532 n.*853*

William Oliver (1811-1895) – distant relative, **6:** 145 n.*221*

Dodgson (of London):

Elizabeth Ada Mary née Smythe – cousin's wife, **8:** 318 n.*522*, 408; **9:** 120 n.*209*

James Hume, Mr. (1845-1912) – cousin, **1:** 106 n.*120*; **2:** 50;

3: 136 n.*199*, 137, 174; **4:** 30; **5:** 78 n.*121*, 95, 96, 170, 250; **6:** 385; **7:** 28 n.*36*; **8:** 57, 141 n.*229*, 318 n.*522*, 408; **9:** 120 n.*209*
Maud "Maudie" Bailey (b. 1886), **8:** 318 n.*522*, 408; **9:** 120 n.*209*

Dodgson, Charles Lutwidge:
Accounts, **2:** 79
Acrostics, **5:** 252 n.*413*; **6:** 245, 427 n.*704*, 428, 462 n.*761*; **7:** 22
Advertising for London photographic studio, **6:** 428
Agreement with Macmillan and Company, **7:** 546 n.*880*
Amateur theatricals, **1:** 124 (Wilcox); **2:** 47 (Mitford); **4:** 151 (Pattison), 205 (Brasenose), 263 (Christ Church), 317, 318 (Benefit for Female Artists); **5:** 41 (Wilcox), 51 (Price), 153 (St. Johns), 253 (St. Johns); **6:** 36 (St. Johns), 67 (Christ Church Choristers), 104 (Synge), 133 (Price), 161 (MacDonald), 188 (Hatch), 224 (MacDonald), 249 (Simpson), 274 (Parker), 444 (Head); **7:** 95 (Lathbury), 158 (Fendall), 194 (MacDonald), 511 (Simpson), 527 (Woodhouse); **8:** 78 (Cecil), 372 (Guildford School); **9:** 118 (St. Nicholas' Hall, Guildford), 121 (Holywell Music Room, Oxford), 207 (Mrs. Barber's School), 296 (Hatch), 303 (Borough Hall, Guildford)
Anagrams, **6:** 64 n.*93*, 65
Argument with brother Wilfred, **3:** 18
Artist's lay figures, **6:** 206 n.*321*; **7:** 118 n.*221*
Attends Oxford assizes, **4:** 219, 275; **5:** 52 n.*73*, 53 n.*74*, 118 n.*154*, 119 n.*186*; **7:** 21 n.*19*, 121 n.*228*
Battels, **8:** 602 n.*956*
Betting, **2:** 50, 52; **3:** 55, 56 n.*85*, 147; **5:** 182, 183 n.*301*, 184 n.*302*
Bodley Oration, **4:** 134, 135 n.*112*
Book buying, **1:** 85, 120; **2:** 33, 47; **3:** 158; **5:** 131, 145; **8:** 579; **9:** 329

Books (any title mentioned in the *Diaries*):
Aids to Reflection (Samuel Coleridge), **1:** 56, 116; **3:** 147
Alec Forbes of Howglen (George MacDonald), **5:** 125
Algebraic Geometry (George Salmon), **3:** 15
Alton Locke (Charles Kingsley), **2:** 8, 10-12
Angel in the House (Coventry Patmore), **1:** 115
Aurora Leigh (Elizabeth Barrett Browning), **3:** 148, 149
Austrian Dungeons in Italy (Felice Orsini), **3:** 9
Away with Melancholy (John Morton), **1:** 128, 132; **2:** 56, 103; **3:** 45, 85
Baby's Grandmother, The (Lucy Walford), **8:** 573
Bachelor of the Albany (Marmion Savage), **1:** 90, 91
Ballads of Crewe (Bon Gaultier), **2:** 44
Bar Sinister, The (Charles Collins), **8:** 15; **9:** 190
Cathedral (Isaac Williams), **1:** 98
Chamber's Euclid, **1:** 82
Chance of Acquaintance, A (William Howells), **8:** 15

Chances (Augustus De Morgan), **3:** 158
Church Dictionary (Walter Hook), **1:** 60
Clinical Lectures (James Paget), **7:** 56
Compendium of Algebra (John Ward), **1:** 81 n.*82*
Con Cregan (Charles Lever), **1:** 109
Cranford (Elizabeth Gaskell), **3:** 169
David Copperfield (Charles Dickens), **1:** 26
David Elginbrod (George MacDonald), **4:** 160
Demosthenes, **3:** 156
De Quincey's Works, **3:** 130, 148, 149, 156, 164
Dictionary of Dates (Joseph Haydn), **2:** 36
Differential Calculus (Bartholomew Price), **1:** 57
Diversions of Hollycot (Christian Isobel Johnstone), **1:** 27
Diversions of Purley (John Horne Tooke), **1:** 52
Done Brown (Henry Craven), **2:** 88; **3:** 85
Dream of the Atonement, A (Anon), **7:** 517
Dred (Harriet Stowe), **2:** 99
Ecclesiastical History (Edward Burton), **1:** 80, 85
Edwin the Fair (Henry Taylor), **4:** 128
Elergy (Thomas Gray), **1:** 51
Elsie's Expedition (Frederick Weatherly), **8:** 579
Exposition of the Creed (John Pearson), **2:** 117
Fairies, The (William Allingham), **8:** 596
Fair Saxon, A (Justin McCarthy), **8:** 15
Fallen Leaves (Wilkie Collins), **7:** 285
Finite Differences (Henry Kuhff), **1:** 69
First Hebrew Book (Thomas K. Arnold), **5:** 131
Foundations of Geometry (Edward Dixon), **8:** 555
Frank Hilton, or the Queen's Own (James Grant), **1:** 114
Friends in Council (Arthur Helps), **1:** 75
From Nowhere to the North Pole (Tom Hood), **8:** 579
Games (Edmund Hoyle), **3:** 151
Gilfillan's Poets, **2:** 33
Goblin Market and Other Poems (Christina Rossetti), **4:** 66
Green Pastures and Piccadilly (William Black), **7:** 285, 286
Guardian Angel, The (Oliver W. Holmes), **9:** 190
Handbook of Physiology (William Kirke), **3:** 165, 167
Head of the Family (Dinah Mulock), **1:** 68, 69, 92, 93; **3:** 141
Health (Thomas Mayo), **8:** 94
Heartsease (Charlotte Yonge), **2:** 57
Hebrew Grammar (Friedrich Gesenius), **5:** 131
Henry IV (William Shakespeare), **1:** 68
Henry VIII (William Shakespeare), **1:** 125, 128
Hidden Depths (Felicia Skene), **8:** 514
Hillyars and the Burtons, The (Henry Kingsley), **5:** 125

Hints for Emergencies (John South), **2:** 47
History of England (David Hume), **2:** 65; **3:** 46, 156
History of England (Thomas Macaulay), **1:** 26
History of Europe (Archibald Alison), **1:** 27
History of Latin Christianity (Henry Milman), **3:** 8
History of the Conquest of England by the Normans (Jacques Thierry), **1:** 23
Horace Complete Works in Latin, **2:** 35
House on the Marsh, The (Florence Warden), **8:** 189
House out of Windows (William Brough), **2:** 56
Hypatia (Charles Kingsley), **3:** 7, 8
Indian Summer (William Howells), **9:** 190
John Halifax, Gentleman (Dinah Mulock), **3:** 141
Lady of Aroostook, The (William Howells), **8:** 15
La Petite Fadette (George Sand), **7:** 351
Lectures on Church History (Edward Burton), **1:** 80
Lectures on Modern History (William Smyth), **1:** 73
Les Malheurs de Sophie (Sophaletta Rostopchine), **7:** 486
Life for a Life, A (Dinah Mulock), **9:** 190
Life, Letters & Literary Remains of John Keats (Richard Milnes), **1:** 55
Life of Benjamin Robert Haydon (Tom Taylor), **1:** 51, 52
Life of Charlotte Brontë (Elizabeth Gaskell), **3:** 85, 86, 90
Little Dorrit (Charles Dickens), **2:** 37, 52
Mabel in Rhymeland (Edward Holland), **8:** 579
Manual of Artistic Anatomy (Robert Knox), **3:** 168
Margaret Fuller (Thomas Higginson), **7:** 426
Maud and Other Poems (Alfred Tennyson), **1:** 119, 120, 129, 134; **2:** 9; **3:** 112, 113
Meditationes Algebraicæ (Edward Waring), **1:** 70, 79
Memoirs (Charles Mathews), **2:** 9
Moral Philosophy (William Paley), **3:** 156
Mr. Smith (Lucy Walford), **8:** 573
My Haunts (Edmund Yates), **2:** 61
New Sketches of Everyday Life (Mary Howitt), **2:** 17
North and South (Elizabeth Gaskell), **1:** 131
Notices to Correspondents (Anon), **3:** 158
Ogilvies, The (Dinah Mulock), **1:** 92, 93
Old Kensington (Anne Thackeray), **8:** 15
On Certainty in Religion (Edward White), **8:** 455
Origin and Progress of Writing (Thomas Astle), **1:** 63
Othello (William Shakespeare), **1:** 85
Our Mutual Friend (Charles Dickens), **5:** 379
Parish Musings (Henry Mansel), **1:** 120
Paul Ferroll (Caroline Clive), **3:** 82
Philosophical Essays (Isaac Watts), **1:** 76

Poem on Routh (John Burgon), **1:** 59
Poems (Elizabeth Barrett Browning), **3:** 158
Poems (George Herbert), **2:** 28
Poems (James Lowell), **4:** 244
Poems (John Moultrie), **4:** 244
Poems (Thomas Hood), **1:** 66
Pre-Raffaelitism (Edward Young), **3:** 44, 45
Pride and Prejudice (Jane Austen), **8:** 15
Principles of Harmony & Contrast of Colours (Michel Chevreul), **1:** 54
Ravenshoe (Henry Kingsley), **5:** 125
Rejected Addresses (James and Horatio Smith), **1:** 59
Ruskin's Poems (ed. James Wright), **7:** 518
Ruth (Elizabeth Gaskell), **1:** 131
Scenes from Clerical Life (George Eliot), **3:** 155
Search After Proserpine (Aubrey De Vere), **4:** 244
Second Hebrew Book (Thomas K. Arnold), **5:** 131
Selections from Shakespeare (Samuel Brandram), **7:** 418
Shadows of the Clouds (James Froude), **1:** 97
Stones of Venice (John Ruskin), **1:** 118
Story of a Nursery Rhyme, The (C. B.), **8:** 20, 579
System in Logic, A (John Stuart Mill), **3:** 156
Tasso, **1:** 84, 85; **2:** 28
Theory of Equations (Isaac Todhunter), **4:** 242
Thoughts in Past Years (Isaac Williams), **1:** 52
Thoughts on Personal Religion (Edward Goulburn), **8:** 250
Thucydides, **2:** 35
Trip to Blunderland, A (Jean Jambon), **8:** 579
Valentine Vox (Henry Cockton), **1:** 57
Vice-Versâ (F. Anstey), **8:** 189
Virgin Widow (Henry Taylor), **4:** 128
Wanted – A King (Maggie Browne), **8:** 579
White Doe of Rylstone (William Wordsworth), **3:** 155
White Swans, The (Hans Christian Andersen), **8:** 253
Works (David Ricardo), **3:** 158
Wuthering Heights (Emily Brontë), **2:** 74

Book-selling terms, **9:** 176, 177
Bostock Scholarship, **1:** 97, 98 n.104; **3:** 20 n.*24*
Boulter Scholarship, **1:** 44
Brewer Street home, **8:** 505 n.*811*
Calendars and dates, **3:** 8 n.*4*, 127, 128 n.*185*
Cases for papers, **7:** 417 n.*695*
Caterer in Hall, **1:** 59 n.*31*
Charades, **1:** 123-125, 128, 129; **2:** 81, 88; **5:** 376; **6:** 107, 108; **8:** 78
Chess, **5:** 172, 173, 189 n.*310*, 283, 349

Choral Society membership, **3:** 60, 61 n.*92*, 144
Ciphers, **2:** 42 n.*83*, 52; **3:** 158 n.*235,* 159-164; **8:** 181; **9:** 55
Circular Letters:
Christ Church biographical records, **7:** 264 n.*477*
Colour of counters for *Game of Logic*, **8:** 293 n.*489*
Dramatic School of Art, **7:** 404 n.*685*, 405
Dymes family support, **8:** 72 n.*117*
Purchaser or tenant for a house, **8:** 232 n.*394*
Shakespeare for girls, **7:** 422 n.*705*
Circulars:
Bode's election for professorship of poetry, **3:** 42
Bouverie's Bill exempting Fellows from conforming to liturgy, **4:** 202
Common Room membership, **8:** 126 n.*205*, 380, 381 n.*625*
Copies of the *Alice* books for Hospitals, **6:** 473 n.*780*; **7:** 44 n.*68*
Dean Emly's election for professorship of poetry, **5:** 248
Testimonial to Faulkner (Christ Church cook), **7:** 238 n.*440*
Clôture, **7:** 420 n.*702*
Composing verses, **6:** 348 n.*577*, 356
Conjuror, **1:** 20
Contributions to University Commission, **3:** 21, 86, 87 n.*135*
Correspondence numbers, **4:** 44-46
Court action to recover a debt, **7:** 17
Court appearance to recover missing facsimiles of *Alice's Adventures Under Ground*, **8:** 301
Cricket, **1:** 27, 42; **7:** 468
Croft School accounts, **6:** 78 n.*113*, 83
Croquêt, **4:** 69, 94, 112, 195-198, 220 n.*240*, 245, 303, 308, 309, 319, 322, 336, 339, 348, 355; **5:** 108, 169; **6:** 90, 149, 153, 252

Curator of the Common Room:
Alterations, **8:** 213 n.*364*, 282 n.*473*, 284
Appointments, **8:** 214 n.*365*
Audit, **8:** 93, 167, 261, 382, 498 n.*800*, 551, 608
Cellars, **8:** 60 n.*97*, 282 n.*473*, 284, 498 n.*800*
Circular, **8:** 126 n.*205*
Conduct, **8:** 61 n.*98*, 346
Ledgers, **8:** 12, 54, 61, 65, 86, 152 n.*248*
Mediation, **8:** 257, 258
Meetings, **8:** 119 n.*190*, 121 n.*194*, 167 n.*278*, 277 n.*465*, 282 n.*473*, 458, 459 n.*737*
Membership, **8:** 119 n.*190*, 121 n.*194*, 126 n.*205*, 136, 380, 381 n.*625*
Notices, **8:** 57 n.*87*, 83 n.*133*, 84 n.*135*, 119 n.*192*, 265, 277, 433 n.*699*, 501 n.*805*, 503 n.*808*, 537 n.*861*, 538 n.*862*, 605 n.*961*
Resignation, **8:** 599, 605 n.*960*, 608 n.*965*
Wine-Committee, **8:** 65, 92, 93, 276, 459

Cut pages from Diary, see Missing pages
Cycle-Book, **7:** 257
Cycling, **7:** 478-480, 495; **8:** 221
Day-book, **2:** 26 n.*51*
Death of his father, **6:** 38-41
Declining social-invitations, **8:** 104, 124, 156, 202, 326; **9:** 152, 224, 229
Dentist visits, **4:** 65; **7:** 243, 358, 454, 455; **8:** 41, 192, 345, 402
Dies cretâ notandus, **6:** 487; **7:** 47, 61, 86, 106, 112, 142, 160, 206, 363, 466, 474; **8:** 25, 378; **9:** 97, 101, 123, 341
Dies faustus, **8:** 23
Dies mirabilis, **2:** 79; **3:** 115
Dies notabilis, **3:** 122
Dinner parties in his rooms, **4:** 73, 82, 83, 259; **6:** 66, 149, 150, 327, 395, 396; **7:** 52, 115, 346, 423, 424, 427, 489; **8:** 62, 94, 200, 216, 267, 315, 455, 458, 469, 472, 514, 516, 566, 594, 629; **9:** 35, 39, 62, 67, 70, 108, 109, 127, 135, 142, 145, 150, 154, 182, 195, 187, 198, 223, 232, 239, 243, 252, 280, 281, 287, 294, 298-300, 318-321, 324, 354
"Directions regarding my Funeral, etc.," **6:** 279 n.*459*
Disapproval of printing outcomes, **5:** 97 n.*151* (*Alice's Adventures*); **8:** 307 n.*509* (*Games of Logic*), 483 n.*783* (*The Nursery "Alice"*); **9:** 105, 106 n.*190* (60th thousand *Looking-Glass*)
Donation of seat-backs to St. Mary's, Oxford, **7:** 521, 523, 534, 545; **8:** 22 n.*17*
Drawing, **1:** 53, 118, 126; **7:** 187 n.*349*, 388; lessons **8:** 12; sketching from life **6:** 143, 201, 343, 356, 358, 359, 361, 375, 412, 422, 481, 482, 484; **9:** 99
Drawing on wood, **4:** 220, 221; **6:** 267

Drawings made by Dodgson of:

Bell, Helen Frances, **7:** 260 n.*471*
Boy and Goose, **7:** 88 n.*154*
Christie, Dora, **7:** 54 n.*85*
Cowie, Helen E. M, **7:** 300 n.*543*, 301 n.*545*
Duckworth, Beatrice, **7:** 45 n. *69*
Dymes, Ruth and Tommy, **7:** 204 n.*381*
Gordon, Violet, **7:** 58, 59
Hare, Maggie, **7:** 290 n.*525*
Hull, Agnes, **7:** 66 n.*105*
Hull Children, **7:** 187 n.*349*
Macwilliams, Agnes, **7:** 292 n.*528*
Nash, Edith, **8:** 26 n.*27*
Richards, Marion, **7:** 363 n.*633*
Waddy, Louisa, **7:** 50 n.*79*

Dreaming, **2:** 38 n.*76*; **7:** 175, 335
Editor of *College Rhymes*, **4:** 71 n.*13*, 89, 121 n.*93*, 136 n.*113*, 142 n.*122*, 144 n.*126*, 146, 148, 149 n.*133*, 169 n.*162*, 173 n.*169*, 177 n.*174*
Election theory, **6:** 306 n.*507*, 307, 345, 440, 447; **7:** 428 n.*715*, 433, 434, 436; see also Works, *Proportional Representation*
Electric pen, **7:** 43 n.*66*, 44, 45, 54, 88, 238 n.*440*, 242 n.*444*, 242 n.*445*, 245, 246 n.*450*, 247 n.*452*, 247 n.*453*, 252, 262 n.*474*, 264 n.*477*, 265 n.*479*
Elocution, **5:** 201
Estate of Aunt Lucy, **7:** 324 n.*575*, 335
Examinations taken for BA degree, **1:** 45, 47-49, 50 n.*2*, 54 n.*13*
Executors' accounts, **6:** 71 n.*104*, 78, 93 n.*145*, 127, 178
Financial problems reducing his support for family, **9:** 173
Genealogy, **2:** 43, 62 n.*124*
Globe, **5:** 232 n.*371*
Gloves, **8:** 415, 416 n.*673*
God-children, **6:** 11 n.*1*
Godparent, **5:** 185 n.*304*
Handbells, **1:** 50

Holidays:
Europe and Russia, **5:** 255-369
Isle of Wight, **4:** 14-19, 343-356; **6:** 296-299, 342-344, 356-363, 411-413, 416-425, 477-485; **7:** 345, 526
Lake District, **2:** 89-99; **3:** 107-119
Proposed trip to France (for photography), **3:** 68
Proposed trip to the Holy Land, **2:** 97 n.*189*
Scotland, **3:** 94-107; **6:** 179-186; **7:** 448-452
see also Bognor, Eastbourne, Margate, and Whitby

Homeopathic (herbal) medicine, **7:** 90 n.*161*, 105, 206, 214 n.*395*, 221, 237 n.*437*, 238, 295, 491 n.*799*; **8:** 431, 432 n.*695*
Hospital circular, **6:** 473 n.*780*; **7:** 44 n.*68*

Illnesses:
Ague, **7:** 338; **8:** 12 n.*3*, 13, 67, 147, 288, 353, 539; **9:** 136, 189
Boil on left wrist, **8:** 482, 483
Bronchitis, **9:** 189, 355 n.*567*
Cold, **7:** 99, 105, 237, 238, 320, 545; **8:** 327; **9:** 49, 50, 135, 136, 189-191, 355 n.*567*
Cough, **6:** 137-139, 191
Cystitis, **8:** 12 n.*3*, 13, 539
Deafness, **1:** 29; **2:** 83 n.*165*; **4:** 182 n.*177*
Diarrhea, **9:** 30
Epileptiform, **8:** 255, 549-553

Erythema, **7:** 490
Fainting, **8:** 549
Feeling unwell, **3:** 69; **6:** 366; **9:** 302
Fever, **7:** 339, 343; **8:** 67, 147, 288, 353; **9:** 355 n.*567*
Headache, **6:** 190, **8:** 67, 255, 288, 549-553
Hooping cough, **1:** 24
Infantile fever, **1:** 29
Influenza, **1:** 61; **9:** 189-191, 355 n.*567*
Lameness, **6:** 462
Liver problems, **9:** 65
Loss of tooth, **9:** 302, see also Dentist visits
Lumbago, **8:** 539, 596; **9:** 52
Mumps, **1:** 28
Neuralgia, **6:** 340
Piles, **8:** 482
Rheumatic attack, **5:** 132; **9:** 169
Sight problems, **2:** 22 n.*41*; **8:** (moving fortifications) 201, 399, 435, 483, 580
Sore throat, **6:** 190; **7:** 99, 320
Sun stroke, **7:** 338
Swollen face, **2:** 95
Synovitis of the knee, **8:** 389-395, 402, 482, 483, 485, 507, 596-598, 600, 601, 603-605, 607; **9:** 61
Vasovagal or Transient Ischaemic attack, **8:** 549-553
Vesical catarrh, **7:** 339

Illumination designs, **1:** 50, 51, 53
Imitating voices, **2:** 128 n.*245*; **3:** 7
Income, **1:** 61, 85, 86, 97, 136; **3:** 20; **5:** 101, 114; **6:** 50, 131; **7:** 244, 248, 349, 375, 377; **8:** 540; **9:** 173
Inquest jury, **6:** 209 n.*328*
Insurance, **3:** 83
Inventions, **3:** 154 (*Court Circular* card game); **4:** 196 (new croquêt game); **6:** 240 (*Arithemtical Croquêt*); **7:** 151 (*Lanrick* board game), 229 (*Syzygies* word game); **8:** 119 (divisibility rules), 432 (postage stamp-case), 434 (logic boards for five and six attributes), 582 (*Nyctograph* for writing in the dark), 633 (new type of riddle); **9:** 107 (Factorial Practice), 129 (Co-operative Backgammon), 187 (number-guessing puzzle), 191 (new type of postal order), 263 (double-sided gummed paper), 351 (rules for long division); see also Ciphers
Invigilating (supervising an examination), **7:** 498
Journeys, cost of, **7:** 212, 281, 453
Junior Mathematical Studentships (elected to Board), **6:** 318, 323
Kissing difficulty, **7:** 240; **8:** 87 n.*141*
Latin theme read in Hall, **1:** 67, 68 n.*52*

Learning languages:
French, **1:** 73, 84; **5:** 250; **7:** 351, 357 n.*624*, 361, 363, 368, 486, 497 n.*812*; **8:** 293
German, **1:** 84; **5:** 275, 280; **7:** 351, 368
Italian, **1:** 73, 84; **2:** 89
Learning to play cards, **3:** 152
Ledger accounts, **7:** 403, 482, 505, 524 n.*848*
Letter in French, **4:** 170 n.*163*
Letter-register, **4:** 44, 45

Letters from:
Alice, Princess, **8:** 469 n.*759*; **9:** 21 n.*25*, 89 n.*161*, 98 n.*178*
Ashley-Cooper, Anthony, Lord Shaftesbury, **8:** 133 n.*216*
Barratt, Wilson, **7:** 533 n.*864*; **8:** 229 n.*387*
Beerbohm Tree, Herbert, **8:** 616 n.*976*
Bickersteth, Robert, **5:** 57 n.*82*
Bramwell, Frederick Joseph, **6:** 69 n.*102*
Brough, Lionel, **7:** 542 n.*875*; **8:** 63 n.*100*
Calverley, Charles S., **7:** 325 n.*576*
Cecil, Lord Eustace, **8:** 321 n.*530*
Charles, Prince (Duke of Albany), **9:** 21 n.*25*, 89 n.*161*
Clarke, Henry Savile, **8:** 421 n.*681*
Clifton, Robert Bellamy, **9:** 113 n.*198*
Dalmeny, Lord, **5:** 48 n.*63*; **6:** 5
Darwin, Charles, **6:** 244 n.*388*
Denman, George, **8:** 560 n.*892*
Denman, Grace, **6:** 191 n.*297*
Duchess of Albany, **8:** 479 n.*776*
Eastern Telegraph Company, **8:** 190 n.*321*
Emlyn, Lord, **5:** 48 n.*63*
Fawcett, Henry, **7:** 508 n.*552*
Fison, Frederick W., **9:** 112 n.*197*
Gathorne Hardy, Gathorne, **5:** 251 n.*411*; **7:** 405 n.*687*; **8:** 398 n.*647*
Gatty, Alfred, **4:** 46
Gatty, Margaret, **4:** 47
Gilbert, W. S., **7:** 90 n.*162*
Grimston, Margaret "Daisy" K., **8:** 401 n.*653*
Grossmith, George, **7:** 323 n.*573*, 352 n.*615*
Helen, Duchess of Albany, **9:** 35 n.*62*
Holiday, Adela Maria née Mileham, **9:** 223 n.*353*
Hutchinson, J. and Son, **8:** 506 n.*814*
Kendal, Margaret "Madge" née Robertson, **8:** 401 n.*653*
King, Edward, **8:** 550 n.*877*
Kingsley, Henry, **4:** 349 n.*457*
Knight, Andrew Rouse Boughton, **7:** 373 n.*648*

Laverty, Wallis Hay, **7:** 103 n.*192*
Leighton, Frederick, **7:** 190 n.*353*, 277 n.*504*
Lewis, Arthur James, **7:** 393 n.*671*
Liddell, Henry G., **4:** 269 n.*312*, **5:** 187 n.*307*; **6:** 65 n.*94*
Liddon, Henry Parry, **8:** 397 n.*646*, 400 n.*652*, 515 n.*831*
Lowe, Edward J., **4:** 57
MacDonald, George, **5:** 81 n.*126*
Macmillan, Frederick, **7:** 409 n.*689*
Marchioness of Granby, Marion Margaret Violet Manners née Lindsay, **8:** 463 n.*746*
Maskelyne, Nevil Story, **8:** 384 n.*630*
Maurice, Frederick D., **4:** 165 n.*159*, 167 n.*161*
Max Müller, Friedrich, **6:** 70 n.*103*
Millais, John Everett, **6:** 77 n.*112*
Munro, Alexander, **4:** 242 n.*271*
Needham, Francis Charles, (Lord Newry), **6:** 143 n.*217*
Northcote, Stafford Henry, **7:** 337 n.*593*, 411 n.*691*, 420 n.*702*
Paget, Francis, **9:** 189 n.*312*
Paget, James, **8:** 595 n.*949*
Patmore, Coventry, **8:** 534 n.*859*
Percy, Lady Edith Campbell née Douglas, **9:** 304 n.*483*
Percy, Lord Henry George, **8:** 597 n.*952*; **9:** 267 n.*423*
Potts, Robert, **4:** 49-51; **7:** 167 n.*316*, 306 n.*551*
Prendergast, Thomas, **7:** 41 n.*62*
Price, Bartholomew, **9:** 113 n.*198*, 115 n.*200*
Proctor, John, **6:** 59 n.*89*
Reed, Priscilla, **7:** 422 n.*705*
Ritchie, Anne Isabella née Thackeray, **8:** 617 n.*978*
Robinson, Hercules, **8:** 54 n.*80*
Rossetti, Christina, **7:** 492 n.*803*, 505 n.*824*; **8:** 67 n.*107*, 198 n.*336*; **9:** 99 n.*180*
Rossetti, Dante Gabriel, **5:** 130 n.*209*, 199 n.*322*
Ruskin, John, **6:** 302 n.*498*, 435 n.*716*; **7:** 518 n.*839*, 537 n.*870*
Sant, James, **5:** 145 n.*234*, 171 n.*284*; **6:** 76 n.*110*, 89 n.*136*; **7:** 367 n.*639*
Seymour, Lord Victor Alexander, **7:** 83 n.*141*
Sketchley, Arthur, **4:** 287 n.*343*
Smith, Henry J. S, **6:** 439 n.*721*
Spottiswoode, William, **5:** 133 n.*212*, 133 n.*213*, 198 n.*321*, 372 n.*552*, 377 n.*559*
Stanley, Arthur P., **5:** 80 n.*124*
Stanley, Augusta, Lady, **5:** 122 n.*193*
Stout, George Frederick, **9:** 160 n.*275*
Taylor, Henry, **6:** 211 n.*329*, 218 n.*343*
Tenniel, John, **5:** 56 n.*80*; **6:** 115 n.*178*, 127 n.*197*

Terry, Benjamin, **5:** 92 n.*142*
Todhunter, Isaac, **6:** 453 n.*745*; **7:** 167 n.*316*, 287 n.*521*
Waldegrave, Lady Mary Dorothea née Palmer, **8:** 622 n.*985*
Ward, Edward M., **5:** 161 n.*266*
Wilberforce, Samuel, **4:** 21
Wilcox, Arthur, **6:** 383 n.*629*
Wolmer, Lady Beatrix Maud née Cecil, **8:** 455 n.*731*

Letters to:
Alderson, Florence, **8:** 222 n.*380*
Alderson, Frederick Cecil, **8:** 77 n.*120*
Alice, Princess, **8:** 513 n.*827*; **9:** 85 n.*154*
Argles, Agnes "Dolly," **6:** 97 n.*152*, 106 n.*165*
Atkinson, Francis Home, **9:** 87 n.*157*
Badcock, Elizabeth "Bessie" H., **9:** 130 n.*228*
Balfour, Georgina, **5:** 115 n.*180*
Baly, Alice Mary née Richards, **9:** 48 n.*84*
Baly, Gladys, **9:** 186 n.*307*, 231 n.*366*
Barber, Charles Burton, **9:** 79 n.*146*
Barber, Charlotte Lucy née Plume, **9:** 185 n.*306*, 208 n.*337*
Barber, Mary "May" Lucy, **9:** 182 n.*303*, 348 n.*558*
Bayne, Thomas Vere, **6:** 116 n.*180*
Bell, George Charles, **8:** 344 n.*568*
Bell, Hilda Rotherwick, **9:** 97 n.*176*
Bell's Life:
Betting, **3:** 55, 56 n.*85*
Beringer, Aimée "Amy" née Daniell, **8:** 407 n.*661*
Blakemore, Sarah Elizabeth née King, **8:** 124 n.*200*
Bowles, Thomas Gibson, **8:** 569 n.*908*
Bowman, Isabella "Isa," **8:** 446 n.*716*, 526 n.*843*
Boyd, William, **6:** 451 n.*742*
Boyes, Charlotte, **8:** 560 n.*893*
Brain, Mary A., **8:** 574 n.*917*
Brooks, Henry Samuel, **9:** 33 n.*56*
Burrows, Esther Elizabeth née Bliss, **7:** 47 n.*72*
Butler, Arthur Gray, **9:** 36 n.*63*, 38 n.*66*, 77 n.*143*
Butler, Harriet Jessie née Edgeworth, **9:** 36 n.*63*, 41 n.*71*, 53 n.*91*, 135 n.*237*
Butler, Olive Harriet, **9:** 40 n.*70*
Capes, B. E. J., **8:** 548 n.*874*
Chambers, Maria, **7:** 110 n.*204*
Chase, Percy Drummond, **8:** 448 n.*717*
Collins, Sir Robert Hawthorn, **9:** 329 n.*528*
Commin, J. G., **9:** 275 n.*438*
Cooke, Kathella née Palmer, **8:** 322 n.*531*

Daniel, Charles Henry Olive, **8:** 396 n.*643*
Dingley, Emma Louisa née Waddy, **9:** 100 n.*181*
Diocesan Registrar, Oxford, **4:** 55
Dodgson, Alice Jane née Donkin, **9:** 248 n.*392*
Dodgson, Edith Alice, **8:** 505 n.*811*; **9:** 274 n.*437*
Dodgson, Elizabeth, **4:** 306 n.*376*
Dodgson, Frances Jane, **8:** 388 n.*633*
Dodgson, Frances Menella "Nella," **9:** 352 n.*564*
Dodgson, Hassard, **6:** 384 n.*631*
Dodgson, Louisa, **5:** 310 n.*480*; **9:** 190 n.*313*, 279 n.*445*
Dodgson, Lucy Caroline, **8:** 141 n.*228*
Dodgson, Mary C., **4:** 28-32, 47-49, 60-63; **5:** 218 n.*347*, 229 n.*366*
Dodgson, Skeffington Hume, **8:** 91 n.*148*
Dodgson, Wilfred Longley, **7:** 373 n.*648*
Dodgson Family, **4:** 40-44
Draper, Dorothy "Dolly" Ellen, **7:** 19 n.*15*; **8:** 623 n.*986*
Draper, Edward Thompson, **7:** 29 n.*39*
Drury, Sophia Louisa née Bousfield, **7:** 156 n.*294*
Duckworth, Robinson, **4:** 264 n.*309*
Du Maurier, George, **8:** 319 n.*523*
Dyer, Caroline, **7:** 445 n.*736*; **8:** 16 n.*10*, 68 n.*110*, 592 n.*944*, 611 n.*968*; **9:** 91 n.*167*, 265 n.*418*, 315 n.*503*
Dymes, Ethel, **8:** 103 n.*172*
Dymes, Ruth, **8:** 42 n.*59*, 79 n.*122*, 142 n.*230*, 148 n.*241*, 310 n.*513*
Egerton Allen, "Georgie" née Wilcox, **9:** 240 n.*378*
Ellis, Dymphna, **5:** 99 n.*157*
Ellis, Edwin John, **8:** 20
Falle, Albina "Lily," **8:** 111 n.*183*, 314 n.*517*
Feilden, Ellinor née Hornby, **6:** 450 n.*739*
Few, Charles Edward, **7:** 480 n.*781*
Fison, Frederick W., **9:** 112 n.*197*
Fitzgerald, Percy, **6:** 242 n.*386*
Fowler, E. S., **9:** 237 n.*374*
Fuller, Mary "Minnie" Frances née Drury, **9:** 283 n.*448*
Gaussen, Ella, **8:** 240 n.*403*
Gee, William H., **8:** 489 n.*792*
Gerrans, Anna Elizabeth née English, **9:** 279 n.*444*, 293 n.*464*
Greenidge, Edith Elizabeth née Lucy, **9:** 191 n.*315*, 242 n.*383*
Griffiths, Beatrice, **9:** 276 n.*441*
Harcourt, Augustus Vernon, **6:** 202 n.*314* (verse-invitation)
Hargreaves, Alice Pleasance née Liddell, **8:** 598 n.*954*
Hatch, Bessie Cartwright née Thomas, **7:** 101 n.*188*; **8:** 87 n.*141*, 105 n.*174*
Hatch, Ethel, **8:** 605 n.*961*
Heurtley, Jane, Mrs., **7:** 834 n.*865*

Hull, Agnes and Jessie (Christmas Cards), **7:** 502 n.*819*
Hunt, Gertrude E., Mrs., **7:** 280 n.*51*
Hussey, Elizabeth née Ley, **7:** 312 n.*558*
Illustrated London News:
Where Does the Day Begin?, **3:** 29 n.*42*
Jackson, Florence "Florrie" Annie, **9:** 18 n.*17*
Jebb, Edith, **6:** 327 n.*542*
Jeffery, Mr. (Bookseller), **9:** 336 n.*539*
Johnson, William J., **8:** 540 n.*865*
Kish, Thomas, **7:** 398 n.*677*, 470 n.*774*; **8:** 446 n.*716*
Kitchin, Alice Maud née Taylor, **6:** 282 n.*465*, 290 n.*479*, 298 n.*492*, 469 n.*774*; **7:** 240 n.*443*, 274 n.*498*; **8:** 552 n.*881*
Knowledge:
Divisibility by Seven, **8:** 121 n.*193*
Langton Clarke, Margaret "Margie," **8:** 177 n.*291*
Lascelles, Brian Piers, **8:** 554 n.*883*
Leathart, James, **5:** 227 n.*362*
Lewis, Arthur James, **6:** 135 n.*208*; **7:** 261 n.*472*
Liddell, Henry George, **6:** 492 n.*815*; **8:** 590 n.*940*
Liddell, Lorina Hannah née Reeve, **8:** 70 n.*115*; **9:** 104 n.*189*
Liddell, Violet Constance, **8:** 394 n.*639*
Liddon, Henry Parry, **6:** 178 n.*274*
Lucy, Alice née Jennings, **9:** 184 n.*305*, 324 n.*519*
Lutwidge, Lucy, **5:** 134 n.*215*, 159 n.*262*
MacDonald, George, **6:** 30 n.*37*
MacDonald, Lilia, **5:** 190 n.*311*
MacDonald, Louisa née Powell, **4:** 230 n.*254*, 250 n.*286*
MacDonald, M., Esq., **8:** 92 n.*149*
MacDonald, Mary, **5:** 125 n.*199*
Mackenzie, Alexander Campbell, **8:** 20 n.*14*
Macmillan, Alexander, **5:** 33 n.*37*, 76 n.*116*, 117 n.*184*, 173 n.*288*, 198 n.*321*, 207 n.*331*, 232 n.*370*, 374 n.*555*; **7:** 342 n.*599*; **8:** 21 n.*15*
Mallalieu, Margaret Ellen née Smith, **8:** 587 n.*938*, 616 n.*977*
Merriman, Henry Gordon, **8:** 346 n.*571*
Mileham, Mary née Livock, **8:** 210 n.*361*
Miller, Edith Mary, **9:** 24 n.*32*, 25 n.*34*, 28 n.*43*, 86 n.*155*, 153 n.*266*
Miller, Louisa Maria née Smith, **7:** 457 n.*754*
Miller, Marion "May" Louisa, **9:** 93 n.*169*
Morrell, Harriette Anne née Wynter, **6:** 304 n.*504*; **8:** 509 n.*820*; **9:** 74 n.*136*
Morrell, Margaret "Margie" Cecil Louisa, **9:** 62 n.*114*, 74 n.*136*
Murdoch, Annie née Wilcox, **8:** 571 n.*910*
Nicholson, Edward Williams Byron, **9:** 108 n.*192*
Nicoll, William Robertson, **7:** 496 n.*808*
Observer,

Christ Church, **7:** 342 n.*598*
Olivier, Edith Maud, **9:** 281 n.*446*
Ottley, Alice, **9:** 14 n.*7*
Oxford University Herald:
Woodstock Election, **6:** 60 n.*92*
Pall Mall Gazette:
Architecture in Oxford, **6:** 366 n.*600*, 367 n.*602*
Betting System, **5:** 183 n.*301*, 184 n.*302*
Clerical Fellowships, **7:** 39 n.*57*
Natural Science at Oxford, **7:** 35 n.*49*, 36,
Organisation of Charity, **5:** 194 n.*318*
Original Research, **6:** 364 n.*599*
Vivisection, **6:** 381 n.*624*, 382
Patmore, Coventry, **9:** 120 n.*210*
Percy, Muriel Evelyn Nora, **9:** 354 n.*567*
Pickard, Henry Adair, **9:** 103 n.*188*
Powell, Frederick York, **7:** 519 n.*841*
Price, Amy Eliza née Cole, **9:** 111 n.*196*, 115 n.*200*
Price, Bartholomew, **5:** 207 n.*330*; **9:** 71 n.*130*, 113 n.*198*, 310 n.*493*
Purey-Cust, William, **8:** 492 n.*796*
Riadore, Ethel and Gwendolen, **8:** 241 n.*404*
Riadore, Gwendolen Jemima, **9:** 20 n.*21*
Rigaud, John, **6:** 398 n.*652*
Rivers, Henry, **6:** 330 n.*546*; **9:** 125 n.*219*
Roberts Brothers, **8:** 483 n.*783*
Rogers, Ann née Reynolds, **8:** 537 n.*861*
Rolleston, George, **6:** 459 n.*755*
Rossetti, Christina, **7:** 505 n.*824*
St. James's Gazette:
Children in Theatres, **8:** 349 n.*574*
Clôture, **7:** 420 n.*702*
Education for the Stage, **7:** 411 n.*691*, 415 n.*694*
Election Gains and Losses, **8:** 251 n.*423*
Franchise Bill, **8:** 132 n.*216*
Hydrophobia Curable, **8:** 242 n.*407*
Lawn Tennis Tournaments, **7:** 450 n.*747*; **8:** 14, 17 n.*12*, 26 n.*28*
Messrs. John Smith and William Brown, **8:** 475 n.*771*
Proportionate Representation, **8:** 106 n.*175*, 108 n.*179*, 116 n.*189*, 119 n.*192*
Purity of Election, **7:** 331 n.*589*
Traitors in the Camp, **7:** 388 n.*669*
Tristan da Cunha, **8:** 391 n.*637*
Vivisection Vivisected, **8:** 172 n.*289*
What Shall We Call A Telephone-Message?, **8:** 443 n.*711*
Whoso Shall Offend One Of Those Little Ones, **8:** 222 n.*381*

Sadler, Mary, **8:** 509 n.*820*
Sadler, Michael Ernest (Steward of Christ Church), **8:** 445 n.*713*, 488 n.*790*, 503 n.*808*, 542 n.*866*
Sandford, Charles, **5:** 370 n.*548*
Scribner, Messrs., **6:** 233 n.*366*
Sharpe, Alfred, **6:** 204 n.*316*
Sheepshanks, Katharine Evelyn, **9:** 264 n.*417*
Skene, Lorina Charlotte née Liddell, **8:** 571 n.*911*
Skene, William Baillie (Treasurer of Christ Church), **8:** 502 n.*806*, 560 n.*892*
Sligo (Lord), **6:** 391 n.*642*
Smith, Henry J. S., **6:** 439 n.*721*
Smith, Mr., **9:** 213 n.*341*
Smith, Muriel A. Howard, **8:** 497 n.*799*
Snow, Walter Francis, **8:** 93 n.*151*
Snow, William M., **8:** 605 n.*961*
Sotheran, Messrs. H., **8:** 542 n.*866*
Standard:
Eight Hours Movement, **8:** 525 n.*842*
Stevens, Edith née Headland , **9:** 79 n.*146*, 126 n.*222*
Stevens, Enid Gertrude, **9:** 67 n.*121*, 244 n.*387*
Stubbs, William, **8:** 553 n.*882*
Swain, Joseph, **8:** 245 n.*410*
Symonds, Ann, Mrs., **8:** 414 n.*671*
Symonds, Miss, **8:** 192 n.*322*
Taylor, Eliza A., **7:** 381 n.*656*
Taylor, Louise "Louie," **8:** 386 n.*631*
Taylor, Tom, **4:** 101 n.*158*, 271 n.*315*
Tennyson, Emily née Sellwood, **4:** 20
Tennyson, Hallam, **4:** 58
Thompson, Henry Lewis, **9:** 322 n.*514*
Thompson, John Barclay, **8:** 61 n.*98*
Thoms, Mr., **9:** 336 n.*539*
Thresher, Sarah, **6:** 419 n.*687*
Tidy, Kathleen, **4:** 52-53
Times, The,
Clerical Fellowships, **7:** 37, 38 n.*55*
Rules for Reckoning Postage, **8:** 29 n.*33*
Todhunter, Isaac, **6:** 331 n.*548*; **7:** 102 n.*191*
Valpy, Arthur Sutton, **9:** 49 n.*85*
Van der Gucht, Marie, **9:** 17 n.*15*
Vicars, Mrs., **5:** 248 n.*406*
Walker, Gladys Hope, **8:** 623 n.*986*
Walters, Lucy, **8:** 80 n.*124*, 330 n.*544*, 392 n.*638*, 511 n.*823*
Walton, Dorothy "Dolly" Ellen née Draper, **9:** 79 n.*146*

Watson, Leili, **7:** 530 n.*859*; **8:** 281 n.*471*, 300 n.*500*, 336 n.*555*
Watson, Walter, **7:** 402 n.*682*; **8:** 184 n.*313*, 262 n.*442*, 292 n.*488*
Welton, James, **9:** 137 n.*239*
Whelpton, Henry Robert, **7:** 70 n.*113*
Wilcox, Fanny née Rooney, **7:** 489 n.*797*
Wilcox, Isabella Lucy, **7:** 437 n.*725*
Wilcox, William, **4:** 15-19
Wolmer, Lady Beatrix Maud née Cecil, **8:** 274 n.*463*
Wordsworth, Elizabeth, **8:** 502 n.*806*
Yonge, Charlotte Mary, **7:** 100 n.*187*

Letter writing, **4:** 103, 114, 164, 167, 170 n.*163*, 177; **5:** 98 n.*154*, 227 n.*362*; **6:** 53; **7:** 325, 461, 530; **8:** 95
Library, **2:** 28 n.*55*, 34 n.*66*, 35 n.*69*, 36 n.*71*, 44 n.*89*, 47 n.*93*, 117 n.*223*; **4:** 24
Literary (Reading) Machine, **8:** 257, 258, 261, 264, 272
Logic, **1:** 129; **6:** 463, 464 n.*764*; **8:** 153 n.*250*, 154-158, 162, 180 n.*300*, 238-240, 242, 246, 248, 250, 271, 283, 308, 314, 320, 327, 332, 434, 436-438, 505 n.*810*; **9:** 50, 51, 136 n.*238*, 143 n.*247*, 148 n.*254*, 149 n.*256*, 151 n.*260*, 152 n.*264*, 155 n.*268*, 158, 180, 181, 184, 185, 189, 193, 199, 212-214, 216, 229, 259, 265, 275 n.*439*, 276, 278, 279, 289, 295
Logic lessons, **8:** 235, 241, 265, 277, 279, 280, 282, 283, 287, 289, 293, 295, 297-299, 328, 331, 332, 334-337, 341 n.*562*, 394; **9:** 25, 29, 127 n.*223*, 129, 131, 134, 136, 141-143, 150, 154, 155, 169, 170, 176-178, 181-183, 243, 245, 259-263, 265, 267, 290-293, 338
Magic lantern, **2:** 31 n.*61*, 119 n.*227*, 123, 126-128; **3:** 7, 143, 146; **9:** 49
Marionettes, **1:** 19, 81, 82, 110, 111; **2:** 31 n.*61*
Marking system, **2:** 71 n.*143*
Marriage, **3:** 83, 84 n.*129*
Master of Arts degree, **3:** 20 n.*24*, 143
Mathematical assistant lecturer, **5:** 113
Mathematical examiner, **4:** 258 n.*302*, 260, 265, 275 n.*321*; **5:** 51 n.*71*, 81, 189, 207
Mathematical lectureship, **1:** 49, 62, 70, 79, 86, 88, 94, 121 n.*150*, 132, 135, 136; **2:** 25, 26 n.*52*, 27-29, 31 n.*60*, 33, 41, 48, 64 n.*128*, 106, 113, 114 n.*220*, 115, 116, 119, 129; **3:** 10, 27, 142, 158; **4:** 10, 11, 26, 37, 78, 79, 87, 158, 197, 202; **5:** 28, 59, 74, 76, 79, 112-116, 152, 179 n.*297*, 189, 197, 250, 370 n.*548*, 375; **6:** 83, 131, 139, 141, 146, 147, 241, 245, 426, 453, 460, 492; **7:** 88, 103, 110, 228, 239, 251, 372, 381, 384; **8:** 592, 593
Mathematical papers, **4:** 76, 83, 103, 106, 107, 110, 113, 114, 116, 117, 148, 185, 192, 202, 205, 213, 217, 218, 257 n.*298*, 262, 267, 306; **5:** 207; **7:** 200 n.*375*, 306, 323-325, 536
Mathematical problems, **6:** 69 n.*102*; **8:** 179-181, 324, 504, 505 n.*810*;

9: 71 n.*130*, 346, 351, 354
Mathematical scholarship, **1:** 58, 61, 70, 73, 77 n.*73*, 78, 79; **4:** 58, 110
Mathematical study, **3:** 90, 117, 141, 156; **4:** 242, 267; **5:** 44
Mathematical teaching, **1:** 58, 60, 63, 65, 66, 70, 76, 84-89, 91, 96, 97, 109, 111, 112; **2:** 28, 29, 32, 36, 37, 42, 44, 122; **3:** 158; **4:** 37; **8:** 239, 240, 293; **9:** 15
Mathematical tutor, **3:** 30; **4:** 10, 11, 63, 294
Mathematical writing, **4:** 13, 24, 26, 37, 44, 47, 58, 148

Mathematics:
Algebra, **1:** 70, 79; **2:** 28, 29; **4:** 87; **5:** 114 n.*178*; **7:** 200
Algebriac Geometry, **1:** 97-99, 101; **4:** 13, 24, 37, 48; **7:** 418 n.*697*; **8:** 539, 540; **9:** 258
Alligation, **1:** 70 n.*59*, 71
Arithmetic, **2:** 27, 28, 71, 122; **4:** 257 n.*298*, 262, 267; **6:** 176; **7:** 306, 536; **8:** 239, 240, 293, 387
Calculating Machines, **5:** 192 n.*316*, 226 n.*360*
Calculus, **1:** 57, 63, 78; **2:** 28, 113, 115; **3:** 117
Circle-Squaring, **7:** 203 n.*380*, 204-206, 351, 352, 423 n.*706*, 425 n.*708*, 426; **8:** 180
Co-ordinate Geometry, **1:** 58
Direction Theory, **8:** 505 n.*811*, 555, 559, 560
Divisibility Rules, **8:** 121; **9:** 341, 342 n.*546*, 344, 346, 350, 351, 353
Dynamics**1:** 78
Euclid, **1:** 41, 70, 76, 77, 82-84, 91, 97 n.*102*, 99 n.*107*, 111, 112; **2:** 28, 29, 64, 65; **3:** 158; **4:** 10, 37, 38, 49-52, 79, 144 n.*125*, 174 n.*170*, 213, 218 n.*235*; **5:** 375 n.*556*; **6:** 134 n.*205*, 148 n.*227*, 200 n.*311*, 331, 345; **7:** 82 n.*13*, 83, 323-325, 350, 487, 536; **8:** 95, 152, 169, 179, 180, 192, 306, 368, 387-390
Finite Differences, **1:** 69
Fourth Dimension, **4:** 24
Geometric Conic Sections, **5:** 375 n.*556*, 378; **6:** 201 n.*312*; **7:** 20
Geometric Problems, **7:** 322 n.*572*; **8:** 324, 504, 505 n.*810*
Grills, **8:** 560 n.*890*
Imaginary Plane, **1:** 75
Infinities and Infinitesimals, **8:** 178-180
Limits for π, see value of π
Logarithms, **2:** 48; **8:** 179
Long Multiplication in one Line, **7:** 214; **8:** 180; **9:** 353
Mathematics (general), **1:** 23, 26, 29, 50, 53, 54 n.*13*, 56
Memoria Technica used for Mathematical Terms, **7:** 102, 103; **8:** 181
Probability, **2:** 44, 45 n.*90*; **7:** 487, 488 n.*793*; **8:** 365
Pythagoras, **9:** 354 n.*566*
Roman Numeral Multiplication, **2:** 33 n.*64*
Series, **6:** 146 n.*222*, 201 n.*312*, 203; **7:** 200

Solid Geometry: **1:** 51, 55, 59, 60, 63, 64, 67, 74, 76, 80, 81, 83-86, 109, 120; **2:** 28
Spherical Trigonometry, **2:** 28, 113, 115
Theory of parallels, **8:** 151 n.*247*, 169, 178, 192, 390, 391, 452, 500, 505, 555
Trigonometry, **1:** 96; **2:** 28; **6:** 426, 435-437; **7:** 12, 13; **8:** 179
Value of π, **7:** 37, 102, 103 n.*193*, 203-206, 424, 425 n.*708*, 426; **8:** 128, 129, 180

Matriculation report, **6:** 301 n.*496*
Meal times, **9:** 302, 348
Mechanical bear, **7:** 53
Mechanical frog, **7:** 283, 291, 295
Medical library, **8:** 93 n.*153*
Memorising, **3:** 143
Meryls (Nine Men's Morris), **6:** 97 n.*151*, 389, 421; **7:** 467; **8:** 421; **9:** 127, 177, 205, 347
Metallic Diary, **6:** 269 n.*435*
Micro-photographs, **4:** 95, 175 n.*172*, 177
Microscope, **4:** 331; **5:** 59
Miscellanea Note-book, **2:** 32 n.*63*
Missing pages from *Diary* and alterations, **1:** 120; **3:** 64 n.*97*; **4:** 175 n.*171*, 193 n.*190*, 214 n.*227*; **7:** 177 n.*327*, 403 n.*683*; **8:** 213 n.*363*, 435 n.*700*
Moderating honour-papers, **6:** 35, 36
Money Orders, **7:** 308 n.*552*
Monograms, **2:** 55, 67 n.*133*
Musical boxes, **4:** 272; **7:** 284
Natural botany, **2:** 89
Nude studies, **8:** 217 n.*370*, 218; **9:** 99 n.*179*
Observes epilepsy, **2:** 46 n.*91*; **7:** 55, 454
Observes hospital operation, **3:** 138, 139 n.*204*
Orguinette, **7:** 295 n.*533*, 301, 302, 360; **9:** 45, 165, 166, 296
Original research, **6:** 364 n.*599*
Oxford Union membership, **3:** 26 n.*37*, 144
Paintings and illustrations commissioned, **6:** 14, 19, 27, 37, 56, 71, 72, 81, 82, 314, 321, 338, 368; **8:** 164 n.*269*
Paper folding, **2:** 113 (boats); **6:** 380 (boats); **7:** 65 (fishing boats); **9:** 21 n.*25* (pistols), 178 (fishing boat), 293 (pistol and boat), 316 (fishing boat), 317 (pistols), 335 (fishing boat)
Parlour-croquêt, **4:** 143, 146
Passport, **5:** 253 n.*418*

Photographs taken by Dodgson:
Acland Family, **4:** 33, 35

Adair, Alexander W., **6:** 33
Alice (niece of Miss Blagrave), **6:** 92
Allen Family, **4:** 216; **5:** 153 n.*248*
Ambrose Family, **6:** 465
Andrews, Septimus, **4:** 33, 336
Argles Family, **6:** 97, 99
Arnold Family, **6:** 152, 203, 217, 273, 284, 286, 328, 389, 400, 470; **7:** 88 n.*156*, 109 n.*203*
Bainbridge Family, **2:** 104, **4:** 36
Balfour Family, **4:** 325, **5:** 12
Bamlet, Robert, **4:** 22
Barker Family, **4:** 305
Barry Family, **4:** 36, 235
Bayne, Thomas Vere, **5:** 163 n.*268*, 244 n.*396*
Beadon, Frederick, **7:** 113 n.*209*
Bennie Family, **6:** 54
Benson, Richard, **4:** 33
Beresford, Selina, **6:** 29
Beyer, Helene, **4:** 254
Bickersteth Family, **5:** 105, 106 n.*164*, 107
Blücher Children, **7:** 274 n.*498*
Bode, Edith, **6:** 85
Bolster, John, **4:** 34
Bosanquet, Samuel, **4:** 33
Bostock, Phoebe, **4:** 27
Bourke, Walter, **4:** 325
Bowlby Children, **4:** 35
Bowles, Thomas, **7:** 163 n.*307*
Bradley Family, **6:** 154, 204, 205
Bray, Teresa "Tiny," **6:** 54
Brine, Katie, **5:** 155 n.*250*
Brodie Family, **4:** 54, 55, 111, 219
Brooke Family, **6:** 406
Bruce, Lily, **6:** 273
Burnett Children, **4:** 355
Cameron, Ewen, **4:** 127
Campbell, Margaret, **4:** 228
Cayley, Charles, **4:** 251
Cecil Family (Lord Salisbury), **6:** 120, 121, 125, 404
Chamberlain, Thomas, **4:** 33
Chambers Family, **6:** 29
Chataway Family, **6:** 488, 489
"Chestnuts, The," **6:** 57
"Children & Fishes" (E. G. Thomson drawing), **7:** 162 n.*304*
Christ Church Cathedral, **2:** 65

Christ Church Deanery, **2:** 66
Christie Family, **6:** 290
Cockburn Family, **5:** 170 n.*281*
Cole, Miss, **4:** 22
Cole, William, Earl of Enniskillen, **4:** 35
Collyns, John Martyn, **2:** 68
Combe, Thomas, **4:** 35
Conybeare Family, **6:** 330, 394
Coote Family, **7:** 108 n.*200*, 115 n.*214*
Craigie Family, **6:** 95, 99, 101
Craik, Dorothy, **7:** 165, 166 n.*312*
"Dane" (Xie Kitchin), **6:** 276 n.*453*, 290 n.*479*, 313, 317, 318, 320, 321, 388
Darnley Family, **4:** 326
Darvall, Henry, **4:** 331
Denman Family, **4:** 327, 328; **6:** 284
Desanges Family, **5:** 168 n.*278*; **6:** 126
De Vere, Aubrey, **4:** 126
Dindorf, Karl, **4:** 34
Dodgson Family, **4:** 22, 34, 37, 128; **7:** 116
Donkin Family, **4:** 33, 131, 132, 219; **5:** 149 n.*240*
Douglas, Angus, **4:** 252
Drage Family, **7:** 189, 190 n.*352*, 280 n.*511*
Drewett, Miss, **7:** 116, 117 n.*218*
Drewitt, Frederick, **7:** 150 n.*283*
Drury Family, **6:** 95, 126, 339
Dubourg, Evelyn, **6:** 289
Duckworth, Robinson, **6:** 466
Du Maurier Children, **6:** 405
Dykes Family, **4:** 129
Ellis Family, **5:** 99 n.*157*
Ellison Family, **4:** 120
Erskine Family, **3:** 169
Evans Family, **6:** 29, 331, 469
Fane Family, **6:** 156, 277
Faraday, Michael, **4:** 34
Farringford, Isle of Wight, **4:** 352, 355
Farringford Servants, **4:** 354
Faussett, Maud, **6:** 338; **7:** 432 n.*721*
Fearon Children, **6:** 209
Feilden, Helen, **6:** 260; **7:** 143 n.*264*
Fell Family, **3:** 109
Forshall, May, **7:** 86, 87 n.*151*
Franklin Family, **4:** 352, 353, 355
Frederick, Crown Prince of Denmark, **4:** 261

Furnivall, Alice, **6:** 92, 94
Gandall Family, **4:** 100, 106
Gatey, Margaret, **3:** 117 n.*163*
Gathorne Hardy, Gathorne, **5:** 248 n.*404*
Gatty, Alfred, **4:** 325
Gilliat Family, **4:** 331
Godfrey, Georgie, **5:** 82 n.*127*
Goff, John & William, **4:** 116
Goode, Miss, **4:** 235
Gordon, Osborne, **4:** 35
Granville Family, **4:** 298, 307
Gray, Lily, **6:** 487, 488, 489; **7:** 116 n.*217*, 119 n.*224*
Greenall, Richard, **4:** 27
Hackman, Alfred, **4:** 298
Harcourt, Edith, **6:** 289
Harington Family, **3:** 168 n.*244*, **4:** 105, 210; **6:** 123
Harrison, James & Matthew, **4:** 35
Harvey Family, **6:** 465
Hatch Family, **6:** 209, 286, 287, 331; **7:** 42 n.*63*, 101 n.*188*, 196 n.*365*, 275 n.*500*
Haydon Family, **6:** 100-102
Heaphy Family, **6:** 126; **7:** 125 n.*235*
Heard, Mr., **4:** 356
Henderson Family, **7:** 144 n.*267*, 190, 191 n.*354*, 192 n.*357*, 193 n.*360*, 195 n.*364*, 271 n.*489*, 273 n.*496*, 276 n.*502*
Henley Family, **4:** 123, 340
Hermon, Mary, Mrs., **6:** 492
Hicks-Beach, Michael, **4:** 92
Hill, Edward, **4:** 35
Holiday Family, **6:** 126
Holman Hunt Family, **4:** 34, 308; **6:** 226
Hoskyns, Emma, **4:** 73
Houghton, Mary, **4:** 27
Houses of Parliament, **4:** 336
Howard, Lydia, **6:** 324
Hughes Family, **4:** 256, 340; **6:** 126
Hull Family, **7:** 142, 143 n.*263*
Hulme Family (Oxford), **5:** 235 n.*378*
Hulme Family (Stoke), **6:** 101
Hussey, Elizabeth "Bessie," **6:** 155
Huxley, Thomas, **4:** 34
"I Zingari" (Dodgsons and Pooles), **4:** 128 n.*102*
Jackson, John, **4:** 34
Jackson, Julia (portrait), **4:** 127
Jackson, Mary, **4:** 217

Jacobson Family, **4:** 216
Jebb Family, **5:** 177 n.*294*; **6:** 327
Jelf, George, **4:** 33; **5:** 163 n.*268*
Jenkins, John, **5:** 163 n.*268*
Johnson Family, **4:** 327
Jones, Miss, **6:** 268
Junior, Mrs., **7:** 119 n.*223*
Keane Family, **4:** 36, 235
Keates Family, **6:** 99
Keyser, Marian, **5:** 252 n.*412*
Kitchin Family, **4:** 219; **6:** 87, 124, 218, 273, 276, 279, 282, 330, 337, 400, 471, 472; **7:** 43 n.*65*, 125 n.*234*, 272 n.*492*
Lake District, **2:** 90 n.*182*, 91, 97
Lambert Family, **4:** 355
Langton Clarke Family, **5:** 12
Latham Family, **4:** 308; **5:** 244 n.*396*
Lawrie, Rose, **6:** 402, 406
Legros, Alphonse, **4:** 251
Liddell Children, **2:** 77, 112, 116 n.*222*; **3:** 64, 66, 73; **4:** 11, 12, 33, 35, 211; **5:** 122 n.*192*, 122; **6:** 121
Liddon, Henry P., **5:** 165 n.*273*
"Little Red Riding-hood" (Agnes Grace Weld), **3:** 89 n.*138*, 108 n.*156*, 140, 148 n.*214*, 172 n.*252*
Lloyd, Catharine, **5:** 155 n.*250*; **6:** 85
Longley Family, **2:** 104, **4:** 22, 23, 324-327, 330
Lushington, Franklin, **3:** 118 n.*165*
Lutwidge Family, **3:** 109, 110 n.*158*; **4:** 22, 37; **6:** 217
MacDonald Family, **4:** 226-228, 255, 256, 331; **6:** 126
Majendie, Dulcie, **6:** 491
March-Phillipps, Geraldine, **6:** 261
Marshall Family, **3:** 118 n.*165*, 119
Marsham, Robert, **4:** 33
Mason Family, **6:** 267, 268, 276
Maurice, Frederick D., **4:** 226
Mayhew Family, **7:** 177 n.*326*
Mayor, Robert, **4:** 34
McDermott, **7:** 127 n.*240*
Merriman, Janet, **6:** 95
Metcalfe Family, **5:** 79; **6:** 85
Millais Family, **5:** 96, 97, 98 n.*153*
Milman, Susan, Mrs., **7:** 109 n.*201*
Minnie Morton (picture), **5:** 165 n.*273*
Mitchell, Henry, **4:** 237, 240
Monier Williams, **5:** 151 n.*243*, 163 n.*268*, 164 n.*271*; **7:** 119
Morley, Edith, **6:** 404

Morrell Family, **6:** 276, 282, 461
Mowbray, John, **6:** 329
Müller Family, **5:** 247 n.*402*, 254 n.*419*; **6:** 123, 124
Munro, Alexander and Mary, **4:** 252
Munro's Sculpture, **4:**, 21, 22, 247
Murchison, Roderick, **4:** 35
Murdoch Family, **2:** 83
"No lessons today" (Flora Rankin), **6:** 244 n.*388*
Ottley Family, **4:** 27
Ouseley, Frederick, **4:** 33
Owen Family, **4:** 213; **5:** 254 n.*419*; **6:** 29, 123
Parker Family, **6:** 275
Parkes, Annie, **4:** 352
Parnell Family, **4:** 327
Peabody, George, **5:** 253 n.*415*
Pember, Edward, **7:** 146 n.*275*
"Penelope Boothby" (Xie Kitchin), **6:** 471, 472 n.*778*
Peters, Mary and daughter, **4:** 94
Petherick, John, **4:** 34
Phillips, John, **5:** 165 n.*273*
Picture in Christ Church Library, **3:** 124, 125 n.*179*
Plomer, Laura, **6:** 419
Pollock Family, **5:** 170 n.*282*; **7:** 122 n.*229*
Poole Family, **2:** 106, 128
Powell Family (MacDonald in-laws), **4:** 255
Powell Family (Sharow), **4:** 235
Prescott, Emily, **4:** 127
Price Family, **4:** 278; **6:** 209
Prince Leopold, **6:** 396
Raikes Family, **6:** 403
Randall, James, **4:** 34
Randall, Mrs., **4:** 331
Randolph, **4:** 35
Ranken, William, **4:** 35, 106
Rankin Children, **4:** 228
Read, Louisa and Thomas, **4:** 237, 240
Reynolds Family, **4:** 340
Rich, John, **4:** 33
Ripon Bishop's Palace, **5:** 107
Rogers Family, **4:** 217
"Roman Girl" (Miss Ward), **6:** 275
Rossetti drawings, **4:** 253
Rossetti Family, **4:** 251, 252
Rowden Family, **4:** 219, 296
Royal bedstead, **4:** 211

Rumsey Family, **6:** 33, 34, 37
Ruskin, John, **6:** 396
Russell, Henry, **5:** 177 n.*294*
Salmon, Robert, **4:** 35
Sampson, Edward, **6:** 156
Samuels, Gertrude, **6:** 403
Sant Family, **5:** 167 n.*275*, 168, 169 n.*279*, 170; **6:** 126
Saunders, Augustus, **4:** 33
Self-portrait (assisted), **3:** 66, **7:** 18, 19 n.*15*
Sells, Hubert, **6:** 102
Sherwit Children, **2:** 106
Shirley Family, **4:** 294, 298; **6:** 31
"Shot" (dog's name), **5:** 177 n.*294*
Simpson Children, **6:** 217
Skeletons, **4:** 36, 38
Slatter Family, **4:** 35
Smith, Ada, **7:** 190 n.*353*
Smith, Goldwin, **6:** 338
Smith, Laura, **6:** 98
Smith, Samuel, **7:** 145 n.*270*
Smith, William Slayter, **3:** 170
Smith Family, **3:** 85; **4:** 22
Southey, Reginald, **2:** 68, **4:** 33
Spencer, Lady Sarah, **6:** 336
Standen Family, **6:** 99, 285
Stanley, Arthur, **4:** 35
Stogden, Edith, **4:** 309
Stone, Edith, **5:** 82 n.*127*
Strong Family, **4:** 255
Synge Family, **6:** 99, 101
Tait, Archibald, **7:** 273 n.*497*
Talbot, Eleonora, Mrs., **6:** 336
Tate Family, **2:** 88; **4:** 232
Taylor, Christie, **6:** 92, 95
Taylor Family (Henry), **4:** 126, 127
Taylor Family (James), **7:** 191, 192 n.*356*, 192 n.*358*
Taylor Family (Tom), **4:** 249, 250
Tennyson Family, **3:** 118 n.*165*, 119
Terry Family, **5:** 91, 93 n.*144*, 94 n.*146*, 95 n.*149*; **6:** 126, 405
Thompson, Henry L., **5:** 234 n.*377*
Thompson, Mr. & Mrs. John Barclay, **6:** 209; **7:** 117 n.*220*, 146 n.*273*
Thresher Family, **6:** 415
Tidy, Kathleen, **3:** 169, 170
Todd Family, **6:** 475
Tolhurst, Beatrix, **6:** 90

Treacher Family, **5:** 163 n.*268*
Trimmer, Mary, **6:** 102
Tristram, Henry, **4:** 34
Turnbull, Elizabeth, **5:** 98 n.*153*
Twiss, Quintin William Francis, **3:** 69 n.*108*
Tyrwhitt, Richard St. John, **2:** 108
Unspecified sitters, **2:** 72, 97
Vicars Family, **4:** 306
Villiers Family, **6:** 32
Walker, John, **3:** 116 n.*162*
Ward Family, **5:** 168 n.*278*, 169 n.*280*, 170; **6:** 275
Watkin Family, **4:** 246
Watson Children, **6:** 99, 101, 102
Webster Family (Cumberland), **2:** 90 n.*181*, 91; **3:** 116, 117 n.*163*
Webster Family (Malvern), **4:** 118, 119
Weld Family, **3:** 87, 88, 89 n.*138*; **4:** 355
Westmacott Family, **4:** 330, 331
Wethered, Mrs, **4:** 209
White, Maria, **4:** 331
White, Mrs., **4:** 296
Whiteside, Daisy, **6:** 404
Wilberforce, Samuel, **4:** 34
Wilcox Family, **4:** 23, **5:** 12, 164 n.*270*; **6:** 92, 469; **7:** 109 n.*202*
Willatson Family, **5:** 80
Wilson, Edward (Henry VIII), **4:** 246
Wilson Todd, **5:** 103, 104 n.*161*
Winteringham Church and Rectory, **4:** 240
Wood, Amy, **4:** 240
Woodhouse Family, **7:** 269 n.*484*
Woodroffe Family, **7:** 143, 144 n.*266*
Woodward, Benjamin, **4:** 35
Woolner, Thomas, **4:** 35
Yonge, Charlotte and her mother, **5:** 147 n.*237*

Photography:

Acquires photographs, **3:** 26 (portraits of Robson), 134 n.*194* (Mayall's portrait of Tennyson), 139 n.*206* (paintings in Manchester Exhibition), 155, 157 ("Children's Play" by Munro), 173 ("Juliet" by Henry Peach Robinson); **4:** 317, 341 (photos by Clementina, Lady Hawarden); **5:** 62 n.*92* (double exposures), 85 n.*132* (Terrys), 121 (Mount Charles), 137 n.*221* (Rejlander prints), 278 (Russian prints), 345, 349 (daughter of Prince Galitzine of Russia); **7:** 72 (Agnes Hull by Eastbourne photographer), 429 n.*716* (Coleman drawings by Robinson), 455 (Marion Richards by Kent), 457 n.*754* (May and Edith Miller by Kent), 461 (Evie and Jessie Hull by Kent), 468

(Winnie Howes and Clare Turton by Kent), 469 (Alice Hull and Winnie Howes by Kent), 471 (Agnes Hull by Kent), 474 (Jessie Hull by Kent)
Albums, **3:** 31 n.*45* (offer to Common Room), 134 n.*194*, 148 n.*214*, 153; **4:** 205, 206 (gift to Prince of Wales); **5:** 200 n.*326* (for cartes of Senior Students); **6:** 401 n.*658* (gift to Henry Holiday), 475 (Dodgson family album)
Arranging photographs, **3:** 48, **4:** 121, 265, 332; **6:** 410, 489; **7:** 120, 122, 124 n.*233*, 276 n.*501*, 279
Badcock's Yard studio, **4:** 194 n*193*, 216, 261, 321
Cameras, **2:** 53, 54, 67; **4:** 322, 352; **6:** 161
Cases made for apparatus, **4:** 341 (Thomas)
Chemicals, **2:** 67, 68, 70; **4:** 229, 247; **5:** 167
Collodion, **2:** 68; **3:** 65 n.*98*; **4:** 47
Colouring photographs, **2:** 120; **4:** 19, 20, 139, 140, 276
"Convex" photograph, **7:** 290 n.*526*
Debenham's Studio, Ryde, Isle of Wight, **6:** 419 n.*688*
Erasing negatives, **4:** 247 (Cundalls); **7:** 120, 279
Exhibitions:
London, **2:** 19, 22, 23
Photographic Gallery, London, **3:** 13
Photographic Society of London, **2:** 24 n.*45*, 56 n.*112*, 118 n.*226*; **3:** 139 n.*205*, 148 n.*214*, 149, 171, 172 n.*252*, 174; **4:** 25, 314, 315
Ryman's, Oxford, **3:** 22
Failed photographs, **2:** 72, 108; **3:** 74, 76, 109, 116, 169; **4:** 246, 308; **5:** 96, 177; **6:** 487
Ghost pictures, **4:** 219
Gives up photography, **7:** 280 n.*511*
Glacial Acetic Acid, **2:** 68
Gutta Percha Bath, **2:** 70 n.*139*
Horne and Thornethwaite's collodion, **4:** 210
Ideas about photography, **1:** 51 n.*6*; **2:** 129
Kent, William – Eastbourne photographer, **7:** 455 n.*753*, 457 n.*754*, 461, 468, 469, 471, 474
List of girls photographed or to be photographed, **4:** 178-181
Meeting photographers:
Cameron, Julia Margaret, **4:** 345, 356
Clementina, Lady Hawarden, **4:** 317
Cotton, William C., **3:** 68
Diamond, Hugh W., **2:** 24 n.*45*
Holder, Colonel, **4:** 343
Rejlander, Oscar, **4:** 183
Wallich, George C., **5:** 143 n.*230*
Whiting, Mr., **4:** 249
Photographic costumes, **5:** 122, **6:** 152, 205, 213, 276, 279, 282, 284,

286, 287, 333, 402, 405, 406; **7:** 42, 109 n.*203*, 110, 118, 162, 189, 190 n.*352*, 192 n.*356*
Photographic equipment, **2:** 26 n.*49*, 53, 80, 97, 102, 105; **3:** 94, 107
Photographic expeditions, **1:** 130 n.*160* (Richmond), 133 (Marsden); **3:** 68 (proposed trip to France), 127 (proposed trip with Southey), 174 (Munro's offer to photograph in his studio); **4:** 22 (Bishop Auckland), 27 (Richmond), 27 (Daresbury), 36 (Whitby), 118 (Malvern), 234 (Whitby), 237 (Winteringham), 312, 322, 324 (Lambeth), 326 (proposed trip to Little Holland House), 352 (Farringford)
Photographic lessons given, **6:** 328 n.*543*, 390, 394
Photographic printing, **2:** 89; **4:** 229, 251, 257, 332 n.*426*, 341, 356 (by Cundalls), 295 (by Hills and Saunders); **5:** 171 n.*283* (by Cundalls); **6:** 289, 397 (by Robinson and Cherrill), 410, 488, 490; **7:** 18, 19 n.*15* (by Robinson), 45, 193, 196, 276, 279, 280
Photographic processes, **6:** 393 (Wortley's method); **7:** 279 (Forshaw and Coles starch process for mounting photos)
Photographic registering, **6:** 408, 409 n.*670*, 410, 411, 475
"Photography Extraordinary," **1:** 132
Portrait taken, **4:** 183 (by Rejlander); **5:** 145 n.*233* (by Wallich); **6:** 18 n.*17* (by Wallich)
Proposed photographs (not all came to fruition):
Acland Family, **2:** 111-112; **3:** 33 n.*50*
Andrews, Septimus, **4:** 333
Archbishop of York, **4:** 316
Archer, Maggie, **5:** 215
Arnold Family, **6:** 268
Bainbridge Family, **2:** 102
Baughan, Edith, **5:** 234
Browning, Robert, **4:** 247
Chataway, Gertrude, **6:** 470
Christ Church Cathedral, **3:** 23
Clerke, Charles C., **3:** 25
Conybeare, Ethel "Linda," **6:** 393
Crofts Family, **6:** 263
Currey Family, **4:** 123
Darnley Family, **4:** 239
Duchess of Malborough's Children, **4:** 215
Ellison Family, **4:** 116
Erskine Family, **3:** 168
Fane Children, **6:** 155
Fellowes Family, **3:** 73
Gilchrist, Connie, **7:** 29, 30
Hall, Miss, **6:** 339
Harrington Family, **3:** 154, 167; **7:** 110
Hatch Family, **7:** 191

Hughes Family, **4:** 254, 339
Hull, Agnes, **7:** 137
Hulme Family, **6:** 101
Iffley Church, **3:** 54
Jacobson, William, **3:** 25
Kean, Charles, **4:** 46
Kitchin Family, **6:** 85, 264
Leslie Family, **4:** 279
Liddell Family, **2:** 110; **3:** 62; **4:** 214
"Little Miniatures," **5:** 205
MacDonald Family, **4:** 223
Mason, Alice, **6:** 266
Mayhew Family, **7:** 147, 163 n.*306*
Merriman, Janet, **6:** 90
Millais Family, **5:** 88
Munro Sculptures, **3:** 157, 174; **4:** 12, 241
Neal Family, **4:** 77
Newman, John Henry, **7:** 272
Norris Family, **3:** 34
Parnell Family, **4:** 239, 311
Peel, Miss, **6:** 339
Prince Leopold, **6:** 393
Prince of Wales, **4:** 24, 39-42
Princess Beatrice, **4:** 329
Reynolds Children, **4:** 339
Rossetti Family, **4:** 243, 244
Rumsey Family, **4:** 77; **6:** 33
Samuels, Gertrude, **6:** 402
Shirley Family, **4:** 294
Skeletons, **3:** 62 n.*93*
Slatter Family, **4:** 102
Smith Family, **2:** 85
Stanley, Lady Augusta, **4:** 333
Talbot, May, **7:** 270, 271
Taylor, Henry and Family, **4:** 92, 122, 125
Taylor, James and Family, **7:** 191 n.*355*
Taylor, Tom and Family, **4:** 246, 271
Taylor Gallery, **3:** 22
Tennyson Family, **3:** 108, 111
Terry Family, **4:** 224, 243, 358; **5:** 62
Thackeray, William M., **3:** 123 n.*176*
Tidy, Kathleen, **3:** 169
Traill, Brenda, **6:** 335
Ugly Boy, **4:** 30
Warburton Family, **4:** 77, 87, 103

Watkin, Harriet, **4:** 246
Willets, Miss, **7:** 162 n.*305*
Willshire Family, **4:** 291
Proposed studio in London, **5:** 162
Pyro gallic acid, **2:** 68
Rooftop studio, Tom Quad, **6:** 38, 186 n.*289*, 203 n.*315*, 404, 487; **7:** 42; **8:** 201, 217
Selling photographs, **3:** 69 n.*108*, 70, **4:** 36; **5:** 81 n.*126*, 130 n.*209*
Showing others how to mount photographs, **5:** 186
Showing photographs, **2:** 85, 108, 118, 125; **3:** 26, 33 n.*50*, 35, 39, 41, 61, 73, 113, 114, 123, 153, 154, 157; **4:** 14, 15, 17, 94, 187, 195, 251, 258, 260, 272, 278, 279, 296, 333, 337, 340, 345, 347, 350, 355, 357; **5:** 20, 35, 144, 148, 233; **6:** 32, 33, 52, 77, 142, 143, 148, 164, 172, 268, 273, 292, 323, 370, 394-396, 399, 416-419, 421, 423, 446, 451, 460, 478, 482; **7:** 34, 54, 61, 68, 71, 73, 74, 80, 82, 86, 119, 137, 147, 167, 191, 207, 213, 216-218, 225, 226, 228, 252, 260, 283, 301, 302, 336, 347, 358, 367, 383, 395, 417, 424, 453, 455-457, 460, 464, 467, 473, 474, 492, 497, 500, 516, 520, 524, 534; **8:** 12, 24, 33, 37, 51, 62, 96, 111, 129, 136, 138, 139, 178, 196, 200, 206, 209, 215, 231, 232, 245, 292, 299, 327, 341, 376, 377, 390, 417, 424, 428, 594; **9:** 30, 160, 165, 253, 256
Southey's photographs, **1:** 66 n.*50*, 65, 68-70; **3:** 127, 139 n.*205*
Supplying photographs, **3:** 64 (Longley), 86 (Liddell), 89 (Weld), 93 (Tennyson), 93 (Liddell), 170 (Erskine); **4:** 40-43 (Prince of Wales), 140 (Henry Taylor), 206 n.*215* (Prince of Wales's album), 279 (Holman Hunt), 325 (MacDonalds), 332 (Tom Taylor), 337 (Watts), 343 (Hawarden), 358 (Terrys); **5:** 23 (Denmans), 30 (Burnetts), 98 (Terrys), 171 n.*284* (Sants); **7:** 148 (Hendersons), 224 (Arnolds, Hatches & Taylors)
University fund for photography, **3:** 21 n.*26*
Verses for albums, **3:** 148 n.*214*
Viewing art to assist in photographic composition, **3:** 51
Viewing work of other photographers, **3:** 28 (Fenton), 125 n.*180* (Anon), 156 (Thomson), 173 (Robinson); **4:** 25 (Fenton), 25 (Mudd), 25 (Robinson), 25 (Watkins), 60, 315, 335, 345 (Cameron), 183 (Rejlander), 315, 317, 343 (Hawarden); **5:** 65 (African images), 188 (images of the Liddells)

Physiology and Anatomy, **6:** 245; **7:** 351
Plans and lists of work in hand, **7:** 150, 351, 368; **8:** 179-183
Pocket barometer, **4:** 251
Postal Order invention, **9:** 191
Post Office improvements, **6:** 345, 346 n.*573*

Presentation copies of Dodgson's works:

Alice's Adventures in Wonderland, **5:** 17 n.*12*, 19, 20, 93 n.*145*, 122, 122 n.*193*, 140, 231 n.*368*, 251 n.*411*; **6:** 43, 53, 54, 83, 91, 93, 116, 124, 171, 185, 192, 254, 256, 295, 363, 385, 407, 477; **7:** 22, 61, 64, 66, 206, 269 n.*484*, 293, 355, 504; **8:** 28 n.*31*, 98, 293, 359, 361 n.*589*, 402 n.*654*, 420 n.*680*, 522 n.*838*; **9:** 164, 165 n.*282*, 322 n.*514*
Alice's Adventures Under Ground, **5:** 243 n.*395*; **8:** 310 n.*513*, 313 n.*516*, 361 n.*589*, 419 n.*678*, 468, 469 n.*759*, 479 n.*776*, 497 n.*799*; **9:** 44 n.*76*, 97 n.*176*, 111 n.*196*
Charade, A, **8:** 497 n.*799*
Curiosa Mathematica, Part II, Pillow-Problems, **9:** 65 n.*119*, 81 n.*148*
Doublets, **7:** 206
Easter Greeting, **7:** 87 n.*151*
French *Alice*, **5:** 243 n.*395*, 251 n.*411*; **6:** 92 n.*142*, 205, 407; **7:** 355; **8:** 526 n.*843*
Game of Logic, The, **8:** 300 n.*501*, 320 n.*528*, 321 n.*530*, 322 n.*531*, 324 n.*537*; **9:** 130 n.*228*
German *Alice*, **5:** 243 n.*395*; **6:** 80 n.*116*, 83; **8:** 521 n.*837*
Hunting of the Snark, The, **6:** 486; **7:** 293, 520
Italian *Alice*, **6:** 260 n.*415*
Mischmasch, **8:** 29
Nursery "Alice," The, **5:** 243 n.*395*; **8:** 469 n.*759*, 472 n.*764*, 507 n.*817*, 508 n.*818*, 527 n.*844*, 581 n.*926*, 585 n.*934*, 595 n.*948*; **9:** 254 n.*400*
Phantasmagoria, **6:** 72, 73 n.*107*, 75
Rhyme? and Reason?, **5:** 243 n.*395*; **8:** 67 n.*109*, 68 n.*110*, 70 n.*115*, 87 n.*141*; **9:** 218 n.*347*
Sylvie and Bruno, **5:** 243 n.*395*; **8:** 494 n.*797*, 495 n.*798*, 500 n.*804*, 503 n.*807*; **9:** 125 n.*219*, 271 n.*428*
Sylvie and Bruno Concluded, **5:** 243 n.*395*; **9:** 116 n.*201*, 117 n.*202*, 118 n.*203*, 125 n.*219*
Symbolic Logic, **9:** 238 n.*375*, 241 n.*379*, 261 n.*413*, 276 n.*441*
Tangled Tale, A, **8:** 254 n.*427*
Through the Looking-Glass, **5:** 243 n.*395*; **6:** 190 n.*296*, 192, 246, 254, 256, 295, 324, 385, 418, 421; **7:** 61, 87 n.*151*, 250; **8:** 137 n.*223*, 264, 297 n.*495*, 324 n.*537*, 405 n.*658*, 585 n.*935*; **9:** 258 n.*406*, 322 n.*514*
Wonderland Postage-Stamp Case, **8:** 497 n.*799*

Printing-Press, **1:** 51, **3:** 33, 34
Profit on *Alice's Adventures*, **6:** 50 n.*72*
Proposed idea to collect plans of English Abbeys, **2:** 96
Proposed paper on Betting, **2:** 52
Proposed paper on Cipher, **2:** 42 n.*83*, 52
Proposed paper on Nursery Songs, **2:** 52
Proposed paper on Paradoxes, **2:** 52

Proposed system for managing carriages at Covent Garden, **5:** 46
Proposed trip to France, **3:** 68
Proposed trip to Germany (Rhine Valley), **3:** 68 n.*105*
Proposed trip to Lake District, **3:** 24 n.*31*
Proposed trip to Scotland, **3:** 24 n.*31*
Pro-Proctor, **5:** 252 n.*414*, 375, 376 n.*557*

Pseudonyms:
"Dares," **2:** 37 n.*74*
"Dynamite," **8:** 132 n.*216*
"Edgar Cuthwellis," **2:** 39
"Edgar U. C. Westhill," **2:** 39
"Lewis Carroll," **2:** 39 n.*79*
"Louis Carroll," **2:** 39
"Rusticus Expectans," **6:** 364
"R.W.G.," **2:** 39 n.*79*

Purchase of theatrical dresses, **7:** 118
Purchasing pictures, see commissioning paintings
Railways, **1:** 18, 19, 25
Reading scheme, **1:** 73, 74; **2:** 34, 35 n.*69*, 41, 89, 114, 129; **3:** 130, 131, 156, 158; **6:** 103
Reduction in salary proposed, **6:** 131; **7:** 239, 244 n.*448*, 248
Registering *Alice* books as dramas, **6:** 241 n.*384*, 242
Relationship with father, **1:** 44, 45

Religious matters:
Assisting at church services, **4:** 122, 128 n.*103*, 160, 163, 170, 231, 278, 295, 304; **5:** 206, 211, 228; **8:** 184, 446, 459, 502, 509, 600; **9:** 212
Baptism performed, **4:** 163, 231 n.*255*
Bible reading, see Scripture reading
Broad Church, **4:** 11, 82 n.*35*
Church duty, **4:** 141
Divinity reading, **2:** 114, 129; **3:** 90, 158
Funeral service performed, **4:** 129 n.*104*
Ministry, **3:** 18
Ordination, **1:** 73; **3:** 18 n.*20*, 37 n.*58*, 38, 142; **4:** 20, 21, 55, ordained deacon 57, 78 n.*28*, 137 n.*115*, 138; **5:** 102, 103 n.*160*, 131 n.*210*, 228
Prayers, **3:** 142; **4:** 67, 78, 84, 101, 103, 106, 108, 136, 141, 148, 152, 155, 158, 159, 171, 184, 185, 198, 204, 217, 218, 232, 242, 258, 259, 265-267, 274, 276, 295, 299, 305, 321, 322, 352; **5:** 12, 15, 26, 29, 40, 41, 68, 73, 79, 81, 82, 98, 102, 111, 112, 114, 117, 122, 124, 129, 132, 146, 152, 163, 165, 166, 172, 174, 177, 187, 189, 190, 191, 196, 197, 199, 207, 228, 245, 247, 251, 373, 376, 377, 378, 381; **6:** 28, 31, 39,

42, 52, 60, 70, 77, 103-106, 113, 128, 132, 137-139, 141, 146, 152, 156, 169, 171, 172, 187, 194, 202, 204, 212-214, 229, 267, 269, 308, 318, 426, 442, 496; **7:** 11, 171, 314, 321, 371, 395, 504, 512; **8:** 76, 86, 256, 303, 372, 604, 612, 615; **9:** 301

Preaching, **4:** 73-75, 76 n.*22*, 78 n.*28*, 107, 141, 154, 161, 163, 170, 174, 231, 232, 237, 259, 277, 295, 304, 308; **5:** 26, 50, 54, 55, 56, 58, 68, 73, 75 n.*114*, 79, 81, 84, 96, 101, 103, 107, 110, 111, 113, 124, 134, 206; **7:** 324, 341, 342 n.*597*; **8:** 312, 328, 346, 375, 434, 439, 440, 459, 502, 509, 540, 546, 549, 612, 615, 629; **9:** 13, 38, 40, 50, 63, 66, 69, 92, 94, 105, 118, 127, 175, 217, 285, 290, 293, 297, 298 n.*472*, 346

Reading in church service, **3:** 23, 48; **5:** 25, 56, 58, 73, 76, 84, 107, 113, 124, 134, 163, 233; **6:** 211; **9:** 123, 151

Ritualists, **7:** 388 n.*669*

Scripture reading, **3:** 158; **4:** 158

Sunday duty, **5:** 44

Views on Spurgeon preaching, **3:** 46

Resignation of lectureship, **7:** 349 n.*610*, 371, 372 n.*646*, 373, 375, 377-379, 381, 382 n.*658*

Resolutions:

To be a competent mathematical lecturer, **3:** 142; **4:** 158

To be punctual, **2:** 73; **3:** 142

To deny himself sleep, **4:** 159

To do something worthy in life, **4:** 267

To leave old habits behind, **5:** 29

To make progress in photography, **2:** 129

To prepare sermons, **4:** 159

To read the Bible daily, **4:** 158

To work hard, **2:** 129; **3:** 142

Returned mail, **9:** 350

Rifle-shooting scores, **4:** 102 n.*65*

River trips, **2:** 77-79; **3:** 32, 56, 62; **4:** 12, 24, 69 n.*11*, 81 n.*33*, 88, 94, 95 n.*53*, 111, 112, 114, 115, 192, 195, 200, 204, 213; **5:** 77

Rooms, **2:** 64 n.*128*, 67-69, 121, 125; **4:** 63, 64, 147 n.*131*; **5:** 29 n.*30*, 130 n.*208*; **6:** 38, 59, 90, 291; **7:** 323, 326; improvements, **8:** 84 n.*135*, 123, 124, 153, 155-157, 324, 499, 500, 548

Royalty payments, **9:** 171

Russian Journal, **5:** 255-369; **6:** 169

Sailing, **6:** 182

Sandown sketch-book, **7:** 45

School prizes, **1:** 23, 29

Scout, **2:** 71 n.*141*, 85; **8:** 323, 325, 602; **9:** 268, 287

Second-hand bookshops, **4:** 121

Set of bones, **6:** 245

Shaving without soap, **6:** 427
Shopping, **4:** 161; **5:** 123, 212, 226, 366, 367, 380; **6:** 13, 20, 49, 97, 177
Showing pictures, **8:** 85, 163, 202, 275, 335, 341, 342, 359, 382, 385, 433, 491, 558, 620; **9:** 196
Skating accident, **1:** 61
Song writing, **5:** 42 n.*53*
Sound, composition of, **8:** 249
Speech at Censors' Dinner, **7:** 501; **8:** 156
Speech hesitation, **4:** 21, 122 n.*94*, 141 n.*120*, 161, 170; **5:** 233; **7:** 324; **8:** 397; **9:** 123
Speech in Congregation, **4:** 56; **7:** 436; **8:** 94 n.*154*, 246, 303 n.*503*
Spiritualism and the supernatural, **3:** 127; **5:** 229; **6:** 71, 376, 391, 427
Star maps, **7:** 353 n.*616*
Steamer and ship journeys, **2:** 51; **3:** 104; **4:** 340; **5:** 296, 361; **6:** 296, 357, 360, 415, 424, 484; **7:** 290, 447, 452; **8:** 478; **9:** 29, 82
Steamship investments, **6:** 417 n.*684*; **7:** 89 n.*158*; **8:** 258, 259, 293, 521, 540 n.*865*
Stock taking of personal property, **9:** 206
Story-telling:
  "Bird caught on thorn," **9:** 340, 343
  "Bruno and the Foxes," **7:** 105, 198
  "Bruno's Picnic," **7:** 95, 300, 471; **8:** 111, 146, 208, 338, 346, 468, 476, 496, 522, 574, 587, 624; **9:** 97, 101, 129, 250, 269, 278, 313, 339, 340, 342-344, 346
  "Cophetua and the Beggar-Maid," **6:** 472, 473 n.*779*
  "Hobgoblin and Blacksmith," **6:** 246, 269, 280, 363, 376, 378, 425; **7:** 290, 361, 471
  "Jenny Lind singing," **9:** 343
  "Lame Shepherd-Dog," **9:** 340, 343
  "Little Christel," **9:** 242, 340, 343
  "MOWS," **9:** 339, 343
  "Mr. C. and Mr. T.," **9:** 129, 242, 293, 313, 316, 340, 342, 343, 346
  "Mr. M. etc.," **9:** 129
  "Mr. O'Grady," **4:** 60
  "Old Goose," **9:** 129, 316, 343
  "Pixies, The (Three Little)," **5:** 169, 377; **6:** 101 n.*158*, 102, 246, 280, **7:** 73; **9:** 242
  "Prince Uggug," **6:** 376, 377
  "Sermon-Story," **9:** 168
  "Soup, The" (based on Russian fable), **6:** 426
  "Three Little Foxes," **7:** 70, 72
  "Two Sisters," **6:** 452
  "Victor and Arnion," **9:** 333, 335
Student of Christ Church, **1:** 17, 45, 47, 98 n.*104*, 135; **4:** 20, 137 n.*115*
Stylographic pen, **7:** 224 n.*410*

Sub-Librarian, **1:** 61 n.*34,* 72, 76, 78, 79, 85, 93, 100, 101; **3:** 20 n.*24*
Teaching Harry Liddell sums, **3:** 16 n.*17*, 17, 23
Teaching (non-mathematical), **1:** 108, 111, 112, 114; **2:** 30; **3:** 90
Telescope, **4:** 207; **6:** 55

Theatre performances seen:
1863 (Henry Byron), **4:** 270
Adelphi (Terence), **3:** 140
Adventures of a Love-Letter (Charles Mathews), **4:** 270
Adventures of Fritz, The (J. K. Emmet), **7:** 199
After Dark (Dion Boucicault), **7:** 75
Agamemnon at Home (Aeschylus), **5:** 253
Alabama (Augustus Thomas), **9:** 215, 219, 220
Alabama, The (Albert Smith), **4:** 281
Aladdin and his Wonderful Lamp (Frank Green), **7:** 313
Aladdin and the Wonderful Lamp (Anon), **5:** 311, 313
Aladdin and the Wonderful Lamp (John Morton), **3:** 14
Alfred the Great (Robert Brough), **4:** 263
Alice in Fairy-Land (Elliston Family, adapt. Carroll), **7:** 138
Alice in Wonderland (Henry Savile Clarke, adapt. Carroll), **8:** 311, 313, 316, 318, 348, 439
Alice in Wonderland (Kate Freiligrath-Kroeker, adapt. Carroll), **8:** 496
All in the Wrong (Arthur Murphy), **3:** 79
Always Intended (Horace Wigan), **5:** 63
Amber Heart, The (Alfred Calmour), **8:** 406
Ample Apology, An (George Roberts), **5:** 64
A Pas de Fascination (Anon), **5:** 123
Area Belle, The (William Brough & Andrew Halliday), **4:** 337
Arrah na Pogue (Dion Boucicault), **5:** 64
As You Like It (William Shakespeare), **5:** 220; **8:** 418
Athens Club, The (Anon), **7:** 194
At the Seaside (Richard Corney Grain), **7:** 131
Away with Melancholy (John Morton): **1:** 105
Awful Rise in Spirits, An (Tom Taylor), **4:** 248
Barefaced Imposters (John & Richard Doe and John Noakes), **4:** 205
B.B. (Francis Burnand), **4:** 279
Beauty and the Beast (Anon), **7:** 234
Beauty and the Beast (Eliza Keating), **7:** 95
Beauty and the Beast (James Planché), **5:** 42
Behind Time (Benjamin Webster), **5:** 137
Belles of the Kitchen, The (Anon), **8:** 285
Belle's Stratagem, The (Hannah Cowley), **7:** 326
Betsy Baker (John Morton), **4:** 263
Birthplace of Podgers, The (John Hollingshead), **8:** 574
Birds in Their Little Nests Agree (Charles Rae), **7:** 23

Black Eyed Susan (Francis Burnand), **5:** 232
Black-Eyed Susan (Roy Redgrave, adapt. Douglas Jerrold), **9:** 332, 333
Blue-Beard (Henry Byron), **5:** 157
Bootle's Baby (Hugh Moss), **8:** 405, 485
Boots at the Swan (Charles Selby), **3:** 153, 171
Born to Good Luck (Tyrone Power), **4:** 358
Bottle of Smoke, A (Anon), **2:** 80
Box and Cox (John Morton), **4:** 225
Box B (Richard Corney Grain), **9:** 88
Broken Hearts (W. S. Gilbert), **7:** 442
Broken Melody, The (Herbert Keen & James Leader), **9:** 277
Brother Sam (John Oxenford, Edward Sothern & John Buckstone), **5:** 88, 92
Burgomaster's Wedding, The (Anon), **5:** 313
Butler, The (Herman Merivale), **8:** 333
Butterfly's Ball and the Grasshopper's Feast (Edward Blanchard), **2:** 23
Case of Conscience, A (John Oxenford), **3:** 132
Charity Begins at Home (B. C. Stephenson & Clement Scott), **8:** 632
Charles I (William Wills), **6:** 253; **7:** 185; **9:** 78
Children of the King, The (Carl Armbruster & Arthur Rushton), **9:** 347
Chili Widow, A (Arthur Bourchier & Alfred Sutro), **9:** 219
Cinderella (Anon), **5:** 45
Cinderella (Frank Green), **7:** 153, 156, 159
Cinderella (Horace Lennard), **9:** 122
Cinderella (Louisa MacDonald), **4:** 324
Claudian (Henry Herman), **8:** 81, 103, 108
Cleft Stick, A (John Oxenford), **5:** 117
Clerical Error, A (Henry Jones), **7:** 540; **8:** 52
Clito (Sydney Grundy), **8:** 274
Clôches de Corneville (Henry Farnie, Robert Reece and Robert Planquette), **7:** 369; **8:** 135, 136, 363
Cochin China (Anon), **5:** 311
Commission, A (Weedon Grossmith), **9:** 303
Comrades (Brandon Thomas & B. C. Stephenson), **7:** 513
Conjugal Lesson, A (Henry Danvers), **4:** 300
Constance (Frederick Clay), **5:** 45
Cool as a Cucumber (William Jerrold), **4:** 270
Corsican Brothers, The (Dion Boucicault, adapt. Dumas), **7:** 318; **8:** 567
Cousin Joe (John Oxenford), **9:** 331
Cox and Box (Francis Burnand & Arthur Sullivan), **5:** 240
Crinoline (Robert Brough), **3:** 12
Cup, The (Alfred Tennyson), **7:** 317, 326
Cymberline (William Shakespeare), **5:** 23
Daddy Hardacres (John Simpson), **3:** 51

Daisy's Escape (Arthur Pinero), **8:** 614
Danischeffs, The (Lord Newry), **7:** 536
David Garrick (C. P. Colnaghi & Eustae Ponsonby), **8:** 478; **9:** 274, 313
David Garrick (Thomas Robertson), **4:** 300; **5:** 160
Deaf as a Post (John Poole), **4:** 309
Dearest Mamma (Gordon Walter), **9:** 119
Delicate Ground (Charles Dance), **3:** 12
Devil-May-Care (Henry Besley), **9:** 87
Diplomacy (Clement Scott), **7:** 96; **9:** 57
Doge of Duralto, The (Robert Brough), **3:** 153
Done Brown (Henry Craven), **1:** 133
Don Pasquale (Donizetti), **3:** 98
Dorothy (B. C. Stephenson and Alfred Cellier), **8:** 367, 523, 524; **9:** 212
Dot (Dion Boucicault), **8:** 374
Doubleday's Will (Anon), **7:** 131
Duke's Motto, The (John Brougham), **4:** 182, 221
East Lynne (John Oxenford), **9:** 331
Editha's Burglar (Frances Burnett & Stephen Townsend), **8:** 440
Engaged (W. S. Gilbert), **7:** 97-99, 387
Esmeralda (Pugni), **3:** 50
Faces in the Fire (Leicester Buckingham), **5:** 72
Faint Heart Never Won Fair Lady (James Planché), **3:** 120
Faithful James (B. C. Stephenson), **9:** 26
Far From the Madding Crowd (Joseph Carr, adapt. Hardy), **7:** 468
Fascinating Individual, A (Henry Danvers), **2:** 82
Faust (William Wills), **8:** 273; **9:** 146
Faust and Marguerita (Dion Boucicault), **3:** 105
Favourite of Fortune, A (John Marston), **5:** 139
Fee, Fo, Fum (Anon), **5:** 379
Flying Dutchman (Edward Fitzball), **2:** 80
Follow the Leader (Charles Rae), **7:** 23
Game of Romps, A (John Morton), **3:** 52, 81
Girl I Left Behind Me, The (David Belasco & Franklin Fyles), **5:** 37, 85
Glaucus (F. T. Traill), **5:** 95
Gli Ugonotti (Meyerbeer), **5:** 156
Golden Ladder, The (George Sims), **8:** 381
Gondoliers, The (Gilbert and Sullivan), **8:** 522
Good For Nothing (John Buckstone), **5:** 17; **7:** 186
Good Night Signor Pantalon (John Oxenford), **2:** 80
Goody Two Shoes (Anon), **7:** 13
Green Bushes, The (John Buckstone), **5:** 47
Hamlet (William Shakespeare), **2:** 20; **4:** 312; **7:** 156, 159; **8:** 168, 424, 616; **9:** 280
Hans the Boatman (Clay Greene), **9:** 272
Heart Strings and Fiddle Strings (David Fisher), **5:** 64

Henry IV (William Shakespeare), **1:** 133; **4:** 281 (part 1), 291
Henry VIII (William Shakespeare), **1:** 105, 106; **2:** 21, 22, 83; **8:** 619
Henry Dunbar (Tom Taylor), **5:** 123
Hidden Hand, The (Tom Taylor), **5:** 37
High Life Below Stairs (James Townley), **5:** 71, 156
H. M. S. Pinafore (Gilbert and Sullivan) – children's version, **7:** 316
Honesty is the Best Policy (Mark Lemon), **3:** 101
Honour (Maurice Barrymore), **7:** 369
Hoodman Blind (Henry Jones & Wilson Barrett), **8:** 234
Hook and Eye (Eille Norwood), **9:** 274, 313
Hornet's Nest, The (Henry Byron), **7:** 123
Hunchback, The (James Knowles), **5:** 155
Hundred Thousand Pounds, A (Henry Byron), **5:** 156; **9:** 119
Hussar's Daughter, The (Anon), **5:** 311
Ici On Parle Francais (Thomas Williams), **4:** 151
Idler, The (Charles Chambers), **8:** 562; **9:** 23, 24
Il Barbiere di Seviglia (Rossini), **1:** 104
Il Flauto Magico (Mozart), **5:** 98
Il Trovatore (Verdi), **4:** 341; **8:** 577
In The Pigskin (John Morton), **5:** 69
Iolanthe (Gilbert and Sullivan), **7:** 503, 540, 543
Iphigenia (Edward Nolan), **5:** 153
Irish Diamond, An (Anon), **9:** 332
Irish Tiger, An (John Morton), **4:** 337
Ixion (Francis Burnand), **4:** 315
Jack and Jill (Anon), **8:** 160
Jack and the Beanstalk (Frank Green), **7:** 92, 152
Jack the Giant-Killer (Robert Soutar), **7:** 233
Jane Shore (William Wills), **7:** 114; **8:** 586
Janet Pride (Dion Boucicault), **2:** 123; **4:** 337
John Dobbs (John Morton), **4:** 151, 152
Jones the Avenger (Anon), **2:** 123
Joseph's Sweetheart (Robert Buchanan), **8:** 412, 425
Judah (Henry Jones), **8:** 527
Kenilworth (Thomas Dibdin), **5:** 168
King Lear (William Shakespeare), **9:** 44
King Réne's Daughter (Frederick Weatherley), **9:** 162
Kiss in the Dark, A (John Buckstone), **5:** 109
La Cigale (Francis Burnand and Edmond Audran), **8:** 565; **9:** 163, 166
Ladies' Battle, The (Thomas Robertson), **7:** 183
Lady Barbara's Birthday (Miss Barker), **7:** 515
Lady of Lyons, The (Henry Byron), **5:** 109; **7:** 356
La Famille Benoiton (Victorien Sardou), **5:** 364
La Figlia di Reggimento (Donizetti), **3:** 49
La Fille de Madame Angot (Lecocq), **8:** 287, 288

Lavater (Henry Coape), **5:** 210
La Vie (Offenbach), **8:** 38
Lawrence's Love Suit (John Wooler), **5:** 47
Leading Strings (Adolphus Troughton), **3:** 133
Lend Me Five Shillings (John Morton), **5:** 220
L'Enfant Prodigue (Voltaire), **8:** 556
Les Deux Aveugles (Offenbach), **5:** 241
Lesson for Life (Tom Taylor), **4:** 225, 356
Level Crossing, The (George Sims), **9:** 20
Liar, The (Samuel Foote), **5:** 210, 253
Liberty Hall (Richard Carton), **9:** 56, 58, 60, 91
Lights o'London, The (George Sims), **8:** 208
Little Doctor Faust (Henry Byron), **7:** 140
Little Don Giovanni (Henry Byron), **5:** 125
Little King Pippin (Edward Blanchard), **5:** 127, 128
Little Minister, The (James M. Barrie), **9:** 352
Little Red Riding-Hood (Anon), **7:** 510
Little Squire, The (Dora Greet), **9:** 138
Little Toddlekins (Charles Mathews), **4:** 205, 206
Littletop's Christmas Party (Anon), **5:** 193
Little Treasure, The (Augustus Harris), **2:** 23, 24
Lord Dundreary Married and Done For (Henry Byron), **5:** 160
Lost Keys, The (Anon), **7:** 194
Lost to the World (Mrs. Talbot Hunter), **9:** 26
Lottery Ticket, A (Samuel Beazley), **8:** 333
Louis XI (Dion Boucicault), **3:** 120
Love Chase, A (James Knowles), **5:** 69
Love in Idleness (Parker & Goodman), **9:** 310
Lurette (Offenbach), **7:** 541
Macbeth (William Shakespeare), **8:** 456
Macfarlane's Will (Joseph Mackay), **7:** 396
Madame Favart (Offenbach), **7:** 193, 212, 220, 232
Magic Toys (John Oxenford), **4:** 291
Magistrate, The (Arthur Pinero), **8:** 199
Maid and the Magpie (John Payne), **2:** 21
Maid of Honour (John Wooler), **4:** 309
Margate Sands (Wilmot Harrison), **4:** 272
Marquesa, The (John Uniacke), **8:** 473
Masaniello (Robert Brough), **3:** 79, 133; **4:** 310
Masks and Faces (Tom Taylor), **9:** 335
Matched and Mated (Francis Burnand and Thomas German Reed), **7:** 57
May Queen, The (John Buckstone), **9:** 20
Mazurka (Henry Byron), **4:** 309
Meg's Diversion (Henry Craven), **5:** 232

Merchant of Venice (William Shakespeare), **7:** 236, 442, 540; **8:** 68, 336, 338; **9:** 21, 73, 75, 203, 204
Middleman, The (Henry Jones), **8:** 486
Midsummer Night's Dream, A (William Shakespeare), **2:** 124; **3:** 14, 153; **8:** 417, 501
Mignon (Thomas), **5:** 366
Mikado, The (Gilbert and Sullivan), **8:** 210, 269, 280, 282; **9:** 286
Money (Edward Bulwer Lytton), **5:** 157; **7:** 540
Mother Goose (Sarah Thorne), **8:** 609
Mountebanks, The (W. S. Gilbert and Alfred Cellier), **8:** 631; **9:** 24
Mrs. Green's Snug Little Business (Charles Cheltnam), **5:** 47
Mrs. White (Richard Raymond), **4:** 300
Mrs. Willis' Will (Emile Souvestre), **7:** 194
Much Ado About Nothing (William Shakespeare), **7:** 493, 508; **8:** 126, 342; **9:** 205
Mumbo Jumbo (Anon), **4:** 317
Music Hath Charm (David Fisher), **3:** 106
My Aunt's in Town (Richard Corney Grain), **8:** 481
My Friend from Leatherhead (N. H. Harrington & Edmund Yates), **3:** 101, 102, 120
My Heart's in the Highlands (William Brough & Andrew Halliday), **4:** 291
My Little Girl (Dion Boucicault), **7:** 438
My Poll and My Partner Joe (John Haines), **3:** 101
My Sweetheart (Frederick Maeder), **8:** 229
My Wife's Bonnet (John Morton), **5:** 37
My Wife's Mother (Charles Mathews), **5:** 88
My Wife's Party (Richard Corney Grain), **8:** 632
My Wife's Relations (Walter Gordon), **4:** 223
My Wife's Second Floor (John Morton), **4:** 221
Nance Oldfield (Charles Reade), **8:** 567
Nancy Sikes (Cyril Searle, adapt. Dickens), **7:** 122
New Men and Old Acres (Augustus Dubourg and Tom Taylor), **7:** 15
New Sub, The (Seymour Hicks), **8:** 618; **9:** 12, 26
Niobe (Harry Paulton), **9:** 16
Norma (Bellini), **1:** 103; **4:** 104, 282
No Song, No Supper (Prince Hoare), **5:** 32, 88
Number One, Round the Corner (William Brough), **4:** 263
Number 204 (Francis Burnand and Thomas German Reed), **7:** 57
Odd Pair, An (T. Malcolm Watson), **9:** 88
O'Flahertys, The (Anon), **5:** 23
Old Guard, The (Henry Farnie and Robert Planquette), **8:** 569
Old Song, An (Freeman Wills & A. Fitz King), **9:** 162
Olivette (Henry Farnie and Edmond Audran), **7:** 304
Olivia (William Wills), **7:** 106, 110; **8:** 209, 565

Only a Halfpenny (John Oxenford), **2:** 24
Orange-Blossoms (John Wooler), **4:** 272
Organ-Grinder (Maria Edgeworth), **7:** 95
Orpheus and Eurydice (James Planché), **4:** 272
Our Boys (Henry Byron), **8:** 131, 140
Our Eldorado (Frank Scudamore), **9:** 164
Our Flat (Mrs. H. Musgrave), **8:** 530
Our Mary Anne (John Buckstone), **5:** 32
Ours (Thomas Robertson), **7:** 231
Our Table d'hôte (Richard Corney Grain), **7:** 57
Our Wife (John Morton), **2:** 124
Pan (Henry Byron), **5:** 69
Pantomime of the White Cat (Charles Kean), **3:** 153
Pantomime Rehearsal, A (Cecil Clay), **8:** 618; **9:** 12, 26, 303
Paper Chase, The (Charles Thomas), **8:** 428
Partners (Robert Buchanan), **8:** 460, 584
Parvenu, The (George Godfrey), **7:** 438
Patience (Gilbert and Sullivan), **7:** 394, 431, 441, 461, 477; **8:** 138
Paul Jones (Henry Farnie), **8:** 589
Paul Pry (Douglas Jerrold), **8:** 574
Paw Clawdian (Francis Burnand), **8:** 112
Perfection (Thomas Bayly), **5:** 221
Pilgrim's Progress (Louisa MacDonald), **7:** 179, 183, 193, 279
Pirates of Penzance (Gilbert and Sullivan), **8:** 161, 164
Polyeuctus (Pierre Corneille), **7:** 473
Poor Piano (Richard Corney Grain), **9:** 88
Poor Pillicoddy (John Morton), **7:** 158
Popping the Question (John Buckstone), **5:** 51
Port Admiral, The (Thomas Bowles), **4:** 318
Prince Camaralzaman (Henry Bellingham & William Best), **5:** 117
Prince for an Hour, A (John Morton), **2:** 83
Prince Karl (A. C. Gunter), **8:** 440
Princess Primrose (Henry Bellingham), **5:** 145
Professor's Love-Story, The (J. M. Barrie), **9:** 225, 230, 243
Pygmalion and Galatea (W. S. Gilbert), **7:** 23; **8:** 190
Real Little Lord Fauntleroy, The (Frances Hodgson Burnett), **8:** 400, 405, 409, 441, 471
Red Riding Hood (Anon), **7:** 75
Retribution (Tom Taylor), **2:** 82
Richard II (William Shakespeare), **3:** 52
Richard III (William Shakespeare), **8:** 451, 454
Richelieu (Edward Bulwer Lytton), **8:** 628
Rip Van Winkle (Dion Boucicault & Joseph Jefferson), **5:** 123
Rip Van Winkle (Henry Farnie and Robert Planquette), **7:** 532; **8:** 34
Rivals, The (Richard Sheridan), **5:** 153; **7:** 540

Robert Macaire (Charles Selby), **8:** 406; **9:** 162
Robin Hood (Anon), **7:** 91, 97
Rob Roy (Anon), **7:** 449
Romantic Attachment (Arthur Wood), **5:** 139, 160
Romantic Idea, A (James Planché), **5:** 210
Rory O'Mare (Samuel Lover), **5:** 17
Rosencranz and Guildenstern (W. S. Gilbert), **8:** 618; **9:** 12
Rose and the Ring, The (Henry Savile Clarke), **8:** 546
Royal Bride, The (Anon), **7:** 511
Rumplestiltskin (Francis Burnand), **4:** 315
Ruth's Romance (Frederick Broughton), **8:** 285
Scholar, The (John Buckstone), **3:** 105
School (Thomas Robertson), **7:** 278, 319
School For Scandal (Richard Sheridan), **5:** 32
Serf, The (Tom Taylor), **5:** 85, 94, 97
Settling Day (Tom Taylor), **5:** 59, 63, 71
Sheep in Wolf's Clothing, A (Tom Taylor), **3:** 51; **5:** 115, 117, 241
She Stoops to Conquer (Oliver Goldsmith), **9:** 22, 273
Shocking Events (John Buckstone), **5:** 139
Silver Gilt (W. Warham), **8:** 59
Silver King, The (Henry Jones and Henry Herman), **7:** 525; **8:** 52, 198, 457, 587; **9:** 173
Simpson and Co. (John Poole), **5:** 85
Society (Thomas Robertson), **5:** 125
Solon Shingle (Anon), **5:** 96
Somnambula (Henry Byron), **5:** 156
Sonnambula (Bellini), **5:** 253
Sorcerer (Gilbert and Sullivan), **7:** 96
Sowing the Wind (Sydney Grundy), **9:** 100
Squire, The (Arthur Pinero), **8:** 412
Statue Bride, The (Anon), **2:** 123
Stay at Home (George Lewes), **2:** 82
Streets of London (Dion Boucicault), **4:** 358
Sunlight and Shadow (Richard Carton), **8:** 577
Sweethearts (W. S. Gilbert), **7:** 186
Sweet Lavender (Arthur Pinero), **8:** 477; **9:** 15, 123
Sylvius (Anon), **5:** 193
Taking it Easy (Anon), **8:** 112
Taming of the Shrew, The (William Shakespeare), **9:** 121
Taps, The (Lionel Brough & Willie Edouin), **8:** 237
Teddy the Tiler (George Rodwell), **5:** 17
Tempest, The (William Shakespeare), **3:** 81, 126, 132
Thieves, Thieves (Anon), **3:** 51
Thousand (Anon), **7:** 528
Three Furies, The (George Roberts), **5:** 73

Through Fire and Water (Walter Gordon), **5:** 96, 137
Ticket-of-Leave Man (Tom Taylor), **4:** 223, 226, 248, 249, 279, 310; **5:** 63, 145
Ticklish Times (John Morton), **3:** 171
Timothy to the Rescue (Henry Byron), **4:** 309; **5:** 168
Tom Noddy's Secret (Thomas Bayly), **8:** 478
Toodles, The (Richard Raymond), **5:** 96
To Parents and Guardians (Tom Taylor), **7:** 369
Tragedy Queen, The (N. R. Fournier), **3:** 153
Trial of Effie Deans (Dion Boucicault), **4:** 159
Trying a Magistrate (John Toole), **7:** 442
Turn Him Out (Thomas Williams), **4:** 272
Twelfth Night (William Shakespeare), **7:** 315; **8:** 131, 423; **9:** 132
Twenty Minutes under an Umbrella (Augustus Dubourg), **7:** 194
Two Little Vagabonds (George Sims and Arthur Shirley), **9:** 283, 284, 303
Two Orphans, The (John Oxenford), **7:** 141
Uncle's Will (S. Theyre Smith), **7:** 183
Uncle Tom's Cabin (George Rowe), **7:** 142
Ulysses (Francis Burnand), **5:** 72
Upper Crust (Henry Byron), **8:** 112
Utopia (Limited) (Gilbert and Sullivan), **9:** 118
Venus and Adonis (Francis Burnand), **4:** 300
Vicarage, The (Clement Scott), **7:** 319
Vice Versa (Edward Rose), **8:** 59
Waiting Consent (Mrs. R. Fairbairn), **8:** 374
Walker, London (James M. Barrie), **8:** 614
Water Babes, The (Edward Bowles), **9:** 251
Wedding Breakfast (John Parry), **5:** 157
Wep-Ton-No-Mah (Go-Won-Go-Mohawk), **9:** 277
What Will They Say in Brompton? (Joseph Coyne), **3:** 133
While There's Life There's Hope (Anon), **4:** 221
White Lie, A (Sydney Grundy), **9:** 54
Whittington and his Cat (Anon), **7:** 399
Whittington and his Cat (A. Henry), **7:** 504
Windsor Castle (Francis Burnand & Montague Williams), **5:** 92, 93
Winter's Tale (William Shakespeare), **2:** 82, 83, 124
Wives as They Were (Elizabeth Inchbald), **2:** 123
Woman's Revenge, A (Henry Pettitt), **9:** 213
Woman's Secret, A (Anon), **5:** 313
Wonderful Woman, A (Charles Dance), **4:** 205; **5:** 42
Wreck Ashore, The (John Buckstone), **5:** 137
You Can't Marry Your Grandmother (Thomas Bayly), **3:** 171
Yachting Cruise, A (Francis Burnand), **5:** 157
Yeoman of the Guard (Gilbert and Sullivan), **8:** 453

Young and Handsome (James Planché), **3:** 12

Theatre trips, **1:** 102, 105, 133; **2:** 20, 23, 80, 82, 83, 108, 109, 123, 124; **3:** 12, 14, 49, 51, 52, 76, 79, 81, 91, 93, 98, 101, 103, 105, 131, 133, 146, 153, 171; **4:** 21, 25, 64, 104, 109, 153, 157, 159, 182, 207, 221, 223, 225, 269, 272, 279, 281, 282, 290, 291, 300, 309, 310, 312, 337; **5:** 16, 23, 32, 37, 41, 45, 47, 63, 64, 69, 71, 72, 85, 88, 92, 94, 96, 98, 99, 109, 117,122, 123, 125, 127, 137, 155, 156, 159, 160, 168, 201-205, 210, 220, 231, 232, 240, 281, 311, 313, 356, 364, 366, 379; **6:** 27, 36, 112, 121, 130, 135, 156, 169, 180; **7:** 13, 15, 17, 23, 75, 76, 91-93, 96, 97, 99, 105, 110, 114, 122, 123, 140-142, 152, 153, 155, 156, 159, 183, 185-187, 193, 199, 212, 220, 231-233, 236, 304, 313, 316, 317, 319, 326, 356, 369, 387, 394, 399, 431, 438, 441, 442, 444, 449, 468, 477, 492, 493, 503, 504, 508, 510, 513, 515, 525, 532, 536, 539, 541, 543, **8:** 34, 38, 52, 59, 80, 103, 108, 112, 125, 131, 135, 136, 138, 140, 160, 161, 164, 168, 190, 198, 199, 208-210, 229, 234, 237, 269, 273, 274, 280, 282, 285, 287, 288, 311, 313, 316, 318, 333, 338, 342, 348, 363, 367, 374, 381, 400, 405, 406, 409, 412, 417, 418, 423-425, 428, 439-441, 451, 453, 454, 456, 457, 471, 473, 477, 478, 485, 486, 501, 522-524, 527, 530, 546, 556, 562, 565, 567, 569, 574, 577, 584, 586, 587, 589, 609, 614, 618, 619, 628, 631; **9:** 12, 15, 16, 20-24, 26, 44, 54, 56-58, 60, 73, 75, 78, 91, 100, 121-123, 132, 139, 146, 162-166, 173, 203-205, 212, 213, 215, 219, 220, 225, 230, 243, 251, 272-274, 277, 280, 283, 284, 286, 310, 313, 331-333, 335, 347, 352

Trust Fund for Dodgson sisters, **8:** 606, 607 n.*962*, 611

Typewriting – see Hammond Typewriter

Vaccination, **4:** 198; **6:** 186

Velociman (cycle) improvements, **7:** 435 n.*722*, 436, 481-483, 485, 486, 488, 494

Ventilating lamp, **7:** 323

Views on:

Booksellers' profits, **8:** 21 n.*15*

Dinner parties, **7:** 433, 471, 472, 488

Listening to music, **1:** 127, 128

Mathematics at Oxford, **3:** 58 n.*89*, 60

Slavery, **4:** 287

Smoking, **4:** 18

Visiting the sick, **6:** 147 n.*224*; **7:** 161 n.*301*, 223, 226, 228, 245, 257, 263, 274; **8:** 170 n.*284*, 215, 256-258, 260, 261, 264, 266, 268, 270, 272, 275, 364, 373, 374, 378, 403, 406, 429, 441, 472, 486, 503, 547

Vivisection, **6:** 381 n.*624*, 382, 390; **8:** 171, 172 n.*288*

Voting procedures, see Election theory

Walks (alone), **5:** 90; **7:** 118, 126, 158, 204, 216, 248, 252, 330, 335, 337, 531; **8:** 102, 188, 320, 329, 378; **9:** 61, 67, 93, 95, 97, 101, 159, 161, 163, 171, 173-175, 179, 181, 183, 185, 193, 199, 220, 223, 224, 234,

238, 239, 252, 264, 275, 277-279, 302, 307, 312-314, 323, 326, 328-330, 336
Weight, **7:** 458
White Stone Days, **1:** 129, 133; **2:** 54, 65 n.*129*, 79; **3:** 66, 73, 109; **4:** 94, 204, 266, 291, 359; **5:** 32, 36, 64, 95, 205; **6:** 101, 181; **7:** 516; **8:** 472, 597; **9:** 32, 36, 64, 95, 205
Wire puzzles, **7:** 201, 287, 459; **9:** 172, 173

Works by Dodgson:
A Disputed Point in Logic, **9:** 137 n.*239*, 138
"After Three Days," **4:** 55
"Alfred the Great" (marionette play), **1:** 110
Algebra (10), **7:** 44 n.*67*
Algebra (13), **7:** 45
Algebraical Formulae for Responsions, **6:** 31 n.*40*
Alice dramatised, **6:** 236, 241, 242, 260, 301, 369, 379, 457 n.*752*, 463, 465, 467
Alice's Abenteuer im Wunderland, see German *Alice*
Alice's Adventures in Wonderland, **1:** 11, 20, 34, 57 n.*22*, 122 n.*151*; **3:** 60 n.*91*, 61 n.*92*, 129 n.*186*; **4:** 25, 81 n.*33*, 95 n.*53*, 110 n.*79*, 217 n.*232*, 220, 221, 271 n.*315*, 284, 297 n.*359*, 298, 311, 312, 347 n.*453*; **5:** 9, 10, 11 n.*1*, 15 n.*8*, 16 n.*10*, 22 n.*17*, 26 n.*25*, 29 n.*31*, 33, 36 n.*43*, 56 n.*80*, 64 n.*94*, 70, 76 n.*115*, 76 n.*116*, 93 n.*145*, 97 n.*151*, 100, 101 n.*158*, 115 n.*180*, 117 n.*184*, 122, 130 n.*209*, 140, 143, 145 n.*234*, 151 n.*245*, 173 n.*288*, 199 n.*322*, 207 n.*331*, 231, 242; **6:** 50 n.*72*, 75, 120, 189, 224; **7:** 44, 466; **8:** 99 n.*164*, 137, 307, 369 n.*606*, 370, 371, 373; **9:** 106, 275 n.*440*, 326 n.*523*, 340
Alice's Adventures Under Ground, **1:** 14, 20; **4:** 35, 93 n.*51*, 95, 96 n.*54*, 110 n.*79*, 115, 142 n.*121*, 172 n.*167*, 197 n.*198*, 229, 297 n.*359*; **5:** 11 n.*1*, 56 n.*80*; **8:** 169 n.*283*, 170, 182 n.*305*, 183, 186, 187, 219-221, 234, 242, 247, 299, 302, 303, 307, 308 n.*510*, 309; **9:** 44 n.*76*
"Alice's Hour in Elfland," **4:** 95
Alice's Puzzle-Book, **6:** 381, 382 n.*627*
Alphabet Cipher, **2:** 42 n.*83*
American Telegrams, **5:** 49 n.*66*
Analysis of Responsions, **7:** 404, 405, 409 n.*689*
"Anharmonic Ratio," **4:** 13
Arithmetical Croquêt, **2:** 34 n.*67*; **6:** 240 n.*382*; **9:** 244
Arithmetical Dominoes, **6:** 379 n.*622*, 380
Art-Repository, **1:** 52 n.*8*, 55
"Asymptotes," **4:** 47
"Atalanta in Camden Town," **5:** 254 n.*420*
"Authors and Booksellers" – paper, **8:** 26
Aventures d'Alice au Pays des Merveilles, see French *Alice*

"Beatrice," **4:** 149 n.*133*
Behind the Looking-Glass, see *Through the Looking-Glass*
"Besides the salt sea-wave," **4:** 143 n.*123*, 144
Blank Cheque, The, **6:** 318 n.*528*, 321
"Blot Backgammon," **5:** 378
"Books to read," **7:** 404
"Brief Method of Dividing a Given Number by 9 or 11," **9:** 341, 342 n.*546*, 351 n.*562*
"Bruno and the Foxes," **7:** 105, 198
"Bruno's Picnic," **7:** 95, 300, 471; **8:** 111, 146, 208, 338, 346, 468, 476, 496, 522, 574, 587, 624; **9:** 49, 93, 97, 101, 129, 134, 178, 250, 259, 269, 278, 313, 337-340, 342-344, 346
Bruno's Revenge, **4:** 46; **5:** 251 n.*410*, 370 n.*547*, 374 n.*554*, 375; **7:** 47 n.*72*, 85, 104 n.*194*
Burlesque on Ancient Tragedy, **2:** 49 n.*98*
"Candidates for Responsions," **6:** 65 n.*94*
Castle Croquêt, see *Croquêt Castles*
Christmas Greeting, **6:** 428 n.*705*
"Circle-Squaring," **9:** 81 n.*148*
Circular Billiards, **8:** 507 n.*816*
Comet, The (family magazine), **1:** 30, 31, 35, 38
"Complete Postage Guide, A," **8:** 29 n.*33*
Condensation of Determinants, **5:** 132 n.*211*, 133 n.*212*, 133 n.*213*, 147, 149, 152 n.*246*
Co-operative Backgammon, **9:** 126 n.*221*, 129 n.*226*, 131, 134 n.*235*
"Court Circular" (card game) **3:** 154 n.*224*; **5:** 26 n.*24*
"Croft Railway Game," **1:** 18-19
Croquêt Castles, **4:** 196 n.*196*, 197, 198, 220, 352; **5:** 84, 88, 90, 94, 108, 162, 170; **6:** 227; **8:** 531, 627, 629; **9:** 12, 71
"Crundle Castle," **1:** 31
Curiosa Mathematica, Part I, A New Theory of Parallels, **8:** 180 n.*298*, 180 n.*299*, 390 n.*635*, 391, 452, 500
Curiosa Mathematica, Part II, Pillow-Problems, **7:** 380 n.*655*; **8:** 179, 180 n.*297*, 324 n.*536*; **9:** 17 n.*14*, 44 n.*75*, 50, 61, 65
Curiosa Mathematica, Part III, Numbers, **9:** 351 n.*562*
Cycle for Working Examples, **4:** 48, 158 n.*147*, 161
"Day of Week for Any Given Date," **8:** 323 n.*532*, 323 n.*533*; **9:** 144, 169, 266
"Dear Gazelle, The," **1:** 113 n.*133*, 120
"Deserted Parks, The," **5:** 246 n.*400*; **7:** 177 n.*328*
"Differential Calculus (from Price)," **4:** 49
"Difficulties," **1:** 35-37
"Difficulties of the Four Gospels, The," **8:** 360 n.*587*
"Direction-Theory as applied to Pairs if Lines," **8:** 505 n.*811*, 555 n.*884*, 559

Discussion of Procedure in Elections, **6:** 306 n.*507*, 307
"Disillusionised," **4:** 65 n.*1*
Divisibility rules, **8:** 119 n.*191*, 121 n.*193*; **9:** 341,344, 346, 350, 351 n.*562*, 353
Doublets, **7:** 102, 165, 170-172, 174, 175, 196 n.*367*, 197 n.*368*, 206, 224 n.*413*, 252, 259, 260 n.*471*, 306; **8:** 195, 196 n.*331*, 556; **9:** 178
Dynamics of a Parti-cle, **5:** 80 n.*124*, 81, 91 n.*141*
Easter Greeting, **6:** 428 n.*705*, 446, 452
Eight or Nine Wise Words, see *Wise Words*
"Election Gains and Losses," **8:** 251 n.*423*
Elections to the Hebdomadal Council, The, **5:** 181 n.*299*, 181 n.*300*; **6:** 66 n.*96*
Elementary Treatise on Determinants, An, **5:** 112 n.*176*, 125, 132, 133 n.*213*, 198 n.*321*, 206, 207 n.*330*, 229, 370, 372 n.*552*, 374 n.*555*
"Ellipse," **4:** 44
Endowment of the Greek Professorship, **4:** 56; **5:** 28 n.*29*
Enunciations of Euclid, Books I & II, The, **4:** 257 n.*300*
Enunciations of Euclid I-VI, The, **6:** 245 n.*389*
"Epitaph for Jock," **3:** 86, 147
"Equivalent Algebraical Expressions," **4:** 47
Essays on Theology, **8:** 183
"Eternal Punishment," **9:** 201 n.*329*
Euclid and His Modern Rivals, **4:** 52; **6:** 491 n.*810*, 495, 496 n.*819*; **7:** 11 n.*1*, 64, 65 n.*103*, 67, 72, 73 n.*117*, 75, 79, 81 n.*135*, 83, 84, 86 n.*150*, 103, 129, 130, 134, 136, 143, 150, 162, 163, 167 n.*316*, 282 n.*512*, 350, 368, 380; **8:** 179 n.*296*, 192, 203, 219, 240, 248
Euclid, Book V, Proved Algebraically, **6:** 245 n.*390*; **8:** 95 n.*155*, 180 n.*298*, 500
Euclid Books I, II , **6:** 331 n.*548*, 345; **7:** 329 n.*584*, 346, 350, 368, 379, 405, 410, 487 n.*792*, 495, 520; **8:** 152 n.*249*, 156, 182 n.*308*
Euclid Papers for Matriculation, **7:** 324 n.*574*, 325, 329
"Euclid's Theory of Parallels," **8:** 151 n.*247*, 152
Examination Statute, **4:** 273 n.*319*
Examples in Arithmetic, **6:** 383 n.*629*
"Faces in the Fire," **1:** 15; **4:** 26
"Factorial Practice," **9:** 107 n.*191*
Fame's Penny Trumpet, **6:** 476, 477 n.*788*
Feeding the Mind, **8:** 148 n.*240*
Fifth Book of Euclid Treated Algebraically, The, **1:** 99 n.*107*; **4:** 10, 26; **5:** 378, 379 n.*561*
Formulae of Plane Trigonometry, The, **4:** 48, 49
"Four Seasons," see *Sylvie and Bruno*
French *Alice*, **5:** 10, 231, 232 n.*370*, 370 n.*549*, 380 n.*563*; **6:** 82 n.*121*, 92 n.*142*
"Game of Fives, A" **7:** 521 n.*845*, 534

Game of Logic, The, **1:** 129 n.*159*; **8:** 183, 285 n.*479*, 287, 289, 293 n.*489*, 295, 303, 306, 307 n.*509*, 320 n.*527*, 337; **9:** 29, 128
"Games and Puzzles," **7:** 380 n.*655*; **8:** 181 n.*302*; **9:** 351 n.*562*
Garland of Rachel, The – contribution, **7:** 372 n.*647*
"General Equation of Second Degree: Asymptote," **4:** 54
General List of Subjects, and Cycle for Working Examples, **4:**101 n.*64*, 158 n.*147*, 161; **5:** 28 n.*28*
"Geometry for Boys," **8:** 183
German *Alice*, **5:** 10, 227 n.*361*, 231, 232 n.*370*; **6:** 53 n.*76*, 78 n.*113*, 80 n.*116*, 82, 83
"Girls' Own Shakespeare," **7:** 418, 421, 422 n.*705*; **8:** 89 n.*145*, 182 n.*306*, 187
"Grills," **8:** 559, 560 n.*890*
Guida di Bragia, La, **1:** 82 n.*84*
Guide to the Mathematical Student, A, **5:** 28 n.*28*
Guildford Gazette Extraordinary, The, **6:** 104 n.*163*
"Harmonic Pencils," **4:** 13
"Hiawatha's Photographing," **2:** 52 n.*104*; **3:** 126 n.*182*, 147; **4:** 26
"Hints on Etiquette", **1:** 131
"Hospital Circular," **6:** 473 n.*780*; **7:** 44 n.*68*, 45
Hunting of the Snark, The, **6:** 348 n.*577*, 368 n.*604*, 427-433, 445, 448, 449 n.*737*, 452, 453, 455
"Hydrophobia Curable," **8:** 242 n.*407*
Index to "In Memoriam," An, **4:** 59, 60, 99 n.*61*, 244
Isa's Visit to Oxford, **8:** 409 n.*663*
Italian *Alice*, **6:** 260 n.*415*
"Lady of the Ladle, The," **1:** 48, 54 n.*13*, 110 n.*128*
La Guida di Bragia, **1:** 19; **2:** 128 n.*245*
"Lang Coortin', The," **4:** 142 n.*122*; **7:** 23, 103, 104 n.*194*
Lanrick, **2:** 57 n.*115*; **7:** 151 n.*287*, 159, 160, 162-164, 171, 336 n.*592*, 377, 466; **9:** 19 n.*19*, 29, 37, 39, 58, 70, 72, 73, 77, 94, 126, 133, 170, 174, 176, 248, 256, 292, 304
Lawn Tennis Tournaments, **7:** 361 n.*630*, 450 n.*747*; **8:** 13 n.*4*, 16, 21, 26 n.*28*
"Lays of Sorrow," **1:** 32, 33, 37
Legend of "Scotland," The, **1:** 26, 93 n.*97*; **2:** 10 n.*10*; **3:** 86 n.*134*, 151, 152 n.*220*
"Life's Pleasance," **4:** 173 n.*169*
Ligniad, The, **1:** 66 n.*48*; **2:** 64 n.*128*
"Limits of Circle-Squaring," **7:** 351 n.*613*, 368, 380 n.*655*, 423 n.*706*
Limits of π, **8:** 128 n.*209*, 129, 180
"Little Christel," **9:** 242, 340
"Logarithms By Lightning: A Mathematical Curiosity," **6:** 431 n.*712*
"Logical Paradox, A" (Allen and Co.), **9:** 143 n.*247*
"Lonely Moor, The" **4:** 61

"Long Multiplication in a Single Line," **7:** 214 n.*396*, 223 n.*409*, 495; **8:** 376; **9:** 68 n.*124*, 178, 262, 338, 353
"Lory, The," **1:** 34, 35
"Lyceum, The," **7:** 318 n.*568*
"Maggie's Visit to Oxford," **8:** 469 n.*760*
"Majesty of Justice, The" **4:** 169 n.*162*
"Melancholetta," **3:** 45 n.*72*, 146
Memoria Technica, **3:** 143; **6:** 428 n.*706*, 429, 430 n.*708*, 431, 436 n.*717*, 436 n.*718*; **7:** 36 n.*53*, 37, 45 n.*70*, 102, 103 n.*193*, 380 n.*655*; **8:** 128, 181, 336; **9:** 68 n.*124*, 72, 173, 177 n.*298*, 230, 262, 291, 293, 294, 313, 338, 343
Method for taking Votes, **6:** 451 n.*740*
"Miracles – why they have ceased," **7:** 257 n.*468*
Mischmasch (family magazine), **1:** 30, 31, 48, 52 n.*8*, 111 n.*129*, 116, 122 n.*151*; **2:** 14 n.*20*, 89 n.*179*, 105 n.*201*; **3:** 45 n.*72*, 53 n.*80*; **4:** 25, 26
Mischmasch (word game), **7:** 286 n.*519*, 304 n.*548*, 499, 516, 524; **8:** 39, 293, 338; **9:** 41, 170, 176, 230, 235, 238, 244, 255, 278, 292, 294, 296, 301, 306, 339
"Miss Jones," **3:** 36 n.*56*; **4:** 139 n.*117*, 154, 196, 203, 204 n.*212*, 234, 287 n.*343*; **7:** 323 n.*573*
"Moans from the Miserable," **1:** 32, 33
"Morning Clouds" – draft play, **5:** 127 n.*203*, 128, 129 n.*207*, 132, 136, 162, 242 n.*393*
"MOWS," **9:** 339 n.*543*, 343
"Mr. C. and Mr. T.," **8:** 533; **9:** 129 n.*225*, 176, 242, 259, 289, 293, 313, 316, 338, 340, 342, 343, 346
"Mr. M. etc.," **9:** 129 n.*225*
"My Uncle," **2:** 105 n.*202*, 107
"My Uncle's Papers," **2:** 105 n.*202*
"Natural Selection" – see *Lanrick*
New Belfry of Christ Church, Oxford, The, **6:** 214 n.*333*, 263 n.*422*
New Method of Evaluation, The, **5:** 54 n.*76*, 56, 57, 77 n.*119*
New Theory of Parallels, see *Curiosa Mathematica*
Notes by an Oxford Chiel, **6:** 326 n.*541*, 339
"Notes on Salmon," **4:** 37
Notes on the First Part of Algebra, **4:** 48, 49
Notes on the First Two Books of Euclid, **4:** 38, 48
"Nothing," **2:** 112 n.*218*
Novelty and Romancement, **2:** 26 n.*48*, 52 n.*104*, 99, 100 n.*192*, 105
Numerical Croquêt, see Arithmetical Croquêt
Numerical (or Arithmetical) Dominoes, **6:** 379 n.*622*, 380
Nursery "Alice," The, **7:** 322 n.*572*, 326 n.*577*, 397 n.*675*; **8:** 181 n.*303*, 186, 219, 242, 439, 443, 448, 453, 506 n.*812*, 558 n.*888*; **9:** 171

"Nursery Songs," **2:** 105; **3:** 123 n.*174*, 147
Objections, Submitted to the Governing Body, **6:** 364 n.*598*
"Old Goose," **9:** 129 n.*225*, 316, 343
"Organisation of Charity, The," **5:** 194 n.*318*
Palace of Humbug, The, **2:** 14 n.*20*, 34 n.*68*; **3:** 52, 53 n.*80*, 61, 64, 146
Papers on Logic, **8:** 283 n.*474*
"Parabola," **4:** 44
Path of Roses, The, **2:** 49 n.*99*, 52 n.*104*, 61
"Peter and Paul," **7:** 418 n.*696*, 529, 530; **8:** 182, 187, 189, 202, 235, 245, 554 n.*883*
Phantasmagoria, **1:** 55 n.*17*, 110 n.*127*; **2:** 89 n.*179*; **4:** 26, 37, 55, 65 n.*1*, 66 n.*3*; **6:** 37, 38 n.*53*, 59 n.*90*, 72, 73 n.*107*, 75, 262 n.*419*, 338, 349, 434, 435, 448; **7:** 22, 85, 108, 326, 351, 368, 380 n.*655*, 439, 521
Photographer's Day Out, A, **4:** 25
Photographic Exhibition, **4:** 25
Photographs, **4:** 35
"Photography Extraordinary," **1:** 132
Pillow Problems, see *Curiosa Mathematica*
"Pixies, The (Three Little)," **5:** 22 n.*16*, 377; **9:** 242
"Poet's Farewell, The," **1:** 37
Postal Problem, A, **8:** 560 n.*892*
Proctorial Cycle, **8:** 206 n.*354*, 207, 244 n.*408*, 245 n.*409*, 246 n.*411*, 247 n.*412*, 247 n.*413*, 248, 249 n.*417*
Professorship of Comparative Philology, The, **6:** 446 n.*733*, 448, 449
Prologue (for Hatch play), **6:** 188 n.*292*
Proportional Representation (also *Parliamentary Elections*), **8:** 103, 106 n.*175*, 108 n.*179*, 116 n.*189*, 118, 119 n.*192*, 126 n.*204*, 149, 150, 151 n.*247*, 156, 158 n.*255*, 162, 163 n.*265*, 166 n.*277*, 182 n.*307*
"Purity of Elections," **7:** 326 n.*578*, 330, 331 n.*589*, 336
"Puzzles from Wonderland," **6:** 127 n.*198*, 134
"Rectification of Curves," **4:** 44
Rectory Magazine, The (family magazine), **1:** 30, 38
Rectory Umbrella, The (family magazine), **1:** 19, 30-33, 37; **3:** 29 n.*42*, 30; **8:** 222 n.*379*, 234, 242
"Redistribution," **8:** 147, 148 n.*240*
"Remarks on the Victims," **7:** 137 n.*252*, 202 n.*378*
Report on Finance Committee, **8:** 261 n.*440*, 262
Resident Women-Students, **9:** 244 n.*385*
Rhyme? and Reason?, **1:** 55 n.*17*, 110 n.*127*, 113 n.*133*; **2:** 89 n.*179*; **7:** 326 n.*577*, 329 n.*583*, 351, 368, 380 n.*655*, 439, 521 n.*845*, 534, 535 n.*866*; **8:** 13, 44 n.*65*, 67
Roll of Senior Students, Ch. Ch., The, **6:** 381 n.*625*
"Romantic Problems," **7:** 265 n.*478*
Rosebud, The (family magazine), **1:** 30, 31

Rules for Court Circular, **4:** 26, 59
"Russian Sons" (puzzle), **8:** 633 n.*1003*
"Sailor's Wife, The," **2:** 52 n.*104*, 113 n.*219*; **3:** 30 n.*43*, 54 n.*83*, 146
"Scholarships at Oxford," **6:** 201 n.*312*
"Schoolroom Shakespeare," see "Girls' Own Shakespeare"
"Sea Dirge, A," **4:** 37, 48, 49
"Select Passages from the *Bible*," **8:** 449 n.*718*
"Sequel to The Shepherd of Salisbury Plain," 59
"Series," **7:** 200 n.*376*, 380 n.*655*
"Serious Poems," see *Three Sunsets and Other Poems*
"She's all my fancy painted him," **1:** 122 n.*151*
"Solid Geometry," **4:** 49
Solitude, **2:** 36 n.*70*, 37, 38 n.*77*, 52 n.*104*
"Some popular fallacies about vivisection," **6:** 390 n.*641*
Song for *Poor Pillicoddy*, **7:** 158 n.*296*
Song for *Puss in Boots*, **6:** 444 n.*729*
"Sonnet" ("Full many a flower" for Mary's poetry album), **2:** 12 n.*15*, 40 n.*80*; **3:** 41 n.*64*, 146
"Sport, Morality of," **9:** 93, 94 n.*170*
"Stage, and the Spirit of Reverence, The," **8:** 395 n.*641*
Star, The (family magazine), **1:** 30, 31
"Stolen Waters," **4:** 65 n.*1*
"Storm, The," **1:** 33
"Study from English Poets," **1:** 122 n.*151*
Suggestions as to Election of Proctors, see *Proctorial Cycle*
Suggestions for the Committee Appointed to Consider Senior Studentships, **6:** 148 n.*226*, 154 n.*236*, 155
Supplement to "Euclid and His Modern Rivals," **8:** 179 n.*295*, 186, 191
Supplement to "Twelve Months in a Curatorship," **8:** 92 n.*150*
Syllabus of Plane Algebraical Geometry, **1:** 97 n.*102*; **4:** 37, 48; **5:** 27, 28 n.*28*
Sylvie and Bruno, **1:** 20, 31; **3:** 39 n.*60*; **6:** 249, 250, 321, 376; **7:** 329 n.*583*, 351, 368, 380 n.*655*, 418 n.*696*, 456; **8:** 143 n.*231*, 183 n.*309*, 229, 230, 285, 305, 306 n.*506*, 355 n.*581*, 359, 370, 384, 415, 416, 434, 445, 449, 475, 481, 483, 487-495; **9:** 125, 171, 176
Sylvie and Bruno Concluded, **8:** 434, 521, 522, 604; **9:** 16, 17 n.*14*, 54, 83, 93, 94 n.*170*, 101, 102, 105-111, 116, 125, 126 n.*222*, 171, 176; dedicatory poem, **9:** 102
Symbolic Logic, **1:** 129 n.*159*; **8:** 180 n.*300*, 246, 285 n.*478*, 355; **9:** 50-52, 54, 128 n.*224*, 136 n.*238*, 157, 181, 183, 191 n.*315*, 229-231, 235, 237, 239, 241 n.*379*, 244, 256 n.*405*, 261 n.*413*, 273
Symbols and Abbreviations for Euclid, **5:** 128 n.*206*
Syzygies, **7:** 228 n.*422*; **8:** 556, 557 n.*886*, 564, 567, 571, 577, 601
Syzygies and Lanrick, **9:** 51
Tangled Tale, A, **2:** 57 n.*115*; **7:** 265 n.*478*, 329 n.*583*, 410 n.*690*, 498,

546; **8:** 162 n.*264*, 180 n.*301*, 218 n.*371*, 219, 254 n.*427*
Telegraph Cipher, **2:** 42 n.*83*; **6:** 28 n.*32*
"Tema Con Variazion," see "The Dear Gazelle"
"Theorem of Tangents," **4:** 26
Three Sunsets and Other Poems, **4:** 65 n.*1*; **7:** 380 n.*655*; **8:** 181 n.*304*; **9:** 197
"Three Voices, The," **1:** 110 n.*127*; **2:** 52 n.*104*, 89 n.*179*, 105 n.*201*, 107; **7:** 104 n.*194*, 106
"Thrillings," **1:** 31
Through the Looking-Glass, **1:** 12, 20, 36; **2:** 99 n.*191*; **4:** 173 n.*169*; **5:** 192 n.*314*, 379 n.*561*; **6:** 20 n.*22*, 22, 30, 37 n.*32*, 59, 76 n.*111*, 79 n.*115*, 112, 121, 139 n.*211*, 140, 145, 146, 164, 179, 187-190, 200; **7:** 44; **8:** 369 n.*606*, 371, 373; **9:** 105, 106 n.*190*, 107, 115 n.*200*, 134 n.*235*, 275 n.*440*, 326 n.*523*, 340
"Time and Tide," **1:** 120, 121, 122 n.*151*
To All Child-Readers of Alice, **6:** 189 n.*293*
"Tommy's Dead," **3:** 141 n.*209*, 147
Tragedy of King John, The, **1:** 81, 82 n.*84*
"Treatise on Order of Religious Ideas," **8:** 472 n.*765*
Twelve Months in a Curatorship, **8:** 71, 72, 90 n.*147*
"Unknown One, The," **1:** 29
"Upon the Lonely Moor," **2:** 52 n.*104*, 99 n.*191*; **3:** 181
Useful and Instructive Poetry (family magazine), **1:** 30, 31
"Vernon Gallery, The," **1:** 35
Verse riddles, see "Puzzles from Wonderland"
"Victor and Arnion," **9:** 333, 334 n.*534*, 335
Vision of the Three T's, The, **6:** 265 n.*426*, 267 n.*430*, 273, 275
"Vivisection Vivisected," **8:** 172 n.*289*
"Walking-Stick of Destiny, The," **1:** 35
"Ways and Means" (game), **1:** 126 n.*155*; **4:** 114 n.*83*
"Where does the day begin?" **1:** 35, 36; **3:** 29 n.*42*, 54, 146; **4:** 57; **8:** 190 n.*321*
"Whoso Shall Offend One Of Those Little Ones," **8:** 222 n.*381*
"Wilhelm von Schmitz," **1:** 48, 54 n.*13*, 110 n.*128*, 116
Will-o'-the-Wisp, The (family magazine), **1:** 30, 31
"Will you walk a little faster," **2:** 17 n.*30*
Wise Words, **8:** 518 n.*834*
"Woes," **1:** 32
Wonderland Postage Stamp-Case, **8:** 432 n.*696*, 518 n.*834*
"Word-Links" – see *Doublets*
"Word-Music," **3:** 36 n.*56*, 146
"Ye Carpette Knyghte," **1:** 55 n.*17*; **2:** 37, 52 n.*104*
"Ye Fatalle Cheyse," **1:** 33
"Zoological Papers," **1:** 35

Writing table purchase, **6:** 420 n.*689*

Dodgson Motto, **2:** 42, 43 n.*84*
Dods (of Tynterfield, Sale, Cheshire):
Agnes Allen, Mrs. (b. 1842), **6:** 172 n.*268*, 176
Harriet (b. 1857), **6:** 172 n.*268*, 176
Mary (b. 1860), **6:** 172 n.*268*, 176
Peter, Lt. Col. (b. 1829), **6:** 172 n.*268*, 176, 426
Dodson (of Abingdon, Berkshire):
Frances A. (b. 1830), **5:** 55 n.*78*, 86
Mary Ann née Wapshare, **5:** 55 n.*78*
Nathaniel, Rev. (1787-1867), **5:** 55 n.*78*
Dodson, Mr., **6:** 110, 111 n.*173*
Doge of Duralto, The (dr. Robert Brough), **3:** 153 n.*223*
Doig, Henry (b. 1813) – agent for Sir Joseph Noël Paton, **6:** 181 n.*282*, 185
Dolby, see Sainton-Dolby
Dominique's Restaurant, Nevski, St. Petersburg, **5:** 340
Dommett (of Penge, Surrey):
Charles W., Mr. (b. 1839) – solicitor, **7:** 209 n.*388*, 210
Clara E. (b. 1873), **7:** 208, 209 n.*388*, 213
Frances Emily (b. 1870), **7:** 208, 209 n.*388*, 213
Isabel J. (b. 1867), **7:** 208, 209 n.*388*, 213
Mary F., Mrs. (b. 1834), **7:** 209 n.*388*, 210
William (b. 1869), **7:** 209 n.*388*
Donaldson (of Chiswick, London):
Alyce (b. 1876), **8:** 557 n.*887*
Frances, Mrs. (b. 1847), **8:** 557 n.*887*
John, Mr. (b. 1842) – civil engineer, **8:** 557 n.*887*
Thornycroft (b. 1873), **8:** 557 n.*887*
Donaldson, Margaret (b. 1864) – teacher, **9:** 176 n.*296*, 207, 278
Doncaster, Yorkshire, **5:** 191, 369; **6:** 55, 56, 108, 110
Done Brown (dr. Henry Craven), **1:** 133 n.*168*; **2:** 88 n.*177*; **3:** 85 n.*132*, 146
"Don Giovanni" (in *Faust*), **3:** 106
Donizetti, Gaetano (1797-1848) – composer, **3:** 50 n.*76*, 98 n.*147*
Donkin (of Oxford):
Alice Emily (1850-1900?), **4:** 33, 219; **5:** 149 n.*240*; **6:** 149, 388; **7:** 179, 180 n.*333*
Arthur Edward (b. 1848), **6:** 149, 304 n.*303*, 317; **8:** 454 n.*728*
Harriet née Hawtrey (1815-1876), **6:** 218, 388
William Fishburn, Prof. (1814-1869) – professor of astronomy, **4:** 131 n.*106*, 260; **5:** 149 n.*240*; **6:** 52 n.*74*, 67
William Frederick (b. 1846), **6:** 149
Donkin (of Barmby Moor and Sleights):
Alice Jane (1851-1929), see Dodgson

Edward (b. 1854?), **4:** 131 n.*106*, 131 n.*107*, 134
Edward, Mr. (b. 1827) – land agent, **4:** 130, 131 n.*106*, 134, 231, 298, 299; **6:** 52 n.*74*, 171
Francis "Frank" H. (b. 1852), **4:** 131 n.*106*, 131 n.*107*, 134; **7:** 446 n.*737*
Henry (b. 1859), **4:** 131 n.*106*, 131 n.*107*, 134
Mary Eleanor "Polly" (b. 1856?), see Smith
Mary née Watt (b. 1824), **4:** 130, 131 n.*106*, 134, 231 n.*256*, 298, 299; **6:** 52 n.*74*, 171, 239
Don Pasquale (Donizetti) – opera, **3:** 98 n.*147*
Dora (pic. Edwin Long), **6:** 73 n.*108*
Dorcas – Mrs. Dyer's maid at Eastbourne, **8:** 128
Dorchester, Oxfordshire, **4:** 195; **5:** 90, 135; **7:** 335
Dorking, Surrey, **6:** 43, 45, 225, 295
Dorothy (B. C. Stephenson and Alfred Cellier) – operetta, **8:** 367 n.*601*, 523, 524; **9:** 212, 213 n.*340*
Dot (dr. Dion Boucicault), **8:** 373, 374 n.*616*
Dotheboy's Hall from *Nicholas Nickleby* (bk. Charles Dickens), **2:** 98
Doubleday's Will (dr. Anon), **7:** 131 n.*245*
Douglas, Angus (b. 1855?) – artists' model, **4:** 252 n.*291*
Douglas (of Stanway, Gloucestershire):
Anne Frederica Anson, Lady Elcho (d. 1896), **4:** 342 n.*444*
Francis Richard, Lord Elcho (1818-1914), **4:** 342 n.*444*
Doull – pupil of Henry Barclay, **8:** 160 n.*260*
Dover, Kent, **5:** 254, 255, 369; **6:** 185, 186, 466
Down Place, Compton, Surrey, **7:** 11, 344
Dowsing's, see Trafalgar Hotel
Dowson, John, Dr. – physician, **2:** 46 n.*91*
Doyle, Francis Hastings (1810-1888) – professor of poetry, **5:** 249 n.*407*
Doyle, Richard (1824-1883) – illustrator, **4:** 16; **5:** 25, 192 n.*315*; **8:** 168 n.*279*
Doyne (of Oxford):
Gertrude Irene Hope née Hollings (b. 1865), **8:** 265 n.*445*, 273, 274
Robert Walter, Dr. (1857-1916) – opthalmist, **8:** 265 n.*445*, 268, 269, 273, 275, 389
Drage (of Somerset):
F. Gertrude, Mrs. (b. 1842), **7:** 190 n.*352*
Gerida (b. 1865), **7:** 189, 190 n.*352*, 274, 280 n.*511*
Gertrude (b. 1864), **7:** 189, 190 n.*352*, 274, 280 n.*511*
William Henry, Maj. (1828-1921) – army officer, **7:** 190 n.*352*
Drage (of Hatfield, Hertfordshire):
Geoffrey (1860-1955) – politician, **8:** 55 n.*83*
Lovell (b. 1858) – physician, **8:** 55 n.*83*
Dramatic Recitations, **9:** 20 n.*22*
Dramatic School of Art, **7:** 404 n.*685*, 405, 410, 411 n.*691*, 415 n.*694*
Draper (of Alfreton, Derbyshire):

Charlotte Edith née Denman (1855-1884), **4:** 36, 179, 319 n.*405*, 327, 328 n.*417*, 328 n.*418*; **5:** 19, 88; **6:** 20; **7:** 113 n.*208*, 187, 188, 330, 343, 344, 376 n.*651*, 395, 396, 516 n.*836*, 517; **8:** 143 n.*232*, 146, 147, 160 n.*258*
William Henry, Rev. (1855-1933), **7:** 516 n.*836*; **8:** 143 n.*232*, 146
Draper (of Crouch End, Middlesex):
Dorothy "Dolly" Ellen (b. 1863), see Walton
Edward Thompson, Mr. (1825-1887) – agent for the Royal Marines, **7:** 29 n.*39*
Ellen, Mrs. (b. 1835), **7:** 29 n.*39*
Roger Edward (b. 1867), **7:** 29 n.*39*
"Draw the sword, Scotland" (James Planché) – song, **5:** 225, 226 n.*359*
"Dreaded independent MA" – member of Christ Church Common Room, **7:** 321, 322 n.*571*
Dreaming of Fairy-land (pic. Thomas Heaphy), **6:** 15 n.*9*, 27 n.*31*, 71, 82 n.*120*
Dream of the Atonement, A (bk. Anon), **7:** 517 n.*838*
Dred (bk. Harriet Beecher Stowe), **2:** 99 n.*190*
Dresden, Germany, **5:** 354-357; **6:** 410
Dresden Picture-Gallery, **5:** 355, 357 n.*530*
Drew (of Eton, Buckinghamshire):
Frederic, Mr. (1836-1891) – teacher, **9:** 183 n.*304*
Frederic Henry (b. 1880), **9:** 183 n.*304*
Helen (1881-1927), **9:** 183 n.*304*, 254
Leslie (b. 1891), **9:** 183 n.*304*
Mabel (b. 1877), **9:** 183 n.*304*
Sara Constance, Mrs. (b. 1847), **9:** 183 n.*304*, 254
Drew, Mrs. – friend of the Lucys, **9:** 254 n.*399*
Drewitt (of Kensington, London):
Caroline Mary, Mrs. (d. 1940), **7:** 149 n.*282*
Frederick George Dawtrey, Dr. (1848-1942) – physician, **7:** 149 n.*282*, 150 n.*283*
Drewitt, Miss – friend of the Barclay Thompsons, **7:** 116, 117 n.*218*
Driver (of Oxford):
Mabel née Burr (b. 1867), **8:** 608 n.*964*; **9:** 309 n.*490*
Samuel Rolles, Rev. Dr. (1846-1914) – professor of Hebrew, **8:** 259 n.*438*
Dr. Mark's Little Men – juvenile theatre group, **3:** 91 n.*141*, 93
Drownings, **6:** 209, 355
Druce, Amy Laura (b. 1861), **9:** 125 n.*220*, 127, 143
Druitt, Robert (b. 1847) – solicitor, **6:** 168 n.*262*
Drury (of Radnor Place, London):
Emily "Emmie" Henrietta (1864-1930), see Wyper
Isabella "Ella" Maude (1862-1884), see Fischer
James Samuel, Dr. (1822-1865) – physician, **6:** 91 n.*140*, 356
Mary "Minnie" Frances (1859-1935), see Fuller

Sophia Louisa née Bousfield (1830-1886), **6:** 91 n.*140*, 94, 122, 196, 200, 220, 223, 256, 260, 317, 333, 339, 352, 356, 411; **7:** 155, 156 n.*294*, 186, 187, 230, 234, 235, 315, 316, 319, 350, 368, 369, 415, 422, 453, 515; **8:** 48 n.*70*, 58, 108, 110-112, 115, 125, 140, 165, 189, 219, 268, 299
Dryden, John (1631-1700) – poet and dramatist, **3:** 60
Dry Sandford, Oxfordshire, **3:** 46
Dublin Castle (ship), **7:** 314
Dublin Pantomime, **9:** 55
Dubourg (of Alfred Place West, London):
Augustus Henry (b. 1859), **7:** 15, 96, 256, 278; **8:** 345
Augustus William, Mr. (1830-1910) – civil servant and dramatist, **6:** 86 n.*129*, 255 n.*407*, 258, 286, 288, 289, 300, 310, 311, 313, 315-317, 335, 336, 349, 353, 359, 360, 397, 398, 414, 466; **7:** 13, 14 n.*8*, 15, 17, 95, 97, 111, 114, 117, 122, 140, 158, 159, 180, 194, 256, 277, 328, 396, 404, 441, 447, 541; **8:** 66 n.*105*, 68-70, 113, 345, 411, 412, 456, 581, 619; **9:** 55 n.*96*
Charles, **6:** 310; **7:** 15
Ellen née Nightingale (b. 1829), **6:** 86 n.*129*, 258, 286, 288, 289, 313, 315-317, 335, 349, 353, 359, 360, 397, 398, 414, 466; **7:** 95, 97, 111, 114, 117, 122, 140, 158, 159, 180, 194, 256, 277, 328, 396, 441, 442, 541; **8:** 66 n.*105*, 110, 113, 165, 345, 410, 411, 456, 581, 619; **9:** 55 n.*96*
Evelyn "Evey" Sophia (1861-1917), see Alexander
Kathleen, **6:** 86 n.*129*, 397
Seymour James (b. 1856), **6:** 86 n.*129*, 288; **7:** 15
Du Cane (of Eastbourne, Sussex):
Katherine (b. 1863), **8:** 39 n.*54*
Louisa F. (b. 1861), **8:** 39 n.*54*
Louisa T., Mrs. (b. 1827), **8:** 39 n.*54*
Duckworth (of Lambeth, Surrey):
Ada Gertrude (b. 1872), **6:** 483 n.*796*, 484
Beatrice E. (b. 1874), **6:** 483 n.*796*, 484; **7:** 45 n.*69*
Edith R. (b. 1870), **6:** 483 n.*796*, 484
Isabel (b. 1879), **6:** 483 n.*796*
Philip (b. 1880), **6:** 483 n.*796*
Phillippa I., Mrs. (b. 1845), **6:** 483 n.*796*, 484; **7:** 124, 142
William M. (b. 1876), **6:** 483 n.*796*, 484
William M., Mr. (b. 1845) – journalist, **6:** 483 n.*796*, 484; **7:** 124, 142
Duckworth, Robinson, Rev. (1834-1911), **1:** 43; **3:** 61 n.*92*; **4:** 24, 81 n.*33*, 82 n.*34*, 83, 88, 94, 195, 196, 201, 298; **5:** 25, 56 n.*80*, 371 n.*551*; **6:** 393 n.*644*, 466; **8:** 99 n.*164*, 232 n.*394*
Du Croz - or Du Crow (of London and West Hoathly, Sussex):
Miss, **6:** 377 n.*616*
Mr., **6:** 377 n.*616*

Mrs., **6:** 377 n.*616*
Violet, **7:** 312 n.*557*
Duff Gordon (of Walsingham House, Piccadilly, London):
Alexander Cornewall, Sir (1811-1872), **4:** 246 n.*279*
Urania "Ranie" (d. 1877), **4:** 246 n.*279*, 248 n.*283*
Duggan (of Eastbourne, Sussex):
Joseph (b. 1875), **8:** 230, 231 n.*390*
Kathleen (b. 1877), **8:** 230, 231 n.*390*
Duggan, Mary "Maggie" (1860-1919) – actress, **8:** 285, 286 n.*480*
Duke (of Chichester, Sussex):
Francis, Rev. (b. 1840), **6:** 231 n.*363*
Laura, **6:** 231 n.*363*
Lilian Augusta? "Gussie" (b. 1863), **6:** 231 n.*363*
Mary A., Mrs. (b. 1839), **6:** 231 n.*363*
Duke (of Chichester, Sussex):
Francis (b. 1840), see above
Mary R., Mrs. (b. 1804), **6:** 231 n.*363*
William, Mr. (b. 1807) – bailiff and solicitor, **6:** 231 n.*363*
Duke of York's Column, London, **4:** 109
Dukes, Edward Rowland (1817-1883) – tutor and rhetoric reader, **4:** 212 n.*223*; **7:** 115 n.*213*, 321; **8:** 43 n.*62*
Duke's Motto,The (dr. John Brougham), **4:** 182 n.*177*, 221
Dulwich College, Surrey, **3:** 150
Dulwich Gallery, **2:** 22
Dumas, Alexandre (1802-1870) – writer, **4:** 248 n.*282*
Du Maurier (of Hampstead, London):
Beatrix C. J. (1864-1913), **5:** 380 n.*563*; **6:** 19 n.*18*, 316, 404 n.*664*, 405 n.*665*
Emma B. née Wightwick (b. 1841), **5:** 380 n.*563*; **6:** 19 n.*18*, 114, 316, 404, 405; **7:** 104
George Louis Palmella Busson, Mr. (1834-1896) – novelist, actor, artist, **5:** 36 n.*44*, 141 n.*225*, 240 n.*389*, 370 n.*549*, 380 n.*563*; **6:** 18, 19 n.*18*, 114, 262 n.*419*, 316, 404, 405; **7:** 104 n.*195*; **8:** 319 n.*523*
Guy (1865-1915), **5:** 380 n.*563*; **6:** 316; **7:** 104 n.*195*
Marie "May" D. (b. 1869), **6:** 316, 405 n.*665*
Sylvia J. (b. 1867), **6:** 316, 405 n.*665*
Dundas, Misses – friends of the Argles, **6:** 109
Dunkeld, Scotland, **6:** 184
Durrant (of Kensington, London):
Alice Mabel (b. 1871), **7:** 528 n.*854*
Arabella, Mrs. (b. 1846), **7:** 528 n.*854*
Edith M. (b. 1868), **7:** 528 n.*854*
Frederick William, Mr. (b. 1824) – estate agent, **7:** 528 n.*854*
Helen "Nellie" M. (b. 1870), **7:** 528 n.*854*
Dusseaux's Restaurant, St. Petersburg, **5:** 346

Duval, Mary (b. 1827) – lodging-house keeper, **7:** 462
Duverger, Théophile Emmanuel (1821-1901?) – artist, **5:** 224 n.*357*
Dyce, William (1806-1864) – artist, **3:** 78 n.*122*
Dyer (of Lushington Road, Eastbourne, Sussex):
Benjamin, Mr. (b. 1849) – postman, **7:** 51 n.*81*, 463
Caroline, Mrs. (b. 1847) – lodging-house keeper, **7:** 51 n.*81*, 127, 140, 181, 198, 281, 282, 296, 298, 350, 354, 368, 454, 467, 480; **8:** 16 n.*10*, 68 n.*110*, 128, 218, 345, 411, 569, 592 n.*944*, 611 n.*968*; **9:** 79 n.*146*, 82, 91 n.*167*, 265 n.*418*, 271 n.*429*, 315 n.*503*, 325 n.*521*, 328
"Dorcas" (maid), **8:** 128
Emma (b. 1873), **7:** 51 n.*81*
"Jane" (maid), **7:** 480
John F. (b. 1875), **7:** 51 n.*81*, 140, 296
William (b. 1876), **7:** 51 n.*81*, 140, 296
Dyer-Edwardes (of Prinknash Park, Gloucestershire):
Clementina Georgina Lucy Drummond née Villiers, **8:** 212 n.*362*, 318, 335
Noëlle Lucy Martha (1878-1956), **8:** 212 n.*362*, 318, 335
Thomas, Mr. (1847-1926), **8:** 212 n.*362*
Dykes (of St. Oswald's, Durham):
Caroline Sybil (b. 1856), **4:** 129 n.*105*
Ernest Huntingdon (1851-1924), **4:** 129 n.*105*
Ethel Susan (b. 1859), **4:** 129 n.*105*
George Lionel Andrew (b. & d. 1857), **4:** 129 n.*105*
Gertrude Kingston (b. 1854), **4:** 129 n.*105*
John Arthur St. Oswald (b. 1863), **4:** 129 n.*105*
John Bacchus, Rev. (1823-1876) – hymn-tune composer, **4:** 129 n.*105*
Mabel Hey (1860-1870), **4:** 129 n.*105*
Mary E. (b. 1852), **4:** 129 n.*105*
Susannah née Kingston (b. 1827), **4:** 129 n.*105*
Dymes (of Eastbourne, Sussex):
Amelia, Mrs. (b. 1835), **7:** 49 n.*77*, 50, 55, 58, 61, 64, 67, 70, 73, 74, 128, 132, 134, 181, 203, 209, 218, 219, 283, 352, 354, 358, 368, 454, 462, 466; **8:** 22, 23 n.*20*, 38, 62, 63, 65, 66, 72, 212, 304, 406, 409
Amelia May "Mamie" (b. 1863), **7:** 49 n.*77*, 73, 128, 181, 218, 219, 302, 358, 458, 463, 470; **8:** 48, 87
Beatrice Laura (b. 1871), **7:** 49 n.*77*, 63, 73, 74, 181, 218; **8:** 38-41, 62, 165, 373
Ethel D. (b. 1864), **7:** 49 n.*77*, 73, 128, 181, 202, 204, 205, 218, 283, 454, 459, 479; **8:** 26, 103 n.*172*, 406
Helen (b. 1872), **7:** 49 n.*77*, 63, 74, 135, 138, 181, 218, 282; **8:** 62, 409
Margaret "Margie" Henrietta (1868-1957), **7:** 49 n.*77*, 59, 61, 62, 64-66, 72-74, 128-130, 132, 134-138, 181, 200, 208, 210, 213, 218, 219, 282, 356, 362, 366, 367, 455, 458-461, 468, 471, 473, 477, 478; **8:** 22 n.*18*, 26, 27, 38-41, 48, 56, 60-62, 65, 83, 85, 89, 91, 94, 131, 144-146, 304,

366, 367, 373, 413, 415, 475
Maud S. (b. 1874), **7:** 49 n.*77*, 73, 74, 181, 218, 286, 287; **8:** 62, 409
Ruth Hester (1869-1940), **7:** 49 n.*77*, 59, 61, 62, 64-66, 72-74, 128, 130, 132, 134, 137, 138, 181, 198, 202-204, 213, 218, 286, 287, 297, 362, 366, 455, 458-461, 472, 477, 478; **8:** 22 n.*18*, 29, 33, 34, 40, 41, 42 n.*59*, 65, 79 n.*122*, 142 n.*230*, 144-146, 148 n.*241*, 165, 373, 374
Thomas Jamieson, Mr. (1831-1913) – teacher, **7:** 49 n.*77*, 50, 58, 61, 64, 67, 73, 74, 128, 132, 134, 203, 209, 218, 352, 358, 454, 458, 462, 466; **8:** 22, 23 n.*20*, 33 n.*39*, 36, 48, 62, 63, 65, 66, 72, 165, 212, 304, 406, 409, 570, 571
Thomas "Tommy" A. (b. 1866), **7:** 49 n.*77*, 63, 72, 204, 218
"Dynamite" (pseudonym), **8:** 132 n.*216*
Dyster, Frederick Daniel (1810-1893) – physician, **4:** 187, 188 n.*183*

Ealing, Middlesex, **5:** 151, 159; **6:** 344; **7:** 77, 376
Earle (of Norham Gardens, Oxford):
Beatrice "Bee" Anne (1868-1938), **7:** 35 n.*50*, 499; **8:** 43 n.*60*, 85, 102, 252, 281, 282, 556, 561, 563, 621; **9:** 56 n.*99*, 62
Charles Chretien (b. 1865), **7:** 35 n.*50*, 499
Dorothy "Dolly" Charlotte (1874-1942), **7:** 35 n.*50*, 499; **8:** 85; **9:** 57, 257
Jane née Rolleston (1834-1911), **7:** 35 n.*50*; **8:** 43 n.*60*, 85, 188, 218, 252, 268, 281, 343, 595; **9:** 56 n.*99*, 57, 133
John, Rev. (1824-1903) – professor of Anglo Saxon, **6:** 486 n.*801*; **7:** 35 n.*50*, 36, 163, 175, 262, 432, 499; **8:** 43 n.*60*, 85, 268, 281, 595; **9:** 56 n.*99*, 57
John Rolleston (1865-1933), **7:** 35 n.*50*, 499
Katherine Margaret "Maggie" (1872-1934), **7:** 35 n.*50*, 499; **8:** 43 n.*60*, 85, 86, 92, 111, 188, 252, 333, 334
Mary Rosamond "Sissie" (1867-1927), **7:** 35 n.*50*, 499; **8:** 85, 86, 92, 94, 218, 230, 252, 265, 268, 281, 319, 343, 373, 376, 453, 559
Earle (of Newington, Surrey):
Clara Elizabeth née Johnstone (b. 1855), **8:** 583 n.*931*, 614, 615; **9:** 16 n.*11*, 55, 59, 106, 215
Clara Maria (b. 1879), **8:** 583 n.*931*, 592, 614, 615, 633; **9:** 16 n.*11*, 55, 122, 138, 140, 215
Eliza "Lizzie" (b. 1884), **8:** 583 n.*931*, 592, 614, 615, 633; **9:** 55, 215
Lilian "Lillie" or "Lily" (b. 1882), **8:** 583 n.*931*, 614, 633; **9:** 55, 59, 215
Robert John (b. 1876), **8:** 583 n.*931*, 614
Robert John, Mr. (b. 1850) – mercantile clerk, **8:** 583 n.*931*; **9:** 16 n.*11*, 59
Earle (of Harrow, Middlesex):
Frances, Mrs. (b. 1847), **6:** 411, 412 n.*673*
Frederick, Mr. (b. 1841) – schoolmaster, **6:** 411, 412 n.*673*
Earley, Berkshire, **6:** 96
Earl's Court, London, **7:** 110

Earl's Terrace, London, **5:** 21
Earp, Mary S. (b. 1860) – teacher, **9:** 259 n.*408*
Easby, Yorkshire, **4:** 231
Easington, Yorkshire, **1:** 124 n.*153*; **2:** 118 n.*226*
East Bergholt, Suffolk, **1:** 107

Eastbourne:
Abergeldie, **7:** 469
Albion Hotel, **9:** 161, 334, 335
All Saints Church, **8:** 418
All Souls' Church, **8:** 293, 294
Athletic Sports, **7:** 64
Beach Services, **7:** 67
Beachy Head, **7:** 27, 50, 51, 65, 136, 138, 204, 216, 290, 364, 455, 470; **8:** 33, 35, 39, 143, 144, 228, 233, 367, 416, 428, 429, 478, 481, 485, 520, 569; **9:** 14, 83, 93, 95, 101, 159, 171, 174, 330, 331
Blackwater Road School, **8:** 38 n.*52*, 39
Bourne Street, **7:** 52
Burlington Hotel, **7:** 27
Burlington Place Chapel, **7:** 130
Christ Church, **7:** 130, 132-137, 198, 202, 212, 282, 300, 455, 456, 459, 461, 466, 470, 472, 473; **8:** 22, 40, 228, 358, 421, 426, 476, 485, 529, 568, 578; **9:** 15, 30, 91, 94, 157, 211, 271, 272, 274, 328, 331, 333-335, 340, 341
Christ Church National Schools, Whitley Road, **9:** 337-339, 342, 343
College, **7:** 49 n.*77*
Compton Place (Flower Show), **7:** 356, 460 n.*759*; **8:** 24, 230, 358, 420, 479, 526, 573; **9:** 25, 90, 159, 273, 332
Cycle Tournament, **8:** 476
Devonshire Club, **7:** 55
Devonshire Park, **7:** 69, 130, 199, 201, 203, 216, 218, 219, 286, 354-357, 359, 360, 363, 366, 457-459, 461, 463-465, 467, 469-471, 473-475, 478, 479; **8:** 22, 24, 26-29, 33-37, 39, 129, 137, 139, 140, 144, 145, 227, 232, 236, 237, 286, 291, 293, 354, 357, 361, 367, 415, 417, 421, 422, 427, 476, 480, 573, 585; **9:** 15, 20, 22, 24, 26, 28, 29, 91, 92, 212, 213, 272, 273, 331
Devonshire Park Baths, **8:** 228, 235 n.*397*, 480
Devonshire Park Theatre, **8:** 138, 229, 287, 357, 363, 423, 478, 485, 523, 530, 572, 589; **9:** 15, 91, 161-163, 273, 274, 335
Devonshire Pavilion, **7:** 68, 134
Diplock's Assembly Rooms, **7:** 138
Dirleton, Jevington Road School, **8:** 295, 299
Dog Show, **7:** 359
Donnington (School), Enys Road, **8:** 413
Fort, **8:** 138

Gildridge Road, **8:** 22, 101
Grand Hotel, **9:** 160
Grosvenor House Hotel, **7:** 27
Holywell, **9:** 95
Illuminated Fête (Devonshire Park), **8:** 232, 236, 289, 360, 422, 423, 480, 572
Library, **7:** 291
Lighthouse, **9:** 93
Lodgings, **8:** 16, 22, 101, 218, 284, 345, 519; **9:** 13, 20, 28, 82 n.*150*, 101, 153, 207, 265, 271 n.*429*, 328, 334
Lushington Road, **7:** 51 n.*81*, 127, 135, 198, 282, 297; **8:** 25, 26
Marine Parade, **7:** 52, 53, 58, 59, 62, 69, 70, 205, 206
Marionette Entertainment, **7:** 367
Murrells Workshops, **7:** 478
Ocklynge Mission-Room, **9:** 92, 94, 97, 175
Parade, **8:** 522
"Paradise," **7:** 66, 72; **8:** 27, 41, 232, 355, 357, 359, 475
Pavilion, see Devonshire Pavilion
Pier, **7:** 52, 55, 58, 60, 61, 65, 66, 69, 74, 128-130, 132, 133, 136, 198, 208, 210, 213, 215, 216, 282-284, 287, 458, 470; **8:** 26, 234, 289, 293, 414, 415, 485, 526, 528; **9:** 164, 272
Postmaster, **9:** 278
Post Office, **7:** 129
Procession of Roses, **9:** 207
Queen's Hotel, **7:** 466
Regatta, **7:** 57, 132, 363
Rink, **7:** 128, 201, 205, 295, 353, 472-474, 476
St. Andrew's, Norway Schools, **9:** 340, 342 n.*547*, 343
St. Anne's Church, Upperton, **8:** 418, 421, 423, 426, 476
St. Peter's Church, **8:** 22, 529; **9:** 91
St. Saviour's Church, **7:** 60-62, 67, 129, 134, 136, 139, 200, 212, 461, 462, 466; **8:** 286, 423, 529; **9:** 14
Sea Side Road Theatre, **8:** 135, 285, 428, 569, 577, 586; **9:** 26, 164, 166, 212, 213, 272, 277, 331, 332
Sunday School Union, **8:** 345
Sussex Hotel, **9:** 92
Swimming Entertainment, **9:** 273, 332
Town, **6:** 128; **7:** 27, 28, 48, 127, 181, 197, 212, 217-219, 281, 289, 295, 303, 305, 350, 360, 362, 367, 444, 453, 454, 461, 469, 473, 477, 480, 487, 545; **8:** 16, 22, 32, 101, 127, 192, 222, 227, 229, 236, 237, 240, 242, 284, 290, 297-299, 345, 354, 357, 362, 367, 402, 413, 420, 472, 520, 568, 576; **9:** 14, 24, 27, 32, 82, 156, 159, 207, 271, 328
Town Hall, **8:** 354, 425, 485, 521, 529, 583; **9:** 20, 28
Trinity Church, **7:** 52, 54, 67, 132, 300
Upperton, **9:** 97

Wish Tower, **8:** 231, 426

East Dean, Sussex, **7:** 138, 470
Easter and Act Term, **2:** 60
Easter eggs, **2:** 56
Eastern Telegraph Company, **8:** 190 n.*321*
Easthampstead, Berkshire, **6:** 87
Eastlake, Mary (1856-1911) – actress, **7:** 525 n.*849*, 540; **8:** 59, 80, 81 n.*125*, 113, 168, 208, 234, 274, 381
East Lynne (dr. John Oxenford), **9:** 331, 332 n.*530*
East Meon, Hampshire, **7:** 116 n.*216*
East Sheen, London, **4:** 122, 183, 314; **5:** 73
East Terrace, Whitby, **2:** 15 n.*25*, 102
Eaton, Berkshire, **3:** 165
Eaton (of Alvechurch, Worcester):
Dorothy Charlotte (b. 1879), **7:** 346 n.*607*
John Richard Turner, Rev. (b. 1825), **7:** 346 n.*607*
Julia Mary, Mrs. (b. 1837), **7:** 346 n.*607*
Mary Rosamond (b. 1872), **7:** 346 n.*607*
Eaton Square Chapel, London, **6:** 198, 251, 257
Ecclesiastical Commission, **5:** 15
Eckersall, Charles, Rev. (1797-1863), **1:** 95 n.*98*, 96; **2:** 15 n.*24*
Eclipse of moon, **7:** 64
Eden (of Weekley, Northampton):
Fanny H., Mrs. (1843), **8:** 206 n.*352*
Frederick Morton, Mr. (b. 1829) – barrister and land agent, **8:** 206 n.*352*
Edens (of St. Aldates, Oxford):
Ellen, Mrs. (b. 1843), **9:** 287 n.*454*
George, Mr. (b. 1846) – lodging-house keeper, **9:** 287 n.*454*
Edgbaston High School for Girls, **8:** 89 n.*145*, 122; **9:** 263, 306
Edgemonde, Shropshire, **6:** 387
Edgeworth (of Banda, India):
Christina née Macpherson, **7:** 148, 149 n.*281*
Michael Pakenham, Mr. (1812-1881) – botanist and civil servant, **7:** 148, 149 n.*281*
Edgeworth, Maria (1767-1849) – novelist, **7:** 149 n.*281*
Edinburgh, Scotland, **3:** 94, 97-104, 144; **6:** 179, 183, 184, 186
Edinburgh Castle, **3:** 97
Edinburgh Cathedral, **7:** 448
Edinburgh National Gallery, **3:** 102
Edison's Phonograph, **8:** 523 n.*840*, 524
Editha's Burglar (dr. Frances Hodgson Burnett and Stephen Townsend), **8:** 440 n.*705*
Edmond, J. – dramatist, **5:** 38 n.*46*
Edmonds, Emily – actress, **2:** 22 n.*40*

"Edmund Hyde, Lord Clarendon" – article for *The Train* (Frederick Arnold), **2:** 84 n.*167*
Edmunds, Mr. – actor, **4:** 315
Edouin (of London):
Rose, Mrs. (1845-1925), **8:** 237 n.*399*
Willie, Mr. (1846-1908) – dramatist and theatre manager, **8:** 237 n.*399*, 530
Educational Times, **7:** 223 n.*409*; **8:** 172 n.*289*; **9:** 342 n.*546*
Edwardes (of Banbury Road, Oxford):
Avice K. (b. 1880), **9:** 181, 182 n.*302*, 183
Edward, **9:** 182 n.*302*
Ela G. (b. 1876), **9:** 182 n.*302*
Ellen, Mrs. (b. 1850), **9:** 182 n.*302*
Ethel, **9:** 181, 182 n.*302*, 183
Stephen, Rev. (1826-1886) – bursar of Merton College, **4:** 308 n.*382*; **9:** 182 n.*302*
Sybil (b. 1883?), **9:** 179 n.*300*, 181, 182 n.*302*, 183
Edwardes (of Streatham, Surrey):
Mrs., **4:** 308 n.*382*
Stephen (1826-1886), see above
Edwards, Edward John (b. 1851) – domestic chaplain, **8:** 466 n.*756*
Edwards, Mary Ellen (1839-1908?) – artist, **5:** 86 n.*134*
Edwards, Percy – child actor and singer, **8:** 417 n.*675*
Edwards, S., Mr. – believer in a non-commercial world, **8:** 491 n.*794*
Edwin and Morcar, Earls, **1:** 11
Edwin the Fair (bk. Henry Taylor), **4:** 128 n.*101*
Egerton (of Burwash, Sussex):
Caroline Augusta "Gussie" (1876-1951), **9:** 130 n.*227*, 133, 137, 178
Helen Mary (1878-1961), **9:** 130 n.*227*, 133, 145, 178
Helen née Breach (b. 1852), **9:** 130 n.*227*, 133, 145
Jack (b. 1885), **9:** 133
John Coker, Rev. (1831-1888), **9:** 130 n.*227*, 145
Katherine "Kitty" (b. 1881), **9:** 133 n.*233*, 178
Sybil (b. 1880), **9:** 133 n.*233*, 178
Egerton, Jane Sophia (fl. 1840-1856) – artist, **2:** 75 n.*151*
Egerton Allen (of Tenby, Pembrokeshire)
Charles Francis, Mr. (1847-1927), **8:** 549 n.*875*, 558; **9:** 76
Elizabeth Georgina "Georgie" née Wilcox (1848-1934) – cousin, **1:** 124 n.*154*, 129; **2:** 88 n.*178*; **5:** 174 n.*289*; **6:** 344, 348, 349, 355, 361, 362, 465, 495; **7:** 303, 396, 415; **8:** 30 n.*36*, 330, 353, 357, 452 n.*724*, 549 n.*875*, 558; **9:** 57 n.*103*, 76, 203, 239, 256
Egyptian Hall, London, **4:** 139, 153, 159; **8:** 114
Elaine (sculpture by Thomas Woolner), **6:** 14 n.*8*
Elcho, Lord, see Douglas
"Electric Lady" – magic trick, **8:** 529

Elegy (bk. Thomas Gray), **1:** 51
Elementary Geometry (bk. Olaus Henrici), **7:** 282 n.*512*
Elementary Geometry (bk. James Wilson), **6:** 134 n.*205*
Elements of Euclid, The (bk. edited by Robert Simson), **4:** 51
Elements of the Calculus of Finite Differences (bk. Henry Kuhff), **1:** 69 n.*56*
Elements of the Philosophy of the Human Mind (bk. Dugald Stewart), **1:** 74 n.*67*
Elger (of Brighton, Sussex):
Catherine, Mrs. (b. 1811), **7:** 92 n.*165*
John, Mr. (b. 1802) – land owner, **7:** 92 n.*165*
Elihu Burritt's Miscellaneous Writings, **1:** 134 n.*169*
Eliot, George (1819-1880) – writer, **3:** 155 n.*227*
Elisha raising the son of the Shunammite (pic. Frederick Leighton), **7:** 317 n.*566*
Ellice (of London):
Mrs., **8:** 425 n.*687*, 431
Pauline (b. 1877) – pianist, **8:** 425 n.*687*, 429, 431
Elliot, Louisa Charlotte (b. 1866) – friend of the Jebbs, **6:** 387 n.*634*
Elliott Brothers, London – opticians and scientific instrument makers, **5:** 226; **7:** 502 n.*820*; **8:** 408
Ellis (of Cranbourne, Berkshire):
Bertha S. (b. 1858), **4:** 178, 292, 293 n.*351*, 320; **5:** 99 n.*157*
Conyngham, Rev. (1817-1891), **4:** 292, 293 n.*351*, 320; **5:** 83, 84 n.*131*, 99, 100
Frances Dymphna Harriet (1854-1930), **4:** 179, 293 n.*351*, 320; **5:** 19, 96, 99 n.*157*
Jane (b. 1862?), **4:** 293 n.*351*, 320
Katherine "Kate" (b. 1860), **4:** 180, 293 n.*351*, 320; **5:** 99 n.*157*
Mary (b. 1856), **4:** 181, 292, 293 n.*351*, 320; **5:** 99 n.*157*
Sophia Isabella née Babington (1829?-1893), **4:** 292, 293 n.*351*, 320
Ellis, Edwin John (1841-1895) – artist, **8:** 20 n.*13*
Ellis, Vera (b. 1876?) – friend of Mrs. Shute, **8:** 619 n.*981*
Ellison (of Seymour Street, London):
Catherine Margaret née Cresswell (b. 1822), **4:** 119 n.*88*
George Thomas, Mr. (b. 1811) – landowner, **4:** 119 n.*88*
Ellison (of Windsor, Berkshire):
Constance Margaret (b. 1856), **4:** 117 n.*86*, 119, 120 n.*90*, 179, 184; **5:** 19; **6:** 389
Dorothy Frances (b. 1859), **4:** 117 n.*86*, 119, 120 n.*90*, 179, 291
Douglas (1863-1942), **4:** 117 n.*86*
Gerald Francis (b. 1861), **4:** 117 n.*86*, 119, 120 n.*90*, 291
Henry Blomfield (b. 1868), **4:** 117 n.*86*
Henry John, Rev. (1813-1899), **4:** 116, 117 n.*86*, 119, 120 n.*90*, 184, 291, 320; **5:** 82, 108 n.*168*, 109, 177; **6:** 372, 373 n.*612*

John Henry Joshua (1855-1944), **4:** 117 n.*86*, 119, 120 n.*90*, 184
Mary Beatrice (b. 1857), **4:** 117 n.*86*, 119, 120 n.*90*, 149 n.*133*, 178, 184, 291; **6:** 389
Mary Dorothy née Jebb (1832-1870), **4:** 116, 117 n.*86*, 119, 120 n.*90*, 184, 209 n.*218*, 291, 320; **5:** 82, 108 n.*168*, 108 n.*169*, 109, 177; **6:** 389
Ellison (of Melsonby, Yorkshire):
Henry, Rev. (1820-1905?), **1:** 108
Julia Esther née Paul (b. 1818), **1:** 108
Elliston (of Brighton, Sussex):
Clara, **7:** 92 n.*166*, 128 n.*242*, 138, 140, 153-155, 182, 199, 200, 313; **8:** 37, 38 n.*50*, 130
Edith (b. 1871), **7:** 128 n.*242*, 138, 154, 199, 313; **8:** 38 n.*50*, 130
Maud (b. 1869), **7:** 128 n.*242*, 138, 313
Mrs., **7:** 128 n.*242*, 138, 154; **8:** 37, 38 n.*50*, 130
Elm Lodge, Hampstead (MacDonalds), **4:** 225, 226, 359
Elsdon, Northumberland, **1:** 9
Elsfield, Oxfordshire, **9:** 252
Elsie's Expedition (bk. Frederick Weatherly), **8:** 579 n.*925*
Emberlin, William G. (b. 1833) – stationer, **3:** 131; **7:** 417 n.*695*; **8:** 355 n.*579*, 518
Emerson (from the United States of America):
Ellen, **6:** 275 n.*450*
Ralph Waldo, Mr. (1803-1882) – writer, **6:** 275 n.*450*
Emerton, Wolseley Partridge (b. 1843) – barrister, **7:** 321, 322 n.*571*
Emery, Isabel Winifred Maud (1863-1924) – actress, **8:** 400, 401 n.*653*
Emery, Samuel Anderson (1817-1881) – actor, **2:** 82 n.*162*
Emery, Winifred, see Maude
Emlyn, Lord, see Vaughan
Emmerson, Miss – governess to the Smedleys, **4:** 190
Emmet, J. K. (1841-1891) – actor, **7:** 199, 200 n.*374*
Ems, Germany, **5:** 359-361
Encyclopedia Metropolitana, **1:** 74 n.*68*
Engadine, Switzerland, **7:** 198
Engaged (dr. William S. Gilbert), **7:** 78 n.*126*, 97-99, 387
English, Ida (b. 1864) – sister of Mrs. Gerrans, **9:** 324 n.*518*
"English Counties" – topic for study, **7:** 150
English Gentleman, The (dr. Henry Byron), **6:** 169 n.*264*
Ennerdale, Cumberland, **2:** 93
Enniskillen, Earl, see Cole
"Enoch Arden" (Alfred Tennyson) – poem, **5:** 139
Enraged Musician, The (dr. Thomas German Reed), **2:** 119
Ensham, Oxfordshire, see Eynsham
"Epigram on a Toad" (Charles Dodgson Snr.) – poem, **2:** 41 n.*81*
Epilepsy, **2:** 46 n.*91*; **7:** 55, 344, 345, 454, 458; **8:** 255 (epileptiform)
Episode in the Life of Margaret of Anjou, An (pic. James Hayllar), **6:** 22,

23 n.*23*
Ericksen (of London):
Dora, **6:** 252 n.*400*, 378
Nellie, **6:** 252 n.*400*, 378
"Erl King" (Schubert), **1:** 26
Erskine (of Ripon, Yorkshire):
Anne Agnes (1825-1912), see Fowler
Caroline Stuart (1818-1890), **5:** 179 n.*296*; **6:** 222 n.*350*, 292, 294, 442; **7:** 18 n.*14*, 140, 142, 193; **8:** 333 n.*548*, 338, 362, 375, 382, 413, 443, 450, 471, 487, 495, 509
Harriet Frances (b. 1814), **2:** 9, 10 n.*9*, 56, 58; **3:** 169, 170; **5:** 179 n.*296*; **6:** 222 n.*350*; **7:** 142
Henry David, Very Rev. (1786-1859) – dean of Ripon, **2:** 10 n.*9*; **3:** 169, 170; **5:** 179 n.*296*
Eryholme, Yorkshire, **1:** 131; **2:** 99
Escaped Nun, **7:** 365
Eschwege (of Lewisham, Kent):
Elizabeth Letitia née Foot (b. 1844), **7:** 197 n.*369*, 232, 284, 454, 456, 457, 461; **8:** 129, 576
Fritz (b. 1880?), **8:** 576
Herman, Mr. (b. 1831) – merchant, **7:** 197 n.*369*, 232, 284, 286, 419, 454-456, 461; **8:** 129 n.*210*, 576
Ida "Dolly" (b. 1870), **7:** 197 n.*369*, 232, 455, 457, 461, 464; **8:** 129, 576
Kathleen Lilian (1867-1934), **7:** 197 n.*369*, 223, 232, 286, 419, 421, 455, 457, 458, 461; **8:** 129, 576
Nina "Ninty" (b. 1875), **7:** 197 n.*369*, 232, 457, 461, 462, 464; **8:** 129, 576
Esmeralda (Pugni) – opera, **3:** 49, 50 n.*76*
Esmond, Annie (b. 1874) – actress, **9:** 166, 167 n.*284*
Essay on Elementary Geometry (bk. Isaac Todhunter), **7:** 80, 83
Essay on Probabilities, An (bk. Augustus De Morgan), **3:** 158 n.*234*
Esson, William (1838-1916) – mathematical lecturer, **7:** 225, 226 n.*415*
Eton College, Buckinghamshire, **8:** 479
Etonian, The, **1:** 30
Etty, William (1787-1849) – artist, **3:** 102 n.*150*
Euan Smith (of Park Lane, London):
Charles Bean, Col. Sir (1842-1910) – army officer, **8:** 466 n.*754*, 467, 468; **9:** 56 n.*100*, 76
Edith née Alexander, **8:** 466 n.*754*, 468, 471; **9:** 33 n.*56*, 56 n.*100*, 76
Hilda (b. 1878), **8:** 466 n.*754*, 467, 469, 471; **9:** 33 n.*56*, 56 n.*100*
Euclid's Elements of Geometry (bk. edited by Robert Potts), **4:** 50-52
Euston Station, London, **8:** 405, 615
Evangeline (pic. Henry Barraud), **2:** 18 n.*31*
Evans (of Battersea, Surrey):
Augustus, Mr. (b. 1844) – wine merchant, **8:** 145 n.*234*

Irene "Lina" B. (b. 1874), **8:** 145 n.*234*, 146, 149
Irene M. B., Mrs. (b. 1855), **8:** 145 n.*234*
Sydney B. (b. 1873), **8:** 145 n.*234*, 146
Willie "Jolly" B. (b. 1877), **8:** 145 n.*234*, 146
Evans (of Godalming, Surrey):
Edmund, Mr. (b. 1826) – engraver and colour printer, **8:** 443 n.*710*, 506, 518 n.*834*
Herbert (b. 1872), **8:** 443 n.*710*
Mary, Mrs. (b. 1840), **8:** 443 n.*710*
Evans (of Whitbourne Hall, Herefordshire):
Edward Bickerton, Mr. (1819-1893), **7:** 268 n.*483*
Margaret née Fleming (d. 1909), **7:** 268 n.*483*
Evans (of Oxford):
Evan, Rev. Dr. (1813-1891) – master of Pembroke College, **6:** 29 n.*35*, 33, 275, 303, 304, 491; **7:** 81 n.*137*, 84, 117, 227, 248, 309; **8:** 273, 469
Mary "Molly" Beatrice (b. 1870), **6:** 331, 469, 489; **8:** 178 n.*294*, 327, 341, 391, 394, 516, 517, 556; **9:** 243 n.*384*
Mary Sophia, Mrs. (b. 1843), **6:** 29 n.*35*, 33, 275, 303, 304, 331, 469, 489, 491; **7:** 81 n.*137*, 84, 117, 227, 248, 421, 513; **8:** 178 n.*294*, 273, 391, 469, 516, 517, 558, 593, 594; **9:** 243 n.*384*
Evans, May (b. 1868?) – orphan, **7:** 532 n.*861*
Evans, Polly (b. 1867) – circus performer, **7:** 287 n.*520*
"Evan's Hotel" – proposed article by Albert Smith, **2:** 52 n.*104*
Eve (pic. Anna Merritt), **8:** 199 n.*338*
Evelyn, John (1620-1706) – writer, **9:** 304 n.*483*
Evening Herald, **5:** 64
Evie (bk. Georgie Wilcox), **8:** 452 n.*724*
Ewing (of St. John's, Oxford):
Alice J. née Bayly (1851-1906), **7:** 165 n.*311*
Robert, Mr. (1847-1908) – lecturer, **7:** 165 n.*311*
Exeter College, Oxford, **3:** 9, 60, 97, 124 n.*177*; **4:** 83; **5:** 79; **6:** 476; **7:** 64, 99, 144; **8:** 51, 537, 559; **9:** 241, 347
Exeter College Chapel, **7:** 269, 453
Exeter Hall, London, **2:** 54, 122 n.*237*; **5:** 67; **6:** 18; **7:** 26
Exhibition of British Artists, **3:** 50
Exhibition of Female Artists, **5:** 201
Exhibition of French and Flemish Artists, **6:** 22
Exhibition of Modern Painters, **3:** 52
Exposition of the Creed, An (bk. John Pearson), **2:** 117 n.*223*
Expression of Emotions, The (bk. Charles Darwin), **6:** 244 n.*388*
Eynsham (or Ensham), Oxfordshire, **3:** 63; **9:** 127 n.*223*
Eynsham Hall, Oxfordshire (Masons), **6:** 276
Eyre, Ada (b. 1855), **9:** 329 n.*527*
Eyre, Ernest (1860-1882) – undergraduate at Christ Church, **7:** 421, 422 n.*704*

Eytinge, Rose (1835-1911) – actress, **7:** 122, 123 n.*231*
Eyton, Robert, Rev. (b. 1845), **8:** 395 n.*642*
Faber, Beryl (d. 1912) – actress, **9:** 23 n.*28*
Faces In The Fire (dr. Leicester Buckingham), **5:** 72, 73 n.*110*
Faed, Thomas (1826-1900) – artist, **2:** 75 n.*151*; **7:** 538, 539 n.*871*
Faint Heart Never Won Fair Lady (dr. James Planché), **3:** 120 n.*170*
Fairbairn (of Waltham St. Lawrence, Berkshire):
  Adam Henderson, Rev. (b. 1837), **6:** 358 n.*592*, 360, 363, 368
  Adam Maitland (b. 1866), **6:** 358 n.*592*, 360
  Anna Gertrude, Mrs. (b. 1844), **6:** 358 n.*592*, 363
  Frances Gertrude (b. 1865), **6:** 358 n.*592*, 360, 362, 363
  Hilda Margaret (b. 1868), **6:** 358 n.*592*, 360, 362, 363
Fairbairn (of Petworth, Sussex):
  Allison née Callaway (d. 1907), **5:** 64 n.*96*
  Florence (b. 1858), **5:** 64 n.*96*
  James Brooke (b. 1863), **5:** 64 n.*96*
  Mary Allison Dorothy (1860-1936), **5:** 64 n.*96*
  Reginald (1856-1921), **5:** 64 n.*96*
  Thomas, Sir (1823-1891), 2nd Bart., **5:** 64 n.*96*
  Thomas Gordon (1854-1931), **5:** 64 n.*96*
Fairbairn, May née Holt – dramatist, **8:** 374 n.*616*
Fairbrother, Sydney, alias Mrs. Percy Buckler (b. 1872) – actress, **9:** 283, 284 n.*449*, 288, 352
"Fairest of the Fair, The" (William Brough and Thomas German Reed) – song, **2:** 108, 109 n.*211*
Fairfax House, Putney, Surrey (Bullars), **2:** 81 n.*159*
Fairfield:
  Mr. A. – illustrator, **6:** 431 n.*710*, 433, 434
  Mr. E. – illustrator, **6:** 431 n.*710*, 433, 434
Fairford, Gloucestershire, **6:** 476
Fairford Windows, **6:** 476 n.*787*
Fairies, The (bk. William Allingham), **8:** 596 n.*950*
Fairlawn, Sharow, Yorkshire, **2:** 14 n.*22*
Fair Saxon, A (bk. Justin McCarthy), **8:** 15 n.*9*
"Fairview," near Guildford, **7:** 40, 279, 328
"Fairyland," near Guildford, **6:** 225 n.*354*, 295; **7:** 117
Fairy Raid, A (pic. Joseph Noël Paton), **5:** 238 n.*385*
Faithful James (dr. B. C. Stephenson), **9:** 26 n.*36*
Faithfull (of Leicester):
  Frances E., Mrs. (b. 1842), **8:** 40 n.*55*
  James Arthur, Rev. (b. 1847), **8:** 40 n.*55*
Faithfull (of Cheshunt, Hertfordshire):
  Frances R., Mrs. (b. 1826), **8:** 23 n.*21*, 40
  James Grantham, Rev. (1818-1873), **8:** 23 n.*21*
Falcon Family (bk. Marmion Savage), **1:** 90 n.*94*

Falle (of St. Saviour, Jersey):
Albina "Lily" Bertram (b. 1859), **6:** 170 n.*265*; **8:** 98, 111 n.*183*, 314 n.*517*, 341
Bertram Godfray (1859-1948), **6:** 170 n.*265*; **8:** 341 n.*561*
Joshua George, Hon. (1820-1903) – judge, **6:** 170 n.*265*; **8:** 98 n.*161*
Mary Elizabeth née Godfray (1832-1917), **6:** 170 n.*265*; **8:** 98
Rozel (b. 1857), **6:** 170 n.*265*; **8:** 98
Fallen Leaves (bk. Wilkie Collins), **7:** 285 n.*517*
Falls of Moness, near Aberfeldy, Scotland, **6:** 184
Fane, Blanche (d. 1858) – actress, **2:** 23 n.*43*
Fane (of Stokenchurch, Oxfordshire):
Catherine Elizabeth Agnes (b. 1863), **6:** 155 n.*238*, 156
Eleanor, Mrs. (b. 1830), **6:** 155 n.*238*, 277
Isabel (b. 1866?), **6:** 155 n.*238*, 156, 277
John Augustus, Capt. (b. 1831), **6:** 155 n.*238*
Fane, Francis William Henry (1825-1891), Earl of Westmorland, **6:** 468 n.*770*
Faraday, Michael (1791-1867) – scientist, **4:** 34
Far from the Madding Crowd (dr. Thomas Hardy and J. W. Comyns Carr), **7:** 468 n.*769*
Farley, Henry, Rev. (b. 1845), **6:** 369 n.*605*
Farmer (of Oxford):
Miss E., **9:** 121, 122 n.*213*
Miss P., **9:** 121, 122 n.*213*
Farnham, Surrey, **6:** 445, 472; **7:** 118; **9:** 179, 193, 234
Farnie, Henry Brougham (d. 1889) – dramatist, **7:** 305 n.*549*, 370 n.*643*, 532 n.*862*; **8:** 34 n.*41*, 38 n.*51*, 569 n.*907*, 589 n.*939*
Farrances Restaurant, London, **4:** 325
Farrar, Adam Storey, Rev. Dr. (1826-1905), **8:** 188 n.*316*
Farren, Nellie, later Mrs. Robert Soutar (1848-1904) – actress, **5:** 72 n.*108*; **6:** 197 n.*307*; **7:** 140 n.*258*
Farren, William (1826-1908) – actor, **5:** 32 n.*35*
Farringford, Isle of Wight, **3:** 175; **4:** 14, 20, 344, 349, 352, 353 n.*459*, 354-356
Farringford Journal of Emily Tennyson, 1853-1864, The, **4:** 14
Fascinating Individual, A (dr. Henry Danvers), **2:** 82 n.*162*
Fasti Ecclesiæ Hibernicæ (*Calendar of the Irish Church*), **2:** 62 n.*124*, 63
Faucit, Helen (1819-1898), see Martin
Faulkner, Charles Joseph (b. 1834) – mathematical lecturer, **6:** 254 n.*404*
Faulkner, Frank (b. 1856) – cook at Christ Church, **7:** 238 n.*440*; **8:** 552 n.*880*
Faulkner, Robert & Company, Photographer, **6:** 161 n.*250*
Faussett (of Oxford):
Anne (d. 1868), **5:** 58 n.*83*
Bryan (1811-1898), **5:** 58 n.*83*

Edward (1833-1841), **5:** 58 n.*83*
Godfrey (1813-1887), **5:** 58 n.*83*
Godfrey, Dr. (1780-1853) – professor of divinity, **5:** 58 n.*83*
Henry Godfrey (1824-1878), see Faussett-Osborne
John Toke (1835-1893), **3:** 70 n.*109*; **5:** 58 n.*83*, 125, 136; **6:** 156 n.*241*, 370, 433, 435
Marianne Elizabeth née Bridges (d. 1820?) – first wife, **5:** 58 n.*83*
Robert Godfrey (1827-1908), see below
Sarah (1831-1928), **5:** 58 n.*83*; **7:** 273 n.*495*
Sarah née Wethered (1790-1875) – second wife, **5:** 58 n.*83*
Susan (d. 1893), **5:** 58 n.*83*
Thomas Godfrey, see below
William (1825-1913), **5:** 58 n.*83*

Faussett (of Cassington, Oxfordshire):
Ellen Anne née Wethered (1847-1900), **7:** 100, 273, 404, 499, 500; **9:** 64, 65 n.*118*, 127
Mary (b. 1873), **9:** 65 n.*118*, 127
Robert Godfrey, Rev. (1827-1908) – lecturer, steward, and treasurer of Christ Church, **1:** 47, 49, 62 n.*36*, 69; **2:** 68 n.*135*; **3:** 70 n.*109*; **4:** 196, 205; **5:** 24, 51 n.*71*, 53, 57, 58 n.*83*, 73, 91, 113, 116, 118, 122, 123, 125, 128, 132, 136, 148, 179 n.*297*, 181, 215, 253; **6:** 28, 152, 153, 299, 325, 4077**:** 34 n.*47*, 100, 148, 257, 258 n.*469*, 264, 265 n.*479*, 273, 329, 346, 404, 440, 499; **8:** 202 n.*345*, 261 n.*440*, 262 n.*441*, 263, 265 n.*446*, 284; **9:** 64, 127

Faussett (of Canterbury, Kent):
Lucy Jane née Woodcock (b. 1841), **5:** 58 n.*83*
Thomas Godfrey (1829-1877), **5:** 58 n.*83*

Faussett-Osborne (of Hartlip Place, near Sittingbourne, Kent):
Helen Melville née Sandys-Lumsdaine (d. 1913), **7:** 432 n.*721*
Henry Godfrey, Rev. (1824-1878), **5:** 58 n.*83*; **6:** 338 n.*561*; **7:** 432 n.*721*
Margaret Lilias Godfrey (b. 1860), **7:** 432 n.*721*
Maud Isabel Godfrey (b. 1862), **6:** 338 n.*561*; **7:** 432 n.*721*

Faust (dr. William Wills), **8:** 273 n.*461*; **9:** 139, 146
Faust and Marguerita (dr. Dion Boucicault), **3:** 106 n.*154*

Favell (of Derwent Lodge, Portinscale, Cumberland):
Anne Elizabeth née Cayley (1789-1871), **2:** 91 n.*183*
Elizabeth (b. 1818), **2:** 91
James, Mr. (1775-1852), **2:** 91 n.*183*
Rosellen (b. 1816), **2:** 91

Faviell (of Down Place, Compton, Surrey):
Arthur Ernest (b. 1854), **6:** 91 n.*139*
Edith Beatrice (b. 1860), **6:** 90, 91 n.*139*; **7:** 11 n.*3*
Eveline "Effie" Alice (b. 1850), **6:** 91 n.*139*; **7:** 11 n.*3*
Frederick Henry (b. 1852), **6:** 91 n.*139*
Inez, **7:** 11

Nora Constance (b. 1858), **6:** 90, 91 n.*139*
Percy Ralph (b. 1861), **6:** 91 n.*139*
Sarah Oliver, Mrs. (1824-1879), **6:** 90, 91 n.*139*
William Frederick, Mr. (b. 1823) – farmer, **6:** 90, 91 n.*139*; **7:** 11 n.*3*, 344 n.*602*
Favourite of Fortune, A (dr. John Marston), **5:** 139 n.*223*
Favourite Padre, The (pic. John Burgess), **6:** 73 n.*108*
Fawcett (of Springfield, Ripon, Yorkshire):
Eliza Rose née Wood (b. 1843), **2:** 13 n.*18*; **5:** 104 n.*162*, 179 n.*296*; **8:** 220 n.*375*
Rowland Hill, Lt. Col. (d. 1914) – army officer, **5:** 104 n.*162*
Fawcett, Henry (1833-1884) – postmaster general, **7:** 508 n.*552*
Fearon (of Lexham Gardens, London):
Beatrice, see Alexander
Daniel Robert, Mr. (1835-1919) – barrister, **6:** 209
Margaret née Price (1838-1909), **6:** 213; **7:** 118, 119, 124, 171, 181, 194, 256, 387
Maud (b. 1864?), **6:** 209, 213, 369; **7:** 76 n.*121*, 95, 97, 111, 118, 119, 124, 171, 181, 183, 184, 194, 256, 387; **8:** 49 n.*73*
"Feast of Belshazzar, The," (Edwin Arnold) – poem, **1:** 46
Featherston, Master, **1:** 26
Fechter, Charles Albert (1824-1879) – actor, **4:** 182 n.*177*, 312
Fee Fo Fum (dr. Anon), **5:** 379
Feilden (of Kirkby Stephen, Westmorland):
Catherine Maud (b. 1861), **8:** 433 n.*698*
Ellinor Georgina Katherine née Hornby (1834-1910), **6:** 260 n.*414*, 450 n.*739*; **7:** 82 n.*138*, 143, 492; **8:** 60 n.*96*, 264, 278 n.*467*
Helen Arbuthnot (1859-1947), see Mason
Henry Arbuthnot, Rev. (1828-1909), **6:** 260 n.*414*; **7:** 82 n.*138*, 143, 223
Feldon, Ellen (b. 1865) – artists' model, **7:** 429 n.*716*
Fell (of Ambleside, Westmorland):
Edmund (b. 1847), **3:** 109 n.*157*
Frances Irton (b. 1853), **3:** 109 n.*157*
Joseph Lyon (b. 1846), **3:** 109 n.*157*
Maria, Mrs., **3:** 109 n.*157*
Richard Irton (b. 1852), **3:** 109 n.*157*
Samuel Irton, Rev. (1801-1868?), **3:** 109 n.*157*
Fell, Edwin Frederick Berry (b. 1866) – undergraduate at Christ Church, **9:** 312 n.*495*
Fell, Messrs. – ship brokers, **7:** 172, 178
Fellowes (of East Tuddenham, Norfolk):
Louisa Adela Maud "Maudie" (1857-1892), **4:** 98 n.*59*
Pleasance Elizabeth née Reeve (1823-1898), **2:** 43 n.*86*; **3:** 73 n.*114*, 178; **4:** 39, 98 n.*59*
Thomas John Lyon, Rev. (1818-1881), **2:** 43 n.*86*; **4:** 98 n.*59*

Fellowes, Rosamond Sophie (b. 1878), **8:** 192 n.*322*, 195, 269
Fellows (of Rickmansworth, Hertfordshire):
Caroline P. (b. 1855), **8:** 293, 294
Harriet, Mrs. (b. 1823), **8:** 290 n.*486*, 294
Harvey W., Mr. (b. 1827) – solicitor, **8:** 290 n.*486*, 294, 295, 299, 300
Felpham, near Bognor, Sussex, **6:** 228, 230, 234
Fenchurch Street Station, London, **8:** 365
Fendall (of Woodcote House, Windlesham, Surrey):
Charles B., Mr. (b. 1835) – teacher, **6:** 192 n.*298*, 226, 269, 353; **7:** 158 n.*296*
Frances, Mrs., **6:** 192 n.*298*, 226, 227, 269, 353
Georgina "Georgie," **7:** 158 n.*296*
Mary Eleanor (b. 1863), **6:** 192 n.*298*, 226; **7:** 158 n.*296*
Fenians at Manchester, **5:** 372, 373 n.*553*
Fenn:
Mr., **6:** 345 n.*572*, 350, 362 n.*596*, 363
Mrs., **6:** 362, 363
Fenner, Augusta (b. 1867) – governess, **8:** 631 n.*998*
Fenny Compton, Warwickshire, **9:** 255
Fenton, Nellie – actress, **8:** 160 n.*259*
Fenton, Roger (1819-1869) – photographer, **2:** 56 n.*112*; **3:** 28 n.*40*; **4:** 25
Fenwick, Samuel Dr. (1821-1902) – physician, **6:** 232 n.*365*
Fereman, George, Rev. (1824-1877), **3:** 41 n.*65*
Ferguson (of Sunderland, Durham):
Bertha (1863-1919), **6:** 208 n.*325*
Eleanor (b. 1861), **6:** 208 n.*325*
Elizabeth "Bessie" Jane née Wilcox (b. 1828) – cousin, **1:** 122 n.*152*; **3:** 119, 120 n.*168*; **5:** 377 n.*558*; **6:** 207, 208 n.*325*, 333; **8:** 30 n.*36*
Marion (b. 1862), **6:** 208 n.*325*
William Bramwell, Dr. (1818-1885) – wine merchant, **1:** 122 n.*152*; **5:** 377 n.*558*; **6:** 207, 208 n.*325*, 333; **8:** 30 n.*36*
Ferguson (of Eastbourne, Sussex):
Capt., **7:** 138, 139 n.*255*
Mrs., **7:** 138, 139 n.*255*
Ferguson, Miss – governess, **8:** 290 n.*486*, 292-294
Fergusson, James Ranken, Sir (1835-1924), 2nd Bart., **2:** 29 n.*56*
Fernandez, James (1835-1915) – actor, **8:** 584 n.*933*; **9:** 215 n.*343*
Ferrar, Ada (1867-1951) – actress, **9:** 21 n.*24*, 22
Ferrier, Miss – governess to the Shaw-Stewarts, **6:** 314
Ferro, Angelita Helena "Nellie" De Silva (1865-1949), see Martin-Harvey
Few (of Seal, Kent):
Charles Edward, Rev. (b. 1842), **7:** 476 n.*778*, 480; **9:** 146 n.*251*
Dora M. (b. 1870), **7:** 476 n.*778*, 480
Eleanor "Nellie" L. (b. 1873), **7:** 476 n.*778*, 480; **9:** 146 n.*251*

Evelyn (b. 1868), **7:** 476 n.*778*, 480
Margaret Irene "Bob" (b. 1877), **7:** 476 n.*778*, 480; **9:** 146 n.*251*
Mary, Mrs. (b. 1842), **7:** 476 n.*778*, 480
Ffolkes, Olive, **9:** 183 n.*304*
Ffoulkes (of St. Giles', Oxford):
Anne née Strange (1831-1915), **7:** 145 n.*272*, 273
Edmund Salisbury, Rev. (1819-1894), **7:** 145 n.*272*, 273, 324, 534
Sophia Louisa (b. 1870), **7:** 145 n.*272*
Ffoulkes (of London?):
Fred, **7:** 230, 231 n.*424*, 315
Howard, **7:** 230, 231 n.*424*, 315
Field, Kate (b. 1871) – violinist, **9:** 242 n.*381*
Field, The, **7:** 450
Fielding, Mr. – teacher (?) at Richmond School, **1:** 21
Fiennes (of Broughton Castle, near Banbury, Oxfordshire):
Augusta Sophia née Hay, Lady (d. 1915), **7:** 34 n.*48*
Eustace Edward (b. 1864), **6:** 314
John Twisleton Wykeham, Lord (1830-1907), Baron Saye and Sele, **7:** 34 n.*48*
Fife (of Hood Street, Newcastle, Northumberland):
Anne (d. 1895), **3:** 171 n.*251*
Elizabeth, see Crawshay
James George (1824-1894), **3:** 171 n.*251*
John (1822-1875) – army officer, **3:** 171 n.*251*
John, Sir (1795-1871) – surgeon, **3:** 171 n.*251*
Joseph Bainbridge (1821-1891) – surgeon, **3:** 171 n.*251*
William Henry (1819-1874), see above
Fife (of Newcastle, Northumberland):
Caroline Jane née Lennard – second wife, **3:** 171 n.*251*
William Henry, Mr. (1819-1874) – surgeon, **3:** 171 n.*251*
Lucy née Cookson – first wife, **3:** 171 n.*251*
Fife (of Scotland, and Newcastle, Northumberland):
George (b. 1808?), see below
John (1795-1871), see above
William, Mr. (d. 1839) – surgeon, **3:** 171 n.*251*
Fife (of Saville Row, Newcastle, Northumberland):
George, Dr. (b. 1808?) – physician, **1:** 121 n.*149*; **3:** 171 n.*251*
Fifth Book of Hooker's Ecclesiastical Polity, The (bk. Richard Hooker), **5:** 103 n.*160*
Figgis, John Neville, Rev. Dr. (1866-1919) – historian, **8:** 533 n.*856*
Figlia di Reggimento, La (Donizetti) – opera, **3:** 49, 50 n.*76*
Fildes, Samuel Luke (1843-1927) – artist, **8:** 561 n.*894*
Fille de Madame Angot, La (Lecocq) – opera, **8:** 287 n.*483*, 288
Fincher, Lily – friend of Evelyn Dubourg, **6:** 297 n.*490*
Finding of the Saviour in the Temple, The (pic. William Holman Hunt),

6: 258 n.*411*
Fine-Art Society Exhibition, **7:** 533 n.*863*, 541
Fire extinguisher demonstration, **7:** 491, 492
Fireworks, **2:** 76 n.*152*, 77, 78
Firle, Walther (b. 1859) – artist, **8:** 422 n.*682*
First Classical Maps (bk. James Tate), **1:** 115 n.*139*
First Communion, The (pic. Théophile Duverger), **5:** 224 n.*357*
First Hebrew Book, The (bk. Thomas K. Arnold), **5:** 131 n.*210*
Firth (of Brighton, Sussex):
  Dora, Mrs. (b. 1857), **7:** 468 n.*770*
  Walter A., Rev. (b. 1851), **7:** 468 n.*770*
Firth (of Guildford, Surrey):
  Emma R., Mrs. (b. 1836), **9:** 139, 140 n.*241*
  Raywood, Rev. (b. 1835), **9:** 139, 140 n.*241*
Fischer (of Madras, India):
  Isabella "Ella" Maude née Drury (1862-1884), **6:** 91 n.*140*, 94, 95 n.*148*, 122, 126, 159, 177, 196, 200, 259, 317, 339; **7:** 192, 193, 230, 231, 236, 350, 415, 453 n.*749*
  Robert, Mr. – barrister, **7:** 453 n.*749*; **8:** 126 n.*203*
Fisher (of Hove, Sussex):
  Adeline (b. 1871), **9:** 299 n.*474*
  Charles Dennis (b. 1878), **9:** 299 n.*474*
  Cordelia (b. 1880), **9:** 299 n.*474*
  Edward (b. 1872), **9:** 299 n.*474*
  Emmaline (b. 1869), **9:** 299 n.*474*
  Florence (b. 1864), **9:** 299 n.*474*
  Henry (b. 1874), **9:** 299 n.*474*
  Herbert William, Mr. (1827-1903) – barrister, **4:** 127; **5:** 160, 161 n.*265*; **9:** 299 n.*474*
  Mary L. née Jackson (b. 1842), **9:** 299 n.*474*
  William (b. 1875), **9:** 299 n.*474*
Fisher, Annie (b. 1859?), **6:** 123, 124 n.*190*
Fisher, David Nunn (1816-1887) – actor and dramatist, **2:** 124 n.*240*; **3:** 105, 106 n.*154*; **5:** 64 n.*95*
Fisher, Frederic Horatio, Rev. (1837-1915), **8:** 531
Fisher, Miss – governess to the Jebbs, **5:** 178
Fisher, Wilfred, Rev. (b. 1833), **1:** 84 n.*88*, 85
Fisk, George, Rev. (d. 1873?), **4:** 120 n.*89*
Fitzball, Edward (1782-1873) – dramatist, **2:** 80 n.*158*
Fitzgerald (of Kerry, Ireland):
  Aubrey Whitestone (b. 1876) – actor, **9:** 333 n.*533*
  Caroline née Wilson, **9:** 333 n.*533*
  Richard, Dr. – physician, **9:** 333 n.*533*
Fitzgerald, Percy (1834-1925) – writer and theatre critic, **6:** 242 n.*386*, 251, 255

Fitzgerald, Walter (b. 1848) – exhibitioner at Christ Church, **8:** 35 n.*44*
Fitzroy Square, London (Sants), **5:** 208
Fletcher (of Oxford):
Agnes C. (b. 1862), **7:** 432 n.*719*
Agnes W., Mrs. (b. 1835), **7:** 432 n.*719*
Carteret John Halford, Rev. (b. 1828), **7:** 432 n.*719*
Dorothy H. (b. 1879), **9:** 296 n.*469*
Ethel H. (b. 1866), **7:** 432 n.*719*
Margaret (b. 1863), **7:** 432 n.*719*
Fletcher (of Eastbourne, Sussex):
Agnes née Fancourt (b. 1838), **8:** 300 n.*501*, 423
Edith E. (b. 1868), **8:** 330 n.*543*, 332, 334, 335, 423
Eleanor "Nellie" (b. 1871), **8:** 300 n.*501*, 302, 303, 330, 420, 428
John Brunsden, Rev. (1840-1925), **8:** 300 n.*501*, 420, 423, 526
Fletcher, William, Dr. (1872-1938) – physician, **9:** 228 n.*362*
Fleuss, H., Mr. – drawing teacher, **5:** 136, 137 n.*219*
Flight into Egypt (pic. Edwin Long) – see *Anno Domini*
Flint, Mrs., **4:** 292 n.*350*
Floral Hall, London, **7:** 118, 120 n.*225*
Florence (pic. James Sant), **6:** 16, 17 n.*14*
Floyd, Charles Greenwood, Rev. (b. 1830), **4:** 134 n.*111*
Flying Dutchman, The (dr. Edward Fitzball), **2:** 80 n.*158*
Flyter, Caroline Lily (b. 1875) – pupil at Mrs. Drury's school, **8:** 110 n.*181*, 315, 316
Folkington Manor, Sussex (Gwynnes), **7:** 133, 134
Follow the Leader (dr. Charles Rae), **7:** 23 n.*24*
Fontaine, Miss – singer, **5:** 109 n.*171*
Fontmell Rectory, Shaftesbury, Dorset, **6:** 233, 236, 237
Foote, Lydia (1843-1892) – actress, **4:** 248 n.*282*; **5:** 213, 231
Foote, Samuel (1721?-1777) – dramatist, **5:** 210 n.*336*
Forbes, Helen D., Mrs. (b. 1855), **9:** 186 n.*307*
Forbes Robertson, Ian (1859-1936) – actor, **7:** 438 n.*727*; **8:** 620 n.*982*; **9:** 57 n.*104*
Forbes Robertson, Johnston (1852-1937) – actor, **7:** 494 n.*804*; **9:** 218 n.*346*
Forde, Mr. – actor, **9:** 15 n.*10*
Foregate Station, Worcester, **6:** 239
Foregate Street, Worcester, **4:** 120
Foreign Office, London, **8:** 254
Forester, Frank – pupil at King's College, **2:** 24 n.*45*
Forest Leaves (pic. Sophie Anderson), **4:** 290 n.*346*
Formby, Miss, **8:** 628
Formes, Karl Johann (1810-1889) - singer, **1:** 104
Forrest, Eva – actress, **9:** 15 n.*10*
Forshall (of Hornsey, Middlesex):
Frances Maria née Scrimgeor, **7:** 85 n.*147*

Frances Mary "May" (1867-1937), **7:** 85 n.*147*, 86, 87 n.*151*
Francis Hyde, Dr. (b. 1834) – physician, **7:** 27 n.*34*, 85 n.*147*, 86
Theodore (b. 1874), **7:** 85 n.*147*
Forshaw, William (b. 1842) – photographer, **6:** 487; **7:** 279 n.*509*; **8:** 183 n.*311*, 565
Fortnightly Review, The, **6:** 390 n.*641*
Foster, Mary née Prickett (1833-1916) – governess to the Liddells, later proprietor of the Mitre, Oxford, **2:** 111 n.*216*, 113; **3:** 16 n.*17*, 20, 23, 24, 28, 44, 48, 59 n.*90*, 62; **4:** 13, 169, 173-175, 177, 186, 187, 192-196, 200, 204, 211, 298, 307; **5:** 57, 74 n.*112*, 78 n.*122*, **6:** 152 n.*232*
Foster, Miss – artist, **8:** 96 n.*157*
Foster, Miss – governess to the Fairbairns, **6:** 362
Foulkes, Miss – friend of the Drurys, **7:** 155 n.*292*
Found (pic. Dante G. Rossetti), **7:** 505 n.*824*
Foundations of Geometry, The (bk. Edward Dixon), **8:** 555 n.*884*
Four Lane Farm, Basing, Hampshire, **6:** 437, 438
Fournier, N. R. – dramatist, **3:** 153 n.*223*
Fowler, Alfred, Rev. (1835-1880), **6:** 49 n.*71*
Fowler:
Anne Agnes née Erskine (1825-1912), **2:** 58; **3:** 169, 170; **6:** 490 n.*808*
Robinson, Mr. (d. 1895) – barrister, **6:** 490 n.*808*
Fowler, Reginald (b. 1849) – Roman Catholic priest, **7:** 232 n.*426*
Fowler, Thomas, Rev. Dr. (1832-1904), **1:** 43, 49, 64 n.*41*, 89, 98, 99 n.*107*; **2:** 26 n.*50*, 39, 47, 50, 63, 97, 120; **3:** 24, 37, 39, 57, 69, 123, 129; **4:** 70 n.*12*, 134, 151, 175 n.*171*, 176, 196; **5:** 56; **6:** 147 n.*225*, 201, 297, 298, 326; **7:** 18 n.*12*, 309, 414, 498; **8:** 125 n.*202*, 250, 492, 516
Fowler, William Warde (1847-1921) – writer, **8:** 492 n.*796*
Fox (of Tranmere, Birkenhead, Cheshire):
Elsie (b. 1882), **8:** 534 n.*858*, 536
Mrs. née Bragger?, **8:** 534 n.*858*
Stanley, **8:** 534 n.*858*
Francis (of St. Aldates, Oxford):
Matilda, Mrs. (b. 1839), **9:** 45 n.*79*
William, Mr. (b. 1839) – verger at Christ Church, **9:** 45 n.*79*
Franco-Prussian War, **6:** 138 n.*210*
Frank Fairleigh (bk. Frank Smedley), **1:** 110 n.*127*
Frank Hilton (bk James Grant), **1:** 114 n.*135*
Frankland, Mr. & Mrs. – friends of the Ellis family, **5:** 99 n.*156*
Franklin (of Freshwater, Isle of Wight):
Charles Trigance, Col. (1822-1895), **4:** 352, 356; **5:** 111 n.*174*
Lucy née Haywood (1829-1922), **4:** 346, 347-349, 353 n.*459*, 356; **5:** 111 n.*174*
Rose Lucy (1857-1934), **4:** 181, 347, 352, 353 n.*459*, 355 n.*464*; **5:** 111 n.*174*
Vernon (b. 1860?), **4:** 352

Fraser (of Bayswater, London):
Emilie, Mrs. (b. 1815), **6:** 455 n.*748*
John Christian (1856-1899), **6:** 454, 455 n.*748*, 460
John Mattison, Mr. (b. 1806) – colonial broker, **6:** 455 n.*748*
Freeborn (of Oxford):
Clara C. (b. 1851), **7:** 514, 515 n.*834*
Richard Fernandez, Dr. (b. 1822), **4:** 198 n.*200*
Freemason's Concert, Oxford, **3:** 71
Freemason's Fête, Oxford, **4:** 92, 307; **5:** 153, 252; **8:** 343
Freiligraph-Kroeker, Käthe "Kate" (1845-1904) – dramatist, **7:** 233 n.*429*; **8:** 496
Fremantle, Stephen James (1845-1874) – tutor, **6:** 209 n.*328*
French (performing bicyclist family from France):
Henri (b. 1874), **7:** 353, 354 n.*617*, 355, 399, 400
Marie (b. 1873), **7:** 353, 354 n.*617*, 355, 399, 400
Minnie (b. 1875) – cousin?, **7:** 353, 354 n.*617*, 399, 400
Mr., **7:** 399
Mrs., **7:** 400
Nellie (b. 1878), **7:** 353, 354 n.*617*, 400
French and Flemish Artists' Exhibition, London, **4:** 315; **5:** 72, 159, 222
French Gallery, London, **6:** 335; **7:** 93, 189, 460; **8:** 113, 422
Freshwater, Isle of Wight, **4:** 14, 15, 20, 60, 61, 343, 344, 348, 356; **5:** 141
Freud, Sigmund (1856-1939) – psychoanalyst and writer, **1:** 44
Frewen Hall, Oxford, **4:** 24, 41, 42
Friar-Crag, Cumberland, **2:** 91
Friends in Council (bk. Arthur Helps), **1:** 75 n.*70*
Frilford, Berkshire, **7:** 531
Friston, Sussex, **7:** 470
Frith, Sarah A. (b. 1842) – governess to the Threshers, **6:** 415 n.*680*
Fritillaries, **7:** 330, 331 n.*588*
Frodingham, Lincolnshire, **4:** 241 n.*269*
Froggy would a-wooing go (dr. Frank Green), **6:** 377 n.*617*
Frome, Somerset, **5:** 51 n.*70*
From Nowhere to the North Pole (bk. Tom Hood), **8:** 579 n.*925*
Frost, Ada (b. 1874), see Dixon
Frost, Arthur Burdett (1851-1928) – illustrator, **2:** 89 n.*179*; **7:** 104 n.*194*, 106, 108, 112, 329 n.*583*, 380, 521 n.*845*; **8:** 24 n.*23*, 142, 181 n.*301*, 219
Froude, James Anthony (1818-1894) – historian and writer, **1:** 97 n.103
Froude, Richard Hurrell (1803-1836) – friend of John Henry Newman and Tractarian, **9:** 175 n.*295*
Fryer (of Chatteris, Cambridgeshire):
Herbert F. (b. 1854) – farmer, **9:** 322 n.*515*
John, Mr. (b. 1816) – farmer, **9:** 322 n.*515*
Sarah, Mrs. (b. 1832), **9:** 322 n.*515*
Fuller (of London):

Audrey (b. 1885), **9:** 218 n.*347*, 225, 243, 283, 347, 348
Charles Drury (b. 1889), **9:** 218 n.*347*, 243, 283, 347
Herbert Henry, Mr. (b. 1857) – land surveyor, **7:** 369 n.*640*; **8:** 190; **9:** 218 n.*347*, 225, 348
Mary "Minnie" Frances née Drury (1859-1935), **6:** 91 n.*140*, 94, 95 n.*148*, 122, 126, 159, 196, 200, 256, 259, 317, 339, 352, 411; **7:** 156, 192, 193, 230, 315, 316, 319, 368, 369, 415; **8:** 190, 207, 268; **9:** 218 n.*347*, 225, 243, 283 n.*448*, 347, 348
Fun, **6:** 21
Furius – steamship, **8:** 259 n.*436*
Furniss (of St. George's Square, London):
Dorothy (b. 1880), **8:** 186 n.*314*
Frank (b. 1879), **8:** 186 n.*314*
Harry, Mr. (1854-1925) – illustrator, **1:** 20; **8:** 169 n.*283*, 170, 181, 182, 183 n.*309*, 186 n.*314*, 189, 204, 235, 245, 305, 338 n.*557*, 359, 370, 375, 416, 449, 481 n.*780*, 482, 487, 488, 490; **9:** 16, 79 n.*146*, 252 n.*395*, 253, 254 n.*398*
Marion née Rogers (b. 1853), **8:** 186 n.*314*, 375
Furniss, Maud – clerk at Royal Observatory, Greenwich, **8:** 533 n.*857*
Furnivall (of Quarry Street, Guildford):
Alice Eveline (b. 1859), **6:** 90, 91 n.*139*, 92 n.*143*, 94 n.*146*, 138, 296
Bryan (b. 1862?), **6:** 91 n.*139*
Charles John, Mr. (b. 1827?) – farmer, **6:** 91 n.*139*, 138
Edith Mary (b. 1855), **6:** 91 n.*139*
George Frederick (b. 1860), **6:** 91 n.*139*
John Graham Maul (b. 1856), **6:** 91 n.*139*
Katherine Eliza, Mrs., **6:** 91 n.*139*, 138
Fursdon (of Paddington; Dodgson writes "Thursden"):
Charlotte Mary née Nicholl (b. 1863), **9:** 120 n.*207*
George, Mr. (b. 1860) – bank cashier, **9:** 120 n.*207*
Furse (of Westminster, London):
Charles Wellington, Canon (1821-1900), **8:** 390 n.*636*
Edith (b. 1875), **8:** 390 n.*636*
Elizabeth D. (b. 1863), **8:** 390 n.*636*
Margaret W. (b. 1872), **8:** 390 n.*636*
Furtado, Teresa (1845-1877), later Mrs. Clarke – actress, **5:** 123 n.*195*; **6:** 27 n.*30*
"Fury" (Hull's dog), **7:** 187, 439
Fyffe, Charles Alan (1845-1892) – historian, **8:** 250 n.*419*
Fyfield, Berkshire, **7:** 531
Fyles, Franklin (1847-1911) – dramatist, **5:** 38 n.*46*, 85 n.*133*

Gabb, James Percy Alwyne, Dr. (1853-1934) – physician, **9:** 302 n.*479*
Gadsden, Blanche Marie (1870-1961), **8:** 53 n.*79*, 62, 86
Gaisford (of Mid Lavant, Sussex):

Agnes, Mrs. (b. 1835), **7:** 401 n.*680*
Arthur (b. 1870), **7:** 401 n.*680*
Ernest C. (b. 1875), **7:** 401 n.*680*
Evelyn (b. 1870), **7:** 401 n.*680*; **8:** 17
Francis (b. 1861), **7:** 401 n.*680*
George, Rev. (1828-1903), **5:** 55 n.*78*; **7:** 400, 401 n.*680*; **8:** 17 n.*11*
Reginald (b. 1870), **7:** 401 n.*680*
Gaisford (of Christ Church, Oxford):
George (1828-1903), see above
Thomas, Dr. (1779-1855) – dean of Christ Church, **1:** 100 n.*110*; **3:** 16 n.*15*
Galitzine (Dodgson writes "Golicen"):
Constantine, Prince (1832-1879), **5:** 349 n.*519*
Olga (1861-1901), **5:** 349 n.*519*
Gallery of Illustration, London, **2:** 123
Gallery of the British Artists, London, **1:** 104
Galli-Marié, Celestine née Marié del'Isle (1840-1905) – singer, **5:** 367 n.*544*
Galton, Blanche (1845-1936) – singer, **5:** 157 n.*255*
Gambier-Parry (of Chelsea, London):
Grace "Gracie" née Denman (1858-1935), **4:** 180, 319 n.*405*, 326, 327, 328 n.*417*, 340; **5:** 70; **6:** 20; **7:** 113 n.*208*, 235; **8:** 216 n.*369*; **9:** 172 n.*288*
Sidney (1859-1948) – architect, **9:** 172 n.*288*
Gamelin, Mrs., **6:** 228
Game of Romps, A (dr. John Morton), **3:** 52 n.*79*, 81
Games (bk. Edmund Hoyle), **3:** 152 n.*220*
Gamlen (of Oxford):
Florence Mostyn née Owen (1856-1952), **7:** 116 n.*215*; **8:** 624 n.*987*, 627, 629, 630, 632
Florence Ruth (1882-1964), **8:** 624 n.*987*, 627, 629, 632, 633, 634; **9:** 12 n.*2*, 40, 41, 46, 58, 59, 70, 71, 144, 244, 261, 324
William Blagdon, Mr. (1844-1919) – editor, **7:** 116 n.*215*; **8:** 624 n.*987*, 629, 632
Gandell (of Holywell Lodge, Church Street, Oxford):
Florence (b. 1860?), **4:** 100 n.*63*, 106; **5:** 164 n.*271*
Louisa Caroline, Mrs. (1826-1880), **4:** 148; **5:** 164 n.*271*, 186; **7:** 102 n.*190*
Robert, Prof. (1817-1887), **4:** 100 n.*63*, 148; **5:** 78 n.*121*, 164 n.*271*, 186 n.*306*; **7:** 102 n.*190*, 383; **8:** 67 n.*108*
Shomberg Frederick (b. 1859), **4:** 100 n.*63*, 106; **5:** 164 n.*271*
Gandy, Charity Courtis née Ross (1814-1881), **4:** 156 n.*144*
Garfield, James Abram (1851-1881) – President of the United States, **7:** 362 n.*631*
Garrick Club, London, **6:** 253, 259

Garvagh, see Canning
Garvey, Willie – child actor and singer, **8:** 287
Gaselee, Serjeant Stephen (1807-1873) – politician, **3:** 43 n.*68*
Gaskell (of Kiddlington Hall, Oxfordshire):
Alice Cunliffe née Brooks (d. 1872), **7:** 198 n.*370*
Henry Lomax, Mr. (1813-1889), **7:** 198 n.*370*
Gaskell, Elizabeth Cleghorn neé Stevenson (1810-1865) – writer, **1:** 131 n.*163*; **3:** 86 n.*133*, 90, 169 n.*247*
Gassier, Josefa née Fernandez (1821-1866) – singer, **3:** 19, 20 n.*22*
Gateskill (of Guildford, Surrey):
Mrs., **9:** 187 n.*309*
Nellie (b. 1883), **9:** 187 n.*309*
Gatey, Margaret – friend of the Websters, **3:** 117 n.*163*; **4:** 39
Gathorne-Hardy (of Hemsted Mansion, Brenenden, Kent):
Alfred Erskine (1845-1918), **6:** 185 n.*287*
Charles Gathorne (1841-1919), **6:** 185 n.*287*
Edith Elizabeth (1843?-1875) **6:** 185 n.*287*
Emily Blanche (1848-1912), **6:** 185 n.*287*; **7:** 71, 216
Gathorne (1814-1906), 1st Earl of Cranbrook, **5:** 91 n.*140*, 215, 248 n.*404*, 251 n.*411*, 371 n.*550*; **6:** 12 n.*4*, 41 n.*56*, 48, 119 n.*182*, 185 n.*287*, 186, 219, 345; **7:** 39 n.*57*; **8:** 398 n.*647*
Harold (1850-1881), **6:** 185 n.*287*
Jane Isabel (1842?-1862), **6:** 185 n.*287*
Jane née Orr, Lady Cranbrook (1815-1897), **6:** 185 n.*287*; **7:** 66 n.*107*, 70, 71, 216
John Stewart (1839-1911), **6:** 185 n.*287*
Margaret Evelyn (1858-1943), **5:** 20, 251 n.*411*; **6:** 185 n.*287*; **7:** 70-72, 216
Mary Katherine (1852-1911), **6:** 185 n.*287*; **7:** 70, 71, 216
Gatty (of Ecclesfield, Sheffield, Yorkshire):
Alfred, Rev. (1813-1903), **4:** 46, 238 n.*266*, 325 n.*412*
Margaret née Scott (1809-1873), **4:** 46, 238 n.*266*, 239; **5:** 370
Gauss, Carl Friedrich (1777-1855) – mathematician, **1:** 75 n.*69*
Gaussen (of Broughton Hall, Oxfordshire; and Bayswater, London):
Arratoon William David "Toddy" (b. 1875), **8:** 166 n.*275*, 266
Charles Louis (b. 1869), **8:** 166 n.*275*
David, Mr. (b. 1834), **8:** 166 n.*275*, 212, 266
Elizabeth S. née Apcar (b. 1848), **8:** 166 n.*275*, 200, 212, 260, 266, 280, 334, 342, 379, 551
Ella Sophy (b. 1867), **8:** 166 n.*275*, 200, 240 n.*403*, 260, 266, 267, 269, 270 n.*453*, 280, 281, 334, 342, 379, 405, 604
James Robert (1871-1959), **8:** 166 n.*275*
Nannie Isabella (b. 1873, twin), **8:** 166 n.*275*, 212, 266, 267, 280, 334, 342, 551
Nina Alice (b. 1873, twin), **8:** 166 n.*275*, 212, 266, 267, 280, 334, 342

Gavazzi, Alessandro (1809-1889) – orator, **2:** 63 n.*126*
Gaye, Herbert Charles, Rev. (b. 1856), **8:** 547 n.*872*
Gee, William H. (b. 1838) – Oxford bookseller, **8:** 489 n.*792*
Geissler's Tubes, **6:** 72 n.*106*
General Elections, **3:** 43 n.*68*, 66 n.*99*, 144; **4:** 91 n.*48*; **6:** 64 n.*93*, 319 n.*529*; **7:** 254 n.*463*, 258 n.*469*, 267 n.*480*, 330, 331 n.*589*; **8:** 281 n.*471*
General Fairfax and His Daughter (pic. Thomas Heaphy), **5:** 219 n.*350*, 231; **6:** 15 n.*9*
Genesis of Species (bk. George Mivart), **6:** 366, 367 n.*601*
Gengembre (of South Boston, United States of America):
  Mary, **4:** 181; **5:** 126 n.*201*
  Mrs., **5:** 126 n.*201*
George, Alice B. née Cole (b. 1845), **6:** 354, 385
George, Henry (1848-1908) – actor, **8:** 587 n.*938*
Gérardy, Jean (1877-1929) – violoncellist, **8:** 587 n.*937*
German Bazaar, Portland Place, London, **2:** 123
German Reed (of Fairfax Road, Teddington, London):
  Priscilla née Horton (1818-1895), **2:** 108 n.*210*, 109 n.*211*, 123, 128; **3:** 11 n.*9*, 103 n.*151*; **6:** 259 n.*412*, 304, 379; **7:** 131; **9:** 24 n.*30*
  Thomas, Mr. (1817-1888), **2:** 108 n.*210*, 109 n.*211*, 119; **3:** 103 n.*151*; **6:** 259 n.*412*, 260, 304; **9:** 24 n.*30*
German Reed Entertainment, **2:** 108 n.*210*, 109 n.*211*, 123, 128; **4:** 109 n.*77*, 233, 234, 322, 323 n.*409*; **5:** 157; **6:** 259 n.*412*, 286; **7:** 57, 131, 354; **8:** 481, 632; **9:** 24, 88
Gerothwohl, Mr. – artist, **7:** 271 n.*490*
Gerrans (of St. John Street, Oxford):
  Anna Elizabeth née English (1858-1946), **9:** 201 n.*330*, 204, 268, 269, 279 n.*444*, 293 n.*464*, 294, 324 n.*518*
  Henry Tresawna, Mr. (1858-1921) – lecturer, **4:** 13; **9:** 201 n.*330*
Ghost Lady (pic. Thomas Heaphy), **6:** 71
Giani, Eve née Berry (1803-1876), **6:** 236 n.*376*
Gibbs (of Aldenham Park, Hertfordshire):
  Alban George Henry (1846-1936), see below
  Kenneth Francis (1856-1935), **7:** 449 n.*743*, 494
Gibbs (of Portland Place, London):
  Alban George Henry, Mr. (1846-1936), **7:** 449 n.*743*, 494; **8:** 114, 115 n.*187*
  Bridget née Beresford-Hope (1853-1896), **8:** 114, 115 n.*187*
  Catherine "Katie" Louisa (b. 1875), **8:** 114, 115 n.*187*
  Gerald Henry Beresford (1879-1939), **8:** 114, 115 n.*187*
  Mildred Dorothea (b. 1876), **8:** 114, 115 n.*187*
Gibbs (of Bayfordbury Place, Hertfordshire):
  Edith (b. 1857), **6:** 83 n.*124*
  Elizabeth, Mrs. (b. 1820), **6:** 83 n.*124*

Henry John (b. 1859), **6:** 83 n.*124*
John, Mr. (b. 1820) – land steward, **6:** 83 n.*124*
Gielgud (of Kensington, London):
Arthur John (1904-2000), **9:** 156 n.*270*
Francis “Frank” Henry, Mr. (1860-1949) – stockbroker, **9:** 156 n.*270*
Kate née Lewis (1868-1958), **5:** 233 n.*375*; **6:** 113, 194 n.*301*, 256, 312; **7:** 93 n.*169*, 140, 156, 185, 194, 304, 305, 348, 388, 396, 398, 430, 514, 515; **8:** 319; **9:** 156 n.*270*
Lewis Evelyn (1894-1953), **9:** 156 n.*270*
Val Henry (1900-1981), **9:** 156 n.*270*
Giessen, Germany, **5:** 358
Giffard, Effie née Neef, **7:** 226 n.*416*, 385
Giffard, Henry Alexander (1838-1927), **4:** 150, 151 n.*136*; **8:** 504 n.*809*, 560
“Gift, The” (Frederick Weatherley) – song, **8:** 531
Gilbert (of Kensington, London):
Lucy Agnes née Turner (b. 1848), **7:** 514
William Schwenk (1836-1911) – dramatist and illustrator, **6:** 21 n.*23*, 486; **7:** 78 n.*126*, 90 n.*162*, 96, 97 n.*179*, 97 n.*180*, 186 n.*348*, 316 n.*565*, 387 n.*667*, 394 n.*672*, 442 n.*732*, 503 n.*822*, 516; **8:** 618 n.*980*, 631 n.*999*; **9:** 13 n.*5*, 118 n.*204*
Gilby (of Essex House, Barnes, Surrey):
Minnie b. 1868), **6:** 424
Thomas, Mr. (b. 1813) – manufacturer, **6:** 425
Gilchrist (of Hampstead, London):
Constance “Connie” MacDonald (1865-1946) – actress, **7:** 13, 14 n.*8*, 22 n.*22*, 29 n.*38*, 30, 45, 46 n.*71*, 75 n.*120*, 76, 78, 82, 91, 140 n.*258*, 429 n.*716*
Matilda, Mrs. (b. 1829), **7:** 22, 29 n.*38*, 76, 78
Miss, **7:** 29, 78
Gilding, Mrs., **9:** 188 n.*311*
Giles, Mrs., **6:** 94 n.*147*
Gilfillan, George (1813-1878) – writer, **2:** 33 n.*66*
Gilfillan's Poets, **2:** 33, n.*66*
Gill, William – dramatist, **8:** 230 n.*388*
Gilliat, Algernon (b. 1837) – landowner, **4:** 292. 293 n.*351*
Gilliat (of The Cedars, Chorleywood, Rickmansworth, Hertfordshire):
John Saunders, Mr. (1829-1912) – banker, **4:** 284 n.*338*, 286, 292, 293 n.*351*, 325
Louisa Anne Fanny née Babington, **4:** 284 n.*338*, 286, 292, 293 n.*351*, 325, 331
Mabel Fanny (b. 1861), **4:** 181, 284 n.*338*, 325
Rose Babington (b. 1865?), **4:** 284 n.*338*
Gilling, Mary née Rowley (b. 1838), **7:** 94 n.*171*
Gillmore, Frank (1868-1943) – actor, **8:** 426 n.*688*

Gilstrap (of Winthorpe, Nottinghamshire):
Anna Sophia (1863-1940), **5:** 70 n.*105*
George, Mr. (b. 1822), **5:** 70 n.*105*
Isabella, **5:** 70 n.*105*
Jane née Fothergill (d. 1864), **5:** 70 n.*105*
Josephine, **5:** 70 n.*105*
Gilter Head, Tenby, Pembrokeshire, **4:** 190
Ginsburg (of Egham, Surrey):
Christian David, Dr. (1831-1914) – Biblical scholar and writer, **9:** 295 n.*467*
Emilie Catherine (b. 1869), see Mackinder
Emilie née Hausburg (b. 1843), **9:** 295 n.*467*
Ethel M. (b. 1866), **9:** 295 n.*467*
Hildegarde B. (b. 1872), **9:** 295 n.*467*, 296
Sybil G. (b. 1880), **9:** 295 n.*467*, 320
Giraud, Herbert John, Dr. (1817-1888) – chemist and botanist, **6:** 341 n.*567*, 342, 343, 345, 354, 417, 478, 486; **7:** 46, 345 n.*605*, 430, 444, 445, 525; **8:** 576
Girdlestone, Charles, Rev. (1797-1881), **3:** 39 n.*60*
Girdlestone, Robert Baker, Rev. (1836-1923), **2:** 109 n.*213*, 110 n.*213*; **3:** 39 n.*60*; **7:** 520
Girl I Left Behind Me, The (dr. David Belasco and Franklin Fyles), **5:** 37, 38 n.*46*, 85
Girl with Lilac (pic. Sophie Anderson), **4:** 312 n.*389*, 337 n.*435*; **5:** 89 n.*137*
Girton College, Cambridge, **8:** 233
Gittens (or Giddings), Ursula (b. 1872), **9:** 231 n.*366*, 232, 263
Giuglini, Antonio (1827-1865) – singer, **3:** 98 n.*147*; **4:** 341 n.*443*
Gladstone (of Hawarden, North Wales; and London):
Agnes (1842-1931), **4:** 21
Catherine née Glynne (1812-1900), **6:** 286
Helen (1849-1925), **4:** 21; **8:** 56 n.*86*
Mary (1847-1927), **4:** 21
William Ewart, The Hon. (1809-1898), **3:** 17 n.*18*, 66 n.*99*, 144; **4:** 284; **5:** 91 n.*140*, 216; **6:** 12, 13 n.*6*, 28, 29 n.*34*, 64 n.*93*, 65, 264 n.*424*, 268; **7:** 337, 370, 371 n.*645*, 425, 426; **8:** 46, 56, 58, 279 n.*468*, 280, 543 n.*868*; **9:** 34 n.*59*, 64, 124 n.*217*
Gladstone (of Bowden Park, Chippenham, Cambridgeshire):
John Evelyn (1855-1945), **4:** 284 n.*337*
John Neilson, Capt. (1807-1863) – navy officer, **4:** 284 n.*337*
Glanville, John Usher, Rev. (b. 1846), **6:** 438 n.*720*
Glasgow, Scotland, **3:** 104, 144; **6:** 182, 184
Glasgow Cemetery, **3:** 106
Glaucus (dr. F. T. Traill), **5:** 95 n.*147*
Glazebrook (of Harrow, Middlesex):

Ethel née Brodie (1856-1926), **4:** 54, 112 n.*80*, 194, 219, 220; **6:** 46; **7:** 365 n.*637*
Michael George, Rev. (1854-1926) – teacher, **7:** 365 n.*637*
Glenalmond (Trinity College), Scotland, **3:** 24 n.*31*, 90, 91, 93, 94, 95 n.*145*, 96, 97, 144
Glenfinlas – ship, **6:** 411
Glenkill House, Lamlash, **6:** 182
Glenn, Mr. – American confederate sympathiser, **4:** 277 n.*325*
Glen Sannox, Scotland, **6:** 184
"Glorious Apollo" (Samuel Webbe) – song, **2:** 87 n.*174*
Gloucester, **4:** 191
Glover, Charles W. (1806-1863) – composer, **1:** 26
Glyn (of Chester Square, London):
Edward Carr, Rt. Rev. Hon. (1843-1928), **6:** 109 n.*171*
W. (Hon.), **6:** 109 n.*171*
Glynne Jones, Charles Griffith (b. 1856) – undergraduate at Christ Church, **6:** 492 n.*814*
Goblin Market (bk. Christina Rossetti), **4:** 66 n.*4*
Godalming, Surrey, **6:** 355; **7:** 158; **8:** 269, 372; **9:** 192, 289, 293
Godby (of Petersham, Surrey):
Catherine "Katie" M. (b. 1876), **7:** 292 n.*530*, 305
Charles Vincent, Mr. (b. 1846) – teacher, **7:** 292 n.*530*
Eleanor "Nellie" M. (b. 1875), **7:** 292 n.*530*, 305
John (b. 1880), **7:** 292 n.*530*
Mary E., Mrs. (b. 1843), **7:** 292 n.*530*
Phyllis (b. 1877), **7:** 292 n.*530*, 305
Godfrey (of Abingdon, Berkshire):
Catherine Susan (b. 1847), **5:** 74, 75 n.*113*
Charlotte Emma (b. 1841), **5:** 74, 75 n.*113*
Daniel H., Mr. (1799-1876?) – solicitor, **5:** 55 n.*79*, 56, 74, 75 n.*113*, 82
Elizabeth Milligen (b. 1839), **5:** 74, 75 n.*113*
Georgina F. (b. 1855), **4:** 180; **5:** 55 n.*79*, 56, 74, 75 n.*113*, 82 n.*127*
Helen, Mrs. (b. 1813), **5:** 74, 75 n.*113*
Louisa Helen (b. 1838), **5:** 75 n.*113*, 82
Mary Fanny (b. 1852), **5:** 74, 75 n.*113*
Godfrey, George William (1844-1897) – dramatist, **7:** 438 n.*727*
Godfrey (of the United States):
Lily Alice (b. 1872), **7:** 292 n.*531*, 296, 300, 301, 305
Mrs., **7:** 296, 301
"Godiva" (Alfred Tennyson) – poem, **8:** 530
Godiva, Lady – wife of Leofric, Earl of Mercia, **1:** 11
Godstow, Oxfordshire, **1:** 14; **3:** 60 n.*91*; **4:** 94, 115, 142
Godwin (of Hampstead, London):
Charlotte P. née Powell (b. 1815), **4:** 227 n.*251*, 256, 359; **5:** 144 n.*231*
John H., Rev. (b. 1810) – lecturer, **4:** 227 n.*251*, 256

Godwin-Austen, see Austen
Goff, Herbert C. J. (b. 1849) – barrister's clerk, **7:** 445 n.*735*
Goff, James S. (b. 1847) – barrister's clerk, **7:** 445 n.*735*
Goff (of Monkstown, Dublin, Ireland):
John Crosbie (b. 1840) – undergraduate at Christ Church, **4:** 116 n.*85*
William (b. 1842) – undergraduate at Christ Church, **4:** 116 n.*85*
Golden Ladder, The (dr. George Sims), **8:** 381, 382 n.*626*
Golden Square Hospital, London, **7:** 76
Golding (of Walton Street, Oxford):
Alice, **4:** 89 n.*46*
Mrs. – lodging-house keeper, **4:** 80 n.*31*, 89 n.*46*
Thomas – shop-keeper, **4:** 80 n.*31*
Goldsmith, Oliver (1730-1774) – poet and dramatist, **5:** 246 n.*400*; **9:** 22 n.*26*
Golicen, see Galitzine
Gomes, Alice – singer, **8:** 364 n.*594*
Gondoliers, The (Gilbert and Sullivan) – operetta, **8:** 522 n.*839*
Goodall, Frederick (1822-1904) – artist, **5:** 235 n.*379*
Goode (of Ripon, Yorkshire):
Anne Emily (b. 1844)
Mary Caroline (b. 1839), **4:** 235 n.*262*; **6:** 128; **7:** 77 n.*124*; **8:** 81 n.*128*, 342, 356, 433; **9:** 205 n.*334*
William, Rev. (1810-1868), **4:** 235 n.*262*
Goodeve, Louis Arthur (b. 1841) – barrister, **4:** 171 n.*166*
Good for Nothing (dr. John Buckstone), **5:** 17 n.*11*; **7:** 186 n.*348*
Goodman, Edward J. – dramatist, **9:** 310 n.*493*
Goodman, Maude (b. 1853) – artist, **7:** 253, 254 n.*462*
Good-night (pic. Arthur Hughes), **5:** 211 n.*339*
"Good Night" (Hugh Collis) – song, **7:** 510
Good Night Signor Pantalon (dr. Anon), **2:** 80 n.*158*
Goodwin, Harvey, Rt. Rev. (1818-1891), **8:** 208 n.*357*
Goody Two Shoes (dr. Trudy West), **6:** 250 n.*397*, 257; **7:** 13, 14 n.*8*
Gordon, Adam Hay (1846-1894), MA Christ Church, **6:** 290 n.*478*
Gordon, Arthur Pitman, Rev. (1837-1904), **2:** 29 n.*56*
Gordon, Henry Evans (b. 1863) – undergraduate at Christ Church, **5:** 119 n.*186*
Gordon, Miss – friend of Lady Wolmer, **8:** 615
Gordon, Osborne, Rev. (1813-1883), **1:** 47, 58 n.*26*, 100; **2:** 33 n.*64*, 40, 41, 77; **3:** 15, 16 n.*15*, 17, 62; **4:** 38, 54; **5:** 25; **6:** 87, 88 n.*131*, 89, 116, 438
Gordon, Walter, real name William Aylmer Gowing (1823-1892) – dramatist, **4:** 223 n.*245*; **5:** 96 n.*150*, 137 n.*220*
Gordon-Lennox (of Goodwood Park, Chichester, Sussex):
Amy Mary née Ricardo, Lady (d. 1879), **7:** 57, 58 n.*92*, 194
Charles Henry (1870-1935), "Mr. Granite"?, **7:** 194, 195 n.*362*
Charles Henry, Sir (1845-1928), 2nd Duke of Gordon, **7:** 56 n.*89*

Emily (1869-1879?), **7:** 57, 59, 74
Violet Mary (1874-1946), **7:** 57-59, 74
Gore, Charles, Rev. (1853-1932), **8:** 188 n.*316*
Goring, Oxfordshire, **4:** 102, 185; **5:** 148
Gosforth, Cumberland, **2:** 92
Goss, Ellen – actress and dancer, **9:** 163, 164 n.*279*
Gott, John, Rev. (1831-1906), **7:** 17, 18 n.*12*
Gough House, Victoria Hospital, Chelsea, **5:** 30
Goulburn, Edward Meyrick, Rev. Dr. (1818-1897), **4:** 331 n.*423*; **8:** 250 n.*420*
Gould (of Culford Gardens, London):
Beatrice (b. 1889), **9:** 218 n.*346*, 233
Dorothy Sybil Mary (b. 1891), **9:** 218 n.*346*, 233
James Nutcombe, Mr. (1849-1899) – actor, **8:** 419 n.*679*, 424, 562; **9:** 218 n.*346*, 233, 256
Mrs., **9:** 233, 256
Olive (b. 1883), **9:** 218 n.*346*, 233
Winifred "Winnie" (b. 1884), **9:** 218 n.*346*, 233
Gounod, Charles Francois (1818-1893) – composer, **4:** 283 n.*335*
Gowan, Col. – American, **4:** 145 n.*128*
Goward Twins (of London?):
Bella – singer and dancer, **7:** 14 n.*8*
Weevie – singer and dancer, **7:** 14 n.*8*
Gower Street Station, London, **6:** 27
Go-Won-Go-Mohawk – dramatist, **9:** 277 n.*443*
Graeme (of Graemeshall, Orkney):
Alexander Malcolm Sutherland, Lt. (1845-1908) – navy officer, **6:** 228 n.*360*, 234, 236
Margaret Isabel née Neale (1854-1909), **6:** 228 n.*360*, 234
Grafton Gallery, London, **9:** 59
Graham, Cissy (Theatre Company), **9:** 197 n.*323*
Graham, James, Lord (1799-1874), Duke of Montrose – postmaster general, **6:** 48 n.*68*
Grain, Richard Corney (1844-1895) – entertainer, **6:** 304 n.*502*; **7:** 57 n.*90*, 131, 354 n.*618*; **8:** 481 n.*779*, 485, 632 n.*1001*; **9:** 24 n.*30*, 88 n.*159*
Granby, see Manners
Grande Place, Brussels, Belgium, **5:** 261
Granite, Mr., see Gordon-Lennox
Grant, Cyril Fletcher, Rev. (1845-1916), **9:** 245, 246 n.*388*, 290
Grant, James (1822-1887) – historian and writer, **1:** 114 n.*135*
Grant, Major, **7:** 316 n.*563*
Grant, Miss – governess to Lord Listowel's children, **7:** 289
Grant, William Thorold (b. 1862) – undergraduate at Christ Church, **7:** 498 n.*814*
Grantoff (of Ealing, Middlesex):

Caroline (b. 1824), **7:** 40 n.*59*
Ellen (b. 1826), **7:** 40 n.*59*
Granville (of Sandford on Thames, Oxfordshire):
Algernon (b. 1858), **4:** 298 n.*362*, 308
Augustus Kerr Bozzi, Rev. (1818-1884), **4:** 298, 303, 308, 322; **5:** 113 n.*177*
Ellen Elizabeth née Read (b. 1824), **4:** 303, 308, 322; **5:** 113 n.*177*
Ellen Evelyn (b. 1857), **4:** 298 n.*362*, 307, 308 n.*379*, 308; **5:** 113 n.*177*
Emma Violet (b. 1855), **4:** 298 n.*362*, 308; **5:** 113 n.*177*
Mabel (b. 1861), **4:** 298 n.*362*, 308
Mary Elizabeth (b. 1849), **4:** 298 n.*362*, 307, 308 n.*379*, 308
Graphic, The, **6:** 441
"Grass from the Battlefield" (Sydney Dobell) – poem, **4:** 14
Grattan Children – performers, **7:** 13, 14 n.*8*
Gray (of Kensington, London):
Agtia W. (b. 1879), **6:** 416 n.*683*
Anna Celia (b. 1880), **6:** 416 n.*683*
Hilda Mary (b. 1871), **6:** 416 n.*683*, 420
Horace William, Mr. (b. 1843) – civil servant, **6:** 416 n.*683*
Julia née Smyth (b. 1845), **6:** 416 n.*683*, 419
Mary Julia (b. 1876), **6:** 416 n.*683*
Maurice S. (b. 1877), **6:** 416 n.*683*
Millicent E. (b. 1874), **6:** 416 n.*683*
Monica Frances (b. 1872), **6:** 416 n.*683*
Gray (of Brafferton, near Ripon, Yorkshire):
Ann Elizabeth (b. 1816), **4:** 45
Ann Elizabeth née Howard, **4:** 45
Jane (b. 1819), **4:** 45
Lucy (b. 1822), **4:** 45
Margaret Haydon (b. 1825), **4:** 46
Samuel (1820-1890, **4:** 45
William (1815-1885), **4:** 45
William, Canon (1785-1863), **4:** 45
Gray (of Beaumont Street, Oxford):
Basil (b. 1875), **6:** 484 n.*798*
Edward Benjamin, Dr. (1832-1916) – physician, **6:** 420 n.*690*, 483, 485, 488, 489; **7:** 102 n.*189*; **8:** 501 n.*805*
Ethel (b. 1877), **6:** 484 n.*798*; **8:** 84 n.*134*
Herbert Edward (b. 1873), **6:** 484 n.*798*
Lilian "Lily" Amelia (1871-1924), **6:** 483, 484 n.*798*, 487-490; **7:** 102 n.*189*, 116 n.*217*, 119 n.*224*, 124 n.*233*; **8:** 84 n.*134*
Percival (1874-1894), **6:** 484 n.*798*
Stephanie née Carter (1838-1924), **6:** 483, 484 n.*798*, 485, 487-489; **7:** 102 n.*189*, 124
Gray (of Sharow, near Ripon, Yorkshire):

Edmund, Rev. (1826-1890), **2:** 16 n.*26*; **4:** 46
Mary née Gray (1825-1891), **2:** 16 n.*26*
Gray, Hamilton, see Gray, Warwick
Gray, John Durbin (b. 1845) – Radley school pupil, **4:** 74, 75 n.*21*
Gray, Robert Henry, Rev. (1817-1885), **6:** 273 n.*442*
Gray, Sophie (b. 1843) – John Millais' sister-in-law, **5:** 212 n.*340*, 213
Gray, Thomas (1716-1771) – poet, **1:** 34; **2:** 47
Gray's Bard – set to music, **2:** 47
Gray, Warwick (Children's Opera Company), **8:** 287 n.*483*, 288, 363 n.*593*
Great Exhibition (1851), London, **1:** 45
Great Gable, Cumberland, **2:** 92, 95
Great Northern Railway, **2:** 55; **3:** 82; **4:** 98
Great Ormond Street Childrens' Hospital, London, **5:** 29
Greek dress, **7:** 110 n.*204*
Greek language, **2:** 35 n.*69*, 41 n.*81*, 89 n.*180*, 122
Greek Lexicon (bk. Henry Liddell and Robert Scott), **1:** 101 n.*111*
Greek Slave (pic. Hiram Powers), **7:** 316 n.*563*; **8:** 59 n.*91*
Green, Charles H. (b. 1848) – cook at Christ Church, **9:** 138, 229 n.*364*
Green (of Balliol College, Oxford):
Charlotte B., Mrs. (b. 1843), **6:** 308
Thomas Hill, Dr. (1836-1882) – professor of moral philosophy, **6:** 308
Green, George Robert (b. 1832) – headmaster, **8:** 570 n.*909*
Greenall (of Walton Hall, Daresbury, Cheshire):
Bertha (1871-1945), **8:** 205 n.*350*
Gilbert, Sir (1806-1894), 1st Baron Daresbury, **8:** 205 n.*350*
Susannah (b. 1869), **8:** 205 n.*350*
Susannah née Rapp (b. 1832), **8:** 205 n.*350*
Greenall (of Stretton, Warrington, Cheshire):
Eliza Mary née Lyon (d. 1878), **4:** 27
Richard, Rev. (1806-1867), **4:** 27
Greenaway, Catherine "Kate" (1846-1901) – illustrator, **7:** 510, 537 n.*870*
Green Bushes, The (dr. John Buckstone), **5:** 47 n.*62*
Greene, Clay M. (1850-1933) – dramatist, **8:** 604 n.*959*; **9:** 272 n.*431*
Greenidge (of Blackhall Road, Oxford):
Abel Hendy Jones, Mr. (1865-1906) – lecturer, **9:** 196 n.*320*, 199
Edith Elizabeth née Lucy (1871-1907), **8:** 338 n.*558*, 339, 341, 359, 368, 397, 399, 427, 508, 526, 528, 552, 629; **9:** 39 n.*68*, 44, 105, 108, 121, 130, 131, 133-136, 141, 145, 182, 191 n.315, 196, 199, 200, 230, 242 n.*383*, 247, 250, 300, 315, 320
Greenlees, Alexander (b. 1843) – distiller, **8:** 258, 259 n.*436*, 293
Greenock, Scotland, **7:** 447, 448
Green Pastures and Piccadilly (bk. William Black), **7:** 285, 286 n.*518*
Greenside, Miss, **1:** 26
Greenwich Observatory, **8:** 533
Greenwood (of Ripon, Yorkshire):

Caroline (b. 1797), **1:** 50 n.*4*; **4:** 158 n.*146*
Elizabeth (b. 1802), **1:** 50 n.*4*; **4:** 158 n.*146*
Henry (b. 1791), **1:** 50 n.*4*; **4:** 158 n.*146*
Greenwood, Frederick (1830-1909) – editor of *Pall Mall Gazette*, **6:** 449 n.*737*; **7:** 326 n.*578*, 330, 336, 388; **8:** 14 n.*6*, 17, 119
Greet, Dora Victoire née Graves (1857?-1946) – dramatist, **9:** 139 n.*240*
Greet, Philip Ben (1857-1936) – actor and manager, **8:** 417 n.*675*; **9:** 158, 335, 336 n.*537*
Gregorian chants, **7:** 129
Gregory, C. S., Rev., **7:** 520 n.*844*
Gregory, Francis Hood, Maj. (b. 1837) – army officer, **2:** 29 n.*56*
Gregson (of Paddington, London):
Jane (b. 1846) – teacher, **8:** 315 n.*518*
Margaret (b. 1844) – teacher, **8:** 315 n.*518*
Grenside, Eleanor Frances (b. 1841) – nurse, **7:** 26 n.*30*; **8:** 612 n.*971*, 615; **9:** 55 n.*98*
Grenville-Wells (of Westbourne Square, London):
Allada K., Mrs. (b. 1831), **9:** 331 n.*529*
Benita C. (b. 1865), **9:** 331 n.*529*, 334, 335, 340
C., Col. (b. 1822) – army officer, **9:** 331 n.*529*
Nigel G. (b. 1870), **9:** 331 n.*529*
Gresham, Herbert (1853-1921) – actor, **9:** 132 n.*231*
Gresley (took part in a trial at Guildford Assizes):
Miss, **6:** 349, 351
Mrs., **6:** 349, 351
Greville, Sidney Robert, Hon. Sir (1866-1927) – civil servant, **8:** 466 n.*753*
Grey (of Norton-on-Tees, Durham):
Elizabeth née Hogg (d. 1848), **2:** 84 n.*168*
Thomas Robinson, Lt. Col. (1767-1833) – army officer, **2:** 84 n.*168*, 85 n.*169*
Grey, Major, **2:** 84, 85 n.*169*
Grey, Richard, Dr. (1694-1771) – writer, **6:** 429 n.*707*
Griffin, Ethel, **8:** 194, 195 n.*328*, 208
Griffin, Miss – aunt of Ruth Mayhew, **7:** 147, 148 n.*278*
Griffith (of Ripon, Yorkshire):
James, Mr. (b. 1797) – barrister, **2:** 14 n.*21*, 16
John Charles (b. 1852), **2:** 14 n.*21*
Katherine (b. 1850), **2:** 14 n.*21*, 16
Katherine, Mrs. (b. 1827), **2:** 14 n.*21*
Mary Frances (b. 1853), **2:** 14 n.*21*
Griffiths (of Sandown, Isle of Wight):
Agnes (b. 1868), **6:** 343 n.*568*
Elias, Mr. (b. 1829) – lodging-house keeper, **6:** 343 n.*568*
Sarah, Mrs. (b. 1831) – lodging-house keeper, **6:** 343 n.*568*
Griffiths, Beatrice – amateur dramatist, **9:** 276 n.*441*

Griffiths, Dr. – physician, **4:** 349
Griffiths, Misses – cousins of Mrs. Percy Keane, **8:** 232 n.*392*
Grimble, Alice née Ward (b. 1850), **5:** 161 n.*266*, 170 n.*282*; **7:** 430 n.*717*
Grimes (of Shanklin, Isle of Wight):
  Emily (b. 1818), **7:** 526 n.*850*
  Henrietta Louisa (b. 1848) – niece, **7:** 526 n.*850*
Grimston, see Kendal
Grisi, Guilietta (1812-1869) – singer, **1:** 104 n.*115*
Grizzett, Mr. – friend of Septimus Andrews, **4:** 272, 273 n.*318*
Grose, Thomas Hodge (b. 1845) – lecturer, **9:** 327 n.*525*
Grossmith (of London):
  George (1848-1912) – actor and singer, **7:** 97 n.*179*, 323 n.*573*, 352 n.*615*, 503; **8:** 485 n.*784*, 529; **9:** 20, 28
  Weedon (1852-1919) – actor, **8:** 406 n.*660*, 618; **9:** 26 n.*36*, 303 n.*482*
Grosvenor Gallery, London, **7:** 50, 123, 185, 253, 280, 349, 431, 442, 539, 541; **8:** 110, 112, 125, 167, 197, 204, 229, 333, 404, 457
Grove Lodge, London (Pooles), **7:** 12, 40
Gruggen (of Pocklington Grammar School, Yorkshire):
  Emily Eustatia née Morgan, **4:** 131, 132 n.*108*, 133
  Frederick James, Rev. (1820-1872) – headmaster, **4:** 131, 132 n.*108*, 133
Grundy, Charles Henry, Rev. (b. 1845), **6:** 445 n.*732*, 448
"Grundy, Mrs.," **8:** 236, 293, 339; **9:** 35
Grundy, Sydney (1848-1914) – dramatist, **8:** 274 n.*462*; **9:** 54 n.*92*, 101 n.*182*
Guardian, The, **4:** 275; **5:** 11, 12 n.*2*; **7:** 409 n.*689*
Guardian Angel, The (bk. Oliver Wendell Holmes), **9:** 190 n.*314*
Guernsey, **4:** 346; **8:** 96
Guggenheim, Amelia (b. 1862), **8:** 593 n.*946*
Guido, Reni (1575-1642) – artist, **1:** 118 n.*144*

Guildford:
  Assizes, **6:** 345 n.*572*, 349, 350
  Borough Hall, **9:** 303
  Castle, **9:** 14
  Cemetery, **7:** 117
  Election, **8:** 250, 251 n.*421*; **9:** 14 n.*8*
  Nurses' Training Institution, **9:** 346
  School Board, **7:** 526
  Schools, **8:** 372, 450; **9:** 119, 345, 346

Guildhall, Doncaster, **6:** 109
Guillemots, **7:** 182 n.*339*
Gulf of Finland, **5:** 296
Gumfreston, Pembrokeshire, **4:** 190 n.*187*
Gunn, Sophy (b. 1866), **6:** 412 n.*674*

Gunter, A. C. (1848-1907) – dramatist, **8:** 440 n.*705*
Gurney, Archer Thompson, Rev. (1820-1887), **5:** 362 n.*535*, 363
Gurney (of London):
Emelia née Batten, **6:** 221 n.*348*
Russell, Mr. (1804-1878) – barrister, **4:** 318 n.*402*; **6:** 221 n.*348*, 223
Guy's Cliff House, Warwick, **8:** 177
Gwynne (of Folkington, Polegate, Sussex):
Dorothy B. E. (b. 1878), **7:** 135 n.*250*
Evelyn M. (b. 1866), **7:** 134, 135 n.*250*
James Eglington Anderson, Mr. (1832-1915) – civil engineer and farmer, **7:** 133 n.*248*, 134, 135 n.*250*, 438
Mary Earle née Purvis (b. 1844), **7:** 133 n.*248*, 134, 135 n.*250*, 438
Neville (b. 1869?), **7:** 135 n.*250*
Reginald John (b. 1863), **7:** 134, 135 n.*250*
Rupert Sackville (b. 1873), **7:** 135 n.*250*
Violet K. E. (b. 1872), **7:** 135 n.*250*
Gymnasium, Edinburgh, **6:** 181

Hackman, Alfred (1811-1874), **2:** 118 n.*225*; **3:** 68 n.*106*; **4:** 107, 108 n.*75*, 134, 298; **5:** 44 n.*57*, 46, 47, 75 n.*114*
Hadland, Samuel (b. 1838) – gas fitter, **8:** 123 n.*199*
Haig-Brown, Miss – teacher, **9:** 292 n.*462*
Hailey – pupil of Ranken, **6:** 476
Hailsham, Sussex, **9:** 173, 329
Haines, John Thomas (1799?-1843) – dramatist, **3:** 101 n.*149*
Hairsine, Samuel (b. 1830) – teacher, **2:** 58 n.*117*
Haithwaite, William (1862-1914) – scout at Christ Church, **8:** 325 n.*538*
Hakluyt, Richard (1552?-1616) – writer, **2:** 67 n.*132*, 76
Hale, Edwin Moses, Dr. (1829-1899) – physician and homeopath, **4:** 28
Hall (of Dunglass, Haddington, Scotland):
Adelaide Catherine née Elliot, Lady (1841-1926), **6:** 338, 339 n.*562*
Basil Francis, Lord (1832-1909), 7th Bart., **6:** 338, 339 n.*562*
Hall, Alexander William (1838-1919) – politician, **6:** 329 n.*544*; **7:** 267 n.*480*; **8:** 202 n.*345*, 249, 250 n.*419*, 256
Hall (of Maidstone, Kent):
Edward Pickard, Mr., **4:** 65, 66 n.*3*
Edward Vine (b. 1837) – composer and writer, **4:** 66 n.*3*
Mrs., **4:** 65, 66 n.*3*
Hall, Miss – friend of Henrietta Dodgson, **8:** 362 n.*591*
Hall, Owen, alias James Davies (1853-1907) – dramatist, **9:** 197 n.*323*
Hallé (of London and Manchester):
Charles, Sir (1819-1895) – musician, **5:** 226 n.*359*; **6:** 281 n.*462*; **7:** 84 n.*144*; **8:** 442 n.*708*
Wilhelmine, Lady (1839-1911), formerly Madame Norman Neruda – violinist, **6:** 281 n.*462*; **7:** 84 n.*144*; **8:** 442 n.*708*

Halliday, Andrew (1831-1877) – dramatist, **4:** 291 n.*348*, 337 n.*436*; **7:** 200 n.*374*
Halloway House, Hastings (MacDonalds), **6:** 270 n.*437*
Halton, John Foster (b. 1837) – undergraduate at University, **2:** 71 n.*142*
Halton Castle, Cheshire, **1:** 13
Ham, Surrey, **2:** 51
Hambledon, near Godalming, Surrey, **6:** 170 n.*266*, 227, 228; **9:** 235
Hamer, Sam Hield (d. 1941) – editor of *Little Folks*, **9:** 294, 295 n.*466*
Hamilton, Frederick Alexander Pollock (1852-1878) – judge's marshal and mounted policeman, **7:** 21 n.*18*, 22
Hamilton, Mr. – friend of Edwin Dodgson, **6:** 227 n.*358*
Hamilton (of Chichester, Sussex):
Mr., **6:** 444 n.*727*
Mrs., **6:** 444 n.*727*
Hamilton, William Rowan, Sir (1805-1865) – mathematician, **1:** 80 n.*81*
Hamilton Russell (of Burwarton House, Bridgenorth, Shropshire):
Gustavus Frederick, Lord (1797-1872), 7th Viscount Boyne, **6:** 144 n.*219*, 166 n.*258*
Gustavus Russell (1830-1907), 8th Viscount Boyne, **6:** 144 n.*219*, 166 n.*258*; **7:** 311 n.*556*
Katharine Frances, Lady Boyne (d. 1903), **7:** 311 n.*556*
Hammersmith, Middlesex, **4:** 312, 337; **6:** 21, 222
Hammond, Charles Edward (b. 1837) – mathematical lecturer, **5:** 376
Hammond Typewriter, **8:** 394 n.*640*, 396 n.*643*, 398, 424, 428, 556; **9:** 45
Hampton Court Gardens, Middlesex, **5:** 140
Hanbury (of Shobdon, Herefordshire):
Arthur Allen Bateman, Rev. (1829-1919), **7:** 273 n.*495*, 404
Arthur Davenport (b. 1867), **7:** 273 n.*495*
Constance Mary (b. 1863), **7:** 273 n.*495*
Edith (b. 1860), **7:** 273 n.*495*
Mary Beatrice (b. 1874), **7:** 273 n.*495*
Mary Ward née Davenport (d. 1895), **7:** 273 n.*495*, 404
Winifred Kathleen (b. 1879), **7:** 273 n.*495*
Hanbury, Dorothy (b. 1880) – actress, **9:** 139 n.*240*
Handbook of Physiology (bk. William Kirke), **3:** 165 n.*238*, 167
Handel, George Frederick (1685-1759) – composer, **3:** 32 n.*47*
Handel Festival, **6:** 157 n.*242*
Hanger, Miss – lodging-house keeper, **6:** 228
Hankey, Miss – friend of Ethel Barclay, **8:** 130 n.*211*
Hannah (Glenalmond, Scotland):
Anne Sophia née Gregory, **3:** 97
John (1818-1888) – warden of Glenalmond Trinity College, **3:** 96 n.*146*
"Hanson Lewis,"see Becker
Hans the Boatman (dr. Clay Greene), **8:** 604 n.*959*; **9:** 272 n.*431*
Happy Arcadia (dr. W. S. Gilbert & Frederick Clay), **6:** 259 n.*412*

Harcourt (of Eltham, Kent):
Alice née Brandreth (1845-1919), **7:** 224
Leveson Francis. Mr. (1839-1907) – civil engineer, **7:** 496 n.*809*
Harcourt (of Nuneham Courtenay, Oxfordshire):
Aubrey (1852-1904), **6:** 271 n.*439*
Edith (1855-1944), **6:** 271 n.*439*, 289
Edward William, Mr. (1825-1891) – politician, **4:** 113 n.*81*; **5:** 77 n.*118*; **6:** 271 n.*439*, 289
Emily Julia, Miss (d. 1913), **5:** 77 n.*118*
Susan Harriet née Holroyd (d. 1894), **6:** 271 n.*439*
Harcourt (of Cowley Grange, Oxfordshire):
Augustus George Vernon, Mr. (1834-1919) – reader in chemistry, **4:** 23, 110 n.*79*, 111-115, 213; **5:** 49, 50 n.*67*, 77 n.*117*; **6:** 12 n.*3*, 18, 29 n.*35*, 149, 154, 189, 217, 219, 273, 302 n.*499*, 306, 370, 371, 394, 409, 458, 470, 471; **7:** 144, 175, 224, 384, 385, 426, 434, 440, 489, 490 n.*798*, 496, 500, 501 n.*818*; **8:** 155 n.*254*, 296
Bernard Francis (b. 1877), **7:** 385 n.*664*
Cecil Violet (b. 1875), **7:** 385 n.*664*
Doris Margaret (b. 1883), **7:** 385 n.*664*
Helen Dorothea (b. 1876), **7:** 385 n.*664*
Isabel Marcia (b. 1887), **7:** 385 n.*664*
Janet Isabel (b. 1879), **7:** 385 n.*664*
Mabel Frances (b. 1874), **7:** 385 n.*664*
Mildred Edith (b. 1874), **7:** 385 n.*664*
Rachel Mary née Bruce (b. 1849), **6:** 302 n.*499*, 370, 371, 390, 394, 410, 458; **7:** 113, 144, 224, 384, 385 n.*664*, 426; **8:** 155 n.*254*, 267, 393
Simon Evelyn (b. 1882), **7:** 385 n.*664*
Winifred Rachel (b. 1886), **7:** 385 n.*664*
Harcourt (of Chelsea, London):
Augustus George Vernon (1834-1919), see above
Emily Anne (b. 1837), **7:** 224
Frederick Edward Vernon, Admiral (1790-1883) – navy officer, **7:** 224
Leveson Francis (1839-1907), see above
Marcia Elizabeth (1834-1898), **7:** 224
Harcourt, Egerton Vernon (1803-1883) – magistrate, **7:** 426 n.*710*
Harcourt, Sydney – actor, **8:** 311, 312 n.*514*
Harcourt, William George Granville Venables Vernon "Historicus," Sir (1827-1904) – politician, **6:** 34 n.*47*; **7:** 257, 258 n.*469*, 261, 262 n.*473*, 264, 267 n.*480*, 337
Harcourt Amory Collection, Harvard, **1:** 31, 71 n.*60*, 83 n.*87*, 111 n.*129*, 115 n.*139*
Harding (of Reigate, Surrey):
Alice M. (b. 1876), **7:** 205 n.*383*, 206
Bernard C. (b. 1872), **7:** 205 n.*383*
Charles Davis, Mr. (b. 1828) – paper merchant, **7:** 205 n.*383*, 206

Florence M. (b. 1870), **7:** 205 n.*383*, 206, 213
Henry P. (b. 1873), **7:** 205 n.*383*
Mary J., Mrs. (b. 1839), **7:** 205 n.*383*, 206, 215
Hardinge, Henry, Viscount (1785-1856) – Commander-in-Chief of the British Army, **2:** 19 n.*32*
Hardinge, William Money (1854-1916) – writer, **6:** 387 n.*633*
Hardman (of London):
Ann née Wreford (1821-1881), **7:** 235 n.*433*, 236
Frances Anne de Rougemont (b. 1866), **7:** 235 n.*433*, 236, 315, 429, 511
Frederick, Mr. (1814-1874) – writer and journalist, **7:** 235 n.*433*
Hardwick (of Grosvenor Lodging House, Eastbourne, Sussex):
Jane, Mrs. (b. 1833), **7:** 27 n.*34*, 303, 353, 455
John, Mr. (1831-1882) – lodging-house manager, **7:** 27 n.*34*, 48, 182, 303, 455
Hardwicke, Philip Yorke (1690-1764) – writer, **7:** 536
Hardy, Mary Evelyn (b. 1859) – teacher, **8:** 531, 532 n.*852*
Hardy, see Gathorne-Hardy
Hardy, Thomas (1840-1928) – writer, **7:** 468 n.*769*
Hare (of London):
Beatrice Mary (b. 1872?), **7:** 289 n.*523*, 290, 305
Charles Ambrose (1875-1885), **7:** 289 n.*523*, 290, 305
Ernestine Mary née Bruce, Lady (d. 1936), **7:** 289 n.*523*
Margaret "Maggie" Ernestine Augusta (b. 1869), **7:** 289 n.*523*, 290, 305
Richard Granville (1866-1931), **7:** 289 n.*523*
William, Lord (1833-1924), 3rd Earl of Listowel, **7:** 289 n.*523*
Hare, John (1844-1921) – actor and manager, **5:** 125, 126 n.*200*, 231; **7:** 15, 16 n.*10*; **9:** 57 n.*104*
Harford, Frederick Kill, Rev. (1832-1906), **6:** 340 n.*565*; **8:** 44 n.*64*; **9:** 152 n.*263*
Hargreaves (of Cuffnells, Hampshire):
Alice Pleasance née Liddell (1852-1934), **1:** 101 n.*111*, 126 n.*155*; **2:** 65 n.*129*, 111 n.*216*, 112; **3:** 44, 45, 55, 65, 73, 121, to Madeira with parents 129; **4:** 11, 15, 19, 24, 33, 35, 42, 44, 48, 57, 69 n.*11*, river trip to Nuneham 81 n.*33*, 83, 84, 88, river trip to Godstow 93-96, 98, 103, 110-115, 136, 139, 141, 146, 149, 153, 162, 163, 169, 170 n.*163*, celebrations for the Prince and Princess of Wales 171-173, 175-178, meeting at Cheltenham 185 n.*180*, 186 n.*181*, 187, 192, sprained leg 193, 195-200, 204, visit by the Prince and Princess of Wales 208, last river trip 210-213, 257 n.*299*, aloofness 264 n.*309*, 266, 298, superfluous caution 299 n.*364*, 307; **5:** 9, 10, 11 n.*1*, presentation copy of *Alice* listed 19, 60 n.*87*, awkward stage of transition 74 n.*112*, 86, 122 n.*192*, 180 n.*298*, 243 n.*395*; **6:** last photograph 121 n.*184*, 146 n.*223*, presentation copy of *Looking-Glass* 190, presentation of Italian edition of *Alice* 260, 274; **7:** marriage 296 n.*535*; **8:** 99 n.*164*, asks to borrow *Alice* manuscript for facsimile 169 n.*283*, 170, 182,

192 n.*322*, 297 n.*496*, meets Alice's husband 432, visit 598 n.*954*
Reginald Gervis, Mr. (1852-1926) – magistrate, **7:** 296 n.*535*; **8:** 432 n.*697*
Harington (of Oxford):
Alice Margaret (1854-1901), **3:** 154 n.*226*, 167, 168 n.*244*; **4:** 43, 44, 105, 106 n.*72*, 180, 209, 210 n.*220*; **6:** 123; **7:** 110 n.*204*
Beatrice Cecilia (1852-1936), **1:** 108; **3:** 154 n.*226*, 167, 168 n.*244*; **4:** 43, 44, 105, 106 n.*72*, 178, 209, 210 n.*220*; **6:** 123; **7:** 110 n.*204*; **9:** 349 n.*559*
Cecilia née Smith (d. 1844) – first wife, **2:** 110 n.*214*
Mary née Paul (1815?-1886) – second wife, **1:** 108; **3:** 154 n.*226*, 167, 168 n.*244*; **4:** 83 n.*36*, 84, 140; **5:** 120 n.*187*; **7:** 110 n.*204*, 163
Robert "Bob" (1851-1855), **1:** 108
Richard (1835-1911), see below
Richard, Rev. Dr. (1800-1853) – principal of Brasenose, **1:** 87, 88 n.*91*; **2:** 110 n.*214*
Harington (of Bredenbury, Herefordshire):
Charles (1862-1921), **7:** 267, 268 n.*481*
Edward (1863-1937), **7:** 268 n.*481*
Frances Agnata née Biscoe, Lady (1836-1915), **7:** 41, 267, 268 n.*481*, 405, 485
Frances "Fanny" Cecilia (b. 1874), **7:** 268 n.*481*
John "Johnnie" (b. 1873), **7:** 268 n.*481*
Margaret "Meg" Agnata (b. 1871), **2:** 110 n.*214*; **7:** 268 n.*481*, 405, 485
Richard (1861-1931), **7:** 268 n.*481*, 272; **8:** 610
Richard, Sir (1835-1911) – judge, **2:** 68 n.*135*, 74, 10 n.*214*; **3:** 161 n.*236*; **6:** 306, 340, 438; **7:** 41, 228, 242, 246, 267, 268 n.*481*, 310, 322, 384, 405, 485, 501; **8:** 70 n.*114*, 156, 253, 308, 517, 560, 610; **9:** 152 n.*261*
Robert (1868-1933), **7:** 268 n.*481*
Harker, Mr. – song-writer, **3:** 101 n.*149*
"Harlequin" (in harlequinade), **2:** 22
Harley, John Pritt (1786-1858) – opera singer, **2:** 124 n.*240*; **3:** 14, 81, 82 n.*127*
Harley Street, London, **2:** 53
Harper (of Calcutta, India):
Eleanor "Topsy" (b. 1865), **6:** 341 n.*567*
Minnie "Nina" (b. 1867), **6:** 341 n.*567*, 416
Mrs. née Giraud, **6:** 341 n.*567*; **8:** 576 n.*919*
Harper (of Oxford):
Hugo Daniel, Rev. Dr. (b. 1821) – principal of Jesus College, **7:** 146, 147 n.*276*
Margaret A. (b. 1861), **7:** 147 n.*276*
Mary (b. 1857), **7:** 147 n.*276*
Mary C., Mrs. (b. 1830), **7:** 146, 147 n.*276*
Harper's Magazine, **8:** 516 n.*832*

Harrington, N. H. – dramatist, **3:** 101 n.*149*, 120 n.*170*
Harris, Alexander Charles, Hon. (1872-1927) – civil servant, **8:** 592 n.*945*
Harris, Augustus Glossop (1825-1873) – actor and manager, **2:** 23 n.*43*
Harris, Florence "Florry" (b. 1858) – governess to the Bruntons, **7:** 464 n.*763*, 467, 472
Harris, Henry, Rev. (b. 1819), **6:** 317 n.*526*
Harris, L., Miss – singer, **5:** 98 n.*155*
Harrison (of Thornhill, Sunderland, Durham):
Alfred Reid Clanny (b. 1816) – engineer, **5:** 39 n.*48*
Charles Henry (1824-1867), see below
Elizabeth Anna Maria née Hall, **5:** 39 n.*48*
John Thornhill (1815-1891), **5:** 39 n.*48*
Thomas Elliott (1808-1888), see below
William, Mr. - shipbroker, **5:** 39 n.*48*
William Gorst (1803-1891), see below
Harrison (of Hart, Durham):
Beatrice Mary (b. 1855), **5:** 39 n.*48*
Clara Crawford (b. 1839), **5:** 39 n.*48*
Emily Plenderleith (b. 1844), **5:** 39 n.*48*
Gertrude (b. 1837), **5:** 39 n.*48*
Julia Louisa (b. 1845), **5:** 39 n.*48*
Kathleen Courtland (b. 1842), **5:** 39 n.*48*
Margaret Crawford (b. 1853), **5:** 39 n.*48*
Rachel Arbuthnot (b. 1850), **5:** 39 n.*48*
Sophia Park (b. 1847), **5:** 39 n.*48*
Susan (b. 1838), **5:** 39 n.*48*
Susan Arbuthnot Crawford née Auston (b. 1826), **5:** 39 n.*48*
William Gorst, Rev. (1803-1891), **5:** 39 n.*48*
Winifred (b. 1848), **5:** 39 n.*48*
Harrison (of Whitburn, Durham):
Catherine "Dolly" Charlotte (b. 1868), **5:** 39 n.*48*; **8:** 31 n.*37*, 32, 41
Emily Cecilia (b. 1860), **4:** 178; **5:** 39 n.*48*; **8:** 31 n.*37*
Frances Mary, see Langton Clarke
John Collinson (b. 1870), **5:** 39 n.*48*
Julia Mildred (b. 1866), **5:** 39 n.*48*; **8:** 31 n.*37*
Margaret Adair née White – first wife, **5:** 39 n.*48*
Sophia Agneta (b. 1864), **5:** 39 n.*48*; **8:** 31 n.*37*
Sophia née Collinson (1826-1891) – second wife, **5:** 39 n.*48*; **8:** 31 n.*37*
Thomas Elliott (b. 1869?), **5:** 39 n.*48*
Thomas Elliott, Mr. (1808-1888) – engineer, **5:** 12 n.*3*, 39 n.*48*, 159 n.*261*; **8:** 31 n.*37*
Harrison (of Whitburn, Durham):
Charles Augustus (b. 1848), **5:** 39 n.*48*; **8:** 32 n.*38*
Charles Henry, Lt. Col. (1824-1867) – army officer, **5:** 39 n.*48*; **8:** 32 n.*38*
Edith C. (b. 1858), **4:** 179; **5:** 39 n.*48*, 41, 377; **8:** 32 n.*38*

Emily Louisa "Loui" (b. 1851), **5:** 39 n. *48*, 41 n.*49*, 377; **8:** 32 n.*38*
Louisa Elizabeth née Barretto (1825-1906), **5:** 39 n.*48*; **8:** 32 n.*38*
Rose Margaretta (b. 1855), **5:** 39 n.*48*, 41, 377; **8:** 32 n.*38*
Harrison (of Mickley, near Ripon, Yorkshire):
Emily Eliza (b. 1825), **4:** 274 n.*320*; **9:** 227 n.*360*
John Walker, Rev. (1789-1857), **4:** 274 n.*320*
Harrison (of London):
Ethel née Harrison (d. 1916), **8:** 132
Frederic, Mr. (1831-1923) – writer, **8:** 48 n.*70*, 63, 79, 132, 166
Harrison, Henry Leland (b. 1837), **2:** 113
Harrison:
James Park, Mr. (1817-1901) – architect, **4:** 35
Matthew J. (b. 1847), **4:** 35
Harrison, Miss – model for James Sant picture, **5:** 142
Harrison, Sara C. (b. 1864) – art student, **8:** 80 n.*124*
Harrison, Wilmot – dramatist, **4:** 273 n.*318*
Harrison Family (of Richmond), **7:** 348
Harrisons of Ripon – printer and bookseller, **1:** 54 n.*11*
Harrogate, Yorkshire, **1:** 53, 54 n.*15*
Harrow, Middlesex, **6:** 323, 334; **7:** 78
Harrow School, **8:** 554
Hart, A., Mr. – theatrical agent, **8:** 615 n.*975*
Hart, Adelaide "Ada" Elizabeth Jane (d. 1880), see Wilcox
Hart, Durham, **5:** 39 n.*48*
Hart (of Dublin, Ireland):
Elizabeth Anna née Smedley (1822-1890?), **3:** 58, 60; **4:** 188 n.*184*; **6:** 459
Thomas Barnard (1804-1886) – army surgeon, **4:** 188 n.*184*, 190, 191; **6:** 459
Hart (of Kilderry, Ireland):
George Vaughan, Commander RN (1805-1895), **4:** 188 n.*184*, 190, 191
Jane Maria née Hart, **4:** 188 n.*184*
Harte, Francis Bret (1839-1902) – writer, **7:** 260, 261 n.*472*
Harvey (of Whitby, Yorkshire):
Bissel, Lieut.-Col. (1775-1854) – army officer, **2:** 15 n.*25*
Mary, Mrs. (b. 1778), **2:** 15 n.*25*
Mary Agnes (b. 1812), see Bainbridge
Harvey (of St. Giles', Oxford):
Blanche Barbara, Mrs. (b. 1836), **6:** 325, 409, 465; **7:** 116 n.*215*, 329
Henry Auber, Rev. (1825-1910), **6:** 325, 409 n.*671*, 465, 475; **7:** 116 n.*215*, 329
Harvey, Herbert, Rev. (1835-1899), **3:** 70 n.*109*
Harvey, see Martin-Harvey
Harwood, Dorothy – actress, **8:** 584 n.*933*
Harwood, Thomas Eustace, Rev. (b. 1837), **2:** 29 n.*56*

Hassall (of Oxford):
Arthur, Mr. (1853-1930) – lecturer and writer, **8:** 90 n.*146*, 245, 259, 340, 382, 491; **9:** 148, 149 n.*255*, 286 n.*453*
Mary Anne Fergusson née Clarke-Preston, **8:** 90 n.*146*, 245, 334, 340, 382, 383, 491; **9:** 328 n.*526*
Hastie, Messrs. & Co. – solicitors, **8:** 297-299, 301, 302
Hastings, F., Miss – actress, **8:** 59 n.*92*
Hastings, Maud – sister of Mrs. Sanday, **9:** 309 n.*492*, 310, 313
Hastings, Sussex, **1:** 115 n.*138*; **3:** 42 n.*66*; **4:** 27, 53; **6:** 116 n.*180*, 231, 238, 245, 270, 280, 281; **7:** 198, 204, 286, 289, 290, 299, 302, 475; **8:** 145, 230, 360, 425, 478, 481, 485, 520, 524, 534, 536, 578, 585; **9:** 25, 29, 91, 163, 175, 176, 207, 328-330, 333, 334, 336, 340
Hastings Castle, **9:** 25, 29, 207, 334
Hastings Orpheus Glee Union, **7:** 459
Hastings Regatta, **7:** 289
Hatch (of Clevedon House, Park Town, Oxford):
Arthur Herbert (1864-1910), **6:** 133 n.*204*, 151, 209 n.*328*, 261; **8:** 572, 573
Beatrice "Bee" Sheward (1866-1947), **6:** 133 n.*204*, sketches 143, 151, 188 n.*292*, 209, 261 n.*418*, nude studies 286, 287, 289, 331 n.*328*, 487, 490; **7:** 42 n.*63*, 191, 196 n.*365*; **8:** 89, 125, 217, 377, 490, living with the Sandays 625, 632; **9:** 12 n.*4*, 39, 64, 67, 129, 154, 161, trip to Eastbourne 163-165, 198, 200, 223, 232, 233, 236, 238, 241, 253, 260, dines with 283, 284, writes play 294, 296, 297, 315, 321, 324, 347, 348
Bessie Cartwright née Thomas (1839-1891), **6:** 133 n.*204*, 142, 151, 188, 261; **7:** 42 n.*63*, 191, 196, 224, 264, 275, 419; **8:** 87 n.*141*, 105 n.*174*, 564, 573, 595
Edwin, Rev. (1835-1889) – vice-principal of St. Mary Hall, **6:** 133 n.*204*, 142, 188; **7:** 191, 224, 246, 376; **8:** 87 n.*141*, 125, 490 n.*793*
Ethel Charlotte (1869-1975), **6:** 133 n.*204*, 151, 188 n.*292*, 209 n.*328*, 286, 331; **7:** 42 n.*63*, 191, 196 n.*365*, 264; **8:** 87 n.*141*, 103, trip to London 108, 564-566, trip to Eastbourne 572, 573, 595, 605 n.*961*, 619; **9:** 12 n.*4*, 140, 234, 284, 285, 315, 347, 348
Evelyn Maud (1871-1951), **6:** 133 n.*204*, 151; **7:** nude study 196 n.*365*, 264, 275 n.*500*; **8:** 87, 89, 564, 565, 567, 568, 619, 632; **9:** 12 n.*4*, 13, 135, logic lecture 143 n.*248*, 144, 195, 198, 223, 232, 233, 281, 347
Wilfred Stanley (1865-1956), **6:** 133 n.*204*, 143, 151, 188 n.*292*, 209 n.*328*, 261 n.*418*
Hatfield Church, Hertfordshire, **6:** 220 n.*347*
Hatfield House, **6:** 118 n.*181*, 132, 135, 139, 161-165, 220, 246, 248-250, 373, 375, 441, 442; **7:** 100 n.*186*; **8:** 76, 78 n.*121*, 461, 486
Hatton (of London):
Bessie F. (b. 1875) – actress, **8:** 451 n.*722*, 453, 527, 628
Mrs., **8:** 453 n.*726*
Hatton, John Liptrot (1809-1896) – composer, **3:** 71 n.*111*

Haughton, John (b. 1839) – barrister, **3:** 66, 67 n.*101*
Havell, Edmund Jr. (1819-1894) – artist, **2:** 75 n.*151*
Havelock, Henry, Sir (1795-1857) – army commander, **3:** 149 n.*215*
Havers, see Morgan
Haverstock Hill, London, **7:** 106
Haviland, William (1860-1917) – actor, **9:** 162 n.*277*
Hawarden (of Princes Gardens, South Kensington, London):
  Clementina née Elphinstone-Fleeming, Lady (1822-1865), **4:** 315 n.*395*, 317, 318, 341, 343
  Cornwallis Maude, Lord (1817-1905), **4:** 315 n.*395*, 317, 331, 341, 343
Haweis, Hugh Reginald, Rev. (1838-1901) – writer, **7:** 112 n.*207*
Hawke (of Comeragh Road, West Kensington, London):
  John Anthony (1869-1941) – barrister, **8:** 564 n.*899*; **9:** 158 n.*273*
  Winifred "Winnie" Edith Laura née Stevens (1872-1958), **8:** 334 n.*550*, 336, 337, 368, 373, 552, 556, 557, 564 n.*899*, 597, 611, 620, 621, trip to London and Guildford 627-629; **9:** 12 n.*2*, 35, 37, 38, 49, 58, 109, 142, 156, marriage 158
Hawkins (of Oriel College, Oxford):
  Edward, Dr. (1789-1882) – Provost of Oriel, **3:** 121 n.*171*; **5:** 77 n.*118*
  Margaret (1835?-1870), **5:** 77 n.*118*
  Mary Ann née Buckle (1805-1892), **5:** 77 n.*118*
  Mary Frances (1838-1908), **5:** 77 n.*118*
Hawthornden Castle, near Edinburgh, **3:** 99, 100 n.*148*; **6:** 183
Hawtrey (of Frimley, Surrey):
  Ida Florence (b. 1880), **7:** 360
  Jane Mary née Blackburn (b. 1856), **7:** 283 n.*513*, 284, 286, 360
  Mary, **7:** 300, 360
Haydn, Franz Joseph (1732-1809) – composer, **3:** 66
Haydn, Joseph (1786?-1856) – editor, **2:** 36 n.*71*
Haydon, Benjamin Robert (1786-1846) – artist, **1:** 51 n.*5*, 52, 56, 57, 112
Haydon (of Guildford, Surrey):
  Dodsworth, Mr. (1829-1901) – lawyer, **6:** 57, 58 n.*87*, 77, 102, 316, 344, 349, 354, 357, 411; **7:** 13 n.*7*, 160
  Edith Georgiana (b. 1863), **6:** 58 n.*87*, 80, 100-102, 356; **7:** 159
  Eleanor Georgiana née Dudding (b. 1839), **6:** 58 n.*87*, 77, 102, 316, 319, 344, 354, 357, 411; **7:** 159, 160
  Ethel Dodsworth (b. 1867), **6:** 58 n.*87*, 102, 316, 356, 411, 481; **7:** 159
  Katharine Isabella (1864-1868), **6:** 58 n.*87*, 356; **7:** 159
  Mary "May" Eleanor (1862-1944), **6:** 58 n.*87*, 80, 100-102, 316, 356; **7:** 159
  Thomas "Tommy" Horatio (b. 1865), **6:** 58 n.*87*, 102, 316, 356; **7:** 159
  Walter Dodsworth (b. 1861), **6:** 58 n.*87*, 80, 356; **7:** 159
Hayes, Thomas, Rev. (b. 1840), **4:** 78 n.*27*
Haygarth, Henry William, Rev. (b. 1821), **4:** 120, 121 n.*91*
Hayllar (of Castle Priory, Wallingford St. Peter, Berkshire):

James, Mr. (1829-1920) – artist, **5:** 239 n.*386*; **6:** 22
Jessica Ellen (1858-1940) – artist, **8:** 413 n.*669*
Hayman, Charles Norton, Dr. (b. 1853) – physician, **7:** 55, 56 n.*88*
Haynes, Annabel S., Mrs. (b. 1833), **8:** 87 n.*140*
Hayter, William Goodenough (1792-1878) – politician, **6:** 88 n.*132*
Head, Agnes, Mrs. (b. 1831), **6:** 444 n.*729*
Headington, Oxfordshire, **5:** 187; **6:** 326, 450; **9:** 252
Headington Hill Hall, **5:** 69 n.*103*
Headington Lunatic Asylum, **4:** 210, 216
Headlam, Stewart Duckworth, Rev. (1847-1924), **7:** 173 n.*321*
Head of the Family (bk. Dinah Mulock), **1:** 68, 69 n.*55*, 92, 93; **3:** 141
Health (bk. Thomas Mayo), **8:** 94 n.*154*
Heaphy (of London):
Archibald, **7:** 122 n.*230*, 393 n.*670*, 397, 398, 439; **8:** 164, 431
Eliza née Bradstreet (b. 1815?), **5:** 231 n.*368*; **6:** 292 n.*482*, 333; **7:** 122 n.*230*, 125, 397, 398, 439, 494; **8:** 11 n.*2*, 100, 131, 164, 431, 578; **9:** 16 n.*12*, 176
George (b. 1838), see below
Leonora "Leo" (b. 1862), see Le Bouvier
Theodosia "Theo" Laura (1858-1920), see Russell-Morris
Thomas Frank, Mr. (1813-1873) – artist, **5:** 219 n.*350*, 229 n.*366*, 230, 231 n.*368*; **6:** commissions picture14, 15 n.*9*, 22, 23 n.*23*, 27, 56, 68, 71, 79, 81, two commissioned pictures nearly complete 82 n.*120*, supports publication of *The Likeness of Christ* 292 n.*482*
Heaphy (of Hastings, Sussex):
Emma M., Mrs. (b. 1838), **8:** 578 n.*923*, 585
George, Mr. (b. 1838) – dentist, **8:** 578 n.*923*, 585; **9:** 336 n.*538*
Heard, Charles (b. 1828) – Tennyson's gardener and head man, **4:** 356 n.*466*
Heartsease (bk. Charlotte Yonge), **2:** 57 n.*115*
Heart Strings and Fiddle Strings (dr. David Fisher), **5:** 64 n.*95*
Heath, Caroline (1835-1887) – actress, **2:** 20 n.*36*
Heathcote, William (1801-1881) – politician, **3:** 66 n.*99*; **5:** 91 n.*140*
Heatherbell – ship, **6:** 484
Heather-Bigg, Miss, **9:** 96 n.*175*
Heatherley (of Newman Street Studio, London):
Frank (b. 1862), **6:** 333 n.*550*
Lois (b. 1864), **6:** 333 n.*550*; **7:** 398 n.*676*
Thomas, Mr. (1825-1914) – artist , **6:** 333 n.*550*, 402; **7:** 388 n.*668*, 394, 397, 443, 492, 502, 503, 523; **8:** 47, 48 n.*69*, 53, 100, 108, 163, 167, 199, 204, 212, 216
Heathfield, Miss – distant relative, **9:** 103, 104 n.*189*
Heaton, Mary (d. 1873) – friend of the Munros, **4:** 319 n.*404*
Hebrew Grammar (bk. Friedrich Gesenius), **5:** 131 n.*210*
Hebrew Lexicon (bk. Friedrich Gesenius), **5:** 131 n.*210*

Hedley (of Ripon, Yorkshire):
Mary, **7:** 49 n.*75*, 57, 74
Thomas, Rev. (1822-1899), **7:** 49 n.*75*, 57, 74
Hektograph, see Chromograph
Held, Anna (1873-1918) – actress, **9:** 333 n.*532*
Helena Nursing Home, Reading, **8:** 547
Helps, Arthur, Sir (1813-1875) – writer, **1:** 75 n.*70*
Helps Family of Brighton, **7:** 92 n.*165*
Helvellyn, Cumberland, **2:** 95
Henderson (of Headington Hill, Oxford):
Annie Gray Wright (1871-1951), **7:** 144 n.*267*, 148, 190, nude studies 191 n.*354*, 192, 193 n.*360*, 195 n.*364*, 271 n.*489*, 273 n.*496*, 275, 276, 276 n.*502*, 417, 483; **8:** 105, 214, 217, 557, 564, 593, 611; **9:** 62 n.*115*, 198, 228
Ann Wood née Gray (1844-1899), **7:** 144 n.*267*, 148, 190, 192, 193, 221, 222, 271 n.*489*, 275, 276, 376, 483; **8:** 105, 214, 215, 218, 245, 545, 557, 593, 629; **9:** 145, 228, 240, 243, 252, 320
Hamilton Frances (b. 1872), see Petersen
Jeanette (b. 1881), **7:** 144 n.*267*
Lilian "Lily" Janet Wright (1880-1966), **7:** 144 n.*267*; **8:** 105, 214, nude sketches 217, 218, 377, 545, 557, 564, 593, trip to London 621; **9:** 145, 228, 240, 243, 258
Patrick Arkley Wright, Rev. (1841-1922) – tutor, **7:** 144 n.*267*, 192, 221, 222, 306, 309, 419; **8:** 89 n.*143*, 214, 215, 218, 338, 339, 446, 503, 629; **9:** 198, 252, 258, 320
Robert Wright (b. 1875), **7:** 144 n.*267*; **8:** 105, 545
Henderson, James, Rev. (1840-1935), **5:** 172 n.*287*
Henderson's donkey, **1:** 27
Hendschel, Albert Louis Ulrich (1834-1883) – artist, **6:** 434, 435 n.*716*, 439, 448
Henley (of Shotover Lodge, near Headington, Oxfordshire):
Agnes (b. 1852), **6:** 326 n.*540*
Agnes Walwyn née Walrond (1822-1911), **6:** 326 n.*540*
Emily Augusta (b. 1851?), **6:** 326 n.*540*
Georgina Caroline (b. 1850), **6:** 326 n.*540*
Joseph Arthur (b. 1856), **6:** 326 n.*540*
Joseph John, Mr. (1821-1910) – local government officer, **6:** 326 n.*540*
Henley (of Putney, Surrey):
Arthur Keith (b. 1863), **4:** 123 n.*96*; **7:** 544 n.*877*
Beatrice Mary (1859-1941), **4:** 123 n.*96*, 178, 340 n.*442*; **7:** 544; **8:** 531 n.*851*
Charles Beauclerk (1869-1945), **4:** 123 n.*96*
Constance Laura (1857-1930), **4:** 123 n.*96*, 179, 340 n.*442*; **7:** 544
Emily Louisa née Aldridge (1831-1893), **4:** 123 n.*96* , 340; **6:** 359, 422-424; **7:** 544; **8:** 531 n.*851*

Ethel Maud (1865-1931), **4:** 123 n.*96*; **6:** 360 n.*595*, 422; **7:** 544; **8:** 531 n.*851*
Mabel Augusta (1871-1966), **4:** 123 n.*96*; **8:** 531 n.*851*
Mildred Caroline (1867-1951), **4:** 123 n.*96*; **6:** 360 n.*595*, 422
Robert, Rev. (1831-1910), **4:** 122 n.*94*, 123 n.*96*, 340; **6:** 359, 422-424
Robert Eden (1861-1933), **4:** 123 n.*96*; **7:** 544 n.*877*
Henley, Oxfordshire, **6:** 228
Hennell (of Ventnor, Isle of Wight):
Annie T., Mrs. (b. 1817), **6:** 478 n.*790*
Catherine A. (b. 1843), **6:** 478 n.*790*
Henri, Jenny – actress, **5:** 193, 202, 203, 205
Henrici, Olaus M. F. E., Dr. (1840-1918) – mathematician, **7:** 282 n.*512*; **8:** 179 n.*295*
Henry, Abraham (b. 1825) – dramatist, **7:** 504 n.*823*
Henry Dunbar (dr. Mary Braddon, adapt. Tom Taylor), **5:** 123 n.*196*
Henwick, Worcestershire, **4:** 121
Hepworth, Clare – singer, **2:** 122
Herbert, Gwynne – actress, **9:** 87 n.*157*
Herbert, Louisa Ruth (1832-1921), later Mrs. Crabbe – actress, **5:** 72, 73 n.*110*
Herbert, Mary, Lady (d. 1935), **6:** 125 n.*193*
Herbert, Robert George Wyndham, Rt. Hon. Sir (1831-1905) – politician, **8:** 45 n.*67*
Herbert's Island, Derwent Water, Cumberland, **2:** 94
Herbert's Poems (bk. George Herbert), **2:** 28 n.*55*
Hereford, **7:** 127
Hereford Assizes, **7:** 127
Herkomer (of Bushey, Hertfordshire):
Elsa (1877-1938), **8:** 471 n.*763*
Hubert von, Mr. (1849-1914) – artist, **8:** 330 n.*544*, 377, 470, 471 n.*763*, 559, 607 n.*963*, 624, 625 n.*988*
Herman, Henry (1832-1894) – dramatist, **7:** 525 n.*849*; **8:** 81 n.*125*; **9:** 173 n.*290*
"Hermione" (in *Henry VIII*), **2:** 83 n.*164*
Hermitage, The, St. Petersburg, **5:** 294, 338
Hermit's Cave, Holy Island, Scotland, **6:** 183
Hermon (of Albany House, Byfleet, Surrey):
George Edward, Mr. (b. 1852) – undergraduate at Christ Church, **6:** 141, 142 n.*214*, 491, 492
Mary née Newson (b. 1854), **6:** 491 n.*812*, 492
Herodotus (485-424 BC) – Greek historical writer, **1:** 41
Heron, George (d. 1780) of Daresbury Hall, Cheshire, **1:** 13
Heron, Miss, **7:** 86 n.*149*
Heron-Maxwell, Beatrice Ethel (1855-1939) – lady in waiting, **8:** 466 n.*755*, 467, 469, 513

Herring, John Frederick (1795-1865) – artist, **1:** 131 n.*162*
Herring, Miss – singer, **7:** 465 n.*765*
Hertford College, Oxford, **7:** 275, 544; **9:** 199
Hervey, Selina Catherine née Meade, Lady (1832-1911), **8:** 165 n.*272*
Hessey (of London):
  Anne (b. 1825), **5:** 55 n.*78*
  Catherine Mary (b. 1820), **5:** 55 n.*78*
  D., Miss, **5:** 55 n.*78*
  Robert Falkner (1826-1911), see below
Hessey (of Basing, Hampshire):
  Charles D. (b. 1873), **6:** 335 n.*554*, 437
  Emma née Dodson (b. 1833), **5:** 55 n.*78*, 74; **6:** 335 n.*554*
  Fanny D. (b. 1875), **6:** 335 n.*554*
  Francis "Frank," **6:** 335 n.*554*, 437
  James "Jemmie" (b. 1867), **6:** 335 n.*554*, 437
  Robert, **6:** 335 n.*554*, 437
  Robert Falkner, Rev. (1826-1911), **4:** 234 n.*261*, 304; **5:** 55 n.*78*, 56, 86; **6:** 335 n.*554*, 437, 466
Hetherington (of St. Pancras, London):
  Clarice, **8:** 316 n.*519*, 364, 368
  Dorothy "Dot" (used stage name Alberti) – actress, **8:** 316 n.*519*, 364, 369
  Henry, **8:** 316 n.*519*, 364
  Henry, Mr. (b. 1846) – actor, **8:** 316 n.*519*
  Hetty, Mrs. (b. 1836), **8:** 316 n.*519*
Hetton Lawn, Charlton Kings, Gloucestershire, **4:** 185 n.*180*, 186, 187
Heurtley (of Christ Church, Oxford):
  Charles Abel, Dr. (1806-1895) – professor of divinity, **1:** 91 n.*95*; **2:** 109 n.*212*, 117 n.*223*, 125; **3:** 23 n.*30*, 42, 49, 124, 125 n.*179*, 135; **7:** 19, 20 n.*16*, 164, 226, 440; **8:** 44 n.*63*, 124, 127, 358; **9:** 124, 194 n.*319*
  Ellen (b. 1851), **7:** 19, 20 n.*16*, 488; **9:** 195
  Frances (b. 1852), **7:** 19, 20 n.*16*, 488
  Jane, Mrs. (b. 1809), **7:** 19, 20 n.*16*, 226; **8:** 124, 358
Heward, Mrs. – teacher, **8:** 413 n.*670*
Hewett (of The Red House, Chilworth, near Romsey, Hampshire):
  Anna (d. 1884), **6:** 244 n.*387*, 246
  Clara née Von Pochhammer, Lady (d. 1867), **6:** 244 n.*387*
  Edbert Ansgar (1860-1915), **6:** 244 n.*387*, 246
  George Henry (1865-1930), **6:** 244 n.*387*, 246
  George John Routledge, Sir (1818-1876), 3rd Bart., **6:** 244 n.*387*, 246
  Harald George (1858-1949), **6:** 244 n.*387*, 246
  Helga Louisa (d. 1954), **6:** 244 n.*387*, 246
  Hilda Henrietta (d. 1945), **6:** 244 n.*387*, 246
  Hulda Emilie (d. 1928), **6:** 244 n.*387*, 246
  Mary Ethelinda (d. 1873), **6:** 244 n.*387*, 246

Hewett (of Eastbourne, Sussex):
Mrs., **9:** 31
William Henry, Rev. (1853-1934), **8:** 581 n.*928*; **9:** 30 n.*47*, 94, 211, 212, 328, 333, 337, 340
Hewgill & Company – architects, **6:** 341
Hewitt, James Francis Katharinus (1836-1908) – civil servant, **2:** 68 n.*135*; **9:** 200 n.*327*
Hibberd, Shirley (1825-1890) – journalist, **4:** 57
Hicks, George Elgar (1824-1914) – artist, **7:** 539 n.*872*
Hicks, Seymour (1871-1949) – dramatist, **8:** 618 n.*980*; **9:** 13 n.*5*
Hicks-Beach (of Coln St Aldwyn's, Fairford, Gloucestershire):
Eleanor "Nelly" Lucy (b. 1875), **8:** 630 n.*995*
Lucy Catherine née Fortescue (b. 1851), **8:** 630 n.*995*
Michael Edward, Sir (1837-1916), 9th Bart., **4:** 92, 93 n.*50*; **8:** 517 n.*833*, 630; **9:** 211 n.*338*
Susan Evelyn (b. 1878), **8:** 630 n.*995*
Victoria "Tora" Alexandrina (b. 1879), **8:** 630 n.*995*
Hickson, K., Miss – actress and manager, **5:** 109 n.*172*
Hidden Depths (bk. Felicia Skene), **8:** 514 n.*828*
Hidden Hand, The (dr. Adolphe Dennery & J. Edmond, adapt. Tom Taylor), **5:** 37, 38 n.*46*
Higginson, Thomas Wentworth (1823-1911) – writer, **7:** 427 n.*712*
Higgs, Jessie (b. 1871), **6:** 297 n.*489*
Higher Plane Curves (bk. George Salmon), **1:** 63 n.*40*
Highgate School, Middlesex, **2:** 44
Highlander, The (Alexander Munro) – statue, **6:** 13 n.*7*
Highland Nurses (pic. Edwin Landseer), **2:** 75 n.*151*
High Life Below Stairs (dr. James Townley), **5:** 71, 72 n.*108*, 156
High Wickham (Wycombe), Buckinghamshire, **2:** 80
Hilda Terrace, Whitby, **2:** 15 n.*25*, 102, 104
Hildebrand, Emiliar (b. 1842) – friend of the Osborns, **6:** 111 n.*173*
Hildyard, Miss – royal governess, **4:** 156 n.*144*
Hill, Annie (d. 1943) – actress, **9:** 123 n.*216*
Hill, Edward, Rev. (1809-1900), **3:** 67 n.*102*; **4:** 35; **6:** 370 n.*608*, 438
Hill, Elsie Evelyn – actress, **9:** 166, 167 n.*284*
Hill (of Shanklin, Isle of Wight):
Mr., **6:** 417
Mrs., **6:** 417, 418 n.*686*; **8:** 301 n.*502*
Hill (of Timsbury, Somerset):
Mrs., **6:** 302
Richard, Rev. (1816-1883), **6:** 302
Hill, Richard Humphrey, Rev. (b. 1825), **8:** 626 n.*990*
Hill, Rowland (1795-1879) – postmaster general, **3:** 132 n.*192*
Hill, William Byron, Mr. (b. 1828) – surgeon, **4:** 247
Hill Norris, Dr. – photographer, **4:** 211

Hills (of Guildford, Surrey):
Acicia, Mrs. (b. 1827), **9:** 290 n.*456*
Dora M. (b. 1867), **9:** 290 n.*456*
Lucy E. (b. 1864), **9:** 290 n.*456*
Mary A. (b. 1858), **9:** 290 n.*456*
William Jeffreys, Rev. (b. 1829), **9:** 290 n.*456*
Hills, Miss – companion to Mrs. Bayne, **7:** 529 n.*856*; **8:** 165 n.*273*
Hills & Saunders, Oxford – photographers, **4:** 295; **6:** 214, 409 n.*670*, 487
Hillyars and the Burtons, The (bk. Henry Kingsley), **5:** 125 n.*199*
Hindle, John (1807-1872) – solicitor, **3:** 147 n.*211*
Hine (of Kensington, London):
F. A., Mrs. (b. 1850), **6:** 215, 216; **8:** 214 n.*366*
George Thomas Arrowsmith (1838-1916) – architect, **4:** 203 n.*211*, 204; **6:** 215 n.*336*, 216; **8:** 214 n.*366*
Muriel F. (b. 1874), **8:** 214 n.*366*
Thomas G. M. (b. 1872), **8:** 214 n.*366*
Hingston, Alfred Nottage, Rev. (b. 1832), **3:** 49 n.*75*
Hinksey, Berkshire, **4:** 175, 194, 195, 199
Hints for Emergencies (bk. John South), **2:** 47 n.*93*
Hippisley, Robert William, Rev. (b. 1818), **7:** 527 n.*852*
Histoire d'Angleterre (bk. Paul Rapin-Thoyras), **1:** 72 n.*64*
Histological data, **7:** 38 n.*56*
"Historicus," see Harcourt, William G. G. V. V.
History, **2:** 35 n.*69*, 65 n.*130*
History of Cheshire (bk. George Ormerod), **1:** 12
History of England (bk. James Froude), **1:** 97 n.*103*
History of England (bk. Thomas Macaulay), **1:** 26
History of England, The (bk. David Hume), **2:** 65 n.*130*; **3:** 46, 156 n.*230*
History of England, The (bk. Henry White), **1:** 114 n.*137*
History of Europe (bk. Archibald Alison), **1:** 27
History of Europe (bk. Christophe Koch), **1:** 24
History of Latin Christianity (bk. Henry Milman), **3:** 8 n.*4*
History of the Christian Church (bk. Edward Burton), **1:** 80 n.*80*, 84, 85
History of the Christian Church (bk. James Robertson), **5:** 103 n.*160*
History of the Popes (bk. Leopold von Ranke), **1:** 24
Hitchcock (of West Dulwich, Surrey):
Clara Menella née Wilcox (1855-1896) – cousin, **1:** 124 n.*154*; **2:** 101 n.*195*; **5:** 179 n.*296*; **6:** 208 n.*327*, 362, 363, 495; **7:** 45, 47, 48, 423; **8:** 30 n.*36*, 32, 51-57, 131 n.*215*, 307, 327, 353, 370, 371, 375, 450, 458, 461, 562, 596; **9:** 62 n.*114*, 126, 203, 272 n.*432*
William Hume Lane (b. 1884), **8:** 131 n.*215*, 353, 450, 562; **9:** 62 n.*114*
William Lane, Mr. (1860-1886) – teacher, **8:** 30 n.*36*, 131 n.*215*, 132
Hitchcock (of Whitburn, Durham):
Margaret, Mrs. (b. 1833), **8:** 370 n.*607*
Mary Ellen (b. 1865), **8:** 370 n.*607*; **9:** 30 n.*49*

William Lane (1860-1886), see above
William M., Rev. (b. 1836), **8:** 370 n.*607*
Hitchin, Hertfordshire, **6:** 495
Hitchings, George Charles Henry, Dr. (b. 1822) – physician, **2:** 46 n.*91*
Hit or Miss (dr. Francis Burnand), **6:** 27 n.*30*
Hoare (of Islington, London):
Emma, Mrs. (b. 1835), **8:** 457 n.*734*, 550
Leonard, Mr. (b. 1835) – wine merchant, **8:** 457 n.*734*
Mabel (b. 1872) – child actress, **8:** 457 n.*734*, 550, 633
Hoare, Prince (1754-1834) – dramatist, **5:** 32 n.*35*, 88 n.*136*
Hobart, Charles O., Lt. Col. (b. 1808) – army officer, **8:** 360 n.*588*
"Hobgoblin and Blacksmith" (modified from a Russian story) – see also Dodgson, Charles Lutwidge, story-telling, **6:** 187 n.*291*
Hobhouse (of Oxford):
Mary Violet née McNeill (d. 1901), **8:** 374 n.*615*, 376, 593; **9:** 144 n.*249*
Neil (b. 1888?), **9:** 144 n.*249*
Walter, Rev. (1862-1928) – writer and tutor, **8:** 374 n.*615*, 376; **9:** 144 n.*249*
Hobson (of Spalding, Lincolnshire):
Alfred, Mr. (b. 1830) – draper, **8:** 135 n.*219*, 139, 140
Harriet "Hettie" Mary (b. 1874), **8:** 135 n.*219*, 137-139, 149, 232, 234
Helen "Nellie" (b. 1876), **8:** 135 n.*219*, 137-139, 149, 232, 234
Mary, Mrs. (b. 1833), **8:** 135 n.*219*, 137, 139, 140, 232
Hobson (of Croft-on-Tees, Yorkshire):
Henry, Mr. (1819-1873) – teacher, **1:** 108 n.*123*, 111, 112; **6:** 346 n.*575*, 347, 348
Sarah Gordon née Cockfield (1823-1877) – teacher, **1:** 108 n.*123*
Hodern, Alice, **8:** 631 n.*998*
Hodgkins, Frances M. (b. 1813) – friend of Miss Lloyd, **8:** 398 n.*649*
Hodgson, John Evan (1831-1895) – artist, **6:** 86 n.*129*
Hodgson (of Oxford):
Miss – teacher, **9:** 119 n.*205*, 292 n.*461*, 305
Mrs., **9:** 292 n.*461*, 305
Hodgson, Nelly (b. 1873), **8:** 563 n.*897*
Hodgson, Richard Greaves (1845-1931) – teacher, **5:** 189 n.*309*
Hoffmann, Heinrich (1809-1874) – physician and writer, **4:** 140 n.*119*
Hoffmeister, William C., Dr. (b. 1818) – physician to the Royal Family, **6:** 394, 395 n.*646*
Hogarth's Prints, **7:** 421 n.*703*
Hoghton (of Hoghton, Lancashire):
Adam de (b. 1200), **1:** 10
Richard de, Sir (1279-1341) – Knight of the Shire , **1:** 11
Richard de, Sir (1570-1630), 1st Bart., **1:** 11
Sybell neé de Lea (b. 1283), **1:** 11
Hoghton (of Hoghton Tower, near Preston, Lancashire):

Charles, Sir (1643- 1710) – very distant relative, **1:** 10
Mary née Skeffington (d. 1732), **1:** 10
Holborn (Royal) Amphitheatre, **6:** 156 n.*241*
Holder (met at Plumbley's Hotel, Isle of Wight):
Colonel – photographer, **4:** 343, 344 n.*446*, 345, 346
Helen Agnes, **4:** 180, 345
Holding, Mr. – solicitor, **8:** 130 n.*212*
Holdsworth (of London?):
Alice L. (b. 1864), **6:** 114 n.*176*
Alicia F. née Lewis (b. 1834), **6:** 114 n.*176*
Eleanor Kathleen Lewis (b. 1862), **6:** 114 n.*176*
Hole, Samuel Reynolds, Canon (1819-1904), **8:** 147 n.*239*; **9:** 32 n.*53*
Holiday (of Paddington, London):
Adela Maria née Mileham (1843-1920), **8:** 140 n.*227*, 164, 228, 268, 269, 274, 280, 358, 427; **9:** 206 n.*335*, 223 n.*353*
Charles Gilbert J. (b. 1879), **8:** 140 n.*227*, 164, 358
Chrystabel (b. 1883?), **8:** 140 n.*227*, 164, 358, 427
Climène Mary (1875-1965), **8:** 140 n.*227*, 164, 212, 219, 226-229, 268, 274, 279, 313, 358, 427; **9:** 206 n.*335*
Francis A. (b. 1874), **8:** 140 n.*227*, 164, 229
Frederick "Fritz" Charles, Mr. (1843-1930) – civil servant, **8:** 140 n.*227*, 164, 192, 212, 228, 269, 274, 280; **9:** 206 n.*335*
Marie E. H. (b. 1881), **8:** 140 n.*227*, 164, 314
Holiday (of Manningham, Yorkshire):
Alfred, Mr. (1841-1905) – manufacturer, **6:** 126 n.*195*
Elizabeth "Lily" A. née Atchison (b. 1839), **6:** 126 n.*195*
Dora (b. 1869), **6:** 126
Holiday (of Hampstead, London):
Catherine "Kate" née Raven (1840-1925), **6:** 124 n.*192*, 126, 314, 316, 336, 397, 401, 408, 433; **7:** 183
Henry George Alexander, Mr. (1839-1927) – artist, **6:** 124 n.*192*, 126, 303, 314, 316, 321, 336, 337, 341, 344, 368, 370, 397, 401 n.*658*, 403, 408, 427, 429, 433, 434; **7:** 79 n.*131*, 183, 184 n.*343*, 253, 254 n.*462*
Winifred "Winnie" R. (1865-1949), **6:** 126 n.*195*, 314, 316, 336, 402, 404 n.*664*; **7:** 183; **8:** 392
Holiday, Climène née Gerber (1804-1897), **8:** 227 n.*385*
Holiday House (bk. Catherine Sinclair), **4:** 57
Holland, Edward – writer, **8:** 579 n.*925*
Holland (of Wimbledon, Surrey):
Henry Scott, Rev. (1847-1920) – lecturer, **6:** 137 n.*209*, 209 n.*328*, 449; **7:** 225, 269, 270, 386, 403, 405, 434, 440, 500, 501 n.*818*, 511 n.*829*; **8:** 56 n.*86*
Lawrence Gifford, Mr. (b. 1850) – actor, **7:** 377, 378 n.*652*
Hollingshead, John (1827-1904) – dramatist and theatre manager, **7:** 140 n.*258*; **8:** 574 n.*916*

Hollin Hall, Ripon, Yorkshire, **2:** 13 n.*17*, 13 n.*18*, 58 n.*117*; **3:** 152 n.*221*
Hollyer, Fred (1837-1933) – photographer, **8:** 441 n.*706*, 556
Holman (of Eastbourne, Sussex):
Albert B. (b. 1872), **7:** 209 n.*389*
Alice M. L. (b. 1871), **7:** 209 n.*389*, 213, 214, 218
Annie M. (b. 1880), **7:** 209 n.*389*
Edwin C. (b. 1873), **7:** 209 n.*389*
Emily Mary "Daisy" (b. 1864), **7:** 209 n.*389*, 213, 214
Florence Rode Frances (b. 1869), **7:** 209 n.*389*, 213, 214, 217, 218, 283, 454
Helen Maude (b. 1865), **7:** 209 n.*389*, 213, 218
Kathleen M. (b. 1878), **7:** 209 n.*389*
Mary Louisa née Carter (b. 1841), **7:** 209 n.*389*, 213, 215, 283
Stanley G. (b. 1876), **7:** 209 n.*389*
Thomas, Capt. (b. 1837) – army officer, **7:** 209 n.*389*, 213, 215, 463, 464
Holman Hunt (of Warwick Gardens, Kensington, London):
Cyril Benone (b. 1867), **6:** 226 n.*355*
Fanny née Waugh (1833-1866), **5:** 143 n.*229*
William, Mr. (1827-1910) – artist, **2:** 75 n.*151*; **3:** 33 n.*51*, 68 n.*106*, 144; **4:** 31, 34, 47, 55, 79 n.*29*, 109 n.*77*, 244, 245 n.*275*, 279, 280, 287-289, 302, 308 n.*381*, 318; **5:** 64 n.*96*, 76 n.*115*, 137, 143 n.*229*; **6:** 226 n.*355*, 258; **8:** 197 n.*335*, 204, 535, 568; **9:** 198 n.*325*
Holmes, Henry (b. 1840) – violinist and composer, **6:** 402 n.*659*
Holmes, Oliver Wendall (1809-1894) – poet and writer, **3:** 180; **4:** 54; **9:** 190 n.*314*
Holmes, Ralph (b. 1808) – farmer, **1:** 127
Holmrook Hall, Cumberland, **1:** 9, 10, 12, 102 n.*112*; **7:** 210-212
Holroyd (of Leeds, Yorkshire):
Annie – singer, **3:** 11 n.*9*, 103 n.*151,* 146
Mr. – merchant, **3:** 11
Sophie – singer, **3:** 11 n.*9*, 103 n.*151,* 146
Holy Island, Scotland, **6:** 183
Holy Land, **1:** 117; **2:** 96, 97 n.*189*
Holyrood Palace, Edinburgh, **3:** 97
Holyrood Terrace, Malvern, Worcestershire, **4:** 119
Holywell Green, Oxford, **4:** 88
Holywell Lodge, Oxford, **7:** 383
Holywell Music Rooms, Oxford, **4:** 206 n.*216*; **5:** 153; **9:** 121
Holywell Penitentiary, Oxford, **6:** 142
Home and Homeless (pic. Thomas Faed), **2:** 75 n.*151*
Home from Work (pic. Arthur Hughes), **4:** 252 n.*290*; **5:** 15 n.*6*
Homeopathic (herbal) medicine, **7:** 90 n.*161*, 105, 206, 214 n.*395*, 221, 237 n.*437*, 238, 295, 491 n.*799*
Homer (between 1200 and 850 BC) – poet, **3:** 9; **4:** 16
Home Rule Bill, **8:** 279 n.*468*, 280, 543 n.*868*; **9:** 64

"Home, sweet home" (John Payne and Henry Bishop) – song, **5:** 225
Home Words, **9:** 340 n.*544*
Honesty is the Best Policy (dr. Mark Lemon), **3:** 101 n.*149*
Honey, George (1822-1880) – actor, **4:** 221 n.*242*, 272; **5:** 231 n.*369*; **6:** 397 n.*649*; **7:** 97 n.*180*, 387
Honour (dr. Maurice Barrymore), **7:** 369 n.*641*
Hood (of London):
Thomas, Mr. (1799-1845) – poet, **1:** 66 n.*47*;
Tom (1835-1874) – humorous writer, **8:** 579 n.*925*
Hood, Walter J. (b. 1822) – magistrate, **7:** 470 n.*774*
Hoodman Blind (dr. Henry Jones and Wilson Barrett), **8:** 234 n.*396*
Hood's Poems (bk. Thomas Hood), **1:** 66 n.*47*
Hooe, Sussex, **9:** 220
Hook (of Chichester, Sussex):
Cecil, Rev. (1844-1938), **6:** 227 n.*359*
Edith née Turner (b. 1851), **6:** 227 n.*359*
Hook (of Chichester, Sussex):
Cecil (1844-1938), see above
Walter (1839-1899), **3:** 157 n.*233*
Walter Farquhar, Dr. (1798-1875) – dean of Chichester, **1:** 60 n.*32*; **3:** 33 n.*48*, 157 n.*233*; **6:** 227 n.*359*
Hook and Eye (dr. Eille Norwood), **9:** 274 n.*435*, 313
Hooker, Richard (1554?-1600) – theologian, **5:** 103 n.*160*
Hoole (of Clerkenwell, London):
Charles Holland (1837-1902) – tutor at Christ Church, **4:** 162 n.*155*, 170, 212, 278; **5:** 21 n.*14*, 56, 59; **6:** 137, 153, 218; **7:** 440
William Holland (b. 1829) – financier, **6:** 218 n.*341*
Hooper, Isabel "Ella" Mary, **8:** 25 n.*24*, 26-28, 41
Hooper, Miss – lodging-house keeper, **7:** 353
Hooping-cough, **2:** 51
Hope (of Chelsea, London):
Adrian Charles Francis, Mr. (1858-1904), **9:** 90 n.*164*
Jacqueline L. R. (b. 1890), **9:** 90 n.*164*, 253
Laura Elizabeth Rachel née Troubridge (1858-1929) – writer, **9:** 90 n.*164*, 94, 172, 253
Hope, Miss, **9:** 253, 260 n.*410*, 261
Hopkins (met at Eastbourne, Sussex):
Miss M., **7:** 132-134
Mrs. – cousin of Miss Lloyd, **7:** 132
Hopkinson (of East Retford, Nottinghamshire):
Ann (b. 1856), **6:** 54 n.*78*
Jane, Mrs. (b. 1818), **6:** 54 n.*78*
Thomas, Mr. (b. 1826) – master builder, **6:** 54 n.*78*
Hopley (of Westham, Sussex):
Evelyn "Eva" (b. 1875), **9:** 217 n.*345*

Howard, Rev. (1829-1922), **9:** 217 n.*345*
Mabel (b. 1874), **9:** 217 n.*345*
Maud (b. 1877), **9:** 217 n.*345*
Hop-o'-my-Thumb (dr. Frank Green), **6:** 309 n.*512*
Horace (65-8 BC), **1:** 79 n.*78*; **2:** 35 n.*69*; **4:** 16
"Horatius" (Thomas Macaualay) – poem, **1:** 33
Horne Tooke, see Tooke
Hornet's Nest, The (dr. Henry Byron), **7:** 123 n.*232*
Horsley, John Callcott (1817-1903) – artist, **2:** 75 n.*151*; **3:** 79 n.*125*
Horticultural Fête, Oxford, **6:** 36, 339
Horticultural Gardens, London, **4:** 85, 317, 343; **6:** 158 n.*244*, 177
Horticultural Show, Worcester Gardens, Oxford, **2:** 77
Horton, see German Reed
Hoskyns (of Aston Tyrrold, Wallingford, Berkshire):
Emma (1854-1933), **4:** 71 n.*15*, 73
John Leigh, Rev. (1817-1911), 9th Bart., **4:** 71 n.*15*
Phillis Emma née Strutt Peyton (1818-1914), **4:** 71 n.*15*

Hotels abroad:
Bellevue, Brussels, **5:** 259
D'Angleterre, Ems, **5:** 360
D'Angleterre, Warsaw, **5:** 350
De Prusse, Leipzig, **5:** 358
De Russie, Berlin, **5:** 265
De Saxe, Dresden, **5:** 354
Des Deux Mondes, Paris, **5:** 366
Deutsches Haus, Königsberg, **5:** 278
De Ville, Brussels, **5:** 261
Du Louvre, Paris, **5:** 366
Du Nord, Cologne, **5:** 263
Dusaux, Moscow, **5:** 300
Golden Goose, Breslau, **5:** 352
Gostinitsa Klee, Petersburg, **5:** 284, 337
Rappe, Giessen, **5:** 358
Smimovskaya, Nijni Novgorod, **5:** 308
Victoria, Bingen, **5:** 362

Hotels and Inns:
Albion, Eastbourne, **9:** 161, 334, 335
Bell Vue, Bournemouth, **4:** 348
Bell Vue, Cheltenham, **4:** 186, 191
Bell Vue, Malvern, **4:** 118
Brodick, Arran, **6:** 184
Burlington, Eastbourne, **7:** 27
Castle, Hastings, **6:** 238

Charing Cross, London, **5:** 117
Clarendon, London, **6:** 217
Clarendon, Oxford, **4:** 213; **6:** 66, 324; **7:** 108, 269, 535; **9:** 39 n.*69*
Clarendon, Redcar, **5:** 102
Cliftonville, Margate, **6:** 399; **8:** 419, 424
Cobourg, Tenby, **4:** 187, 189
Davis's, London, **7:** 453
Douglas, Aberfeldy, **6:** 184
Full Moon Inn, Bath, **7:** 250
Garland's, London, **7:** 40
Golden Cross, London, **2:** 122
Grand, Brighton, Sussex, **6:** 414; **7:** 199
Grand, Eastbourne, **9:** 160
Great Northern, Doncaster, **5:** 191
Great Northern, London, **4:** 153, 231; **5:** 100, 377; **6:** 44, 49, 205
Great Western, London, **4:** 87, 134, 273; **5:** 21; **6:** 29, 239; **7:** 142, 368, 387, 494, 522; **8:** 57, 131, 207, 217, 405
Grosvenor, London, **6:** 415; **7:** 179
Grosvenor House, Eastbourne, **7:** 27
Imperial, Malvern, **4:** 118, 119
King's Cross Station, London, **6:** 495
King's Head, Sandown, **6:** 295, 332, 341, 354, 355
Lord Warden, Dover, **5:** 255
Marina, Shanklin, **8:** 576
Mitre, The, Oxford, **5:** 78 n.*122*
Needles, Isle of Wight, **4:** 350
Norfolk Square, London, **4:** 87, 134; **8:** 209, 216
North Eastern, York, **6:** 494
Northumberland, London, **2:** 121, 122
North Western, Stafford, **7:** 210
Old Hummums, Covent Garden, London, **1:** 102; **3:** 12, 49, 76, 82, 153, 171; **4:** 31, 182, 183, 221, 279, 309, 322, 325, 356; **5:** 30 n.*32*, 32, 35, 45, 59, 61, 69, 84, 91, 95
Parkhurst's Clerical, London, **7:** 12
Plumbley's, Freshwater, **4:** 14, 343
Prince's Gate, London, **7:** 96
Queen's, Eastbourne, **7:** 466
Queen's, Glasgow, **6:** 182, 184
Queen's, Southsea, **6:** 361
Railway, Reading, **6:** 103
Randolph, Oxford, **5:** 180; **6:** 267
Royal, Bath, **7:** 249
Royal, Edinburgh, **6:** 179, 180, 185; **7:** 448
Royal, Whitby, **6:** 172
Star and Garter Inn, Worcester, **4:** 120; **6:** 239

Star Inn, Oxford (later the Clarendon Hotel), **2:** 108, 109
Sussex, Eastbourne, **9:** 92
Temperance, Guildford, **7:** 140
Trafalgar (Dowsing's, Spring Gardens), London, **5:** 122, 125, 136, 155, 166, 208, 221, 229
Union, London, **7:** 166
United, Charles Street, London, **5:** 379; **6:** 12, 26, 48, 67, 156, 169, 170, 209, 221, 250, 253, 255, 258, 281, 288, 378, 407, 443, 486; **7:** 23, 26, 75, 93, 105, 110, 140, 293, 327, 524, 532, 538; **8:** 98, 113, 198, 228, 273
Wellington, London, **1:** 104
Westminster Palace, London, **4:** 269
White Hart, Guildford, **6:** 56, 121
White Hart, Salisbury, **6:** 278
White Hart, Windsor, **4:** 184, 293, 321; **5:** 82
White Lion, Banbury, **8:** 609
White Lion, Guildford, **6:** 56, 137, 139, 355, 407, 477, 485; **7:** 26, 125, 325, 326, 328, 399, 531; **8:** 82, 220
York, Ryde, **6:** 295
York, Sandown, **6:** 411, 412

Hotten, John Camden (1832-1873) – publisher, **4:** 113, 114 n.*82*
Houghton, Mary née Cliff (b. 1822), **4:** 27
Household Words (ed. Charles Dickens) – magazine, **2:** 13 n.*16*
Houseman (of Bayswater, London):
Edward "Teddy" S. (b. 1871), **6:** 424 n.*697*, 442
Eva M. (b. 1866), **6:** 424 n.*697*, 454
Gertrude H. (b. 1867), **6:** 424 n.*697*, 442, 454
Henrietta F., Mrs. (b. 1839), **6:** 424 n.*697*, 442, 443, 454, 465
Henry, Mr. (b. 1837) – solicitor, **6:** 424 n.*697*, 442, 443, 465
Jane "Janie" A. (b. 1869), **6:** 424 n.*697*, 442, 454
House of Austria (bk. William Coxe), **1:** 24
House on the Marsh, The (bk. Florence Warden), **8:** 189 n.*318*
House out of Windows (dr. William Brough), **2:** 56 n.*110*
Houses of Parliament, London, **4:** 336 n.*433*; **6:** 12, 28, 219, 222; **7:** 39 n.*57*, 321 n.*570*; **8:** 477 n.*772*
Hove, Sussex, **8:** 235
Howard, A., Mr. – creditor, **7:** 17 n.*11*
Howard (of Compton Place, Eastbourne, Sussex):
Fanny, Lady (b. 1810), **7:** 460 n.*759*
Frederick J., Sir (b. 1814), **7:** 460 n.*759*
Howard, Henry R., Capt. (1815-1895) – illustrator, **5:** 141 n.*226*
Howard (of Portsea, Hampshire):
Lydia (b. 1864) – child actress, **6:** 236 n.*375*, 324
Lydia, Mrs. (b. 1841) – dressmaker, **6:** 236 n.*375*, 324

Mr., **6:** 236 n.*375*, 324
Howard, Maud L. (b. 1877) – artists' model, **8:** 522 n.*838*, 536
Howden (of Church Bank, Bowden, Cheshire):
Jane Hewit née Clark (b. 1821), **6:** 172 n.*268*, 176
Jane "Jeannie" Heaton Cunnynham Clark (b. 1861), **6:** 172 n.*268*, 176
John Augustus, Mr. (b. 1818) – surgeon, **6:** 172 n.*268*, 176
Howden, R. – poet, **3:** 100 n.*148*
Howden, Yorkshire, **5:** 111
Howe, Annie M. (b. 1861) – headmistress, **9:** 342 n.*548*
Howe, Henry H. (1813-1896) – actor, **8:** 620 n.*982*
Howell, Messrs. – booksellers, **7:** 518
Howell & James – photographic stationer, **4:** 206
Howells, William Dean (1837-1920) – writer, **8:** 15 n.*9*; **9:** 190 n.*314*
Howes (of Penge, Surrey):
Edgar M. (b. 1878), **7:** 458 n.*755*; **8:** 101
Edmund, Mr. (b. 1842) – wine merchant, **7:** 458 n.*755*, 471; **8:** 40, 101, 143, 144
Eleanor Winifred "Winnie" (b. 1874), **7:** 458 n.*755*, 460, 465, 466, 468, 469, 471, 480; **8:** 27, 28 n.*30*, 33, 34, 37, 101, 102, 143, 144, 232
Elizabeth R. née McMaster (b. 1849), **7:** 458 n.*755*, 465, 466, 469, 471; **8:** 28 n.*30*, 32, 40, 101, 143, 144
Howes, Maria (b. 1862) – Margaret Wilcox's maid, **7:** 146 n.*274*, 148
Howitt (of Uttoxeter, Staffordshire):
Mary née Botham (1799-1888) – writer and poet, **2:** 17 n.*30*
William, Mr. (1792-1879) – writer, **2:** 17 n.*30*
How Long? (pic. Herbert Schmalz), **7:** 539 n.*872*
Hoyle (of Hornsey, Middlesex):
Agnes M. (b. 1870), **6:** 234 n.*370*
Blanche E. J. (b. 1866), **6:** 234 n.*370*
Cecilia, Mrs. (b. 1840), **6:** 234 n.*370*
Cecilia Ellen Savile (b. 1865), **6:** 234 n.*370*
Dudley (b. 1868), **6:** 234 n.*370*
Ida F. (b. 1874), **6:** 234 n.*370*
Mr., **6:** 234 n.*370*
Hoyle, Edmund (1672-1769) – writer on games, **3:** 152 n.*220*
Hudson, Charles (d. 1897) – actor, **8:** 381, 382 n.*626*
Hughes (of London):
Agnes (1859-1945), **4:** 178, 224 n.*246*, 256 n.*296*, 270, 282, 339, 340 n.*441*; **5:** 66 n.*98*, 158; **6:** 112, 126, 352, 378
Amy (1857-1915), **4:** 178, 224 n.*246*, 270, 339, 340 n.*441*; **5:** 19, 66 n.*98*, 158, 211; **6:** 112, 126, 378
Arthur, Mr. (1830-1915) – artist, **3:** 26 n.*37*, 127 n.*184*; **4:** 55, 99 n.*60*, 223, 224 n.*246*, 229, 230, 254, 256 n.*296*, 270, 281, 339, 340; **5:** 14 n.*5*, 66 n.*98*, 86, 95, 158, 170, 211 n.*339*; **6:** 16 n.*13*, 19, 112, 225, 352
Arthur Foord (1856-1934), **4:** 224 n.*246*, 270, 324, 339, 340 n.*441*;

5: 66 n.*98*, 158; **6:** 112
Edwin (1861-1862), **5:** 66 n.*98*
Emily (1861-1949), **4:** 179, 224 n.*246*, 270, 339; **5:** 66 n.*98*, 158, 211; **6:** 112
Godfrey (b. 1865), **5:** 66 n.*98*, 158; **6:** 352
Tryphena née Foord (b. 1831), **4:** 324, 339, 340 n.*441*; **5:** 66 n.*98*, 95, 158, 211; **6:** 19, 112, 352
Hughes, Annie (1869-1954) – actress, **8:** 486 n.*787*; **9:** 225, 226 n.*357*
Hughes (of Battersea, Surrey):
Henry "Harry" (1862-1896), **6:** 249 n.*395*
William Hastings, Mr. (1833-1909) – sherry importer, **6:** 249 n.*395*
Hughes, Thomas (1822-1896) – writer, **1:** 27, 28; **6:** 249 n.*395*, 454 n.*747*
Huleatt (of Shalford, near Guildford, Surrey):
Blanche M. (b. 1873), **9:** 291 n.*458*, 292
Cornelia S., Mrs. (b. 1834), **9:** 291 n.*458*, 292
Hugh, Rev. (1823-1897?), **9:** 291 n.*458*, 293
Irene (b. 1882), **9:** 291 n.*458*, 292
Hull (of Kensington, London):
Agnes Georgina (1867-1936), **7:** 62 n.*98*, 64, 66, 68, 69, 71-74, 76, 93, 134, 137, 139, 142, 143, 186, 188, 194, 202, 205, 210, 214, 216-220, 236, 280, 286, 295, 299, 300, 317, 318 n.*568*, 319, 327 n.*579*, 357, 359, 363, 364, 387, 430, 443, 460, 462, 463, 465-467, 471-474, 485, 515, 517, 536; **8:** 101, 102
Alice Frances (1863-1952), **7:** 62 n.*98*, 66, 74, 76, 136, 142, 186, 188, 194, 199, 200, 203, 210, 212, 216-220, 236, 296, 299, 300, 304, 357, 359, 360, 363, 364, 387, 431, 439, 441, 460-462, 467, 469, 472, 473, 536; **8:** 101, 102
Charles Patrick Amyatt (1865-1920), **7:** 62 n.*98*, 65, 68, 76, 136, 194, 214, 215, 232, 252, 253 n.*461*, 287, 361, 460; **8:** 101
Eveline "Evie" Isabella (1868-1944), **7:** 62 n.*98*, 64-66, 68, 69, 71, 73, 74, 76, 93, 134, 139, 186, 188, 194, 202, 208, 212, 216, 218-220, 256, 284, 286, 299, 304, 305, 317, 319, 349, 361, 364, 396, 430, 453, 461, 462, 467, 473-475, 515, 536; **8:** 101, 102
Frances Amelia née Law (1833-1883), **7:** 62 n.*98*, 64, 67, 68, 72, 76, 93, 124, 130, 135, 137, 139, 142, 182, 185-189, 194, 199, 209, 214-216, 218-220, 231-234, 236, 252, 256, 286, 287, 291, 295, 296, 298, 301, 304, 305, 348, 350, 356, 357, 363, 364, 387, 392, 396-398, 430, 431, 439, 441-443, 463, 466, 467, 472, 474-476, 478, 508, 515, 536; **8:** 22, 23 n.*20*
Henry Charles, Mr. (1833-1902) – barrister, **7:** 62 n.*98*, 64, 67, 72, 73, 76, 93, 124, 130, 135, 137-139, 182, 185-189, 194, 199, 214-216, 218-220, 225, 231-234, 236, 256, 286, 287, 296, 298, 301, 304, 305, 341, 348, 350, 356, 357, 363, 364, 387, 392, 396-398, 430, 431, 439, 441-443, 467, 469, 470, 472, 475, 478, 480, 508, 543; **8:** 22, 23 n.*20*, 36, 101, 102, 231, 289, 299, 302, 445, 482

Jessie Madeline (1871-1953), **7:** 62 n.*98*, 64-66, 68, 69, 71-74, 76, 93, 136, 139, 186, 188, 194, 202, 208, 210, 216-218, 219, 231, 256, 278, 286, 291, 295, 298-300, 304, 305, 317, 319, 349, 357, 359, 361, 363, 364, 392, 396-398, 430, 443, 453, 461-463, 467, 469, 472-476, 479, 485, 515, 536; **8:** 101

Hull (of Eastbourne, Sussex):

Henry William, Mr. (1804-1890) – formerly a curate, **7:** 62 n.*98*, 76, 136, 217; **8:** 36 n.*46*, 101

Julia (b. 1841), **7:** 68

Mary Phillipps née Amyatt (b. 1803), **7:** 62 n.*98*

Hull (Kingston upon Hull), Yorkshire, **4:** 236

Hulme (of Oxford):

Alice (b. 1862), **5:** 235 n.*378*

Catherine "Kate" M. (b. 1859), **5:** 235 n.*378*

Elizabeth "Bessie" G. (b. 1852), **5:** 19, 235 n.*378*

Jane née Tanner (b. 1826), **5:** 235 n.*378*

Samuel Joseph, Rev. (1824-1886), **5:** 235 n.*378*

Hulme (of Guildford, Surrey):

Amelia, Mrs. (b. 1828?), **6:** 100 n.*156*

Anne E. (b. 1857), **6:** 100 n.*156*, 101

Edith B. (b. 1862), **6:** 100 n.*156*, 101

Edward Charles, Dr. (b. 1821) – physician, **6:** 100 n.*156*; **7:** 79 n.*128*

Edward Wyndam (b. 1860), **6:** 100 n.*156*; **7:** 79 n.*128*

Helen A. (b. 1859), **6:** 100 n.*156*, 101

Mary Florence (b. 1863), **6:** 100 n.*156*, 101

Hume, David (1711-1776) – historian, **2:** 65 n.*130*; **3:** 46, 156 n.*230*

Hume, Emma née Sykes (b. 1825), **5:** 148 n.*238*

Hume (of James Street, Westminster, London):

James, Mr. (1743-1819), customs officer – great-great-uncle , **1:** 9

Lucy (1775-1818), see Dodgson

Mary (1786-1868), see Smedley

Hume, Menella (1805-1896) – distant cousin, **6:** 352 n.*583*, 361; **7:** 415

Hummums, see Hotels, Old Hummums

Humphrey, Mr. – friend of the Ellisons, **5:** 109 n.*171*

Humphry Ward (of Tring, Hertfordshire):

Arnold Sandwith (1876-1950), **8:** 376 n.*619*

Janet (b. 1879), **8:** 376 n.*619*

Mary Augusta née Arnold (1851-1920) – writer, **6:** 145 n.*220*, 209 n.*328*; **7:** 358 n.*626*, 523; **8:** 376 n.*619*

Thomas, Mr. (1845-1926) – writer, **7:** 358 n.*626*, 523

Hunchback, The (dr. James Knowles), **5:** 155, 156 n.*252*

Hundred Thousand Pounds (dr. Henry Byron), **5:** 156 n.*253*; ***9:** 119 n.*206

Hunt (of Ore, near Hastings):

Amy Henrietta (b. 1857), **4:** 178

James, Dr. (1833-1869) – speech therapist, **4:** 28, 30, 31, 53, 60,

141 n.*120*, 203 n.*211*
James Sidney (b. 1859), **6:** 288 n.*472*
Hunt (of New York, United States):
Catherine née Howland, **5:** 336, 349, 366
Richard Howland (1862-1931), **5:** 336
Richard Morris, Mr. (1827-1895) – architect, **5:** 336, 349
Hunt, George Ward (1825-1877) – politician, **5:** 216 n.*345*; **6:** 12 n.*5*, 28, 67 n.*99*
Hunt, Jessie (b. 1857) – schoolmistress, **7:** 541
Hunt, Lady, **5:** 213
Hunt, Miss, **9:** 305 n.*484*
Hunter (of Bute, Scotland):
Cecil Stuart (1882-1935), **8:** 470 n.*762*
Eveleen Mary (1876-1961), **8:** 470 n.*762*, 523, 629
Harriet "Hartie" Buchanan (1877-1962), **8:** 470 n.*762*, 629
Morag Una Fionghal (1879-1971), **8:** 470 n.*762*, 629
Sarah Agnes Matilda née Anderson (1851-1934), **8:** 470 n.*762*, 629
William, Dr. (1846-1892) – physician, **8:** 470 n.*762*
Hunter, Mrs. Talbot – dramatist, **9:** 26 n.*35*
Huntingdon, Huntingdonshire, **5:** 15
Hunton, Mrs. – Whitby landlady, **5:** 108 n.*167*
Hurd, Mr., see Heard
Hurley, Buckinghamshire, **5:** 57, 58 n.*83*
Hurlstone, Frederick Yeates (1800-1869) – artist, **6:** 79 n.*114*
Hurrell, Mr. (b. 1814?), **9:** 175 n.*295*, 176, 220, 330, 340
Hursley, Hampshire, **3:** 137 n.*201*
Hurworth, Durham, **1:** 117, 134
Hurworth Rectory, **5:** 172 n.*287*
Husband in Clover, A (dr. Hermon Merivale), **6:** 315 n.*523*
Hussar's Daughter, The (dr. Anon), **5:** 311
Hussey (of St. Aldates Street, Oxford):
Edward Law, Mr. (1816-1899) – surgeon, **7:** 329 n.*582*, 343; **8:** 13 n.*5*
Maria, Mrs. (b. 1827), **7:** 329 n.*582*
Hussey (of Oxford):
Elizabeth "Bessie" Ley (1852-1919), **4:** 296 n.*355*; **6:** 155; **7:** 312, 328, 377, 427; **8:** 88 n.*142*, 90, 91, 218, 272, 375
Elizabeth née Ley (1810-1896), **4:** 295; **6:** 155; **7:** 312 n.*558*, 313, 328, 329 n.*582*, 377, 427; **8:** 88 n.*142*, 90, 100, 218, 268, 272, 337, 375, 510, 548
Robert, Dr. (1803-1856) – professor of ecclesiastical history, **2:** 120 n.*230*; **3:** 125 n.*179*
Hussey (of Great Ringstead, Norfolk):
George (b. 1865), **8:** 88 n.*142*, 272 n.*459*
John (b. 1866), **8:** 272 n.*459*
William Law, Canon (1813-1893), **8:** 272 n.*459*

Hutchinson, Alice (b. 1866), **8:** 597 n.*951*
Hutchinson (of Northam, Devon):
Augusta D. (b. 1850), **8:** 512, 619, 628
Edith Letitia (1858-1952), see Shute
Mrs., **8:** 424, 589, 619, 628
William Nelson, Gen. (b. 1804) – army officer, **8:** 43 n.*61*, 357, 417, 589, 619, 628
Hutchinson, James – writer of educational books for the home, **1:** 27
Hutchinson, James L. (1846-1919) – circus manager, **7:** 287 n.*520*
Hutchinson, J. and Son, Throgmorton Street, London, **8:** 506 n.*814*
Hutchinson, see Washington
Hutchinson & Tayleure's Circus, **7:** 286, 287 n.*520*
Huth-Walters, Edmund, Rev. (b. 1846), **7:** 497 n.*810*
Hutton (of Ormskirk, Lancashire):
Ellen née Garth (b. 1818), **9:** 324 n.*520*
Ellen P. (b. 1853), **9:** 324 n.*520*
Mary J. (b. 1858), **9:** 324 n.*520*
Thomas, Mr. (b. 1817) – newspaper proprietor, **9:** 324 n.*520*
Thomasine A. (b. 1851), see Baynes
Huxley (of Westbourne Square, London):
Julia "Judy" Frances née Arnold (1862-1908), **6:** 145 n.*220*, 152, 192, 201, 203, 209 n.*328*, 213, 217 n. *338*, 226, 268, 273, 275, 284, 286, 306, 317, 322, 325, 328, 369, 389, 400, 412, 426, 430, 451, 452, 470; **7:** 18 n.*13*, 80, 87, 88, 99, 109 n.*203*, 111, 160, 162, 177, 189, 228, 380, 383, engagement 405 n.*686*, 419, 424, 497, 512, 524; **8:** 69, 100 n.*165*, 168, marriage 188, 372
Leonard, Mr. (1860-1933), **7:** 405 n.*686*, 524; **8:** 100 n.*165*, 372
Huxley (of Marlborough Place, London):
Leonard (1860-1933), see above
Thomas Henry, Prof. (1825-1895) – scientist, **4:** 34; **7:** 38 n.*56*
Hyde, Mrs., **7:** 251 n.*458*, 252
Hyde Park, London, **5:** 166 n.*274*, 168
Hypanis, Richmond, Yorkshire, **1:** 130 n.*161*; **2:** 86
Hypatia (370?-415) – philosopher, **2:** 49, 84 n.*167*
Hypatia (bk. Charles Kingsley), **3:** 7 n.*3*, 145

Ici On Parle Francais (dr. Thomas Williams), **4:** 151, 152 n.*137*
Idler, The (dr. Charles Chambers), **8:** 562 n.*896*; **9:** 22, 23 n.*28*, 24
Idyll (pic. Frederick Leighton), **7:** 317 n.*566*, 347, 348
Iffley, Oxfordshire, **1:** 42; **2:** 120; **3:** 48, 49, 54; **4:** 69, 74, 82, 88, 196, 200; **6:** 474
Iffley Rectory, **4:** 76, 87, 176
Iffley Road, Oxford, **5:** 234
Ignatius, Rev. Father, real name Joseph Leycester Lyne (1837-1908), **7:** 87 n.*153*

Il Flauto Magico (Mozart) – opera, **5:** 98 n.*155*
Illington, Marie (1856-1927) – actress, **7:** 114 n.*211*
Illuminations at Oxford, **2:** 77; **4:** 171 n.*165*, 173
Illustrated London News, The, **1:** 112 n.*130*, 117; **3:** 29 n.*42*, 54, 146; **5:** 11, 12 n.*2*
Illustrated Times, The, **4:** 25; **5:** 11, 12 n.*2*
Il Trovatore (Verdi) – opera, **4:** 341 n.*443*
Impey, Miss, **9:** 266 n.*419*
Ince (of Oxford):
Mary Anne née Eaton (b. 1824), **7:** 239; **8:** 55 n.*83*
William, Dr. (1825-1910) – professor of divinity, **2:** 64 n.*127*; **7:** 144 n.*269*, 164, 239, 434, 436, 437, 440; **8:** 55 n.*83*, 296, 510, 594
Inchbald, Elizabeth (1753-1821) – dramatist, **2:** 123 n.*239*
Incident in Luther's Life, An (pic. Henry O'Neil), **5:** 236 n.*382*
Incurable Hospital, Oxford, **7:** 161 n.*301*
India, **3:** 149; **5:** 135
Indian Civil Service, **7:** 492 n.*802*
Indian dresses, **7:** 119 n.*223*
Indian Summer (bk. William Howells), **9:** 190 n.*314*
In Die Malo (pic. Joseph Noël Paton), **7:** 449 n.*744*
In Disgrace (pic. Henry Schlesinger), **6:** 22
Influenza Epidemic, **8:** 602, 603
Inge, William (1829-1903) – Provost of Worcester College, **9:** 47 n.*82*
Ingoldsby Legends, The, **1:** 33
Ingram, Herbert (1811-1860) – publisher, **1:** 112 n.*130*, 117
In Memoriam (bk. Alfred Tennyson), **4:** 99 n.*61*, 353; **8:** 533, 535
International Bazaar, **4:** 64, 97 n.*56*
International Dateline, **8:** 190 n.*321*
International Exhibition, London, **4:** 64, 85, 97 n.*57*, 98, 100; **6:** 177, 272, 289, 354, 415
In The Hayloft (pic. Helen Allingham), **7:** 533 n.*863*
In The Pigskin (dr. John Morton), **5:** 69 n.*104*
Introduction, The (pic. James Archer), **5:** 214
Inveraran, Scotland, **6:** 184
Inverness, Scotland, **4:** 229
Inversnaid, Stirling, Scotland, **3:** 104
Invitations (dr. Edmund Yates), **4:** 153, 154 n.*140*
Iolanthe (Gilbert and Sullivan) – operetta, **7:** 503 n.*822*, 540, 543
Iostephane (pic. Frederick Leighton), **7:** 188 n.*350*
Iphigenia (dr. Edward Nolan), **5:** 153 n.*248*
Irish Church Bill, **6:** 13 n.*6*, 28, 29 n.*34*
Irish Coercion Bill, **7:** 321 n.*570*
Irish Diamond, An (dr. Anon), **9:** 332 n.*531*
Irish Land League, **7:** 370, 371 n.*645*
Irish Tiger, The (dr. John Morton), **4:** 337 n.*436*

Irish University Bill, **6:** 264 n.*424*, 268
Iron Church, Whitby, Yorkshire, **6:** 54
Irvine, John William (1836-1906) – undergraduate at Christ Church, **2:** 29 n.*56*
Irving, Henry (1838-1905) – actor, **6:** 253, 254 n.*403*, 272, 315; **7:** 156 n.*294*, 318, 327, 494, 516; **8:** 113, 126, 209 n.*359*, 273, 338, 406, 456, 529, 565, 567, 619, 628; **9:** 44 n.*77*, 73, 78
Irving, Laurence (1872-1914) – actor, **8:** 614 n.*974*
Irvingism, **4:** 329 n.*420*
Irvingite Church, Albury, Surrey, **6:** 225 n.*354*
Irwin, Phoebe née Thomas, formerly Bostock (b. 1812), **4:** 27
Isaacson, John Frederick, Rev. (1801-1886), **4:** 344 n.*447*, 346, 349, 355, 356
Isis, River, Oxford, **1:** 14
Isle of Man, **1:** 11
Isle of Wight, **4:** 14, 15, 59, 342; **6:** 345, 354
Islington, London, **3:** 50
Islip, Oxfordshire, **4:** 278; **9:** 67
Israel in Egypt (Handel), **6:** 158 n.*245*
It is Never Too Late to Mend (bk. Charles Reade), **2:** 107 n.*208*
Ivan Tower, Moscow, **5:** 307
Ixion (dr. Francis Burnand), **4:** 315, 316 n.*396*

Jabberwock (pic. E. Fairfield), **6:** 431
"Jabberwock" (Augustus Vansittart) – Latin translation, **6:** 455
Jack and Jill (dr. Anon), **8:** 160 n.*259*
Jack and the Beanstalk (dr. Frank Green?), **7:** 92 n.*166*
Jackson (of Saxonbury, near Frant, Sussex):
  Adeline Maria (b. 1838), **4:** 127 n.*100*
  Julia (b. 1846), **4:** 127 n.*100*
Jackson (of Lincoln; and London):
  Agnes Jeune (b. 1851), **7:** 248 n.*455*
  Beatrice (b. 1862), **7:** 248 n.*455*
  Bertha Mary (b. 1846), **7:** 248 n.*455*
  Eliza (b. 1848), **7:** 248 n.*455*
  Emily Kaye (b. 1853), **7:** 248 n.*455*
  Frances Eliza (b. 1841), **7:** 248 n.*455*
  Helen Mackenzie (1852-1879?), **7:** 248 n.*455*
  Henry John Blomfield (b. 1859), **7:** 248 n.*455*
  John, Rt. Rev. (1811-1885) – bishop of Lincoln, and London, **4:** 34; **7:** 248 n.*455*
  Lucy Ellen (b. 1844), **7:** 248 n.*455*
  Margaret Sophia (b. 1843), **7:** 248 n.*455*
  Marion Faith (b. 1854), **7:** 248 n.*455*
  Mary (b. 1839), **7:** 248 n.*455*

Mary Anne Frith née Browell (d. 1874), **7:** 248 n.*455*
Jackson (of Bardwell Road, Oxford):
Amelia née Staines (1843-1925), **9:** 241 n.*380*, 347
William Walrond (1838-1931) – rector of Exeter College, **9:** 241 n.*380*, 347
Jackson, Cyril (1746-1819) – dean of Christ Church, **9:** 76 n.*140*
Jackson (of Barnes, Surrey):
Florence Annie (b. 1876), **8:** 486 n.*788*, 489, 531; **9:** 18 n.*17*
Mary Louise (1874-1959), **8:** 486 n.*788*, 489, 531
Jackson (of Oxford):
Margaret E., Mrs. (b. 1820), **4:** 217
Mary L. (b. 1854), **4:** 216 n.*231*, 217 n.*233*
Robert, Dr. (1810-1887) – physician, **3:** 122 n.*172*; **4:** 216 n.*231*, 217
Jackson, Thomas Graham (1835-1924), 1st Bt., and Company, Architects, **6:** 340; **7:** 419 n.*699*
Jackson's Oxford Journal, **3:** 37 n.*57*, 43 n.*68*; **4:** 13, 59, 91 n.*48*, 100 n.*62*; **5:** 52 n.*73*, 53 n.*74*, 78 n.*120*, 91 n.*140*, 118 n.*185*, 119 n.*186*, 371 n.*550*; **7:** 174, 338
Jack the Giant-Killer (dr. Robert Soutar), **7:** 233 n.*428*
"Jack the Ripper," **8:** 576 n.*919*
Jacob, Ella (b. 1858) – friend of Miss Lloyd, **8:** 60 n.*95*
Jacobson (of Oxford):
Eleanor Jane née Turner (b. 1812), **3:** 61; **4:** 216
William, Dr. (1804-1884) – professor of divinity, **2:** 44 n.*88*; **3:** 25 n.*33*, 28 n.*40*, 35, 42, 54, 58, 61, 62; **4:** 216; **5:** 29 n.*30*, 30, 221
Jambon, Jean, alias John Hay Athol Macdonald, Lord Kingsburgh (1836-1919) – writer, politician and judge, **8:** 579 n.*925*
James (of Burwarton, Shropshire):
Alethea Fanny (1867-1879), **6:** 165 n.*257*
Alfred, Rev. (1832-1897), **6:** 165 n.*257*; **7:** 311 n.*556*, 312, 446; **9:** 43 n.*74*
Basil (1883-1889), **6:** 165 n.*257*
John Henry (1863-1892), **6:** 165 n.*257*
Lucy Caroline (1868-1879), **6:** 165 n.*257*
Lucy née Woodward (b. 1843), **6:** 165 n.*257*
Margaret Beckwith (1870-1884), **6:** 165 n.*257*
Mary Elizabeth (b. 1864), **6:** 165 n.*257*; **9:** 43 n.*74*
Phillip Henry (1875-1917), **6:** 165 n.*257*
Robert Rutson (b. 1881), **6:** 165 n.*257*
Ruth Evangeline (1878-1892), **6:** 165 n.*257*
Samuel Woodward (1865-1882), **6:** 165 n.*257*
William Ashton (b. 1871), **6:** 165 n.*257*
James, Kate (1854-1913) – actress, **8:** 473 n.*768*
James, Marion J. (b. 1831) – writer, **6:** 402 n.*659*
James (of Sandwich, Kent):

Sarah Caroline née Ellison, Lady (1814-1890), **5:** 175 n.*291*
Walter Charles (1816-1893), 1st Lord Northbourne, **5:** 175 n.*291*
Walter Henry (1846-1932), **5:** 175 n.*291*
Jameson (of Bordighera, Italy):
Caroline Grace née MacDonald, **4:** 99 n.*60*, 180, 222, 225, 228 n.*253*, 272, 280, 292, 324; **5:** 21, 157, 193; **6:** 27; **7:** 350 n.*612*
Kingsbury, Rev. (1856-1943), **7:** 350 n.*612*
Jameson (of Cleasby, Yorkshire):
Joseph, Rev. (1794?-1875), **2:** 13 n.*17*
Nancy Matilda Wood née Schaak, **2:** 13 n.*17*
James Street, Oxford, **5:** 234
Jane Eyre (bk. Charlotte Brontë), **3:** 82
Jane Shore (dr. William Wills), **7:** 108, 114 n.*211*, 115; **8:** 586 n.*936*
Janet Pride (dr. Dion Boucicault), **2:** 123 n.*238*; **4:** 337 n.*436*
Janion (of Lansdowne Road, Kensington, London):
Elizabeth (b. 1823) – teacher, **4:** 326 n.*413*
Maria (b. 1842) – teacher, **4:** 326 n.*413*
Janus – part of the Dodgson crest, **2:** 42
Jarrow, Durham, **3:** 9, 90
Jarrow Church, **5:** 175 n.*291*
Jarvis, Frances Jane née Clarke (b. 1830), **5:** 159 n.*261*
"Jeanette and Jeanot" (Charles Glover and Charles Jefferys) – song, **1:** 26
Jebb (of Firbeck Hall, Rotherham, Yorkshire):
Alvary Frederick Richard (1860-1871), **5:** 109 n.*171*, 177, 178
Edith Fanny Maud (1858-1942), **4:** 179; **5:** 19, 109 n.*171*, 177, 178, 191, 234; **6:** 108 n.*168*, 110, 233, 326-328, 386; **7:** 91, 92 n.*165*, 94, 179, 279, 444
Emma Louisa née Ramsden (1821-1901), **5:** 109 n.*171*, 177, 191, 369; **6:** 233, 326, 328, 386, 387; **7:** 91, 92 n.*165*, 94, 118, 179, 183, 278, 444; **8:** 355 n.*580*, 357, 358, 511
Eustace Henry Ramsden (1855-1871), **5:** 109 n.*171*, 177 n.*293*, 191; **6:** 108
Florence Emma Dorothy (1854-1925), **5:** 109 n.*171*, 177, 178, 191; **6:** 233, 386; **7:** 179, 444; **8:** 511
Henry Gladwin, Rev. (1826-1898), **5:** 108 n.*169*, 109 n.*171*, 177, 178, 369; **6:** 55, 56 n.*82,* 108, 233, 386, 387; **7:** 91, 92 n.*165*, 94, 118, 179, 183, 278, 444, 546; **8:** 511
Henry "Harry" Scrope Frescheville (1867-1939), **5:** 109 n.*171*, 177 n.*293*; **6:** 233, 386; **7:** 94, 444; **8:** 355 n.*580*
Jebb (of Boston, Lincolnshire):
Avery (1842-1917), **6:** 55, 56 n.*82*
Frances Dorothy (1828-1902), see Oliphant
Henry Gladwin, see above
Marianne (b. 1829), **5:** 108 n.*169*
Susannah Gladwin (b. 1827), **5:** 108 n.*169*

Jebb (from overseas):
Isabel – pupil at Mrs. Drury's school, **8:** 110 n.*181*, 126, 165, 190, 219
John, Mr. **8:** 165, 166 n.*274*
Jebb, Mr. – related to the Jebbs of Firbeck Hall, **8:** 59 n.*91*
Jefferson (of Sharow, near Ripon, Yorkshire):
Eliza (b. 1822) – teacher, **2:** 58 n.*117*; **6:** 491 n.*809*
Joseph (1818-1882) – teacher, **2:** 58 n.*117*; **6:** 491 n.*809*
Jefferson, Joseph (1829-1905) – actor and dramatist, **5:** 123 n.*195*; **7:** 199
Jeffery, Mr. – bookseller, **9:** 336 n.*539*
Jefferys, Charles (1807-1865) – lyricist, **1:** 26
Jeffreys, Henry Anthony, Rev. (1821-1898), **5:** 128 n.*205*
Jehu (pic. Kate Smith), **5:** 201 n.*327*
Jekyll (of St. Martin's in the Fields, London):
Edward Hill, Capt. (1804-1876) – army officer, **1:** 75, 76 n.*71*
Joseph (1802-1841), MA Christ Church, **1:** 75, 76 n.*71*
Jelf (of Oxford; and London):
Alice Emmy (d. 1921), **3:** 25
Emily Clara (b. 1840), **3:** 25
Emmy, Countess Schlippenbach (1802-1878), **4:** 220; **6:** 149
George Edward (1834-1908), see below
Richard William, Dr. (1798-1871) – principal of King's College, London, **3:** 25 n.*33*; **4:** 218 n.*234*, 220; **6:** 149
Jelf (of Saffron Walden, Essex):
Arthur Selborne (b. 1876), **8:** 626 n.*991*
Charles Gordon (1886-1915), **8:** 626 n.*991*; **9:** 31 n.*52*
Dorothy F. E. (b. 1879), **8:** 626 n.*991*; **9:** 31 n.*52*, 106
Frederica "Freda" (b. 1881), **8:** 626 n.*991*; **9:** 31 n.*52*
George Edward, Rev. (1834-1908), **3:** 26 n.*34*, 60, 134; **4:** 33; **5:** 163 n.*268*, **6:** 147 n.*225*, 445, 446; **8:** 626 n.*991*; **9:** 31 n.*52*, 32
Katharine "Kitty" (b. 1883), **8:** 626 n.*991*; **9:** 31 n.*52*
Katherine France née Dalton, **6:** 445 n.*732*, 446; **8:** 626 n.*991*; **9:** 31 n.*52*
Meriet (b. 1890), **8:** 626 n.*991*; **9:** 31 n.*52*
Philip "Phil" (b. 1884?), **8:** 626 n.*991*; **9:** 31 n.*52*
Jelf, William Edward, Rev. (1811-1875) – tutor and Greek scholar, **6:** 153 n.*235*
Jenkins (of Bognor, Sussex):
Gwendolen, **6:** 235 n.*372*
Mr., **6:** 235 n.*372*, 236
Mrs., **6:** 235 n.*372*
Jenkins, John David, Rev. (1828-1876), **5:** 163 n.*268*, 165
Jennings, Mabel E. (b. 1840), **9:** 297 n.*471*
Jenoure, Aida – actress, **8:** 631 n.*999*
Jephthah's Daughter (pic. John Millais), **5:** 213 n.*341*
Jermyn, Katie née Chambers, **6:** 348
Jermyn Street, London, **5:** 201

Jerrold, Douglas William (1803-1857) – dramatist, **8:** 574 n.*916*; **9:** 332 n.*531*
Jerrold, William Blanchard (1826-1884) – dramatist, **4:** 270 n.*313*
Jersey, **8:** 96, 97
Jervis, Mr. – stage manager, **7:** 504 n.*823*, 509, 512
Jessop's Wine Shop, Oxford, **7:** 274
Jeune (of Whaddon Manor, Gloucestershire):
Caroline Margaret Noel or Noëlle, (b. 1880), **8:** 404, 405 n.*658*, 409
Caroline née Lawless (d. 1881), **8:** 405 n.*658*
Evan "Evie" Browell, Col. (b. 1852) – army officer, **8:** 405 n.*658*
Jeune (of Oxford):
Evan "Evie" Browell (b. 1852), see above
Francis, Rt. Rev. (1806-1868) – master of Pembroke, **3:** 17 n.*18*; **4:** 200 n.*204*; **6:** 34 n.*45*
Francis "Frank" Henry (1843-1905), **7:** 81 n.*137*
John Frederick "Fritz" Symons (1849-1925), see above
Margaret Dyne née Symons (1816-1891), **4:** 148; **7:** 81 n.*137*, 226, 385; **8:** 404, 405 n.*658*, 409
Margaret "Meggie" Symons (b. 1840), **6:** 34 n.*45*
Jeune (of Old Windsor, Berkshire):
Frances Susannah née Bunbury (d. 1915), **7:** 81 n.*137*, 82
John Frederick "Fritz" Symons, Mr. (1849-1925) – barrister, **7:** 81 n.*137*, 82
Jewish Synagogue, Berlin, **5:** 270, 271
Jewitt, Orlando (1799-1869) – engraver, **4:** 222
Jex-Blake, Thomas William (1832-1915) – fellow of Queen's, **2:** 77 n.*154*
Joachim, Joseph (1831-1907) – violinist, **7:** 156 n.*293*
Joan of Arc (pic. Henrietta Ward), **5:** 216, 217 n.*346*, 227 n.*362*
Joan of Arc (pic. John Millais), **5:** 86 n.*134*
Joberns, Charles Henry (b. 1835), **4:** 150 n.*135*
Joel, Elsie – actress, **8:** 161 n.*263*, 164
John Bull Magazine, **5:** 11, 12 n.*2*
John Dobbs (dr. John Morton), **4:** 151, 152 n.*137*
John Halifax, Gentleman (bk. Dinah Craik), **1:** 69 n.*55*; **3:** 141, 142 n.*210*, 145
Johnson (of Llandaff House, Boys' School, 2 Regent Street, Cambridge):
Alice (b. 1861), **6:** 378
Augustine Henry (b. 1865), **6:** 378
George William (1857-1926), **6:** 378
Harriet Brimley née Macmillan (b. 1830), **6:** 378
Harriet M. (b. 1855), **6:** 378
Reginald Brimley (b. 1867-1932), **6:** 378
William Ernest (1858-1931), **6:** 378
William Henry Farthing, Mr. (1825-1901) – schoolmaster, **6:** 378
Johnson (of Oxford):
Arthur Henry, Rev. (1845-1927) – lecturer, **6:** 303 n.*501*; **9:** 327 n.*525*
Bertha Jane née Todd (1846-1927), **6:** 303 n.*501*; **9:** 327 n.*525*

Johnson (of London?):
Edith (b. 1860?), **4:** 179, 328 n.*417*
Mrs., **4:** 327, 328 n.*417*
Johnson, Edward Ralph, Rev. Dr. (1829-1911) – bishop of Calcutta, **8:** 560 n.*891*
Johnson (of Stapleton, near Croft, Yorkshire):
Elizabeth, Mrs. (b. 1814?), **2:** 8 n.*3*
William, Mr. (1794-1875) – farmer, **2:** 8 n.*3*
Johnson (of Brighton, Sussex):
Henry William Robinson Luttmann (1800-1868), **7:** 508 n.*825*
James L. (b. 1801), **7:** 508 n.*825*
S. E. Luttmann (b. 1807), **7:** 508 n.*825*; **8:** 529, 530 n.*848*
Johnson, Maggie (b. 1874), alias Byron – friend of Isa Bowman, **9:** 33 n.*55*
Johnson, William J. (b. 1833) – insurance agent, **8:** 540 n.*865*
Johnson Scholarships, **1:** 77 n.*73*, 79
Johnstone (of Brighton, Sussex):
Anna, Mrs. (b. 1833), **8:** 130 n.*211*
William, Dr. (b. 1813) – army surgeon, **8:** 130 n.*211*
Johnstone (of Eastbourne, Sussex):
Caroline M. (b. 1860), **7:** 465, 466 n.*766*, 469, 471, 479
Louisa, Mrs. (b. 1825), **7:** 465, 466 n.*766*, 467
Louisa M. (b. 1865), **7:** 465, 466 n.*766*, 469, 471, 479
Johnstone, Charles Frederick, Rev. (b. 1841), **4:** 346 n.*451*, 356
Johnstone (of Lambeth Road, London):
Clara Elizabeth (b. 1855), see Earle
Eliza, Mrs., **8:** 583 n.*931*; **9:** 55
John, Mr., **8:** 583 n.*931*
Johnstone, Eliza (1836-1899) – actress, **8:** 575 n.*918*, 583, 615
Johnstone (of Kensington, London):
Harriet Selina, Mrs. (b. 1844), **7:** 364 n.*634*, 365, 367
John Brown, Mr. (b. 1845) – tailor, **7:** 364 n.*634*, 366
Julia Margaret (b. 1871), **7:** 364 n.*634*, 365, 366-368
Jones, Alfred Vivian (b. 1846) – teacher, **7:** 508 n.*825*
Jones, Alice – amateur actress, **6:** 310
Jones, Alice – friend of Monier-Williams family, **7:** 32 n.*42*
Jones (of Headington, Oxfordshire):
Charles, Capt. (b. 1825) – army officer, **6:** 266 n.*428*, 268
Miss, **6:** 266 n.*428*, 268
Jones, Henry, Dr. (1831-1899) alias "Cavendish" – authority on whist, **8:** 17 n. *12*
Jones, Henry Arthur (1851-1929) – dramatist, **7:** 525 n.*849*; **8:** 486 n.*787*; **9:** 173 n.*290*
Jones, Miriam C. (b. 1825) – lodging-house keeper, **7:** 359
Jones, Owen Carter (1809-1874) – designer and book illustrator, **1:** 51
Jones the Avenger (dr. Anon), **2:** 123 n.*239*

Jorden, Mrs. (b. 1809), **9:** 269 n.*425*
Joseph's Sweetheart (dr. Robert Buchanan), **8:** 412 n.*667*, 425
Jotcham, Mildred Maud (b. 1869), **8:** 337 n.*556*
"Journeys of St. Paul" – topic for study, **7:** 150
Jowett, Benjamin, Dr. (1817-1893) – professor of Greek, **3:** 180; **4:** 55, 56, 59, 63, 82 n.*35*, 163, 164 n.*158*, 262 n.*307*, 276 n.*322*; **5:** 54 n.*76*; **7:** 519, 521, 523
Joyce (of Harrow-on-the-Hill, Middlesex):
Adela (b. 1871), **6:** 334 n.*552*
Amy M. (b. 1873), **6:** 334 n.*552*
Emily née Barclay (b. 1835), **6:** 334 n.*552*
Francis Hayward, Rev. (1829-1906), **3:** 46, 47 n.*73*, 48, 56 n.*85*, 57, 59, 62, 124 n.*178*, 125, 131-3, 145, 164 n.*237*; **4:** 54, 57, 60, 61, 89 n.*46*; **6:** 323, 334 n.*552*; **7:** 53 n.*84*, 211 n.*394*, 498 n.*813*; **9:** 203 n.*332*
George Hayward (b. 1864), **6:** 334 n.*552*; **7:** 211 n.*394*
Gilbert Cunningham (b. 1867), **6:** 334 n.*552*; **7:** 211 n.*394*
Laura (b. 1868), **6:** 334 n.*552*
Rachel Eleanor (b. 1870), **6:** 334 n.*552*
Robert Barclay (b. 1863), **6:** 334 n.*552*; **7:** 498 n.*813*
Joyce, Herbert (1830-1897) – civil servant, **3:** 126 n.*181*, 131, 132; **4:** 61
Joyce, James Wayland, Rev. (1812-1887), **6:** 168 n.*261*
Joyce, Sidney (1834-1911) – tutor, **2:** 46, 66 n.*131*; **3:** 46, 47 n.*73*; **6:** 323 n.*536*, 335; **7:** 424
Jubilee Day, **9:** 320, 321 n.*513*
Judah (dr. Henry Jones), **8:** 527 n.*845*
Juggernaut, **2:** 11
Julian, R., Mr. – veterinary surgeon, **7:** 439, 440 n.*729*
Juliet in Friar Lawrence's Cell (pic. Edward Ward), **5:** 216, 217 n.*346*
Jullien, Louis Antoine (1812-1860) – musician, **3:** 19, 20 n.*22*
Junior, Mrs. W., **7:** 119 n.*223*
Junius Brutus (dr. Edward Bulwer Lytton), **8:** 168
Jupiter – planet, **6:** 55
Jury, The (pic. Frederick Barnard), **7:** 538, 539 n.*871*
Juvenile Drama (bk. George Speaight), **1:** 19

Kane, Richard Nathaniel, Rev. (1835-1922?), **9:** 69 n.*126*
Karney (of Shanklin, Isle of Wight):
Arthur B. L. (b. 1875), **6:** 480 n.*793*
Emma S., Mrs. (b. 1835), **6:** 479, 480 n.*793*, 481
Evelyn S. (b. 1869), **6:** 480 n.*793*, 484
Gilbert Sparshott, Rev. (b. 1837), **6:** 479, 480 n.*793*, 481
Margaret "Daisy" A. (b. 1864), **6:** 480 n.*793*, 481, 484
Mary "May" (b. 1866), **6:** 480 n.*793*, 481, 484
Kavanagh, Carrie – child actress and singer, **8:** 287
Kean (of London):

Charles (1811-1868) – actor and manager, **1:** 105 n.*117*, 125; **2:** 19 n.*34*, 20 n.*36*, 82, 83 n.*164*; **3:** 14 n.*13*, 80, 81, 153 n.*222*; **4:** 46
Ellen née Tree (1806-1880) – actress, **1:** 105 n.*119*, 125; **2:** 33, 83 n.*164*
Keane (of West Terrace, Whitby, Yorkshire):
Elizabeth Fryer née Thomas (d. 1908), **2:** 102 n.*196*; **5:** 108
Hilda Elizabeth (b. 1857), **4:** 180
Jane "Janie" Maria Colpoys (b. 1858), **4:** 180
John "Johnnie" Thomas (b. 1854), **5:** 108
Marcus William Allatson (1861-1889), **4:** 235 n.*262*; **5:** 108
William, Rev. (1818-1873), **2:** 102 n.*196*; **4:** 36, 235 n.*262*; **5:** 108 n.*170*, 178, 179; **6:** 54, 55 n.*80*, 172
Keane (of Ireland):
Isabella Louisa "Louise" or "Loui," **8:** 231 n.*391*, 232, 233, 235-237, 239, 240, 242, 245, 271, 273, 274, 288-291, 293, 295, 298, 302, 321, 424, 425, 427, 428
Mary Frances née Ellis, **8:** 231 n.*391*, 232, 245, 271, 273, 288, 289, 291, 412, 424
Percival William, Mr. (b. 1848), **8:** 231 n.*391*
Keary (of Wetherby, Yorkshire):
Annie (1825-1879) – writer, **6:** 252 n.*399*
Eliza (1828-1914) – writer, **6:** 252 n.*399*
Keates (of Quarry Street, Guildford, Surrey):
Ann J., Mrs. (b. 1831), **6:** 99 n.*155*
Gertrude W. (b. 1859), **6:** 99 n.*155*
Lucia F. (b. 1862), **6:** 99 n.*155*
Keats, John (1795-1831) – poet, **1:** 51 n.*5*, 55 n.*16*
Kebbel, Thomas Edward (b. 1827) – barrister, **1:** 40
Keble, John (1792-1866) – professor of poetry, **3:** 137 n.*201*; **4:** 10, 47, 109, 136, 303 n.*368*
Keble College, Oxford, **6:** 119 n.*182*, 336, 385, 410, 491; **7:** 48, 225, 306, 453; **8:** 56, 121, 125, 196, 248, 315, 409, 598; **9:** 46 n.*81*, 251, 258
Keble College Chapel, **6:** 460 n.*756*, 461, 469, 474, 475, 490; **7:** 100, 104, 143, 225, 269, 346
Keed, Mrs. – lodging-house keeper, **6:** 229
Keeley, Louise (1836-1877) – actress, **5:** 32 n.*35*
Keen, Herbert – dramatist, **9:** 277 n.*442*
Keene (of Barnes, Surrey):
Amy, Mrs. (b. 1861), **7:** 459 n.*758*
Charles Vernon Peacock, Mr. (b. 1855) – lawyer, **7:** 459 n.*758*
Keith, Thomas (b. 1828) – surgeon, **8:** 329, 330 n.*542*
Kelly, Charles, see Wardell
Kelly (of New York, United States of America):
Edmond, Mr. (1851-1909) – lawyer, **7:** 336 n.*591*
Mrs., **7:** 336 n.*591*
Kelly, Thomas J., Col. (b. 1833) – Fenian, **5:** 373 n.*553*

Kemble (of London):
Charles, Mr. (1775-1854) – actor, **1:** 62 n.*37*
Frances “Fanny” Anne (1809-1893) – actress, **1:** 62 n.*37*
Kemble, Henry (1848-1907) – actor, **7:** 438 n.*727*; **8:** 584 n.*933*, 616
Kemp, Master – pupil at Richmond School, **1:** 21
Kemp, Thomas R. (1836-1905) – politician, **7:** 254 n.*463*
Kemp Town Station, Brighton, **7:** 362
Kendal, formerly Grimston (of Harley Street, London):
Margaret “Daisy” K. (b. 1872), **8:** 401 n.*653*
Margaret “Madge” née Robertson (1848-1935) – actress, **6:** 258 n.*410*, 289, 315 n.*522*; **7:** 183 n.*342*, 187, 238, 315, 540; **8:** 165 n.*271*, 400, 401 n.*653*, 412, 413; **9:** 54 n.*92*
William Hunter (1843-1917) – actor, **5:** 221 n.*351*; **6:** 258 n.*410*, 315 n.*522*; **7:** 183, 540; **8:** 165 n.*271*; **9:** 54 n.*92*
Kenilworth (dr. Thomas Dibdin adapt. Walter Scott), **5:** 168 n.*277*
Kenilworth (dr. William Synge adapt. Walter Scott), **6:** 104 n.*163*
Kennedy, David (1825-1886) – singer, **4:** 159 n.*149*
Kennedy, William (1779-1871) – poet, **3:** 107 n.*155*
Kensington, London, **4:** 244, 250, 332; **5:** 66, 70, 145, 193; **7:** 348, 514, 515, 523, 532
Kensington Gardens, **8:** 219
Kensington Museum, **3:** 76, 171; **4:** 287, 317, 331; **5:** 137
Kensington Park, **7:** 113
Kent, William (b. 1820) – photographer, **7:** 455 n.*753*, 457 n.*754*, 461, 469, 471, 474; **8:** 357 n.*583*, 423
Kentish Town, London, **5:** 62
Kenyon, George Thomas, Capt. (1840-1908) – politician, **4:** 263 n.*308*
Keppel Taylor, Mrs., **4:** 347 n.*454*, 349, 352, 356
Keswick, Cumberland, **1:** 55 n.*18*, 107; **2:** 89-91; **3:** 9 n.*6*, 93, 109, 115, 117, 119, 145; **6:** 41
Kettenus, Aloys (1823-1887) – Belgian violinist and conductor, **8:** 286 n.*482*
Kew, Surrey, **5:** 159
Key Haven, Hampshire, **4:** 348
Keynes, John Neville (1852-1949) – lecturer, **9:** 152 n.*264*, 180
Keyser (of Warren House, Stanmore, Middlesex):
Charles, Mr. (1814-1892) – stockbroker, **5:** 252 n.*412*
Margaret née Blore (b. 1824), **5:** 252 n.*412*
Marian Charlotte, **5:** 252 n.*412*
Khilkoff, Gregoire, Prince, **5:** 318 n.*491*
Kibworth-Beauchamp, Leicestershire, **6:** 110
Kidlington, Oxfordshire, **1:** 77; **7:** 198
Kidston (of Hampton Poyle, Oxfordshire):
John Wallace, Rev. (1851-1926), **7:** 452 n.*748*, 527; **8:** 111 n.*182*
Mona Margaret Noël née Paton (1860-1928), **6:** 182, 183 n.*285*, 336, 481;

7: 448 n.*742*, 527; **8:** 111 n.*182*
Kielhorn, Franz, Dr. (1840-1908) – professor of oriental languages, **6:** 151
Kilburn, Burleigh Dunbar (b. 1861) – barrister, **7:** 248 n.*454*
Killarney, Kerry, Ireland, **4:** 354 n.*461*
King, A. Fitz – dramatist, **9:** 162 n.*277*
King (of Christ Church, Oxford; later of Lincoln):
Annie née Heberden (b. 1806), his mother, **7:** 137
Edward, Dr. (1829-1910) – professor of pastoral theology, **6:** 277 n.*454*, 373, 458, 459; **7:** 86 n.*148*, 136, 137, 244, 269, 345, 385, 440; **8:** 66 n.*106*, 97, 542, 543 n.*867*, 550 n.*877*
King, Edith – child actress, **8:** 381, 382 n.*626*
King (of South Parks Road, Oxford):
Emily Clara née Jelf (b. 1840), **6:** 302; **7:** 161 n.*303*
Godfrey J. (b. 1871), **7:** 161 n.*303*
Hugh C. (b. 1873), **7:** 161 n.*303*
John Richard, Rev. (1835-1907) – lecturer, **6:** 147 n.*224*, 302; **7:** 161 n.*303*
Madeline A. (b. 1869), **7:** 161 n.*303*
King, George (b. 1824) – cabinet maker, **8:** 548
King, Lily – cousin of Marion Richards, **8:** 132, 134 n.*218*, 137, 496
King, Mr., **2:** 18
King, Mrs. – grandmother of the Welchmans, **6:** 297, 299
Kingdon, Hollingworth Tully, Rev. (1835-1907), **7:** 275 n.*499*
Kingerlee, Thomas Henry (b. 1843) – builder and politician, **9:** 206 n.*336*
"King of Otaheite's Tea Party, The" (R. Topliff) – song, **2:** 100
King Réne's Daughter (dr. Frederick Weatherley), **9:** 162 n.*277*
King's College, London, **2:** 24
King's Cross Station, London, **6:** 48, 161, 162, 206, 225, 250, 292, 348, 495; **9:** 140, 226
Kingsford, Philip, Rev. (1828-1901), **4:** 118 n.*87*
King's Idylls (bk. Alfred Tennyson), **4:** 14, 16
Kingsland, Glanville – child actor and singer, **8:** 287
Kingsley (of Holne, Devon; and Barnack, Northamptonshire):
Charles (1819-1875) – writer, **2:** 8 n.*5*, 10; **3:** 7 n.*3*; **4:** 136; **6:** 74, 75 n.*109*
Henry (1830-1876) – writer, **4:** 349 n.*457*, 350; **5:** 25, 90; **6:** 196 n.*305*
Kingsley, Miss – possibly Charlotte, sister of Charles Kingsley, **5:** 24
King's Palace, Berlin, **5:** 269
Kingston, Arthur, Rev. (1860-1936?), **9:** 188 n.*311*, 290, 311, 312
Kingston, Gertrude (1866-1937) – actress, **8:** 618 n.*980*
Kingston-Bagpuize, Berkshire, **7:** 531
Kington, see Oliphant
Kinsey (of Stoke or Merrow, near Guildford, Surrey):
Daisy (b. 1872), **8:** 76 n.*119*
Helen (b. 1875), **8:** 76 n.*119*

Mrs., **8:** 75, 76 n.*119*
Kipling, Frances Ada (1851-1924), see Wilcox
Kirke, William Senhouse (1823-1864) – physician, **3:** 165 n.*238*, 167
Kirk Fenton (Church Fenton), Yorkshire, **4:** 68 n.*7*
Kish (of Sunderland, Durham):
Edward (b. 1868) – shipbroker, **8:** 259 n.*436*, 521 n.*836*
James (b. 1864) – shipbroker, **8:** 259 n.*436*, 521 n.*836*
Thomas, Mr. (b. 1836) – shipbroker, **7:** 178 n.*330*, 398 n.*677*, 470; **8:** 258, 259 n.*436*, 289, 446 n.*716*, 521 n.*836*
Kiss, August Karl Eduard (1802-1865) – sculptor, **5:** 266
Kiss in the Dark, A (dr. John Buckstone), **5:** 109 n.*172*
Kitchin (of Oxford):
Alexandra "Xie" Rhoda (1864-1925), see Cardew
Alice Maud née Taylor (1844?-1930), **4:** 260, 261; **6:** 87 n.*130*, 300, 307, 308, 313, 317, 321, 339, 471; **7:** 164, 177, 240 n.*443*, 244, 251, 272, 274 n.*498*; **8:** 201 n.*342*, 203, 268, 382, 552 n.*881*; **9:** 140
Brook Taylor (1869-1940), **6:** 226 n.*356*, 321, 400 n.*657*, 472
Dorothy Maud Mary (1874-1953), **7:** 272 n.*492*; **8:** 201 n.*342*, 392
George Herbert "Ben" (b. 1865), **6:** 124 n.*191*, 264, 273, 300, 305, 321, 325, 400 n.*657*
George William, Rev. (1827-1912) – lecturer at Christ Church, **1:** 49, 67, 85 n.*90*, 86, 87, 88 n.*91*, 89, 94, 95, 99 n.*107*, 132, 134; **3:** 135 n.*196*, 137, 140 n.*208*, 147, 161, 174; **4:** 59, 82, 134, 219 n.*237*, 220, 258 n.*302*, 260, 261; **6:** 218 n.*340*, 307, 308; **7:** 79, 164, 177, 240, 244, 329, 376; **8:** 201 n.*342*, 203, 268, 400; **9:** 140
Hugh Bridges (1867-1945), **6:** 321, 400 n.*657*, 472
Kitchin (of Ipswich, Suffolk):
George William (1827-1912), see above
Isaac, Rev., **3:** 135 n.*196*
James, **3:** 135 n.*196*, 138 n.*203*
Joseph (b. 1824), **3:** 135 n.*196*
Mary née Bardgett, **3:** 135 n.*196*
Thomas Millward (b. 1832), **3:** 135 n.*196*
Knight, Cyrus Frederic, Rev. (1831-1891) – American cleric, **4:** 5
Knight (of Canon Gate, Jedburgh, Roxburgh, Scotland):
Annie (b. 1862), **8:** 30 n.*36*, 53, 58, 193, 203, 353, 377
Mary "May" (b. 1857), **6:** 333; **8:** 95 n.*156*, 198
Mary née Wilcox (b. 1834) – cousin, **6:** 333; **8:** 30 n.*36*, 193, 203, 353
Valentine, Mr. (b. 1812) – civil servant, **8:** 30 n.*36*, 193
Knight (of Kingston upon Thames, Surrey):
Edith A. (b. 1868), **7:** 527, 528 n.*854*
Eva (b. 1875), **7:** 527, 528 n.*854*
Knight (of Lewisham, Kent):
Elizabeth Sarah, Mrs. (b. 1854), **8:** 418, 419 n.*678*
Ellen "Nellie" Elizabeth (1876-1955), **8:** 418, 419 n.*678*, 429

John Lewis, Mr. (1852-1934) – clerk, **8:** 419 n.*678*
Sydney (b. 1880), **8:** 418, 419 n.*678*
Knight (related to the Burtons):
Miss, **7:** 60 n.*95*, 61
Mrs., **7:** 60 n.*95*, 61
Knight, Mr. – chemist, **7:** 250
Knightwick, Worcestershire, **7:** 267, 268
Knightwick Station, **9:** 66, 69
Knole House, Sevenoaks, Kent, **6:** 270 n.*436*
Knollys, William Frederick Erskine, Rev. (b. 1816), **6:** 319 n.*530*, 320
Knollys, William Thomas, Gen. (1797-1883) – royal administrator, **6:** 320 n.*531*
Knop, Fraülein – governess, **7:** 461; **8:** 129
Knott, James (b. 1855) – shipbroker, **8:** 293 n.*490*
Knowbury, Shropshire, **7:** 84, 126
Knowledge, **8:** 121 n.*193*, 151 n.*247*
Knowles, James Sheridan (1784-1862) – dramatist, **5:** 69 n.*104*, 156 n.*252*
Knox, Robert (1791-1862) – physician, **3:** 168 n.*243*
Knubley (of Portinscale, Cumberland):
Margaret, Mrs. (1816-1865) – lodging-house keeper, **2:** 96 n.*187*
Richard, Mr. (b. 1816) – carpenter, **2:** 96 n.*187*
Knuckle-bone Player (pic. Frederick Leighton), **5:** 238 n.*384*
Koch, Christophe Guillaume de (1737-1813) – historian and writer, **1:** 24
Königsberg, Russia, **5:** 278-282
Kremlin, Moscow, Russia, **5:** 317, 335
Krüg, Fraulein, later Mrs. Weymouth – teacher, **9:** 270 n.*426*, 271
Krylov, Ivan Andreevitch (1768-1844) – writer, **6:** 426 n.*701*
Kuhff, Henry (1804-1842) – mathematician, **1:** 69 n.*56*
Kynaston, Herbert (1809-1878) – teacher, **5:** 249 n.*407*
Kyrle, Harold – actor, **7:** 97 n.*180*

La Bionda (pic. Richard Buckner), **6:** 22, 23 n.*23*
Lablache, Luigi (1794-1858) – singer, **1:** 104
La Cigale (Francis Burnand and Edmond Audran) – operetta, **8:** 564, 565 n.*900*; **9:** 163, 164 n.*279*, 166
Lacy, Walter (1809-1898) – actor, **2:** 20 n.*36*
Lacy twins – child actresses, **5:** 203, 205
Ladies' Battle, The (dr. Thomas Robertson), **7:** 183 n.*342*
Lady, The, **8:** 557 n.*886*, 564, 567, 571, 577, 601
Lady Barbara's Birthday (dr. Miss Barker), **7:** 515, 516 n.*835*
Lady Clancarty (dr. Tom Taylor), **6:** 349 n.*578*, 352, 353
Lady Edith Campbell and the Lord George Campbell, The (pic. James Sant), **2:** 75 n.*151*
Lady Jane Grey refusing the Crown (pic. Henrietta Ward), **6:** 17 n.*15*
Lady Margaret Hall, Oxford, **8:** 85 n.*136*, 170, 233, 277, 280, 282, 283,

306, 332, 334, 335, 507, 516, 537, 539, 545; **9:** 135
Lady of Aroostook (bk. William Howells), **8:** 15 n.*9*
Lady of Lyons, The (dr. Henry Byron), **5:** 109 n.*172*; **7:** 356 n.*623*
"Lady of Shalott, The" (Alfred Tennyson) – poem, **4:** 18
Lady of Shalott, The (pic. Dante Gabriel Rossetti), **4:** 20
Lady with the Lilacs, The (pic. Arthur Hughes), **4:** 230 n.*254*, 256
La Famille Benoiton (dr. Victorien Sardou), **5:** 364 n.*539*
Lagrua, Madame Emma – opera singer, **4:** 282 n.*333*
Laing, Catherine J. – editor, **7:** 309, 310 n.*553*
Laing, Mrs. – friend of the Craiks, **6:** 254 n.*404*
Lake (of Eastbourne, Sussex):
  Frederick (b. 1852) – merchant, **8:** 581 n.*926*
  Miss – lodging-house keeper, **8:** 581 n.*927*
Lake (of St. Ebbe's, Oxford):
  Mrs., **2:** 36 n.*72*, 40, 41
  Stephen, **2:** 36 n.*72*, 37, 40, 41
Lake, William Charles, Rev. (1817-1897), **3:** 17 n.*18*
Lake District, **1:** 55 n.*18*, 65 n.*44*; **2:** 85, 90 n.*182*; **3:** 24; **4:** 14
Lalla Rookh (bk. Thomas Moore), **1:** 113 n.*133*
Lamb, Beatrice (b. 1866) – actress, **9:** 16 n.*13*
Lamb (of Tottenham, London):
  Blanche, **8:** 580, 581 n.*926*, 592, 633
  Eleanor M., Mrs. (b. 1855), **8:** 580, 581 n.*926*
  Gwendolen Florence, **8:** 580, 581 n.*926*, 591, 633
  Thomas, Mr. (b. 1850) – commercial traveller, **8:** 581 n.*926*
Lambert, Alfred J., Rev. (b. 1844), **6:** 109 n.*171*
Lambert, Mr. – tutor, **6:** 247 n.*392*
Lambert (of Plumbley's Hotel, Freshwater, Isle of Wight):
  William T. (b. 1857), **4:** 355 n.*464*
  William T., Mr. (b. 1830) – hotel proprietor, **4:** 355 n.*464*
Lambeth, Surrey, **7:** 105
Lambeth Palace, **4:** 280, 311, 312, 322, 324-327, 330, 331, 336, 339, 340; **5:** 80 n.*125*, 245
Lamlash, Isle of Arran, Scotland, **6:** 182, 183, 184
Lancashire Election, **6:** 64 n.*93*
Lancashire Witch, Residing at Bolton-le-Sands, A (pic. John Horsley), **2:** 75 n.*151*
Lancaster, **1:** 11
Lancaster Gate, London, **5:** 209
Landergan, Henry (b. 1839) – organist, **6:** 110, 111 n.*173*
Landseer, Edwin Henry (1802-1873) – artist, **2:** 75 n.*151*; **3:** 129 n.*186*; **5:** 200 n.*325*, 221
Landslip, Isle of Wight, **6:** 296, 299, 343, 360, 362, 478
Lane (of Aylesbury, Buckinghamshire):
  Arthur Graham (b. 1879), **8:** 426 n.*689*

George, Mr. (b. 1849) – gas engineer, **8:** 426 n.*689*
Letitia Mary (b. 1880), **8:** 426 n.*689*
Mary, Mrs. (b. 1848), **8:** 426 n.*689*
Lane, Charlton George, Rev. (1836-1892), **8:** 299 n.*499*
Lane Fox, Miss – violinist, **8:** 531, 532 n.*852*
Laneton Parsonage (bk. Elizabeth Sewell), **1:** 27
Lang, Andrew (1844-1912) – writer, **1:** 42
Lang, Cosmo Gordon, Rev. (1864-1945), **9:** 153 n.*265*, 252, 278
Lange (of West House, Whitburn, Durham):
Emma Juliana (b. 1830), **5:** 13 n.*4*, 41
William James Montague (b. 1819), **5:** 13 n.*4*, 41
Langham Hall, London, **7:** 193
Langley, Algernon A. (b. 1863) – agricultural student, **7:** 311 n.*555*
Langston, James H. (1796-1863) – politician, **3:** 43 n.*68*
Langton Clarke (of Ealing, Middlesex; and Leamington, Warwickshire):
Algernon E. (b. 1864), **5:** 12 n.*3*; **8:** 31 n.*37*, 177
Alice Gertrude (b. 1863), **5:** 12 n.*3*; **7:** 77 n.*125*; **8:** 31 n.*37*, 177
Ann "Annie" (b. 1865), **5:** 12 n.*3*; **7:** 77 n.*125*; **8:** 31 n.*37*, 177
Charles Langton "Robin" (b. 1859), **5:** 12 n.*3*, 35; **8:** 31 n.*37*, 177
Diana Elizabeth (b. 1862), **4:** 179; **5:** 12 n.*3*, 35; **7:** 77 n.*125*; **8:** 31 n.*37*, 177
Frances Mary née Harrison (b. 1835), **5:** 12 n.*3*, 39 n.*48*; **8:** 31 n.*37*, 177
James, Rev. (1833-1916), **4:** 24; **5:** 12 n.*3*, 34, 35, 151 n.*244*, 152, 159; **7:** 77 n.*125*, 376 n.*650*; **8:** 31 n.*37*, 32, 177
James Francis (b. 1875), **5:** 12 n.*3*; **8:** 31 n.*37*, 177
Lionel (b. 1871), **5:** 12 n.*3*; **8:** 31 n.*37*, 177
Margaret "Margie" Frances (b. 1860), **4:** 180; **5:** 12 n.*3*, 19, 35; **7:** 77 n.*125*, 377; **8:** 31 n.*37*, 32, 177 n.*291*
Maurice Harrison (b. 1873), **5:** 12 n.*3*; **8:** 31 n.*37*, 177
Noel Massington (b. 1866), **5:** 12 n.*3*; **8:** 31 n.*37*, 177
Olive Augusta (b. 1880), **5:** 12 n.*3*; **8:** 31 n.*37*, 177
Reginald Adair (b. 1869), **5:** 12 n.*3*; **8:** 31 n.*37*, 177
Theresa Cecil (b. 1876), **5:** 12 n.*3*; **8:** 31 n.*37*, 32, 41, 177
Thomas Elliott (b. 1879), **5:** 12 n.*3*; **8:** 31 n.*37*, 177
La Notte (pic. Antonio Correggio), **5:** 357 n.*530*
La Petite Fadette (bk. George Sand), **7:** 351 n.*613*
Laroche, see Sylvester
Lascelles, Brian Piers (1859-1922) – teacher, **8:** 554 n.*883*
Lascelles, Miss – singer, **1:** 53
La Sonnambula (Bellini) – opera, **3:** 101 n.*149*; **5:** 253 n.*417*
Last Chapter, The (pic. Robert Martineau), **4:** 334 n.*430*
"Last Hackney-Coach, The" in *The Train* (W. Moy Thomas), **3:** 30 n.*44*
Last Kiss, The (pic. Mary Edwards), **5:** 86 n.*134*
Last Parting of Marie Antoinette and Her Son, The (pic. Edward Ward), **2:** 75 n.*151*

"Last Rose of Summer, The" (Thomas Moore) – song, **5:** 153
Latham (of Adelaide Road, Hampstead, London):
Annie, Mrs. (b. 1830), **4:** 308 n.*380*; **5:** 244 n.*397*
Beatrice M. (b. 1861), **4:** 308 n.*380*; **5:** 19, 244 n.*397*
Henry, Mr. (1829-1871) – barrister, **4:** 308; **5:** 244 n.*397*
Latham, Henry (1821-1902) – lecturer, **9:** 338, 339 n.*541*
Latham, Peter Wallwork, Dr. (1832-1923) – physician, **8:** 399 n.*651*
Latham, Susannah (b. 1870), **8:** 563 n.*897*
Lathbury (of Charles Street, London):
Annie, Mrs. (b. 1833), **7:** 95 n.*173*
John A., Capt. (b. 1833) – army officer, **7:** 95 n.*173*
Latin, **2:** 35 n.*69*, 41, 43 n.*84*, 59 n.*118*, 71 n.*143*, 120, 122
Lauraine Family (skaters), **7:** 64 n.*102*
Laurie, Miss – friend of the Shutes, **8:** 209 n.*358*
Lavater (dr. Henry Coape), **5:** 210 n.*336*
Lavender Sweep, Wandsworth, London (Tom Taylor's), **5:** 136
Laverty, Wallis Hay, Rev. (1847-1928), **7:** 87 n.*152*, 103 n.*192*
La Vie (Offenbach) – operetta, **8:** 38 n.*51*
Lavie, Germain (1836-1901) – solicitor, **1:** 87, 88 n.*91*; **2:** 126 n.*244*; **7:** 381 n.*657*
Lavis, Mr. – Eastbourne photographer, **8:** 305, 306 n.*506*
Law, Alexander Patrick (1832-1895), MA New Inn Hall, **7:** 68 n.*111*, 199
Law, Edward, Dr. (1791-1868) – chaplain to British Embassy, St. Petersburg, Russia, **3:** 58 n.*88*
Law, Frederick Henry, Rev. (1827-1907), **6:** 42 n.*58*, 49, 83
Law, Miss, **7:** 236
Law; or Marriage with a Deceased Wife's Sister (bk. Joseph Middleton), **2:** 57 n.*114*
Lawn Tennis Courts, Norham Gardens, Oxford, **7:** 269
Lawrence, George Alfred (1827-1876) – writer, **4:** 266 n.*310*
Lawrence, Ida – actress, **9:** 284 n.*449*, 285
Lawrence, John Robert, Rev. (b. 1851), **6:** 447 n.*735*
Lawrence, Mrs., **8:** 525 n.*842*
Lawrence, Thomas, Sir (1769-1830) – artist, **2:** 17 n.*29*, 69 n.*137*
Lawrence, William, Sir (1783-1867) – surgeon, **3:** 138, 139 n.*204*
Lawrence's Love Suit (dr. John Wooler), **5:** 47 n.*62*
Lawrie, Rose (b. 1860?) – friend of Holidays, **6:** 402 n.*660*, 406 n.*667*, 431
Lawson (of Richmond, Yorkshire):
Arthur W. (1862-1949), **7:** 209 n.*390*
Frances née Smurthwaite (b. 1830), **7:** 209 n.*390*
Norton G. (1858-1946), **7:** 209 n.*390*
William Norton, Mr. (1830-1911) – lawyer, **7:** 209 n.*390*
Lawson, Francis Wilfred (1842-1935) – artist, **6:** 433 n.*715*, 434, 435
Lawson, Miss – sister of Mrs. Archer, **5:** 214 n.*343*
"Lay of the Last Minstrel, The" (Walter Scott) – poem, **6:** 263 n.*422*

Leader, James, see Tanner
Leading Strings (dr. Adolphus Troughton), **3:** 133 n.*193*
Leah the Forsaken (Mosenthal), **6:** 221 n.*349*, 311
Leamington, Warwickshire, **4:** 32; **6:** 228, 345, 410, 491; **7:** 116 n.*216*; **8:** 177
Leamon, Elizabeth E. (b. 1828) – lodging-house keeper, **7:** 297 n.*537*, 299, 300
Lear and Cordelia (pic. Ford Maddox Brown), **5:** 15 n.*6*
Leathart (of Bracken Dene, Gateshead, Durham):
Anna Hilda (b. 1873), **5:** 14 n.*5*
Charles Bowkstead (b. 1880), **5:** 14 n.*5*
Constance Maria (b. 1871), **5:** 14 n.*5*
Edith Mary (b. 1860), **4:** 180; **5:** 14 n.*5*, 19, 176, 227 n.*362*
James, Mr. (1820-1895) – manufacturer, **4:** 252 n.*290*; **5:** 14 n.*5*, 176, 227 n.*362*
James Gilbert (b. 1875), **5:** 14 n.*5*
Margaret (b. 1862), **4:** 180; **5:** 14 n.*5*, 176, 227 n.*362*
Maria née Hedley (b. 1840), **5:** 14 n.*5*, 86, 227 n.*362*
Mary Beatrice (b. 1864?), **4:** 178; **5:** 14 n.*5*, 177, 227 n.*362*
Percival Wilson (b. 1876), **5:** 14 n.*5*
Thomas Hedley (b. 1877), **5:** 14 n.*5*
William Bell Scott (b. 1879), **5:** 14 n.*5*
Leatherhead, Surrey, **5:** 99
Lebra, Adele, see Purvis
Le Bouvier, Leonora "Leo" née Heaphy (b. 1862), **5:** 231 n.*368*; **6:** 15 n.*9*, 71, 126; **7:** 122 n.*230*, 125 n.*235*, 397, 398; **9:** 16 n.*12*
Le Breton, William Corbet, Very Rev. (b. 1816), **8:** 99 n.*163*
Lechertier, Barbe & Company – artists' suppliers, **6:** 206 n.*321*
Lechlade, Gloucestershire, **8:** 266
Leckhampton Hill Gloucestershire, **4:** 186
Leclerque, Carlotta (1838-1893) – actress, **2:** 124 n.*240*; **3:** 14 n.*13*, 82 n.*127*, 105, 106 n.*154*; **8:** 451 n.*722*
Lecocq, A. C. (1833-1918) – composer, **8:** 287 n.*483*
Lectures on Modern History (bk. William Smyth), **1:** 73 n.*65*
Lectures upon the Ecclesiastical History of the First Three Centuries (bk. Edward Burton), **1:** 80 n.*80*, 84, 85
Ledwich, Roger de (fl. 1210) – very distant relative, **1:** 11
Lee, Emma (b. 1823) – governess to the Longleys, **2:** 56 n.*111*, 58, 104
Lee, Lillie (b. 1860?) – child actress, **5:** 193, 203, 204
Leech, John (1817-1864) – illustrator, **4:** 103 n.*68*; **5:** 45 n.*59*
Leeds, **1:** 129, 130; **2:** 43; **3:** 157; **9:** 153
Lees, Florence (b. 1869) – logic pupil, **8:** 300 n.*501*, 302, 303
Leeson, Dan – actor., **4:** 160
Legard (of Stokesley, Yorkshire):
Francis Digby, Rev. (1829-1883), **7:** 175 n.*323*

Jane née Harcourt (d. 1875), **7:** 175 n.*323*
Legard, Mr. – friend of Stuart Collingwood, **9:** 303 n.*480*
Legendre, Adrien Marie (1752-1833) – mathematician, **8:** 387 n.*632*
Le Geyt:
Janet P., **6:** 32 n.*42*, 33, 36; **8:** 138 n.*224*, 139, 140, 144, 145, 454
Mrs., **8:** 138 n.*224*, 140, 144, 145, 454
Leggatt (of London):
Edward Owen, Col. (1825-1902) – army officer, **8:** 28 n.*32*, 29, 32, 60, 378
Evelyn C. O. (b. 1870), **8:** 28 n.*32*, 29, 32, 33, 41
Gertrude Winifred "Winnie" (b. 1871), **8:** 28 n.*32*, 29, 32, 33, 41
Mrs., **8:** 28 n.*32*, 29
Oswell, **8:** 28 n.*32*
Legge (of Barnack, Northamptonshire):
Alfred, Rev. (1840-1931), **6:** 25 n.*28*
Katherine L., Mrs. (b. 1836), **6:** 25 n.*28*
Legge (of Oxford):
Anna G. (b. 1865), **7:** 162 n.*305*
Hannah Mary née Hull (b. 1823), **7:** 167
Helen E. (b. 1860), **7:** 162 n.*305*
James, Prof. (1815-1897) – professor of Chinese, **7:** 162 n.*305*
James G. (b. 1862), **7:** 162 n.*305*
Thomas M. (b. 1863), **7:** 162 n.*305*
Legh, Charles Henry Frederick Americus (1858-1885) – undergraduate at Christ Church, **7:** 18 n.*14*
Legros, Alphonse (1837-1911) – artist and sculptor, **4:** 251 n.*288*
Le Hay, John (1854-1926) – actor and entertainer, **8:** 546 n.*870*
Leicester, **6:** 53 n.*77*, 110
Leicester, Ernest (1866-1939) – actor, **9:** 283, 284 n.*449*
Leicester Square, London, **1:** 104
Leigh, Ada, **5:** 104 n.*162*
Leigh, Gilbert Henry Chandos, Hon. (1851-1884), **6:** 162, 163 n.*252*, 164
Leighton, Alexes (d. 1926) – actress, **8:** 417 n.*675*
Leighton, Baldwin (1836-1897), 8th Bart. – politician, **1:** 70 n.*57*, 76, 85
Leighton, Catherine, Mrs. (b. 1819), **6:** 120
Leighton, Frederick, Sir (1830-1896) – artist, **1:** 98; **4:** 55; **5:** 236 n.*380*, 238 n.*384*; **7:** 46 n.*71*, 187, 188 n.*350*, 190 n.*353*, 253, 254 n.*462*, 317, 319, 502, 523; **8:** 216 n.*368*, 220
Leipzig, Germany, **5:** 358
Leisure Hours (pic. John Millais), **4:** 301 n.*367*
Leitch, George (1841-1907) – actor, **6:** 309 n.*512*, 377, 444
Leith, Edinburgh, **3:** 103; **6:** 184; **7:** 450
Le Jeune, Henry (1819-1904) – artist, **2:** 75 n.*151*; **3:** 76 n.*116*; **4:** 55
Le Maistre (of Brighton, Sussex):
Augusta, Mrs. (b. 1837), **7:** 508 n.*825*

Edward A. (b. 1871), **7:** 508 n.*825*
George John, Rev. (b. 1830) – teacher, **7:** 508 n.*825*
Helena A. (b. 1876), **7:** 508 n.*825*
Madeline K. (b. 1877), **7:** 508 n.*825*
Mary L. J. (b. 1868), **7:** 508 n.*825*
Victor (b. 1869), **7:** 508 n.*825*
William (b. 1864), **7:** 508 n.*825*
Lemmens-Sherrington, Helen (1834-1906) – singer, **5:** 226
Lemon, Mark (1809-1870) – dramatist, editor of *Punch*, **3:** 101 n.*149*; **5:** 241 n.*390*, 254 n.*420*
Lempriere, William, Rev. (1818-1895), **8:** 98 n.*160*
Lend Me Five Shillings (dr. John Morton), **5:** 220, 221 n.*351*
L'Enfant du Régiment (pic. John Millais), **2:** 75 n.*151*
L'Enfant Perdu (pic. Arthur Hughes), **5:** 211 n.*339*
L'Enfant Prodigue (dr. Voltaire), **8:** 556 n.*885*
Lennard, Horace (d. 1920) – dramatist, **9:** 122 n.*214*
Lennon, Florence Becker née Tanenbaum (1895-1984) – biographer, **1:** 44
Leofric the Great (d. 1057), **1:** 11
Leonide or Leonidas, Lev Vasil'evich Krasnoppekov (1817-1876) – bishop of Moscow, **5:** 302, 303 n.*472*, 315, 317, 333-335
Le Pigou (of Spencer House, St. John's Park, St. Helens, Hampshire):
Arthur, Major-Gen. (b. 1826), **4:** 224 n.*248*
Elizabeth E. (b. 1863), **4:** 224 n.*248*
Frederica E. M. (b. 1857), **4:** 224 n.*248*
Henrietta J. (b. 1859), **4:** 224 n.*248*
Jemima F., Mrs. (b. 1826), **4:** 224 n.*248*
Mary B. (b. 1860), **4:** 224 n.*248*
Les Deux Aveugles (Offenbach) – operetta, **5:** 241, 242 n.*391*
Leslie, Charles Robert (1794-1859) – artist, **3:** 174 n.*255*
Leslie, Fred (1855-1892) – actor, **7:** 532 n.*862*; **8:** 34 n.*41*
Leslie, George Dunlop (1835-1921) – artist, **7:** 179 n.*332*
Leslie, Henry (1830-1881) – actor, **3:** 12 n.*10*
Leslie, Henry David (1822-1896) – musician and composer, **5:** 153 n.*247*
Leslie, John, Sir (1822-1916), 1st Bart. – politician, **4:** 279, 280 n.*329*
Les Malheurs de Sophie (bk. Sophaletta Rostopchine), **7:** 486 n.*790*
Lesson For Life, A (dr. Tom Taylor), **4:** 225 n.*249*, 356
Letchworth (of Guildford, Surrey):
Henry Howard, Rev. (1836-1921), **6:** 284 n.*467*, 463 n.*763*; **8:** 358 n.*584*
Mrs., **8:** 358 n.*584*
Level Crossing, The (dr. George Sims), **9:** 20 n.*22*
Lever, Charles James (1806-1872) – writer, **1:** 109 n.*126*
Lever (of Iffley, Oxfordshire):
Florence, Mrs. (b. 1849), **7:** 270 n.*486*; **8:** 90 n.*146*, 245
Reginald Croft, Capt. (b. 1838) – army doctor, **7:** 270 n.*486*; **8:** 90 n.*146*, 245

Lewes, George Henry (1817-1878) – dramatist, **2:** 82 n.*162*
Lewes, Sussex, **9:** 274
Lewes Castle, **9:** 274
Lewin, Dr. – speech therapist, **6:** 215 n.*336*, 216, 218, 219
Lewis, Ada (1875-1925) – actress, **9:** 132 n.*231*
Lewis, Arthur Edward (b. 1862) – undergraduate at Christ Church, **7:** 379 n.*654*
Lewis (of Moray Lodge, London):
Arthur James, Mr. (1844-1924), **5:** 24, 31 n.*33*, 233 n.*375*, 240, 379; **6:** 19 n.*19*, 114, 122 n.*187*, 223, 312; **7:** 93 n.*169*, 186, 256, 278, 366, 515, 529
Elizabeth Murray Kate née Terry (1844-1924) – actress, **3:** 14 n.*13*, 81, 82 n.*127*, 132; **4:** 182 n.*177*, 224 n.*247*, 225, 230, 243, 246, 357 n.*467*, 358; **5:** 20-22, 24, 30, 31 n.*33*, 32 n.*34*, 35, 37, 62, 63, 85, 85 n.*133*, 91, 92 n.*142*, 93 n.*144*, 94 n.*146*, 99, 115 n.*179*, 117, 118, 123, 127, 129, 130, 136, 155, 156 n.*252*, 157, 162, engagement 233 n.*375*, 240, 241 n.*390*, first visit to Moray Lodge 379; **6:** 19 n.*19*, 84, 114, 194 n.*301*, 220, 221, 223, 256, 312, 313, 466; **7:** 93 n.*169*, 140, 185, children 194, 238, 256, 278, 304, 305, 348, 388, 398, 430, 515, 516, 529; **8:** 220, 319, 368, 406, 556, 617; **9:** 190, 215
Janet Marion (1869-1945), **5:** 233 n.*375*; **6:** 194 n.*301*, 256, 312, 341; **7:** 93 n.*169*, 140, 156, 185, 194, 304, 305, 348, 388, 396, 398, 430, 514, 515; **8:** 50, 51 n.*75*, 315, 556; **9:** 190
Kate "Katie" (1868-1958), see Gielgud
Lucy Maud (1871-1962), **5:** 233 n.*375*; **6:** 194 n.*301*; **7:** 93 n.*169*, 140, 156, 185, 194, 304, 305, 348, 388, 396, 398, 430, 514, 515; **8:** 50, 51 n.*75*, 319, 406, 556, 617; **9:** 215
Mabel Gwynedd (1872-1957), **5:** 233 n.*375*; **6:** 194 n.*301*; **7:** 93 n.*169*, 140, 156, 185, 194, 304, 305, 348, 388, 396, 398, 430, 514-516, 529; **8:** 50, 51 n.*75*, 319, 368, 406, 556, 617; **9:** 190
Lewis, Clive Staples, Dr. (1898-1963) – writer, **1:** 44
Lewis, E., real name Solomon – child actor, **5:** 202
Lewis, Emily – listed to be photographed, **4:** 179
Lewis, Frederick Christian (1779-1856) – engraver, **2:** 17 n.*29*, 69 n.*137*
Lewis, Gerrard, Rev. (b. 1830), **6:** 400 n.*656*
Lewis, Helen – friend of the Bowmans, **8:** 474 n.*770*
Lewis, James Edward (b. 1851), BA Merton, **7:** 225 n.*414*, 226
Lewis, Jessie (b. 1866) – friend of the Drapers, **7:** 29 n.*39*
Lewis, John Delaware (1828-1884) – writer and politician, **6:** 329 n.*544*
Lewis, Misses, **8:** 442 n.*708*
Lewis, Waller Augustus, Dr. (1817-1882) – physician, **6:** 288 n.*473*
Lexham Gardens, London, **7:** 76, 118
Ley, Jacob, Rev. (1803-1881) – tutor, **7:** 228 n.*421*, 328, 329 n.*582*
Ley, William, Mr. (1806-1869) – surgeon, **5:** 50 n.*69*
Liar, The (dr. Samuel Foote), **5:** 210 n.*336*, 253

Liardet, Jane (b. 1844) – sister of Mrs. Gateskill, **9:** 187 n.*309*
Liberal Unionists, **8:** 509 n.*819*
Liberty, Miss A. – artist, **2:** 75 n.*151*
Liberty Hall (dr. Richard Carton), **9:** 56 n.*101*, 58, 60, 91
Liddell (of Ravensworth Castle, Gateshead, Durham):
  Adolphus Frederic Octavius (1818-1885), see below
  Anne Elizabeth (1802-1878), see Williamson
  Maria Susannah née Simpson (d. 1845), **2:** 100 n.*193*
  Thomas Henry (1775-1855), 1st Baron Ravensworth, **1:** 123 n.*153*; **2:** 100 n.*193*
Liddell (of Ravensworth Castle, Gateshead, Durham):
  Adolphus Frederic Octavius, Sir (1818-1885), **1:** 123 n.*153*
  Adolphus George Charles (1846-1920), **1:** 123 n.*153*
  Frederica Elizabeth neé Lane-Fox (d. 1867), **1:** 123 n.*153*
  Frederica Maria (1848-1891), **1:** 123 n.*153*, 125, 128, 133
  Gertrude Frances Elizabeth (1852-1916), **1:** 123 n.*153*, 133
  Marcia Kathleen Anne (d. 1907), **1:** 123 n.*153*
  Mary Beatrice Caroline (1859-1951), **1:** 123 n.*153*
  Walter Bertram (1857-1864), **1:** 123 n.*153*
Liddell (of Christ Church, Oxford):
  Albert Edward Arthur (b. and d. 1863), **4:** 200, 201
  Alice Pleasance (1852-1934), see Hargreaves
  Edith Mary (1854-1876), **1:** 101 n.*111*, 126 n.*155*; **2:** 65 n.*129*, 111 n.*216*, 112; **3:** 44, 45, 73, 121, 129, 178; **4:** 11, 24, 33, 35, 40, 42, 44, 48, 57, 69 n.*11*, 81 n.*33*, 83, 84, 88, 93, river trip to Godstow 94, 96, 98, 103, 110-115, 136, 139, 141, 146, 149, 153, 162, 163, 169, 171-177, 179, 185 n.*180*, 186 n.*181*, 187, 191-200, 204, 208, 210-213, 257 n.*299*, 264 n.*309*, 266, 272, 298, 299 n.*364*, 307; **5:** 19, 60 n.*87*, 86, 243 n.*395*; **6:** 187 n.*290*, death from peritonitis 469 n.*771*, 471 n.*777*, 492 n.*815*; **8:** 99 n.*164*
  Edward Henry "Harry" (1847-1911), **1:** 101 n.*111*; **2:** 43 n.*86*, 48 n.*95*, 65 n.*129*, 66, 68, 69 n.*136*, 70 n.*140*, 73, 77, 78, 108, 112, 116, 120 n.*232*, 122, 125, 126; **3:** taught sums 16 n.*17*, 17, 20, 22-24, 28, 32, 36, 44, 45, river trip 48, 56, 59, 62, 63, 65, 73, 121, 129, meeting at Twyford School 136 n.*199*, 137; **4:** 142, 152, 192
  Henry George (1811-1898) – dean of Christ Church, **1:** 88 n.*91*, 101 n.*111*, 124 n.*153*; **2:** 25, discusses lectureship 27, 29, 33, 43 n.*86*, 67, 70, 73, 78, 100 n.*193*, at Torquay for health 107 n.*206*, 108, 110, 111 n.*217*, 122, 125, to Madeira for health 126; **3:** 16 n.*15*, 16 n.*17*, 22 n.*27*, 24, 29 n.*41*, 36, 37 n.*57*, 59 n.*90*, 65, return to Christ Church 66, 72 n.*112*, 73, 74, 86, 94, 121, 125, 129, 144, 145; **4:** 13, 23, 39, 50, 59, 63, 78, 79, 103, enquiry about Holy Orders 137 n.*115*, 138, 145 n.*127*, 149, High Table changes 152, 192, 200, 206, river trip to Nuneham 213, 266, disagreement over Junior Studentships 268, 269; **5:** 86, changes introduced at tutors' meeting 187 n.*307*, 207; **6:** 131,

274, 492 n.*815*; **7:** 227, 244, 320, 440; **8:** 123, 127, resignation as dean 590 n.*940*, 607 n.*963*; **9:** 76 n.*141*
James Arthur Charles (1850-1853), **1:** 101 n.*111*; **3:** 22 n.*27*, 29 n.*41*
Lorina Hannah neé Reeve (1826-1910), **1:** 101 n.*111*; **2:** 43 n.*86*, 70, children only photographed as a group 116 n.*222*, 120, 122, 125, 126; **3:** 16 n.*17*, 20, 24, 59 n.*90*, 66, 73, 74, 86, 93, 94, 121, 123, 129; **4:** 13, 42, 103, 136, 139, 143, 146, 185 n.*180*, 192, 198, death of child at Deanery 201, 206, 213, 214, 264 n.*309*, 266, 299 n.*364*; **5:** 188, 207, 242, 243 n.*395*; **6:** 121, 260, 274, photos of Edith 492; **7:** 320; **8:** 70 n.*115*, 513, 514, 515 n.*830*, 597, 607; **9:** 104 n.*189*, 224
Lorina "Ina" Charlotte (1849-1930), see Skene
Rhoda Caroline Anne (1859-1949), **4:** 181, 193, 208, 213, 299 n.*364*, 307; **8:** 370, 513, visited rooms 597, 598
Violet Constance (1864-1927), **4:** 277 n.*324*; **8:** 370, 394 n.*639*, 513, 597
Liddell (of Hetton Lawn, near Cheltenham, Gloucestershire):
Amelia Frances, **4:** 186 n.*181*, 187
Charlotte Mary Elizabeth, **4:** 186 n.*181*, 187
Charlotte née Lyon (d. 1871), **4:** 185 n.*180*, 186 n.*181*
Henry George, Rev. (1787-1872), **1:** 124 n.*153*; **2:** 118 n.*226*; **4:** 185 n.*180*, 186 n.*181*, 213
Liddell (met at Hetton Lawn):
Charles (1813-1894), **3:** 72 n.*112*, 121; **4:** 186, 196
Marion née Hesketh (1842?-1910), **3:** 72 n.*112*
Liddell & Scott, Newcastle – drapers and outfitters, **3:** 125 n.*180*
Liddon (of Whitehall Place, London, and Wimbledon, Surrey):
Agnes (b. 1873), **7:** 77 n.*123*
Annie Elizabeth (b. 1876), **7:** 77 n.*123*
Annie Strickland, Mrs. (b. 1844), **7:** 77 n.*123*
Dorothy (b. 1875), **7:** 77 n.*123*
John, Mr. (b. 1835) – barrister, **1:** 68 n.*54*, 71, 89 n.*93*; **2:** 73 n.*147*, 77, 122; **3:** 54 n.*83*, 61, 130, 153; **4:** 223, 279; **5:** 70, 85, 159, 212, 220; **6:** 178 n.*274*; **7:** 77 n.*123*
John P. (b. 1877), **7:** 77 n.*123*
Louisa Mabel (b. 1872), **7:** 77 n.*123*
Matthew Glennis (b. 1880), **7:** 77 n.*123*
Liddon (of Christ Church, Oxford; and Amen Court, Ludgate, London):
Henry Parry (1829-1890), **1:** 43; **2:** 25 n.*46*, 73 n.*147*; **4:** 141, 170, 201, 260; **5:** 25, 26 n.*26*, 131 n.*210*, 135, 165 n.*273*, 228 n.*363*, 253, 254 n.*421*, trip to Russia 255-369; **6:** 66, 119 n.*182*, 120, 178, 220, 221, 247, 277, 303, 373, 395, 464 n.*765*, 465; **7:** 164, 189, 225, 238, 244, 440, 448; **8:** 11 n.*1*, 77, 127, 171, 201 n.*343*, 346, 397 n.*646*, 400 n.*652*, 515 n.*831*, death 527 n.*846*, memorial portrait 537 n.*861*, 559; **9:** 235
John (b. 1835), see above
Life and Adventures of Valentine Vox, the Ventriloquist, The (bk. Henry Cockton), **1:** 56, 57 n.21

Life and Letters of Lewis Carroll (bk. Stuart D. Collingwood), **1:** 13, 18, 20, 27-29, 32, 35, 41, 45, 47, 135
Life for a Life, A (bk. Dinah Craik), **9:** 190 n.*314*
Life, Letters and Literary Remains of John Keats, The (bk. Richard Milnes), **1:** 55 n.*16*
Life of Benjamin Robert Haydon, The (bk. Tom Taylor), **1:** 51 n.*5*, 52, 56, 57, 112
Life of Charlotte Brontë (bk. Elizabeth Gaskell), **3:** 85, 86 n.*133, 90*, 145
Life of Marcus Tullius Cicero, The (bk. Conyers Middleton), **1:** 24
Life of Lorenzo de Medici, The (bk. Thomas Roscoe), **1:** 24
Light and Shade (pic. Arthur Lewis), **6:** 19 n.*19*
Lightfoot, John Prideaux, Dr. (1803-1887) – rector of Exeter College, **4:** 134, 135 n.*112*
Light of the World, The (pic. William Holman Hunt), **4:** 109 n.*77*
Lights o' London, The (dr. George Sims), **8:** 208 n.*355*
Light Princess, The (bk. George MacDonald), **4:** 99 n.*60*
Light thrown on a dark passage (pic. James Sant), **5:** 142, 143, 149
Likeness of Christ, The (bk. Thomas Heaphy), **5:** 219 n.*350*, 230 n.*367*; **6:** 292, 293 n.*483*, 294, 301-303
Lille, France, **5:** 258
Lilleshall Abbey, Newport, Shropshire, **6:** 387 n.*634*
Lily (b. 1857) – child at Whitby, **6:** 55
Lime burning (pic. George Cole), **5:** 219 n.*350*
Lincoln College, **1:** 89, 98, 99 n.*107*; **2:** 26, 39, 47, 120; **3:** 24, 25, 37, 57, 69, 123; **7:** 309; **8:** 492
Lincoln's Inn, London, **7:** 187
Lind, Jenny (1820-1887), Madame Johanna Maria Goldschmidt – singer, **2:** 50 n.*101*, 54 n.*106*; **4:** 318, 319 n.*404*
Linden, Marie (b. 1862) – actress, **8:** 112, 113 n.*184*
Lindley, Nathaniel, Rt. Hon. (1828-1921) – judge, **7:** 21 n.*18*, 22
Lindon, Clement Hemery (b. 1854) – barrister, **7:** 235 n.*434*
Lindsay, Charles Hugh, Col. (1816-1889) – sat for Millais' *Jephthah*, **5:** 213 n.*341*
Lindsay, Coutts, Sir (1824-1913) – artist, **7:** 253, 254 n.*462*
Lindsay (of Cowley, Oxfordshire):
  Major – army officer, **9:** 127
  Mrs., **9:** 111 n.*196*, 115 n.*200*, 127, 205
  Ruby (b. 1884?), **9:** 111 n.*196*, 115 n.*200*, 127, 205
Lingard, Mr., **4:** 245 n.*277*
Linnell (of Redhill, Surrey):
  Constance "Connie" (b. 1883?), **8:** 584, 585 n.*934*, 586, 587, 592, 633; **9:** 24 n.*31*
  Dorothy "Dolly" (b. 1885), **8:** 585 n.*934*, 586, 587, 592, 633
  Elizabeth M. R., Mrs. (b. 1840), **8:** 585 n.*934*, 586, 587; **9:** 24 n.*31*
  James Thomas, Mr. (1820-1905) – artist, **8:** 585 n.*934*, 586; **9:** 24 n.*31*

Linnell, John (1792-1882) – artist, **8:** 585 n.*934*
Lion, Messrs., Russell Place, London – photographic dealers, **4:** 175 n.*172*
Lionel-Smith (of Oxford):
Arthur, Mr. (1850-1924) – history tutor, **9:** 145 n.*250*
Dorothy (b. 1886?), **9:** 145 n.*250*
Molly (b. 1885?), **9:** 145 n.*250*
Lister, John Moore, Rev. (1840-1919), **6:** 33, 34 n.*45*
Liston, Effie – actress, **8:** 575 n.*918*
Literary Churchman, The, **5:** 11, 12 n.*2*
Little, Ethel M. (b. 1874), **9:** 347 n.*556*
Little, John Fletcher, Dr. (b. 1844) – physician, **9:** 193 n.*318*
"Little Christel" – story, **9:** 65
Little Doctor Faust (dr. Henry Byron), **7:** 140 n.*258*
Little Don Giovanni (dr. Henry Byron), **5:** 125, 126 n.*200*
Little Dorrit (bk. Charles Dickens), **2:** 37 n.*75*, 52
Little Ella – circus performer, **3:** 76, 77 n.*119*
Little Folks, **9:** 295 n.*466*
Little Holland House, Kensington, London, **4:** 334, 336; **5:** 34 n.*39*
Little King Pippin (dr. Edward Blanchard), **5:** 127 n.*203*, 128, 129 n.*207*
Little Lord Fauntleroy, The Real (dr. Frances Hodgson Burnett), **8:** 400, 401 n.*653*, 405, 409, 427, 441, 442, 471, 517; **9:** 83
Little Minister, The (dr. James M. Barrie), **9:** 352 n.*564*
Littlemore Asylum, Oxford, **5:** 50 n.*69*
Little Plays for Children: The Grinding Organ (dr. Maria Edgeworth), **7:** 95 n.*174*
Little Red Riding-Hood (dr. Anon), **7:** 510
Little Red Riding-Hood and Bo-Peep (dr. Frank Green?), **6:** 316 n.*525*
Little Squire, The (dr. Dora Greet and Horace Sedger), **9:** 138, 139 n.*240*
Littlethorpe, Yorkshire, **3:** 169 n.*246*, 170
Little Thumb (bk. Hans Christian Andersen), **9:** 89 n.*161*, 90 n.*164*
Little Toddlekins (dr. Charles Mathews), **4:** 205 n.*214*, 206
Littletop's Christmas Party (dr. Anon), **5:** 193 n.*317*
Little Treasure, The (dr. Augustus Harris), **2:** 23 n.*43*, 24
Litton (of Long-Wall Street, Oxford):
Anne née Carus-Wilson (1821-1901), **2:** 121 n.*234*
Edith Alice (1849-1919), **4:** 179
Edward Arthur, Rev. (1813-1897), **1:** 68 n.*53*
Liverpool, Lancashire, **7:** 302
Liverpool Street Station, London, **8:** 373
Living Marionettes, **7:** 68
Living Miniatures, **5:** 193 n.*317*, 200-205
Livingstone, Robert George, Rev. (1838-1935), **7:** 144 n.*268*, 163, 246, 309
Llandudno, North Wales, **4:** 215 n.*228*
Llewelyn (of Swansea, Glamorgan, Wales):
John Dillwyn, Mr. (1810-1882) – photographer, **2:** 118 n.*226*

John Talbot Dillwyn (1836-1927), see below
Llewelyn (of Swansea, Glamorgan, Wales):
Caroline Julia née Hicks-Beach (1840-1917), **8:** 630 n.*996*
John Talbot Dillwyn, Mr. (1836-1927) – railway director and politician, **2:** 118 n.*226*; **8:** 630 n.*996*
Lloyd (of Holywell Street, Oxford):
Catharine Eliza (1824-1898), **5:** 155 n.*250*, 188 n.*308*; **6:** 85 n.*127*, 260, 301, 397, 461, 465; **7:** 80 n.*134*, 84, 85, 108, 110, 115-117, 127, 130-133, 244, 269, 346, 381, 530, 535, 536, 543; **8:** 56 n.*85*, 60-62, 85, 94, 218, 258, 306, 398, 490, 538, 591, 593, 629; **9:** 90 n.*163*, 91, 103, 123, 126, 144, 232, 251, 320
Charles (1824-1862), **1:** 132 n.*165*, 134; **2:** 29 n.*56*, 33, 66 n.*131*, 67, 76 n.*152*, 122; **3:** 36, 47, 60, 64; **4:** 63
Charles, Rt. Rev. (1784-1829) – bishop of Oxford, **5:** 188 n.*308*
Lloyd, Charles Harford (1849-1919) – composer, **8:** 444 n.*712*
Lloyd, Miss – nurse, **8:** 547
Loan of a Lover, The (dr. James Planché), **6:** 188 n.*292*
Loch Katrine, Scotland, **3:** 104
Loch Lomond, Scotland, **6:** 184
Locker, Arthur (1828-1893) – editor of *The Graphic*, **6:** 441
Locker, Frederick (1821-1895) – poet, **7:** 372 n.*647*
Lockey, Charles (fl. 1846-1859) – singer, **2:** 54
Lockhart (of Cleghorn, Lanarkshire):
Allan Eliott, Mr. (1803-1878) – barrister, **2:** 81
Charles "Charlie" Walter (1850-1889), **2:** 81
Jane Margaret "Maggie" (b. 1848), **2:** 81 n.*160*; **4:** 123 n.*95*
Mary Dora (b. 1846), **2:** 81 n.*160*; **4:** 123 n.*95*
Miss, either Matilda (b. 1832) or Marianne (b. 1836), **2:** 81
Lockit, Misses – child actresses, **8:** 439, 440 n.*704*
Loftus, Marie Cecilia "Cissie" (1876-1940) – actress, **9:** 347, 348 n.*557*
Logan (of London):
Katie (b. 1864) – child actress, **6:** 250 n.*397*, 253, 254, 256, 259, 260, 262, 272, 281, 310, 311, 378
Helen "Nellie," Mrs. (b. 1845) – actress, **6:** 250 n.*397*, 253, 256, 272, 310
Lombardi & Company, Brighton – commercial art and photographic firm, **7:** 71 n.*115*
London Bridge, **6:** 415
London Bridge (pic. William Holman Hunt), **4:** 280 n.*330*
London Docks, **6:** 411
London Institute, **6:** 95 n.*149*
London Review, The, **5:** 11, 12 n.*2*
Long – pupil of Rev. T. C. Barker, **4:** 304
Long, Edwin Longsden (1829-1891) – artist, **6:** 73 n.*108*; **8:** 115 n.*188*; **9:** 58 n.*106*, 75, 78
Long, Mr. – friend of the Terrys, **5:** 62 n.*91*

Longfellow, Henry Wadsworth (1807-1882) – poet, **2:** 17, 18 n.*31*, 54 n.*106*
Longley (of Ripon; Bishop Auckland; and Lambeth Palace, London):
Arthur (1841-1920), **2:** 55 n.*109*; **3:** 85
Caroline Georgiana (1843-1867), **2:** 10 n.*10*, 55-6, 58, 104; **3:** 85, 86, 151, 152 n.*220*; **4:** 22; **5:** 179 n.*296*
Caroline Sophia née Parnell (d. 1858), **1:** 93; **2:** 8 n.*4*; **3:** 85, 166 n.*240*
Charles Thomas, Rev. Dr. (1794-1868) – eventually archbishop of Canterbury, **1:** 93 n.*97*; **2:** 8 n.*4*, 9 n.*7*, 10, 55, 56, 101, 102 n.*197*, 119 n.*228*; **3:** 64 n.*96*, 151, 152 n.*220*; **4:** 22, 313, 326 n.*415*, 327; **5:** 158 n.*260*, 179 n.*296*
Frances "Fanny" Elizabeth (b. 1840), **2:** 10 n.*10*, 55, 104; **3:** 85, 151, 152 n.*220*; **4:** 312 n.*390*, 326; **5:** 179 n.*296*
George (1835-1892), **1:** 93; **2:** 8 n.*4*, 55, 66 n.*131*
"Jock" (dog), **3:** 86
Mary Henrietta, see Bourke
Rosamond Esther Harriet (1844-1936), see Parker
Longley (of London):
Diana Elizabeth née Davenport (1838-1917), **4:** 313 n.*391*, 325, 330 n.*422*
Henry, Sir (1832-1899), **1:** 93 n.*97*; **2:** 9 n.*7*, 55, 66 n.*131*; **3:** 161 n.*236*; **4:** 330 n.*422*; **6:** 214 n.*332*, 340 n.*565*, 370, 380; **8:** 435, 436 n.*701*
John Augustine (b. 1867), **8:** 435, 436 n.*701*, 514
Longman, Thomas Norton (1849-1930) – publisher, **8:** 559 n.*889*
Lonsdale (of Littlehampton, Sussex):
Claude (b. 1859), **7:** 469 n.*771*
Mr., **7:** 465 n.*764*; **8:** 32, 37
Philip, **7:** 469 n.*771*; **8:** 33 n.*40*
Looking-Glass Biscuit Tin, **9:** 71 n.*131*
"Lord Dundreary" (in *Our American Cousin*), **5:** 88 n.*136*
Lord Dundreary Married and Done For (dr. Henry Byron), **5:** 160 n.*264*
Lords' Cricket Ground, St. John's Wood, London, **1:** 103
Losely House, near Guildford, **6:** 170 n.*266*
Lost Keys, The (dr. Anon), **7:** 194, 195 n.*362*
Lost Plum-Cake, The (bk. Elizabeth G. Wilcox), **9:** 239, 240 n.*378*, 256
Lost to the World (dr. Mrs. Talbot Hunter), **9:** 26 n.*35*
Lott (of Bampton Lew, Oxfordshire):
Frederick Barnes (b. 1854), **3:** 25, 27
Frederick Edwin, Rev. (1813-1869), **3:** 24 n.*32*, 25
Elizabeth née Barnes (b. 1817), **3:** 24, 25, 27; **6:** 338
Mary Elizabeth (b. 1855), **3:** 25, 27; **4:** 89 n.*46*, 180
Theophilus (b. 1856), **3:** 25, 27
Lottery Ticket, A (dr. Samuel Beazley), **8:** 333, 334 n.*549*
Louis XI (dr. Dion Boucicault), **3:** 120 n.*170*
Love, Mabel (1875-1953) – actress, **8:** 565 n.*900*
Love Chase, The (dr. James Knowles), **5:** 69 n.*104*

Love in Humble Life (dr. John Payne), **6:** 312 n.*516*, 313
Love in Idleness (dr. Louis Parker & Edward Goodman), **9:** 309, 310 n.*493*
Lovely Sisters, The (pic. Thomas Lawrence), **2:** 69 n.*137*
Lover, Samuel (1797-1868) – dramatist, **5:** 17 n.*11*
Lowdore, Cumberland, **2:** 92
Lowe, Alfred, Rev. (b. 1854), **6:** 387 n.*633*
Lowe, Edward Jackson, Rev. (b. 1825), **4:** 56, 57
Lowe, Robert (1811-1892), Viscount Sherbrooke – politician, **5:** 215 n.*344*, 244 n.*398*; **6:** 119 n.*182*
Lowell, James Russell (1819-1891) – American poet, **4:** 244 n.*274*
Lower Brailes, Warwickshire, **7:** 375
Lowestoft, Suffolk, **3:** 28
Lowthorpe (of Park St, London; and Edinburgh):
Beatrice Maude (b. 1867), **4:** 84 n.*37*; **7:** 28 n.*36*, 40 n.*60*, 211, 527
Charles Evelyn St. Quintin (b. 1860), **4:** 84 n.*37*; **7:** 28 n.*36*, 211, 527
Charolotte Lizzie (d. 1856), **4:** 84 n.*37*
Elizabeth "Lizzie" Lucy née Raikes (1832-1888), **2:** 108 n.*209*; **3:** 173 n.*254*; **4:** 84 n.*37*; **7:** 28 n.*36*, 211, 527 n.*852*; **8:** 418 n.*676*
Ernest Frederick Cecil Fletcher (1865-1927), **4:** 84 n.*37*; **7:** 28 n.*36*, 40 n.*60*, 211, 527
James William Frederick, Mr. (b. 1830), **2:** 108 n.*209*; **3:** 173 n.*254*; **4:** 84 n.*37*; **7:** 28 n.*36*, 211, 270, 527
William "Willie" Frederick Raikes (1857-1864), **4:** 84 n.*37*
Lowthorpe (of Kingston-upon-Hull, Yorkshire):
Lady, née Riddell, **2:** 108 n.*209*
William, Sir (b. 1794) – magistrate, **2:** 108
Loys Weedon, Towcester, Northamptonshire, **5:** 207
Lubbock, John, Rt. Hon. Sir (1834-1913) – banker and writer, **8:** 106, 107 n.*176*
Lucas, Harry, alias John Davis (b. 1837) – wheelwright, **5:** 52 n.*73*
Lucas, Mr. – theatre manager, **9:** 254 n.*401*
Luccombe Chine, Isle of Wight, **6:** 296
Lucette, see Rhys
Lucretius, Titus Carus (98-55 BC) – philosopher and poet, **4:** 17
Lucy (of Putney, Surrey):
Alice née Jennings (b. 1841), **8:** 338 n.*558*, 339, 341, 343, 359, 362, 399, 528; **9:** 39 n.*64*, 131, 184 n.*305*, 196, 236, 238, 239, 246, 247, 250, 254, 257, 258, 264, 266, 269, 297, 324 n.*519*
Catherine "Katie" Susanna (1870-1934), **8:** 338 n.*558*, 339, 341, 360 n.*586*, 362 n.*592*, 363-365, 368, 397, 427, 508, 556, 626; **9:** 141, 145
Edith Elizabeth (1871-1907), see Greenidge
William, Mr. – ironfounder, **8:** 338 n.*558*
William Theodore (b. 1866), **8:** 338 n.*558*, 362, 528; **9:** 324 n.519
Ludlow, Shropshire, **6:** 165, 167, 219, 237, 385; **7:** 48, 125-127, 150
Luke, George Rankine (1836-1862) – tutor at Christ Church, **4:** 23, 59

Lukis (of Wath, near Ripon, Yorkshire):
Augusta Georgina Frances (1859-1894), **5:** 43 n.*56*
Frederick William Fellowes (b. 1853), **5:** 43 n.*56*
Gertrude A. D. (b. 1867), **5:** 43 n.*56*
Lucy Adelaide née Fellowes (b. 1831), **5:** 43 n.*56*
Marguerita Wilhelmina (b. 1852), **5:** 43 n.*56*
Mary Adelaide (1855-1875), **5:** 43 n.*56*
Mildred L. J. (b. 1861), **5:** 43 n.*56*
Sidney Elizabeth Mary (1862-1879), **5:** 43 n.*56*
Walter Du Bois F. (b. 1857), **5:** 43 n.*56*
Wilfrid Ravenshaw Fellowes (b. 1864), **5:** 43 n.*56*
William Collings, Rev. (1817-1892) – archaeologist, **5:** 43 n.*56*
Lulsley, Worcestershire, **9:** 69
"Lulu" El Nino Farini – acrobat, **6:** 156 n.*241*
Lumsdaine, Francis Gordon Sandys, Rev. (1828-1873), **2:** 74 n.*148*
Lunacy Commission, **7:** 438, 439 n.*728*, 444 n.*734*
Lupton, Sydney (b. 1850) – teacher, **6:** 263 n.*421*
Lurette (Offenbach) – operetta, **7:** 541 n.*874*
Lusada, Miss – friend of the Owens, **6:** 218
Lushington (of Park House, Maidstone, Kent):
Cecilia née Tennyson (d. 1909), **3:** 118 n.*166*; **4:** 353 n.*460*
Edmund Law (1811-1893), **3:** 118 n.*166*
Lushington (of Park House, Maidstone, Kent):
Edmund Henry, Mr. (1766-1839) – barrister, **3:** 118 n.*165*
Edmund Law (1811-1893), see above
Ellen Eliza (b. 1817), **3:** 118 n.*166*
Emily (b. 1818), **3:** 118 n.*166*
Franklin (1823-1901), **3:** 118 n.*165*
Maud Catherine (b. 1816), **3:** 118 n.*166*
Sophia née Philips (1779-1841) – second wife, **3:** 118 n.*165*
Lust-Garten, Berlin, Germany, **5:** 274

Lutwidge:

Lutwidge (of Tunbridge Wells, Kent):
Anne Louisa neé Raikes (1797-1877) – aunt, **1:** 12
Charles Henry, Rev. (1800-1843) – uncle, **1:** 12
Caroline Louisa (1837-1877) – cousin, **7:** 26 n.*32*, 28 n.*36*
Charles Robert Fletcher (1835-1907) – cousin, **1:** 12, 109 n.*125*, 111; **2:** 67 n.*133*; **3:** 72 n.*113*; **4:** 303 n.*369*; **6:** 238, 278, 279, 385; **7:** 26 n.*32*, 28, 40, 210-212, 527
Lutwidge:
Charles (1722-1784) – great-great-uncle, **1:** 11
Henry (1724-1798) – great-grandfather, **1:** 11, 12, 102 n.*112*
Henry Thomas (1780-1861) – great-uncle, **1:** 12; **2:** 95 n.*186*, 96; **3:** 107,

109, 110 n.*158*
Lucy née Hoghton (1694-1780) – great-great-great-aunt, **1:** 10, 11
Mary née Taylor (d. 1860) – great-aunt, **2:** 96 n.*188*; **3:** 109, 110 n.*158*
Skeffington (1779-1854) – great-uncle, **1:** 12
Skeffington, Admiral (1737-1814) – great-great-uncle, **1:** 12
Thomas (1670-1745) – great-great-great-uncle, **1:** 10, 11
Lutwidge (of Hull, Yorkshire):
Charles (1768-1848) – grandfather, **1:** 9, 11, 12, 102 n.*112*, 109 n.*125*
Charlotte Menella (1807-1857) – aunt, **3:** 63 n.*94*, 76, 134 n.*195*
Elizabeth Anne née Dodgson (1770-1836) – grandmother, **1:** 9, 12
Frances Jane (1803-1851) – mother, see Dodgson
Henrietta Mary (1811-1872) – aunt, **4:** 22, 28; **6:** 231, 237 n.*379*, 238
Lucy (1805-1880) – aunt, **1:** 23-25, 28, 39, 60 n.*33*, 80; **2:** 14, 56; **3:** 171; **4:** 22, 37, 80, 81, 97, 109; **6:** 47-49, 51, 58, 69, 169 n.*263*, 186, 205, 238, 245, 270, 279, 280, 308, 332, 344, 362, 370, 386, 465, 477; **7:** 11, 25, 39, 45, 74, 104, 125, 150, 166, 170, 189, 219, 229, 256, 281, 293, 294 n.*532*, 324 n.*575*
Margaret Anne (1809-1869) – aunt, **3:** 76; **4:** 22, 28
Robert Wilfred Skeffington (1802-1873), barrister and commissioner in lunacy – uncle, **1:** 12, 26, 47, 51, 102 n.113, 107, 130, 131, 132; **2:** 18, 24, 26, 51 n.*103*, 83, 123; **3:** 13, 52, 63 n.*94*, 76, 80, 132, 144, 172; **4:** 84, 85, 271, 279, 284, 314, 322, 331, 343; **5:** 25, 33, 36, 78 n.*122*, 79, 89, 136, 137, 145, 170, 180, 208; **6:** 15, 47, 49, 74, 75, 84, 93, 112, 127, 130, 157, 160, 161, 165, 172, 177, 178, 181, 183, 184, 194, 195 n.*303*, 196, 206, 217, 220, 222-224, 237, 238, 251, 256, 257, 269, 272, 278, 279, 346; **7:** 438, 439 n.*728*

Lyall, Mr. – friend of the Drurys, **7:** 235 n.*434*
Lych-Gate (pic. Henry Darvall), **5:** 86 n.*134*
Lygon, Frederick (1830-1891), Earl Beauchamp – politician, **6:** 67 n.*99*
Lymington, Hampshire, **4:** 348
Lynam, Charles Cotterill (b. 1859) – teacher, **9:** 262, 263 n.*414*
Lynch, Margaret (b. 1879) – amateur actress and singer, **9:** 303 n.*482*
Lynn, Dr. – illusionist, **7:** 68 n.*112*; **8:** 146 n.*235*
Lyon, Lucy Sarah (b. 1842), **7:** 441 n.*731*
Lyons, Edmund, Admiral Sir (1790-1858) – navy officer, **2:** 79 n.*156*
Lytton, Edward Bulwer, Lord (1803-1873) – writer and dramatist, **5:** 109 n.*172*, 157 n.*255*; **7:** 540 n.*873*; **8:** 628 n.*994*

Mabel in Rhymeland (bk. Edward Holland), **8:** 579 n.*925*
Macallam, Hamilton (1841-1896) – artist, **4:** 320 n.*406*
Macan (of Oxford):
Mildred Elizabeth née Healey (1859-1955), **7:** 383 n.*660*; **9:** 285 n.*450*
Reginald Walter, Mr. (1848-1941) – lecturer, **7:** 383 n.*660*, 440, 489, 490 n.*798*; **8:** 123 n.*198*, 213, 296; **9:** 285 n.*450*

Macaulay (of Great Shelford, Cambridgeshire):
Emilie Rose (1881-1958), **9:** 259 n.*409*, 262
George Campbell, Mr. (1852-1915) – teacher, **9:** 259 n.*409*, 262
Grace Mary, Mrs. (b. 1856), **9:** 259 n.*409*, 261, 262
Jean (b. 1883), **9:** 259 n.*409*, 262
Margaret Campbell (b. 1880), **9:** 259 n.*409*
Macaulay, Miss – cousin of the writer (see below), **8:** 538 n.*863*
Macaulay, Thomas Babbington (1800-1859) – writer, **1:** 27; **6:** 427
Macbride (of Oxford):
John David, Dr. (1778-1868) – principal of Hertford College, **3:** 44 n.*71*
Miss, **3:** 44 n.*71*
MacDonald (of Museum Villas, Oxford):
Alexander, Mr. (1839-1921) – artist, **8:** 624, 625 n.*988*; **9:** 122 n.*213*
Ellen "Nellie" (b. 1865), **9:** 121, 122 n.*213*
MacDonald (of various addresses in London and Hastings):
Bernard Powell (1865-1928), **4:** 99 n.*60*; **7:** 186
Caroline Grace (1854-1884), see Jameson
George, Dr. (1824-1905) – writer and poet, **1:** 44; **4:** 27, 28, 98, 99 n.*60*, 105, 109, 124, 160, 222, 223, 226, 228 n.*253*, 230, 244, 250, 254-256, 272, 302, 310, 312, 317, 318, 320, 324, 325, 331, 336, 341, 359; **5:** 21 n.*15*, 23, 47, 61, 63, 81 n.*126*, 143-145, 157, 210, 214, 215, 232; **6:** 21, 22 n.*24*, 26, 27, 30, 126 n.*196*, 161, 179 n.*277*, 187, 222, 224, 270, 271; **7:** 78, 179-181, 183-186, 193, 194, 222, 350, 473
George MacKay (1867-1909), **4:** 99 n.*60*
Greville Matheson (1856-1944), **3:** 176, 177; **4:** 33, 99 n.*60*, 105, 197 n.*198*, 222, 228 n.*253*, 255 n.*294*, 257, 272, 280, 312, 324, 341; **5:** 21; **6:** 27; **7:** 78, 350
Irene (1857-1939), **4:** 99 n.*60*, 105, 180, 183, 225, 228 n.*253*, 272, 276, 312, 317, 318, 324, 331 n.*425*; **5:** 67, 126, 157; **6:** 27; **7:** 78, 180, 186
Jane (George's half-sister), **4:** 310 n.*385*, 324, 325
Lilia "Lily" Scott (1852-1891), **4:** 99 n.*60*, 180, 222, 228 n.*253*, 255 n.*294*, 256, 272, 324, 325, 332; **5:** 21, 63, 145, 190 n.*311*, 193, 214; **6:** 15, 19, 27, 84, 162, 225; **7:** 78, 180 n.*334*, 185, 195
Louisa (George's half-sister), **4:** 310 n.*385*
Louisa née Powell (1822-1902) – dramatist, **4:** 99 n.*60*, 105, 197 n.*198*, 222, 225-227, 230 n.*254*, 244, 250, 254, 255, 272, 302, 310, 312, 317, 318, 320, 324, 325, 331, 336, 341, 359; **5:** 21, 47, 61, 63, 143, 145, 157, 210, 214, 215, 232; **6:** 15 n.*11*, 21, 26, 27, 30, 84, 126 n.*196*, 161, 162 n.*251*, 222, 224, 270, 271; **7:** 78, 179-181, 183-186, 193, 194, 222, 350, 473
Mary Josephine (1853-1878), **3:** 176, 177; **4:** 34, 99 n.*60*, 181, 183, 222, 228 n.*253*, 229-231, 255 n.*294*, 272, 280, 312, 317, 318, 324, 325, 331 n.*425*, 332; **5:** 19, 21, 63, 145, 157; **6:** 19, 27, 270; **7:** 78, 181 n.*336*
Maurice (1864-1879), **4:** 99 n.*60*; **6:** 126 n.*196*; **7:** 181 n.*336*
Nelly (George's niece), **4:** 228 n.*253*

Robert "Bob" Falconer (1862-1913), **4:** 99 n.*60*, 105 n.*71*, 228 n.*253*, 272, 280; **6:** 126 n.*196*; **7:** 185
Ronald (1860-1933), **4:** 99 n.*60*, 228 n.*253*, 255 n.*294*, 272, 318, 324; **5:** 23; **6:** 126 n.*196*; **7:** 78, 488 n.*796*, 489
Winifred Louisa (1858-1946), **4:** 99 n.*60*, 105, 181, 222, 228 n.*253*, 255 n.*294*, 272, 280, 312, 324; **5:** 67; **6:** 27; **7:** 78, 180, 186
MacDonald, Thomas Mosse, Mr. (1856-1910) – teacher, **7:** 519 n.*841*; **8:** 92 n.*149*
MacDonald, William Henry (b. 1836) – teacher, **7:** 496 n.*808*
Mace, Frances – artists' model, **7:** 429 n.*716*
Macey, see Macy
MacFarland, James E. – American Army Secretary, **4:** 286 n.*341*
Macfarlane Family, **8:** 442 n.*708*
Macfarlane's Will (dr. Joseph Mackay), **7:** 396 n.*674*
Mackarness (of Cuddesdon Palace, Oxford):
Alethea Buchanan née Duke (1827-1909), **9:** 297 n.*470*, 299
John Feilder, Rev. Dr. (1820-1889) – bishop of Oxford, **8:** 253 n.*426*
Mackarness (of Hambleden, Buckinghamshire):
George Evelyn, Capt. (b. 1852) – farmer, **9:** 299 n.*475*
Jessie Alethea (b. 1881), **9:** 299 n.*475*
Kathleen May (b. 1880), **9:** 299 n.*475*
Marie Sidney née Campbell (b. 1860), **9:** 299 n.*475*
Mackay, Joseph (b. 1850) – dramatist, **7:** 396 n.*674*
Mackenzie, Alexander Campbell (1847-1935) – composer, **8:** 15 n.*8*, 20 n.*14*, 23, 102, 105, 183
Mackenzie, Louisa Stewart (b. 1854) – friend of the Haydons, **6:** 481 n.*794*
Mackershaw, Yorkshire, **2:** 58 n.*116*
Mackinder, Emilie Catherine née Ginsburg., **9:** 295 n.*467*, 296, 298, 313, 320
Mackinder and Winefield – theatre managers, **9:** 254 n.*401*
Mackintosh, Margaret, Mrs. (b. 1810), **8:** 130, 131 n.*213*
Mackintosh, Muriel E. M. (b. 1877), **8:** 130, 131 n.*213*
Maclaren, Archibald (b. 1818) – headmaster, **7:** 104 n.*195*
Maclean (of Oxford):
Elfrida "Friday" (b. 1886) **9:** 313 n.*499*
Mrs., **9:** 313 n.*499*
Olive (b. 1885), **9:** 313 n.*499*
Maclise, Daniel (1806-1870) – artist, **2:** 20 n.*37*; **3:** 76 n.*117*
Macmillan (of Knapdale, Streatham, Surrey):
Alexander, Mr. (1818-1896) – publisher, **4:** 311 n.*387*, 349; **5:** 15 n.*8*, 25, 26 n.*25*, 33 n.*37*, 45, 64, 70, 76 n.*116*, 97 n.*151*, 100, 115 n.*180*, 117 n.*184*, 143, 151, 173 n.*288*, 227 n.*361*, 231, 232 n.*370*; **6:** 251, 252 n.*399*, 293, 378
Caroline née Brimley (d. 1871) – first wife, **6:** 252 n.*399*
Emma née Pignatel (b. 1843) – second wife, **6:** 251, 252 n.*399*, 378
George Augustin (1855-1936), **6:** 252 n.*399*, 253, 378

John Victor (1877-1956), **6:** 252 n.*399*
Malcolm Kingsley (1853-1889), **6:** 251, 252 n.*399*
Margaret (b. 1857), **6:** 252 n.*399*, 253, 378
Mary (b. 1875), **6:** 252 n.*399*
Olive (1858-1926), **6:** 252 n.*399*, 253, 378
William Alexander (1864-1867), **6:** 252 n.*399*
Macmillan (of London):
Arthur Daniel (1857-1877), **6:** 252, 378
Catherine "Katie" C. (b. 1855), **6:** 252
Daniel, Mr. (1813-1857) – publisher, **6:** 252 n.*399*
Frances née Orridge (d. 1867), **6:** 252 n.*399*
Frederick Orridge (1851-1936) – publisher, **6:** 252 n.*399*; **9:** 54 n.*95*, 106, 107, 171, 172
Maurice Crawford (1853-1936), **6:** 252 n.*399*
Macmillan and Company, **4:** 258 n.*301*; **5:** 9, 89, 93, 101 n.*158*, 140; **6:** 72, 74-76, 189, 190, 349, 427, 429-433, 453; **7:** 93, 196 n.*367*, 322, 342, 397, 546 n.*880*; **8:** 21 n.*15*, 186, 218, 269, 303, 307 n.*509*, 313, 321, 359, 361, 402, 404, 438, 443, 487, 488 n.*789*, 494, 495, 558 n.*888*, 620; **9:** 44, 54, 105, 106 n.*190*, 107, 111, 112, 116, 117, 173, 176, 237 n.*373*, 326, 340
Macnaghten (of Hampstead, London):
Alfred Hill, Mr. (1848-1915) – tea merchant, **8:** 296 n.*492*, 302
Arabella Marie née Betts (1849-1931), **8:** 296 n.*492*, 305
Ella Margaret (b. 1877), **8:** 296 n.*492*, 303, 305
Macwilliam (of Leatherhead, Surrey):
Agnes (b. 1874), **7:** 292 n.*528*, 295, 305
Annie (b. 1871), **7:** 295, 305
Margaret, Mrs. (b. 1846), **7:** 292 n.*528*, 295
William Banks, Rev. (b. 1836), **7:** 295
Macy (of Oxhill, Warwickshire):
Edith T. (b. 1863), **7:** 71 n.*114*, 128 n.*241*
Lilian "Lily" (b. 1864), **6:** 444 n.*726*; **7:** 91 n.*164*, 92, 93; **8:** 193 n.*323*, 226
Mehetabel Sarah, Mrs. (b. 1834), **7:** 71 n.*114*, 74, 128 n.*241*
Vincent Hardwicke, Rev. (b. 1833), **8:** 193 n.*323*
Vincent Travers (b. 1867), **6:** 444 n.*726*; **7:** 91 n.*164*, 92
Madame Favart (Offenbach) – operetta, **7:** 193, 194 n.*361*, 212, 220, 232, 304
Madame Tussaud's Waxworks, London, **3:** 172
Madan (of Oxford):
Arthur Cornwallis (b. 1850) – tutor, **7:** 171 n.*319*; **9:** 76 n.*141*, 315
Falconer (1851-1935) – librarian, **1:** 27-29, 99 n.*107*; **7:** 309, 310 n.*553*
Henry George (1839-1901) – teacher, **6:** 180 n.*279*
Maddock, Ellen (b. 1869) – niece of Mrs. Smith of Brighton, **8:** 226 n.*382*
Madeira, Island of, **2:** 111 n.*217*, 125, 126; **3:** 16 n.*17*, 22 n.*27*, 73 n.*114*, 86, 121, 129, 145

Madonna della Seggiola (pic. Raphael), **2:** 16 n.*27*
"Mad Tea-party" (dramatised by the Arnolds), **6:** 369 n.*607*
Maeder, Frederick George (1841-1891) – dramatist, **8:** 230 n.*388*
Magdalen College, Oxford, **2:** 107 n.*207*; **4:** 234 n.*261*, 298; **6:** 142, 150, 317, 389, 426; **7:** 85, 108, 346, 445, 453, 535; **8:** 62, 121, 196, 215, 216, 248, 275, 339, 396, 409, 482, 511, 544, 554, 568, 591, 619; **9:** 153, 223, 232, 255, 322
Magdalen College Chapel, **6:** 327, 389; **7:** 109, 244, 269, 346, 424
Magdalen College School, **7:** 244
Magdalene (pic. Emanuel Benner), **8:** 366 n.*599*
Magee, William Connor, Rev. (1821-1891), **7:** 227, 341 n.*596*
Maggie, you're cheating (pic. James Archer), **5:** 214
Magic Lantern, **2:** 31 n.*61*, 119 n.*227*, 123, 126-128; **3:** 7, 13
Magic Toys, The (dr. John Oxenford), **4:** 291 n.*348*
Magistrate, The (dr. Arthur Pinero), **8:** 199 n.*339*
Magrath, John Richard, Rev. Dr. (1839-1930) – Provost of Queen's College, **8:** 86 n.*139*
Maid and the Magpie, The (dr. John Payne), **2:** 21 n.*39*
Maiden Bradley, Wiltshire, **1:** 72 n.*63*; **4:** 137
Maidens' Race, The (pic. John Weguelin), **7:** 538, 539 n.*871*
Maid of Honour, The (dr. John Wooler), **4:** 309 n.*384*
Maister (of Littlethorpe, near Ripon, Yorkshire):
  Arthur, **3:** 169 n.*246*
  Catherine, Mrs. (1789-1861), **3:** 169 n.*246*
  Catherine, see Tidy
  Everetta Catherine (b. 1806), **3:** 169 n.*246*
  Frances, **3:** 169 n.*246*
  Harriet (b. 1810), **3:** 169 n.*246*
  Henry, **3:** 169 n.*246*
  Jane, see Bean
  John, Lt. Gen. (1788-1852) – army officer, **3:** 169 n.*246*
  Mary Anne, **3:** 169 n.*246*
Majendie (of Elvetham, Hampshire):
  Arthur, Rev. (1838-1895), **6:** 421 n.*693*, 490
  Bernard J. (b. 1876), **6:** 421 n.*693*
  Dulcebella, Mrs. (b. 1839), **6:** 421 n.*693*, 490, 491
  Dulcie S. (b. 1868), **6:** 421 n.*693*, 422, 425, 490, 491
  Lionel R. (b. 1872), **6:** 421 n.*693*
Majoribanks, Fanny Octavia Louisa née Spencer, Lady (d. 1904), **8:** 511 n.*824*
Malakoff Tower, Sebastopol, Russia (Crimean War), **1:** 104, 130
Malchus – biblical slave, **2:** 10
Malet, Clement Drake Elton (1845-1930) – pupil at Twyford, **3:** 137 n.*202*
Malet (of Wilbury Park, Salisbury, Wiltshire):
  Henry Charles Eden, Sir (1835-1904), 3rd Bart., **8:** 563 n.*898*

Laura Jane Campbell née Hamilton (d. 1922), **8:** 563 n.*898*
Vera Jean Hamilton (1881-1951), **8:** 563 n.*898*, 591, 633
Maling, Edward Allen, Mr. (b. 1839) – surgeon, **6:** 208 n.*326*
Mallalieu (of Shepherd's Bush, London):
George William "Willie" (1873-1948), **8:** 587 n.*938*; **9:** 27
Margaret Ellen née Smith, **8:** 587 n.*938*, 616 n.*977*, 632; **9:** 27
Mary Elizabeth Agnes "Polly" (b. 1880) – actress, **8:** 587 n.*938*, 592, 632, 634; **9:** 14 n.*9*, 15, 16, 27
William, Mr. (1846-1927) – actor and comedian, **8:** 587 n.*938*, 632; **9:** 14 n.*9*
Mallam (of Iffley, Oxfordshire):
Agnes (b. 1879), **9:** 244 n.*387*, 294
Alice née Phillips (b. 1845), **9:** 244 n.*387*, 294, 296, 300, 320
Dorothea (b. 1875), **9:** 244 n.*387*, 294
Gertrude (b. 1877), **9:** 244 n.*387*, 294
Grace (b. 1883?), **9:** 244 n.*387*
James Thomas, Mr. (b. 1850) – surveyor, **9:** 244 n.*387*, 294, 320
Ursula (1886-1977), **9:** 244 n.*387*, 294, 296, 320
Malton, Yorkshire, **5:** 190
Malvern, Worcestershire, **4:** 116, 118, 224; **7:** 531
"Mamillius" (in *The Winter's Tale*), **2:** 83 n.*164*, 124
Man and Wife (bk. Wilkie Collins), **6:** 141 n.*212*
Manchester, **3:** 90, 119, 145; **7:** 98, 106, 107
Manchester Exhibition, **3:** 120 n.*169*, 139 n.*206*
Mangles (of Woking, Surrey):
Georgiana, Mrs. (b. 1814), **6:** 94 n.*147*; **7:** 400 n.*679*
Grace, **7:** 400 n.*679*
Manisty, Henry, Sir (1808-1890) – judge, **7:** 121 n.*227*
Manners (of Avon Tyrrell, Christchurch, Hampshire):
John Thomas, Lord (1852-1927), 3rd Bart., **6:** 441, 442 n.*724*
Lydia Sophia, Lady (d. 1916) – his mother, **6:** 441, 442 n.*724*
Manners (of Croydon, Surrey):
Louisa (b. 1864), **8:** 252 n.*424*, 474
Mary Emmeline (1858-1941) – writer and poet, **8:** 252 n.*424*, 474, 477 n.*773*
Rachel (niece), **8:** 252 n.*424*
Manners (of Belvoir Castle, Grantham, Lincolnshire):
Henry John Brinsley, Marquess (1852-1925), 8th Duke of Rutland, **8:** 463 n.*746*
Marion Margaret Violet née Lindsay (1856-1937), Marchioness of Granby, **8:** 463 n.*746*, 471
Robert Charles John (1885-1894), Lord Haddon, **8:** 463 n.*746*, 464
Victoria Marjorie Harriet (1883-1946), **8:** 463 n.*746*, 464, 468, 469, 486
Mannings, Henry Jacob (b. 1846) – pupil at Twyford, **3:** 137 n.*202*
Manorbier Castle, Pembrokeshire, **4:** 190

Mansel (of Oxford):
  Henry Longueville, Dr. (1820-1871) – professor of ecclesiastical history, **5:** 197; **6:** 34 n.*45*, 67 n.*99*
  Mrs., **6:** 34 n.*45*
Mansell (of Shroton, Dorset):
  Edward B. (b. 1866), **6:** 237 n.*377*
  Laura (b. 1857), **6:** 236, 237 n.*377*
  Loubel (b. 1860?), **6:** 236, 237 n.*377*
  Richard C. (b. 1867), **6:** 236, 237 n.*377*
Mansell's Booksellers, Oxford, **3:** 52
Mansen, Ethel – friend of the Napiers, **6:** 358
Mansfield, Richard (1854-1907) – actor and manager, **8:** 433 n.*699*, 440, 442, 451
Mansfield, William David, Lord (1806-1898), 4th Earl, **3:** 95
Mansfield Street, London, **6:** 161, 169
Mansion House, London, **5:** 255
Manual of Artistic Anatomy (bk. Robert Knox), **3:** 168 n.*243*
Mapleton (of Chapel Allerton, Yorkshire):
  David, Rev. (b.1823), **7:** 190 n.*352*
  Mary Ann, Mrs. (b. 1830), **7:** 190 n.*352*
  Mary "May" (b. 1866), **7:** 189, 190 n.*352*
Map of London, **7:** 165 n.*310*
Marcham (or Marsham), Berkshire, **3:** 43; **7:** 531
"March of the Cameron Men" (Mary Maxwell Campbell) – song, **2:** 100
March-Phillipps (of London):
  Georgina née Dashwood, **6:** 260, 261 n.*416*
  Geraldine (b. 1865), **6:** 261 n.*417*
  Henry (b. 1855), **6:** 260, 261 n.*416*
Marcon, Charles Abdy, Rev. (1854-1953) – teacher, **9:** 47 n.*83*
"Margaret" (Alfred Tennyson) – poem, **4:** 14, 15, 17
Margaret Fuller (bk. Thomas Higginson), **7:** 426 n.*711*
Margaret Street, London, **5:** 211
Margate, Kent, **6:** 128 n.*199*, 129-131, 399; **8:** 418, 424; **9:** 218
Margate Grotto, **6:** 130
Margate Infirmary, **5:** 29
Margate Sands (dr. Wilmot Harrison), **4:** 272, 273 n.*318*
Margetts, Oxford – furniture suppliers **4:** 309
Marionette Theatre (for Kitchins), **6:** 307, 308, 321, 325
Marius, C. D. (1850-1896) – actor and singer, **7:** 194 n.*361*, 304, 305 n.*549*, 541
Markby, Robert Brenner (1842-1908) – actor, **6:** 349 n.*579*
Markenfield Hall, Yorkshire, **3:** 149 n.*216*
Marlborough – see Spencer-Churchill
Marlborough College, **3:** 136; **5:** 136; **7:** 495
Marlow, Buckinghamshire, **5:** 57, 58 n.*83*

Marmion – steamship, **7:** 452
Marochetti, Baron Carlo (1805-1868) – sculptor, **4:** 36, 97 n.*55*, 328 n.*418*
Marquesa, The (dr. John Uniacke), **8:** 473 n.*768*
Marriott, Charles, Rev. (1811-1858), **1:** 64 n.*42*
Marriott, Mr. – subject of benefit concert at Hastings, **7:** 475 n.*777*
Marsden, Yorkshire, **1:** 133
Marsh (of Guildford area):
Selina Rose Catherine née Morgan, **6:** 94 n.*147*, 96
William Nathaniel Tilson, Rev. (1816-1881), **6:** 94 n.*147*
Marshal, Mary (b. 1857), **6:** 116 n.*179*
Marshall (of Monk Coniston Park, Ambleside, Westmorland):
Constance Eleanor (d. 1853), **3:** 112 n.*160*
James Aubrey Garth (1844-1873?), **3:** 112 n.*160*
James Garth (1802-1873) – industrialist, **3:** 111, 112 n.*160*, 117, 118 n.*165*, 119, 173, **4:** 47, 92 n.*49*
Julia Mary Garth (1845-1907), see O'Brien
Mary Alice Pery née Rice Spring (1812-1875), **3:** 111, 112 n.*160*, 113, 117, 118 n.*165*, 119, 173; **4:** 47, 92 n.*49*
Victor Alexander Garth (1841-1928), **3:** 111, 112 n.*160*, 117; **6:** 263 n.*421*
Marshall (of Pyrton, Oxfordshire):
Ellen (b. 1862), **7:** 279 n.*508*
George, Rev. (1817-1897) – public examiner and moderator, **1:** 71 n.*61*; **2:** 66 n.*131*, 70, 76 n.*152*, 126; **3:** 31, 64, 67; **6:** 153, 215, 370 n.*608*, 438; **7:** 279 n.*508*; **8:** 438 n.*702*; **9:** 299 n.*474*
Sophia B., Mrs. (b. 1826), **7:** 279 n.*508*
Walter Langley (b. 1865), **7:** 279 n.*508*
Marshall Family, near Whitburn, **5:** 41
Marsham, Robert Townshend (1834-1914) – diplomat, **4:** 33
Marston, John Westland (1819-1890) – dramatist, **5:** 139 n.*223*
Marston, Oxfordshire, **6:** 278; **9:** 252
Marston Meysey, Gloucestershire, **6:** 476
Martin, Charles (b. 1841) – teacher, **4:** 294 n.*353*
Martin (of Marylebone, London):
Edith (b. 1880) – child actress, **8:** 383 n.*629*, 403; **9:** 173 n.*290*
Georgina (b. 1876) – child actress, **8:** 383 n.*629*
Laura, Mrs. (b. 1842), **8:** 383 n.*629*, 403
Martin (of Onslow Square, London):
Helen née Faucit, Lady (1819-1898) – actress, **5:** 23, 24 n.*21*; **6:** 220 n.*346*, 352
Theodore (1816 -1909), pseud. Bon Gaultier – solicitor and writer, **2:** 44 n.*89*
Martin, Joseph (b. 1838) – barrister, **7:** 24 n.*26*
Martin, Miss, friend of the Terrys, **5:** 94
Martineau (of Heckfield, Hampshire):

John, Mr. (1834-1910) – barrister, **6:** 423 n.*695*
Louisa Amabel née Adeane (1841-1894), **6:** 423 n.*695*
Violet Isabel (1865-1948), **6:** 423 n.*695*, 425
Martineau, Robert Braithwaite (1826-1869) – artist, **4:** 333 n.*429*, 334, 335, 337
Martin-Harvey (of East Sheen, Surrey):
Angelita Helena "Nellie" De Silva née Ferro (1865-1949) – actress, **6:** 483 n.*797*; **9:** 146 n.*252*, 161, 162 n.*277*, 163, 204
Margaret Muriel del Melfort (b. 1895), **9:** 204 n.*333*
John, Mr. (1863-1944) – actor and manager, **9:** 162 n.*277*, 163, 204, 347
Martyn (of Long Melford, Suffolk):
Adelaide M. (b. 1867), **6:** 296 n.*488*
Arthur (b. 1868?), **6:** 296 n.*488*
Beatrice J (b. 1871), **6:** 296 n.*488*
Catherine Elizabeth née Harrison (1830-1882), **6:** 296 n.*488*, 354
Catherine "Kate" Clarissa (b. 1859), **6:** 296 n.*488*
Charles Harrison (b. 1861), **6:** 296 n.*488*
Charles John, Rev. (1836-1901), **6:** 296 n.*488*, 354; **7:** 49 n.*76*
Constance (b. 1865), **6:** 296 n.*488*
Harry (b. 1870?), **6:** 296 n.*488*
Lucy Jane (b. 1860?), **6:** 296 n.*488*
Marwood (of Busby Hall, Yorkshire):
Alice (d. 1867), **7:** 257 n.*467*
Arthur Pierson (1868-1916), **7:** 257 n.*467*
Charles Metcalfe (1874-78), **7:** 257 n.*467*
Clara Charlotte (1870-1910), **7:** 257 n.*467*
Ellinor Edith (b. 1861), **7:** 257 n.*467*
Emily "Emmie" Caroline (b. 1857), **7:** 257 n.*467*; **8:** 30 n.*36*
Frances A. née Peel (b. 1832) – wife of cousin, **7:** 257 n.*467*
Frances Mary (b. 1856), **7:** 257 n.*467*
George Frederic (1858-1898), **7:** 257 n.*467*
George, Mr. (1808-1882) – cousin, **7:** 257 n.*467*
Henry (b. 1864), **7:** 257 n.*467*
Lilian (b. 1872), **7:** 257 n.*467*
Lucy Susanna (b. 1860), **7:** 182 n.*341*, 257 n.*467*
Rose (b. 1873), **7:** 257 n.*467*
William Francis (b. 1863), **7:** 257 n.*467*
Marwood, Frances "Fanny" (d. 1886) – cousin, **1:** 133 n.*166*
Marwood, George, Rev. (1746-1827) – second husband of Dodgson's grandmother, **1:** 10, 133 n.*166*
Marx-Goldschmidt, Berthe, Madame – pianist, **8:** 583 n.*932*
Mary Barton (bk. Elizabeth Gaskell), **1:** 131 n.*163*
Marylebone Cricket Club (MCC) – cricket match with Oxford, **2:** 73
Marylebone Tenants (John Ruskin's charity), **6:** 162 n.*251*
Masaniello (dr. Robert Brough), **3:** 79, 80 n.*126*, 133 n.*193*; **4:** 310 n.*386*

Maskelyne, Mervyn Herbert Nevil Story (1823-1911) – scientist, photographer and politician, **8:** 384 n.*630*
Maskelyne and Cooke – entertainers, **6:** 467, 468 n.*769*
Masks and Faces (dr. Charles Reade and Tom Taylor), **6:** 443 n.*725*; **9:** 335, 336 n.*537*
Mason (of Northleigh, Oxfordshire):
Alice E. (b. 1866), **6:** 266 n.*428*, 267, 268, 276, 322
Caroline "Carry" Isabel (b. 1863), **6:** 266 n.*428*, 268, 276, 322
Ida F. (b. 1868), **6:** 266 n.*428*, 267, 276
Isabel née Barry (b. 1833), **6:** 266 n.*428*, 267, 268, 276, 321
James, Mr. (1824-1903) – magistrate, **6:** 266 n.*428*, 267, 276
Rita G. (b. 1872), **6:** 266 n.*428*, 276
Rose S. (b. 1869), **6:** 266 n.*428*, 276
Mason (of Chislehurst, Surrey):
Fanny Thornton née Amoore (1851-1919), **8:** 81 n.*128*
Henry Alfred, Rev. (1851-1939), **8:** 81 n.*128*
Mason (of Eden Place, Kirkby Stephen, Westmorland):
Helen Arbuthnot née Feilden (1859-1947), **6:** 260 n.*414*; **7:** 82 n.*138*, 143 n.*264*, 492; **8:** 60 n.*96*, 264, 391, 433, 551
Henry Paul, Col. (1855-1924) – army officer, **8:** 60 n.*96*, 551
Mason, James Murray (1798-1871) – American Confederate Commissioner, **4:** 286 n.*341*
Mason, John (1859-1919) – actor, **8:** 562 n.*896*; **9:** 215 n.*343*
Mason, John M., Rev. (1820-1899), **5:** 175 n.*291*
Mason College, Birmingham, **9:** 259 n.*408*
Masonic Fête, Oxford, **6:** 36, 118, 155, 340
Massey, Gerald (1828-1907) – poet, **4:** 109
Master Henry Kemble (pic. Miss A. Liberty), **2:** 75 n.*151*
Matched and Mated (dr. Francis Burnand and Thomas German Reed), **7:** 57 n.*90*
Mathematical Problems (bk. Joseph Wolstenholme), **7:** 487, 488 n.*793*
Mathematical Recreations (bk. Walter Ball), **9:** 307 n.*487*
Matheson (of London):
Greville Ewing (d. 1872) – Bank of England clerk, **4:** 227 n.*251*
William (1834?-1891), **4:** 226 n.*250*, 228, 330
Matheson (of London):
Greville Ewing Jnr. (b. 1847?), see below
Thomas (b. 1845), **4:** 324; **5:** 210
Matheson (of Church Row, Hampstead, London):
Greville Ewing Jnr., Mr. (b. 1847?), **4:** 310 n.*385*, 324, 330; **5:** 210 n.*337*
Antoinette "Netty" A. née Smart (1847-1923), **4:** 310 n.*385*, 330; **5:** 210 n.*337*
Mathews (of Kentish Town, London):
Charles, Mr. (1776-1835) – actor, **2:** 9 n.*6*
Charles James (1804-1878), see below

Anne née Jackson, second wife – actress, **2:** 9 n.*6*
Mathews (of Belgrave Road, London):
Charles James, Mr. (1804-1878) – architect, actor and dramatist, **4:** 205 n.*214*, 270 n.*313*; **5:** 72, 73 n.*110*, 88 n.*136*, 210 n.*336*; **6:** 27 n.*30*
Lizzie née Davenport (d. 1899), second wife – actress, **4:** 270; **5:** 72, 73 n.*110*, 210
Matley (or Mattey) Family of Eastbourne, **7:** 296 n.*536*
Matthews (or Merton, Surrey):
Florence M. Medham (b. 1871), **7:** 204, 205 n.*382*, 213
Martha, Mrs. (b. 1845), **7:** 204, 205 n.*382*
Matthews, Frank (1807-1871) – actor, **3:** 14 n.*13*, 81, 82 n.*127*
Matthews, James Pardo, Rev. (1803-1885), **4:** 67, 68 n.*7*
Matty – pupil of William Ranken, **6:** 476
Maud and Other Poems (bk. Alfred Tennyson), **1:** 72, 119 n.*145*, 129, 134; **2:** 9 n.*8*; **3:** 112, 113
Maude (of Cleveland Gardens, London):
Cyril Francis, Mr. (1862-1951) – actor, **9:** 100, 101 n.*182*, 352
Isabel Winifred Maud née Emery (1863-1924) – actress, **9:** 100, 101 n.*182*, 352
Maul, Richard Graham, Rev. (1820-1895), **6:** 288 n.*473*, 349
Maund, Henry, Dr. (1828?-1879) – physician, **6:** 420 n.*690*
Maurice (of Brunswick Place, London):
(John) Frederick Denison, Rev. (1805-1872), **4:** 82 n.*35*, 105 n.*70*, 160, 163, 164 n.*158*, 165 n.*159*, 167 n.*161*, 222, 226, 228 n.*253*, 309; **5:** 157 n.*257*, 210 n.*337*; **6:** 15 n.*11*; **7:** 203
Georgiana née Hare-Naylor (b. 1810), **4:** 160
Mawley, Master – pupil at Richmond School, **1:** 21
Max Müller, see Müller
May (of St. Pancras, London):
A. E. (b. 1873), **7:** 522 n.*847*
Alfred, Mr. (b. 1843) – carpenter, **7:** 522 n.*847*
Ellen "Nellie" B. (b. 1871), **7:** 522 n.*847*, 523; **8:** 114 n.*185*
E. V. (b. 1878), **7:** 522 n.*847*
J. F. S. (b. 1880), **7:** 522 n.*847*
Martha, Mrs. (b. 1849), **7:** 522 n.*847*
May, Amelia R. (b. 1836) – friend of the Threshers, **6:** 414 n.*677*
May, Jane – actress, **8:** 556 n.*885*
Mayall, John Edwin (1810-1901) – photographer, **3:** 14 n.*12*, 88, 134 n.*194*
Mayhew (of Oxford):
Anthony Arnold (b. 1874), **7:** 147 n.*277*
Anthony Lawson, Rev. (1842-1917) – lecturer, **7:** 147 n.*277*, 149, 163, 176; **9:** 248
Arthur Innes (1878-1948), **7:** 147 n.*277*
Charles L. (b. 1876), **7:** 147 n.*277*

Ethel Innes (1867-1919), **7:** 147 n.*277*, 149, 160, 163 n.*306*, 176, 177 n.*326*, 191; **8:** 85 n.*138*
Jane Innes née Griffin (1846-1916), **7:** 147 n.*277*, 149, 163, 176; **9:** 248
Janet Evelyn (1872-1891), **7:** 147 n.*277*, 163 n.*306*
Margaret Dorothea (1883-1971), **7:** 147 n.*277*; **9:** 77 n.*143*, 229, 243, 248, 250, 255, 320, 347, 348
Mary Ruth (1866-1939), **7:** 147 n.*277*, 149, 160, 163, 176, 177 n.*326*, 191; **9:** 182
Mayhew, Charles (b. 1841) – pupil-teacher, **2:** 30
May Morris (pic. Dante Gabriel Rossetti), **7:** 513
Mayne (of Guildford, Surrey):
Evelyn Caroline (b. 1875), **9:** 119 n.*205*
Lilian Rachel (b. 1873), **9:** 119 n.*205*
William Otway, Mr. (b. 1852) – officer of the House of Commons, **9:** 119 n.*205*
Mayne, Richard, Sir (1796-1868) – police commissioner, **5:** 166 n.*274*
Mayo (of Wimpole Street, London):
Charles Thomas (1834-1895), **2:** 72 n.*144*
Robert (b. 1832), **1:** 77 n.*74*, 84, 85; **2:** 20 n.*35*, 25, 44; **3:** 67 n.*101*; **4:** 89 n.*45*, 89 n.*46*
Thomas, Dr. (1790-1871) – physician, **2:** 20 n.*35*; **8:** 94 n.*154*
Mayor, Robert Bickersteth (1820-1898) – teacher, **1:** 26, 58 n.*25*; **4:** 34
Mayow, Mayow Wynell, Rev. (b. 1811), **4:** 97
May Queen, The (dr. John Buckstone), **9:** 20 n.*22*
Mazourka (dr. Henry Byron), **4:** 308 n.*384*
McCallum, Andrew (1821-1902) – artist, **5:** 214 n.*342*
McCleod, Herbert (b. 1841) – professor of science, **6:** 375 n.*614*
McConnell, William (fl. 1850-1865) – illustrator, **2:** 100 n.*192*; **3:** 30 n.*44*
McDermott, Miss – friend of Miss Lloyd, **7:** 127 n.*240*
McLaren, Alexander (b. 1826) – Baptist minister, **8:** 135 n.*221*
McLeod, Flora A. (b. 1851) – governess, **7:** 311 n.*555*, 446
McLewer, Mrs., **7:** 76, 77 n.*122*
McMaster, Mr. – grandfather of Winnie Howes, **7:** 469 n.*772*
McNair, Ruby (b. 1883), **9:** 292 n.*461*, 305
McNeil, Mary (b. 1819), **8:** 98 n.*160*
McSwiney, John Henry Herbert, Rev. (1827-1899), **5:** 340, 341 n.*511*, 342; **8:** 399 n.*650*
Mead, Tom (1820-1889) – actor, **3:** 105, 106 n.*154*
Meade, Robert Henry, Sir (1835-1898) – civil servant, **8:** 45 n.*67*
Meadows, Drinkwater (1795-1869) – actor, **2:** 9
Measor, Adela (1860-1933) – actress, **7:** 180 n.*335*, 369 n.*641*, 387
Meath, Ireland, **1:** 11
Mechanical Tortoise – gift for the Liddells, **2:** 125
Mechanics' Institutes, **2:** 100 (Whitburn, Durham); **4:** 25 (South Shields, Durham)

Medd, Charles Septimus (1838-1909) – barrister, **4:** 151 n.*136*
Meditationes Algebraicae (bk. Edward Waring), **1:** 70 n.*58*, 79
Medley, Dudley Julius (1861-1953) – history lecturer, **9:** 46 n.*81*, 47
Medlicott, Miss, **9:** 293 n.*463*
Medora (engraving, possibly of Medora Leigh (1814-1849) – alleged daughter of Lord Byron), **4:** 23
Meeres, Charles, Dr. – physician, **6:** 420 n.*689*
Meg's Diversion (dr. Henry Craven), **5:** 232, 233 n.*372*
Meifod, Montgomeryshire, Wales, **8:** 339, 340 n.*560*
Meldrun, Miss – governess to the Cootes, **7:** 98
Mellon, Sarah née Woolgar (1824-1909) – actress, **4:** 337 n.*436*; **5:** 17 n.*11*, 69, 96 n.*150*, 137
Melsomby, Yorkshire, **1:** 108
Melville, Leander (fl. 1840-1855) – actor, **1:** 133
Memling, Hans (c. 1430-1499) – artist, **5:** 276 n.*443*
Memoirs (bk. John Horne Tooke), **1:** 73 n.*66*
Memoirs of Charles Mathews (bk. Mrs. Anne Mathews), **2:** 9 n.*6*
Menai Bridge, North Wales, **1:** 14
Mendel, Blanca (b. 1869), **7:** 94, 95 n.*172*, 96
Mendelssohn, Jacob Ludwig Felix (1809-1847) – composer, **3:** 60
Mentone, resort on French Riviera, **6:** 69
Menzies, Frederick, Rev. (b. 1815), **6:** 268
Merciful Knight, The (pic. Edward Burne Jones), **5:** 15 n.*6*
Merivale, Herman Charles (1839-1906), alias Felix Dale – dramatist, **8:** 334 n.*549*
Merriman (of Royal Grammar School, Guildford, Surrey):
  Harry Moubray (b. 1857), **6:** 90 n.*137*
  Henry Gordon, Dr. (1823-1887) – headmaster, **6:** 90 n.*137*, 100; **8:** 286 n.*481*, 346 n.*571*
  Jane Augusta née Edmonds (b. 1829), **6:** 90 n.*137*, 100; **8:** 286, 346 n.*571*
  Janet Gertrude (1859-1907), **6:** 90 n.*137*, 95 n.*148*; **8:** 346 n.*571*
  Mabel Georgiana (b. 1867), **6:** 90 n.*137*; **8:** 346 n.*571*
  Mary H. (b. 1854), **6:** 90 n.*137*, 104 n.*163*; **8:** 346 n.*571*
  Maude E. (b. 1853), **6:** 90 n.*137*; **8:** 346 n.*571*
Merriott (of Eton College, Buckinghamshire):
  Caroline, Mrs. (b. 1842), **8:** 479 n.*775*, 480
  John Hepburne, Rev. (b. 1841) – teacher, **8:** 479 n.*775*, 480
Merrow, near Guildford, Surrey, **6:** 45
Merry (of Lincoln College, Oxford):
  Alice Elizabeth née Collings (d. 1914), **4:** 147
  William Walter, Rev. (1835-1918) – tutor and moderator, **4:** 147 n.*130*
Merryman's Monthly, **5:** 207 n.*331*
"Merry Swiss Boy" (Ignaz Moscheles) – song, **2:** 100
Merryweather, George, Dr. (b. 1794) – physician, **1:** 95 n.98
Merton, near Wimbledon, Surrey, **7:** 205

Merton College, Oxford, **2:** 65; **4:** 163; **6:** 363; **7:** 225; **8:** 552
Meryls (Nine Men's Morris board game), **6:** 97 n.*151*, 389, 421; **7:** 467; **8:** 421; **9:** 127, 177, 205, 347
"Mesostic" (type of Acrostic), **9:** 126 n.*222*
Messiah (Handel), **2:** 50 n.*101*, 54 n.*106*, 122 n.*237*; **5:** 67; **6:** 18 n.*16*; **7:** 25, 26 n.*29*
Metamorphoses (bk. Ovid), **1:** 79 n.*78*
Metcalfe (of St. Giles', Oxford):
Frances R. H. (b. 1860), **4:** 180; **5:** 79 n.*123*, 186; **6:** 85 n.*127*
Frederick, Rev. (1815-1885), **5:** 79 n.*123*, 186; **6:** 85 n.*127*, 486 n.*801*
Rosamond M. U. (b. 1859), **4:** 181; **5:** 79 n.*123*, 186; **6:** 85 n.*127*
Methley, Mr. – friend of the Fews, **7:** 481 n.*782*
Metropolitan Railway, London, **4:** 336 n.*434*; **7:** 112, 304, 537; **9:** 58
Metzler, Joseph (b. 1835), and Company – musical instrument supplier, **7:** 294
Meyerbeer, Giacomo (1791-1864) – composer, **5:** 156 n.*254*
Meysey Hampton, Gloucestershire, **6:** 476
Michaelangelo Buonarroti (1475-1564) – artist, **1:** 65
Michell, Richard, Rev. (1805-1877), **5:** 185 n.*303*; **6:** 67 n.*99*, 266
Mickley, near Ripon, Yorkshire, **4:** 274 n.*320*
Middleman, The (dr. Henry Jones), **8:** 486 n.*787*
Middlesex Volunteers, **7:** 112
Middleton, Conyers (1683-1750) – historian and writer, **1:** 24
Middleton, Joseph (fl. 1850-1855) – dramatist, **2:** 57 n.*114*
Middleton, May – friend of the Arnolds, **7:** 383 n.*661*
Mid Lavant, Sussex, **8:** 240
"Midshipmite, The" (Clement Scott) – poem, **7:** 540 n.*873*
Midwinter (of Ahmednagar, India):
Henry Nathaniel, Rev. (b. 1848), **9:** 174 n.*292*, 179
Mrs., **9:** 174 n.*292*, 179
Muriel (b. 1884), **9:** 174 n.*292*, 178, 179, 329
Mignon (Thomas) – opera, **5:** 366, 367 n.*544*
Mikado, The (Gilbert and Sullivan) – operetta, **8:** 210 n.*360*, 220, 268, 269, 280, 282, 404, 573; **9:** 286
Mileham (of Chislehurst, Surrey):
Charles Henry Money, Mr. (1837-1917) – artist and architect, **8:** 134 n.*217*, 136, 139, 210, 314
Christopher "Christo" (b. 1883), **8:** 134 n.*217*, 139
Mary "May" Livock (1874-1939), **8:** 134 n.*217*, 136-140, 149, 210, 314
Mary née Livock (1850-1914), **8:** 134 n.*217*, 139, 210 n.*361*, 314
Miles (of Guildford, Surrey):
Agatha – amateur actress, **9:** 119 n.*206*
G. Frank (1852-1891) – artist, **9:** 119 n.*206*
Miles (of Stainsbridge House, Malmesbury, Gloucestershire):
Edward Peach William, Mr (1829-1889) – magistrate, **6:** 353

Olivia Beatrice Adelaide (b. 1862), **6:** 226 n.*357*, 353
Miles, William (b. 1833) – servant, **8:** 602, 603 n.*957*
Milford Haven, Pembrokeshire, **4:** 187
Milford Junction, Yorkshire, **5:** 111
Milky Way, **5:** 369
Mill, John Stuart (1806-1873) – economist, **1:** 74 n.*67*; **3:** 156 n.*230*
Millais (of Cromwell Place, London):
Alice Sophia Caroline "Carrie" (1862-1936), **4:** 179, 289 n.*345*; **5:** 212, 213 n.*341*; **6:** 73
Effie Gray (1858-1912), **4:** 179, 289 n.*345*; **5:** 19, 45, 96, 97 n.*152*, 98 n.*153*, 212, 213 n.*341*; **6:** 73
Euphemia "Effie" Chalmers née Gray (1828-1897), **4:** 287, 289 n.*345*; **5:** 70 n.*106*, 72, 96, 97 n.*152*, 98 n.*153*, 212, 213; **6:** 86
Everett (1856-1897), **4:** 289 n.*345*
George Gray (1859-1878), **4:** 289 n.*345*
John Everett (1829-1896) – artist, **1:** 98, 102; **2:** 75 n.*151*; **3:** 33 n.*51*, 74, 75 n.*115*; **4:** 36, 78, 79 n.*29*, 287, 288, 289 n.*345*; **5:** 45, 70 n.*106*, 88, 96, 97, 98 n.*153*, 137, 212-214; **6:** 73, 77 n.*112*, 80, 86, 398; **7:** 278 n.*506*
Mary Hunt (1860-1944), **4:** 181, 289 n.*345*; **5:** 45, 70, 96, 97 n.*152*, 98 n.*153*, 212, 213 n.*341*, 240; **6:** 73, 80, 237
Millais, William Henry (1828-1899) – artist, **5:** 212 n.*340*, 213
Millais Exhibition, **7:** 327 n.*580*
Millard (of Church Street, Basingstoke, Hampshire):
Dora Frances née Sclater (1835-1920), **6:** 423 n.*696*, 425, 438
James Elwin, Rev. Dr. (1823-1894), **6:** 423 n.*696*, 425, 437, 438
Magdalen (1867-1921), **6:** 423 n.*696*, 425; **9:** 89 n.*162*
Miller, Agnes (b. 1871) – actress, **9:** 215 n.*343*, 219, 222, 223
Miller (of Eastbourne, Sussex):
Edith Mary (1870-1929), **7:** 355 n.*620*, 357-359, 368, 456, 457 n.*754*, 475; **8:** 40, 101, 130, 510; **9:** 20 n.*20*, 21, 22, 24 n.*32*, 25 n.*34*, 26, 27, 28 n.*43*, 29, 82, 83, 86 n.*155*, 91, 93, 95, 97, 98, 153 n.*266*, 163, 164, 166, 214, 228-230, 238, 253, 260, 353
Henry, Mr. (1840-1873) – stockbroker, **7:** 355 n.*620*
Louisa Maria née Smith (1844-1919), **7:** 355 n.*620*, 357, 358, 456, 475, 476; **8:** 22, 23 n.*20*, 40, 101, 193, 228, 510; **9:** 20 n.*20*, 21, 22, 82, 159, 163, 216
Marion "May" Louisa (1868-1946), **7:** 355 n.*620*, 357-359, 368, 456, 457 n.*754*, 475-477; **8:** 40, 101, 129, 130, 193, 227, 228, 510; **9:** 20 n.*20*, 32, 82, 84-86, 88, 91, 92, 93 n.*169*, 95, 97, 101, 102, 108, 157, 159, 163, 166, 216, 236-240
Miller (of Wheatley, Oxfordshire):
James, Col. (1829-1909) – army officer, **9:** 312 n.*497*
Sarah Dorothy née Evans (1837-1911), **9:** 312 n.*497*
Miller (of Melcombe Place, London):

Mary J. R., Mrs. (b. 1846), **7:** 93 n.*167*
William Edwards, Mr. (1852-1903) – artist, **7:** 93 n.*167*
Millett, Maude (1868-1920) – actress, **8:** 486 n.*787*, 562, 577; **9:** 56 n.*101*, 58
Mills, Charles, Sir (1825-1895) – civil servant, **8:** 49, 50 n.*74*, 52, 53
Millward, Jessie (1861-1932) – actress, **7:** 494 n.*804*; **9:** 20 n.*22*
Milman (of Westminster, London):
Archibald John Scott (1834-1902), see below
Arthur (1829-1913), see below
Henry Hart, Rev. Dr. (1791-1868) – dean of St. Paul's, **3:** 8 n.*4*
William Henry (1825-1908), **3:** 8 n.*4*; **6:** 223, 224 n.*352*
Milman (of Southwell Gardens, Kensington, London):
Archibald John Scott, Mr. (1834-1902) – civil servant, **7:** 109 n.*201*
Susan Augusta Carter née Hanbury (1847-1928), **7:** 109 n.*201*
Milman (of The Grove, Kensington, London):
Arthur, Mr. (1829-1913) – clerical administrator, **2:** 72 n.*145*; **3:** 8 n.*4*; **6:** 223, 224 n.*352*
Frances Mary née Tatham (b. 1849), **6:** 224 n.*352*
Milman (of Cranley Place, Kensington, London):
Bertha Mary (1860-1931), **6:** 84 n.*125*, 196
Henry Salusbury, Mr. (1821-1893) – barrister, **6:** 84 n.*125*, 195, 196, 223, 257
Margaret Anne (1859-1954), **6:** 84 n.*125*, 196
Matilda Julia (1861-1938), **6:** 84 n.*125*, 196, 253
Milman, Frances Maria (1824-1888), **7:** 100 n.*186*, 102, 109, 432
Milman, Miss – in charge of Dr. Wolston's children, **8:** 37 n.*49*, 132
Milne, Francis Alexander (b. 1854) – barrister, **6:** 374 n.*613*
Milner (of Vale Lodge, Woodside, Winkfield, Berkshire):
Adelaide (b. 1797), **5:** 99 n.*156*
Frances H. (b. 1813), **5:** 99 n.*157*
Louisa H. F. (b. 1839) – niece, **5:** 99 n.*157*
Susan (b. 1795), **5:** 99 n.*156*
Milner, Florence (1855-1950) – writer and editor, **1:** 31, 111 n.*129*
Milner, Miss – singer, **3:** 10 n.*7*
Milnes, Richard Monckton (1809-1885) – writer and poet, **1:** 55 n.*16*
Milton, Berkshire, **7:** 279
Milton, John (1608-1674) – poet, **1:** 73
Mind, **9:** 143 n.*247*
Minin or Bamina Tower, Nijni Novgoroda, Russia, **5:** 312
Minnie Morton (pic. Sophie Anderson), **5:** 61 n.*88*, 67, 89 n.*137*, 165 n.*273*; **6:** 81 n.*119*, 85
Minuet, The (pic. John Millais), **5:** 213 n.*341*
Mirrielees (of St. Petersburg, Russia):
Archibald, Mr. (1798-1877) – merchant in Russia, **5:** 294 n.*462*
Jane née Muir (1810-1875), **5:** 294 n.*462*

William (b. 1828), **5:** 294 n.*462*, 296, 297
Miss Cicely Fane (pic. Lady Charles Newton), **5:** 86 n.*134*
"Miss Edith" (possibly Bret Harte) – verse recitation, **8:** 530
Miss Harriet Dickens (pic. Jane Egerton), **2:** 75 n.*151*
Miss Lily's Return from the Ball (pic. James Hallyar), **5:** 238, 239 n.*386*
"Miss Snowberry" (voice imitation), **2:** 128
Mitcham, Surrey, **4:** 318
Mitchell, Elizabeth (b. 1835) – lodging-house keeper, **7:** 354
Mitchell (of Winteringham, Lincolnshire):
Henry, Rev. (1829-1907), **4:** 237 n.*265*, 240, 261
Fanny, Mrs. (b. 1844), **4:** 261
Mitcheson (of Oxford):
Mrs. née Ley, **8:** 71 n.*116*, 548, 558
Richard Edmund, Mr. (b. 1860) – tutor, **8:** 71 n.*116*
Mitford, Algernon Bertram (b. 1837) – civil servant, **2:** 48, 109 n.*213*
Mitford, John Thomas Freeman (1805-1886), Earl of Redesdale – politician, **7:** 82 n.*138*
Mitford's Harmonic Parties, **2:** 47
"Mitre," The High, Oxford, **2:** 106 n.*205*; **4:** 277
Mivart, George Jackson, Sir (1827-1900) – barrister, biologist and writer, **6:** 367 n.*601*
Moberly (of Christ Church, Oxford):
Alice Sidney née Hamilton (b. 1852), **9:** 262, 263 n.*414*, 309, 318, 319
Robert Campbell, Canon (1845-1903) – professor of pastoral theology, **9:** 262, 263 n.*414*, 317
Moberly, Charlotte Anne Elizabeth (1846-1937) – principal of St. Hugh's, **9:** 135 n.*236*, 143, 180
Modern History (bk. Thomas Arnold), **1:** 23
Modjeska, Helena née Opid (1840-1909) – Polish actress, **8:** 38
Moffatt, George (1806-1878) – politician, **5:** 216 n.*345*
Moldau River, **5:** 275
Molly's Ball Dress (pic. Kate Perugini), **8:** 199 n.*338*
Molyneux:
Agnes Elizabeth Sophia – pianist, **6:** 295 n.*487*, 296
Mrs., **6:** 295 n.*487*, 296
Violet Mary Ann Eliza – pianist, **6:** 295 n.*487*, 296
Molyneux, Capel, Rev. (1804-1877), **4:** 86 n.*41*
Monbijon Palace, Berlin, Germany, **5:** 274
Monck, Henry Power Charles Stanley (1849-1927) – undergraduate at Christ Church, **6:** 153 n.*233*
Monckton, Lady (1837-1920) – actress, **8:** 562 n.*896*; **9:** 57 n.*104*
Money (dr. Edward Bulwer Lytton), **5:** 157 n.*255*; **6:** 397 n.*649*, 406, 407; **7:** 540 n.*873*
Money, Miss, **8:** 101 n.*167*
Monier-Williams (of Oxford):

Clive (b. 1863?), **5:** 146 n.*235*, 163 n.*268*
Ella Chlora Faithfull (1859-1954), see Bickersteth
Julia née Faithfull, **5:** 146 n.*235*, 148, 151, 163 n.*268*, 207, 376; **6:** 302, 342; **7:** 32 n.*42*, 119, 174, 262; **8:** 23 n.*21*
Monier, Prof. (1819-1899) – professor of Sanskrit, **5:** 146 n.*235*, 148, 163 n.*268*, 207, 376; **6:** 302 n.*497*, 342; **7:** 174
Outram Faithfull (b. 1855?), **5:** 146 n.*235,* 163 n.*268*
Stanley Faithfull (b. 1857), **5:** 146 n.*235*, 163 n.*268*
Monk, Edwin George (1819-1900) – musician, **2:** 47 n.*94*
Monk, William Henry (1823-1889) – composer, **6:** 95 n.*149*
Monkhouse, Harry (1854-1901) – actor, **8:** 631 n.*999*
Monsell (of Guildford, Surrey):
Harriett, Mrs. (b. 1812), **6:** 316
John Samuel Bewley, Dr. (1811-1875) – cleric, poet and composer, **1:** 120 n.*147*; **6:** 192, 193 n.*299*, 316, 386 n.*632*; **9:** 214 n.*342*
Montgomery, Walter S. (1827-1871) – actor, **4:** 281 n.*331*; **5:** 126 n.*200*
Monthly Packet, The, **5:** 11, 12 n.*2*; **6:** 14 n.*8*; **7:** 265 n.*478*, 410 n.*690*; **8:** 162 n.*264*, 492 n.*796*
Monthly Register, **4:** 253
Monument, near Sandown, Isle of Wight, **6:** 298, 299, 343, 363
Moodie, Louise (1846-1934) – actress, **8:** 473 n.*768*
Moody (of Frensham, Surrey):
Ambrose (b. 1893), **9:** 214 n.*342*
Basil (b. 1890), **9:** 214 n.*342*
Clement (b. 1891), **9:** 214 n.*342*
Katherine (b. 1895), **9:** 214 n.*342*
Rachel, Mrs. (b. 1852), **9:** 214 n.*342*
William Herbert, Rev. (b. 1848), **9:** 214 n.*342*
"Mooney and Spooney," **2:** 128 n.*245*
Moor (of Holland Road, Hove, Sussex):
Mr., **6:** 309 n.*511*
Sarah, Mrs. (b. 1839), **6:** 309 n.*511*
Moor, The, Cleedownton, Shropshire (home of Wilfred Dodgson), **6:** 166 n.*258*, 239, 308, 452, 478; **7:** 48, 125, 126, 232
Moore (of Italy and London):
Andrew, **6:** 398
Arthur C. (b. 1866), **6:** 397, 398 n.*650*
John Collingham, Mr. (1829-1880) – artist, **2:** 75 n.*151*; **6:** 397, 398 n.*650*, 455
Maggie, **6:** 397
Mrs., **6:** 398
Moore (of Oxford):
Annie née Mackenzie (1858-1906) – second wife, **9:** 125 n.*220*
Edward, Dr. (1835-1916) – principal of St. Edmund Hall, **6:** 277 n.*456*, 288, 303; **9:** 47 n.*83*, 125 n.*220*

Katherine Edith née Stogden (1848-1878) – first wife, **6:** 277 n.*456*, 303
Mary Beatrice (b. 1880), **9:** 125 n.*220*
Moore, Aubrey Lackington (1848-1890) – lecturer, **6:** 449 n.*738*, 490; **7:** 309, 436 n.*723*
Moore (of Brighton, Sussex):
Decima (b. 1871) – actress, **8:** 618 n.*980*; **9:** 12, 13 n.*5*, 26, 219 n.*348*
Edward H., Mr. (b. 1824) – chemist, **9:** 219 n.*348*
Emily (b. 1857) – professor of singing, **9:** 219 n.*348*
Emily, Mrs. (b. 1830), **9:** 219 n.*348*
Eva (b. 1868), **9:** 219 n.*348*
Lilian (b. 1872), **9:** 219 n.*348*
Moore, Eleanora "Nelly" (1845-1869) – actress **4:** 300 n.*366*; **5:** 32 n.*35*, 222
Moore (of St. John's Road, Oxford):
Margaret (b. 1878?), **9:** 309 n.*489*, 310
Mrs., **9:** 309 n.*489*
Moore, Miss – friend of the Fullers, **9:** 283
Moore, Thomas (1779-1852) – poet, **1:** 113 n.*133*
Moray Lodge, London (Lewis family), **5:** 379; **6:** 19, 85, 113, 114, 194, 256, 312, 344, 352, 398; **7:** 78, 140, 156, 185, 186, 194, 256, 278, 304, 305, 348, 388, 396, 398, 430, 514, 515, 529; **8:** 368, 406, 556, 617
More, Thomas, Sir (1478-1535) – statesman and writer, **3:** 71 n.*111*
More free than welcome (pic. William Crawford), **5:** 236, 237 n.*383*
Moreton, Oxfordshire, **5:** 90
Morgan (of Kensington, London):
Alice Mary née Havers (1850-1890) – artist, **7:** 533 n.*863*; **8:** 253 n.*425*, 254, 279 n.*469*, 405, 481 n.*780*
Frederick, Mr. (1856-1927) – artist, **7:** 105 n.*196*; **8:** 253 n.*425*
Lilian "Lily" E. (b. 1875), **8:** 253 n.*425*, 254, 405
Morgan (of Edinburgh, Scotland):
Jane Ellen "Nellie" (b. 1880), **7:** 449 n.*745*
Jane "Jeannie" Heaton Cunnynham Clark née Howden (b. 1861), **7:** 449 n.*745*
John J., Rev. (b. 1840), **7:** 449 n.*745*
Morgan (of Brighton, Sussex):
Helen "Nellie" (b. 1874?), **8:** 420 n.*680*
Marie P. (b. 1878?), **8:** 420 n.*680*
Morley (of Upper Park Road, Hampstead, London):
Edith Caroline (1864-1945), **6:** 356 n.*588*, 357, 404 n.*663*
Henry, Mr. (1822-1894) – professor of literature, **6:** 356 n.*588*, 357
Margaret "Maggie" (b. 1860), **6:** 356 n.*588*, 357
Mary (b. 1859?), **6:** 356 n.*588*, 357
Mary Anne née Sayer (d. 1892), **6:** 356
Morley, John, Viscount (1838-1923) – journalist, **6:** 390 n.*641*; **9:** 264 n.*416*
Morning (pic. William Dobson), **7:** 538, 539 n.*871*

Morning Kiss, The (pic. William Bouguereau), **5:** 223 n.*355*
Morning Post, **4:** 275; **7:** 512 n.*830*
Morphany Lane, Daresbury, Cheshire, **4:** 27
Morrell (of East Indies):
Baker, Rev. (1841-1887) – chaplain, **6:** 461 n.*758*
Edith Frances née Brett (d. 1887), **6:** 461 n.*758*
Rachel Emilia Louisa (b. 1869), **6:** 461 n.*758*
Morrell (of Headington Hill, Oxford):
Emily Alicia (b. 1854), see below
James, Mr. (1810-1863), **5:** 69 n.*103*
Morrell (of Headington Hill, Oxford):
Emily Alicia née Morrell (b. 1854), **5:** 69 n.*103*
George Herbert, Mr. (b. 1845) – magistrate, **5:** 69 n.*103*
Morrell (of Oxford):
Frederic Parker, Mr. (1839-1908) – solicitor, **6:** 275 n.*449*, 304, 323, 461, 491; **7:** 17 n.*11*, 147
Frederica Harriette (b. 1869), **6:** 275 n.*449*, 282
Harriette Anne née Wynter (1843-1924), **6:** 275 n.*449*, 276, 304, 323, 461, 491; **7:** 147; **8:** 53 n.*79*, 509 n.*820*; **9:** 59 n.*108*, 74 n.*136*
Hugh St. John (b. 1872), **6:** 275 n.*449*
Margaret "Margie" Cecil Louisa (b. 1868), **6:** 275 n.*449*, 276, 282; **7:** 163; **9:** 59 n.*108*, 62 n.*115*, 74 n.*136*
Philip Edward (b. 1870), **6:** 275 n.*449*
Morrell, Mrs. Arthur, **6:** 461 n.*758*
Morrell's Brewery, Oxford, **9:** 269
Morris, Edward Henry, Rev. (b. 1862), **7:** 381 n.*657*
Morris (of Campden House Road, London):
Florence "Flo" or "Flossie" Maude née Terry (1856-1896) – actress, **4:** 179, 246, 357 n.*467*, 358; **5:** 16 n.*9*, 21, 22, 30, 35, 62, 65, 91, 92 n.*142*, 93 n.*144*, 94 n.*146*, 95 n.*149*, 99, 115 n.*179*, 117, 118, 123, 127, 162, 169, 240, 241 n.*390*, 379; **6:** 69, 97, 122, 126, 135 n.*208*, 136, 190, 195, 222, 312, 313, 341, 398, 405 n.*665*; **7:** 157 n.*295*, 164, 176, 185, 381, 442, 443, 514 n.*833*, 516; **8:** 127 n.*208*, 165, 271, 315, 368, 410, 539
Geoffrey, **8:** 368 n.*603*
Olive, **8:** 368 n.*603*
William, Mr. – solicitor, **8:** 127 n.*208*
Morris, Marmaduke Charles Frederick (b. 1844) – headmaster, **6:** 168 n.*262*
Morris, William (1834-1896) – artist, **1:** 40; **3:** 26 n.*37*
Morrison, Mr., **5:** 84
Morrison, William (b. 1832) – undergraduate at Christ Church, **1:** 96 n.*101*
Morshead, Ernest Garstin Anderson, Dr. (b. 1861) – physician, **8:** 161 n.*262*, 326
Mortimer (of Bromley, Kent):

Edith M. (b. 1867), **8:** 499 n.*803*
Kate "Katie" (b. 1868), **8:** 300 n.*501*, 302, 303, 499
Mabel (b. 1873), **8:** 499 n.*803*
Mary (b. 1866), **8:** 499 n.*803*
Mary Anne Grey née Harmsworth (b. 1839), **8:** 300 n.*501*, 499
William (b. 1875), **8:** 499 n.*803*
William, Mr. (b. 1837) – stockbroker, **8:** 499 n.*803*
Mortlake, Surrey, **4:** 183
Morton, Agnes (b. 1852) – headmistress, **9:** 292 n.*462*
Morton, John, Dr. (b. 1840) – physician, **6:** 350 n.*581*
Morton, John Maddison (1811-1891) – dramatist, **1:** 105 n.*118*; **2:** 56 n.*110*, 83 n.*163*, 123 n.*240*; **3:** 7 n.*1*, 14 n.*13*, 52 n.*79*, 171 n.*250*; **4:** 152 n.*137*, 222 n.*242*, 225 n.*249*, 263 n.*308*, 337 n.*436*; **5:** 38 n.*46*, 69 n.*104*
Moscheles, Ignaz (1794-1870) – composer, **2:** 100
Moscow, Russia, **5:** 253, 299-307, 312-325, 332-336
Moseley (of Bedale, North Yorkshire; later Buildwas, Shropshire):
Maria Katherine née Anderson (1846-1889), **4:** 232 n.*257*, 233; **6:** 222 n.*350*
Walter, Mr. (1832-1887), **6:** 222 n.*350*
Moses (pic. John Millais), **4:** 289
Moskva River, Russia, **5:** 301
Mosley, Mrs. – northern secretary of SPCA, **6:** 382
Moss, Hugh (1856-1926) – dramatist, **8:** 405 n.*659*
Mother Goose (dr. Sarah Thorne), **8:** 609, 610 n.*966*
Motherwell, William (1797-1835) – poet, **3:** 106, 107 n.*155*
Mott (of Wolvercote, Oxford):
Alice (b. 1887), **8:** 624 n.*987*, 625, 634
Ann, Mrs. (b. 1841), **8:** 625, 626 n.*990*
Mould (of Paddington, London):
George S., Mr. (b. 1834) – War Office clerk, **7:** 55 n.*87*, 283
Gundreda Edith "Trotty" (b. 1868), **7:** 55 n.*87*, 59, 60, 75, 283
Mary "Bilda" P. (b. 1866), **7:** 55 n.*87*, 59, 60, 75, 129, 283
Mary P., Mrs. (b. 1848), **7:** 55 n.*87*, 59
Moultrie, John (1799-1875?) – poet, **4:** 244 n.*274*
Mounsey, Augustus Henry (1834-1882) – school-friend, **2:** 78 n.*155*, 79, 87, 88 n.*176*
Mount Charles, see Conyngham
Mountebanks, The (W. S. Gilbert and Alfred Cellier) – operetta, **8:** 631 n.*999*; **9:** 24 n.*32*
Mowat, John Lancaster Gough (b. 1846) – lecturer, **7:** 499 n.*815*
Mowbray (of Kensington, London):
Annie Maud (b. 1849), **7:** 81 n.*136*
Edith Marian (b. 1857), **7:** 81 n.*136*
John Robert, Sir (1815-1899) – politician, **6:** 67 n.*99*, 329, 370, 438; **7:** 39 n.*57*, 81 n.*136*, 149, 228 n.*421*, 342

Mower, The (pic. Arthur Hughes), **5:** 86 n.*134*
Moxon, Edward (1801-1858) – publisher, **4:** 20, 59, 99 n.*61*, 244
Moxon, Lilian, **9:** 200, 201 n.*328*, 204 n.*333*
Moyle, Emily (b. 1864), **9:** 294 n.*465*
Mozart, Wolfgang Amadeus (1756-1791) – composer, **5:** 98 n.*155*
Mozley, James Bowling, Dr. (1814-1878) – professor of divinity, **6:** 291 n.*480*, 303
Mr. Ames' Children (pic. James Sant), **5:** 86 n.*134*
"Mr. Mite" in *Living Miniatures*, **5:** 202
Mr. Popham's Child (pic. James Sant), **5:** 86 n.*134*
Mrs. Charles Kingsley (pic. Edmund Havell), **2:** 75 n.*151*
Mrs. Coventry Patmore (pic. John Brett), **2:** 75 n.*151*
Mrs. Green's Snug Little Business (dr. Charles Cheltnam), **5:** 47 n.*62*
Mrs. James Leathart and Children (pic. Arthur Hughes), **5:** 86 n.*134*
Mrs. Liddell (pic. Lady Charles Newton), **5:** 86 n.*134*
"Mrs. Mite" in *Living Miniatures*, **5:** 203
Mrs. Roseleaf at the Sea-side (John Orlando Parry) – song, **4:** 322, 323 n.*409*
Mrs. Rutherford's Children (bk. Elizabeth Wetherell), **2:** 125 n.*242*
Mrs. White (dr. Richard Raymond), **4:** 300 n.*366*
Mrs. Willis' Will (dr. Emile Souvestre), **7:** 194, 195 n.*362*
"Mr. Trimmer" (voice imitation), **2:** 128 n.*245*
"Mr. Watkin's Apprentice" (William Brough) in *The Train*, **2:** 52 n.*104*
Mudd, James (1821-1906) – photographer, **4:** 25
Mudie, Charles Edward (1818-1890) – bookseller and librarian, **3:** 148 n.*213*
Muir (of St. Petersburg, Russia):
  Alison "Alice" née Bell (1822-1910), formerly Mrs. William Philip, **5:** 298
  Andrew, Mr. (1817-1899) – merchant in Russia, **5:** 293, 294 n.*462*, 297, 298, 337, 338; **9:** 235 n.*371*
  Meta Alice (1862-1943), **5:** 20, 298
Muir, Mr., **4:** 355 n.*465*
Mulgrave, near Whitby, Yorkshire, **5:** 179
Müller (of Norham Gardens, Oxford):
  Ada (b. 1861), **5:** 247 n.*401*, 254 n.*419*; **6:** 124, 213, 380
  Beatrice Stanley (1865-1902), see Colyer-Fergusson
  Friedrich Max, Prof. (1823-1900) – professor of modern European languages, **4:** 161, 162 n.*154*; **5:** 247 n.*402*; **6:** 151, 275, 321, 446, 449; **7:** 144, 177, 239; **8:** 595 n.*949*
  Georgina Adelaide née Grenfell (1835-1916), **5:** 247 n.*401*; **6:** 151, 275, 321; **7:** 144, 177, 224, 239
  Mary (b. 1862), **5:** 247 n.*401*, 254 n.*419*; **6:** 123, 124, 127, 213, 380; **7:** 535
Müller (of Hastings, Sussex):

Alfred, Prof. (b. 1843) – professor of languages and music, **8:** 521 n.*837*, 524, 526, 534
Lottie (b. 1878), **8:** 521 n.*837*, 524, 526, 534, 536
Mary, Mrs. (b. 1846), **8:** 521 n.*837*, 524, 526, 534
Mulock, see Craik
Mulready, William (1786-1863) – artist, **4:** 287 n.*342*
Mumbo Jumbo (dr. Anon), **4:** 317
Munro (of Belgravia, London):
Alexander, Mr. (1825-1871) – sculptor, **3:** 26 n.*37*, 125 n.*180*, 155, 156 n.*229*, 157 n.*232*, 173, 176; **4:** 12, 21, 22, 33, 55, 223, 229, 230 n.*254*, 241, 242 n.*271*, 243-245, 247, 249, 250, 252 n.*291*, 254, 279, 283, 315, 318, 319, 333; **5:** 70, 86 n.*134*; **6:** 13 n.*7*
John Arthur Ruskin (b. 1864), **8:** 51 n.*76*
Mary née Carruthers (d. 1872), **4:** 229, 243-245, 247, 252 n.*291*, 279, 318, 319
Miss, **4:** 270, 318, 324, 339, 340 n.*441*; **6:** 27
Munro's sculptures, **4:** 21, 22
Murchison, Roderick Impey, Sir (1792-1871) – geologist, **4:** 35
Murdoch (of Edinburgh, Scotland):
Agatha M. (b. 1867), **7:** 284 n.*516*, 290, 448, 537
Alexander D., Rev. (b. 1840), **1:** 122 n.*152*; **6:** 179 n.*276*, 219; **7:** 284 n.*516*, 285, 289, 290, 448, 537, 538; **9:** 47
Anna "Annie" née Wilcox (b. 1831) – cousin, **1:** 122 n.*152*, 124 n.*154*, 129; **3:** 120 n.*168*; **6:** 179 n.*276*, 219; **7:** 284 n.*516*, 285, 289, 290, 448, 537, 538; **8:** 571 n.*910*, 598; **9:** 47, 52, 55, 57
Anna Etheldreda (b. 1865), **7:** 284 n.*516*, 290, 448, 537
George Cuthbert (b. 1872), **7:** 284 n.*516*, 285, 290; **8:** 598 n.*953*; **9:** 46 n.*81*, 47, 52
Mildred Cecilia (b. 1868), **7:** 284 n.*516*, 290, 448, 537
Murdoch (of Putney, Surrey):
Alice Maria (1852-1881), **2:** 81, 82 n.*161*, 83 n.*166*; **4:** 178
Charles Stewart (1838-1908), **2:** 81, 82 n.*161*, 83, 84
Katherine "Katie" Frederica (1840?-1926), **2:** 81 n.*160*, 83; **3:** 112 n.*160*
Millicent "Minnie" Horatia (b. 1842?), **2:** 81, 82 n.*161*, 83
Murillo, Bartolomé Esteban (1617-1682) – artist, **5:** 295 n.*463*
Murley (of Eastbourne, Sussex):
Charles, Mr. (b. 1819) – retired, **8:** 424 n.*685*
Laura C., Mrs. (b. 1848), **8:** 424 n.*685*, 425
Laura "Lily" C. (b. 1878), **8:** 424 n.*685*, 425
Murphy, Arthur (1727-1805) – dramatist, **3:** 80 n.*126*
Murphy, Mrs. – former pupil at Mrs. Drury's school, **7:** 230, 231 n.*424*
Murray, A. – dramatist, **7:** 541 n.*874*
Murray (of Oxford):
Ada Agnes née Ruthven, **8:** 454 n.*729*
James Augustus Henry, Sir (1837-1915) – editor of *Oxford English*

Dictionary, **8:** 454 n.*729*
Murray, D. Greig – aspiring actor, **7:** 447 n.*739*
Murray, Dominick (b. 1840?), real name Moran – American actor, **4:** 358, 359 n.*468*
Murray, George Sholto Douglas (1844-1912) – civil servant, **6:** 69 n.*100*
Murray, G. Lindsay, **7:** 447 n.*739*
Murray, Herbert Harley (1829-1904) – civil servant, **1:** 66 n.*48*
Murska, Ilma di (1834-1889) – Croatian singer, **8:** 354 n.*577*
Murton, C. J. – actor, **8:** 230 n.*388*
Musgrave, Mrs. H. – dramatist, **8:** 530 n.*849*
Musgrave, see Wykeham-Musgrave
"Music Hath Charm" (David Fisher) – song, **3:** 106
Music Party, A (pic. Arthur Hughes), **4:** 301 n.*367*
Mutton-Bird Island, Australia, **1:** 56
My Aunt's in Town (dr. Richard Corney Grain), **8:** 481 n.*779*)
Myers' Circus, **7:** 173, 174 n.*322*
My First Sermon (pic. John Millais), **4:** 288, 289 n.*345*
My Friend from Leatherhead (dr. N. H. Harrington and Edmund Yates), **3:** 101 n.*149*, 120 n.*170*
My Haunts (bk. Edmund Yates), **2:** 61 n.*122*
"My Heart's in the Hielands" (Robert Burns) – song, **2:** 100
My Heart's in the Highlands (dr. William Brough and Andrew Halliday), **4:** 291 n.*348*
My Little Girl (dr. Dion Boucicault), **7:** 438 n.*727*
"My Mother bids me bind my hair" (Mrs. John Hunter and Joseph Haydn) – song, **5:** 225, 226 n.*359*
My Poll and My Partner Joe (dr. John Haines), **3:** 101 n.*149*
My Second Sermon (pic. John Millais), **4:** 301 n.*367*
My Sweetheart (dr. Frederick Maeder and William Gill), **8:** 229, 230 n.*388*
My Wife's Bonnet (dr. John Morton), **5:** 37, 38 n.*46*
My Wife's Mother (dr. Charles Mathews), **5:** 88 n.*136*
My Wife's Party (dr. Richard Corney Grain), **8:** 632 n.*1001*
My Wife's Relations (dr. Walter Gordon), **4:** 223 n.*245*
My Wife's Second Floor (dr. John Morton), **4:** 221 n.*242*

Nairne, Robert, Dr. (1804-1886) – physician, **6:** 195 n.*304*
Nana (pic. Marceli Suchorowski), **8:** 114 n.*186*
Nance Oldfield (dr. Charles Reade), **8:** 567 n.*903*
"Nancie" (Eva Dodgson) – manuscript story, **9:** 294, 295 n.*466*
Nancy Sikes (dr. Cyril Searle), **7:** 118 n.*222*, 122, 123 n.*231*
Napier (of George Street, London):
Ann, Mrs. (b. 1837), **6:** 299 n.*493*, 342, 343, 354, 356, 359, 411, 445, 479
Bertram Harold (b. 1861), **6:** 299 n.*493*
Charlie, **6:** 478
Clive, **6:** 299 n.*493*, 342

Ethel M. (b. 1863), **6:** 299 n.*493*, 342, 343, 360, 411, 420, 422, 445, 478, 479; **7:** 481
Herbert, **6:** 299 n.*493*, 342, 425
Kitty, **6:** 299 n.*493*, 342, 343, 358, 411, 412, 478
Mabel W. (b. 1872)
William D. M. (b. 1871), **6:** 299 n.*493*
William Donald, Dr. (b. 1831) – physician, **6:** 299 n.*493*, 342, 343, 354, 356, 359, 411, 479
Napoleon, Charles Louis (1808-1873) – Emperor of the French, **2:** 16, 17 n.*28*; **3:** 9 n.*5*
Napper (of Stoke, near Guildford, Surrey):
Albert, Mr. (b. 1816) – farmer, **7:** 344 n.*604*
Alice E. (b. 1849), **7:** 344 n.*604*
Anna (b. 1844), **7:** 344 n.*604*
Sarah, Mrs. (b. 1821), **7:** 344 n.*604*
Nash (of Upperswinford, Worcestershire):
Barbara Alice (b. 1877), **8:** 25 n.*24*, 26, 27, 41, 287
Edith Mary (1873-1950), **8:** 25 n.*24*, 26-29, 41, 287, 289; **9:** 18 n.*16*
Fanny Ann née Foxall (b. 1848), **8:** 25 n.*24*, 26, 28; **9:** 18
Isaac, Mr. (b. 1845) – ironware manufacturer, **8:** 25 n.*24*, 26, 27
Nash, Mr. & Mrs. – friends of Tom Taylor, **5:** 65 n.*97*
Nasmyth, Alexander (1758-1840) – artist, **5:** 234 n.*377*
Nathalie, Miss – niece of the Combes, **5:** 314
National Anthem, **5:** 98
National Bank of Charity, **6:** 41, 42 n.*57*
National Gallery, London, **7:** 304, 305, 477; **8:** 162, 439; **9:** 53
National Portrait Gallery, London, **3:** 31 n.*45*
Natural History of the Bible (bk. Henry Tristram), **1:** 98 n.*106*
Natural Science at Oxford, **7:** 35 n.*49*
Nature, **8:** 323 n.*533*
Naughty Boy, The (pic. Jean Béranger), **5:** 222 n.*354*
Naval Schools' Review, Horticultural Gardens, London, **6:** 158 n.*244*
Neal, Charlotte "Shattie" (b. 1863?), **6:** 356, 357 n.*590*
Neale (of Iffley, Oxfordshire):
Emily F. (b. 1856), **4:** 77 n.*26*
Harriet F. née Strong (b. 1829), **4:** 77 n.*26*
Henry A. (b. 1857), **4:** 77 n.*26*
Neale, Lindsay – friend of the Camerons, **4:** 345 n.*450*
Neate, Charles (1807-1879) – politician, **3:** 17 n.*18*, 43 n.*68*, 54 n.*82*
Neate (of Hampstead, London):
John, Mr. (1825-1889) – solicitor, **7:** 167 n.*315*
Raynor Maurice, (1867-1942) – solicitor, **8:** 194, 195 n.*328*, 208; **9:** 96 n.*174*
Sophia, Mrs. (1832-1908), **7:** 167 n.*315*, 184, 542, 543; **8:** 194 n.*326*, 204, 208, 212, 501; **9:** 96 n.*174*

Neate, Mrs. Percy, **8:** 208 n.*356*
Neave, Misses, **9:** 305 n.*485*
Needham (of Mourne Park, Co. Down; Aldford Street, Park Lane, London):
Francis Charles (1842-1915), Viscount Newry, 3rd Earl of Kilmorey, **4:** 68, 68 n.*10*, 139, 213; **5:** 121 n.*191*; **7:** 537 n.*869*
Henry Colville, Hon. (1844-1917), **5:** 119 n.*186*
Needles, Isle of Wight, **4:** 351
Neef – see Giffard
Neill, George J. (b. 1833) – cutler, **7:** 352 n.*615*, 481 n.*783*, 482, 485, 488, 494
Neilson, Julia – actress, **8:** 584 n.*933*
Nell, or the Old Curiosity Shop (dr. Andrew Halliday), **6:** 135 n.*208*
Nelson (of Putney, Surrey):
Emma, Mrs. (b. 1819), **7:** 80 n.*133*
Lydia J. (b. 1849), **7:** 80 n.*133*
Nelson (of Carlisle, Cumberland):
Isabel (b. 1869), **7:** 528 n.*854*
Mary "May" I. (b. 1868), **7:** 527, 528 n.*854*
Nelson, Nina (b. 1883) – friend of Enid Stevens, **9:** 225 n.*355*
Nemesis of Faith, The (bk. James Froude), **1:** 97 n.*103*
Neruda, Wilhelmine Normann, Madame (1839-1911), see Hallé
Nervi, Italy, **7:** 78
Nethersole, Olga (1867-1951) – actress, **9:** 57 n.*104*
Nettlecombe, Somerset, **9:** 63
Nettleship (of Oxford):
Edith M. (b. 1872), **7:** 79 n.*130*
Harry M. (b. 1876), **7:** 79 n.*130*
Henry, Prof. (1839-1893) – professor of Latin literature, **7:** 79 n.*130*, 80
Matilda, Mrs. (1842-1920), **7:** 79 n.*130*, 80
Neuburger (of London):
Meur, Mr. (b. 1834), **7:** 96
Rebecca, Mrs. (b. 1844), **7:** 94, 95 n.*172*, 96
Neville, Henry Gartside (1837-1910) – actor, **4:** 223 n.*245*; **5:** 63 n.*93*, 85
Neville (of London):
Kate (1863-1964) – actress , **7:** 106 n.*197*
Loui – actress, **7:** 106 n.*197*
Nevski, St. Petersburg, Russia, **5:** 288
Newby, Mary Isabel (1880-1960), **9:** 172 n.*289*, 174, 178
Newcastle, Northumberland, **1:** 126, 129; **3:** 125; **5:** 13 n.*4*, 14, 176
New College, Oxford, **3:** 48, 54, 71, 72; **4:** 307; **5:** 153; **6:** 292, 395, 438, 439, 450; **7:** 191, 269, 518, 544; **8:** 14, 60, 226, 264, 409, 410, 625, 629; **9:** 51, 251
Newfoundland dog, **4:** 43; **7:** 359
New Gallery, London, **8:** 404, 413, 457, 566, 568, 622, 632; **9:** 73
Newhaven, Sussex, **7:** 470

New Inn Hall, Oxford, **3:** 67 n.*102*; **7:** 491 n.*801*
New Jerusalem Monastery, Voskresensk, Russia, **5:** 325-330
Newland Downs, near Guildford, Surrey, **6:** 45
Newland's Corner, near Guildford, Surrey, **6:** 82, 90, 227, 308; **8:** 113; **9:** 216
Newlands Lodge, Sevenoaks, Kent (Crofts), **6:** 263 n.*423*, 269, 270
Newman, John Henry, Rev. (1801-1890), **4:** 10; **6:** 60 n.*91*; **7:** 272 n.*491*
New Men and Old Acres (dr. Augustus Dubourg and Tom Taylor), **7:** 15, 16 n.*10*
New Palace, Potsdam, Prussia, **5:** 272
Newport, Isle of Wight, **4:** 352; **6:** 296, 386, 424
Newry, see Needham
New Sketches of Everyday Life (bk. Mary Howitt), **2:** 17 n.*30*
New Sub, The (dr. Seymour Hicks), **8:** 618 n.*980*; **9:** 12, 13 n.*5*, 26
New Testament, **5:** 102
Newton, Ann Mary née Severn, Lady (1832-1866) – artist, **5:** 86 n.*134*
Newton, Margaret J. (b. 1871), **8:** 458 n.*736*, 563, 612
Newton, Mr. – agricultural student, **7:** 446 n.*737*
New York, United States, **9:** 354
New Zealand, **4:** 138 n.*116*; **5:** 163, 164 n.*271*; **8:** 66 n.*104*
Niagara Hall, London, **9:** 58, 59
Niagara Panorama, **8:** 404, 408
Nicholl (of Connaught Square, Paddington, London):
Allen Hume (1866-1941), **8:** 450 n.*721*
Capel Hume (1864-1871), **8:** 450 n.*721*
Cecil Hume (b. 1859), **8:** 450 n.*721*; **9:** 119
Charlotte Mary (b. 1863), see Fursdon
Ella Augusta Mary (b. 1858), **8:** 450 n.*721*
Frances "Fanny" Mary née Tweed (b. 1836), **2:** 85 n.*170*; **8:** 450 n.*721*; **9:** 119, 120 n.*207*
Hume, Capt. (1834-1895) – army officer and magistrate, **1:** 126 n.*156*; **6:** 359, 385; **8:** 141 n.*229*, 450 n.*721*; **9:** 119, 120 n.*207*
Iltyd Arthur Hume (b. 1856), **8:** 450 n.*721*; **9:** 119
Jestyn Hume (b. 1860), **8:** 450 n.*721*
Nicholl (of Ludlow, Shropshire; London; Wimbledon, Surrey):
Charlotte née Hume (1807-1835), **1:** 126 n.*156*; **6:** 359
Hume (1834-1895), see below
Whitlock, Dr. (1786-1838), **1:** 126 n.*156*; **6:** 359
Nicholls (of Oxford):
Agnes (b. 1863) – teacher, **9:** 261 n.*412*
Mary (b. 1872) – teacher, **9:** 261 n.*412*
Nicholls (staying with the MacDonalds in 1879):
Ernest, **7:** 180 n.*334*
Willie, **7:** 180 n.*334*
Nicholson, Edward Williams Byron (1849-1912) – Bodley's

librarian, **9:** 108 n.*192*
Nicholson, Miss, **9:** 261 n.*412*
Nicholson, Mrs. – related to the Shuldhams, **3:** 26 n.*35*
Nicol:
Mr., **7:** 33 n.*45*
Mrs. – niece of Thomas Jones Prout, **7:** 33 n.*45*
Nightingale (of Greenwich, Kent):
Edith (b. 1882), **8:** 594, 595 n.*948*, 634
Florence (b. 1884), **8:** 594, 595 n.*948*, 634
Nightingale, Florence (1820-1910) – hospital reformer, **1:** 94
Nightingale, Miss – sister of Mrs. Dubourg, **6:** 295-297
Nijni Novgorod, Russia, **5:** 307
Nine Men's Morris, see Meryls
Niobe (dr. Harry and Edward Paulton), **9:** 16 n.*13*, 32
Noad, James (b. 1861) – photographer, **8:** 220 n.*377*, 221, 222, 234, 242, 297 n.*496*, 299, 301, 302
Noel, Montague Henry, Rev. (1840-1929), **5:** 135 n.*218*
Noke, Oxfordshire, **4:** 278
Nolan (of Liverpool, Lancashire):
Edward (1846-1870) – dramatist, **5:** 153 n.*248*, 253 n.*417*
Thomas (b. 1844), **5:** 153 n.*248*
Noott, Edgar Frank Cornwallis, Rev. (1860-1905), **8:** 396 n.*644*, 511, 544
Norma (Bellini) – opera, **1:** 103 n.*114*, 104; **4:** 104 n.*69*, 282 n.*333*
Norman Conquest (bk. Jacques Thierry), **1:** 23
Normanton, Derbyshire, **5:** 189
Norris (of Corpus Christi College, Oxford):
Caroline Lydia (b. 1847), **3:** 34; **6:** 349-351, 425
Caroline M. née Hume (b. 1812), **2:** 110; **3:** 39, 41, 42, 121 n.*171*; **4:** 197; **6:** 345
Charlotte (b. 1849), **3:** 34
James, Rev. Dr. (1796-1872) – President of Corpus Christi, **3:** 34 n.*52*, 49, 121 n.*171*, 123, 155; **4:** 197; **5:** 148 n.*238*, 245
Mary (b. 1854?), **4:** 194 n.*191*; **6:** 345 n.*572*, 349-351
William Burrell (b. 1852), **6:** 349-351
Norris (of Penge, Surrey):
Catherine T. (b. 1859) – actress, **7:** 48 n.*73*
Sarah A., Mrs. (b. 1826), **7:** 48 n.*73*
William P., Prof. (b. 1826) – professor of science, **7:** 48 n.*73*
Northallerton, Yorkshire, **4:** 233
Northampton House School, London, **7:** 179
Northampton Mercury, **3:** 127
North and South (bk. Elizabeth Gaskell), **1:** 131 n.*163*
Northcote (of The Elms, Boldre, Hampshire):
Isabella Jane née Weguelin (b. 1843), **6:** 98
Lewis Stafford, Major (1831-1882), **6:** 98

Selina Helena (1844-1901) – sister, **6:** 98
Northcote, Stafford Harry (1869-1926), Viscount St. Cyres, **9:** 76 n.*140*
Northcote, Stafford Henry, Sir (1818-1887) – politician, **5:** 215 n.*344*; **8:** 150 n.*244*
Northern Branch of the Society for the Prevention of Cruelty to Animals, **6:** 382
North Moreton, Oxfordshire, **5:** 135
Northumberland, Dukes of, see Percy
Norton, David Evans, Rev. (b. 1832) – headmaster, **1:** 78 n.*75*
Norwegian Ladies, **9:** 326
Norwood, Eille (1861-1948) – dramatist, **9:** 274 n.*435*
Norwood, Middlesex, **7:** 208
No Song, No Supper (dr. Prince Hoare), **5:** 32 n.*35*, 88
Notices to Correspondents (bk. Elizabeth Barrett Browning), **3:** 158 n.*234*
Nottingham, **6:** 215
Nova Scotia, **2:** 105
Noviss, Esther (b. 1859) – housemaid, **7:** 298 n.*540*
Novo Devichi Monastery, Moscow, Russia, **5:** 325
Number 204 (dr. Francis Burnand and Thomas German Reed), **7:** 57 n.*90*
Number One, Round the Corner (dr. William Brough), **4:** 263 n.*308*
Nuneham, Oxfordshire, **1:** 67, 71; **4:** 73, 81, 113, 193, 194, 204, 213; **5:** 77 n.*117*
Nunn, Mrs. – cousin of Evelyn Dubourg, **7:** 186
Nyctograph, **8:** 582 n.*929*

Oakeley, William Pearce (b. 1860) – undergraduate at Jesus, **7:** 222 n.*407*
Oakley (of Covent Garden, London):
Charles Edward, Rev. (1832-1865), **4:** 327 n.*416*, 339
Mrs., **4:** 327
Oak Tree House, Hampstead (Holidays), **6:** 401
Oberon (Weber) – opera, **3:** 32 n.*47*
Oberthür, Carl or Karl (1819-1895) – harpist, **8:** 594 n.*947*
O'Brien (of Kensington, London):
Edward W., Mr. (b. 1837) – magistrate, **8:** 271 n.*457*
Julia Mary Garth née Marshall (1845-1907), **3:** 111, 112 n.*160*, 118 n.*165*, 119; **4:** 47; **8:** 271 n.*457*, 412
O'Brien, H. – artist, **2:** 21 n.*38*
Observatory (Oxford?), **8:** 545
Observer, **9:** 239
Oddie, John William (1839-1923) – lecturer, **6:** 303 n.*500*
Odd Pair, An (dr. T. Malcolm Watson), **9:** 88 n.*159*
Odd Rode, Cheshire, **6:** 344
"Ode on the Death of the Duke of Wellington" (Alfred Tennyson) – poem, **1:** 119 n.*145*
Oder River, Prussia, **5:** 353

Offenbach, Jaques (1819-1880) – composer, **5:** 242 n.*391*; **7:** 193, 304, 541 n.*874*
Offerton, Durham, **1:** 9
O'Flahertys, The (dr. Anon), **5:** 23, 24 n.*21*
Ogilvie (of Christ Church, Oxford):
Charles Atmore (1793-1873), **2:** 79 n.*157*; **3:** 25 n.*33*, 29, 125; **4:** 71 n.*14*, 206; **6:** 262 n.*420*
Mary Ann Gurnell née Armstrong (d. 1875), **3:** 25
Ogilvies, The (bk. Dinah Craik), **1:** 68 n.*55*, 92 n.*96*
Ogle, Helen P. (b. 1845), **4:** 180
Ogle (of Oxford):
James Adey, Prof. (1793-1857) – professor of medicine, **5:** 155 n.*251*
Octavius (1829-1894), **5:** 155 n.*251*, 156
William (1827-1912), **5:** 155 n.*251*, 156
O'Grady, Geraldine (b. 1877) – pupil of the Dymes, **7:** 454 n.*751*
Old Guard, The (Henry Farnie and Robert Planquette) – operetta, **8:** 569 n.*907*
Old Kensington (bk. Anne Thackerary), **8:** 15 n.*9*
Old Mortality (dr. A. R. Headland and H. A. Treble, adapt. Walter Scott), **6:** 180 n.*280*
Old Poz (dr. Maria Edgeworth), **6:** 104
Old Song, An (dr. Freeman Wills and A. Fitz King), **9:** 162 n.*277*
Old Testament, **5:** 102
Oliphant (of Gask, Perthshire, Scotland):
Frances Dorothy née Jebb (1828-1902), **5:** 108 n.*169*; **6:** 56 n.*82*
Thomas Laurence Kington (1831-1902) – barrister, **6:** 56 n.*82*
Oliphant, Philip Oliphant Kington Blair (1832-1892), **6:** 55, 56 n.*82*
Olive (bk. Dinah Mulock), **1:** 68, 69 n.*55*, 107
Olive Leaves for the People (bk. Elihu Burritt), **1:** 134 n.*169*
Oliver, M. "Patty" (1834-1880) – actress and singer, **5:** 233 n.*372*
Oliver Twist – see *Nancy Sikes*
Olivette (Henry Farnie and Edmond Audran) – operetta, **7:** 304, 305 n.*549*
Olivia (dr. William Wills), **7:** 105, 106 n.*197*, 110; **8:** 209 n.*359*, 565
Olivier, Edith Maud (1872-1948) – friend of Evelyn Hatch, **9:** 281 n.*446*
Olivier, Mr. – actor, **9:** 119 n.*206*
Olliffe, Geraldine – actress, **9:** 283, 284 n.*449*
Olsham, B. – actor, **5:** 193
Omnibus Volume of Lewis Carroll's Works (pub. Nonesuch), **1:** 31, 35, 48
On Certainty in Religion (bk. Edward White), **8:** 455 n.*730*
O'Neil, Henry Nelson (1817-1880) – artist, **5:** 236 n.*382*
O'Neill, Norah, see Quin
Onions (of Drayton in Hayles, Shropshire):
Edith A. (b. 1855), **8:** 339 n.*559*
John Henry (1852-1889) – lecturer, **6:** 494 n.*816*; **7:** 440 n.*730*, 490; **8:** 11 n.*1*, 339, 459 n.*738*

Only a Halfpenny (dr. John Oxenford), **2:** 23, 24 n.*44*
Onslow (of Clandon House, near Guildford, Surrey):
Denzil Roberts (1839-1908) – politician, **6:** 319 n.*529*; **7:** 254 n.*463*
Guildford James Hillier (1814-1882) – politician, **6:** 319 n.*529*
Onslow Square, London, **4:** 86; **5:** 89, 138, 142, 170; **6:** 71, 127, 156, 177, 186, 195, 196, 198, 206, 251, 255-257, 279
On the Divine Philosophy of Labour (bk. Elihu Burritt), **1:** 134 n.*169*
On the Look Out (pic. Henry Le Jeune), **2:** 75 n.*151*
On the Study of Words (bk. Richard Trench), **1:** 73 n.*66*
"Operatic Music" – lecture, **6:** 95
"Ophelia" (in *Hamlet*), **2:** 20, 21
Orange-Blossoms (dr. John Wooler), **4:** 272, 273 n.*318*
Orangesmith (of Beckenham, Kent):
Mr., **6:** 254 n.*404*
Mrs. née Faulkner, **6:** 254 n.*404*
Orations against Aphobus (bk. Demosthenes), **3:** 156 n.*230*
Ore, near Hastings, Sussex, **4:** 28
O'Reilly, Kathleen (b. 1865) – friend of Evelyn Dubourg, **8:** 165 n.*271*
Orford, Emmie – actress, **8:** 630 n.*997*, 631
Orgeni, Anna Maria Aglaja Görger St. Jörgen (b. 1843) – singer and teacher, **5:** 153 n.*247*
Oriel College, Oxford, **4:** 291 n.*347*; **7:** 175; **8:** 169, 192, 196, 306
Oriental Club, London, **9:** 76
Origin and Progress of Writing, The (bk. Thomas Astle), **1:** 63 n.*38*
Orloff (or Orlov), Nikolay Alexeyevich, Prince (1827-1885), **5:** 315 n.*487*
Ormerod, George (1785-1873) – writer, **1:** 12
Orpheus and Eurydice (dr. James Planché), **4:** 272, 273 n.*318*
Orpheus Glee Club, Oxford, **3:** 71; **4:** 209
Orsini, Teobaldus Orsus Felice (1819-1858) – writer, **3:** 9 n.*5*
Orthoscope – French toy, **2:** 123
Osborn (of Kibworth-Beauchamp, Leicestershire):
Catherine Barbara née Marriott (b. 1832), **6:** 111 n.*173*
Catherine Louisa (b. 1865), **6:** 111 n.*173*
Edith (b. 1880), **6:** 111 n.*173*
Francis Wilfrid (b. 1862), **6:** 111 n.*173*
Margaret (1864-1942), **6:** 111 n.*173*
Martha (b. 1869), **6:** 111 n.*173*
Montagu Francis Finch, Rev. (1824-1895), **6:** 110, 111 n.*173*
Montagu John (b. 1869), **6:** 111 n.*173*
Osborn, Emma V., Mrs. (b. 1822) – lodging-house keeper, **6:** 228
Osborn, Mrs. – guest of Mrs. Mackarness, **9:** 299 n.*475*
Osborne, Ralph Bernal (1808-1882) – politician, **5:** 215 n.*344*
"Oscar" (pic. Oscar Rejlander), **5:** 236 n.*381*
Osgood, Emma Aline (1849-1911) – singer, **7:** 366 n.*638*
Osney House, Oxford, **9:** 311 n.*494*

Ossian's Tomb, Glenalmond, Scotland, **3:** 97
Ostlere, Edith – actress, **8:** 485 n.*785*
"O Swallow, Swallow" (Alfred Tennyson) – song, **2:** 121 n.*234*
"Otheroscope" – theatrical optical illusion, **7:** 299 n.*542*
Otter (of Ranby Hall, Lincolnshire):
  Elizabeth née Young (d. 1875), **3:** 87 n.*136*
  Francis (1832-1895) – barrister and politician, **2:** 63 n.*125*
  Francis, Mr. (d. 1875), **3:** 87 n.*136*
Ottewill, Thomas & Company – photographic manufacturer, **2:** 26 n.*49*, 53; **3:** 50, 51 n.*77*
Ottley (of Richmond, Yorkshire):
  Alice (1840-1912) – headmistress, **2:** 86 n.*171*; **3:** 92 n.*142*; **4:** 231 n.*256*, 338; **5:** 42 n.*54*; **7:** 107 n.*199*; **8:** 30 n.*35*; **9:** 14 n.*7*, 33 n.*56*, 42-44, 69
  Caroline Agnes "Aggie" (b. 1849), **2:** 86 n.*171*; **4:** 222; **7:** 57 n.*91*; **8:** 30 n.*35*; **9:** 69 n.*125*
  Charles "Charlie" Langdale (1858-1932), **2:** 86 n.*171*; **4:** 222, 338; **7:** 107 n.*199*
  Constance "Cooie" (1854-1857), **2:** 86 n.*171*
  Edward "Teddie" Bickersteth (1852-1910), **2:** 86 n.*171*; **4:** 222, 338
  Elizabeth née Bickersteth (1817-1902), **2:** 86 n.*171*; **3:** 92; **4:** 222 n.*243*, 226, 229, 338; **7:** 57 n.*91*, 63, 107, 209, 364; **8:** 149 n.*242*
  Emily "Emmie" (1838-1893), **2:** 86 n.*171*; **3:** 92 n.*142*
  Georgiana "Georgie" (b. 1847), see Sewell
  Henrietta Sarah "Sallie" (b. 1836), **2:** 86 n.*171*; **3:** 92 n.*142*
  Henry "Harry" Bickersteth (1850-1932), see below
  Herbert Taylor (b. 1859), **2:** 86 n.*171*; **7:** 107 n.*199*
  John Bickersteth (b. 1845), **2:** 86 n.*171*
  Lawrence, Rev. (1808-1861), **2:** 86 n.*171*; **3:** 92; **4:** 27
  Lawrence "Lawrie" (b. 1843), **2:** 86 n.*171*
  Portia (b. 1839, died in infancy), **2:** 86 n.*171*
  Richard (b. 1842, died in infancy), **2:** 86 n.*171*
  Robert "Robin" Lawrence (1856-1933), **2:** 86 n.*171*; **4:** 222, 338; **7:** 107 n.*199*, 245 n.*449*, 246, 276, 440 n.*730*; **8:** 55 n.*81*, 149, 170, 594; **9:** 314 n.*500*, 320
  Sophie Elizabeth "Bessie" (1841-1854), **2:** 86 n.*171*
Ottley (of Regent's Park, London):
  "Daisy" (b. 1882?), **8:** 573 n.*914*, 589, 634
  Desmond (b. 1884?), **8:** 573 n.*914*, 589
  Fielding Hay Bickersteth (1877-1958), **7:** 107 n.*199*
  Henry "Harry" Bickersteth, Rev. (1850-1932), **2:** 86 n.*171*; **6:** 150 n.*229*; **7:** 107 n.*199*; **8:** 573 n.*914*; **9:** 341 n.*545*
  Marion Florence Carrington née Marriott (b. 1857), **7:** 107 n.*199*; **8:** 573 n.*914*
Our Boys (dr. Henry Byron), **8:** 131 n.*214*, 140
Our Clerks (dr. Tom Taylor), **6:** 197 n.*307*

Our Eldorado (dr. Frank Scudamore), **9:** 164 n.*281*, 165
Our Flat (dr. Mrs. H. Musgrave), **8:** 530 n.*849*
Our Mary Anne (dr. John Buckstone), **5:** 32 n.*35*
Our Mutual Friend (bk. Charles Dickens), **5:** 379
Ours (dr. Thomas Robertson), **7:** 231 n.*425*
Our Table d'hôte (dr. Richard Corney Grain), **7:** 57 n.*90*
Our Wife, or, The Rose of Amiens (dr. John Morton), **2:** 124 n.*240*
Ouseley, Frederick Arthur Gore, Rev. (1825-1889) – musician and warden of St. Michael's College, Tenbury, **4:** 33; **6:** 167 n.*259*, 168; **7:** 53 n.*84*
Outhwaite, Elizabeth (1779-1862), **4:** 129 n.*104*
Outlines of Moral Philosophy (bk. Dugald Stewart), **1:** 74 n.*67*
Overton, John Henry, Rev. (1835-1903), **3:** 129, 130 n.*187*
Ovid (43 BC - AD 17?), **1:** 23, 79 n.*78*
Owen, B. Lloyd, Miss – amateur actress, **8:** 496, 497 n.*799*
Owen (of Bradmore Road, Oxford):
Henrietta "Atty" O'Brien (1862-1953), **5:** 254 n.*419*; **6:** 29 n.*35*, 123, 153, 480, 482, 484; **7:** 240 n.*442*, 246
Lucy "Tinie" O'Brien (b. 1861), **5:** 254 n.*419*; **6:** 29 n.*35*, 123, 153, 482, 484
Mary Ellen née Sewell (1835-1928), **5:** 254; **6:** 29 n.*35*, 144, 351, 480, 481; **7:** 240 n.*442*, 246
Sidney George (b. 1858), **4:** 213 n.*225*; **7:** 240 n.*442*
Sidney James, Mr. (1827-1912), **5:** 254; **6:** 29 n.*35*, 144, 187, 218, 263, 351; **7:** 227, 246, 436, 484 n.*788*, 489, 490
Owen, James Albert (1842-1907) – teacher, **4:** 202 n.*209*
Owen, Mr. – director of London Polytechnic, **7:** 42, 43 n.*64*, 44
Owens, John Edmund (1823-1886) – actor and comedian, **5:** 96 n.*150*
Oxenford, John (1812-1877) – dramatist, **2:** 24 n.*44*, 80 n.*158*; **3:** 132 n.*190*; **4:** 291 n.*348*; **5:** 88 n.*136*, 117 n.*182*; **9:** 84 n.*152*, 332 n.*530*

Oxford:
Art Society, **8:** 624, 625 n.*988*; **9:** 39 n.*69*, 70 n.*129*
Ashmolean Club, **7:** 225
Ashmolean Museum, **3:** 22 n.*28*; **4:** 143; **5:** 163; **6:** 287; **9:** 266 n.*420*
Botanical Gardens, **4:** 200; **8:** 196, 216, 339; **9:** 223
Brigade Depot, **7:** 270
Broad Street, **6:** 66; **9:** 131
Castle, **1:** 40
Choral Society, **3:** 32, 36 n.*56*, 60
Corn Exchange, **4:** 194 n.*191*; **5:** 251; **8:** 461, 509
Court Assizes, **1:** 95 n.*99*; **4:** 219 n.*238*, 275; **5:** 52 n.*73*, 53 n.*74*, 118 n.*185*; **7:** 21 n.*19*, 121 n.*228*
Disturbances (Bread Riots), **5:** 370, 371 n.*550*
Elections, **6:** 329; **8:** 249, 250 n.*419*; **9:** 13 n.*6*, 193 n.*318*, 206 n.*336*

Elementary Schools' Musical Society, **9:** 325 n.*522*
Fires, **6:** 123 n.*188*, 371 n.*609*
High School for Girls, **7:** 32 n.*43*; **8:** 56, 65, 195, 331, 334, 336-339, 341 n.*562*, 345, 346; **9:** 68, 127 n.*223*, 129, 130, 134, 141, 143, 155, 180, 183, 246, 250, 259-261, 265, 267, 269, 270, 301, 319, 327
Holywell Music Rooms, **4:** 206 n.*216*; **5:** 153; **9:** 121
Infirmary, **5:** 30
Jessop's Wine Shop, **7:** 274
Medical Charities and Teachers' Benevolent Funds, **9:** 325 n.*522*
Parks, The, **6:** 144, 153, 276, 426, 463, 488; **7:** 177, 534; **8:** 100, 218
Preparatory School, **9:** 262, 263 n.*414*
Ryman's Gallery, **1:** 67, 94; **2:** 69; **3:** 22, 69, 70, 129; **4:** 79 n.*29*; **9:** 124
Town Hall, **1:** 62; **2:** 63; **3:** 70; **6:** 34; **8:** 68, 605; **9:** 308 n.*488*, 310, 349

Oxford and Cambridge Magazine, **2:** 40 n.*80*
Oxford and Cambridge Volunteer Review, **5:** 78 n.*120*
Oxford Chronicle, **6:** 60
Oxford Critic, The, **2:** 14 n.*20*; **3:** 52, 53 n.*80*, 61, 64, 146
Oxford Movement, **4:** 10
Oxford Union Jubilee, **6:** 300 n.*495*

Oxford University:
Admission of women, **8:** 94 n.*154*, 102 n.*169*; **9:** 242 n.*382*, 244 n.*385*
Amateur Concert, **4:** 88, 305
Bachelor of Civil Law (B.C.L.), **5:** 164 n.*269*
Bampton Lectures, **5:** 228 n.*363*; **6:** 267 n.*429*, 458; **7:** 246; **8:** 188, 395, 510; **9:** 194, 196, 314, 320
Boat Procession, **8:** 342
Bodleian Library, **2:** 39 n.*78*, 62, 118 n.*225*; **4:** 82, 309; **6:** 455; **7:** 104, 346, 347, 520; **8:** 196; **9:** 197
Chancellor of the University, **3:** 21; **6:** 118 n.*181*, 119 n.*182*
Clarendon Press, **3:** 33 n.*51*; **4:** 31, 83, 146, 169, 203, 257, 298; **5:** 97 n.*151*, 140, 143, 229, 372; **6:** 66, 200, 214, 318, 446, 451, 473; **7:** 80, 224, 324, 346, 404, 405; **9:** 61, 239
Clerke's Fund, **8:** 549
Clinical professorship, **3:** 122 n.*172*, 145
Colleges – *Memoria Technica* rhymes, **7:** 37 n.*54*
Commemoration (Encænia), **1:** 46; **2:** 77 n.*153*; **4:** 88, 90, 209, 277, 307; **5:** 153, 254; **6:** 36, 85, 118, 155, 340, 466, 467; **7:** 440, 544; **8:** 343; **9:** 76, 203, 264, 323
Commission, **2:** 31 n.*62*; **3:** 19 n.*21*, 20, 21, 22, 37, 38 n.*59*, 40, 43, 86, 87 n.*135*; **5:** 49 n.*65*, 158 n.*260*; **7:** 82 n.*138*, 113, 227, 230, 237
Congregation, **4:** 56, 193; **5:** 180; **7:** 436; **8:** 94 n.*154*, 206 n.*354*, 245, 246, 247 n.*413*, 303 n.*503*; **9:** 242, 244
Convocation, **4:** 150, 193, 201, 276 n.*322*; **5:** 180; **6:** 449; **7:** 177;

8: 102 n.*169*, 171, 172 n.*288*, 246, 279, 317; **9:** 72
Coronership, **7:** 378 n.*653*
Degree List (Mathematics), **4:** 152
Degrees for Women, **9:** 242 n.*382*, 244 n.*385*, 244 n.*386*
Delegates (of Local Examinations), **4:** 110, 114, 116
Dramatic Society, **7:** 238 n.*439*; **9:** 190
Eights (boat races), **1:** 42; **2:** 66, 68; **3:** 60, 62; **4:** 298; **5:** 77, 79; **9:** 145, 256, 257
Encaenia, see Commemoration
Examination Schools, **9:** 223
Hebdomadal Council, **5:** 180, 181 n.*299*, 181 n.*300*; **8:** 279
Home Students, **9:** 327 n.*525*
Junior Mathematical Scholarship, **2:** 113, 115 n.*221*
Junior Scientific Club, **9:** 258
Member of Parliament, **8:** 202 n.*345*
Moderations (Mods), **2:** 28 n.*54*, 113, 115 n.*221*, 124 n.*241*; **3:** 67, 166 n.*241*; **4:** 58; **5:** 375; **7:** 148, 375, 379, 382, 491; **9:** 46
Moderators' Meeting, **6:** 33
Museum, **1:** 40; **4:** 34, 38, 83, 94, 169, 176, 305; **5:** 59, 79, 207; **6:** 328, 469, 488, 490; **7:** 346, 453; **8:** 409; **9:** 253
Newdigate prize-winner, **7:** 519 n.*841*
Ordination Sermon, **6:** 373
Oxford and Cambridge Boat Race, **5:** 64, 226
Press, see Clarendon Press above
Proctor Cycle, **8:** 206 n.*354*, 207, 279, 303 n.*503*, 317
Proctors, **2:** 64 n.*127*; **3:** 66; **4:** 150, 175 n.*171*, 206, 276, 308; **5:** 244 n.*396*, 252 n.*414*, 375, 376 n.*557*; **8:** 263
Professorship of Anglo-Saxon, **6:** 486; **7:** 35 n.*50*
Professorship of Divinity, **7:** 144 n.*269*
Professorship of Poetry, **3:** 35 n.*54*; **8:** 249 n.*418*
Responsions (Smalls or Little-go), **1:** 89 n.*91*; **5:** 250; **6:** 141, 329, 464, 492 n.*815*; **7:** 31 n.*40*, 103, 148, 245, 246 n.*450*, 247, 323, 375, 384, 404, 405, 409 n.*689*, 436, 491; **8:** 399, 403
Sermons, **4:** 305; **6:** 462; **7:** 142, 225, 236, 269, 341, 346, 371, 431, 537; **8:** 44, 55, 62, 70, 83, 205, 208, 260, 342, 395, 538, 549, 594, 629; **9:** 37, 51, 68, 228, 262, 314, 315, 346
Sheldonian Theatre, **1:** 46; **5:** 252 n.*414*; **9:** 325
Slade Professor of Art, **7:** 497 n.*811*
Slade Scholarships, **2:** 68, 70
Statutes, **4:** 193 n.*189*, 273, 274, 275 n.*321*
Taylor Buildings and Gallery, **1:** 65; **3:** 22 n.*28*, 28; **7:** 22, 537; **9:** 266 n.*420*
Testamur (examination certificate), **3:** 166; **4:** 19
Torpids (boat races), **2:** 43 n.*86*; **4:** 173
Union, **3:** 26 n.*37*, 33 n.*49*, 53, 54 n.*82*, 127 n.*184*, 155; **7:** 89

University Club, **7:** 177
Vice-Chancellor of the University, **3:** 66; **4:** 275 n.*321*; **7:** 22 n. 20, 31, 35, 404 n.*684*, 519, 521, 523; **9:** 38, 72 n.*132*, 254

Oxford University Herald, **6:** 60 n.*92*
Oxonian Advertiser, **1:** 48, 110 n.*128*
Ox roast, **4:** 172

Paddington Station, London, **3:** 133; **5:** 21, 255; **6:** 219; **7:** 46, 112; **8:** 168, 406, 408, 556, 566, 567, 572, 573, 593, 594, 619, 632; **9:** 59, 147, 205, 243, 284, 285, 316, 335, 347, 348, 352
"Paganini Redivivus" – performer, **7:** 528 n.*855*, 529, 531
Page, Cyril William, Rev. (1805-1873), **5:** 128 n.*205*
Page, Herbert William Cobbold (b. 1836) – undergraduate at Christ Church, **2:** 33 n.*65*, 76 n.*152*; **3:** 16 n.*16*
Page, Thomas Douglas (1836-1880) – lecturer, **5:** 365 n.*540*, 366
Paget (of Harewood Place, London):
Catherine (d. 1937), **8:** 402 n.*655*
Francis (1851-1911), see below
James, Sir (1814-1899) – surgeon, **6:** 278 n.*457*, 279; **7:** 80 n.*132*; **8:** 329, 330 n.*542*, 402, 595 n.*949*
Lydia née North, Lady (1815-1895), **8:** 402 n.*655*
Mary Maud (1861-1945), **8:** 402 n.*655*
Paget (of Acton, Middlesex):
Dolly (b. 1883), **8:** 201 n.*343*, 207
Gladys (b. 1880), **8:** 201 n.*343*, 207
Henrietta, Mrs. (b. 1852), **8:** 201 n.*343*
Henry Marriott, Mr. (1856-1936) – artist, **8:** 201 n.*343*, 202, 207, 271
Paget (of Christ Church, Oxford):
Francis, Dr. (1851-1911) – professor of pastoral theology, **6:** 307 n.*508*, 318; **7:** 33 n.*46*, 272, 275, 434, 440, 494; **8:** 266 n.*447*, 390, 400, 409, 459, 515, 559, 560, 590, 604, 607, 632; **9:** 109 n.*194*, 124, 148, 151, 189 n.*312*, 194, 195, 199, 200, 230, 238, 247, 300, 309, 347
Helen Beatrice née Church (1858-1900), **7:** 33 n.*46*; **8:** 266 n.*447*, 383, 390, 409, 558; **9:** 152, 199, 205, 224, 321
Paget (of St. Peter's Terrace, St Mary the Less, Cambridge):
George Edward, Sir (1809-1892) – professor of physics, **8:** 402 n.*655*
Rose Elizabeth (b. 1860), **8:** 402 n.*655*
Violet Emma (b. 1860), **8:** 402 n.*655*
Paggi:
Anita – flautist, **7:** 199 n.*372*
Josephine – violinist, **7:** 199 n.*372*
Paine (of Wallington, Surrey):
Adelaide Beethoven Harriett (1866-1940), **6:** 399 n.*653*
Mary Ann née Little (1844-1899), **6:** 399 n.*653*

William (1835-1916) – manufacturer's agent, **6:** 399 n.*653*
Paisley – pupil of Alexander Webster, **2:** 89, 90 n.*181*
Pakenham, Thomas, Lord (1864-1915), 5th Earl of Longford, **7:** 498 n.*814*
Palestine House, Sandown, Isle of Wight, **6:** 362
Paley, William, Rev. Dr. (1743-1805) – writer, **2:** 10 n.*11*; **3:** 156 n.*230*
Palgrave, Francis Turner (1824-1897) – poet, **3:** 88 n.*137*, 89, 140; **5:** 211 n.*339*; **8:** 249 n.*418*
Palin, Edward, Rev. (1826-1903), **4:** 161 n.*153*
Pall Mall, London, **5:** 136, 148, 215
Pall Mall Gazette, The, **5:** 11, 12 n.*2*, 181, 182, 183 n.*301*, 184 n.*302*, 194 n.*318*; **6:** 364 n.*599*, 365-368, 381, 382, 390, 391, 448, 477; **7:** 35 n.*49*, 36, 39 n.*57*; **8:** 222 n.*381*, 516
Palmer (of Mount Street, London):
Beatrix Maud née Cecil, Lady Wolmer (1858-1950), **6:** 118 n.*181*, 120, 121 n.*183*, 125 n.*194*, 127, 134, 135, 160-162, 165, 169, 200, 221, 222, 224, 225, 248, 250, 286, 336, 374, 375, 398, 441; **7:** 111 n.*206*, 189, 306, 443; **8:** 76, 110, 274, 333, 410, 455 n.*731*, 457, 462, 467, 562, 564, 565, 614, 615, 618, 620-622; **9:** 58 n.*107*, 76, 78, 140, 156
Mabel Laura Georgiana "Wang" (1884-1958), **8:** 410 n.*664*, 455, 462, 468, 469, 562, 565, 615, 618, 620-622; **9:** 58 n.*107*, 76, 78, 156
Robert Stafford Arthur (1888-1916), **9:** 58 n.*107*, 78, 157
Roundell Cecil (b. 1887), **8:** 410 n.*664*, 462, 562, 615, 618, 621, 622; **9:** 58 n.*107*, 157
William Waldegrave, Viscount Wolmer (1859-1942), **8:** 410 n.*664*, 455, 457; **9:** 58 n.*107*, 140
Palmer (of Christ Church, Oxford):
Edwin, Dr. (1824-1895) – archdeacon of Oxford, **7:** 145 n.*271*, 228, 242, 260, 275, 434, 440, 486, 487; **8:** 127 n.*206*, 203, 253, 549; **9:** 222 n.*352*
Edwin J. (b. 1869), **7:** 145 n.*271*
Henrietta, Mrs. (b. 1833), **7:** 145 n.*271*, 228, 275, 486
Lucy D. (b. 1874), **7:** 145 n.*271*
Mary H. (b. 1872), **7:** 145 n.*271*
Palmer, Jane née Robson (d. 1865), **2:** 15 n.*25*
Palmer, Kathella, see Cooke
Palmer, Milly or Minnie (1857-1936) – actress, **5:** 47 n.*62*
Palmer (of Blackmoor, Liss, Hampshire):
Roundell, Lord (1812-1895), 1st Earl of Selborne, **6:** 459 n.*754*
Sophia Matilda (1853-1915), **8:** 615, 622 n.*985*
William Waldegrave (1859-1942), see above
Palmerston, see Temple
Palmerston House, Sandown, Isle of Wight, **6:** 362
Pan (dr. Henry Byron), **5:** 69 n.*104*
Pantomime of the White Cat (dr. Charles Kean), **3:** 153 n.*222*
Pantomime Rehearsal, A (dr. Cecil Clay), **8:** 618 n.*980*; **9:** 12, 13 n.*5*, 26, 303 n.*482*

Pantomimes, **2:** 23, 24 n.*44*, 80; **3:** 14 n.*13*, 153 n.*222*; **4:** 157; **5:** 41, 42 n.*52*, 45 n.*58*, 127 n.*203*, 379; **6:** 112, 250, 253, 257, 309, 311, 314, 316, 376-378, 444; **7:** 13, 17, 23, 75, 76, 91-94, 99, 107, 153-155, 313, 367, 392, 399, 492, 504, 509, 510, 512, 515, 525; **8:** 160 n.*259*, 610 n.*966*; **9:** 122 n.*214*

Paper Chase, The (dr. Charles Thomas), **8:** 428 n.*691*

Papini, Guido (b. 1847) – violinist, **7:** 217, 218 n.*399*

Papworth, Edgar George (1809-1866) – artist, **2:** 75 n.*151*

Parable of the Children in the Market-place, The (pic. William Dobson), **2:** 75 n.*151*

Pares (of Chilworth, Surrey):
- Alice (b. 1859), **6:** 171 n.*267*
- Basil (b. 1869), **6:** 171 n.*267*
- Bernard (b. 1867), **6:** 171 n.*267*
- Constance (b. 1864), **6:** 171 n.*267*, 225
- Ethel (1861-1917), **6:** 171 n.*267*, 225
- George Lancelot (b. 1865), **6:** 171 n.*267*, 225
- Harold (1873-1917), **6:** 171 n.*267*
- John, Mr. (1833-1915) – magistrate, **6:** 170, 171 n.*267*, 225
- Katherine née Back (b. 1831), **6:** 171 n.*267*, 225, 294
- Mabel Austen (b. 1871), **6:** 171 n.*267*
- Margaret "Maggie" (b. 1862), **6:** 171 n.*267*, 225
- Norman (b. 1857), **6:** 171 n.*267*

Parham, Francis (b. 1835) – undergraduate at Christ Church, **1:** 87, 88 n.*91*, 91; **2:** 114 n.*220*, 115

Paris, France, **2:** 17; **5:** 362-368; **6:** 138 n.*210*

Paris (dr. Arthur Sketchley), **4:** 287 n.*343*

Parish (of Stoke, near Guildford, Surrey):
- Alfred, Commander (1817-1903) – shipping service, **7:** 160 n.*300*
- Alice (b. 1854), **7:** 167
- Eleanor Mary née Brandreth (1830-1916), **7:** 160 n.*300*, 166, 167, 230
- Florence (b. 1856), **7:** 167
- Mary "May" Eleanor (1866-1944), **7:** 160 n.*300*, 167, 230

Parish Musings (bk. John Monsell), **1:** 120 n.*147*

Paris International Exhibition, **5:** 250 n.*409*, 363 n.*538*, 366

Park, Eliza – pupil at St. Aldates, **2:** 32

Parker (of Eccleston Paddocks, Chester, Cheshire):
- Cecil Thomas, Hon. (1845-1931), **6:** 151 n.*230*
- Rosamond Esther Harriet née Longley (1844-1936), **2:** 10 n.*10*, 55-56, 58, 104; **3:** 85, 151, 152 n.*220*; **4:** 22, 23, 312 n.*390*, 324 n.*411*, 326; **5:** 179 n.*296*, **6:** 151 n.*230*

Parker, F. J., The Hon. – from Boston, United States of America, **4:** 54

Parker, Francis (1851-1931) – barrister, **7:** 445 n.*735*; **9:** 229 n.*364*

Parker, James and Company, Publishers, Oxford, **3:** 165; **4:** 37, 49; **6:** 190, 393; **7:** 43, 167; **9:** 241

Parker, Louis Napoleon (1852-1944) – dramatist, **9:** 310 n.*493*
Parker, Miss – friend of the Earles, **8:** 343 n.*564*
Parker Family (of Oxford?), **6:** 275
Parkes (of Grove Road, Kingston-on-Thames, Surrey):
Annie (b. 1855), **4:** 178, 351 n.*458*, 352; **5:** 19, 37 n.*45*, 140; **7:** 220 n.*403*, 221
Francis "Frank" (b. 1865), **4:** 351 n.*458*; **5:** 37 n.*45*, 140; **7:** 221
Henry "Harry" (b. 1858), **4:** 351 n.*458*; **5:** 37 n.*45*, 140
Mary Rebecca, Mrs. (b. 1821), **4:** 351 n.*458*, 356; **5:** 37 n.*45*, 88, 140; **7:** 220 n.*403*, 221
William, Mr. (1823-1889) – civil engineer, **4:** 351 n.*458*, 352, 353, 356; **5:** 37 n.*45*, 88, 138, 140; **7:** 220 n.*403*, 221
William Jardyne (b. 1862), **4:** 351 n.*458*; **5:** 37 n.*45*, 140; **7:** 221
Parkes (of Gloucester):
Phoebe (b. 1820), **5:** 37 n.*45*; **7:** 220 n.*403*
William (1823-1889), see above
Parkins & Gotto, Oxford Street, London – stationers, **5:** 200 n.*326*
Park Street, Westminster, **5:** 138
Parliament (The House), **5:** 215 n.*344*
Parnell (of Minstead Lodge, Lyndhurst, Hampshire):
Alfred Bligh (1846-1865), **4:** 328 n.*419*
Caroline Margaret née Dawson (1822-1912) – second wife, **4:** 239 n.*267*, 311 n.*388*, 325, 328, 359; **5:** 66 n.*99*, 93
Elizabeth "Leila" Mary Emily (1859-1936), **4:** 179, 239 n.*267*, 311 n.*388*, 326 n.*415*, 327, 343; **5:** 66 n.*99*
Evelyn Caroline (d. 1861), **4:** 239 n.*267*
Henry William, Lord (1809-1896), 3rd Baron Congelton, **4:** 239 n.*267*, 311 n.*388*, 325, 327-329, 359; **5:** 66 n.*99*, 93
Lionel Charles Nugent (1864-1940), **4:** 239 n.*267*
Louisa "Loui" Anna Maria (1857-1933), **4:** 180, 239 n.*267*, 311 n.*388*, 326 n.*415*, 327, 343; **5:** 66 n.*99*
Mabel Frances Letitia (1862-1947), **4:** 181, 239 n.*267*, 311 n.*388*, 326 n.*415*, 327
Madeline Catherine (1855-1925), **4:** 180, 239 n.*267*, 311 n.*388*, 326 n.*415*, 327; **5:** 66
Sophia née Bligh (d. 1846) – first wife, **4:** 239 n.*267*
Victor Alexander Lionel Dawson (1852-1936), **4:** 239 n.*267*, 311 n.*388*, 326 n.*415*, 327
Parnell (of Minstead Lodge, Lyndhurst, Hampshire):
Caroline Elizabeth née Dawson (d. 1861), **4:** 239 n.*267*
Emma Jane (d. 1884), see Bligh
Henry Brooke (1776-1842), 1st Baron Congelton, **4:** 239 n.*267*
Henry William (1809-1896), see above
Parnell, Charles Stewart (1846-1891) – politician, **7:** 370, 371 n.*645*; **8:** 543 n.*868*

Parratt (of St Giles', Oxford):
Amy T. (b. 1872), **8:** 482 n.*781*, 486
Dorothy T. (b. 1876), **8:** 482 n.*781*, 486
Emma née Gledhill (b. 1843), **8:** 482 n.*781*
Geoffrey T. (b. 1878), **8:** 482 n.*781*
Katherine (b. 1874), **8:** 482 n.*781*, 486
Margaret (b. 1880), **8:** 482 n.*781*, 486
Walter, Sir (1841-1924) – musician, **8:** 482 n.*781*
Parry (of Regent Street, London):
John Orlando (1810-1879) – actor, song-writer and entertainer, **2:** 100; **4:** 109 n.*77*, 203, 204 n.*212*, 234, 322, 323 n.*409*, 337; **5:** 157 n.*256*, 242 n.*392*; **6:** 15 n.*10*
Mrs., **6:** 15
Partners (dr. Robert Buchanan), **8:** 460 n.*739*, 584
Parton, Ernest (1845-1933) – artist, **7:** 539 n.*872*
Parvenu, The (dr. George Godfrey), **7:** 438 n.*727*
Passion (J. S. Bach), **6:** 265, 266 n.*427*
Pastoral (pic. Frederick Leighton), **5:** 236 n.*380*
Patchwork (dr. Howard Paul), **3:** 103 n.*151*
Patey, Janet Monach née Whytock (1842-1894) – singer, **7:** 219 n.*400*, 360
Patience (Gilbert and Sullivan) – operetta, **7:** 394 n.*672*, 397, 431, 441, 461, 477, 503; **8:** 138 n.*225*, 453
Patmore (of The Mansion, Hastings St. Clement, Sussex):
Bertha (b. 1857), **8:** 534 n.*859*, 536
Coventry Kersey Dighton, Mr. (1823-1896) – poet, **1:** 115 n.*138*; **4:** 109; **8:** 534 n.*859*, 535, 536, 571
Francis Epiphanius "Piffy" (b. 1882?), **8:** 534 n.*859*, 536, 571
Gertrude (b. 1859), **8:** 534 n.*859*, 536
Harriet née Robson (b. 1841), third wife, **8:** 534 n.*859*, 536
Paton (of 14 George Square, Edinburgh, Scotland):
Agatha Waller (b. 1875), **7:** 452 n.*748*
Angela Noël (b. 1865), **7:** 452 n.*748*
Aveline Catherine (b. 1872), **7:** 452 n.*748*
Eric Waller (b. 1877), **7:** 452 n.*748*
Kinloch Diarmid (b. 1867), **7:** 452 n.*748*
Margaret, Mrs. (b. 1843), **7:** 452 n.*748*
Nigel Fairholt (b. 1869), **7:** 452 n.*748*
Waller Hugh, Mr. (1828-1895) – artist, **7:** 452 n.*748*
W. Hubert (b. 1864), **7:** 452 n.*748*
Paton (of 33 George Square, Edinburgh, Scotland):
Diarmid Noël (1859-1928), **6:** 183 n.*285*; **7:** 448 n.*742*
Donald R. (b. 1873), **7:** 448 n.*742*
Emilie "Dolly" (b. 1872), **7:** 448 n.*742*
Ernest T. (b. 1867), **6:** 183 n.*285*; **7:** 448 n.*742*
Eva (b. 1876), **7:** 448 n.*742*

Frederick Noël (1861-1914), **6:** 183 n.*285*; **7:** 448 n.*742*
Joseph Noël, Sir (1821-1901) – artist, **3:** 102 n.*150*; **4:** 36, 55; **5:** 238 n.*385*; **6:** 20 n.*22*, 22 n.*24*, 30, 59, 179 n.*277*, 180, 181, 183 n.*285*, 184, 185; **7:** 346 n.*606*, 448, 452; **8:** 111 n.*182*, 203
Lora Hamilton Noël, **6:** 183 n.*285*; **7:** 448 n.*742*
Margaret née Ferrier, Lady (b. 1833), **6:** 183 n.*285*, 184; **7:** 448 n.*742*, 452
Mona Margaret Noël (1860-1928), see Kidston
Ronald A. (b. 1865), **6:** 183 n.*285*; **7:** 448 n.*742*
Victor Albert (b. 1863), **6:** 183 n.*285*; **7:** 448 n.*742*
Patterson Family – friend of the Patons, **6:** 183
Pattinson (of Gateshead, Durham):
Anne, Mrs. (b. 1820), **5:** 211 n.*339*
Edith Anne (b. 1856), **5:** 211 n.*339*
Ethel N. (b. 1861), **5:** 211 n.*339*
Hugh Lee (b. 1853), **5:** 211 n.*339*
Joseph Walter (b. 1850), **5:** 211 n.*339*
Margaret (b. 1846?), **5:** 211 n.*339*
Norman P. (b. 1862), **5:** 211 n.*339*
Victoria (b. 1844), **5:** 211 n.*339*
William Watson, Mr. (b. 1814) – chemical engineer, **5:** 211 n.*339*
Pattinson, Mrs., **1:** 26; **2:** 90 n.*181*
Pattison (of Lincoln College, Oxford):
Emilia Frances née Strong (1840-1904), **4:** 77 n.*26*, 146 n.*129*, 151
Mark (1813-1884) – rector of Lincoln College, **2:** 39 n.*78*; **4:** 146 n.*129*, 161, 162 n.*154*
Pattison (of Paddington, London):
Francis Winn, Mr. (b. 1834) – clerk to HM Customs, **7:** 424 n.*707*
Jane C. (b. 1827) – sister, **7:** 424 n.*707*
Margaret A., Mrs. (b. 1834), **7:** 424 n.*707*
Paul, Dolben, Rev. (b. 1833), **3:** 154 n.*225*; **7:** 329 n.*585*
Paul (of London):
Howard, Mr. (1830-1905) – entertainer, **3:** 103 n.*151*, 146
Isabella Featherstone, Mrs. (1833-1879) – singer, **3:** 103 n.*151*, 146
Paul, Louis Joseph Jerôme (b. 1864), Prince Napoleon, **7:** 543 n.*876*
Paul Ferroll (bk. Caroline Clive), **3:** 82, 83 n.*128*, 145
Paul Jones (dr. Henry Farnie), **8:** 589 n.*939*
Paul Pry (dr. Douglas Jerrold), **8:** 574 n.*916*
Paulton (of Granby Street, St. Pancras, London):
Edward (1866-1939) – dramatist, **9:** 16 n.*13*
Harry (1842-1917) – actor and dramatist, **7:** 540 n.*873*; **8:** 26 n.*26*; **9:** 16 n.*13*
Pavy, Frederick William, Dr. (1829-1911) – physician, **6:** 467 n.*768*
Paw Clawdian (dr. Francis Burnand), **8:** 112, 113 n.*184*
Paxton, Francis Valentine (b. 1836) – undergraduate at Christ Church,

1: 87, 88 n.*91*, 96
Paxton, Sydney (1860-1930) – actor, **8:** 478 n.*774*
Payne (of London):
Frederick (1841-1880) – entertainer and clown, **6:** 112 n.*174*
Harry (1831-1895) – entertainer and clown, **6:** 112 n.*174*
Payne, George – pupil at St. Aldates, **2:** 30
Payne, John W. Howard (1792-1852) – dramatist and poet, **2:** 21 n.*39*; **5:** 225, 226 n.*359*
Payne Smith (of Christ Church, Oxford):
Robert, Dr. (1819-1895) – professor of divinity, **4:** 134, 135 n.*112*; **5:** 197, 200 n.*324*; **7:** 189, 239 n.*441*, 440, 446, 490
William Henry (1852-1944) – lecturer, **6:** 440 n.*722*
Peabody, George (1795-1869) – philanthropist, **5:** 252, 253 n.*415*
Peace Concluded (pic. John Millais), **2:** 75 n.*151*
Pearce, Ethel Muriel (b. 1880) – friend of the Salweys, **9:** 344 n.*550*
Pearce, Mr. – singer, **3:** 10 n.*7*
"Pearl" in *Living Miniatures*, **5:** 203
Pearse, Beachamp Kerr Warren, Rev. (b. 1836), **5:** 99 n.*156*, 100
Pearson, Edward, Dr. (1756-1811) – writer, **5:** 103 n.*160*
Pearson (of Funtington, Sussex):
George Frederick, Rev. (b. 1825), **6:** 228 n.*360*, 230, 235
Mrs., **6:** 230, 235
Pearson, John (1613-1686) – bishop of Chester, **2:** 117 n.*223*
Pearson, Miss – friend of the Ogilvies, **4:** 71
Pearson, Phillippa (Mrs. A. Cyril) – composer, **7:** 467 n.*767*
Peel, Adelaide Frances Isabella, Lady (1836-1917), **6:** 42
Peel (of Easthampstead Park, Wokingham, Berkshire):
Caroline Susan Mary née Stapleton (1847-1916), **6:** 87, 88 n.*131*
Cecil Lennox, Lt. Col. (1830-1910) – army officer, **6:** 87, 88 n.*131*
Peel (of Lewisham, Kent):
Ellen (b. 1843), **8:** 202 n.*345*
Mary (b. 1841), **8:** 202 n.*345*
Peel (of Westlea, Broxbourne, Hertfordshire):
Fanny Agatha Louisa (1868-1915), **6:** 339 n.*564*
Georgiana Adelaide, Lady (d. 1922), **6:** 339 n.*564*
Peel, James (1811-1906) – artist, **2:** 75 n.*151*
Peel, Robert, Sir (1788-1850) – prime minister, **1:** 16
Peerage and Baronetage (bk. Bernard Burke), **1:** 10
Peet (of Shanklin, Isle of Wight):
Henry "Harry" Herbert (b. 1868), **6:** 341 n.*567*
Mrs. née Giraud, see Dabbs
Pember (of Stockwell, Surrey):
Edward Henry (1833-1911), **2:** 45 n.*90*, 48; **3:** 76, 82; **6:** 248 n.*394*, 250; **7:** 146 n.*275*
Frederick (b. 1838), **4:** 57

Pemberton (of India):
Annie G. (b. 1866), **6:** 418 n.*685*, 421, 422
Bobbie (b. 1868?), **6:** 418 n.*685*, 421, 422
Catherine "Katie" (b. 1865), **6:** 417, 418 n.*685*, 421, 422
Evelyn (b. 1863?), **6:** 417, 418 n.*685*, 421, 422
Pembroke College, **3:** 60; **4:** 71, 83 n.*36*, 195, 321, 340; **5:** 150, 152; **6:** 91, 295; **8:** 149, 214, 517, 603; **9:** 72, 111, 231, 233, 247, 318
Pender, John (1815-1896) – MP and pioneer of submarine telegraphy, **4:** 301
Pendulum machine – for drawing curves, **7:** 35
Penley, W. S. (1853-1912) – actor, **7:** 313 n.*559*
Penmorfa, Llandudno, **4:** 215 n.*228*
Pennie, Misses – school mistresses, **3:** 115, 116 n.*162*
Penny (of Russia; and Rotherfield, Sussex):
Elizabeth T., Mrs. (b. 1843), **5:** 306, 317, 325, 335, 336
Robert George, Rev. (1838-1912), **5:** 302 n.*471*, 305, 314, 315, 317, 325, 332, 335, 336; **8:** 280 n.*470*
Penrith, Cumberland, **2:** 89, 97; **3:** 119, 145
Pepper, John Henry (1821-1900) – illusionist, **6:** 271 n.*438*; **7:** 299 n.*542*
Peppercorn, Mr. – solicitor, **6:** 474
Pepper-ghost principle, **6:** 271 n.*438*; **7:** 299 n.*542*
Perceval (of Eccleston Square, London):
Charles Spencer, Mr. (1829-1889) – civil servant, **7:** 444 n.*734*
Dudley (b. 1875), **7:** 444 n.*734*
Edith (b. 1872), **7:** 444 n.*734*
Edward (b. 1877), **7:** 444 n.*734*
Margaret "Margie" (b. 1871), **7:** 444 n.*734*
Mary Elinor Vere née O'Brien (b. 1840), **7:** 444 n.*734*
Percival, Alice (b. 1861) – friend of the Woodhouses, **7:** 220 n.*403*
Percival (of Trinity College, Oxford):
John, Rev. (1834-1918) – President of Trinity College, **7:** 222, 223 n.*408*, 225, 272, 371
Louisa, Mrs. (b. 1831), **7:** 223 n.*408*, 225
Percy (of Albury Park, near Guildford, Surrey):
Alan Ian (1880-1930), **9:** 304 n.*483*, 353 n.*565*
Edith Cambell née Douglas, Lady (d. 1913), **6:** 80 n.*117*; **9:** 304 n.*483*
Eustace Sutherland Campbell (1887-1958), **9:** 304 n.*483*
Henry George, Lord (1846-1918), Baron Warkworth, Earl Percy, **6:** 80 n.*117*; **9:** 123 n.*215*, 267 n.*423*, 304 n.*483*, 353
James (1885-1903), **9:** 304 n.*483*
Mary (1878-1965), **9:** 304 n.*483*
Muriel Evelyn Nora (1890-1956), **9:** 304 n.*483*, 354 n.*567*
William Richard (1882-1963), **9:** 304 n.*483*
Percy (of Alnwick Castle, Northumberland):
Algernon George, Lord (1810-1899), 6th Duke of Northumberland,

6: 80 n.*117*, 162; **9:** 304 n.*483*
Henry George (1846-1918), see above
Louisa née Drummond, Lady (d. 1890), **6:** 80 n.*117*; **9:** 304 n.*483*
Percy, Hugh, Lord (d. 1786), formerly Smithson, 1st Earl Percy, **2:** 62
"Percy Martindale" (in *Heartsease*), **2:** 57 n.*115*
Perfect (of Lewes, Sussex):
Amy Sophia (1875-1960), **9:** 208 n.*337*, 274
Annie (b. 1866), **9:** 274 n.*436*
Arthur Pearson, Rev. (1838-1910), **9:** 208 n.*337*
Beatrice (b. 1862), **9:** 274 n.*436*
Edith (b.1869), **9:** 274 n.*436*
Fanny Maria née Pemberton (b. 1838), **9:** 208 n.*337*
Mildred (b. 1871), **9:** 274 n.*436*
Perfection (dr. Thomas Bayly), **5:** 221 n.*351*
Perth, Scotland, **3:** 94, 97, 144; **6:** 184
Perugini, Kate née Dickens (1839-1929) – artist, **7:** 533 n.*863*; **8:** 199 n.*338*
Petch (of Wellington Square, Oxford):
Agnes (b. 1861), **8:** 472 n.*766*
Anne, Mrs. (b. 1836), **8:** 472 n.*766*
Gertrude M. (b. 1867), **8:** 472 n.*766*
Henrietta (b. 1863), **8:** 472 n.*766*
Katharine (b. 1859), **8:** 472 n.*766*
Peterborough, Northamptonshire, **6:** 24, 26, 106
Peterhof, Russia, **5:** 293, 296
Peters (of Oxford):
Brenda Mary (1885-1922), **9:** 78 n.*145*, 250
Frank Hesketh, Mr. (1849-1900) – lecturer in classics, **9:** 78 n.*145*
Maud Radcliffe née Urlin, **9:** 78 n.*145*
Phyllis Maud (1882-1953), **9:** 78 n.*145*
Peters (of Lympston, Devon):
Eleanor Jane, **4:** 94 n.*52*
Florence Mary, **4:** 94 n.*52*
Frances Lucy (d. 1856), **4:** 94 n.*52*
Harriet Amy Blackburne, **4:** 94 n.*52*
Mary Jane née Levy (b. 1817), **4:** 94 n.*52*
William Henry, Mr. (1814-1896) – magistrate, **4:** 94 n.*52*
Petersburg, see St. Petersburg
Petersen (of India):
Hamilton Frances née Henderson (b. 1872), **7:** 144 n.*267*, 148, 190, 191 n.*354*, 192 n.*357*, 193 n.*360*, 195, 271 n.*489*, 273 n.*496*, 276 n.*502*, 417, 483; **8:** 105, 217, 557, 564, 593; **9:** 34 n.*60*, 145, 228
James Christopher Delphin, Mr., **9:** 34 n.*60*
Petersfield, Hampshire, **6:** 355
Petherick, John (1814-1882) – civil servant, **4:** 34
Petrovski Monastery, Moscow, **5:** 302

Petrovski Palace, Moscow, **5:** 314
Petrovski Park, Moscow, **5:** 333
Pet's Pet, The (pic. James Sant), **2:** 75 n.*151*
Pettitt, Henry (1848-1893) – dramatist, **9:** 213 n.*341*
Pevensey, Sussex, **8:** 236; **9:** 15, 24, 220, 330
Pharaoh's Handmaidens (pic. John Collier), **7:** 539 n.*872*
Phelps (of Camberwell, Surrey):
  Annie M. H. (b. 1867), **7:** 207 n.*385*
  Beatrice "Bertie" C. J. (b. 1869), **7:** 207 n.*385*, 213
  Ethel (b. 1880), **7:** 207 n.*385*
  Florence Ada (b. 1874), **7:** 207 n.*385*
  Frederick G. M. (b. 1871), **7:** 207 n.*385*
  Harriet, Mrs. (b. 1844), **7:** 207 n.*385*
  Philip George, Mr. (b. 1843) - surgeon, **7:** 207 n.*385*
Phelps, Samuel (1804-1878) – actor-manager, **4:** 281 n.*331*; **5:** 24 n.*21*
Philaret, Vasilii Drosdov (1782-1867), metropolitan archbishop of Moscow, **5:** 316 n.*489*, 319
Phillimore, Robert, Sir (1810-1885) – judge, **7:** 24 n.*27*
Phillips (of Hambledon, Surrey):
  Ellen Sarah, Mrs. (b. 1832), **9:** 235 n.*371*
  Miss, **9:** 235 n.*371*
  Richard, Rev. (b. 1832), **9:** 235 n.*371*
Phillips, John (b. 1794) – solicitor, **7:** 302, 303 n.*547*
Phillips, John, Prof. (1800-1874) – geologist, **5:** 165 n.*273*
Phillips, Kate (1856-1931) – actress, **8:** 374 n.*616*, 428
Phillips, Miss, **7:** 66 n.*106*
Phillpotts, Henry, Rt. Rev. (1778-1869) – bishop of Exeter, **6:** 98 n.*154*
Phillpotts, Henry John, Rev. (b. 1834), **9:** 41, 42 n.*72*
Philosophical Essays (bk. Dugald Stewart), **1:** 74 n.*67*
Philosophical Essays on Various Subjects (bk. Isaac Watts), **1:** 76 n.*72*
Philosophy of the Active and Moral Powers, The (bk. Dugald Stewart), **1:** 74 n.*67*
Philothespian Society (OUDS), **8:** 68, 69 n.*111*
Philpott (of Avon Dassett, Warwickshire):
  Alice Ethel Janet (b. 1879), **7:** 217 n.*398*
  Anne née Farmer, Mrs. (b. 1842), **7:** 215, 216, 217 n.*398*, 288
  Frederick G. F. (b. 1875), **7:** 217 n.*398*
  Irene C. (b. 1878), **7:** 217 n.*398*
  Mary Louisa (b. 1878), **7:** 217 n.*398*
  Robert G. K. F. (b. 1876), **7:** 217 n.*398*
  Vaughan Farmer (b. 1873), **7:** 217 n.*398*
  Vaughan Williams, Rev. (1839-1917), **4:** 150 n.*134*, 152; **7:** 215, 216, 217 n.*398*
Philpott, Miss, **7:** 303
Phiz, real name Hablot Knight Browne (1815-1882) – illustrator,

1: 113 n.*132*
Photography, see Dodgson, Charles Lutwidge
Phryne Before The Judges (pic. Jean-Léon Gérôme), **5:** 160 n.*263*
Piccadilly, London, **3:** 133
"Piccard's Rough," Artington, near Guildford, **7:** 344
Piccolomini, Marietta (1834-1899) – singer, **3:** 49, 50 n.*76*, 98 n.*147*
Pickard (of Whitby, Yorkshire):
Adelaide Loftus Joanna (1846-1898), **2:** 103
Ann Adelaide Hippolyta née Harvery, formerly Bainbridge, **2:** 15 n.*25*, 103 n.*199*
George Percy, Capt. RN (1801-1852) – second husband, **2:** 103 n.*199*
Pickard, Henry Adair (b. 1832) – inspector of schools, **1:** 84 n.*88*, 85; **2:** 69 n.*138*; **3:** 35, 45; **4:** 54, 162, 163 n.*156*; **9:** 103 n.*188*
Pickering, Messrs., London – booksellers, **4:** 244, 299
Pickering's Diamond Classics, **2:** 28 n.*55*
Pidcock (of Kensington, London):
Amy (b. 1866), **7:** 355 n.*620*
Elizabeth, Mrs. (b. 1834), **7:** 355 n.*620*; **8:** 27 n.*29*
Mabel (b. 1871), **7:** 355 n.*620*, 361, 368
Millicent, **7:** 355 n.*620*, 361, 368; **8:** 130
Spencer, Mr. (b. 1828) – worked at the Board of Trade, **7:** 355 n.*620*; **8:** 27 n.*29*
Pidgeon, Winter Randell (b. 1860) – undergraduate at Christ Church, **7:** 248 n.*454*
Pierce, Elizabeth (b. 1851) – sextoness, **7:** 363 n.*632*; **9:** 271, 272 n.*430*
Pierpoint (of Eastbourne, Sussex):
Anne née Deare (b. 1811), **7:** 67 n.*109*
Elizabeth G. (b. 1845), **7:** 67 n.*109*
Richard Deare (1838-1929), **7:** 67 n.*109*
Richard William, Rev. (1812-1890), **7:** 67 n.*109*
Pierre, Mr. – singer , **1:** 53
Piggott (of Edgmond, Shropshire):
Catherine, Mrs. (b. 1838), **6:** 387 n.*634*
Charles Francis Corbet, Rev. (b. 1821), **6:** 387 n.*634*
Pigou, Francis, Rev. (1832-1916), **6:** 108 n.*169*, 109
Pigou, see also Le Pigou
Pilgrim's Progress (dr. Louisa MacDonald), **7:** 179, 180 n.*334*, 183, 193, 223, 279, 350
Pimlico, London, **3:** 157
Pimm, Gaius (b. 1835) – grocer, **3:** 63 n.*95*
Pimm, William – house agent, **6:** 57 n.*84*
Pinder, Eva Blanche (b. 1869) – logic pupil, **8:** 300 n.*501*, 301
Pindter, Fraülein – governess, **7:** 399, 400, 512 n.*831*, 513, 518
"Pinehurst," Upper Norwood, London (Smedley), **6:** 157 n.*243*, 179, 198, 205, 209, 219, 284

Pinero, Arthur Wing (1855-1934) – dramatist, **8:** 199 n.*339*, 412 n.*668*, 477 n.*773*, 614 n.*974*; **9:** 15 n.*10*
Pinner, Middlesex, **6:** 334
Pirates of Penzance, The (Gilbert and Sullivan) – operetta, **8:** 161 n.*263*, 164
Pitt, Felix W. (1858-1922) – actor, **9:** 173 n.*290*
Pittar (of Khidderpore, East Indies):
Charles William Erskine (b. 1864), **7:** 492 n.*802*
Kathrine "Kattie" (b. 1869), **7:** 50 n.*78*, 91, 99, 492
Lilian "Lily" (b. 1866), **7:** 50 n.*78*, 91, 99, 492
Margaret "Daisy" (b. 1867), **7:** 50 n.*78*, 91, 99, 492
Mrs., **7:** 49, 50 n.*78*
"Pixies, The," see Dodgson, Charles Lutwidge – Story-telling
Plain Commentary on the Book of Psalms, A (bk. John Burgon), **1:** 59 n.*30*
Plain Commentary on the Four Gospels, A (bk. John Burgon), **1:** 59 n.*30*
Planché, James Robinson (1796-1880) – dramatist, **3:** 12 n.*10*, 120 n.*170*; **4:** 85 n.*39*, 273 n.*318*; **5:** 42 n.*52*, 210 n.*336*
Plane and Spherical Trigonometry (bk. John Snowball), **1:** 65 n.*46*
Planquette, Robert (1851-1903) – composer, **7:** 370 n.*643*; **8:** 569 n.*907*
Playfair, Charles Stuart Macdonald, Rev. (b. 1861), **9:** 311 n.*494*
Playfair, Nigel Ross (1874-1934) – barrister and actor, **9:** 204 n.*333*, 234 n.*369*
Please, have you seen Mother? (pic. Alfred Dever), **5:** 86 n.*134*
Plevna, Turkey, **7:** 88 n.*155*
Plomer (of Chestfield Street, Hanover Square, London):
Helen, Mrs. (b. 1839), **6:** 418, 419, 443, 465; **7:** 234 n.*432*
Laura Isabel (b. 1862), **6:** 412, 413 n.*675*, 416, 418-420, 465; **7:** 234 n.*432*
Plummer (of Heworth, Durham):
Alfred (1841-1926), **5:** 175 n.*291*
Catherine (b. 1839), **5:** 175 n.*291*
Charles (1851-1927), **5:** 175 n.*291*
Emma (b. 1845), **5:** 175 n.*291*
Francis (b. 1843), **5:** 175 n.*291*
Heathcote (b. 1838), **5:** 175 n.*291*
Jane (b. 1848), **5:** 175 n.*291*
Louisa (b. 1835), **5:** 175 n.*291*
Louisa née Powles (b. 1809), **5:** 175 n.*291*
Matthew, Rev. (1809-1898), **5:** 175 n.*291*
Spencer (b. 1837), **5:** 175 n.*291*
Plumptre, Frederick Charles, Dr. (1796-1870) – master of University College, **3:** 121 n.*171*
Pocchini, Carolina – dancer, **3:** 50 n.*76*
Poe, Edgar Allen (1809-1849) – writer and poet, **3:** 83
Poem on Routh, (bk. John Burgon), **1:** 59 n.*30*

Poems (bk. William Bryant), **4:** 24
Poems (bk. William Winter), **7:** 385 n.*665*
Poems, Chiefly Lyrical (bk. Alfred Tennyson), **4:** 299 n.*365*
Poems written for a Child (bk. Menella Smedley and Elizabeth Hart), **6:** 17 n.*14*
Point, The, St. Petersburg, Russia, **5:** 345
Polegate, Sussex, **7:** 133, 134, 458; **8:** 143; **9:** 97, 101, 159, 330
Pollen, John Hungerford (1820-1902) – artist, **3:** 26 n.*37*

Pollock:
Amy Menella née Dodgson (1842-1922) – cousin, **1:** 106 n.*120*, 107; **2:** 24, 51 n.*102*, 80, 81, 110 n.*214*; **5:** 123 n.*197*, 170, 211; **6:** 16 n.*12*, 19, 20, 223 n.*351*, 361; **7:** 127; **8:** 125 n.*201*
Charles Edward, Sir (1823-1897), judge – husband of cousin, **2:** 110 n.*214*; **5:** 123 n.*197*, 158, 170, 211; **6:** 16 n.*12*, 19, 20, 223 n.*351*; **7:** 20, 21 n.*18*, 22, 80, 120 n.*226*, 121, 122 n.*229*, 127, 224; **8:** 125 n.*201*; **9:** 77 n.*142*
Charles Stewart (b. 1864), **8:** 125 n.*201*
Ethel Caroline (b. 1877) – second-cousin, **9:** 62 n.*114*
George Hume (1870-1924) – second-cousin, **2:** 110 n.*214*
Helen (b. 1868) – second-cousin, **8:** 319 n.*524*
Herbert Charles (b. 1852), **6:** 20 n.*20*, 385; **7:** 224 n.*411*
Isabel Amy (b. 1867) – second-cousin, **8:** 319 n.*524*
Joanna de Morlot (1863-1949), **4:** 180; **5:** 123 n.*197*, 158, 170 n.*282*; **6:** 223, 485; **8:** 125; **9:** 77 n.*142*
Kate (b. 1872) – second-cousin, **8:** 319 n.*524*
Margaret Agnata née Harington (b. 1871) – wife of second-cousin, **2:** 110 n.*214*
Margaret Homera (b. 1879) – second-cousin, **9:** 62 n.*114*
Robert (b. 1874) – second-cousin, **9:** 77 n.*142*
William Rivers (1859-1909) – the judge's nephew, **7:** 120 n.*226*, 127

Pollock, Florence E. (b. 1858) – niece of Mrs. Blakemore, **8:** 122 n.*195*
Pollock, Mrs. née McAlpine Lenny, **8:** 241 n.*405*
Polwhele, Mrs., alias Miss Esmond, **9:** 165 n.*282*, 166, 168, 170
Polyeuctus (dr. Pierre Corneille), **7:** 473 n.*776*
Polytechnic (Royal), London, **3:** 13, 52; **6:** 457 n.*752*, 465, 467; **7:** 42, 43 n.*64*
Ponsonby, Eustace (d. 1924) – dramatist, **8:** 478 n.*774*; **9:** 274 n.*435*
Ponti, H., see Collis
Poole, Alfred, Rev. (b. 1826), **4:** 11

Poole:

Poole (of East Bergholt, Essex):
Alice Henrietta (b. 1844) – distant cousin, **4:** 124 n.*97*, 189; **6:** 198, 294; **7:** 12 n.*4*; **8:** 499
Arthur (1841-1900) – distant cousin, **4:** 124 n.*97*; **5:** 211 n.*338*; **6:** 198
Isabella née Hume (1812-1873) – second cousin, **2:** 106; **4:** 124 n.*97*, 189, 190
Margaret "Meta" Frances (1842-1907) – distant cousin, **4:** 124 n.*97*, 189; **5:** 179 n.*296*; **6:** 157 n.*243*, 198; **7:** 12 n.*4*; **8:** 282 n.*472*, 310, 311, 439, 453, 499; **9:** 120 n.*208*
Reginald (b. 1853) – distant cousin, **4:** 124 n.*97*
Skeffington, Col. (1803-1876) – second cousin, **2:** 106; **4:** 124 n.*97*, 128 n.*102*, 187, 189, 190; **5:** 179 n.*296*
Poole (of Stanmore, Middlesex):
Anna (1805-1894) – second cousin, **2:** 96 n.188; **4:** 124 n.*97*
Charles, Mr. (1758-1838) – great-uncle, **1:** 102 n.*112*; **2:** 96 n.188, 105 n.*203*; **4:** 124 n.*97*
Edward (1810-1884) – second cousin, **7:** 28 n.*36*
Henrietta Octavia née Lutwidge (1778-1848) – great-aunt, **1:** 102 n.*112*; **2:** 96 n.*188*, 105 n.*203*; **4:** 124 n.*97*
Henry (1808-1878) – second cousin, see below
Mary (1817-1892) – second cousin, **2:** 96 n.188; **4:** 124 n.*97*; **7:** 211 n.*394*
Skeffington (1803-1876) – second cousin, see above
Poole (of Farfield, Cheshire):
Catherine Lucy (b. 1846) – distant cousin, **2:** 105 n.*203*; **4:** 124 n.*97*
Elizabeth née Noad (1819-1849) – wife of second cousin, **2:** 105 n.*203*; **4:** 124 n.*97*
Henrietta Elizabeth (1842-1881) – distant cousin, **4:** 124 n.*97*
Henry, Mr. (1808-1878) – second cousin, **1:** 102 n.*112*; **2:** 96 n.188, 105 n.*203*; **4:** 124 n.*97*
Henry Skeffington (b. 1844) – distant cousin, see below
Isabel Mary (1840-1868) – distant cousin, **4:** 124 n.*97*
Margaret Ellen (b. 1848) – distant cousin, **2:** 105 n.*203*; **4:** 124 n.*97*; **7:** 211 n.*394*
Mary Annie (b. 1853) – distant cousin, **7:** 211 n.*394*
Poole (of Stoke, near Guildford, Surrey):
Florence Hope Grant née Grey (1849-1923) – wife of distant cousin, **4:** 124 n.*97*
Henry Skeffington, Mr. (b. 1844) – distant cousin, **4:** 124 n.*97*

Poole, Cora – actress, **8:** 614 n.*974*
Poole (of Beaumont Street, Oxford):
Dorothy Joy (1882-1947), **9:** 259 n.*409*, 267, 268, 280

Rachel Emily née Malleson (1860-1937), **9:** 259 n.*409*, 268, 284, 299
Reginald Lane, Mr. (1857-1939) – lecturer, **9:** 259 n.*409*, 268
Poole, Elizabeth (1820-1906) – singer, **3:** 82 n.*127*
Poole, John (1786-1872) – dramatist, **4:** 309 n.*384*; **5:** 85 n.*133*
Poor Piano (dr. Richard Corney Grain), **9:** 88 n.*159*
Poor Pillicoddy (dr. John Morton), **6:** 104; **7:** 158 n.*296*
Pope, Cecilia Mary née Tennyson (1859-1918), **7:** 271 n.*487*; **8:** 178 n.*293*, 191, 196, 271, 272
Pope, Estrella – friend of the Arnolds, **6:** 430
Pope, The, **1:** 49; **2:** 64
Popping the Question (dr. John Buckstone), **5:** 51, 52 n.*72*
Port Admiral, The (dr. Thomas Bowles), **4:** 318 n.*401*
Portal (of Albury, near Guildford, Sussex):
George Raymond, Rev. (b. 1827), **6:** 45 n.*63*, 46, 49, 170, 243
Helen Mary Charlotte née Daubez (b. 1831), **6:** 45 n.*63*, 170, 243
Porter, Richard Ibbetson, Rev. (1837-1896), **5:** 134 n.*216*
Porter's Knot, The (dr. John Oxenford), **9:** 84 n.*152*
Portinscale, Cumberland, **2:** 90, 94-5, 96 n.*187*; **3:** 115
Portland Place, London, **2:** 123
Port Meadow, Oxford, **4:** 203, 212 n.*223*
Portsea Pier, Portsea, Hampshire, **6:** 485
Portsmouth, Hampshire, **6:** 297, 342, 358, 361, 422, 479, 481-485
Postford House, Chilworth, Surrey (Pares family), **6:** 171 n.*267*, 225
Post Office, London, **3:** 132 n.*192*; **6:** 48 n.*68*, 58
Potsdam, Germany, **5:** 272, 273
Pott (of Abingdon, Berkshire):
Alfred, Rev. (b. 1822) – Archdeacon of Berkshire, **2:** 73 n.*147*; **7:** 262 n.*473*
Alfred V. (b. 1874), **7:** 262 n.*473*
Alice (b. 1875), **7:** 262 n.*473*
Emily A., **7:** 262 n.*473*
Emily H., Mrs. (b. 1835), **7:** 262 n.*473*
George S. (1871), **7:** 262 n.*473*
Mary B. (b. 1859), **7:** 262 n.*473*
Potter, Paul M. (1854-1921) – dramatist, **9:** 212 n.*339*
Potter, Paulus (1625-1654) – artist, **5:** 295 n.*465*
Potts, Miss – governess to the Duchess of Albany's children, **8:** 596
Potts, Robert (1805-1885) – mathematician, **4:** 49
Poutiatine, Eugene, Count (d. 1909), **5:** 338, 348
Powell (of The Limes, Clapton, Middlesex):
Angela (b. 1826), **4:** 227 n.*251*; **5:** 23 n.*20*
Caroline "Carrie" Chase (b. 1832), **4:** 227 n.*251*, 255 n.*294*, 256 n.*295*; **5:** 23 n.*20*
Charlotte, **4:** 227 n.*251*, 256
Florentia "Flora" (b. 1830), **4:** 227 n.*251*; **5:** 23 n.*20*

George Holt (1825-1890), see below
James, Mr. (1786-1877) – leather merchant, **4:** 225, 227 n.*251*, 256; **5:** 23 n.*20*
Louisa (1822-1902), see MacDonald
Phoebe (b. 1820?), **4:** 227 n.*251*; **5:** 23 n.*20*
Phoebe née Sharman – second wife, **4:** 227 n.*251*
Powell (of Sharow Lodge, Yorkshire):
Anna Catherine (1841-1911), **4:** 233 n.*259*, 235 n.*262*
Constance – niece, **4:** 233 n.*259*, 235 n.*262*
Louisa Burnaby née Greene (1804-1892), **4:** 233 n.*259*; **5:** 43 n.*55*
Samuel Hopper, Rev. (1805-1902), **4:** 233 n.*259*; **5:** 43 n.*55*
Powell, Frederick York (1850-1904) – lecturer, **7:** 519 n.*841*; **8:** 202 n.*344*, 296, 306
Powell (of Cedar Lawn, Hampstead, London)
George Holt, Mr. (1825-1890) – leather merchant, **4:** 227 n.*251*; **5:** 23 n.*20*
Mary Louisa (b. 1852?), **4:** 227 n.*251*; **5:** 23 n.*20*
Matilda Maynard "May" (b. 1858), **4:** 181, 227 n.*251*; **5:** 23 n.*20*
Powell (of Piccard's Rough, Artington, near Guildford, Surrey):
Mary Elizabeth (b. 1854), **7:** 343, 344 n.*601*
Theodora W. (b. 1871), **7:** 343, 344 n.*601*
Thomas W., Mr. (b. 1819) – stockbroker, **7:** 343, 344 n.*601*
Power (of Bramley, Surrey):
Alice J. (b. 1861), **8:** 452 n.*723*
Blanche S. M. (b. 1855), **8:** 452 n.*723*
Henry Bolton, Rev. (1821-1882), **8:** 452 n.*723*
Katherine M. A. (b. 1856), **8:** 452 n.*723*
Mary (b. 1867), **8:** 452 n.*723*
Mary, Mrs. (b. 1823), **8:** 452 n.*723*, 472; **9:** 179 n.*301*
Maud E. (b. 1859), **8:** 452 n.*723*
Power (of London):
Harold – comic singer, **4:** 139 n.*117*, 153
Tyrone (1797-1841) – actor and dramatist, **4:** 139 n.*117*, 359 n.*468*
Power, Nellie (1855-1887) – actress, **6:** 112 n.*174*
Powers, Hiram (1805-1873) – artist, **7:** 316 n.*563*
Powles, Miss – governess to the Prices of Whitburn, **8:** 353 n.*575*
Powlett, Harry George, Sir (1803-1891), Duke of Cleveland, **7:** 316 n.*564*
Powys (of Cowley Military Barracks, Oxfordshire):
Helen, Mrs. (b. 1845), **7:** 161 n.*302*
Henry, Major (b. 1840) – army officer, **7:** 161 n.*302*
John (b. 1871), **7:** 161 n.*302*
Norah (b. 1873), **7:** 161 n.*302*
Pratt, Alice, **7:** 19 n.*15*
Pratt (of Seal, Kent):
Augusta Georgiana (1845-1908), **7:** 481 n.*782*

Caroline Elizabeth (1839-1929), **7:** 481 n.*782*
Clara Isabella (d. 1930), **7:** 481 n.*782*
Eleanor Margaret (d. 1923), **7:** 481 n.*782*
Elizabeth Louisa (d. 1928), **7:** 481 n.*782*
Frances Sarah Harriet (1837-1917), **7:** 481 n.*782*
George Charles, Lord (1799-1866), 2nd Marquis Camden, **7:** 481 n.*782*
Mary Eleanor Elizabeth (d. 1927), **7:** 481 n.*782*
Theresa Sarah (d. 1924), **7:** 481 n.*782*
Pratt, Jacob Vivour (b. 1857) – undergraduate at Christ Church, **7:** 370 n.*644*, 372
Prayer in the Storm, The (dr. Benjamin Webster), **6:** 379 n.*621*
Preciosa (Weber) – opera, **3:** 70 n.*110*
Preedy, Charles, Rev. (b. 1855), **8:** 254 n.*428*
Prendergast, Thomas (1806-1886) – linguist, **7:** 41 n.*62*, 351 n.*613*; **8:** 293 n.*491*
Pre-Raphaelites, **3:** 26 n.*37*, 33 n.*51*, 68 n.*106*, 78
Pre-Raphaelitism (bk. Edward Young), **3:** 44 n.*70*, 45, 145
Prescott, Emily – neighbour of Henry Taylor, **4:** 127 n.*100*
Prescott, William (b. 1864) – headmaster, **9:** 345 n.*553*
Press, The, **5:** 11, 12 n.*2*
Prestel, Messrs. – agent for artists, **6:** 439
Pretty Baa-Lambs (pic. Ford Madox Brown), **5:** 15 n.*6*
Price (of Norham Gardens, Oxford):
Agnes Florence, **4:** 179; **6:** 303 n.*501*
Bonamy, Prof. (1807-1888) – professor of political economy, **2:** 72 n.*146*; **6:** 209, 303 n.*501*, 320 n.*532*, 487; **7:** 83 n.*140*, 239, 377, 432, 531, 535; **8:** 154 n.*253*
Lydia née Rose (b. 1812), **6:** 303 n.*501*, 320 n.*532*, 427 n.*703*, 487; **7:** 83 n.*140*, 239, 377, 432, 535; **8:** 154 n.*253*
Rosie, **7:** 97
Price (of St. Giles', Oxford):
Alice Margaret (1863-1945), **6:** 144, 273 n.*444*; **7:** 163
Amy Eliza née Cole (1835-1909), **4:** 69, 70 n.*12*, 147, 148, 151, 152 n.*137*, 309; **5:** 52 n.*72*, 147, 187; **6:** 205 n.*319*, 209, 301, 327, 336, 354, 487, 489; **7:** 81 n.*137*, 163, 260, 334; **8:** 195 n.*330*; **9:** 72, 73 n.*133*, 111 n.*196*, 231-233, 247, 298, 300, 318
Amy Maud (1858-1923), **4:** 297 n.*360*; **6:** 144, 209, 276, 278, 487; **7:** 81 n.*137*
Bartholomew, Prof. (1818-1898) – professor of natural philosophy, **1:** 48, 49, 54 n.*13*, 57 n.*22*, 58, 59 n.*28*, 60, 63, 64 n.*41*, 67, 69, 70, 74, 91, 95 n.*98*, 110 n.*128*; **2:** 28 n.*54*, 48, 114, 115 n.*221*,116, 129; **3:** 41 n.*63*, 58 n.*89*, 60, 67; **4:** 49, 66 n.*3*, 69, 70 n.*12*, 114, 116, 134, 147, 148, 150, 151, 260; **5:** 51 n.*71*, 112 n.*176*, 133 n.*212*, 147, 149, 187, 235, 370 n.*548*; **6:** 35, 36, 133, 200, 301, 327, 336, 354, 489; **7:** 81 n.*137*, 163, 165, 260, 334; **8:** 195 n.*330*, 247, 387; **9:** 71 n.*130*, 72, 73 n.*133*,

111 n.*196*, 113 n.*198*, 232, 233, 298, 300, 310 n.*493*, 318
Elinor "Nellie" Rokeby (1868-1956), **9:** 73 n.*133*
Mary Eliza Mabel (1862-1940), **6:** 143, 144, 276, 278
Rose Emelyn (1866-1894), **6:** 144
William Arthur (1860-1954), **4:** 297 n.*360*; **6:** 273 n.*444*
Price (of Sunderland, Durham):
Catherine née Lucette (d. 1892) – actress, **5:** 42 n.*52*
Morton (1824-1876), alias Capt. Horton Rhys (or Reece) – actor and manager, **5:** 42 n.*52*
Price, Charles James Coverly (b. 1838) – mathematical lecturer at Balliol, **4:** 150, 151 n.*136*
Price (of Romford, Essex):
Frances M., Mrs. (b. 1844), **8:** 353 n.*575*
George Frederick, Rev. (1831-1901), **8:** 353 n.*575*
Hamilton (b. 1875), **8:** 353 n.*575*
Sybil (b. 1873), **8:** 353 n.*575*
Wykeham (b. 1880), **8:** 353 n.*575*
Price (of Christ Church, Oxford):
Maude (b. 1857), **4:** 278 n.*326*; **5:** 20
William (1831-1901) – chaplain and schoolmaster, **4:** 278 n.*326*
Price, William Lake (1810-1891) – artist and photographer, **2:** 19 n.*33*
Prichard, James Edward, Dr. (1849-1901) – physician, **8:** 89 n.*143*
Prickett, Mary (1833-1916), see Foster
Pride and Prejudice (bk. Jane Austen), **8:** 15 n.*9*
Priestess of Juno (James Westmacott) – sculpture, **6:** 14 n.*8*
Primrose (of Dalmeny Park, Edinburgh, Scotland):
Archibald Philip (1847-1929), Viscount Dalmeny, 5th Lord Rosebery, **5:** 48 n.*63*; **9:** 152 n.*262*, 156, 255
Hannah née de Rothschild (d. 1890), **9:** 152 n.*262*
Margaret "Peggy" Etrenne Hannah (1881-1967), **9:** 152 n.*262*, 156, 255
Sybil Myra Caroline (1879-1955), **9:** 152 n.*262*, 156, 255
Primrose Day, **8:** 188
Prince Camaralzaman (dr. Henry Bellingham and William Best), **5:** 117 n.*182*
Prince for an Hour, A (dr. John Morton), **2:** 83 n.*163*
Prince Karl (dr. A. C. Gunter), **8:** 440 n.*705*
Princess, The; A Medley (bk. Alfred Tennyson), **2:** 121 n.*234*; **4:** 354 n.*461*
Princess Primrose (dr. Henry Bellingham and William Best), **5:** 145 n.*232*
Principles of Comedy and Dramatic Effect, The (bk. Percy Fitzgerald), **6:** 242
Principles of Harmony and Contrast of Colours and their Applications to the Arts, The (bk. Michel Chevreul), **1:** 54 n.*12*
Principles of Moral and Political Philosophy (bk. William Paley), **3:** 156 n.*230*
Pringle (of Guildford, Surrey):

Bertie, **9:** 303 n.*481*
Isabel, Mrs. (b. 1863), **9:** 303 n.*481*
Prinsep (of Little Holland House, Kensington, London):
Henry Thoby, Mr. (1792-1878) – Indian civil servant, **4:** 334 n.*431*, 336
Valentine Cameron (1838-1904) – artist, **3:** 26 n.*37*
Pritchard, G. – actor, **9:** 20 n.*22*
Pritchard (of Stanmore, Shropshire):
Jane née Gordon, **6:** 87, 88 n.*131*
John, Mr. (b. 1796) – barrister, **6:** 87, 88 n.*131*
Probert, Edward, Rev. (1830?-1891?) – chaplain, **6:** 81 n.*118*, 162, 163 n.*252*
Proceedings of The Royal Society, **5:** 152 n.*246*
Proctor, John (fl. 1879-83) – artist, **6:** 59 n.*89*
Proctor, Mr. – marshal at court, **7:** 21 n.*18*, 22
Professor's Love-Story, The (dr. James M. Barrie), **9:** 225, 226 n.*357*, 230, 243
Prometheus Unbound (bk. Percy B. Shelley), **1:** 53 n.*10*
Proportional Representation Society, **8:** 158, 162, 163 n.*265*
Proscribed Christmas, The (pic. Thomas Heaphy), **6:** 22, 23 n.*23*
Prosperous Days of Job, The (pic. William Dobson), **2:** 75 n.*151*
Prout, Thomas Jones, Rev. (1823-1909), **2:** 27 n.*53*, 66 n.*131*, 125; **3:** 35, 168 n.*243*; **4:** 54, 76 n.*24*, 143 n.*124*; **5:** 26, 27 n.*27*, 48, 49 n.*65*, 50 n.*67*, 246; **6:** 305, 331, 368, 389; **7:** 33, 173, 175, 189, 225, 239, 242, 247, 341, 342, 419, 424, 440, 446, 490, 499, 531; **8:** 11 n.*1*, 54, 252; **9:** 133 n.*234*, 232, 268 n.*424*, 286, 322
Psamathe (pic. Frederick Leighton), **7:** 188 n.*350*
"Psycho" – magic trick, **6:** 468 n.*769*
Publisher's Circular, The, **5:** 11, 12 n.*2*
"Puck" (in *Midsummer Night's Dream*), **2:** 124
Puckle (of Stoke, near Guildford, Surrey):
Louisa H. (b. 1861), **9:** 291 n.*457*, 293, 306, 345
Mr., **9:** 291 n.*457*
Puckle (of Camberwell, Surrey):
Matilda H., Mrs. (b. 1831), **7:** 345
Robert A. (b. 1823) – legal officer, **7:** 344 n.*602*, 345
Puffendorf, Samuel von, Baron (1632-1694) – historian, **5:** 269 n.*436*
Pugni, Cesare (1805-1870) – composer, **3:** 50 n.*76*
Punch, **1:** 112 n.*130*, 113, 116, 117 n.*142*; **2:** 14 n.*20*, 34; **3:** 31 n.*46*, 53 n.*80*; **4:** 59; **5:** 140, 141 n.*225*, 254 n.*420*; **6:** 21, 477; **8:** 147, 169 n.*283*
Purey-Cust, William Arthur, Rev. (1855-1938), **8:** 492 n.*796*
Purvis, K. E., Miss (b. 1847), **7:** 135 n.*250*
Purvis, Rose "Queenie" Lilian, alias Adele Lebra (b. 1880?), **8:** 527 n.*844*, 528-530, 536
Pusey (of Christ Church, Oxford):

Edward Bouverie, Dr. (1800-1882) – professor of Hebrew, **1:** 45; **4:** 10, 82 n.*35*, 88, 150, 151, 163, 164 n.*158*, 201 n.*208*; **5:** 154 n.*249*, 197; **6:** 119 n.*182*, 150; **7:** 236 n.*436*, 440, 471 n.*775*

Philip Edward (1830-1880), **7:** 236 n.*436*

Pusey, Henry Bouverie, Lt. (1837-1869) – army officer, **2:** 29 n.*56*

Pusey House, Oxford, **9:** 314

Puss in Boots (dr. Anon), **6:** 444 n.*729*

Putney, Surrey, **1:** 106; **2:** 23, 24, 50, 79, 81 n.*159*, 82 n.*161*, 83, 123; **3:** 80, 132, 139, 140, 173; **4:** 86, 122, 124, 224, 314, 323, 324, 339, 340, 343; **5:** 65, 95, 97, 99, 123, 157, 170, 211; **6:** 15, 19, 74, 165, 223, 284, 352, 385, 389

Puzzles and Games:

142857 puzzle, **9:** 339 n.*542*, 343

Addition-sum Trick, **2:** 40; **9:** 269

Chess, **4:** 61

Court Circular – card game, **4:** 26, 59

Crocodile Dilemma, **9:** 149 n.*256*

Easter-Day Rule, **9:** 307 n.*487*

Elephant-hunters, **4:** 60

Fifteen Game, **7:** 270 n.*485*

Five Apples – problem, **9:** 316, 317

Froggy's Problem – logic puzzle, **9:** 275 n.*439*

Great-grandsons - problem, **9:** 295 n.*468*

Hare and Hounds – game, **6:** 316

Hendrik, Elias, and the Pigs Problem, **9:** 112 n.*197*

Home-Rule Puzzle, **9:** 89 n.*161*

Lying Problems, **9:** 147, 148 n.*254*, 216, 278

Meryls (Nine Men's Morris), **6:** 97 n.*151*, 389, 421; **7:** 467; **8:** 421; **9:** 127, 177, 205, 347

Money-sum – problem, **9:** 176 n.*296*, 343

Monkey and Weight Problem, **9:** 111 n.*196*, 113 n.*198*, 115 n.*200*

Nine-Trick, **2:** 36, 37 n.*73*

Number-guessing, **9:** 187 n.*308*, 189, 236, 237 n.*374*, 239, 299

Number-repeating, **9:** 293

Pack of Cards – puzzle, **9:** 176, 317

Peg Meryl – game, **9:** 37

Properties of 9 – puzzle, **9:** 338

Puss in the Corner, **6:** 73

Railway game invented at Croft Rectory, **1:** 18, 25

Right-angled Triangles – problem, **9:** 354 n.*566*

Roman Multiplication, **2:** 33 n.*67*

Saying unseen digits, **9:** 269

Sixes and Sevens – game, **6:** 227, 413

Soldier, Monkey, and Nuts – problem, **9:** 112 n.*197*

Sympathy – card game, **2:** 45 n.*90*, 48
Thieves and Apples – puzzle, **8:** 195
Three Bridges, **7:** 246 n.*451*
Ural Mountains, **4:** 115 n.*84*
Word Puzzle, **7:** 310, 311 n.*554*

Pygmalion and Galatea (dr. William S. Gilbert), **7:** 23 n.*24*; **8:** 190 n.*320*; **9:** 16 n.*13*
Pym, Mr. & Mrs. – cousins of the Gilliats, **4:** 286
Pyne, Louisa (1829-1904) – singer, **5:** 225
Pyramid, The (dr. Thomas German Read), **4:** 322, 323 n.*409*

Quakers, **3:** 56 n.*85*, 57
"Quarry, The," Shrewsbury, **7:** 126
Quarry Street, Guildford, Sussex, **6:** 56
Quartermain, Mr. – carpenter, **6:** 147 n.*224*, 149
Queen, The, **1:** 82 n.*84*
"Queen Catherine" (in *Henry VIII*), **2:** 22, 83
Queen's College, Oxford, **2:** 77 n.*154*; **6:** 180; **7:** 452; **8:** 544 n.*869*, 603; **9:** 327
Queen's Drive, Edinburgh, **6:** 181
Queen's Gate, London, **7:** 96
Queen's Room, Hatfield House, **6:** 165
"Quil, Sir John" (in Miss Horton's Entertainment), **2:** 108, 109 n.*211*
Quin (of Peckham Road, Camberwell, Surrey):
Alice Mary (1860-1950), **7:** 40 n.*59*; **9:** 59 n.*109*, 84, 85, 87, 205, 289, 316, 331, 335
Constance Helen (1862-1893), see Woods
Elizabeth Menella "Minna" alias Norah O'Neill (1858-1942), **8:** 579 n.*924*, 609, 610, 614-620, 622, 628, 630; **9:** 27, 50 n.*86*, 53-57, 59, 61, 86, 87, 131, 138-140, 146, 147, 156, 157, 167, 168, 172, 173, 203-205, 231-234, 316, 331, 335, 347
Francis Stanistrate Smythe – cousin by marriage, **1:** 113 n.*134*
Isobel "Belle" Barnard (1870-1951), **7:** 40 n.*59*; **8:** 622, 623 n.*986*, 628, 630, 631; **9:** 81, 82 n.*149*, 87, 131, 146, 153, 154, 157, 172, 207, 265, 316, 331, 335
Marion "Pat" Bruère (b. 1864), **9:** 87 n.*156*, 131, 146, 153, 172, 207, 265, 316, 331, 335
Menella née Wilcox (1829-1886) – cousin, **1:** 113 n.*134*, 114; **7:** 40 n.*59*

Rackett, Thomas (b. 1819) – furniture dealer, **6:** 420 n.*689*
Racquet-courts, **4:** 83, 169
Radcliffe, Misses, **7:** 459 n.*757*
Radcliffe Camera, Oxford, **6:** 305; **7:** 102
Radcliffe Library, Oxford, **6:** 472, 473 n.*781*, 474

Radley, Berkshire, **1:** 28; **6:** 438; **7:** 320; **8:** 329
Radley College, **3:** 37, 39, 40 n.*62*, 124; **4:** 33, 66 n.*3*, 74; **9:** 263
Radnor Place, London, **7:** 155
Ragg (of Malin's Lee, Shropshire):
Frederick William (1845-1929), **9:** 201 n.*328*
Gertrude (b. 1864), **9:** 52 n.*90*
Hilda (b. 1874), **9:** 52 n.*90*
Lonsdale (1867-1945), **9:** 52 n.*90*, 123, 151, 201, 294
Maurice Wilfred (1871-1916), **9:** 52 n.*90*, 181, 200

Raikes:

Raikes (of Onslow Square, London):
Alice Theodora (1862-1945), see Wilson Fox
Arthur Whittington (1877-1921), **8:** 110 n.*180*, 114
Blanche Amabel "Amy" (1866-1904), **6:** 251, 253, 269, 403; **7:** 328; **8:** 110 n.*180*, 114
Cecil Dacre Staveley (1874-1947), **8:** 110 n.*180*
Charlotte Blanche née Trevor-Roper (1838-1922) – distant cousin, **6:** 159 n.*246*, 196, 200, 216, 251, 258, 269, 352, 403, 405; **7:** 277, 278 n.*507*, 328, 396; **8:** 110 n.*180*, 114, 227
Edith Gertrude (1867-1949), **6:** 251, 253, 269, 403; **7:** 328; **8:** 110 n.*180*, 114
Francis Edward (1870-1923), **8:** 110 n.*180*
Henry Cecil, Mr. (1838-1891), postmaster general – distant cousin, **1:** 12; **6:** 159 n.*246*, 196, 269, 352, 405; **7:** 277, 278 n.*507*, 328, 396; **8:** 110 n.*180*, 114, 227, 385
Henry St. John Digby (1863-1943), **8:** 110 n.*180*
Lucy Violet (1868-1937), **7:** 328; **8:** 110 n.*180*, 114
Thomas Algernon (1876-1951), **8:** 110 n.*180*, 114
Raikes (of Welton House, Yorkshire):
Anne Louisa (1797-1877) – aunt, **1:** 12
Thomas (1790-1866), see below
Raikes (of Gordon Square, London):
Charles (1828-1876) – cousin, **3:** 173 n.*253*; **4:** 84 n.*37*
Elizabeth Frances née Lutwidge (1799-1883), second wife – aunt, **1:** 12; **2:** 108 n.*209*; **3:** 173 n.*253*; **4:** 84 n.*37*, 283, 331 n.*423*, 336; **5:** 67 n.*100*, 380; **6:** 130, 407, 443, 466, 467; **7:** 12, 74, 160, 183, 211, 219, 253, 294, 315, 369, 526 n.*851*, 527
Elizabeth Lucy (1832-1888) – cousin, **3:** 173 n.*253*; **4:** 84 n.*37*
Elizabeth née Armstrong (d. 1824), first wife, **4:** 84 n.*37*
Frederick (died young) – cousin, **3:** 173 n.*253*; **4:** 84 n.*37*
Robert (1818-1901), see below
Thomas, Mr. (1790-1866), banker – uncle, **1:** 12; **2:** 108 n.*209*; **3:** 173 n.*253*; **4:** 84 n.*37*, 283, 331 n.*423*, 336; **5:** 67 n.*100*

Raikes (of Treberfydd, Breconshire):
  Robert, Mr. (1818-1901) – cousin, **7:** 28 n.*36*, 211, 527
  Robert Taunton (1843-1919), **7:** 28 n.*36*, 527

Railway Dominoes, **8:** 418
Ralston (of Hampstead, London):
  Dorothy (b. 1879), **7:** 529 n.*857*
  Ethel L. (b. 1877), **7:** 529 n.*857*; **8:** 193
  Grace S., Mrs. (b. 1843), **7:** 529 n.*857*, 541; **8:** 193
  Kate "Katie" E. (b. 1873), **7:** 529 n.*857*, 543; **8:** 193, 305
  Phyllis N. (b. 1881), **7:** 529 n.*857*
  Shirley B. (b. 1875), **7:** 529 n.*857*
  William, Mr. (b. 1842) – artist, **7:** 529 n.*857*, 530, 534, 541; **8:** 193, 194 n.*325*, 305
Ralston, Mr., **7:** 231
Ralston, William Ralston Shedden (1828-1889) – Russian scholar, **6:** 187 n.*291*, 246; **8:** 305 n.*505*
Ramsay, Edward Bannerman, Rev. Dr. (1793-1872), **3:** 103, 104 n.*153*; **6:** 180 n.*281*
Ramsay, Harriet (b. 1854) – schoolmistress, **9:** 344 n.*550*
Ramsay, William Mitchell (1851-1939) – professor of archaeology, **8:** 259 n.*438*
Ramsden (of Carlton Hall, Nottingham):
  Emily Anna (1835?-1913), **7:** 94 n.*170*
  John Plumptre (1832-1906), **7:** 94 n.*170*
Ramsgate, Kent, **6:** 130
Randall (of Abingdon, Berkshire):
  Alice (b. 1863?), **9:** 260, 261 n.*412*
  Ann Harriet née Bruxner (1819-1899), **9:** 260, 261 n.*412*
  Catherine (b. 1857), **9:** 260, 261 n.*412*
  Emily Mina (b. 1860), **9:** 260, 261 n.*412*
  James Leslie, Canon (1828-1922), **9:** 261 n.*412*
Randall, James, Rev. (1790-1888), **4:** 34
Randall, Mrs. – friend of the Gilliats, **4:** 331
Randolph, Herbert, Rev. (1789-1875), **3:** 43, 44 n.*69*; **4:** 35
Randolph, John Leverson (b. 1859) – barrister, **7:** 292 n.*529*
Ranke, Leopold von (1795-1886) – historian and writer, **1:** 24
Ranken (of Brislington, Somerset):
  Catherine A. (b. 1843), **4:** 278; **5:** 112 n.*175*
  Isabella K., Mrs. (b. 1803), **5:** 112 n.*175*
  Miss, later Mrs. Samon (d. 1880?), **4:** 278; **5:** 112 n.*175*
  William Henry (1832-1920), see below
Ranken (of Meysey Hampton, Gloucestershire):
  Frances M., Mrs. (b. 1845), **6:** 476 n.*786*
  William Henry, Rev. (1832-1920), **1:** 43, 49, 59 n.*28*, 60, 102-104;

2: 44 n.*87*, 47, 63; **3:** 24 n.*31*, 39, 40 n.*62*, 61, 124, 130; **4:** 35, 65, 66 n.*3*, 73, 74, 81, 103, 106 n.*73*, 161, 174, 176, 277, 278, 298, 303; **5:** 50 n.*68*, 59; **6:** 216 n.*337*, 475, 476, 492; **7:** 358, 498, 499; **8:** 171 n.*287*

Rankin (of London):

Flora – friend of the MacDonalds, **4:** 228 n.*253*

Mary – friend of the MacDonalds, **4:** 228 n.*253*

Raphael, Raffaello Sanzio (1483-1520) – artist, **1:** 65; **2:** 16 n.*27*; **5:** 295 n.*466*

Rapin-Thoyras, Paul de (1661-1725) – historian and writer, **1:** 72 n.*64*

Rattle, Henry (1835-1869) – undergraduate at Christ Church, **1:** 87, 88 n.*91*, 91; **2:** 113, 114 n.*220*, 124 n.*241*

Rauch, Christian Daniel (1777-1857) – sculptor, **5:** 266 n.*432*

Raven's Crag, Lake District, **3:** 118

Ravenshoe (bk. Henry Kingsley), **5:** 125

Rawlinson, Misses – amateur actresses, **5:** 52 n.*72*

Raymond, Richard John (1818?-1847?) – dramatist, **4:** 300 n.*366*

Raynham, Miss (1844-1871) – actress, **4:** 310 n.*386*; **5:** 47 n.*62*

Read, David Charles (1790-1851) – artist, **5:** 36 n.*42*

Reade, Charles (1814-1884) – dramatist, **2:** 107 n.*208*; **9:** 336 n.*537*

Reade, Mr. – of Murrells' Workshops, Eastbourne, **7:** 478

Reader, The, **5:** 11, 12 n.*2*

Reading, Berkshire, **5:** 90; **6:** 60, 93, 103, 115, 116, 123, 192, 228, 256, 258, 279, 337, 455, 474, 477; **7:** 48, 160, 166, 197, 312, 531

Rebekah (pic. Frederick Goodall), **5:** 235 n.*379*

Recreation Science, **4:** 56, 57

Redcar, Yorkshire, **5:** 102 n.*159*, 172 n.*285*; **6:** 51

Red Cross Knight with Una (pic. George F. Watts), **4:** 334 n.*431*

Reddish, Professor – swimming instructor, **8:** 347, 348 n.*572*

Redesdale, Earl, see Mitford

Red Hill (or Redhill), Surrey, **9:** 14

Red Pike, Cumberland, **2:** 93, 94

Red Riding-Hood (pic. Sophie Anderson), **6:** 22, 23 n.*23*

Red Riding-Hood (dr. Anon), **7:** 75 n.*120*

Reece, Robert (1838-1891) – dramatist, **7:** 370 n.*643*; **8:** 135 n.*220*

Reed, Mrs., **4:** 116

Reed, see also German Reed

Reed, W., Mr., **8:** 420 n.*680*

Rees, Walter Francis (b. 1854) – undergraduate at Christ Church, **6:** 299 n.*494*, 427; **8:** 397 n.*645*

Reeve (of Oulton, Suffolk):

James (1777-1827), **2:** 70 n.*140*

Lorina née Farr (d. 1879), **2:** 70 n.*140*; **3:** 20, 21 n.*25*, 28, 65; **4:** 172, 175; **5:** 188 n.*308*

Reeves, Clara – pupil at St. Aldates, **2:** 32

Reform Act Demonstrations, **5:** 166 n.*274*, 168
Reformation, The, **2:** 35
Reformation of the Church of England, The (bk. John Blunt), **5:** 103 n.*160*
Reform Bill, **5:** 215 n.*344*, **5:** 244 n.*398*
Regent Circus, London (now Piccadilly Circus), **4:** 325
Regent's Park, London, **3:** 133
Regent Street, London, **3:** 52
Rehan, Ada (1861-1916) – actress, **9:** 132 n.*231*
Reid, Cecil Frederick (b. 1842) – undergraduate at Christ Church, amateur actor, **4:** 263 n.*308*
Reigate, Surrey, **7:** 215
Rejected Addresses (bk. James and Horatio Smith), **1:** 59 n.*29*
Rejlander, Oscar Gustav (1813-1875) – photographer, **3:** 13 n.*11*; **4:** 183 n.*178*, 194, 222 n.*244*; **5:** 137 n.*221*, 236 n.*381*
Residence, The, Ripon, **1:** 56; **2:** 8, 57
"Resolution and Independence" (William Wordsworth) – poem, **2:** 99 n.*191*
Retford, Nottinghamshire, **6:** 54 n.*78*
Retford School, **7:** 203
Retribution (dr. Tom Taylor), **2:** 82 n.*162*
Return from Confirmation, The (pic. Jessica Hayllar), **8:** 413 n.*669*
Review of Oxford and Cambridge Volunteers, **4:** 202, 203
"Review of Wilson" – in the *Athenæum* (Augustus De Morgan), **7:** 80, 81 n.135, 83
Rewley House, Oxford, **9:** 311 n.*494*, 313, 326
Reynolds, Amy – friend of the Murdochs, **7:** 289, 290 n.*524*
Reynolds (of Marylebone, London):
  Amy Beatrice (b. 1854), **4:** 339 n.*439*, 340
  Charlotte Ann née Bullock Webster (b. 1819), **4:** 339, 342
  Edith Mary (b. 1848), **4:** 339 n.*439*, 340; **5:** 43 n.*56*
  Henry Revell, Mr. (1800-1866) – solicitor, **4:** 338, 339, 340, 342
Reynolds, Samuel Harvey (1831-1897) – fellow of Brasenose, **1:** 65 n.*43*
Rhine, River, **5:** 361
Rhys (or Reece), see Price
Riadore (of High Road, Mid Lavant, Sussex):
  Geldart John Evans, Rev. (1825-1917), **6:** 230 n.*362*; **7:** 400, 401 n.*680*; **8:** 240, 241 n.*404*, 337
  Gwendoline (or Gwendolen) Jemima (1868-1940), **6:** 230 n.*362*; **7:** 400, 401 n.*680*; **8:** 241 n.*404*, 337, 339; **9:** 19 n.*18*, 20, 86, 87
  James "Jim" (b. 1866), **6:** 230 n.*362*; **7:** 401 n.*680*
  Marion Agatha G. née McAlpine (1834-1924), **6:** 230 n.*362*; **7:** 400, 401 n.*680*; **8:** 240, 241 n.*404*, 337, 339; **9:** 18, 19 n.*18*
  Marion Ethel G. (1864-1933), **6:** 230 n.*362*; **7:** 400, 401 n.*680*; **8:** 240, 241 n.*404*, 337, 339
  Percy (b. 1871), **6:** 230 n.*362*; **7:** 400, 401 n.*680*
Ricardo, David (1772-1823) – writer, **3:** 158 n.*234*

Ricci, Federico (1809-1877) – composer, **1:** 53
Rich, John, Rev. (1826-1913), **4:** 33; **6:** 370 n.*608*; **7:** 89 n.*157*
Richard, Edith A. (b. 1828) – teacher, **8:** 473 n.*767*
Richard, Louis Paul Emile (1795-1849) – mathematician and teacher, **9:** 350 n.*560*
Richards (of Bognor, Sussex):
Frances A. A., Mrs. (b. 1812), **6:** 235 n.*373*
John W., Rev. (b. 1811), **6:** 235 n.*373*
Richards (of Winchester, Hampshire):
Marianne née Robbins (b. 1843), **6:** 414 n.*678*; **7:** 356 n.*622*, 357, 361, 363, 392, 397, 454, 456; **8:** 22, 23 n.*20*, 33, 40, 101, 129, 193, 287, 301, 415; **9:** 95 n.*172*, 98 n.*177*, 159
Marion Gertrude (1870-1956), **6:** 414 n.*678*; **7:** 354, 355 n.*619*, 357, 358, 360-368, 392, 396, 397, 454-456, 473, 474, 476, 478, 479; **8:** 22, 33-35, 40, 41, 101, 129, 132, 136-139, 144-146, 193, 287; **9:** 95 n.*172*, 97-99
Walter Guyon (1869-1946), **6:** 414 n.*678*; **7:** 356 n.*622*, 360, 361, 397, 473; **8:** 136, 138
Richards:
Miss, **8:** 585, 589
Mrs. – mother of Mrs. Baly, **8:** 585
Richardson, Charles (1775-1865) – dictionary compiler, **3:** 131 n.*189*
Richardson, Henry (b. 1846) – teacher, **7:** 495 n.*807*
Richardson, Mrs. – related to Prof. Westwood, **5:** 141 n.*227*
Richardson, Thomas, Father (b. 1820), **9:** 320 n.*512*
Richelieu (dr. Edward Bulwer Lytton), **6:** 315 n.*523*; **8:** 628 n.*994*
Richmond, America, **4:** 286
Richmond (of York Street, Portman Square, London):
Cecilia Sarah (b. 1847), **4:** 319 n.*404*
Edith (b. 1846), **4:** 319 n.*404*
George, Mr. (1809-1896) – artist, **5:** 60 n.*87*, 221 n.*352*, 253 n.*416*
William Blake (1842-1921) – artist, **4:** 42, 319 n.*404*; **5:** 60 n.*87*; **6:** 492 n.*815*; **8:** 197 n.*335*
Richmond, J. – assistant butler in Common Room, **8:** 602, 603 n.*957*
Richmond, Yorkshire, **1:** 17, 20-22, 58 n.*25*, 115, 127, 130; **2:** 26 n.*49*, 86 n.*171*, 99; **3:** 91; **4:** 27, 166,177, 182, 231, 232; **7:** 209
Richmond Castle, Yorkshire, **3:** 91
Richmond Naval School, Surrey, **7:** 532
Richmond Rectory, Yorkshire, **3:** 92
Richmond School, Yorkshire, **2:** 78 n.*155*, 87 n.*173*; **9:** 34 n.*57*
Richmond School Magazine, **1:** 29
Richmond upon Thames, Surrey, **2:** 9, 51, 54; **4:** 284
Riddell (of Putney, Surrey):
Eliza (b. 1863), **8:** 343 n.*566*
Mary A. (b. 1858), **8:** 343 n.*566*
Ridding, George (1828-1904) – fellow of Exeter College, **3:** 124 n.*177*;

4: 134, 135 n.*112*
Rift within the Lute, The (pic. Arthur Hughes), **5:** 15 n.*6*
Rigaud, John (1823-1888) – fellow of Magdalen College, **5:** 381 n.*564*; **7:** 269; **8:** 232 n.*393*
Righton, Edward C. (d. 1899) – actor, **8:** 59 n.*92*
Rignold, George (1838-1912) – actor, **7:** 114 n.*211*
Riley, Thomas (b. 1842) – artist, **8:** 410, 411 n.*665*
Ripley (of Kingston upon Thames, Surrey):
Ella Blanche (b. 1867), **7:** 528 n.*854*
Lucy (b. 1870), **7:** 528 n.*854*
John A., Mr. (b. 1827) – stockbroker, **7:** 528 n.*854*
Marianne, Mrs. (b. 1830), **7:** 528 n.*854*
Ripon, Yorkshire, **1:** 17, 43, 50, 55 n.*19*, 79, 93 n.*97*; **2:** 8, 14 n.*21*, 18, 39 n.*78*, 55-6, 57 n.*113*, 58 n.*116*, 58 n.*117*, 86 n.*171*; **3:** 7, 143, 147, 167, 168; **4:** 13, 24, 25, 44, 46, 52, 58, 157, 267; **5:** 38, 42, 105, 124, 190, 378; **6:** 43, 168, 176, 491; **9:** 227
Ripon & Richmond Chronicle, **3:** 10 n.*7*, 11 n.*9*, 91 n.*141*, 170 n.*249*
Ripon Bishop's Palace, **3:** 150; **4:** 158; **5:** 42, 43, 105, 107, 125, 191, 379
Ripon Deanery, **3:** 168
Ripon Diocesan Church Building Society, **5:** 103, 111
Ripon Residence, **3:** 150, 152
Rip Van Winkle (dr. Dion Boucicault and Joseph Jefferson), **5:** 123 n.*195*
Rip Van Winkle (Henry Farnie and Robert Planquette) – operetta, **7:** 532 n.*862*; **8:** 34 n.*41*
Risley, Edith Elton (b. 1855), **8:** 220 n.*376*, 264
Risque, W. H. (d. 1916) – lyricist, **9:** 197 n.*323*
Ritchie (of Kensington, London):
Anne Isabella née Thackeray (1837-1919), **6:** 100 n.*156*, 196, 197, 199, 258; **7:** 141 n.*260*; **8:** 271 n.*457*, 617 n.*978*; **9:** 60 n.*112*, 64, 65, 180, 182
Hester "Effie" M. (b. 1878), **7:** 141 n.*260*; **8:** 617 n.*978*; **9:** 64 n.*117*, 65, 180-182
Richmond Thackeray Willoughby, Mr. (1854-1912) – politician, **7:** 141 n.*260*
William T. D. (b. 1880), **7:** 141 n.*260*; **8:** 617 n.*978*
Rivals, The (dr. Richard Sheridan), **5:** 153 n.*248*; **7:** 540 n.*873*
Rivers (of Tonbridge, Kent):
Charles "Charlie" H. (b. 1865), **6:** 271 n.*440*, 313
Elizabeth née Hunt (b. 1840), **6:** 271 n.*440*, 288, 313
Ethel Marian (b. 1867), **6:** 271 n.*440*, 313
Henry Frederick, Rev. (1830-1911) – speech therapist, **6:** 271 n.*440*, 288, 292, 296, 299, 313, 321, 330, 332, 369, 414; **7:** 12 n.*5*; **9:** 125 n.*219*
Katharine "Katie" Elizabeth (b. 1871), **6:** 271 n.*440*, 288, 313
William "Willy" Halse R. (1864-1922), **6:** 271 n.*440*, 313
Rivers, Hilda – actress, **9:** 310 n.*493*

Riviere, William (1806-1876) – artist, **3:** 26 n.*37*
Rivington (of Bladon, Oxfordshire):
Beatrix "Patty" Martha Noel Frederica Calthrop (b. 1884), **9:** 203 n.*332*, 301
Dorothea "Dolly" Marie Caroline (1883-1951), **9:** 203 n.*332*, 301, 308-310, 318 n.*509*, 319, 325, 326, 331-335
John Alfred, Rev. (1846-1931), **9:** 203 n.*332*, 313
Mrs., **9:** 203 n.*332*, 308, 313
Rivington, Messrs., Oxford – bookseller, **5:** 131
Rix (of Beccles, Suffolk):
Charlotte "Lottie" Jane (1867-1952), **8:** 204 n.*349*, 217
Edith Mary (1866-1918), **8:** 204 n.*349*, 215-217, 233 n.*395*, 234-236, 304, 305, 315, 316, 372, 373, 440-442, 472, 495, 533, 581, 613; **9:** 259 n.*408*, 300, 301 n.*478*, 318-322, 333-336, 340
Frederic Shelly, Mr. (1836-1933) – solicitor, **8:** 204 n.*349*, 233, 236
Jemima Bostock née Bradley (1831-1902), **8:** 204 n.*349*, 215, 216, 234-236
Shelly William (b. 1873), **8:** 204 n.*349*
Wilton John (1871-1952), **8:** 204 n.*349*
Robarts, Charles Nathaniel (1834-1889) – precentor of Christ Church, **8:** 492 n.*795*
Robert Macaire (dr. Charles Selby), **8:** 406 n.*660*; **9:** 162 n.*277*
Roberts, Arthur (1853-1933) – actor, **8:** 569 n.*907*
Roberts, George (1832-1896) – dramatist, **5:** 64 n.*95*, 73 n.*110*
Roberts, William – pupil at St. Aldates, **2:** 30
Robertson, Elizabeth "Toppy," **7:** 207 n.*384*, 213
Robertson (of St. Giles', Oxford):
James, Mr. (b. 1810), **7:** 148, 149 n.*281*
Mary, Mrs. (b. 1813), **7:** 148, 149 n.*281*
Robertson, James Craigie (1813-1882) – writer, **5:** 103 n.*160*
Robertson, Maud (d. 1930) – actress, **9:** 15 n.*10*
Robertson, Thomas William (1829-1871) – dramatist, **4:** 300 n.*366*; **5:** 45 n.*58*, 126 n.*200*, 231 n.*369*; **7:** 183 n.*342*, 231 n.*425*, 278 n.*505*
Robin Hood (dr. Anon), **7:** 91 n.*163*, 97
Robinson (of Vowchurch, Herefordshire):
Beatrice Mary Gavin (b. 1878), **9:** 287 n.*454*
Edward Lewis Gavin, Mr. (1837-1908) – solicitor, **9:** 287 n.*454*
Harriet Egbertha Lucy née Harrison (b. 1852), **9:** 287 n.*454*
Mabel Frances Gavin (b. 1875), **9:** 287 n.*454*
Margaret Gavin (b. 1880), **9:** 287 n.*454*
Ralph Spencer Gavin (1887-1958), **9:** 287 n.*454*
Sylvia Dorothy Gavin (b. 1879), **9:** 287 n.*454*
Robinson (of Hendon Lodge, Sunderland, Durham):
Caroline (b. 1802), **2:** 87 n.*175*
Dorothy (1798-1831), **2:** 87 n.*175*

George, Mr. (1757-1832) – wine-merchant, **2:** 87 n.*175*
George James (1799-1817), **2:** 87 n.*175*
James Septimus (1811-1872), **2:** 87 n.*175*
Jane née Wall (1754-1792) – first wife, **2:** 87 n.*175*
John Wall (b. 1783), **2:** 87 n.*175*
Mary (1797-1833), **2:** 87 n.*175*
Mary née Clark (1773-1842) – third wife, **2:** 87 n.*175*
Mary née Nesham (1762-1802) – second wife, **2:** 87 n.*175*
Nelson George (b. 1808), **2:** 87 n.*175*
Thomas Temple (b. 1807), **2:** 87 n.*175*
William (1800-1875), **2:** 87 n.*175*
Robinson, Harry Perry (1859-1930) – businessman, **7:** 484 n.*788*
Robinson, Henry Peach (1830-1901) – photographer, **3:** 173, 174 n.*255*; **4:** 25; **7:** 18, 19 n.*15*, 210, 429 n.*716*, 482 n.*784*
Robinson, Hercules George Robert, Sir (1824-1897), 1st Baron Rosmead – civil servant, **8:** 50 n.*74*, 54 n.*80*
Robinson, Mary M. (b. 1835) – teacher, **8:** 204 n.*349*
Robinson & Cherrill, Messrs. – photographers, **6:** 313 n.*518*, 320, 397
Robinson brothers – pupils at Richmond School, **1:** 21
Rob Roy (dr. Anon), **7:** 449 n.*746*
Robson (of London):
Frederick (1847-1919) – actor, **5:** 72, 73 n.*110*
Thomas Frederick, Mr. (1822-1864) – actor, **2:** 82 n.*162*, 123; **3:** 12 n.*10*, 13 n.*11*, 26 n.*36*, 51, 79, 80 n.*126*, 133, 153, 171
Robson (of Stoke, near Guildford, Surrey):
John Henry, Dr. (1842-1921) – teacher, **8:** 75, 76 n.*119*, 79, 81, 220, 443, 615; **9:** 188 n.*311*, 305
Martha B. {Bessie?} (b. 1869), **8:** 76 n.*119*, 328
Martha Elizabeth née Purdue (b. 1840), **8:** 75, 76 n.*119*, 79
Robson, William (1785-1863) – dramatist, **3:** 153 n.*223*
Robust Invalid, The (dr. Charles Reade), **6:** 121, 122 n.*185*
Rochester, Kent, **9:** 31
Rochester Cathedral, **9:** 32
Rochester Garrison Church, **9:** 32
Rocke, Alfred Beale (1833-1887) – undergraduate at Christ Church, **1:** 84 n.*88*, 85; **2:** 31 n.*59*
Rockstro, William Smyth (1823-1895) – composer, **6:** 98 n.*153*
Rodney, Charlotte Georgiana née Morgan, Dowager Lady (d. 1878), **6:** 96 n.*150*
Rodwell, George Herbert Bonaparte (1800-1852) – dramatist, **5:** 17 n.*11*
Roffe, Miss – governess to the Bells, **7:** 495 n.*806*
Rogers (of Beaumont Street, Oxford):
Annie Mary Ann Henley (1856-1937), **4:** 106 n.*74*, 161, 178, 217 n.*233*; **5:** 19, 26; **8:** 86 n.*139*
Ann Susannah Charlotte née Reynolds (1826-1899), **4:** 106 n.*74*, 146,

161, 217 n.*233*, 257; **5:** 80 n.*125*; **6:** 323; **8:** 86 n.*139*
Arthur George Liddon (b. 1864), **4:** 106 n.*74*
Bertram Mitford Heron (1860-1953), **4:** 106 n.*74*
Clement Francis (1866-1949), **4:** 106 n.*74*; **5:** 185 n.*304*; **6:** 11 n.*1*
Henry Reynolds Knatchbull (1858-1876), **4:** 106 n.*74*
James Edwin Thorold, Prof. (1823-1890), **4:** 106 n.*74*, 146, 161, 295; **5:** 24 n.*22*, 26, 51, 80, 185 n.*304*; **6:** 11 n.*1*, 323; **7:** 339 n.*595*
Leonard James (1862-1933), **4:** 106 n.*74*
Rogers, Felix – actor, **4:** 316; **5:** 126
Rogers, William, Rev. (1819-1896), **5:** 196 n.*319*
Roker, Durham, **1:** 125; **2:** 86; **4:** 155-157, 324; **5:** 175; **6:** 175, 208
Rolleston (of Park Grange, South Parks Road, Holywell, Oxford):
George (1829-1881) – anatomist, **3:** 165 n.*238*, 168; **4:** 67 n.*5*, 169, 260; **5:** 59 n.*85*; **6:** 459 n.*755*; **7:** 432 n.*720*
Grace née Davy (1832-1914), **6:** 459 n.*755*; **7:** 432 n.*720*
Rolleston, Lancelot (1847-1941) – undergraduate of Christ Church, **5:** 250 n.*408*
Roman Catholic bookseller, Eastbourne, **9:** 329
Roman Catholics, **4:** 11, 17; **6:** 153, 486
Romance of Two Worlds, A (bk. Marie Corelli), **9:** 208 n.*337*
Romantic Attachment (dr. Arthur Wood), **5:** 139 n.*223*, 160
Romantic Idea, A (dr. James Planché), **5:** 210 n.*336*
Rooney, Frances Rodd (1832-1919), see Wilcox
Rorke (of London):
Kate "Katie" (1864-1945) – actress, **8:** 426 n.*688*; **9:** 57 n.*104*
Mary (1858-1938) – actress, **8:** 451 n.*722*
Rory O'More (dr. Samuel Lover), **5:** 17 n.*11*
Rosa Troupe – actresses, **8:** 311, 312 n.*514*, 412
Roscoe, Thomas (1791-1871) – historian and writer, **1:** 24
Rose:
General – brother of Mrs. Bonamy Price, **6:** 320 n.*532*
Mrs. née Price, **6:** 320 n.*532*
Rose and the Ring, The (dr. Henry Savile Clarke), **8:** 546 n.*870*
Rosebery, see Primrose
Roselle, Percy (b. 1856) – actor, **5:** 127 n.*203*, 128, 129 n.*207*, 130, 136
Rosencranz and Guildenstern (dr. William S. Gilbert), **8:** 618 n.*980*; **9:** 12, 13 n.*5*
"Roses, The," Upper Norwood (Smedley), **6:** 294, 333 n.*551*, 334, 344
Roslin, Midlothian, Scotland, **3:** 99-101; **6:** 180, 183
Roslin Castle, **3:** 100
Ross, Melville George Hope Warrender, Capt. RN (d. 1866), **4:** 155 n.*142*, 156
Rosse, Frederick (1867-1940) – composer, **9:** 197 n.*323*
Rossetti (of Tudor House, Cheyne Walk, Chelsea, London):
Christina Georgina (1830-1894), **4:** 66 n.*4*, 109, 251 n.*288*, 253,

282 n.*332*, 288 n.*344*, 318; **5:** 24, 162, 227 n.*362*; **7:** 127 n.*238*, 492 n.*803*, 513, 523; **8:** 67 n.*107*, 198 n.*336*, 216, 282, 305, 612
Dante Gabriel (1828-1882) – artist, **3:** 26 n.*37*, 33 n.*51*; **4:** 20, 66 n.*4*, 243, 247, 250-254, 316; **5:** 14 n.*5*, 71 n.*107*, 130 n.*209*, 162, 199 n.*322*; **7:** 492 n.*803*; **9:** 28 n.*42*, 99 n.*180*
Frances Mary Lavinia née Polidori (1800-1886), **4:** 252 n.*291*; **5:** 162; **7:** 492; **8:** 198 n.*336*, 282
Maria Francesca (1827-1876), **4:** 252 n.*291*, 253, 318; **5:** 162
William Michael (1829-1919), **4:** 252 n.*290*, 252 n.*291*, 253, 254; **5:** 162
Rossetti Exhibition, Burlington House, London, **7:** 505 n.*824*, 511, 513
Rossi (from Italy):
Ernesto Fortunato Giovanni (1827-1896) – actor, **3:** 98 n.*147*
Giovanni Gaetano (1828-1886) – composer, **3:** 98 n.*147*
Lauro (1810-1885) – composer, **3:** 98 n.*147*
Rossini, Gioacchino Antonio (1792-1868), **1:** 104 n.*116*
Rostopchine, Sophaletta Feodorovna (1799-1874), later Countess de Ségur – writer, **7:** 486 n.*790*
Rosy Morn (pic. Sophie Anderson), **4:** 285 n.*340*, 290 n.*346*
Rotation of the moon, **2:** 60 n.*121*, 61
Rotherwick, Hampshire, **6:** 438; **8:** 255
Round, Miss – friend of the Eschweges, **8:** 576
Rowardennan, Stirling, Scotland, **3:** 104
Rowden (of Oxford):
Edward Wetherall, Mr. (1814-1870) – registrar of New College, **4:** 219, 261 n.*305*
Mary Harriet, **4:** 296 n.*357*
Mrs., **4:** 219, 296
Rowden, Emmie (b. 1876) – amateur actress, **9:** 296 n.*469*
Rowe, George Fawcett (d. 1889) – dramatist, **7:** 142 n.*262*
Rowell (of Alfred Street, Oxford):
Edith Mary (b. 1876), **9:** 142 n.*245*, 299
Emily Bessie (b. 1875), **9:** 142 n.*245*, 143
Emily Sarah née Barrett (b. 1844), **9:** 130 n.*227*, 141, 254, 299
Ethel Maud (1877-1951), **9:** 130 n.*227*, 141, 143, 204, 326
George Joseph, Mr. (b. 1843) – master decorator, **9:** 130 n.*227*
Hettie Leonora (1879-1963), **9:** 142 n.*245*, 143, 254, 299, 313
Hilda Maria (1873-1918), **9:** 142 n.*245*, 143
Rowley (of Brighton, Sussex):
Edwin (b. 1847), **7:** 94 n.*170*
Thomas, Mr. (b. 1807) – optician, **7:** 94 n.*171*
Rowley, Richard, Rev. (1832-1864), **1:** 72 n.*63*, 84, 85; **2:** 66 n.*131*, 74, 75, 103 n.198; **4:** 136, 137 n.*114*, 138, 277
Rowley & Company – agent for artists?, **7:** 537 n.*870*
Royal Academy, London, **1:** 102, 103; **2:** 7 n.*1*, 11 n.*12*, 17 n.*29*, 18 n.*31*, 75 n.*151*, 80, 83, 103 n.198; **3:** 74, 77, 173; **4:** 36, 55, 64, 85 n.*38*, 280,

281, 285, 289, 301, 328, 337; **5:** 86 n.*134*, 89, 148, 208, 209 n.*334*, 211 n.*339*, 218 n.*347*, 221, 235; **6:** 13, 14, 16, 19, 85, 114, 122, 160, 161, 165, 222-226, 284, 286, 407, 467; **7:** 45, 46, 50, 118, 127, 179 n.*332*, 183, 186, 278, 280, 347, 429, 430, 438, 442, 493, 502, 523, 538; **8:** 113, 114, 199, 208, 212, 216, 274, 338 n.*557*, 342, 345, 406, 410, 411, 413, 455, 471, 511, 561, 564, 565, 567, 618, 621, 629, 630; **9:** 12, 73, 78, 146, 204, 205, 255

Royal Artillery, **2:** 19 n.*32*, 25 n.*47*

Royal Bride, The (dr. Anon), **7:** 511

Royal Chamber, Deanery, Oxford, **4:** 205, 211

Royal Family:

Albert, Prince Consort (1819-1861), **1:** 94, 101 n.*111*; **4:** 39, 40, 57, 172 n.*168*, 297

Albert Edward, Prince of Wales, Duke of Saxony (1841-1910), later Edward VII, **4:** 24, 39-43, 171 n.*165*, 173, 184, 201, 206, 207 n.*217*, 208, 210, 262; **5:** 339; **6:** 201 n.*313*, 320; **7:** 534; **9:** 308 n.*488*, 309, 310

Albert Victor, Prince (1864-1892), Duke of Clarence, **8:** 603 n.*958*, 604

Alexandra, Princess of Denmark, Princess of Wales (1844-1925), **4:** 171 n.*165*, 172 n.*168*, 173, 206, 207 n.*217*, 208

Alfred, Prince (1844-1900), Duke of Edinburgh, **4:** 39, 40

Alice, Princess (1843-1878), **4:** 39, 40

Alice Mary Victoria Augusta Pauline, Princess (1883-1981), **8:** 463 n.*745*, 467, 468, 469 n.*759*, 486, 513 n.*827*, 596; **9:** 21 n.*25*, 85 n.*154*, 89 n.*161*, 98 n.*178*, 221 n.*350*

Arthur, Prince (1850-1942), Duke of Connaught, **4:** 282, 283 n.*334*; **6:** 158 n.*244*; **9:** 150 n.*257*

Beatrice, Princess (1857-1944), **4:** 329 n.*421*; **5:** 10, 19, 122 n.*193*; **6:** 80 n.*116*, 83, 92

Frederick, Crown Prince of Denmark (1843-1912), **4:** 261, 262 n.*306*

George III (1738-1820), **3:** 57

George Frederick Ernest Albert, Prince (1865-1936), Duke of York, later George V, **9:** 81 n.*147*

Helena, Princess (1846-1923), **4:** 283 n.*334*

Helen Frederica Augusta, Princess (1861-1922), Duchess of Albany, **8:** 462, 463 n.*745*, 467, 468, 479 n.*776*, 513 n.*827*, 596, 597; **9:** 35 n.*62*, 89 n.*161*, 224

Henry VIII (1491-1547), **1:** 10, 63; **3:** 156 n.*230*

James I, **1:** 11, 26, 27

Leopold Charles Edward George Albert, Prince (1884-1954), 2nd Duke of Albany, **8:** 463 n.*745*, 467, 596; **9:** 21 n.*25*, 89 n.*161*, 225 n.*354*

Leopold George Duncan Albert, Prince (1853-1884), Duke of Albany, **5:** 56 n.*80*, 371 n.*551*; **6:** 393 n.*644*, 394, 395 n.*646*, 396 n.*647*, 397; **8:** 99 n.*163*

Louis, Prince of Hesse-Darmstadt (1837-1892), **4:** 39

Matilda (William the Conqueror's illegitimate daughter), **1:** 11
Victoria, Princess Royal (1840-1901), **1:** 94
Victoria, Queen (1819-1901), **1:** 94, 99; **3:** 13, 14 n.*12*, 177; **4:** 39, 40, 57, 172 n.*168*, 239, 296, 297 n.*358*, 311, 330; **5:** 83 n.*130*, 84; **6:** 80; **8:** 99, 343 n.*565*, 344 n.*567*; **9:** 320
Victoria Mary "May" Augusta, Princess (1867-1953), **9:** 81 n.*147*
William the Conqueror (1025-1087), William I of England, **1:** 11

Royal Marriage (pic. Edward Ward), **6:** 17 n.*15*
Royal Society, **5:** 148, 149, 152 n.*246*
Rozel Manor, Jersey, **8:** 98
Rucker, Miss – friend of the Turtons, **7:** 159 n.*298*
Rudston Read (Winteringham, Lincolnshire):
Barbara Louisa Fell née Thompson (b. 1831) – second wife, **9:** 312 n.*496*
Louisa Lucy née Erskine (1816-1865) – first wife, **4:** 236 n.*264*, 237, 239, 240, 272 n.*316*, 279, 296; **9:** 312 n.*496*
Thomas Frederick, Rev. (1811-1892), **4:** 236 n.*264*, 237, 240; **7:** 99 n.*183*; **8:** 256 n.*431*
Rugby, Warwickshire, **1:** 22-29, 41, 58 n.*25*, 71 n.*60*, 93, 115 n.*139*; **4:** 30, 31
Rugby School, **2:** 72 n.*146*; **4:** 30, 31, 34, 171 n.*165*, 282, 306 n.*376*; **6:** 134 n.*205*
Rumplestiltskin (dr. Francis Burnand), **4:** 315, 316 n.*396*
Rumsey (of Iffley, Oxfordshire):
Elizabeth, Mrs. (b. 1826?), **4:** 74 n.*20*, 77, 161, 260; **6:** 34 n.*46*, 66
Elizabeth F. Cornelia "Leila" (b. 1859), **4:** 74 n.*20*, 179; **6:** 32 n.*42*, 33, 34 n.*46*, 37, 67
James, Rev. (1824-1903), **4:** 74 n.*20*, 77, 161, 260; **6:** 32 n.*42*
John Thomas Medlycott (b. 1855), **4:** 74 n.*20*
Louisa (b. 1866), **4:** 74 n.*20*; **6:** 67
Mary H. (b. 1860), **4:** 74 n.*20*; **6:** 67
Runcorn, Cheshire, **1:** 12
Rushton, Arthur, alias John Plummer – dramatist, **9:** 348 n.*557*
Ruskin, John (1819-1900) – professor of fine art, **1:** 114 n.*136*, 118; **2:** 7 n.*1*, 118; **3:** 39, 114, 122 n.*173*, 125, 127, 145; **6:** 302 n.*498*, 368, 396 n.*648*, 434, 435 n.*716*; **7:** 86, 497 n.*811*, 518 n.*839*, 537; **8:** 62 n.*99*
Ruskin's Poems, **7:** 518 n.*839*
Russ (language), **4:** 146
Russell (of London Road, Woburn, Bedfordshire):
Charles James Fox, Lt.-Col. (1807-1894) – army officer, **5:** 177 n.*294*
George William Erskine (1853-1919), **5:** 177 n.*294*
Henry Charles (1842-1922), **5:** 177 n.*294*
Russell, Henry (1812-1900) – composer and singer, **3:** 23 n.*29*
Russell, John (1792-1878) – 1st Earl Russell, **5:** 177 n.*294*
Russell, John Rutherfurd, Dr. (1816-1866) – homeopathic doctor,

4: 228 n.*252*
Russell, Mr. – manager of Covent Garden Theatre, **5:** 46 n.*60*
Russell, Western Francis (b. 1862) – undergraduate at Christ Church, **7:** 276 n.*503*
Russell-Morris (of Chelsea, London):
Theodosia "Theo" Laura née Heaphy (1858-1920, **5:** 20, 219 n.*350*, 230, 231 n.*368*; **6:** 15 n.*9*, 71, 79, 126, 292, 333; **7:** 122 n.*230*, 159, 388, 393, 394, 397, 398, 430, 439, 443, 444, 453, 486, 493, 502-504, 508-511, 523, 524, 529, 532, 536; **8:** 11 n.*2*, 37, 38, 47, 49, 53, 58, 59, 100-103, 108, 112-115, 131, 163, 164, 167, 168, 184, 187, 189, 190, 199, 200, 204, 209, 212, 216; **9:** 205 n.*334*
Vivian (b. 1890?), **9:** 205 n.*334*
Russia, **3:** 58 n.*88*; **7:** 88 n.*155*, 89 n.*159*; **9:** 235
Russia, Emperor of (Csar Nicholas I), **1:** 67
Russian Folktales (bk. William Ralston), **6:** 187 n.*291*
Russian Princess, **8:** 270 n.*454*
"Rusticus Expectans" (pseudonym), **6:** 364
Ruswarp, near Whitby, Yorkshire, **5:** 178; **6:** 54
Ruth: A Novel (bk. Elizabeth Gaskell), **1:** 131 n.*163*
Ruth's Romance (dr. Frederick Broughton), **8:** 285, 286 n.*480*
"R.W.G." (pseudonym), **2:** 39 n.*79*
Rydal, Westmorland, **3:** 109
Rydal Falls, Westmorland, **2:** 97
Ryde, Isle of Wight, **4:** 346; **6:** 295, 296, 299, 342, 354, 357, 359, 360, 413, 417, 418, 421, 422, 424, 480, 484
Ryder, John (1814-1885) – actor, **3:** 81, 82 n.*127*; **4:** 159; **6:** 281 n.*463*
Ryle, John Charles, Rev. (1816-1900), **7:** 226 n.*417*
Ryman's of Oxford, Stationer and Art Gallery, **1:** 67, 94; **2:** 69; **3:** 22, 69, 70, 129; **4:** 79 n.*29*; **9:** 124
Rymill (or Ryemill), Mr. – solicitor's clerk, **7:** 161 n.*301*, 223, 226, 228, 245, 257, 263, 274

St. Aldates School, Oxford, **2:** 30 n.*57*, 32
St. Bartholomew's Hospital, London, **3:** 138; **4:** 38, 347, 352, 355; **7:** 500
St. Bees, Cumberland, **2:** 92, 93
St. Cecilia, **1:** 50
St. Cecilia (pic. Thomas Heaphy), **6:** 82 n.*120*
St. Cecily (pic. Dante Gabriel Rossetti), **4:** 20
St. Clement's Caves, Hastings, **9:** 25
St. Cyres, Viscount, see Northcote
St. Edmund's Hall, Oxford, **4:** 260; **9:** 47
St. Edward's School, Oxford, **6:** 379
St. George's Hall, London, **6:** 97
St. Giles', Oxford, **1:** 40; **4:** 113, 141, 170
St. Helena (Island in the Atlantic Ocean), **7:** 314

St. Hilda's Terrace, Whitby, **2:** 15 n.*25*
St. Hugh's Hall, Oxford, **9:** 135, 143, 144, 150, 180, 183, 188, 199, 223, 251, 281
St. James's Dining Rooms (Restaurant), London, **4:** 182, 225, 287, 337; **5:** 72, 125
St. James's Gazette, **1:** 64 n.*41*; **7:** 326 n.*578*, 330, 331 n.*589*, 388 n.*669*, 410, 411 n.*691*, 415 n.*694*, 420 n.*702*, 450 n.*747*, 512 n.*830*; **8:** 14, 17 n.*12*, 26 n.*28*, 106 n.*175*, 107 n.*177*, 108 n.*179*, 116 n.*189*, 119 n.*192*, 121, 122, 126 n.*204*, 132 n.*216*, 147, 148 n.*240*, 172 n.*289*, 222 n.*381*, 242 n.*407*, 251 n.*423*, 349 n.*574*, 391 n.*637*, 443 n.*711*, 475 n.*771*, 544 n.*869*
St. James's Hall, Piccadilly, London, **4:** 11; **5:** 225; **6:** 26, 160 n.*248*, 256; **7:** 112, 528
St. James's Park, London, **9:** 58
St. John, Florence (1855-1912) – actress and singer, **7:** 193, 194 n.*361*, 220, 232, 304, 541
St. John's College, Cambridge., **2:** 62; **7:** 336
St. John's College, Oxford, **4:** 150 n.*134*, 206, 307; **5:** 153, 253; **6:** 36, 153, 217, 449, 469, 490; **7:** 48, 108, 227, 270, 453, 538; **8:** 71, 121, 196, 315, 335, 339, 399, 409, 517, 573; **9:** 199, 223, 238
St. Katherine's Wharf, London, **7:** 453
St. Kentigern's, Oxford, **9:** 228 n.*363*, 229, 230
St. Leonards-on-Sea, Sussex, **4:** 29; **6:** 386; **7:** 54, 56, 61, 63, 139, 284, 305; **9:** 161, 175, 220, 275, 277, 333, 334, 338, 343, 344
St. Margaret's, Bethnal Green, **9:** 349 n.*559*
St. Mary Hall, Oxford, **7:** 126 n.*237*, 544
St. Mary's Hospital, Paddington, **9:** 193, 196, 205
St. Michael's School, Bognor, **6:** 234, 235 n.*373*
St. Michael's School, Tenbury, **6:** 167 n.*259*, 168 n.*260*
St. Nicholas Hall, Guildford, **9:** 118
St. Omer, France, **5:** 257
St. Pancras Station, London, **6:** 177; **7:** 441, 442, 444
St. Paul's School, Oxford, **9:** 129, 241
St. Petersburg, Russia, **5:** 282-299, 336-340, 343-349
St. Thomas Schools, Oxford, **9:** 204 n.*333*
St. Vincent's Villa, Ventnor, **6:** 362
Sabbath, a Delight, The (bk. Charles Dodgson Snr.), **2:** 74 n.*149*
Sackville West, see West
Sadler (of Old Headington, Oxford):
  Mary née Harvey (d. 1931), **8:** 379 n.*623*, 385, 509 n.*820*
  Michael Ernest, Mr. (1861-1943) – steward of Christ Church, **8:** 260 n.*439*, 379 n.*623*, 385, 445 n.*713*, 488 n.*790*, 503 n.*808*, 542 n.*866*
Saigeman, Laura (b. 1855), see Tate
Sainton-Dolby, Charlotte Helen (1821-1885) – singer, **2:** 54 n.*106*; **5:** 225

Saker, Horatio (1848-1902) – comedian, **3:** 105, 106 n.*154*
Sale, Mrs., **8:** 59 n.*93*
Salford, Lancashire, **3:** 119
Salisbury, Lord, see Cecil
Salisbury, Wiltshire, **6:** 82, 278, 279
Salisbury Crays, Edinburgh, **3:** 97
"Sally come up" (T. Ramsey and E. W. Mackney) – song, **4:** 93 n.*51*
Salmon, George (1819-1904) – mathematician, **1:** 63 n.*40*, 64, 74, 81, 83; **2:** 28, 113-115; **3:** 15 n.*14*, 136 n.*198*; **4:** 13, 24, 37; **7:** 142
Salmon, Gordon, Rev. (b. 1833), **5:** 38 n.*47*
Salmon, Robert Ingham, Rev. (b. 1834), **4:** 35
Saltburn, Yorkshire, **5:** 102
Salter, William (1804-1875) – artist, **6:** 79 n.*114*
Saltwick Bay, near Whitby, Yorkshire, **5:** 179
Salvation Army, **8:** 568, 569
Salvini, Tomasso (1829-1915) – actor, **6:** 403 n.*661*
Salwey (of Christ Church, Oxford):
Emily née Maxwell (b. 1852), **7:** 488 n.*794*
Herbert, Rev. (1842-1929) – tutor and censor, **6:** 370 n.*608*, 372; **7:** 239 n.*441*, 341, 364, 384, 429, 434, 440, 488 n.*794*; **8:** 371 n.*609*
Salwey (of Blackwater Road, Eastbourne, Sussex):
Geoffrey (b. 1872), **9:** 343 n.*549*, 344
Henry, Rev. (1836-1913), **9:** 343 n.*549*, 344
Lucy Brenda née Christie (b. 1842), **9:** 343 n.*549*, 344
Sambourne, Edward Linley (1845-1910) – illustrator, **6:** 338 n.*560*, 385, 388, 448; **7:** 22 n.*21*, 23, 103, 104 n.*194*
Sampson (of Bristol):
Edith Anne (b. 1849), 307, 333, 339, 352, 356, 357, 359-361
Edward Chaddock, Mr. (1822-1895) –postmaster, **7:** 446 n.*738*
Edward Francis (1848-1918), **1:** 43; **6:** 131 n.*201*, 141, 156, 201, 308, 309, 323, 341, 343, 344, 356-361, 363, 366, 370, 372, 386, 397, 399, 400, 416-418, 420-425, 448, 461, 484, 485, 488, 489; **7:** 20 n.*17*, 26, 27, 48, 64, 65, 85, 86, 90, 117, 136, 137, 162, 225, 269, 270, 276, 320, 321, 325-327, 344, 345, 358-361, 363, 364, 368-370, 375, 377-379, takes over as mathematical lecturer 382, 387, 388, 404, 429, 440, 444, 446, 447, 452, 482, 483, 487, 508, 524, 525, 536, 538, 543; **8:** 11 n.*1*, 26, 27, 29, 30, 54, 55, 90, 96, 110, 111, 139, 206 n.*353*, 245, 276, 295-297, 308, 323, 592, 594, 603; **9:** 111 n.*196*, 113 n.*198*, 148, 149 n.*255*, 248
Ernest (b. 1858), **7:** 446 n.*738*, 526
George (1861-1949), **7:** 446 n.*738*; **9:** 248 n.*391*
Sydney Gerard (1859-1943), **9:** 198 n.*324*
Walter Adam (1856-1913), **7:** 446 n.*738*
Samuel, Saul, Sir (1820-1900) – civil servant, **8:** 64 n.*102*, 65
Samuels, Gertrude Caroline (b. 1865), **6:** 402, 403; **7:** 98 n.*181*, 99, 111
Sand, George (1804-1876) – writer, **7:** 351 n.*613*

Sanday (of Christ Church, Oxford):
Marian C. A. née Hastings (d. 1904), **8:** 625 n.*989*; **9:** 64 n.*117*, 223, 232-234, 236, 260, 309
William, Dr. (1843-1920) – professor of divinity, **8:** 625 n.*989*; **9:** 64 n.*117*, 223, 232-234, 260, 278, 296, 309
Sandeman, Miss – friend of the Owens, **6:** 218
Sanders, Emma (b. 1852) – lodging-house keeper, **7:** 525
Sandford (of Reeves Hall, Essex; and Hanover Square, London):
Alice Ross (b. 1863?), **6:** 247 n.*392*, 248, 255, 373; **7:** 130 n.*243*
Augusta Mary née Greville (b. 1832), **6:** 247 n.*392*, 255, 373; **7:** 129, 130 n.*243*
Blanche Caroline (b. 1865), **6:** 247 n.*392*, 255
Caroline Amabel "Dolly" (b. 1867), **6:** 247 n.*392*, 255
Charlotte Mary "May" (b. 1860?), **6:** 247 n.*392*, 248, 255, 373
Francis Marmaduke Henry (1860-1879), **6:** 247 n.*392*, 248, 255, 373
George Montagu Warren, Mr. (1822-1879) – politician, **6:** 247 n.*392*, 248, 373
Sandford, Charles Waldegrave, Dr. (1828-1903) – tutor and censor at Christ Church, **1:** 66 n.*49*; **2:** 66 n.*131*, 73, 126; **3:** 67, 125; **4:** 54, 72 n.*16*, 92, 134, 211; **5:** 49, 50 n.*67*, 114, 179 n.*297*, 180, 181 n.*299*; **6:** 319, 339
Sandford, Miss – superintendent at Oxford Hospital for Incurables, **7:** 161
Sandford, Oxfordshire, **1:** 71; **2:** 77; **3:** 56, 167; **4:** 73, 74, 81, 161, 174, 219, 277, 298, 303, 308, 322; **5:** 50, 59, 81, 113
Sandford, Richard Forman Manwaring, Lt.-Col. (b. 1834) – army officer, **1:** 58 n.*23*, 65, 66
Sandown, Isle of Wight, **6:** 295-297, 299, 341, 342, 345, 356, 359, 361, 368, 411, 413, 416, 420, 423, 426, 477-479, 482; **7:** 345, 526
Sandown sketch-book, **7:** 45
Sandys, William, Lord (d. 1540), **3:** 71
Sanger's Circus, **4:** 211 n.*222*; **7:** 135
Sankey (of The Turl, Oxford):
Agnes E., Mrs. (b. 1849), **7:** 483 n.*787*
Julius Ottaway, Mr. (b. 1847) – surgeon, **7:** 483 n.*787*
Sankey, Herbert Stuart (b. 1854) – lawyer, **6:** 400 n.*656*
Sans Souci Palace, Potsdam, Germany, **5:** 272, 273
Sant (of Lancaster Gate, Paddington, London):
Ada G. (b. 1859), **4:** 178; **5:** 138 n.*222*, 168 n.*278*, 169, 209; **6:** 16, 69, 75, 126
Eliza née Thomson (1833-1907), **5:** 138 n.*222, 142*, 167, 168, 209, 218; **6:** 69, 75, 158; **7:** 439
Hilda I. F. (b. 1872), **5:** 138 n.*222*
James, Mr. (1820-1916) – artist, **2:** 75 n.*151*; **3:** 76 n.*118*; **4:** 36; **5:** 25, 62 n.*90*, 126, 138 n.*222*, 140, 142, 143, 145 n.*234*, 148, 156, 158, 160, 161, 167 n.*275*, 168-170, 171 n.*284*, 208, 209, 216, 218; **6:** 16, 17 n.*14*, 69, 75, 158; **7:** 439

James "Jimmie" or "Jemmie" (b. 1862), **5:** 138 n.*222*, 169 n.*279*, 209; **6:** 17, 69
Mary Edith (b. 1852), **5:** 138 n.*222*, 142, 167-170, 209; **6:** 17, 69
Minnie Lilla (b. 1854), **5:** 138 n.*222*, 142, 167-169, 209, 225; **6:** 17, 69, 126
Mowbray Lees (b. 1863), **5:** 138 n.*222*, 169, 209; **6:** 17, 69
Sarah Fanny Constance "Tooty" (b. 1856), **4:** 179; **5:** 19, 138 n.*222*, 140, 145 n.*234*, 167 n.*276*, 168-170, 209
Sant, George (b. 1821) – artist, **5:** 138 n.*222*, 209 n.*335*, 218; **6:** 17 n.*14*, 75
Santley, Charles, Sir (1834-1922) – singer, **4:** 341 n.*443*; **5:** 98 n.*155*; **6:** 18 n.*16*; **8:** 427 n.*690*
Sarah Acland Nursing Home, Oxford, **9:** 121 n.*211*
Sarasate, Pablo de (1844-1908) – violinist, **8:** 583 n.*932*
Sardou, Victorien (1831-1908) – dramatist, **5:** 364 n.*539*
Saturday Review, **7:** 276 n.*503*
Saunders (of Priest Gate, Peterborough, Northamptonshire):
Agnes Harriet (b. 1850), **6:** 25 n.*27*
Alfred Robert Henry (1853-1938), **6:** 25 n.*27*
Augustus Page, Very Rev. (1801-1878) – dean of Peterborough, **4:** 33; **5:** 178 n.*295*; **6:** 24 n.*26*, 85
Caroline Louisa (1843-1924), **6:** 25 n.*27*
Cecil Ernest Brassey Pigou (b. 1859) – nephew, **6:** 25 n.*27*
Emma Frances née Walford (1815?-1882), **5:** 178 n.*295*; **6:** 25 n.*27*, 85
Emma Isabella (b. 1841), **6:** 25 n.*27*
Ethel Gertrude (1859-1861), **6:** 25 n.*27*
Florence Matilda (b. 1855), **6:** 25 n.*27*
Margaret (ta) Annie (b. 1848), **6:** 25 n.*27*
Mary Eliza (b. 1846), **6:** 25 n.*27*
Oliver Augustus (1844-1928), **6:** 25 n.*27*
Wilhelmina Blanche (b. 1858) – niece, **6:** 25 n.*27*
Saunders, Silvanus Taylor Hingston (b. 1858), MA Christ Church, **6:** 363 n.*597*
Savage, Marmion W. (1803-1872) – writer, **1:** 90 n.*94*
Scale Force, Cumberland, **2:** 94
Scamps of London, The (dr. Eugene Sue), **5:** 222 n.*353*
Scanlen, Thomas Charles, Sir (1834-1912) – politician, **8:** 52, 53 n.*78*, 58
Scarborough, Yorkshire, **6:** 42, 456, 457, 494, 495; **9:** 225-227
Scarlet fever (at Oxford), **3:** 29 n.*41*
Scaw Fell, Cumberland, **3:** 116
Scenes and Characters (bk. Charlotte Yonge), **4:** 196 n.*197*
Scenes from Clerical Life (bk. George Eliot), **3:** 155 n.*227*
Scheffer, Hendrick (fl. 1839) – artist, **2:** 75 n.*151*
Schlesinger, Henry Guillaume (1814-1893) – artist, **5:** 225 n.*358*; **6:** 22
Schmalz, Herbert Gustave (1857-1935) – artist, **7:** 539 n.*872*; **8:** 220 n.*374*
Schofield, Ethel A. (b. 1869) – logic pupil, **8:** 299 n.*497*, 300 n.*501*
Scholar, The (dr. John Buckstone), **3:** 105, 106 n.*154*

Scholfield (of Fairlawn, Sharow, near Ripon, Yorkshire):
Charles Richard (1832-1902), **2:** 14 n.*22*, 16; **3:** 151 n.*219*
Mary née Champion (b. 1811), **3:** 151 n.*219*
William Edwin Tilt, **3:** 151 n.*219*
William Freer, Mr. (b. 1806) – bank manager, **3:** 151 n.*219*
School (dr. Thomas Robertson), **7:** 278 n.*505*, 319
School Board, **7:** 77
School Edition, Euclid's Elements of Geometry, The (bk. Robert Potts), **1:** 83 n.*87*
School for Scandal, The (dr. Richard Sheridan), **5:** 32 n.*35*; **6:** 250 n.*397*
Schuster (of Haughton Dale, Lancashire):
Edmund Vernon, Rev. (1848-1898), **9:** 168 n.*285*, 169, 207, 213, 217, 273
Harold Vernon (1878-1951), **9:** 168 n.*285*, 169, 170, 282 n.*447*
Isabel Annie née Baynes (1854-1948), **9:** 168 n.*285*, 169, 174, 207, 213, 273
Leonard Walton (1881-1940), **9:** 168 n.*285*, 169
Muriel May (1882-1969), **9:** 168 n.*285*, 169, 171, 173, 178, 207, 217, 220, 274, 332, 334
Violet Isabel (1877-1942), **9:** 168 n.*285*, 169, 170, 178, 212, 219, 276, 335
Winifred "Winnie" Elaine (1879-1947), **9:** 168 n.*285*, 169, 170, 171, 173, 174, 178, 207, 217, 220, 274, 333
Schuster, Mrs., **5:** 188
Scoltock, William (1823-1886) – inspector of schools, **2:** 42 n.*82*, 64, 65, 66 n.*131*, 69, 125; **3:** 20 n.*23*, 26, 32
Scotch Express, **7:** 211
Scotland, **2:** 97; **3:** 24 n.*31*, 94-107
Scott (of Newington, Surrey):
Annie née Leach (b. 1845), **9:** 131 n.*230*
Edward J. W., Mr. (b. 1847) – solicitor's clerk, **9:** 131 n.*230*
Ethel K. (b. 1877), **9:** 151 n.*259*
Mabel Spencer (1874-1949), **9:** 131 n.*230*, 133, 134, 151, 200
Scott (of Eaton Square, London):
Arthur Douglas Bateman (1860-1884), **6:** 164 n.*254*, 220, 247, 373, 375, 441
Catherine "Katie" Matilda Annie Georgina "Pussy" (1859-1937), **6:** 164 n.*254*, 220, 247, 373, 441
Edward William Dolman (1854-1871), **6:** 164 n.*254*, 220
Francis Edward, Sir (1824-1863), **6:** 164 n.*254*
Mabel Augusta (1864-1888), **6:** 164 n.*254*, 220, 247, 373, 441
Mildred Anne, Lady (1829-1909), **6:** 164 n.*254*, 220, 246
Mildred Henrietta (d. 1914), **6:** 164 n.*254*, 220, 247, 441
Scott, Clement William (1841-1904) – author and dramatist, **7:** 320 n.*569*, 540 n.*873*; **8:** 320 n.*525*, 395 n.*641*; **9:** 57 n.*104*, 213 n.*340*
Scott (of Rochester, Kent):
Emma K. H. (b. 1853), **7:** 459 n.*756*, 487
Lilias H. F. (b. 1856), **7:** 459 n.*756*, 487
Mary Agnes (b. 1843), **7:** 459 n.*756*, 487

Mary J. A., Mrs. (b. 1817), **7:** 458, 459 n.*756*
Robert, Rev. Dr. (1811-1887) – dean of Rochester, **1:** 101 n.*111*; **6:** 455 n.*749*; **7:** 458, 459 n.*756*, 461, 470, 487
Walter Folliott (b. 1844), **4:** 192 n.*188*; **5:** 52 n.*72*
Scott, Eric – actor, **8:** 417 n.*675*
Scott, George Gilbert, Sir (1811-1878) – architect, **5:** 175 n.*291*; **6:** 340, 341 n.*566*
Scott (of Kensington, London):
Maud (b. 1872), **8:** 135 n.*221*, 136, 149
Mrs., **8:** 135 n.*221*, 136
Scott, Miss, **9:** 261 n.*412*
Scott (of Oxford):
Mrs., **9:** 254 n.*400*
William Douglas (1893-1917), **9:** 254 n.*400*
Scott, Walter (1771-1832) – writer, **1:** 73
Scott Family of Bracknell, **6:** 88 n.*133*, 96
Scottish songs, **4:** 159 n.*149*
Scott-Siddons:
Mary Frances (1844-1896) – actress, **5:** 220, 221 n.*351*, 222; **6:** 36 n.*50*; **7:** 535 n.*868*; **8:** 82, 83 n.*131*
Thomas Scott, formerly Chanter, RN, **6:** 36
Scratchells Bay, Isle of Wight, **4:** 351
Scrimgeor, Edith (b. 1848) – related to the Forshalls, **7:** 85 n.*147*
Scrivener, see Sinclair
Scudamore, Frank A. (1846-1904) – dramatist, **9:** 164 n.*281*, 165-167
Seaford, Sussex, **7:** 51, 458, 470
Seager, John Lingen, Rev. (1847-1899), **8:** 537 n.*860*
Seal, near Sevenoaks, Kent, **7:** 476, 480
Search after Proserpine (bk. Aubrey De Vere), **4:** 244 n.*274*
Search for Beauty, The (pic. Edwin Long), **9:** 58 n.*106*
Searle, Cyril – dramatist, **7:** 118 n.*222*, 122, 123 n.*231*
Searle, Fanny (b. 1841) – governess to the Woodroffes, **7:** 54 n.*86*
Seascale, Cumberland, **7:** 211
"Sea Serpent, The" (Anon) – comic song, **1:** 26
Sea-Side House, Ventnor (Mrs. Callaway), **6:** 358, 361
Seasons, The (Haydn), **3:** 66
Seathwaite, Lancashire, **2:** 92
Sea-View, Ryde, Isle of Wight, **6:** 295-297, 334, 342, 354, 359, 412, 418
Sebastopol, Russia, **1:** 54 n.*14*, 75, 104, 130; **4:** 145, 146
Second Hebrew Book, The (bk. Thomas K. Arnold), **5:** 131 n.*210*
Sedger, Horace (1853-1917) – dramatist, **9:** 139 n.*240*
Selbourne, Lord, see Palmer
Selby, Charles (1801-1863) – dramatist, **2:** 123 n.*238*; **3:** 153 n.*223*, 171 n.*250*; **8:** 406 n.*660*
Selections from Shakespeare (Samuel Brandram), **7:** 418 n.*698*

Sells (of High Street, Guildford, Surrey):
Charles John (b. 1847) – physician, **6:** 102 n.*161*
Frances D. (b. 1854), **6:** 102 n.*161*
Hubert Thomas - physician, **6:** 102 n.*161*
Thomas Jenner, Dr. (1811-1879) – physician, **6:** 102 n.*161*
Selwyn (of Liverpool, Lancashire):
Edward Carus, Mr. (1853-1918) – principal of Liverpool College, **8:** 100 n.*165*, 188
Lucy Ada née Arnold (1858-1894), **6:** 145 n.*220*, 209 n.*328*; **7:** 87 n.*153*, 88 n.*156*, 177, 228, 264, 496, 497, 522, 523, 531, 536; **8:** 57 n.*88*, 100 n.*165*, 188, 379
Semonof Monastery, Moscow, Russia, **5:** 313, 314
Senior, Jane Elizabeth née Hughes (1828-1877), **4:** 246 n.*279*
Sensations of the Past Season, The, or, 1863 (dr. Henry Byron), **4:** 270 n.*313*
Serf, The, or Love Levels All (dr. Tom Taylor), **5:** 85 n.*133*, 94, 97
Sergeant, Edmund William (b. 1836), MA Balliol, **4:** 163 n.*156*
Serious Family, The (dr. Morris Barnett), **8:** 575 n.*918*
Sermons by XXXIX Living Divines (bk. George Dugard and Alexander Watson), **2:** 74 n.*149*
Sermons on the Christian Sabbath (bk. Charles Dodgson Snr.), **2:** 74
Settling Day (dr. Tom Taylor), **5:** 36 n.*41*, 59, 60 n.*86*, 63 n.*93*, 71
Severne (of Thenfold, Northamptonshire):
Mrs., **5:** 233 n.*374*
Walter Meysey, Mr. (1838-1878), MA Christ Church, **5:** 233 n.*374*
Sewell (of New College, Oxford):
Emma (b. 1818), **6:** 451 n.*741*; **7:** 82 n.*138*, 143
James Edwards, Dr. (1811-1903) – warden of New College, **6:** 292 n.*481*, 450; **7:** 22 n.*20*, 31 n.*40*, 35, 82, 143; **8:** 60 n.*96*, 220, 264
Jane (b. 1820), **6:** 451; **7:** 82 n.*138*, 143
Sewell:
Fitzroy, Mr., **7:** 245 n.*449*
Georgina "Georgie" née Ottley (b. 1847), **2:** 86 n.*171*; **3:** 150 n.*218*; **5:** 75; **7:** 245 n.*449*, 246
Helen, **7:** 245 n.*449*, 246
Sewell, Mrs., **4:** 293
Seymour (of Taunton, Somerset):
Elizabeth née Lloyd (b. 1833), **6:** 301 n.*496*; **9:** 63 n.*116*
Henry Fortescue, Rev. (1827-1900), **9:** 63 n.*116*
Isabel Fortescue (1856-1916), see Weigall
Mary Maud Fortescue (1861-1896), **6:** 301 n.*496*; **7:** 269; **9:** 63 n.*116*, 251
Seymour, Georgiana née Ellice, Lady (d. 1907), **8:** 630 n.*995*
Seys (of Museum Road, Oxford):
Eda Alison (1888-1965), **9:** 317 n.*508*

Evelyn Vaughan née Hughes (1859-1923), **9:** 317 n.*508*, 323
Godfrey, Mr. (1859-1905) – magistrate, **9:** 317 n.*508*
Godfrey William (1885-1963), **9:** 317 n.*508*
Robert Cecil (1883-1921), **9:** 317 n.*508*
Shadow of Death (pic. William Holman Hunt), **6:** 258 n.*411*, 335
Shadows of the Clouds (bk. James Froude), **1:** 97 n.*103*
Shadwell, Charles Lancelot (1840-1919) – undergraduate at Christ Church, **4:** 199 n.*203*, 291 n.*347*; **7:** 440, 485 n.*789*
Shadwell, Mary (or Mabel (b. 1853)), **4:** 181
Shaftesbury, Dorset, **6:** 233
Shaftesbury, Lord, see Ashley-Cooper
Shah of Persia, **6:** 282
Shairp, John Campbell, Prof. (1819-1885) – professor of poetry, **7:** 100 n.*185*
Shakespeare, William (1564-1616) – dramatist, **1:** 62 n.*37*, 68, 73, 85; **3:** 81, 156 n.*230*; **7:** 351

Shakespeare's Plays:
As You Like It, **5:** 220; **8:** 418
Coriolanus, **7:** 368
Cymbeline, **5:** 23; **7:** 368
Hamlet, **2:** 20; **4:** 248, 312; **6:** 403 n.*661*; **7:** 156 n.*294*, 158, 159; **8:** 168, 424, 616 n.*976*; **9:** 280
Henry IV, **1:** 68, 133; **4:** 281 (*Part I*), 291 n.*348*
Henry V, **1:** 62
Henry VIII, **1:** 105, 125, 128; **2:** 9 n.*6*, 19 n.*34*, 20 n.*36*, 21, 22, 83; **8:** 619
Julius Caesar, **8:** 496
King John, **5:** 31 n.*33*; **6:** 281, 282; **8:** 550
King Lear, **6:** 104; **9:** 44 n.*77*
Macbeth, **2:** 47, 48, 100; **4:** 248; **7:** 96, 377, 378, 536; **8:** 456
Merchant of Venice, The, **7:** 236, 442, 540; **8:** 68, 336, 338; **9:** 21 n.*24*, 73, 75, 203, 204
Midsummer Night's Dream, **2:** 123, 124; **3:** 14, 153; **6:** 130; **8:** 417, 500, 501
Much Ado About Nothing, **7:** 493, 494, 508, 516; **8:** 126, 342; **9:** 205
Othello, **1:** 85
Richard II, **3:** 52
Richard III, **2:** 47; **7:** 368; **8:** 449, 451 n.*722*, 454
Romeo and Juliet, **6:** 36
Taming of the Shrew, The, **9:** 121
Tempest, The, **3:** 81, 126, 132; **8:** 182
Twelfth Night, **7:** 315; **8:** 131, 423; **9:** 132 n.*231*
Two Gentlemen of Verona, **7:** 368
Winter's Tale, The, **2:** 82, 124

Shalford, near Guildford, Surrey, **6:** 350; **7:** 117; **8:** 610
Shalford Rectory, **9:** 291
Shand, Thomas Henry Rodie, Rev. (1827-1914), **6:** 35 n.*48*
Shanklin, Isle of Wight, **6:** 295, 341, 342, 354, 360, 416, 417, 478, 480; **7:** 345, 525, 526
Shanklin Chine, **6:** 296, 297, 342, 360
Sharman, Frank – cousin of the Powells, **4:** 256 n.*295*
Sharow, near Ripon, Yorkshire, **5:** 43
Sharp (of Eastbourne, Sussex):
  Martin R., Mr. (b. 1820) – newspaper editor, **8:** 230 n.*389*
  Oliva S., Mrs. (b. 1841), **8:** 230 n.*389*
Sharp, Miss – logic pupil, **8:** 335 n.*551*
Sharpe (of Kensington, London):
  Evelyn A. (b. 1869), **7:** 66 n.*106*, 75
  Gertrude S. (b. 1867), **7:** 66 n.*106*, 75
  Hester F. (b. 1872), **7:** 66 n.*106*
  Louisa M. (b. 1870), **7:** 66 n.*106*
  Sarah Jane, Mrs. (b. 1838), **7:** 66 n.*106*
Sharpe – pupil of Walter Watson, **7:** 182 n.*340*
Shaw, Miss – teacher, **9:** 207, 208 n.*337*, 277
Shaw-Lefevre, Madeline (1835-1914) – principal of Somerville College, **8:** 89 n.*145*, 171
Shaw-Stewart (of Oxford):
  Archibald Claud “George” (1859-1938), **6:** 119 n.*182*, 257, 311, 314
  Constance Angela (1862-1942), **6:** 119 n.*182*, 257, 311, 314
  Constance Mary née Johnston (b. 1850) – third wife, **6:** 119 n.*182*
  Helenor (1858-1946), **6:** 119 n.*182*, 257
  Helenora Margaret Angela née Alexander (d. 1865) – first wife, **6:** 119 n.*182*
  Isabella Barbara née Hume (d. 1883) – second wife, **6:** 119 n.*182*
  John Archibald, Mr. (1829-1900) – magistrate and bursar of Keble, **6:** 119 n.*182*, 162, 164, 196, 206, 213, 216, 220, 257, 306, 311, 312, 314, 460; **7:** 34 n.*48*, 261, 262
Sheard, Thomas Frederick Mason (1866-1921) – artist, **9:** 70 n.*129*
Sheddon (of Kensington, London):
  Caroline. Mrs. (b. 1826), **6:** 55 n.*81*
  Thomas, Mr. (b. 1826) – barrister, **6:** 55 n.*81*
Sheep in Wolf's Clothing, A (dr. Tom Taylor), **3:** 51 n.*78*; **5:** 115 n.*179*, 117, 241 n.*390*
Sheepshanks, Katharine Evelyn (b. 1881) – logic pupil, **9:** 259 n.*409*, 264 n.*417*, 265
Shelley, Frances née Winckley, Lady (d. 1873), **6:** 224 n.*352*
Shelley, Percy Bysshe (1792-1822) – poet, **1:** 53, 118 n.*144*
Shelton, George (1852-1932) – actor, **8:** 113 n.*184*
Shepley Family – friends of the Wilcoxes, **7:** 283 n.*515*, 289

Sheppard, Jack (1702-1724) – executed burglar, **3:** 127
Sheppard, Mr., **7:** 264
Shere, Surrey, **6:** 225, 243
Sheridan, Richard Brinsley (1751-1816) – dramatist, **5:** 32 n.*35*, 153 n.*248*; **7:** 540 n.*873*
Sherrington, see Lemmens-Sherrington
Sherwit (of Alvaston, Derbyshire):
Mary, **2:** 106
Mr. – clerk at Alvaston, **2:** 106 n.*204*
Willie, **2:** 106
Sherwood (of Eastbourne, Sussex):
Arthur Paul, Mr. (1852-1923) – surgeon, **7:** 219 n.*401*, 295; **8:** 288 n.*484*, 482, 483; **9:** 30 n.*48*
Arthur W. (b. 1881), **7:** 219 n.*401*
Katherine D., Mrs. (b. 1858), **7:** 219 n.*401*
She Stoops to Conquer (dr. Oliver Goldsmith), **9:** 22 n.*26*, 273
Shields, Mr., – artist, **7:** 537 n.*870*; **8:** 108 n.*178*
Shippon, Berkshire, **5:** 54 n.*77*, 56, 74
Shirley (of Christ Church, Oxford):
Alice (1857-1911), **4:** 178, 294 n.*354*, 295, 309
Claude (nephew), **4:** 295
Loeta (b. 1862), **4:** 298 n.*361*
Mary (b. 1859?), **4:** 181, 294 n.*354*, 295, 309
Philippa Frances Emilia née Knight (d. 1902), **4:** 294; **6:** 31
Ralph (1865-1946), **6:** 31 n.*39*
Walter Knight (1864-1937), **6:** 31 n.*39*
Walter Waddington, Dr. (1828-1866) – professor of ecclesiastical history, **4:** 294 n.*354*, 298 n.*361*, 305, 309; **5:** 51 n.*71*; **6:** 31 n.*39*
Shirley, Arthur (1852-1925) – dramatist, **9:** 284 n.*449*
Shocking Events (dr. John Buckstone), **5:** 139 n.*223*
"Shoemaker, The" (Beatrice Hatch) – manuscript drama, **9:** 294, 295 n.*466*
Shoreham, near Brighton, Sussex, **6:** 291
Short, Ambrose (b. 1833), MA New College, **3:** 54, 55 n.*84*
Short Course of History (bk. Havilland Chepmell), **1:** 11
"Shortlands," Ryde (home of Benjamin Barrow), **6:** 417, 421
"Shot" (Mr. Russell's dog), **5:** 177 n.*293*
Shotover, Oxfordshire, **9:** 133 n.*234*, 278, 312, 326
Shotover House, **9:** 312 n.*497*
Shrewsbury, Shropshire, **7:** 126, 145 n.*270*, 146, 311
Shrimpton, Messrs. Thomas & George, booksellers, stationers and photographers, Broad Street, Oxford, **4:** 139, 140 n.*118*, 177
Shrub Hill Station, Worcester, **6:** 239
Shuldham (of Seymour Street, London):
Edward Barton, Dr. (b. 1826) – physician and homeopath, **2:** 110 n.*214*; **3:** 26 n.*35*, 34, 61, 64, 68, 123; **7:** 90 n.*161*, 105, 142, 193, 491 n.*799*

Mrs., **7:** 90
Shuldham, John (1794-1884) – Edward Barton Shuldham's uncle, **3:** 34
Shute (of Guildford, Surrey):
Alice, **6:** 104
Eva, **6:** 104 n.*163*
Shute (of Christ Church, Oxford):
Edith Letitia née Hutchinson (1858-1952), **7:** 488 n.*795*, 494; **8:** 43 n.*61*, 83, 85, 96, 178, 196, 209, 245, 264, 357-359, 376-378, 410, 422-424, 511, 512, 522, 589, 619, 628; **9:** 316 n.*505*
Richard L. (1849-1886) – tutor, **6:** 366, 372 n.*611*; **7:** 121 n.*227*, 237, 238, 239 n.*441*, 247, 260, 320, 330, 434, 440, 488 n.*795*; **8:** 43 n.*61*, 83, 96, 195, 209, 263, 264, 296 n.*493*, 417, 421
Sibson, Francis, Dr. (1814-1876) – physician, **6:** 350 n.*581*
Sick Doll, The (pic. Kate Perugini), **7:** 533 n.*863*
Siddons, Sarah née Kemble (1755-1831) – actress, **1:** 105
Siddons, see also Scott-Siddons
Sidgwick (of Woodstock Road, Oxford):
Arthur, Mr. (1840-1920) – tutor, **8:** 94 n.*154*, 626, 627
Charlotte née Wilson (b. 1853), **8:** 624 n.*987*, 626, 627; **9:** 70 n.*128*
Ethel (1877-1970), **8:** 624 n.*987*, 626, 627, 634
Margaret "Margie" (1881-1949), **8:** 624 n.*987*, 627, 629, 634; **9:** 70 n.*128*
Rose (1877-1918), **8:** 624 n.*987*, 627, 629, 634
Sidgwick (of Park Town, Oxford):
Sarah J., Mrs. (b. 1833), **7:** 32 n.*43*
William Carr, Mr. (b. 1834) – lecturer, **3:** 93 n.*144*; **7:** 32 n.*43*
Siedel, Fraülein – governess to the Smiths of Shipton, **9:** 184 n.*305*, 269
Sierra Leone, Africa, **7:** 370 n.*644*, 372
Sigh no more, ladies (pic. Arthur Hughes), **6:** 16 n.*13*
Signal, The (pic. Pierre Coomans), **5:** 223, 224 n.*356*
"Silent Pool, The," near Guildford, **6:** 225 n.*354*, 295; **7:** 117, 344, 442; **8:** 628
Silent Woman, The (dr. Ben Jonson), **6:** 250 n.*396*
Silva (bk. John Evelyn), **9:** 304 n.*483*
Silver Gilt (dr. W. Warham), **8:** 59 n.*92*
Silver King, The (dr. Henry Jones and Henry Herman), **7:** 524, 525 n.*849*; **8:** 52 n.*77*, 59, 197, 198, 199 n.*337*, 457, 587; **9:** 170, 173 n.*290*
Sim, Mr. – Christ Church treasury clerk, **7:** 258 n.*469*, 260
Simcox, Charlotte (b. 1831), "Sister Mary Theresa," **8:** 270 n.*455*, 275
Sime, Donald (b. 1848), MA Worcester, **8:** 306 n.*508*
Simeon, John, Sir (1815-1870) – politician, **4:** 14, 17, 18
Simms, Sarah – pupil at St. Aldates, **2:** 32
Simpson (of Hastings, Sussex):
Arthur C. P. W., Capt. (b. 1874) – army officer, **9:** 188 n.*311*
Kathleen, Mrs. (b. 1872), **9:** 188 n.*311*
Simpson, Charles – pupil at St. Aldates, **2:** 30

Simpson (of Kensington, London):
Charles Turner, Mr. (1819-1902) – barrister, **6:** 199 n.*309*, 223, 309-311; **7:** 235, 315, 397, 511; **8:** 284 n.*477*; **9:** 27 n.*38*
Gaynor Anne (1862-1954), **6:** 199 n.*309*, 217, 221, 249; **7:** 224, 235, 335, 429; **9:** 27 n.*38*
Gaynor Elizabeth née Williams – first wife, **6:** 199 n.*309*
Henrietta Mary Amy (1866-1957), **6:** 199 n.*309*, 217, 221, 250; **7:** 235, 316 n.*561*, 429, 511
Mary Charlotte Mair née Senior (b. 1826) – second wife, **6:** 199 n.*309*, 206, 216, 217, 221, 223, 249, 309-311; **7:** 235, 315, 397, 429, 511; **9:** 27 n.*38*
Reginald Wynne (1858-1936), **6:** 199 n.*309*, 221, 249; **7:** 224 n.*412*, 272, 335, 381
Walter (b. 1856?), **6:** 199 n.*309*, 249
Simpson (of Windsor, Berkshire):
Edith (b. 1870), **5:** 83 n.*129*
Elizabeth Frances Ann (b. 1858), **4:** 180; **5:** 83 n.*129*, 84
Grace H. M. (b. 1868), **5:** 83 n.*129*
Harry W. (b. 1855), **5:** 83 n.*129*
John Percy G. (b. 1861), **5:** 83 n.*129*, 84
Mary Elizabeth, Mrs. (b. 1835), **4:** 320, 321 n.*407*; **5:** 83 n.*129*, 84
Robert A. (b. 1853), **5:** 83 n.*129*
Robert James, Rev. (1823-1900), **4:** 320, 321 n.*407*; **5:** 83 n.*129*, 84, 102, 221, 233
Simpson (of Stoke, near Guildford, Surrey):
Eliza J. M. (b. 1845), **9:** 188 n.*311*
Robert Hamilton, Lt.-Col. (b. 1829) – army officer, **9:** 188 n.*311*
Simpson, John (1790-1870) – farmer, **2:** 8 n.*3*
Simpson, John Palgrave (1807-1887) – dramatist, **3:** 51 n.*78*
Simpson and Co. (dr. John Poole), **5:** 85 n.*133*
Simpson's Restaurant, London, **5:** 122
Sims, George R. (1847-1922) – dramatist, **8:** 208 n.*355*, 382 n.*626*; **9:** 20 n.*22*, 284 n.*449*
Sims, Lizzie – actress, **7:** 153 n.*290*
Sinclair, Catherine (1800-1864) – writer, **4:** 57
Sinclair, or Scrivener, (of London):
Harry (1872-1940), **7:** 98 n.*182*, 158, 186, 542 n.*875*
Jessie Josephine (1865-1952), **7:** 98 n.*182*, 156, 158, 186, 542 n.*875*, 543; **8:** 477, 478, 501; **9:** 96 n.*174*
Joseph Henry, Mr. (1829-1879), real name Scrivener – actor, **7:** 75 n.*120*, 105, 114, 156, 158, 167, 186
Kate "Katie" Jemima (b. 1869), **7:** 98 n.*182*, 158, 184, 542 n.*875*
Maria née Moger (d. 1879), **7:** 98 n.*182*, 105, 114, 156, 158, 167
Sarah "Sally" Caroline, "Little Cerito" (1868-1956) – actress, **7:** 75 n.*120*, 91, 98 n.*182*, 106, 107 n.*198*, 156, 158, 184, 542 n.*875*;

8: 194, 195 n.*328*, 208, 477, 501; **9:** 96 n.*174*
Sinclair, Rose (b. 1882) – friend of the Gamlens, **8:** 632 n.*1002*
Singer, Isaac Merritt (1811-1875), and Company – manufacturer, **8:** 21 n.*16*
Sir Galahad (pic. Arthur Hughes), **5:** 158 n.*259*, 211
Sisters, The (Alexander Munro) – sculpture, **6:** 13 n.*7*
Sisters, The (pic. William Richmond), **5:** 60 n.*87*
Sister's Kiss (pic. Frederick Leighton), **7:** 188 n.*350*
Sister Voices for the Field, Factory and Fire-Side (bk. Elihu Burritt), **1:** 134 n.*169*
Skeffington, John, Viscount Massareene (d. 1695) – distant relative, **1:** 10
Skeffington, William, Sir (d. 1535) – very distant relative, **1:** 10
Skeffington, Mr. – cousin of Edmund Southwell, **8:** 193 n.*324*
Skelton on Ure, Yorkshire, **2:** 14, 15 n.*24*
Skene (of Pitlour House, Fife, Scotland):
Alice Janet (b. 1875), **8:** 323 n.*535*; **9:** 71 n.*131*, 72
Ina Katharine Hilda (b. 1877), **8:** 323 n.*535*; **9:** 71 n.*131*, 72
Lorina Charlotte née Liddell (1849-1930), **1:** 101 n.*111*, 126 n.*155*; **2:** 43 n.*86*, made friends with 49 n.*97*, 65 n.*129*, 66, 73, first boat trip 78, 108, 111 n.*216*, 112, 116, 125, 126; **3:** 20, 28, 44, 45, 48, 62, 65, takes photo of Dodgson 66, 73, 121, 123, leaves for Madeira 129; **4:** 11, 24, 33, 35, 42, 44, 48, 57, 69 n.*11*, river trip to Nuneham 81 n.*33*, 83, 84, 88, 93, river trip to Godstow 94, 96, 98, 103, 110-115, 136, 139, 141, crest books 146, 149, 153, 162, 163, 171-177, 180, Cheltenham invitation 185 n.*180*, 186 n.*181*, 187, 192-200, 204, 206, 208, 210-213, rumours 214 n.*227*, 257 n.*299*, 264 n.*309*, 266, 298, 299 n.*364*, 307; **5:** 19, 57 n.*81*, 60 n.*87*, 86, 122 n.*192*, 188, 243 n.*395*; **6:** last photograph 121 n.*184*, marriage 321 n.*534*; **8:** 99 n.*164*, meets her children 323 n.*535*, 516, 571 n.*911*, tea-party 597; **9:** 71 n.*131*, 72
Lucy Edith (b. 1882?), **8:** 323 n.*535*; **9:** 71 n.*131*, 72
Philip George Moncrieff, **8:** 323 n.*535*
Ruth Mary (1884?-1915), **8:** 323 n.*535*
William Baillie, Mr. (1838-1911) – treasurer of Christ Church, **6:** 321 n.*534*; **8:** 284 n.*476*, 323 n.*535*, 432, 502 n.*806*, 560 n.*892*; **9:** 71 n.*131*, 286 n.*452*
Sketchley, Arthur (1818-1882), real name George Rose – actor, **4:** 287 n.*343*
Skiddaw, Cumberland, **2:** 95
Slade (of Kensington, London):
Alfred Frederic Adolphus, Sir (1834-1890), 3rd Baronet, **7:** 201 n.*377*, 206, 210, 212, 215, 216, 218
Basil Alfred (b. 1865), **7:** 201 n.*377*
Constance Maud (b. 1871), **7:** 201 n.*377*, 202, 213-215, 217, 218
Cuthbert (b. 1863), **7:** 201 n.*377*
Marguerite Irene (b. 1868), **7:** 201 n.*377*, 202, 206, 214, 215, 217, 218
Mary Constance née Cuthbert (b. 1845), **7:** 201 n.*377*, 213, 215-218

Violet Mary (b. 1862), **7:** 201 n.*377*, 216, 217
Slade School, Headington, Oxford, **5:** 81
Slade School of Art, **7:** 360, 442, 443 n.*733*; **8:** 79
Slater (of Chesterton, Cambridge):
Adelaide Margaret (b. 1869), **7:** 312 n.*557*, 313
Francis, Rev. (1837-1897), **6:** 443, 444 n.*726*
Slatter (of Whitchurch, Oxfordshire):
Elizabeth, Mrs. (b. 1812), **4:** 102, 136, 185, 295, 302; **5:** 68, 69, 134 n.*216*, 148; **7:** 252, 427, 531; **8:** 200 n.*341*, 234, 237
Elizabeth "Bessie" Ann (b. 1854), **4:** 35, 102, 136, 178, 185, 295; **5:** 19, 48, 134; **7:** 53, 252, 427, 531; **8:** 200 n.*341*, 234, 236; **9:** 73
John, Rev. (1818-1899), **4:** 35, 43, 72 n.*17*, 102, 135, 185, 295, 302; **5:** 48 n.*64*, 68, 69, 134 n.*216*, 148; **7:** 174, 251 n.*459*, 252, 370, 427, 531; **8:** 200 n.*341*, 234, 237, 303, 487; **9:** 34 n.*58*, 71, 73, 203
Slatter's Bookshop, Oxford, **2:** 33; **5:** 180; **6:** 324
Slaughter, Walter (1860-1908) – composer, **8:** 291 n.*487*, 546
Sleep (Henry Holiday) – sculpture, **7:** 184 n.*343*
Sleeping (pic. John Millais), **5:** 213 n.*341*
Sleeping Princess, The (Alfred Tennyson) – tableaux vivants, **4:** 42
Sleights, Yorkshire, **6:** 52 n.*74*, 171
Sligo, Lord, see Browne
Sloane Square, London, **6:** 198; **7:** 511
Slough, Buckinghamshire, **4:** 294
Smallpeice (of Guildford, Surrey):
Alice (b. 1842), **6:** 90 n.*138*
Alicia, Mrs. (b. 1815), **6:** 90 n.*138*
Frederick (b. 1844), **6:** 90 n.*138*
Grace (b. 1851), **6:** 90 n.*138*
James S. (b. 1853), **6:** 90 n.*138*
Mark, Mr. (b. 1813) – solicitor, **6:** 90 n.*138*, 349
Small-pox, **4:** 198
Smart, Antoinette "Netty" A. (1847-1923), see Matheson

Smedley:

Smedley (of Whitburn, Durham):
Anna – aunt, **4:** 23
Eliza (d. 1859) – aunt, **4:** 23
Smedley (of Tenby, Pembrokeshire):
Clara née Curgenven – wife of second cousin, **4:** 189 n.*186*
Edith (b. 1851) – distant cousin, **4:** 189 n.*186*, 190
Edward Gerard (b. 1844) – distant cousin, **4:** 188 n.*183*
Edward Hume, Mr. (1817-1862), barrister – second cousin, **4:** 189 n.*186*
Egerton Bernard (b. 1850) – distant cousin, **4:** 189 n.*186*
Frances "Fanny" Millicent (b. 1848) – distant cousin, **4:** 189 n.*186*, 190

Mary "Minnie" Hume Craven (b. 1846) – distant cousin, **4:** 189 n.*186*, 190
Winifred "Nellie" (b. 1847) – distant cousin, **4:** 189 n.*186*, 190
Smedley (of Tenby, Pembrokeshire):
Edward, Rev. (1788-1836) – great-uncle, **1:** 9; **4:** 189 n.*186*
Edward Hume (1817-1862) – second cousin, see below
Elizabeth "Honie" (1822-1888) – second cousin, **4:** 189 n.*186*
Mary (b. 1821?) – second cousin, **4:** 189 n.*186*
Mary neé Hume (1786-1868) – great-aunt, **1:** 9, 27, 39, 107 n.*121*, 110 n.*127*; **4:** 188 n.*183*, 189 n.*186*; **5:** 24
Menella Bute (1820-1877), poet and writer – second cousin, **1:** 10, 27, 39, 107 n.*121*, 110 n.*127*, 113; **2:** 13 n.*19*, 40, 110; **4:** 19, 116, 188 n.*183*, 189 n.*186*, 190; **5:** 86 n.*134*; **6:** 83 n.*123*, 84, 157 n.*243*, 189, 198, 199, 205, 209, 219, 294, 333, 334, 344, 350, 361-363, 459, 478; **7:** 12 n.*4*, 36 n.*52*, 67
Smedley (of Westminster, London):
Frances Sarah née Ellison – wife of distant cousin, **4:** 116
Francis, Mr. (1791-1859), bailiff – distant cousin, **4:** 116
Francis "Frank" Edward (1818-1864), writer – distant cousin, **1:** 9, 107 n.*121*, 110 n.*127*, 112, 114, 122, 123, 131, 132; **2:** 14 n.*20*; **3:** 133

Smith – pupil of Wilfred Dodgson, **7:** 125, 126 n.*236*, 311 n.*555*
Smith, A. – actress, **2:** 22 n.*40*
Smith, Ada (b. 1868) – artists' model, **7:** 190 n.*353*
Smith (of Brighton, Sussex):
Agnes Caroline (b. 1867), **7:** 67 n.*110*, 71, 72, 75, 94, 153-155, 215-217, 313, 362
Frances E. née Boddington (b. 1835), **7:** 67 n.*110*, 71, 72, 128, 153, 154, 215-217, 313, 362, 366, 456, 468, 479, 509, 510; **8:** 34 n.*41*, 40, 130, 146, 160, 226, 237, 347, 348, 354, 415, 604; **9:** 272 n.*431*
Gracilla "Grace" (b. 1869), **7:** 67 n.*110*, 72, 75, 94, 153, 215, 216, 362, 456, 468, 473, 510; **8:** 34 n.*41*, 40, 146, 160, 226, 237, 348, 354
Reginald H. (b. 1871), **7:** 67 n.*110*, 71, 94, 153, 215, 468, 510; **8:** 354
Smith, Albert Richard (1816-1860) – writer and dramatist, **1:** 123; **2:** 52 n.*104*, 123 n.*240*; **3:** 120 n.*168*, 173; **4:** 281 n.*331*
Smith, Alexander (1830-1867) – poet, **4:** 109
Smith (of Ripon, Yorkshire):
Alfred, Mr. (d. 1849) – surgeon, **3:** 136 n.*197*, 147 n.*211*
Alfred Fowler (1831-1891) – teacher, **3:** 136 n.*197*, 147 n.*211*, 148, 149
Mary née Hindle, 136 n.*197*
Smith, Alfred Charles, Rev. (b. 1823), **3:** 164 n.*237*
Smith (of Shanklin, Isle of Wight):
Alice, **6:** 355
Helen, **6:** 355, 356
Smith (of Shipton upon Cherwell, Oxfordshire):

Alice "Boozy" (b. 1882?), **9:** 184 n.*305*, 269
Charles "Charlie" (b. 1885?), **9:** 184 n.*305*, 269
Edward "Ted" (b. 1892?), **9:** 184 n.*305*, 269
Herbert (b. 1878), **9:** 184 n.*305*, 269, 314
Herbert (or Harold), Mr. (b. 1860) – clerk, **9:** 250 n.*393*, 269, 283, 286, 314
Mary Eleanor "Polly" née Donkin (b. 1856?), **4:** 131 n.*106*, 131 n.*107*, 132 n.*109*, 134, 181; **6:** 52, 137; **9:** 184 n.*305*, 250 n.393, 269, 283, 286
Stella (b. 1888), **9:** 184 n.*305*, 269
William "Willie" (b. 1890?), **9:** 184 n.*305*, 269
Smith (of Dinsdale, Yorkshire):
Anne Grey (1847-1863), **2:** 84 n.*168*, 85
Fanny Grey (1846-1874), **2:** 84 n.*168*, 85; **4:** 22
Frederick John Grey (b. 1853), **2:** 84 n.*168*
Joanna Grey (1845-1932), **2:** 84 n.*168*, 85; **4:** 22
John William, Rev. (1811-1897), **2:** 84 n.*168*; **3:** 84 n.*130*, 140; **4:** 22
Maria Grey (b. 1843), **2:** 84 n.*168*, 85; **4:** 22
Maria née Grey (1808-1898), **2:** 84 n.*168*; **3:** 84 n.*130*, 140; **4:** 22
William Arthur Grey (1849-1886), **2:** 84 n.*168*, 85; **4:** 22
Smith (of Eastbourne, Sussex):
Caroline Margaret née Cowie (1855-1914), **8:** 422 n.*683*
Irton, Rev. (1856-1933), **8:** 422 n.*683*
Smith, Cicely "Cissie" (b. 1875) – friend of the Albuquerques, **8:** 346 n.*570*
Smith (of Torquay, Devon):
Clement M., Dr. (b. 1828) – military surgeon, **6:** 98 n.*153*
Laura (b. 1861), **6:** 98 n.*153*
Smith (of Oxford):
Eleanor Elizabeth (1823-1896), **4:** 147
Henry John Stephen (1826-1883) – professor of geometry, **4:** 147, 307 n.*378*
Smith, Francis (b. 1823) – auctioneer, **6:** 43, 44 n.*61*
Smith, Gertrude (b. 1858) – sister-in-law to Polly Smith, **9:** 184 n.*305*, 269
Smith, Gilbert Nicholas, Rev. (1796-1877), **4:** 190 n.*187*
Smith (of Oxford):
Goldwin (1823-1910) – fellow of University College, **3:** 164 n.*237*; **5:** 180, 181 n.*299*; **6:** 308, 338, 339, 459 n.*755*
Harriet E. M. Boulton née Dixon (d. 1909), **6:** 459 n.*755*
Smith, Henry – pupil at St. Aldates, **2:** 30
Smith, Henry, Dr. (b. 1827) – physician, **8:** 506 n.*813*
Smith, Herbert – related to the Mallalieus, **9:** 27 n.*40*
Smith (of London):
Horatio (1779-1849) – writer, **1:** 59 n.*29*
James (1775-1839) – writer, **1:** 59 n.*29*
Smith, Isaac Gregory, Rev. (1826-1920), **6:** 267 n.*429*
Smith, J. C. (1808-1888) – actor, **5:** 109 n.*172*

Smith, Kate Alice (fl. 1879) – artist, **5:** 201 n.*327*
Smith, Messrs. H. & J. – offered betting secret, **5:** 183 n.*301*
Smith, Miss – aunt of the Millers, **7:** 355 n.*620*, 357
Smith, Mr., **9:** 213 n.*341*
Smith (of Richmond, Surrey):
Mrs., **7:** 178 n.*329*
Robert Willan Ashby, Rev. (1814-1879), **7:** 178 n.*329*
Smith, Muriel A. Howard (b. 1878) – amateur actress, **8:** 496, 497 n.*799*
Smith, Samuel Albert, Rev. (b. 1848), **7:** 126 n.*237*, 145 n.*270*
Smith, Stella (b. 1882) – niece of Mrs. Miller, **9:** 22 n.*27*, 23, 24, 95
Smith, S. Theyre – dramatist, **7:** 183 n.*342*
Smith, William Slayter, Capt. (1792-1865) – army officer, **3:** 168 n.*245*, 170 n.*249*
Smith Barry, Arthur Hugh (1843-1925) – amateur actor at Christ Church, **4:** 263 n.*308*
Smyth, William (1765-1849) – writer, **1:** 73 n.*65*, 74
Smythe (of Barbavilla House, Collinstown, County Westmeath, Ireland):
Louisa Ellen Lyster, **8:** 318 n.*522*
Lydia Lucy Lyster, **8:** 318 n.*522*
Maud Frances Lyster, **8:** 318 n.*522*
Smythies, Charles Alan, Rt. Rev. (1844-1894), **8:** 517 n.*833*
Smythies, Raymond Brewster (1824-1861) – teacher, **1:** 26
Snow (of Exeter, Devon):
Walter Francis (b. 1861) – wine commercial traveller, **8:** 93 n.*151*, 261
William M., Mr. (b. 1825) – wine merchant, **8:** 93 n.*151*, 605 n.*961*
Snowball, John Charles (d. 1855) – mathematician, **1:** 65 n.*46*
Snowdrop (dr. Louisa MacDonald), **6:** 161, 162 n.*251*
Snub (G. W. Kitchin's dog), **4:** 219 n.*237*
Society (dr. Thomas Robertson), **5:** 125, 126 n.*200*
Society for Propagating the Gospel (SPG), **8:** 44, 45, 298, 514
Society for the Protection of Women and Children, **8:** 512 n.*826*
Sogno, Edgar (b. 1866) – headmaster, **9:** 338 n.*540*, 342
Solomon Children – child actors, **5:** 202
Solomon's, Messrs., London – scientific apparatus **4:** 244, 251
Solon Shingle (dr. Anon), **5:** 96 n.*150*
Solway – steamship, **7:** 447
Somers Cocks (of Queensberry Place, Kensington, London):
Arthur Reginald Carew (b. 1861), **6:** 247 n.*392*, 248, 373
Edward Lygon Somers (b. 1858), **6:** 247 n.*392*, 248, 373
Ethel Mildred "Mimi" Susan (b. 1867), **6:** 247 n.*392*, 248, 373
Isabella Susan née Alderson (d. 1894), **6:** 246, 247 n.*392*, 258, 373, 441
Mary Katherine Agneta (b. 1865), **6:** 247 n.*392*, 248, 373
Walter Carew, The Hon. (1824-1898) – auditor, **6:** 246, 247 n.*392*, 249, 335, 373, 375, 376, 441
Somerset, C. W. (1851-1929) – actor, **8:** 422 n.*707*

Somerset, Raglan George Henry (1831-1924) – undergraduate at Christ Church, **2:** 45, 46 n.*91*; **6:** 340 n.*565*
Somerville Hall, Oxford, **8:** 171; **9:** 68, 306
Somnambula, La (dr. Henry Byron), **5:** 156 n.*253*
Sondes Place, Dorking, **6:** 45, 46
Songs from Alice's Adventures (bk. William Boyd), **6:** 132 n.*203*
Songs from Wonderland (bk. Phillippa Pearson), **7:** 467 n.*767*
*Songs of Innocence and of Experienc*e (bk. William Blake), **4:** 258 n.*301*
Sons of the Rev. J. P. Marriott (pic. John C. Moore), **2:** 75 n.*151*
Sorcerer (Gilbert and Sullivan) – operetta, **7:** 96, 97 n.*179*
Sotheran, Messrs. H. – booksellers, **8:** 542 n.*866*
Sothern, Edward Askew (1826-1881) – actor, **4:** 300 n.*366*; **5:** 88 n.*136*, 139 n.*223*, 160; **6:** 169 n.*264*; **7:** 123 n.*232*
Soulsby (of Oxford):
Lucy Helen Muriel (1856-1927) – headmistress, **9:** 68 n.*124*, 130, 133, 134, 180, 269, 294, 297, 301
Susan S., Mrs. (b. 1834), **9:** 132 n.*232*
Soutar, Robert (1827-1908) – dramatist, **7:** 233 n.*428*; **8:** 428 n.*691*
South, John Flint (1797-1882) – medical writer, **2:** 47 n.*93*
South Africa, **5:** 65
South Bank, Malvern, Worcestershire, **4:** 119
South Boston, United States of America, **5:** 126
South Downs, Sussex, **7:** 460
Southey (of Harley Street, London):
Frances Marian née Thornton (b. 1843), **4:** 309; **6:** 11 n.*1*
Reginald, Dr. (1835-1899) – physician, **1:** 51 n.*6*, 66 n.*50*; **2:** 20 n.*35*, 24, 25, 46, 53, 65, 66 n.*131*, 67-70, 111; **3:** 56, 62, 66, 76, 77, 88, 126, 134, 138, 139, 149, 161 n.*236*; **4:** 12, 33, 38, 68 n.*9*, 69, 304, 309, 347, 349, 352; **5:** 30; **6:** 11 n.*1*, 306; **8:** 278 n.*467*; **9:** 260 n.*411*, 324
Ronald (b. 1865), **6:** 11 n.*1*
Southey, Robert (1774-1843) – writer and poet, **1:** 34, 35
Southey's Monument, Cumberland, **2:** 91
South Kensington, London, **6:** 55
South Kensington Museum, **6:** 258; **7:** 184; **8:** 628
Southsea, Hampshire, **6:** 294, 342, 355, 359, 361, 362, 418, 422
South Shields Amateur Magazine, The, **4:** 25
South Stoke, Oxfordshire, **5:** 134
Southwell (of Bridgnorth, Shropshire; and Kensington, London):
Charles L. (b. 1863), **8:** 520
Edmund Martin (1864-1947), see below
Eliza, Mrs. (b. 1825), **8:** 520
Lionel J. (b. 1870), **8:** 520
Thomas M., Mr. (b. 1823) – carpet manufacturer and magistrate, **8:** 520
William L. (b. 1856), **8:** 520
Southwell (of Bridgnorth, Shropshire):

Edmund Martin, Capt. (1864-1947) – army officer and magistrate, **8:** 176 n.*290*, 193, 386, 460, 519, 520
Ethel Florence née Barclay (1864-1947), **6:** 205 n.*320*, 308, 309, 376, 377, 414, 443; **7:** 28 n.*35*, 71, 72, 91-93, 153-156, 157 n.*295*, 158, 215, 217, 303, 312, 313, 362, 366, 399, 400, 422-425, 441-444, 456, 473, 478, 519; **8:** 37 n.*48*, 130, 160, 176 n.*290*, 193, 385, 386, 519, 520; **9:** 169 n.*286*
Lorna (b. 1888), **8:** 176 n.*290*, 519; **9:** 169 n.*286*
Phyllis (b. 1886), **8:** 176 n.*290*, 519, 520, 536; **9:** 169 n.*286*
Southwell, Messrs., London – photographic dealers, **5:** 85 n.*132*
Southwick, near Sunderland, Durham, **6:** 206-208, 225; **7:** 166, 312, 335, 502; **8:** 353
Souttar, Robinson (1848-1912) – politician, **9:** 13 n.*6*
Souvestre, Emile (1806-1854) – dramatist, **7:** 195 n.*362*
Sowing the Wind (dr. Sydney Grundy), **9:** 100, 101 n.*182*
Sowton, William L. (b. 1877) – actor, **9:** 119 n.*206*
Spanish Military Nun, The (bk. Thomas De Quincey), **3:** 149
Sparkes (of Alfold, Surrey):
Alfred (b. 1850), **7:** 158 n.*297*
Beatrice M. (b. 1864), **7:** 158 n.*297*
Joseph E. (b. 1858), **7:** 158 n.*297*
Maria J. (b. 1861), **7:** 158 n.*297*
Marion, Mrs. (b. 1818), **7:** 158 n.*297*
Richard John, Rev. (b. 1807), **7:** 158 n.*297*
Sparkes (of Brighton, Sussex):
Charles, Mr. (b. 1826) – draper's assistant, **8:** 532 n.*855*
Euphemia, Mrs. (b. 1825), **8:** 532 n.*855*
Marion (b. 1867), **8:** 532 n.*855*
Sparks from the Anvil (bk. Elihu Burritt), **1:** 134 n.*169*
Sparrow, Mr. – friend of the Lewises, **7:** 515 n.*834*
Sparrow Hills, Moscow, Russia, **5:** 301
Speaight, George Victor (1914-2005) – writer, **1:** 19
Spearman (of London):
Cecil Augusta Margaret "Maggie" Isabella (b. 1870), **7:** 289, 290 n.*524*, 305, 528, 541; **8:** 139 n.*226*
Edmund Alexander Malcolm (1862-1896), **7:** 541
Edmund Robert, Sir (1837-1918) – diplomatic service, **7:** 290 n.*524*, 528
Maria Louisa Fitzmaurice, Lady (1838-1917), **7:** 289, 290 n.*524*, 528, 541
Marie Jane Louise (1863-1937), **8:** 139 n.*226*
"Spectacles" (Alice Furnivall's horse), **6:** 94 n.*146*
Spectator, The, **5:** 11, 12 n.*2*
Speeches and Writings (bk. John Horne Tooke), **1:** 73 n.*66*
Speed (of Devonshire Place, London):
Katherine "Kate" G. (b. 1863), **6:** 310 n.*513*
Mabel (b. 1865), **6:** 310 n.*513*

William, Mr. (b. 1814) – barrister, **6:** 310 n.*513*
Spelsbury, Oxfordshire, **4:** 303 n.*370*; **8:** 196, 203, 214, 257, 370; **9:** 13, 69
Spencer, Aubrey John (b. 1853) – barrister, **7:** 445 n.*735*
Spencer, Sarah Isabella, Lady (1838-1919), **6:** 336 n.*558*
Spencer, William Henry (b. 1820) – chaplain at Christ Church, **3:** 41 n.*65*
Spencer-Churchill (of Blenheim Palace, Woodstock, Oxfordshire):
Frances Anne Emily Vane née Stewart (d. 1899), Duchess of Marlborough, **4:** 215 n.*229*
John Winston (1822-1883), Duke of Marlborough, **4:** 215 n.*229*
Spender, Hilda – cousin of the Stevens, **8:** 620 n.*983*
Sphinx, Gizeh, The (pic. William Holman Hunt), **2:** 75 n.*151*
Spier, Mr. – friend of the Pennys, **5:** 325
Spiers, Richard James (1806-1877) – shopkeeper, **4:** 73 n.*18*
Spitalfields Weaver, The (dr. Thomas Bayly), **6:** 197 n.*307*
Spooner (of New College, Oxford):
Frances W., Mrs. (b. 1853), **7:** 143 n.*265*, 377
William Archibald, Mr. (1844-1930) – lecturer and dean of New College, **7:** 143 n.*265*, 377; **8:** 104 n.*173*
Spottiswoode (of Grosvenor Place, London):
Sylvia née Tomlin (b. 1837), **5:** 187
William Hugh, Mr. (1825-1883) – mathematician and publisher, **5:** 112 n.*176*, 133 n.*212*, 187, 198 n.*321*, 372 n.*552*, 377 n.*559*; **6:** 47 n.*67*
Spring, Mr. – teacher, **6:** 192 n.*298*
Spring and Winter (pic. Walther Firle), **8:** 422 n.*682*
Spring Rice (of Mount Trenchard, Foynes, County Limerick, Ireland):
Charles William Thomas (1819-1870), **3:** 118 n.*166*
Edmond Henry Francis Louis (1821-1887), **4:** 125 n.*98*
Mary Alice Pery (1812-1875), see Marshall
Mary-Ann née Marshall, Lady (1800-1889) – second wife, **3:** 118 n.*166*
Theodosia Alicia Ellen Frances Charlotte (1817-1891), see Henry Taylor
Thomas, Lord (1790-1866) – 1st Baron Monteagle, **3:** 118 n.*166*
William Cecil (1823-1880), **4:** 125 n.*98*
Spurgeon, Charles Haddon (1834-1892) – baptist minister, **3:** 46, 47 n.*73*
Spurin, Mr. – merchant, **4:** 220 n.*239*, 272
Spurling (of Norham Road, Oxford):
Clara née Eyton (b. 1843), **9:** 130 n.*227*
Frederick William, Rev. (1844-1914) – lecturer, **9:** 130 n.*227*
Mary (b. 1878), **8:** 627 n.*992*; **9:** 130 n.*227*, 136
Squire, The (dr. Arthur Pinero), **8:** 412 n.*668*, 413
Stabbach, Miss – singer, **3:** 66 n.*100*
Stacy, Miss – friend of the Prices, **9:** 73 n.*133*
Stafford, **7:** 210, 211
Stainley (North), Yorkshire, **2:** 58 n.*117*
Staley, Mr., **9:** 217 n.*345*

Stamp, Miss – related to the Dubourgs, **6:** 316
Stamper, Thomas (d. 1877) – Croft inhabitant, **1:** 27
Standard, The, **5:** 91 n.*141*; **6:** 64; **7:** 512 n.*830*; **8:** 430 n.*693*, 525 n.*842*; **9:** 124, 194
Standen (of Reading, Berkshire):
  Annie Aston née Liddell (b. 1833), **6:** 93 n.*144*, 256, 285, 293; **8:** 98, 99 n.*162*
  Douglas, Lt. Gen. (1830-1903) – army officer, **6:** 93 n.*144*, 96, 256, 285, 293; **8:** 99 n.*162*
  Frances (b. 1862?), **6:** 93 n.*144*
  Helen Melville (1864-1937), **6:** 93 n.*144*, 116, 285
  Henrietta Maud (1857?-1938), **6:** 93 n.*144*, 96, 99 n.*155*, 116, 258, 285 n.*468*; **8:** 98, 99, 170, 261
  Isabel Julia (1859-1941), **6:** 93 n.*144*, 96, 99 n.*155*, 116, 258, 285; **8:** 98, 99, 170, 171 n.*286*, 201, 203, 207, 219, 268
  Katherine "Kitty" Beatrice (b. 1868), **6:** 93 n.*144*
  Lilian M. (b. 1866), **6:** 93 n.*144*
Stanfield, (William) Clarkson (1793-1867) – artist, **2:** 75 n.*151*
Stanger, Florence (b. 1869) – logic pupil, **8:** 300 n.*501*, 302
Stanhope, John Roddam Spencer (1829-1908) – artist, **3:** 26 n.*37*
Stanhope Street, London, **5:** 30, 35
Stanley (of The Deanery, Westminster, London):
  Arthur Penrhyn, Rev. Dr. (1815-1881) – dean of Westminster, **3:** 165 n.*239*; **5:** 80 n.*124*, 239 n.*387*; **7:** 24 n.*25*
  Augusta Frederica Elizabeth Bruce, Lady (d. 1876), **4:** 296, 297 n.*358*, 315, 329 n.*421*, 333; **5:** 24, 122 n.*193*; **6:** 80
Stanley (of Chelsea, London):
  Jack, **8:** 359 n.*585*
  Marion "Madge" (b. 1881), **8:** 359 n.*585*
  Mrs., **8:** 359 n.*585*
Stanley, Miss – friend of the Cecils, **6:** 125
Stanley-Leathes, Miss – friend of the Dubourgs, **8:** 456 n.*732*
Stanwix, Cumberland, **2:** 62
Staplehurst, Kent, **6:** 185
Stapleton, Yorkshire, **2:** 8 n.*3*, 99; **3:** 83
Star, The, **5:** 11
Starling Dodd, Cumberland, **2:** 94
Statue Bride, The, or The Elves (dr. Anon), **2:** 123 n.*238*
Stay at Home (dr. George Lewes), **2:** 82 n.*162*
Stedman, James Remington, Dr. (1817-1891) – physician, **6:** 350 n.*581*; **8:** 255 n.*430*
Stedman's Children's Choir, **8:** 291
Steel, Adelaide M. (b. 1871) – niece of the Nettleships, **7:** 79 n.*130*
Steele (of Marston Lane, Oxford):
  Alice, Mrs. (b. 1838), **7:** 146 n.*274*, 148

Beatrice (b. 1860), **7:** 146 n.*274*
John, Mr. (b. 1836) – joiner, **7:** 146 n.*274*
Steele, Nelly – actress, **8:** 199 n.*337*
Steele, Robert Reynolds - editor of *Medieval Lore*, **4:** 254 n.*292*
Steinway Hall, London, **7:** 233, 234
Sténarithmie (bk. Louis Richard), **9:** 350 n.*560*
Stephen (of Hyde Park Gate South, Kensington, London):
Harriet Marion née Thackeray (1840-1875), **6:** 197 n.*306*, 216, 251, 258
Leslie, Mr. (1832-1904) – editor of *Cornhill Magazine*, **6:** 197 n.*306*, 199
Stephenson, Benjamin C. (1839-1906) – dramatist, **7:** 513, 514 n.*832*; **9:** 26 n.*36*, 57 n.*104*, 213 n.*340*
Stephenson, Charles H. (1824-1905) – actor and dramatist, **4:** 337 n.*436*
Stevens, Alfred Peck (1839-1898), "The Great Vance" – singer and comedian, **7:** 519, 520 n.*842*
Stevens (of Crick Road, Oxford):
Edith née Headland (1841-1919), **8:** 334 n.*550*, 336, 556, 559, 593, 597, 626, 629; **9:** 12 n.*2*, 35, 37, 45, 58, 68, 70, 77, 79 n.*146*, 111, 123, 126 n.*222*, 185, 223, 236, 252, 257, 313, 320, 323
Enid Gertrude (1882-1960), **8:** 334 n.*550*, 552, 556, tea-party alone 557, 564, photographed by Forshaw 565, 591, 593, 618, 619, 624, 625, 627, 629, 631, 632, 633; **9:** 12 n.*2*, 37-39, 45-49, 52, 53, 55, 56, 59, 61, 67 n.*121*, 68-71, 73, 75, 77, 78, 81, dedicatory poem for *Sylvie and Bruno Concluded* 102 n.*184*, sits for chalk-head 104, 105, 108 n.192, 111, 112, 121, 123-125, 126 n.*222*, 131, 142, 156, 183, 185, 223, 225, 229, 236, 243, 244 n.*387*, 250, 252, 257, 280, 299, 320, 323
Winifred "Winnie" Edith Laura (1872-1958), see Hawke
Stevens, Katie – friend of the Toms, **9:** 174 n.*293*
Stevenson, Annie – child actress, **8:** 287, 288, 294
Steventon, Berkshire, **7:** 279
Stewart, Alexander Arthur Grainger (b. 1867) – undergraduate at Christ Church, **8:** 267 n.*450*
Stewart, Dugald (1753-1828) – writer, **1:** 74 n.*67*
Stewart (of Bradmore Road, Oxford):
Helen J. née Macmillan (1849-1925), **6:** 440 n.*723*; **7:** 264; **8:** 93 n.*152*; **9:** 266 n.*419*, 295
John Alexander, Mr. (1846-1933) – lecturer, **6:** 137 n.*209*, 306, 366, 372, 440; **7:** 321, 440 n.*730*, 490; **8:** 93 n.*152*, 163
Stewart, Miss – actress, **3:** 102
Stewart, Miss – governess to Adolphus Liddell's family, **1:** 128
Stirling, Mary Ann "Fanny Clifton" née Kehl (1816-1895), Lady Gregory – actress, **3:** 12 n.*10*, 51; **6:** 27 n.*30*, 95 n.*149*; **7:** 540 n.*873*; **8:** 273 n.*461*
Stirling, Scotland, **3:** 104
Stirling Castle, **3:** 104
Stock, St. George William Joseph (b. 1850) – tutor, **7:** 419, 420 n.*701*
Stockport, Cheshire, **1:** 9

Stogden, Edith – cousin of the Prices, **4:** 309 n.*383*, 332, 333 n.*427*
Stoker, Abraham "Bram" (1847-1912) – barrister, writer, and theatre manager, **9:** 147 n.*253*
Stokes, Miss – friend of the Slatters, **9:** 73 n.*134*
Stone, Edith (b. 1857?) – friend of the Godfreys, **4:** 179; **5:** 82 n.*127*
Stone, Edward James (1831-1897) – astronomer, **7:** 384 n.*663*
Stone (of Streatley, Berkshire):
  Emily née Morrell (1812-1891), **5:** 69 n.*103*, 90 n.*139*
  Miss, **5:** 90 n.*139*
  William Henry, Mr. (1799-1863), **5:** 69 n.*103*, 90 n.*139*
Stone, Henry (b. 1818) – patent box manufacturer, **7:** 417 n.*695*
Stone, Henry – pupil at St. Aldates, **2:** 30
Stone, Samuel John, Rev. (1839-1900), **4:** 320, 321 n.*407*; **5:** 83 n.*128*, 84
Stones of Venice (bk. John Ruskin), **1:** 114 n.*136*, 118
Stopford (of Witley, either Surrey or Worcestershire):
  George (b. 1869?), **6:** 421
  Mabel (b. 1868), **6:** 421
  Mr., **6:** 421 n.*691*
Storey, Fred (1856-1917) – actor, **9:** 87 n.*157*
Storr (of India):
  Carrie (b. 1871), **8:** 23 n.*21*, 24, 25, 27, 41
  Emily Mary née Faithfull, **8:** 23 n.*21*, 37
  Mabel (b. 1873), **8:** 23 n.*21*, 24, 25, 27, 41
  Minnie (b. 1875), **8:** 23 n.*21*, 24, 25, 27, 41
  Vernon Faithfull (1869-1940), **8:** 23 n.*21*, 27
Storrs (of Sandown, Isle of Wight):
  Arthur Noel Coopland (b. 1865), **7:** 345 n.*605*
  George Godwyn Coopland (b. 1868), **7:** 345 n.*605*
  Robert Augustine (1859-1941), **7:** 345 n.*605*
  Sarah, Mrs., **7:** 345 n.*605*
  William Townsend, Rev., **7:** 345 n.*605*
  William Townsend Coopland (1862-1953), **7:** 345 n.*605*
Story (from the United States of America):
  Gwendolyn Marion Waldo (1884-1961), **8:** 471, 472 n.*764*
  Thomas Waldo, Mr. (1854-1915) – American sculptor, **8:** 471, 472 n.*764*
Story of a Nursery Rhyme, The (bk. C.B.), **8:** 20 n.*13*, 579 n.*925*
Stout, George Frederick (1860-1944) – editor of *Mind*, **9:** 160 n.*275*
Stowe, Harriet Beecher (1811-1896) – writer, **2:** 99 n.*190*
Stowell, Hugh, Rev. (1799-1865), **4:** 236 n.*263*
Stowell, Mr. – cotton trader, **8:** 82 n.*130*
Stoyle, J. D. (1831-1889) – actor, **5:** 47 n.*62*
Strachan (of Islington, London):
  Arthur I. (b. 1863), **6:** 286 n.*470*
  Florence M. (b. 1866), **6:** 286 n.*470*, 288, 289
  Hortense, **6:** 286 n.*470*, 289; **8:** 411, 412 n.*666*, 413

Jane née Nightingale (b. 1823), **6:** 286 n.*470*, 289
William, Mr. (b. 1826) – print-master, **6:** 286 n.*470*
Strachey (of Kensington, London):
Jane (b. 1870), **9:** 27 n.*38*
John, Mr. (1823-1907) – civil servant, **9:** 27 n.*38*
Katherine Jane née Batten (1835-1907), **9:** 27 n.*38*, 353
Mary Lawrence (b. 1869), **9:** 27 n.*38*
Nina (1867-1946), **9:** 27 n.*38*
Winifred (1865-1892), **9:** 27 n.*38*
Stramire, Miss – former governess to George Price's family, **8:** 353 n.*575*
Strand Magazine, The, **1:** 37
Strang, Martha, Fräulein (b. 1851) – governess to the Gaussens, **8:** 266 n.*448*, 267, 268
"Strangers yet" (Charlotte "Claribel" Barnard) – song, **5:** 225, 226 n.*359*
Strastnoi Nunnery, Moscow, Russia, **5:** 316
Streatley, Berkshire, **4:** 72 n.*17*, 102, 107, 135, 185, 295; **5:** 68, 90, 134; **7:** 252
Street, Eliza (b. 1854) – school mistress, **9:** 344, 345 n.*551*
Streets of London, The (dr. Dion Boucicault), **4:** 358, 359 n.*468*
Stroganoff, Count, **6:** 295
Strong (of Seymour Street, Marylebone, London):
Alice G. C. Linwood (b. 1852), **4:** 255 n.*294*
Arthur Hugh Linwood (b. 1851?), **4:** 255 n.*294*
Beatrice C. Linwood (b. 1861), **4:** 255 n.*294*
Clement Erskine Linwood (b. 1855), **4:** 255 n.*294*
Fanny Louisa née Erskine (1822-1908), **4:** 255 n.*294*; **7:** 193 n.*359*
Henry Linwood, Mr. (1816-1886) – barrister, **4:** 255 n.*294*
Zoe Sophia B. Linwood (b. 1854), **4:** 255 n.*294*
Strong (of Iffley, Oxfordshire):
Emily Frances, see Pattison
Emily née Weedon (b. 1806), **4:** 77 n.*26*, 146 n.*129*
Harriet, see Neale
Henry, Mr. (b. 1794) – bank manager, **4:** 77 n.*26*, 146 n.*129*
Marian (b. 1844), **4:** 77 n.*26*, 146 n.*129*
Strong, Thomas Banks, Rev. (1861-1944), **8:** 599 n.*955*, 602, 608, 609; **9:** 153 n.*265*, 194, 239, 286 n.*453*, 320
Stronghill, Miss – aunt of Florence Beaton, **6:** 482
Struwwelpeter (bk. Heinrich Hoffmann), **4:** 140 n.*119*
Stuart-Wortley, Archibald Henry Plantagenet (1832-1890) – photographer, **6:** 393 n.*643*
Stubbs:
Henry James Laurie, Mr., **6:** 172 n.*268*
Kathleen, **6:** 172 n.*268*, 176
Miss, **6:** 172, 176
Thomas Walker (b. 1856), **6:** 172 n.*268*, 176, 426 n.*702*

Stubbs (of Chester; and Oxford):
Katherine Isabella (b. 1863), **8:** 89 n.*144*
William, Rt. Rev. (1825-1901), **4:** 313, 314 n.*392*; **8:** 89 n.*144*, 470 n.*761*, 545, 553 n.*882*
"Student's Choice, The" – tableau, **6:** 188
Studies and Exercises in Formal Logic (bk. John Keynes), **9:** 152 n.*264*
Studley, Yorkshire, **1:** 55 n.*19*; **2:** 58 n.*116*
Sturges (of Kensington, London):
Decimus, Mr. (b. 1838) – barrister, **7:** 185 n.*346*, 439, 440 n.*729*
Emma, Mrs. (b. 1841), **7:** 185 n.*346*, 439, 440
Ethel M. (b. 1867), **7:** 185 n.*346*
Helen (b. 1871), **7:** 185 n.*346*
Kate (b. 1869), **7:** 185 n.*346*
Maud E. (b. 1864), **7:** 185 n.*346*, 473, 474
Stylographic pen, **7:** 224 n.*410*
Sue, Eugene (1804-1857) – dramatist, **5:** 222 n.*353*
"Sulla Poppa" (Federico Ricci) – song, **1:** 53
Sullivan, Arthur Seymour (1842-1900) – composer, **5:** 240 n.*389*; **7:** 25 n.*28*, 96, 97 n.*179*, 316 n.*565*, 394 n.*672*, 503 n.*822*; **9:** 118 n.*204*
Sultan Abdul Aziz of Turkey (1830-1876), **5:** 255 n.*422*
Summertown, Oxford, **9:** 70
Sumner, John Bird (1780-1862) – archbishop of Canterbury, **4:** 11
Sunbeams Dance Group, **8:** 485 n.*786*
Sunday Times, **8:** 477 n.*772*; **9:** 239
Sunderland, Durham, **1:** 120, 125, 128, 133; **4:** 155, 157; **5:** 38, 377; **6:** 175, 206-208, 216, 352; **9:** 140
Sunderland Choral Society, **2:** 100
Sunderland Herald, The, **5:** 11, 12 n.*2*
Sunlight and Shadow (dr. Richard Carton), **8:** 577, 578 n.*921*
Sunningdale, Berkshire, **6:** 226
Super (pupils of Thomas Dymes):
Dottin, **7:** 454 n.*751*
Oriana (b. 1875), **7:** 454 n.*751*
Surbiton, Surrey, **5:** 37, 88, 138, 139; **7:** 220, 221, 254, 288, 304, 527, 531; **8:** 82
Surrey County Asylum, **2:** 24 n.*45*
Surridge, Miss – friend of Mary Hitchcock, **9:** 30 n.*50*
Sussex Square, Brighton, **6:** 414; **7:** 93, 154
Sutro, Alfred (1863-1933) – dramatist, **9:** 220 n.*349*
Sutton, John Lucas, Rev. (b. 1826) – lecturer on Tennyson, **1:** 91
Sutton, Misses – friends of the Hopleys, **9:** 217 n.*345*
Sutton Courtney, Berkshire, **5:** 90
Sutton Place, near Guildford, **8:** 79 n.*123*, 132
Swabey, Henry, Rev. (1826-1878), **2:** 30 n.*57*, 37, 40; **3:** 41 n.*63*
Swain, John (b. 1829) – engraver and artist, **8:** 299 n.*498*, 302

Swain, Joseph (1820-1909) – engraver, **6:** 429; **8:** 202, 203 n.*346*, 218, 219, 245, 487, 488
Swainson (of St. Pancras, London):
Annie (b. 1871), **8:** 81 n.*126*
Esther L. (b. 1874), **8:** 81 n.*126*
Lilian (b. 1866), **8:** 80 n.*124*, 81
Margaret H. (b. 1872), **8:** 81 n.*126*
Mary (b. 1863), **8:** 81 n.*126*
Swales, Robert – Darlington bookseller, **1:** 82 n.*85*
Swallow, Swallow (pic. John Millais), **5:** 86 n.*134*
Swanborough, Ada (1845-1893) – actress, **3:** 79, 80 n.*126*
Swann – pupil of William Ranken, **6:** 476
Sweetest Eyes (pic. John Millais), **7:** 349 n.*611*
Sweethearts (dr. William S. Gilbert), **7:** 90 n.*162*, 186 n.*348*
Sweet Lavender (dr. Arthur Pinero), **8:** 477 n.*773*; **9:** 15 n.*10*, 123
Swenden, James (b. 1839) – Henry Hobson's executor, **6:** 346, 348
Swepson, Mrs. (Camden House, Margate) – lodging-house keeper, **6:** 399
Swift, Mr. – singer, **2:** 54
Swinburne, Algernon Charles (1837-1909) – poet, **5:** 71 n.*107*
Swindon, Wiltshire, **7:** 495
Swinton, James Rannie (1816-1888) – artist, **5:** 149 n.*239*
Swire (of Richmond area, Yorkshire):
Edward "Ned" – pupil at Richmond School **1:** 21
William – pupil at Richmond School, **1:** 21
Swire (of The Grove, Littlethorpe, near Ripon, Yorkshire):
Gertrude Elizabeth née Stanton (1836?-1877), **5:** 107 n.*165*
Samuel, Mr. (1819-1892) – magistrate, **5:** 107 n.*165*
Swonnell, Rosie (b. 1866) – friend of the Cootes, **7:** 189 n.*351*
Sydenham, Kent, **3:** 15
Sykes (of Aurungabad, East Indies):
John, Capt. (d. 1815), **4:** 133 n.*110*
Mrs., **4:** 133 n.*110*
Sylvester, William Henry (1815?-1886), alias Sylvester Laroche – photographer, **3:** 13 n.*11*, 26 n.*36*
Sylvia's Home Journal, **8:** 252 n.*424*
Sylvius (dr. Anon), **5:** 193 n.*317*
"Sylvius" in *Living Miniature*, **5:** 203, 204
Symm and Company, Builders, Oxford, **7:** 521 n.*846*
Symonds (of Oxford):
Ann, Mrs. (b. 1824), **6:** 34 n.*45*, 321; **8:** 35 n.*43*, 43, 44, 51, 86, 167, 192, 195, 248, 268, 409, 414 n.*671*, 469, 517, 594
Anne "Annie" Harrison (b. 1853), **6:** 33, 34 n.*45*, 321; **8:** 35 n.*43*, 36, 37, 39, 44, 51, 65, 86, 90, 167, 192 n.*322*, 215, 248, 252, 268-270, 414
Frederick, Dr. (1813-1881) – physician, **6:** 33, 34 n.*45*, 321
Horatio Percy (1851-1923), **6:** 34 n.*45*, 321; **7:** 378 n.*653*; **8:** 167

Margaret (b. 1849), **6:** 33, 34 n.*45*, 321; **8:** 35 n.*43*
Mary “May” G. (b. 1852), **6:** 33, 34 n.*45*; **8:** 35 n.*43*, 36, 37, 39, 44, 51, 65, 86, 90, 167, 192 n.*322*, 215, 248, 252, 268, 269, 414
Symons, Jelinger Cookson (1809-1860) – school inspector and writer, **2:** 60 n.*121*, 61
Synge (of Guildford, Surrey):
Francis “Frank” J. (b. 1847), **6:** 100 n.*156*; **7:** 392; **9:** 98
Henrietta, Mrs. (b. 1831), **6:** 100 n.*156*, 193, 196, 233, 457; **7:** 142 n.*261*, 151, 221, 232, 392, 514, 545; **8:** 24 n.*22*, 33, 39, 242, 286, 287, 346, 414, 520, 569; **9:** 31 n.*51*, 83, 95, 98, 102
Madeline “Middie” (b. 1857?), **6:** 99, 100 n.*156*; **7:** 151; **8:** 346 n.*571*, 414, 569; **9:** 31 n.*51*, 98, 99, 102
Maria Marion A. (b. 1855), **6:** 100 n.*156*, 104; **7:** 151; **8:** 346 n.*571*
Robert Follett (b. 1854), **6:** 100 n.*156*; **7:** 392
William Makepeace Thackeray (1860-1929), **6:** 100 n.*156*, 101, 379; **7:** 392
William Webb Follett, Mr. (1826-1891) – writer and diplomat, **6:** 100 n.*156*, 104 n.*163*, 118, 193, 196, 233, 379, 380, 457; **7:** 142 n.*261*, 151, 221, 229, 232, 392, 514, 545; **8:** 24 n.*22*, 33, 39, 242, 269, 279 n.*469*, 286, 287, 346, 414, 429, 520
Synnot, Robert Harry Inglis (1838-1872) – undergraduate at Christ Church, **2:** 121 n.*234*
Synodon Hill, Oxfordshire, **4:** 195
System of Logic (bk. John Stuart Mill), **1:** 74 n.*67*; **3:** 156 n.*230*

Tait (Lambeth Palace, London):
Agnes Sitwell (b. 1860?), **7:** 273 n.*497*
Archibald Campbell, Rev. Dr. (1811-1882) – headmaster of Rugby School, archbishop of Canterbury, **1:** 25, 28, 29; **7:** 273 n.*497*
Catharine née Spooner (1819-1878), **7:** 273 n.*497*
Craufurd (1849-1878), **7:** 273 n.*497*
Edith Murdoch (b. 1858?), **7:** 273 n.*497*
Lucy Sydney Murray (b. 1856), **7:** 273 n.*497*
Taking it Easy (dr. Anon), **8:** 112, 113 n.*184*
Talbois, Yvo de, Count of Anjou (fl. 1060) – very distant relative, **1:** 11
Talbot (of Warden’s Lodgings, Keble College, Oxford):
Edward Stuart, Rev. (1844-1934) – warden of Keble, **5:** 54 n.*75*; **7:** 146, 147 n.*276*, 228, 377; **8:** 202 n.*345*; **9:** 153 n.*265*, 257
Lavinia née Lyttelton, Hon. (b. 1849), **7:** 146, 147 n.*276*, 264, 270, 377
Mary “May” C. (b. 1876), **7:** 270
Talbot (of Bishops Hatfield, Hertfordshire):
Eleonora Julia née Coventry (b. 1825), **6:** 247 n.*392*, 336 n.*558*
William Whitworth Chetwynd, Rev. (1814-1888), **6:** 247 n.*392*, 336
Talbot, John Gilbert, Rt. Hon. (1835-1910) – politician, **8:** 256 n.*432*
Talboys (of Speedwell Place, Oxford):

Caroline (b. 1850), **3:** 37 n.*57*
David, Mr. (b. 1820) – boat builder, **3:** 36, 37 n.*57*
Talmage, Thomas de Witt, Rev. (1832-1902), **9:** 252 n.*395*, 253
Talon (of Eastbourne, Surrey):
Fernande (b. 1879), **7:** 357 n.*624*
Francis, Monsieur (b. 1846) – teacher of French, **7:** 357 n.*624*, 367
Therese, Madame (b. 1848), **7:** 357 n.*624*
Tanner, James T. (1859-1915), alias James Leader – dramatist, **9:** 197 n.*323*, 277 n.*442*
Tapping, Alfred B. (1851-1928) – actor, **9:** 23 n.*28*
Taps, The (dr. Lionel Brough and Willie Edouin), **8:** 237 n.*399*
Tares (dr. Aimée Beringer), **8:** 457 n.*734*
Tarrant (of St. Leonards-on-Sea, Sussex):
Blanche (b. 1866), **6:** 280 n.*461*, 281
Edith (b. 1864?), **6:** 235 n.*372*, 280, 281
Lily (b. 1871), **6:** 280 n.*461*, 281
Mary (b. 1869), **6:** 280 n.*461*, 281
Mrs., **6:** 235 n.*372*, 280, 281
Nellie (b. 1862?), **6:** 235 n.*372*, 280, 281
Tartar Mosque, Nijni Novgorod, Russia, **5:** 309
Tartessus – steamship, **6:** 417 n.*684*; **7:** 89 n.*158*, 172, 174, 178 n.*330*, 398 n.*677*
Tasso, Torquato (1544-1595) – poet, **1:** 84, 85; **2:** 28 n.*55*
Tate (of Richmond, Yorkshire):
Ann Elizabeth née Simpson (1802-64), **1:** 21, 127; **3:** 92 n.*143*
Charles Grey (1836-1900), see below
Ellen (1833-1842), **2:** 88 n.*177*
James (1834-1897), **1:** 132; **2:** 86, 87 n.*173*, 88 n.*177*; **3:** 69 n.*107*, 92 n.*143*, 93
James, Mr. (1801-1863) – headmaster, **1:** 21, 22, 58 n.*25*, 115 n.*139*, 127, 130; **2:** 55 n.*107*, 87 n.*173*, 88 n.*177*; **3:** 92 n.*143*; **4:** 166 n.*160*, 203 n.*210*
John Samuel (1839-1887), **1:** 115; **2:** 88 n.*177*; **3:** 92 n.*143*
Lucy Hutchinson (1842-1873), **1:** 115; **2:** 88 n.*177*; **4:** 231 n.*256*, 232 n.*258*
Thomas Hutchinson (b. 1837), see below
Tate (of Richmond, Yorkshire):
Charles Grey, Mr. (1836-1900) – architect, **1:** 115; **2:** 55 n.*107*, 88 n.*177*; **4:** 203 n.*210*; **8:** 159 n.*257*, 271, 547
Edith Iona (b. 1864), **8:** 159 n.*257*, 271
Jane née Ion (d. 1864), **4:** 203 n.*210*
Tate (of Canada; and Guildford area):
Daisy, **8:** 159 n.*257*, 269, 547; **9:** 60 n.*110*, 102
Janet née Marshall, **9:** 60 n.*110*, 102, 140
Thomas Hutchinson, Mr (b. 1837), **1:** 115; **2:** 88 n.*177*; **9:** 60 n.*110*, 102,

140
Tate, Emma (b. 1856) – principal of Oxford Home-Students, **9:** 228 n.*363*, 229
Tate, G., Mr. – theatrical agent, **8:** 615 n.*975*
Tate (of Eastbourne, Sussex):
Laura née Saigeman (b. 1855) – swimming instructor, **8:** 235 n.*397*, 289, 367, 479; **9:** 273 n.*433*, 332
Sybil (b. 1890?), **9:** 273 n.*433*, 332
Tauchnitz, Christian Bernhard von, Baron (1816-1895) – publisher, **5:** 25
Taunton, Somerset, **9:** 63
Tayleure (or Taylor), Alanson – circus manager, **7:** 286, 287 n.*520*
Taylor (of St. George's Terrace, Monkwearmouth Shore, Durham):
Alice Henrietta (b. 1857), **6:** 43 n.*59*, 207 n.*324*; **7:** 359, 360 n.*628*, 361, 364, 365; **9:** 158, 179
Caroline Stuart Wortley née Collingwood (b. 1828), **6:** 207 n.*324*
H. H., Dr. – surgeon, **6:** 207 n.*324*
Taylor (of Sunderland, Durham):
Anna Maria (b. 1819), **5:** 65 n.*97*
Arnold Henry John (b. 1825), see below
Elizabeth Jane Eugenia (b. 1823), **5:** 65 n.*97*
Tom (1817-1880), see below
Taylor (of Surbiton, Surrey):
Arnold Henry John, Mr. (b. 1825) – local government officer, **5:** 65 n.*97*
Charlotte, Mrs. (b. 1829), **5:** 65 n.*97*
Taylor (of Uplands, East Sheen, Surrey):
Aubrey Ashworth (1845-1870), **4:** 61, 63, 90, 91 n.*48*, 125 n.*98*, 126 n.*99*, 184 n.*179*, 249, 252, 253, 348
Eleanor Emma Ashworth (1847-1911), **4:** 61, 125 n.*98*, 127 n.*100*, 140 n.*119*, 184 n.*179*, 348
Henry, Sir (1800-1886) – writer, **4:** 90, 91 n.*48*, 92, 108 n.*76*, 109, 122, 125 n.*98*, 126 n.*99*, 127 n.*100*, 140 n.*119*, 183, 249, 314, 334, 337, 346, 348; **5:** 73 n.*111*
Henry "Harry" Ashworth (1854-1907), **4:** 60, 61, 63, 125 n.*98*, 127 n.*100*, 140 n.*119*, 249, 348
Ida Alice Ashworth (1850-1929), **4:** 61, 125 n.*98*, 126 n.*99*, 184 n.*179*, 348
Theodosia Alicia Ellen Frances Charlotte née Spring Rice (1817-1891), **4:** 60, 125 n.*98*, 183, 314, 348
Una Mary Ashworth (1857-1922), **4:** 60, 61, 125 n.*98*, 126 n.*99*, 127 n.*100*, 140 n.*119*, 181, 249, 348; **5:** 19
Taylor (of Threlfall, Oxford):
Colin M. (b. 1881), **7:** 191 n.*355*
Eliza A., Mrs. (b. 1840), **5:** 120; **7:** 161 n.*303*, 224, 264, 275, 377, 383; **8:** 70, 156, 188
James, Mr. (1833-1900) – organist and musician, **5:** 120 n.*189*;

7: 161 n.*303*, 191 n.*355*, 224, 275, 383; **8:** 14 n.*7*, 156
Leila Campbell (b. 1868), **7:** 191 n.*355*, 192 n.*356*, 192 n.*358*, 264, 376, 377, 380, 383, 543
Leonard Campbell (b. 1875), **7:** 191 n.*355*
May Campbell (b. 1871), **7:** 191 n.*355*, 264, 377, 380, 383
Reginald Campbell (b. 1879), **7:** 191 n.*355*
Stewart Campbell (b. 1873), **7:** 191 n.*355*
Taylor, George, Rev. (1828-1887), **6:** 94 n.*147*, 96, 100
Taylor (of York):
Helen "Nellie" R. (b. 1857), **8:** 343 n.*564*, 376, 438
Louisa Frances née Collingwood (1832-1881), **8:** 101 n.*166*, 214, 215, 256, 257, 260, 268, 343, 353, 433, 438
Louisa "Loui" or "Louie" (b. 1866), **8:** 170 n.*284*, 215, 244, 256-258, 260, 261, 264-266, 268-270, 272, 273, 275, 333, 364, 373, 374, 378, 386 n.*631*, 403, 406, 429, 433, 441, 445, 452, 472, 486, 503, 538, 547, 621
Muriel (b. 1872), **8:** 101 n.*166*, 336-338, 343, 353, 368, 373, 376, 438
Taylor (of Guildford, Surrey):
Henry Sharp, Dr. (1817-1896) – physician, **6:** 84 n.*126*, 102, 138, 316; **7:** 415 n.*693*; **8:** 161 n.*262*
Sophia Christiana "Christie" (b. 1859), **6:** 84 n.*126*, 92 n.*143*, 95 n.*148*, 138, 316; **7:** 415 n.*693*
Sophia Russel, Mrs. (b. 1820), **6:** 84 n.*126*, 102, 138, 316; **7:** 415 n.*693*
Taylor, Jessie – sister of Mrs. Kitchin, **7:** 251
Taylor, J. M., Rev. – teacher, **3:** 95 n.*145*
Taylor, John Lowther Du Plat (1829-1904) – civil servant, **3:** 132 n.*192*
Taylor (of Lavender Sweep, Wandsworth, London):
John Wycliffe (1859-1925), **4:** 248 n.*283*, 250, 271; **5:** 65
Laura Wilson née Barker (1819- 1905), **4:** 237, 238 n.*266*, 271; **5:** 63, 65, 140; **6:** 250
Tom, Mr. (1817-1880) – civil servant and dramatist, **2:** 82 n.*162*; **3:** 51 n.*78*; **4:** 223 n.*245*, 224, 225 n.*249*, 230, 246, 248 n.*282*, 248 n.*283*, 249-251, 270, 271, 279 n.*328*, 310, 312, 332, 337, 352, 356, 357 n.*467*, 358; **5:** 25, 34 n.*39*, 35, 36 n.*41*, 59, 60 n.*86*, 63, 65, 85 n.*133*, 95 n.*147*, 115 n.*179*, 123 n.*196*, 128, 129 n.*207*, 132, 136, 139, 140, 145 n.*232*, 156, 162, 216, 218, 220, 240, 241 n.*390*; **6:** 86, 250, 351; **7:** 107, 369 n.*642*; **9:** 336 n.*537*
Taylor Buildings and Gallery, Oxford, **1:** 65; **3:** 22 n.*28*, 28; **7:** 22, 537; **9:** 266 n.*420*
Taylor-Taswell, Stephen Taswell, Rev. (b. 1839), **8:** 335 n.*553*
Teddy the Tiler (dr. George Rodwell), **5:** 17 n.*11*
Tedious Task, The (pic. Henry Schlesinger), **6:** 22
Telfer, Frederick – chemist at Oxford, **2:** 70 n.*139*; **3:** 65
Telling (of St. Ebbe's, Oxford):
Helena (b. 1864), **8:** 65 n.*103*, 602

James, Mr. (b. 1823) – butler of the Common Room, **8:** 65 n.*103*, 167 n.*278*, 383, 602; **9:** 350 n.*561*
Temple, Frederick, Rev. Dr. (1821-1902) – headmaster of Rugby, bishop of Exeter, **4:** 31; **7:** 427 n.*714*
Temple, Henry John (1784-1865), 3rd. Viscount Palmerston, **4:** 91 n.*48*
Temple, K., Miss – niece of Frederick Temple, **7:** 427 n.*714*
Temple, Madge (d. 1943) – actress, **8:** 609, 610 n.*966*, 623, 628, 631
Temple Bar, **4:** 55
Temple District, London, **1:** 102; **2:** 81 n.*159*; **3:** 133; **4:** 326
Templer, Laura S. (b. 1852) – boarding-house keeper, **9:** 236 n.*372*
Tenbury, Worcestershire, **6:** 166, 167
Tenby, Pembrokeshire, **3:** 120; **4:** 187-191, 305; **5:** 179; **6:** 84
Tenn, Mr. – artist, **5:** 86 n.*134*
Tenniel (of Portsdown Road, Paddington, London):
Eliza Maria née Foster (d. 1864), **4:** 338 n.*438*
John, Sir (1820-1914) – illustrator, **1:** 20; **3:** 31 n.*46*; **4:** 271 n.*315*, 272, 284, 297 n.*359*, 302, 304 n.*372*, 310, 312, 338 n.*438*; **5:** 9, 10, 16 n.*10*, 22, 25, 26 n.*25*, 33 n.*37*, 36 n.*43*, 45, 56 n.*80*, 64 n.*94*, 97 n.*151*, 100, 140, 141 n.*225*, 241 n.*390*, 254; **6:** 20 n.*22*, 30 n.*37*, 31, 37 n.*32*, 59, 79 n.*115*, 86, 112, 113 n.*175*, 140, 142, 148, 178, 184, 236 n.*376*, 260, 269, 314, 338, 351, 381, 382, 434; **8:** 147, 181, 219, 242; **9:** 275 n.*440*, 340
Lydia Victoire (b. 1824), sister, **4:** 338 n.*438*
Tennyson (of Somersby, Lincolnshire):
Alfred (1809-1892), see below
Arthur (1814-1899), **4:** 353 n.*460*
Cecilia, see Lushington
Charles, see Turner
Emilia "Emily" (1811-1889), **4:** 353 n.*460*
Frederick (1807-1898), **4:** 353 n.*460*
Horatio (1819-1899), see below
Mary (1810-1884), **4:** 353 n.*460*
Matilda (1816-1913), **4:** 353 n.*460*
Septimus (1815-1866), **4:** 353 n.*460*
Tennyson (of Farringford, Freshwater, Isle of Wight):
Alfred, Lord (1809-1892) – poet, **1:** 55 n.*16*, 65 n.*44*, 72, 91, 110 n.*127*, 119 n.*145*, 122; **2:** 9 n.*8*, 89 n.*179*, 121 n.*234*; **3:** 87 n.*136*, 88, 89, 93, 108 n.*156*, 110-15, 118 n.*165*, 119, 126, 127 n.*183*, 134 n.*194*, 145, 175, 179, 181; **4:** 14-20, 32, 42, 45, 47, 48, 59, 60, 97 n.*57*, 99 n.*61*, 109, 113, 114, 127 n.*100*, 136 n.*113*, 222 n.*244*, 334, 349, 356; **5:** 25; **6:** 190; **7:** 318 n.*567*; **8:** 535, 577; **9:** 32 n.*54*, 78 n.*144*
Emily née Sellwood (1813-1896), **3:** 87 n.*136*, 108, 110, 113, 114, 126, 134 n.*194*; **4:** 14-20, 222 n.*244*, 344
Hallam (1852-1928), **3:** 88 n.*137*, 108 n.*156*, 113, 118 n.*165*, 119; **4:** 16-20, 34, 58, 60, 61, 63, 222 n.*244*, 344

Lionel (1854-1886), **3:** 88 n.*137*, 108 n.*156*, 113, 118 n.*165*; **4:** 17-20, 48, 58, 60, 61-63, 85 n.*38*, 90 n.*47*, 222 n.*244*, 344

Tennyson (of Tenby, Pembrokeshire):

Charlotte Cary née Elwes (d. 1868), **4:** 189 n.*185*

Horatio, Mr. (1819-1899), **4:** 189 n.*185*, 353 n.*460*; **7:** 271 n.*487*

Tent Lodge, Lake District, **3:** 108, 110, 111, 113, 144

Terence (c. 190-159 BC) – dramatist, **3:** 140 n.*207*

Terriss (of London):

Ellaline (b. 1871) – actress, **8:** 618 n.*980*; **9:** 12, 13 n.*5*, 26, 122

William, Mr. (1848-1897) – actor, **7:** 318 n.*567*; **8:** 190 n.*320*, 209, 565, 567, 628; **9:** 20 n.*22*, 78

Terry (of various addresses in London):

Benjamin, Mr. (1818-1896) – actor, **4:** 352, 356, 357 n.*467*, 359; **5:** 16 n.*9*, 20, 22, 31, 62, 91, 92 n.*142*, 93 n.*144*, 94 n.*146*, 98, 118, 123, 127, 162, 169, 379; **6:** 69, 97 n.*151*, 115, 341; **7:** 84 n.*142*, 124, 140, 185, 278, 387, 388, 396, 443, 524; **8:** 141; **9:** 61 n.*113*

Benjamin Henry (b. 1839), **4:** 357 n.*467*; **5:** 21, 22 n.*16*, 30, 35

Charles "Charlie" or "Charley" John Arthur (1858-1933), see below

Elizabeth Murray Kate (1844-1924), see Lewis

Ellen Alice (1847-1928), see below

Florence "Flo" Maude (1856-1896), see Morris

Frederick "Fred" (1863-1933), **4:** 357 n.*467*; **5:** 21, 22, 35, 94 n.*146*, 123, 127, 162, 169; **6:** 79, 97, 312, 352, 398; **7:** 328 n.*581*; **8:** 142, 584 n.*933*

George Edward (1855?-1928), **4:** 357 n.*467*; **5:** 21, 22 n.*16*, 162; **6:** 312

Marion Bessie "Polly" (1854-1930), **4:** 181 225, 246, 356, 357 n.*467*, 358, 359; **5:** 16, 19, 21, 22, 30, 35, 65, 91, 92 n.*142*, 93 n.*144*, 94 n.*146*, 99, 118, 123, 127, 162, 169, 240, 241, 379; **6:** 69, 97, 126, 136, 195, 222, 256, 312, 313, 342, 343, 349, 351, 352, 398, 405 n.*665*, 486; **7:** 23 n.*24*, 78, 97, 141 n.*259*, 156, 157, 176, 185, 231 n.*425*, 278 n.*505*, 319, 348, 387, 430, 438, 442, 443, 494, 513, 514, 516, 536; **8:** 50, 51 n.*75*, 53, 131, 168, 169, 199, 217, 273, 278, 471, 562, 577; **9:** 56 n.*101*, 61, 75, 215 n.*343*, 219, 335

Sarah née Ballard (1819-1892), **4:** 356, 357 n.*467*, 358, 359; **5:** 22, 35, 62, 65, 91, 93 n.*144*, 94 n.*146*, 98, 118, 123, 127, 162, 240, 242; **6:** 69, 79, 97, 115, 136, 195, 222, 312, 341, 352, 398; **7:** 124, 140, 156, 157, 176, 185, 278, 328, 387, 396, 430, 443, 513, 524; **8:** 50, 51 n.*75*, 53, 142, 217, 368; **9:** 61 n.*113*

Thomas "Tom" Walter Alfred (1860-1932), **4:** 357 n.*467*, 358; **5:** 16, 21, 22 n.*16*, 94 n.*146*, 118, 123, 127, 162; **6:** 79, 312; **7:** 78, 234 n.*431*

Terry (of Garonne, France; and London):

Charles "Charlie" or "Charley" John Arthur (1858-1933), **4:** 357 n.*467*, 358, 359; **5:** 16, 21, 22 n.*16*, 65, 93 n.*144*, 94 n.*146*, 118, 123, 127, 162, 169; **6:** 69, 79, 312; **8:** 50, 51 n.*75*, 460, 539; **9:** 54 n.*94*, 163

Horace (b. 1885?), **9:** 163 n.*278*

Margaret née Pratt, **8:** 50, 51 n.*75*, 53

Marguerite"Minnie" (1882-1964), **8:** 50 n.*75*, 368, 405 n.*659*, 460, 539; **9:** 122 n.*214*
Terry, Edward O'Connor (1844-1912) – actor and manager, **7:** 140 n.*258*, 540; **9:** 15, 123, 309, 310 n.*493*
Terry (of West Brompton, London; Tower Cottage, Winchelsea, Sussex):
Charles Clavering Wardell – second husband, see under his name
Edith "Edie" Craig (1869-1947), **7:** 164 n.*309*, 181, 256, 514, 515; **8:** 324 n.*537*, 342; **9:** 56 n.*101*, 60, 138, 156, 163, 316, 334, 335
Edward Gordon Craig (1872-1966), **7:** 164 n.*309*, 181, 256, 514, 515
Ellen Alice (1847-1928) – actress, **2:** 83 n.*164*, 124 n.*240*; **3:** 12 n.*10*, 153 n.*222*; **4:** 127 n.*100*, 224 n.*247*, 225, 230, 243, 246, 301 n.*367*, 312, 335 n.*432*, 357 n.*467*, 358; **5:** 21, 22, 31, 34 n.*39*, 35, 62, 65, 85, 91, 92 n.*142*, 93 n.*144*, 94 n.*146*, 99, 123, 127, 155, 156 n.*252*, 162, 170, 240, 241 n.*390*; **6:** 79, 130, 336, 397 n.*649*, 406, 407, 443; **7:** 15, 105, 106 n.*197*, 156 n.*294*, 164 n.*309*, 181 n.*337*, 185 n.*347*, 234, 256, 318, 327, 396, 397, 430, 494, 516, 522; **8:** 126, 131, 168, 209, 273, 317, 338, 342, 406, 441, 456, 565, 567, 620; **9:** 44 n.*77*, 56 n.*101*, 73, 75 n.*138*, 78, 138, 142, 146, 147, 156, 161, 163, 179, 316, 333, 335
George Frederic Watts – first husband, see under his name
Terry, K., Miss – niece of Benjamin Terry, **7:** 84 n.*142*
Tertullianus, Quintus Septimus Florens (155-222) – early Christian theologian, **4:** 10
Thackeray (of Broxbourne, Hertfordshire):
Anne "Annie" Wynne (1865-1944), **6:** 197 n.*306*, 199
Edward Talbot, Lt.-Col. (1836-1927) – army officer, **6:** 197 n*306*
Margaret "Margie" (1863-1944), **6:** 197 n.*306*, 199
Thackeray (of London):
Anne Isabella (1837-1919), see Ritchie
Harriet Marion (1840-1875), see Stephen
William Makepeace, Mr. (1811-1863) – writer, **3:** 57 n.*86*, 123 n.*174*, 144; **4:** 136
Thackeray, Francis St. John (1832-1919) – teacher, **3:** 123 n.*176*; **4:** 136
Thalberg, Sigismond (1812-1871) – composer, **4:** 48
Thames Embankment, London, **5:** 123
Thames River, **7:** 452
"Thauma" (illusion), **8:** 146, 529
Theatre, The, **8:** 319, 320 n.*525*

Theatres:
Adelphi, London, **2:** 80, 123; **3:** 101; **4:** 337; **5:** 16, 69, 96, 122, 137, 240; **6:** 121, 378; **7:** 13, 23, 75, 77, 91, 93, 99, 114, 492
Astley's, London, **6:** 336
Avenue, London, **7:** 504, 508, 512, 513, 515, 525, 541; **8:** 364; **9:** 53, 54
Bijou, Eastbourne, **7:** 356
Comedy, London, **7:** 532; **9:** 100

Court, London, **6:** 311, 312; **7:** 15, 105, 111, 183, 187, 369, 387, 438, 444, 513, 536; **8:** 199, 618, 621; **9:** 12, 26, 347
Covent Garden, London, **1:** 103; **2:** 53 n.*105*; **4:** 282; **5:** 45, 46; **6:** 112 n.*174*, 314, 316
Criterion, London, **8:** 430
Daly's (American), London, **9:** 132 n.*231*
Devonshire Park, Eastbourne, **8:** 138, 229, 287, 357, 363, 423, 478, 485, 523, 530, 572, 589; **9:** 15, 91, 161-163, 273, 274, 335
Drury Lane, London, **1:** 102; **3:** 76, 146; **4:** 281, 290; **5:** 23, 127, 379 n.*562*; **6:** 257, 376, 403; **7:** 155, 159, 539, 540
Gaiety, London, **6:** 197; **7:** 140, 201
Garrick, London, **9:** 57, 215, 219, 225
Glasgow, **3:** 105, 146
Globe, London, **6:** 378; **7:** 369; **8:** 381, 405, 433, 440, 441, 451, 453, 457, 501
Haymarket, London, **2:** 18, 20 n.*36*, 23; **3:** 49, 146; **4:** 177, 253, 300; **5:** 32, 88, 139, 160, 193, 220, 222; **6:** 169, 253, 486; **7:** 23, 78, 97, 123, 278, 319; **8:** 615; **9:** 233, 352
Her Majesty's Opera House, London, **4:** 341 n.*443*, **5:** 98
Imperial, Westminster, London, **7:** 396
Little Theatre, Moscow, **5:** 313
Lyceum, London, **3:** 102, 120 n.*170*; **4:** 182, 312; **6:** 221, 253, 272, 301, 315; **7:** 156, 185, 236, 317, 327, 494, 508, 522; **8:** 125, 131, 189, 209, 273, 338, 342, 406, 565, 567, 619, 628; **9:** 20, 44, 73, 75, 78, 122, 138, 140, 146, 205, 218
Lyceum, Sunderland, **1:** 133
Lyric, London, **8:** 564, 566, 568, 631; **9:** 138
Manchester, **3:** 120, 146
New Royalty, London, **5:** 232
New Theatre, Oxford, **9:** 123 n.*216*, 280, 313
Nijni Theatre, Nijni Novgorod, Russia, **5:** 311
Olympic, London, **2:** 82 n.*162*, 123; **3:** 12, 51, 76, 79, 133, 146, 153, 171; **4:** 223, 226, 248, 279, 310; **5:** 37, 63, 71, 85, 94, 96, 99, 115, 117, 121, 123, 127, 145, 155, 157, 159, 210; **6:** 27, 135, 255, 258, 312, 349; **7:** 118, 122, 123, 141
Opera Comique, London, **7:** 96; **8:** 473
Opéra Comique, Paris, **5:** 366, 367 n.*544*
Prince of Wales, London, **5:** 125, 156, 231; **6:** 349, 397, 405, 407, 443; **7:** 96, 186, 231; **8:** 309 n.*512*, 311, 367, 546, 556
Princess's, London, **1:** 105 n.*117*, 107; **2:** 9 n.*6*, 19 n.*34*, 20 n.*36*, 23, 82, 123; **3:** 14, 52, 81, 131, 146, 153; **4:** 358; **5:** 64; **6:** 130, 250, 253, 256, 258; **7:** 114, 142, 525; **8:** 52, 80, 168, 208, 228, 234, 274; **9:** 283
Queen's, London, **6:** 130, 281, 313, 314, 335
Royal Garden, Dresden, **5:** 356
Royalty, Soho, London, **4:** 315, 317; **9:** 219

St. James', London, **4:** 225, 269; **5:** 72; **8:** 412, 562; **9:** 56
Sadler's Wells, London, **6:** 310, 311
Savoy, London, **7:** 393, 394, 396, 431, 442, 503; **8:** 161, 164, 210, 220, 281, 453, 523; **9:** 118
Sea Side Road, Eastbourne, **8:** 135, 285, 428, 569, 577, 586; **9:** 26, 164, 166, 212, 213, 272, 277, 331, 332
Shaftesbury, London, **8:** 486; **9:** 233
Strand, London, **4:** 221, 273, 309; **5:** 47, 92, 168; **6:** 398; **7:** 193, 220, 232, 304; **8:** 59, 131; **9:** 16
Surrey, London, **7:** 17, 24
Theatre Royal, Brighton, **7:** 154, 155; **8:** 316 n.*520*, 530; **9:** 173
Theatre Royal, Edinburgh, **3:** 98, 101, 146
Toole's, London, **8:** 112, 317, 322, 333, 373, 374, 614
Vaudeville, London, **8:** 412
Vaudeville, Paris, **5:** 364
Westminster, London, **4:** 159

Theocritus (c. 310-250 BC) – poet, **1:** 78 n.*76*
"Theodora Martindale" (in *Heartsease*), **2:** 57 n.*115*
Theory of Equations (bk. Isaac Todhunter), **4:** 242 n.*270*
They had been boys together (pic. Thomas Faed), **7:** 538, 539 n.*871*
Thicknesse (of Leicester):
Agnes Beatrice Jane "Dolly" née Argles (1857-1944), **6:** 24 n.*26*, 25, 26, 97 n.*152*; **7:** 263 n.*475*; **9:** 192 n.*317*
Francis Henry, Rt. Rev. (1829-1921), **9:** 192 n.*317*
Thierry, Jacques Nicolas Augustin (1795-1856) – writer, **1:** 23
Thieves! Thieves! (dr. Anon), **3:** 51 n.*78*
Thirlwall, John Wade (1809-1875) – composer, **2:** 123 n.*238*
Thomas, Augustus (1857-1934) – dramatist, **9:** 215 n.*343*
Thomas, Brandon (1857-1914) – dramatist, **7:** 513, 514 n.*832*; **8:** 618 n.*980*; **9:** 100, 101 n.*182*
Thomas, Charles – dramatist, **8:** 428 n.*691*
Thomas, Charles Louis Ambroise (1811-1896) – composer, **5:** 367 n.*544*
Thomas (of Preshute, Wiltshire):
Ellinor M. W. (b. 1867), **7:** 495 n.*807*
John S., Rev. (b. 1836) – teacher, **7:** 495 n.*807*
Thomas, Lewis William (b. 1826) – singer, **2:** 47
Thomas, Lily, **4:** 319 n.*405*
Thomas, Richard W., & Co., Ltd., Pall Mall, London – photographic chemist and supplier, **3:** 65 n.*98*; **4:** 229, 247, 304 n.*373*, 322, 324, 341; **5:** 97, 167, 171 n.*283*, 200
Thomas, W. Moy (1829-1910) – dramatist, **3:** 30 n.*44*
Thompson (of Seal, Kent):
Benjamin P., Rev. (b. 1828), **7:** 481 n.*782*
Mrs., **7:** 481 n.*782*

Thompson (of Norham Gardens, Oxford):
Florence née Newson (b. 1859), **7:** 146 n.*273*, 163, 227, 246, 270, 336, 512; **8:** 62; **9:** 35 n.*61*
John Barclay (1845-1936) – tutor, **6:** 209 n.*328*, 219, 245, 302, 317, 327, 366, 372, 410; **7:** 116, 117 n.*218*, 117 n.*220*, 145, 163, 227, 246, 270, 321, 336, 428, 436, 440, 489, 490 n.*798*, 500, 511 n.*829*, 512; **8:** 61 n.*98*; **9:** 35 n.*61*
Thompson, Henry Lewis, Rev. (1840-1905), **5:** 186 n.*305*, 234 n.*377*, 248, 251; **6:** 147; **7:** 85 n.*145*; **8:** 273 n.*460*; **9:** 263 n.*414*, 322 n.*514*
Thompson, Hugh Miller, Rt. Rev. (1830-1902) – bishop of Mississippi, **9:** 315 n.*503*
Thompson, Lydia (1836-1908) – actress, **6:** 378 n.*619*
Thompson, William (1811-1871) – Oxford alderman, **5:** 52 n.*73*
Thoms, Mr. – mathematician, **9:** 336 n.*539*
Thomson, Emily Gertrude (1850-1929) – illustrator, **7:** 151 n.*285*, 162 n.*304*, 184 n.*344*, 186, 188, 190 n.*353*, 192, 280, 347, 380, 533, 537; **8:** 103 n.*171*, 108, 112-114, 181 n.*302*, 181 n.*304*, 260, 381, 382, 448, 546, 567, 611; **9:** 79 n.*146*, 81, 99 n.*179*, 101, 102, 104, 105, 108, 124, 197 n.*322*, 199, 351
Thomson, James, Rev. Dr. (1802-1860) – rector of Lincoln, **3:** 25 n.*33*
Thomson, William, Rev. Dr. (1819-1890) – archbishop of York, **3:** 155, 156 n.*229*; **4:** 316 n.*397*
Thorley (of Banbury Road, Oxford):
George Earlam (1830-1904) – warden of Wadham, **5:** 362 n.*536*, 364; **8:** 125 n.*202*; **9:** 75 n.*137*
Miriam (1837-1912), **9:** 315 n.*502*
Thorn, John Thomas, Rev. (b. 1830), MA Christ Church, **1:** 66 n.*48*
Thorne, Charles (1823-1893) – artist, **7:** 540 n.*873*
Thorne (of London):
Ellen "Nellie" (1875-1960) – child actress, **8:** 609, 610 n.*966*; **9:** 27, 28 n.*41*
Fred, Mr. (1847-1919) – actor, **9:** 28 n.*41*
Mrs., **9:** 27, 28 n.*41*
Thorne, Sarah (1837-1899) – actress and manager, **8:** 419 n.*679*, 579, 609
Thorne, Thomas (1841-1918) – actor and manager, **8:** 425, 426 n.*688*
Thornton, Miss – child actress, **8:** 403
Thorold, George Aubrey William (b. 1847) – solicitor, **7:** 235 n.*434*
Thorold, Miss – former pupil of Mrs. Drury, **7:** 230, 231 n.*424*, 316, 319
Thorpe Mandeville, Northamptonshire, **5:** 112
Thorp Lodge, London (Lewis), **6:** 312
Thoughts in Past Years (bk. Isaac Williams), **1:** 52 n.*9*, 98 n.*105*
Thoughts of the Past (pic. Henry Schlesinger), **5:** 225 n.*358*
Thoughts on Personal Religion (bk. Edward Goulburn), **8:** 250 n.*420*
Thousand (dr. Anon), **7:** 528 n.*854*
Three Furies, The (dr. George Roberts), **5:** 73 n.*110*

"Three Little Foxes," see Dodgson, Charles Lutwidge – Story-telling
Thresher (of Winchester, Hampshire):
Constance Barnaby (b. 1880), **6:** 359 n.*593*
Edith Isabel (b. 1872), **6:** 359 n.*593*
Edward Barnaby (b. 1877), **6:** 359 n.*593*
Elizabeth "Beta" Annie (b. 1868), **6:** 359 n.*593*, 361, 413, 415 n.*681*, 482; **8:** 230
Frances Lydia (b. 1873), **6:** 359 n.*593*
James Henville (1870-1943), **6:** 359 n.*593*
James Henville, Rev. (b. 1843), **6:** 359 n.*593*, 360, 413, 414, 415 n.*681*, 438, 439, 480, 482; **7:** 57, 355
Lucy Mabel (b. 1871), **6:** 359 n.*593*, 361, 413, 415 n.*681*
Mary (b. 1869), **6:** 359 n.*593*, 415 n.*681*
Philip Robert (b. 1879), **6:** 359 n.*593*
Sarah Anne, Mrs. (b. 1845), **6:** 359 n.*593*, 360, 413, 415 n.*681*, 480, 482; **7:** 57, 58 n.*92*, 355
William Harrison (b. 1878), **6:** 359 n.*593*
Through Fire and Water (dr. Walter Gordon), **5:** 96 n.*150*, 137
Thucydides (c. 460–399 BC) – historian and writer, **2:** 35 n.*69*
Thurloe Square, London, **4:** 322
Thursby:
Ethel, **6:** 413 n.*675*, 416, 417, 479, 481
Mabel, **6:** 413 n.*675*, 416, 417, 479, 481
Thursden, see Fursdon
Tichborne trial, **6:** 324 n.*539*
Ticket-of-Leave Man, The (dr. Tom Taylor), **4:** 223 n.*245*, 226, 248, 249, 279, 310; **5:** 63, 145 n.*232*
Ticklish Times (dr. John Morton), **3:** 171 n.*250*
Tidy (of Littlethorpe, near Ripon, Yorkshire):
Arthur Grey (b. 1848?), **3:** 152 n.*221*, 169 n.*246*
Catherine née Maister (b. 1818), **3:** 152 n.*221*, 169 n.*246*
Francis John (b. 1846), **3:** 152 n.*221*, 169 n.*246*
Kathleen Harriet (1851-1926), **3:** 152 n.*221*, 169 n.*246*, 170; **4:** 52, 180
Thomas Holmes, Maj.-Gen. (1809-1874) – army officer, **3:** 152 n.*221*, 169 n.*246*; **4:** 52
Tiens, Miss – friend of Louisa Dodgson, **8:** 532 n.*854*
Till, Laurence William, Rev. (1828-1878), **6:** 49 n.*70*, 58 n.*88*, 77
Times, The, **1:** 101, 120, 126; **2:** 24 n.*44*, 53 n.*105*, 60 n.*121*; **4:** 18, 20, 268 n.*311*, 275; **5:** 10, 11, 12 n.*2*, 26, 27 n.*27*, 31, 32 n.*34*, 116 n.*181*, 185; **6:** 64; **7:** 37, 38 n.*55*, 339 n.*595*, 433, 512 n.*830*; **8:** 29 n.*33*
Timothy to the Rescue (dr. Henry Byron), **4:** 309 n.*384*; **5:** 168 n.*277*
Tinworth, George (1843-1913) – sculptor, **8:** 30 n.*34*
Tinytoe, Annette, real name Solomon – child actress, **5:** 202, 203, 205
"Titania" (in *Midsummer Night's Dream*), **2:** 124 n.*240*
Titian, Tiziano Vecellio (c. 1487-1576) – artist, **5:** 295 n.*464*

Titiens or Tietjens, Therese Johanna Alexandra (1831-1877) – singer, **4:** 104 n.*69*, 341
Todd (of The Grove, Kensington, London):
Ada E. Drummond (1867-1953), **6:** 413 n.*675*, 416, 475; **7:** 234; **8:** 49 n.*73*
Laura Elizabeth née Chamberlain (1834-1914), **6:** 416; **7:** 234
Laura Emma Chamberlain (1864-1948), **6:** 412, 413 n.*675*, 416, 475; **7:** 234; **8:** 49 n.*73*
William Egerton, Col. (1831-1896) – army officer, **6:** 413 n.*675*, 416, 475; **8:** 49 n.*73*
Todd, John, Rev. (1805-1883), **1:** 132 n.*164*
Todd, (John) Spencer Brydges (1840-1921) – civil servant, **8:** 49, 50 n.*74*, 51
Todd, see Wilson Todd
Todhunter, Isaac (1820-1884) – mathematician, **7:** 80, 81 n.*135*, 83, 102 n.*191*
Tolhurst (of Easthampstead, Berkshire):
Charles Edmeades (1828?-1891) – diamond merchant, **6:** 89 n.*135*, 90, 96, 116, 348; **7:** 23, 24 n.*25*, 29, 98, 99, 112
Elizabeth Ann née Geddes, **6:** 89 n.*135*, 90, 96, 116, 348, 352, 402, 403; **7:** 98, 99, 112, 497
Gertrude (1867-1910), **6:** 89 n.*135*
Mary Beatrix (1863-1915), **6:** 89 n.*135*, 90, 116, 351
Tollemache, Lionel Arthur (1838-1919) – writer, **6:** 219 n.*344*
Tolming, Thomas, Rev. (1806-1893), **3:** 117 n.*164*
Tolstoy, Leo, Count (1828-1910), **5:** 344
Tom Brown at Oxford (bk. Thomas Hughes), **1:** 41, 43
Tom Brown's Schooldays (bk. Thomas Hughes), **1:** 27
Tomlinson, Herbert (1845-1931) – scientist, **5:** 54 n.*75*, 199 n.*323*
Tom Noddy's Secret (dr. Thomas Bayly), **8:** 478 n.*774*
Toms (of Eastbourne, Sussex):
Alfred Augustus, Rev. (1856-1922), **9:** 92 n.*168*, 94, 102, 174, 175
Florence née Lanfear (b. 1860), **9:** 92 n.*168*, 174
Irene (b. 1883), **9:** 92 n.*168*, 102, 174, 175
Tommy (b. 1885?), **9:** 92 n.*168*, 102
Tonbridge, Kent (Rivers), **6:** 271, 288, 313, 321
Toodles, The (dr. Richard Raymond), **5:** 96 n.*150*
Tooke, John Horne (1763-1812) – writer, **1:** 52 n.*7*, 73 n.*66*
Tooke (of Pinner, Middlesex):
Mary Agnes, Mrs. (b. 1846)., **6:** 323 n.*537*, 334
William Arthur, Mr. (1843-1884) – barrister, **6:** 323 n.*537*, 334
Toole, John Laurence (1830-1906) – actor, **3:** 101 n.*149*, 102, 120 n.*170*; **4:** 270, 337 n.*436*; **5:** 69 n.*104*, 96 n.*150*, 126, 137; **6:** 197 n.*307*, 335; **7:** 442 n.*732*; **8:** 112, 113 n.*184*, 333, 374, 574, 614
Toon, Mrs. – nurse to Gwendolyn Waldo Story, **8:** 471, 472 n.*764*

Tooting, London, (Macmillans), **6:** 251, 253
To Parents and Guardians (dr. Tom Taylor), **7:** 369 n.*642*
Topliff, R. – song-writer, **2:** 100
Torquay, Devon, **2:** 107; **6:** 97
Totland's Bay, Isle of Wight, **5:** 142
Tournay, Belgium, **5:** 258
Tower (of Earl Shilton, Leicestershire):
Ferdinand Ernest, Rev. (1820-1885), **7:** 415 n.*692*
Mary née Champion, **7:** 415 n.*692*
Townley, James (1714-1778) – dramatist, **5:** 72 n.*108*
Townsend, Stephen – dramatist, **8:** 440 n.*705*
Toynbee, Joseph (1815-1866) – aurist, **2:** 83 n.*165*
Toys, **2:** 123, 125, 127; **5:** 217, 334 n.*505*; **6:** 468 n.*769*; **7:** 53, 283, 291
Tractarianism, **2:** 63; **4:** 10
Trafalgar Square, London, **5:** 166, 200 n.*325*
Tragedy Queen, The (dr. N. R. Fournier, adapt. W. Robson), **3:** 153 n.*223*
Traill (of Blandford Forum, Dorset):
Brenda C. (b. 1870), **6:** 334, 335 n.*553*
Harriett, Mrs. (b. 1842), **6:** 335 n.*553*
Sinclair, Mr. (b. 1837) – solicitor, **6:** 335 n.*553*
Traill, F. T. – dramatist, **5:** 95 n.*147*
Train, The, **1:** 55 n.*17*, 110 n.*127*, 117 n.*142*; **2:** 12, 13 n.*16*, 14 n.*20*, 26, 34, 36, 38 n.*77*, 42, 49 n.*99*, 52 n.*104*, 56 n.*110*, 61 n.*123*, 84 n.*167*, 87, 88 n.*176*, 89 n.*179*, 99 n.*191*, 100 n.*192*, 105, 113 n.*219*; **3:** 30 n.*43*, 30 n.*44*, 45 n.*72*, 53 n.*80*, 54 n.*83*, 123 n.*174*, 126 n.*182*; **4:** 26
Trautschold, William (1815-1875) – artist, **5:** 149 n.*239*
Treacher (of Norham Gardens, Oxford):
Joseph Skipper, Rev. (b. 1816), **5:** 163 n.*268*, 178; **6:** 259, 304, 380; **8:** 89 n.*144*
Misses, **5:** 163 n.*268*, 185 n.*304*; **6:** 380
Treasury, Kremlin Palace, Moscow, **5:** 304
Treatise on Conic Sections (bk. George Salmon), **3:** 15 n.*14*
Treatise on Infinitesimal Calculus, A (bk. Bartholomew Price), **1:** 57 n.*22*
Treatise on the Differential Calculus, A (bk. Bartholomew Price), **1:** 57 n.*22*
Trebeck, James John (1837-1904) – undergraduate at Christ Church, **2:** 104 n.*200*
Tregenna Castle, Cornwall, **8:** 131
Tremlet, Edmund – pupil at Richmond School, **1:** 21
Trench (of Guildford, Surrey):
Amy, **9:** 292 n.*460*
Mr. – bank manager, **9:** 119 n.*206*
Trench, Richard Chenevix (1807-1886) – writer, **1:** 73 n.*66*, 74; **3:** 35 n.*53*
Trevor, Captain – friend of the Riadores, **8:** 241 n.*406*
Trial of Effie Deans,The (dr. Dion Boucicault), **4:** 159, 160 n.*150*
Tricycles:

Devon, **7:** 480
Velociman, see under that name
Trilby (dr. Paul Potter), **9:** 212 n.*339*, 233
Trimmer (of Guildford, Surrey):
Hargood (b. 1852), **6:** 46 n.*65*
Helen (b. 1850), **6:** 46 n.*65*
Helen Sophia, Mrs. (1817-1879), **6:** 46 n.*65*, 77
Mary (b. 1855), **6:** 46 n.*65*, 102; **7:** 343 n.*600*
Robert (b. 1849), **6:** 46 n.*65*
Robert, Rev. (1822-1900), **6:** 46 n.*65*, 48, 49, 77, 205; **7:** 343 n.*600*
Trinity College, Cambridge, **2:** 89
Trinity College, Oxford, **4:** 81 n.*33*, 83, 196; **6:** 440; **7:** 222, 269, 272, 371, 453, 488, 491, 508; **8:** 70, 125, 188, 196, 335, 339, 399, 517; **9:** 223
Trip to Blunderland, Our (bk. Jean Jambon) **8:** 579 n.*925*
Tristan da Cunha, South Atlantic, **7:** 314 n.*560*; **8:** 37, 44-47, 49-53, 56, 58, 63-65, 163 n.*267*, 254, 298, 326, 333, 391 n.*637*, 492 n.*796*
Tristram (of Castle Eden, Durham):
Henry Baker, Rev. (1822-1906), **1:** 98 n.*106*; **4:** 34; **6:** 67 n.*99*
Louisa, **4:** 180
May, **4:** 181
Tristram, Thomas Hutchinson, Hon. (1825-1912) – judge, **1:** 98 n.*106*, 132; **2:** 39 n.*78*; **3:** 49 n.*75*
Triumph of the Innocents (pic. William Holman Hunt), **8:** 197 n.*335*, 204
Troitska or Troitsa, Russia, **5:** 316, 333, 344
Troitska Monastery, **5:** 317, 334
Trollope (travelled widely):
Anthony (1815-1882) – writer, **6:** 104 n.*163*
Rose née Heseltine, **6:** 104 n.*163*
Trossachs, Scotland, **3:** 104
Troubridge, see Hope
Troughton, Adolphus Charles (b. 1814) - dramatist, **3:** 133 n.*193*
Trovatore, Il (Verdi) – opera, **8:** 577 n.*920*
Troy, Asia Minor, **1:** 102
Truscott, Miss – head of Guildford Nurses' Training Institution, **9:** 346 n.*554*
Trying a Magistrate (dr. John Toole), **7:** 442 n.*732*
Tryon, George, Vice-Admiral Sir (1832-1893) – navy officer, **8:** 47 n.*68*
Tucker (of Stoke, near Guildford, Surrey):
Edith (b. 1884), **9:** 305 n.*484*
Mr., **9:** 305 n.*484*
Tucker, Henry William, Rev. (1830-1902) – assistant secretary to the SPG, **8:** 44 n.*66*, 298
Tuckwell (of Oxford):
Henry Matthews (1835-1906) – physician, **4:** 151, 152 n.*137*
William (1829-1919) – teacher and writer, **4:** 38, 151, 152 n.*137*

Tudor (of Eastbourne, Sussex):
Mrs., **7:** 459; **8:** 39, 149
Owen Lechmere, Rev. (b. 1854), **7:** 352 n.*614*, 459; **8:** 39 n.*53*, 149, 239
Tudor Lodge, Albert Street, London, **4:** 98, 183, 225, 231
Tuileries Gardens, Paris, **5:** 362
Tunbridge Wells, Kent, **1:** 109 n.*125*; **4:** 295; **6:** 288, 313, 320, 397; **7:** 210
Tunny-fish (blue-fin tuna), **3:** 62 n.*93*; **4:** 38
Turkish dress, **7:** 42 n.*63*
Turnbull, Elizabeth (b. 1851) – servant and model, **5:** 89 n.*137*, 98 n.*153*, 218
Turner (of Gouray Lodge, Jersey):
Adolphus Hilgrove (1847-1911), **5:** 250 n.*408*; **8:** 98 n.*160*, 99
Elizabeth née McNeil (b. 1820), **8:** 98 n.*160*
Turner (of Caistor, Lincolnshire):
Charles, Rev. (1808-1879), formerly Tennyson – poet, **4:** 353 n.*460*
Louisa née Sellwood (b. 1816), **4:** 353 n.*460*
Turner, Eardley (d. 1929) – actor, **8:** 230 n.*388*
Turner (of St. Giles', Oxford):
Edward Tindal, Mr. (1822-1911) – lecturer, **4:** 201 n.*207*; **6:** 67 n.*99*, 153 n.*234*; **7:** 499 n.*815*
Emily, Mrs. (d. 1917), **6:** 491
Turner, Harry – Christ Church collector of rents, **7:** 258 n.*469*, 260
Turner, H. J. (1806-1891) – actor, **4:** 273 n.*318*
Turner, Joseph Mallord William (1775-1851) – artist, **2:** 64
Turn Him Out (dr. Thomas Williams), **4:** 272, 273 n.*318*
Turton (of Blackheath, Kent):
"Boojum" (brother), **7:** 139, 303, 313
Clare "Bibby" (b. 1871), **7:** 139 n.*256*, 159, 215, 288, 303, 313, 465-469; **8:** 135
Col., **7:** 159 n.*298*
Mrs., **7:** 159 n.*298*
Winifred "Winnie," **7:** 313
Tutor's Assistant, a Compendium of Arithmetic, The (bk. Francis Walkingame), **1:** 71 n.*60*
Twain, Mark (real name Samuel Langhorne Clemens), **7:** 195 n.*363*
Twenty Minutes' Conversation under an Umbrella (dr. Augustus Dubourg), **7:** 194, 195 n.*362*
Twenty Minutes with a Tiger (dr. Anon), **6:** 310 n.*513*
Twinkle, Twinkle, Little Star (dr. Frank Green), **6:** 444 n.*728*
Twiss, Quintin William Francis (1835-1900) – civil servant and actor, **2:** 47 n.*92*, 48; **3:** 69 n.*108*, 70; **5:** 240 n.*389*; **8:** 165 n.*271*
Two Little Vagabonds (dr. George Sims and Arthur Shirley), **9:** 283, 284 n.*449*, 303, 352
Two Orphans, The (dr. John Oxenford), **7:** 141 n.*259*
"Two Voices, The" (Alfred Tennyson) – poem, **1:** 110 n.*127*; **2:** 89 n.*179*

Twyford School, Hampshire, **1:** 88 n.*91*; **2:** 58 n.*117*, 120 n.*232*; **3:** 135 n.*196*, 136-8, 145, 147, 149, 161, 174; **4:** 10; **6:** 360; **7:** 244
Tydd (of Holywell, Oxford):
Mrs., **8:** 591 n.*943*
Thomas Henry, Rev. (b. 1848), **8:** 591 n.*943*
Tylee, Thomas Gerard, Rev. (b. 1851), **6:** 261 n.*418*
Tyler, Frederick H. (b. 1857) – actor, **9:** 215 n.*343*, 225, 226 n.*357*
Tylor (of Oxford):
Anna née Fox, **9:** 300 n.*477*
Edward Burnett, Prof. (1832-1917) – anthropologist, **9:** 300 n.*477*
Gertrude (b. 1859), **9:** 300 n.*477*
Tyndall, Kate, alias Mrs. Gilmer (d. 1919) – actress, **9:** 283, 284 n.*449*, 288
Tynemouth, Northumberland, **1:** 121
Typhlograph – see Nyctograph
Tyrolese Minstrels, **6:** 484
Tyrwhitt (of Banbury Road, Oxford):
Alice Katherine "Kittie" (b. 1864?), **6:** 213 n.*331*
Caroline née Yorke (d. 1883) – second wife, **2:** 11 n.*12*; **4:** 106 n.*74*; **7:** 226, 309
Eliza-Anne née Stanhope (d. 1860) – first wife, **2:** 11 n.*12*
Mary Frances "Polly" (b. 1867), **6:** 213 n.*331*
Richard St. John, Rev. (1827-1895), **2:** 11 n.*12*, 64, 66 n.*131*, 67, 69, 108, 126; **3:** 31, 39 n.*61*, 125, 127, 150, 167; **4:** 67 n.*5*, 106 n.*74*, 121 n.*93*, 266 n.*310*, 305, 350; **5:** 25, 120, 247 n.*401*; **6:** 31 n.*38*, 475; **7:** 226, 309; **9:** 232 n.*367*
Tyrwhitt, Robert P. (b. 1799) – retired police magistrate, **7:** 164

Ugonotti, Gli or *Les Huguenots* (Meyerbeer) – opera, **5:** 156 n.*254*
Ulysses (dr. Francis Burnand), **5:** 72, 73 n.*110*
Uncle's Will (dr. S. Theyre Smith), **7:** 183 n.*342*
Uncle Tom's Cabin (dr. George Rowe), **7:** 142 n.*262*
Uniacke, John – dramatist, **8:** 473 n.*768*
Universities Bill, **7:** 39 n.*57*
Universities Mission to Central Africa (UMCA), **7:** 164 n.*308*
University College, Oxford, **2:** 43; **3:** 58 n.*87*, 60; **4:** 38, 151; **6:** 144, 254, 380, 450, 451; **7:** 495, 535; **8:** 62
Unspoken Sermons (bk. George MacDonald), **1:** 44
Unwin (of Putney, Surrey):
Ludovic, **2:** 81
Mary, **2:** 81
Upper Crust, The (dr. Henry Byron), **8:** 112, 113 n.*184*
Utopia (Limited) (Gilbert and Sullivan) – operetta, **9:** 118 n.*204*

Vale of Lorton, Cumberland, **2:** 94
Valentia, see Annesley

Valpy (of Guildford, Surrey):
Arthur Sutton, Rev. (1849-1909), **8:** 240 n.*401*, 305, 311, 450; **9:** 49 n.*85*
Sophia "Jessie" Margaret, Mrs. (1853-1897), **8:** 240 n.*401*; **9:** 205
Van Biene, Auguste (1850-1913) – actor and cellist, **9:** 277 n.*442*
Vanbrugh, see Barnes
Vance, see Stevens
Van der Gucht (of London):
Charles, Mr. (1830-1883), **8:** 227 n.*384*
Marie (1874-1919), **8:** 227 n.*384*, 229, 268, 269, 290-292, 305, 311; **9:** 17 n.*15*, 19, 212, 213
Rosalie née Hodding (1839-1922), **8:** 227 n.*384*, 229, 305
Van der Meere:
Lola, **8:** 354 n.*578*
Wanda, Madame, **8:** 354 n.*578*
Vane, Helen (1861-1940) – actress, **8:** 426 n.*688*
Vanity Fair, **6:** 447 n.*734*; **7:** 159 n.*299*, 163, 170 n.*317*, 171; **8:** 556, 557 n.*886*
Vansittart, Augustus Arthur (1824-1882) – classicist, **6:** 455 n.*750*
Varsity Match, **1:** 42
Vassilievski or Wassili Ostrov, St. Petersburg, **5:** 292
Vatcher (of St. Helier, Jersey):
Bessie, **8:** 96, 97 n.*158*
Rose E. (b. 1864), **8:** 96, 97 n.*158*, 99, 139
Vaughan, Charles John, Rev. (1816-1897), **7:** 31 n.*41*
Vaughan, Frederick Archibald, Lord Emlyn (b. 1847), **5:** 48 n.*63*
Vaughan, John (b. 1843) – bookseller and stationer, **6:** 393 n.*643*; **7:** 44 n.*67*
Vaughan, Kate (1852-1903) – actress, **7:** 140 n.*258*
Vauxhall Bridge Road, London, **6:** 414
Veley (of Bradmore Road, Oxford):
Lilian Jane née Gould (b. 1861), **9:** 232, 233 n.*368*, 256
Victor Herbert, Mr. (1856-1933) – scientist, **9:** 232, 233 n.*368*
Velociman (Tricycle), **7:** 435 n.*722*, 481, 482, 485, 486, 488, 494; **8:** 21 n.*16*, 217, 221
Venables (of St. Giles', Oxford):
Agnes (b. 1860), **9:** 121 n.*212*; 260, 261
Edith (b. 1862), **9:** 121 n.*212*; 260, 261
Venables (of St. Aldates, Oxford)
Frances, Mrs. (b. 1854) – lodging-house keeper, **9:** 236
Venne, Lottie (1852-1928) – actress, **7:** 438 n.*727*, 541
Ventnor, Isle of Wight, **6:** 295, 298, 343, 358, 362, 368, 424, 478; **7:** 170, 171
Venus and Adonis (dr. Francis Burnand), **4:** 300 n.*366*
Venus Verticordia (pic. Dante G. Rossetti), **4:** 316 n.*398*; **5:** 71 n.*107*
Verdant Green, Mr (bk. Cuthbert Bede), **1:** 41-43, 47

Verdi, Guiseppe (1813-1901) – composer, **4:** 341 n.*443*; **8:** 577 n.*920*
Verdi, Lina – child actress, **9:** 347, 348 n.*557*
Vere Street, London, **4:** 105, 160, 222, 309, 310, 330
Vernon, Thomas Henry (b. 1863) – undergraduate at Christ Church, **7:** 482 n.*785*
Vernon Gallery, London, **3:** 133, 172
Vernon Harcourt, see Harcourt
Verona, Italy, **7:** 460
Verrey's Restaurant, London, **8:** 108, 168, 198, 632
Vesey, Arthur Cyril (b. 1834) – undergraduate at Christ Church, **1:** 65 n.*45*, 67, 68, 71, 87, 88 n.*91*, 96
Vezin, Hermann (1829-1910) – actor, **6:** 486 n.*800*; **7:** 105, 106 n.*197*
Vibart, Henry (b. 1863) – actor, **8:** 586 n.*936*
Vibert, Janet – governess to Lord Rosebery's children, **9:** 255 n.*402*
Vicarage, The (dr. Clement Scott), **7:** 319, 320 n.*569*
Vicars (of Rugby School, Warwickshire):
Caroline A. (b. 1849), **4:** 306 n.*376*
Elizabeth E. (b. 1839), **4:** 306 n.*376*
Emily S. (b. 1844), **4:** 306 n.*376*
Hedley, Mr. (1797-1864) – Rugby schoolteacher, **1:** 26; **4:** 306 n.*376*
Henry George Austin (1833-1867), **1:** 26
Mrs., **1:** 26; **5:** 248 n.*406*
Vice Versâ: or a Lesson to Fathers (dr. Edward Rose, adapt. F. Anstey), **8:** 59 n.*92*, 189 n.*318*
Vickers, Susannah (b. 1803) – related to the Bickersteths, **5:** 105 n.*163*
Victor, F. – actor, **9:** 23 n.*28*
"Victoria" (carriage), **8:** 85 n.*137*
Victoria College, St. Helier, Jersey, **8:** 97 n.*159*
Victoria Docks, London, **7:** 166
Victoria Hospital, Gough House, Chelsea, London, **5:** 30
Victoria Metropolitan Railway, **6:** 467
Victoria Station. London, **4:** 318; **7:** 93, 96, 348, 511; **8:** 290-292, 357, 359, 360, 362, 367, 413, 421, 474, 581, 583, 590; **9:** 21, 23, 31, 157, 331, 335
View from the Mount of Offence (pic. William Holman Hunt), **2:** 75 n.*151*
View near Oxford (pic. H. Ash), **2:** 75 n.*151*
View of Tenby (pic. Mr. Tenn), **5:** 86 n.*134*
Villiers (of Adisham, Kent):
Dorothy (b. 1872), **6:** 32 n.*41*
Frances Adelaide (1862-1934), **6:** 32 n.*41*
Godfrey Robert Randall (b. 1877), **6:** 32 n.*41*
Gwendolen Mary (1865-1941), **6:** 32 n.*41*
Henry Montagu (b. 1863), **6:** 32 n.*41*
Henry Montagu, Rev. (1837-1908), **6:** 32 n.*41*
John Russell (b. 1866), **6:** 32 n.*41*
Katherine Helen (b. 1875), **6:** 32 n.*41*

Mabel Agatha (b. 1874), **6:** 32 n.*41*
Margaret Evelyn (b. 1871), **6:** 32 n.*41*
Rhoda Victoria (1868-1878), **6:** 32 n.*41*
Thomas Lister (b. 1869), **6:** 32 n.*41*
Victoria née Russell, Lady (1838-1880), **6:** 32 n.*41*
Vincent, H. H. (1848-1913) – actor and manager, **5:** 63 n.*93*, 71, 85
Vincent, Joseph – Oxford printer, **4:** 275, 306; **5:** 77 n.*119*, 81, 91, 114, 173, 181, 246
Vineyard, Hatfield House, Hertfordshire, **6:** 163, 221, 376
Vining, George (1824-1875) – actor, **3:** 12 n.*10*
Vinning, Louisa – singer, **2:** 122
Violet and Henry Roberts (Alexander Munro) – sculpture, **5:** 86 n.*134*
"Violet Martindale" (in *Heartsease*), **2:** 57 n.*115*
Virgil (70-19 BC) – poet, **1:** 23; **3:** 9; **4:** 17
Virginia Water, Surrey, **4:** 244
Virgin Widow (bk. Henry Taylor), **4:** 128 n.*101*
"Vision of the Sea, A" (Percy B. Shelley) – poem, **1:** 53 n.*10*
Visitation of Seats and Arms (bk. Bernard Burke), **1:** 13
Vistula River, central Europe, **5:** 276
Vivisection, **6:** 381 n.*624*, 382, 390; **8:** 171, 172 n.*288*
Voice from the Forge (bk. Elihu Burritt), **1:** 134 n.*169*
Vokes Family – performers (of London):
Frederick (1846-1882), **6:** 257 n.*409*, 376
Jessie (d. 1884), **6:** 257 n.*409*, 376
Robert (1856-1912), **6:** 257 n.*409*, 376; **8:** 285, 286 n.*480*
Rosina (1851-1894), **6:** 257 n.*409*, 376
Victoria (1853-1894), **6:** 257 n.*409*, 376; **8:** 285, 286 n.*480*
Walter, **6:** 257 n.*409*, 376; **8:** 285, 286 n.*480*
Volga River, Russia, **5:** 312
Volks Electric Railway, Brighton, **8:** 146 n.*236*; **9:** 85
Voltaire, alias François Marie Arouet (1694-1778) – dramatist, **8:** 556 n.*885*
Volunteer Club, London, **4:** 223
Volunteer Review, Port Meadow, Oxford, **4:** 212 n.*223*
Vowchurch, Herefordshire, **9:** 192 n.*316*, 287 n.*454*, 314
Vox Stellarum (almanac), **1:** 79 n.*77*
Vyvyan, M. Caroline (fl. 1868-1897) – artist, **7:** 517 n.*838*

Waddell, Isabella (b. 1831) – governess to the Prices, **6:** 487 n.*803*
Waddy (of Sheffield, Yorkshire):
Annie, **7:** 48 n.*74*, 49, 74; **8:** 25 n.*25*, 583
Edith **7:** 48 n.*74*, 49, 74; **8:** 25 n.*25*
Emma Louisa "Louie," see Dingley
Emma née Garbutt (d. 1898), **7:** 48 n.*74*, 49; **8:** 25 n.*25*, 29
Henry Turner (1863-1926), **8:** 25 n.*25*, 583
Lucy (cousin), **7:** 48 n.*74*, 74; **8:** 25 n.*25*

Mary "Minnie" Elizabeth (b. 1865?), **7:** 48 n.*74*, 49, 74; **8:** 25 n.*25*
Samuel Danks, Hon. (1830-1902) – judge, **7:** 48 n.*74*, 49; **8:** 25 n.*25*
Wadham College, Oxford, **3:** 49 n.*75*, 60; **4:** 83; **5:** 153; **7:** 269, 309, 419; **8:** 89, 125, 196, 339, 409, 446, 503; **9:** 75, 77, 251, 263, 315
Wadham College Barge, **9:** 258
Wagener or Waagen Gallery, Berlin, **5:** 266 n.*433*
Wainewright, Robert A. (b. 1808) – solicitor, **6:** 57 n.*85*; **7:** 295 n.*533*
Waiting Consent (dr. May Fairbairn), **8:** 374 n.*616*
"Waiting Room, The" in *The Train*, **2:** 99
Waiting to Skate (pic. Alice Donkin), **6:** 388 n.*635*
Wakefield (of Kingston upon Thames, Surrey):
Joan Margery or Marjorie (b. 1878), **8:** 251 n.*422*; **9:** 187 n.*310*
Winifred "Winnie" (b. 1879), **8:** 251 n.*422*; **9:** 187 n.*310*
Wakeman, Edward Maltby, Maj. (1846-1926) – army officer, **7:** 148 n.*280*
Waking (pic. John Millais), **5:** 213 n.*341*, 240
Waldegrave (of Southampton, Hampshire):
Granville Augustus William (1833-1913), 3rd Baron Radstock, **7:** 291 n.*527*
Susan Charlotte née Calcroft (d. 1892), **7:** 291 n.*527*
Waldegrave (of Montague Place, London):
Laura Margaret "Madge" (b. 1880), **8:** 622 n.*985*, 631
Mary Dorothea née Palmer, Lady (1850-1933), **8:** 622 n.*985*, 631
Mary "May" Wilfreda (1875-1947), **8:** 622 n.*985*, 631
William Frederick, Lord (1851-1930), 9th Earl, **8:** 622 n.*985*
Wales, **1:** 114
Walesby, Francis Pearson (1798-1858) – examiner in law, **2:** 39 n.*78*
Walford (of Warwick Square, London):
Alfred Saunders, Mr. (1843-1907) – broker, **8:** 573 n.*915*, 576, 578
Frances Maitland (b. 1873), **8:** 573 n.*915*, 577
Helen "Nellie" Sutherland (b. 1876), **8:** 573 n.*915*, 577
Lucy Bethia née Colquhoun (1845-1915) – novelist, **8:** 573 n.*915*, 576, 577; **9:** 29 n.*45*, 91
Olive Montagu (b. 1874), **8:** 573 n.*915*, 577
Walker (of Norham Gardens, Oxford):
Gertrude A., Mrs. (b. 1857), **8:** 90 n.*146*, 100
James, Mr. (1857-1919?) – lecturer, **7:** 382, 383 n.*659*, 440 n.*730*, 496; **8:** 90 n.*146*, 100, 491
Walker (of Oxford Square, London):
Gladys Hope (1875-1957), **8:** 297 n.*494*, 298, 300 n.*501*, 302, 303, 623 n.*986*
James Douglas, Mr. (1841-1920) – barrister, **8:** 297 n.*494*
Susan Matilda née Foster (b. 1847), **8:** 297 n.*494*
Walker, John (1775-1860?) – gardener, **3:** 116 n.*162*
Walker, John Russell, Rev. (1837-1887), **7:** 400, 401 n.*680*
Walker, London (dr. James M. Barrie), **8:** 614 n.*974*

Walker, Miss – governess to the Fendalls, **7:** 158
Walkingame, Francis (fl. 1751-1785) – mathematical writer, **1:** 71 n.*60*
Wall, Henry, Rev. (1810-1873) – professor of logic, **4:** 161, 162 n.*154*
Wall, Mrs., from India, **7:** 357 n.*625*
Wallace, Miss – actress, **5:** 47 n.*62*
Waller (of Charlbury, Oxfordshire):
Alrured J. (b. 1880), **9:** 270 n.*427*
Elizabeth née Jamieson (1844-1915), **9:** 270 n.*427*
Ida E. (b. 1873), **9:** 270 n.*427*
John Hampden, Gen. (1839-1934) – army officer, **9:** 270 n.*427*
Violet L. (b. 1875), **9:** 270 n.*427*
Wallich (of Campden Hill Road, Kensington, London):
Alice Mary (b. 1857), **4:** 178; **5:** 19, 143 n.*230*, 144
Beatrice H. (b. 1860), **4:** 178; **5:** 143 n.*230*, 144
Caroline, Mrs. (b. 1828), **5:** 143 n.*230*
Charles A. (b. 1854), **5:** 143 n.*230*
George Charles, Dr. (1815-1899) – naturalist and photographer, **5:** 25, 33 n.*36*, 143 n.*230*, 144, 145 n.*233*, 194; **6:** 18 n.*17*
Wallis, Ellen Lancaster (b. 1856) – actress, **7:** 540 n.*873*
Wallis, Henry (1830-1916) – artist, **2:** 75 n.*151*
Walmisley (of Iffley, Oxfordshire):
Alice (b. 1870), **8:** 324 n.*537*, 331
Alice R., Mrs. (b. 1828), **8:** 324 n.*537*
Catherine "Katie" F. (b. 1861), **8:** 324 n.*537*, 331
Horatio, Rev. (1822-1905), **8:** 324 n.*537*, 330
Horatio W. F. (b. 1863), **8:** 324 n.*537*
Mabel E. (b. 1858), **8:** 324 n.*537*, 331
Reginald E. (b. 1859), **8:** 324 n.*537*
Walmsley, Betty (b. 1871) – school mistress, **9:** 271 n.*428*
Walpole, Arthur – friend of the Putney Dodgsons, **2:** 81
Walsh (of Eastbourne, Sussex):
Janet, **7:** 454 n.*752*, 456
Mrs., **7:** 456
Walsh, Mr. – friend of Sampson, **6:** 323
Walter, Gordon (1823-1892), alias William Aylmer Gowing – dramatist, **9:** 119 n.*205*
Walters (of Stoke, near Guildford, Surrey):
Alice, **8:** 161, 328, 500, 501
Amy S. (b. 1855), **7:** 360, 505, 508; **8:** 75 n.*118*, 282, 344, 372, 434, 500, 501; **9:** 150, 188, 284, 345
Florence, **6:** 356, 357 n.*590*; **7:** 477; **8:** 75 n.*118*, 83, 500, 501, 533, 565, 610; **9:** 103 n.*187*
Harriet née Mitchell (b. 1825), **6:** 357 n.*590*, 457; **7:** 142 n.*261*, 360, 477; **8:** 75 n.*118*, 140, 218, 220, 251, 274, 372, 434, 441, 533, 547, 565, 566, 616; **9:** 27 n.*39*, 44, 102, 116 n.*201*, 140, 150, 188, 205, 284, 345

Henry Littlejohn Master, Rev. (1821-1898), **6:** 357 n.*590*; **7:** 232 n.*427*, 477; **8:** 434, 547, 616; **9:** 27 n.*39*, 102, 140, 205
Lucy J. (b. 1856), **7:** 96 n.*178*, 360, 443, 539, 541; **8:** 75 n.*118*, 79, 80 n.*124*, 81, 269, 271, 282, 328, 330 n.*544*, 392 n.*638*, 405, 439, 440, 470, 500, 501, 511 n.*823*, 533, 546, 565, 566, 610; **9:** 102, 118, 150, 188, 303, 345
Waltham Cross, Hertfordshire, **6:** 221
Walthew (of Marylebone, London):
Jane A., Mrs. (b. 1824), **6:** 235 n.*371*
Richard, Mr. (b. 1815) – solicitor, **6:** 235 n.*371*
Walton, Dorothy "Dolly" Ellen née Draper (b. 1863), **6:** 462 n.*761*; **7:** 19 n.*15*, 29 n.*39*; **9:** 79 n.*146*
Walton, Elijah (1833-1880) – artist, **5:** 61 n.*88*
Walton Convalescent Home, Surrey, **5:** 29
Walton-le-dale, Lancashire, **1:** 11
Wandering Heir, The (dr. Charles Reade), **6:** 314 n.*520*, 336
Wandsworth, Surrey, **4:** 223, 229, 248, 270, 281, 324, 340, 342; **5:** 65; **6:** 255
Wandsworth Church, **4:** 270
Wannock, Sussex, **9:** 330
Wantage, Berkshire, **5:** 135
"Wanted a Governess" (John Orlando Parry) – song, **2:** 100
Wanted – A King (br. Maggie Browne), **8:** 579 n.*925*
Warburton (of Iffley, Oxfordshire):
Acton (b. 1867), **4:** 77 n.*25*
Thomas Acton, Rev. (1814-1894), **4:** 77 n.*25*, 103, 176
Warburton (of Aughrim, Ireland):
Anna, Mrs. (b. 1784), **4:** 77 n.*25*, 176
Bartholomew Elliott George (1810-1852), **4:** 16
George Drought (1816-1857), see below
Thomas Acton (1814-1894), see above
William Parsons (1826-1919), **4:** 16
Warburton (of Henley House, Frant, Sussex):
Augusta (1854?-1941), **4:** 77 n.*25*, 176, 178
Elizabeth Augusta née Bateman-Hanbury (b. 1832), **4:** 176
George Drought, Mr. (1816-1857) – writer, **4:** 77 n.*25*
Hansell (b. 1856?), **4:** 77 n.*25*, 176
Ward (of Queens Villas, Osborne Road, New Windsor, Berkshire):
Alice (b. 1850), see Grimble
Beatrice Mary Florence (b. 1860), **5:** 19, 161 n.*266*, 168, 169, 170, 210; **6:** 194; **8:** 378 n.*621*; **9:** 221 n.*350*
Edward Matthew, Mr. (1816-1879) – artist, **5:** 127 n.*204*, 161 n.*266*, 168, 170, 210, 216, 217 n.*346*, 227 n.*362*, 229; **6:** 17 n.*15*, 86
Enid C. V. H., **6:** 194, 275; **8:** 378 n.*621*
Eva Marianna (b. 1852?), **5:** 161 n.*266*, 168, 169 n.*280*, 170, 216,

217 n.*346*, 227 n.*362*, 229; **6:** 73; **7:** 430 n.*717*, 444
Flora Emma Sarah (b. 1853), see Chappell
Henrietta Mary Ada, Mrs. (1832-1924) – artist, **3:** 78 n.*123*; **5:** 127 n.*204*, 161 n.*266*, 170, 210, 216, 217 n.*346*, 227 n.*362*, 229 n.*365*; **6:** 17 n.*15*, 194; **7:** 430 n.*717*, 443; **8:** 378 n.*621*, 577; **9:** 221 n.*350*
Leslie "Spy" (1851-1922), **5:** 161 n.*266*, 229; **6:** 447 n.*734*; **7:** 430 n.*717*; **9:** 221 n.*350*
Wriothesley "Russell" (b. 1858) **5:** 161 n.*266*, 168, 169 n.*280*, 170, 210
Ward, Artemus (1834-1867) real name Charles Farrar Browne – writer and performer, **5:** 191, 192 n.*314*
Ward, Gilbert (b. 1860) – teacher, **7:** 513, 514 n.*833*
Ward, Hettie – actress, **8:** 547 n.*871*
Ward, John (fl. 1680-1700) – mathematical writer, **1:** 81 n.*82*
Ward, Miss – model for Millais, **5:** 213 n.*341*
Ward, see Humphry Ward
Wardell (of Barkstone Gardens, Earl's Court, London):
Charles, stage name Kelly (1839-1885) – actor and manager, **7:** 106 n.*197*, 164 n.*309*, 181, 194, 256, 396, 397, 430, 468 n.*769*; **8:** 189 n.*317*
Ellen Alice née Terry (1847-1928), see Terry
Ward Hunt, see Hunt
Ware, Henry Ryder, Rev. (1836-1905), **7:** 545 n.*879*; **8:** 443 n.*709*, 547, 613; **9:** 102 n.*186*, 116 n.*201*, 179, 188, 290
Waring, Edward (1734-1798) – mathematical writer, **1:** 70 n.*58*, 79
Waring, Herbert (1858-1932) – actor, **8:** 578 n.*921*
Waring (of Guildford, Surrey):
John Edward, Mr. (1794-1865), **6:** 94 n.*147*
Mary, **6:** 94 n.*147*
Susan, Mrs. (1811-1883), **6:** 94 n.*147*
Warner, Charles (1847-1909) – actor, **7:** 114 n.*211*
Warner, Susan Bogert (1819-1885), alias Elizabeth Wetherell – writer, **1:** 99 n.*108*; **2:** 125 n.*242*
Warner (of Crick Street, Oxford):
Rosamund Edith née Bury (b. 1860), **9:** 45 n.*80*, 238
William, Rev. (1851-1921) – lecturer, **6:** 372 n.*610*; **7:** 321, 384 n.*662*, 440, 490; **8:** 257 n.*435*; **9:** 45 n.*80*, 238, 247
War Office, London, **6:** 400
Warren, Thomas Herbert, Dr. (1853-1930) – president of Magdalen, **8:** 591 n.*942*
Warrington, Lancashire, **1:** 12-14
Warsaw, Poland, **5:** 349-351
Warwick, **8:** 177
Warwick Castle, **8:** 177
Washington, George (1732-1799) – US president, **2:** 17
Washington, Henry, Rev. (1856-1912), **7:** 541

Wasthead, Cumberland, **2:** 92
Water Babes, The (dr. Edward Bowles), **9:** 251 n.*394*, 252, 254
Water-Babies, *The* (bk. Charles Kingsley), **4:** 311 n.*387*
Water-Colour Society Exhibition, London, **2:** 80
Water Eaton, Oxfordshire, **9:** 67
Waterer (of Windlesham, Surrey):
  John, Mr. (b. 1837) – nurseryman, **6:** 413 n.*675*
  Kate Godfrey, Mrs. (b. 1844), **6:** 413 n.*675*
  Kate "Katie" Alice (b. 1870), **6:** 412, 413 n.*675*
Waterfield, Mr. – secretary to Lord Rosebery, **9:** 255 n.*403*
Waterloo Station, London, **3:** 138, 139; **5:** 66; **6:** 169, 223, 226, 309, 310, 467, 495; **7:** 166, 183, 193, 236, 256, 397, 477, 505, 539, 541; **8:** 292, 403, 453, 565, 617; **9:** 14, 122, 123, 205, 215
Waters (of Staverton, Northamptonshire):
  Barbara Bass née Vessey (b. 1846), **9:** 198 n.*325*
  Thomas, Rev. (1839-1909), **6:** 370 n.*608*; **8:** 632 n.*1000*; **9:** 198 n.*325*
Watkin (of Rosehull, Northenden, Cheshire):
  Alfred Mellor (1846-1914), **4:** 245 n.*277*
  Edward William, Sir (1819-1901) – politician, **4:** 245 n.*277*
  Harriette Sayer (b. 1850?), **4:** 245 n.*277*, 246
  Mary Briggs née Mellor (1821?-1888), **4:** 245 n.*277*, 246
Watkin and Hill, Charing Cross – retailers, **2:** 123, 126
Watkins (of Durham):
  Henry William, Dr. (1844-1922) – archdeacon, **8:** 510 n.*821*
  Kate Mary Margaret née Thompson, **8:** 510 n.*821*
Watkins, Herbert (b. 1829) – photographer, **4:** 25
Watkins, Lizzie (b. 1873) – actress, **9:** 166, 167 n.*284*
Watson, C., Mr. – engaged to Daisy Tate, **9:** 102 n.*185*
Watson (of Guildford, Surrey):
  Caroline Harriet Leili (1846-1920), **7:** 151 n.*286*, 460, 502; **8:** 30 n.*34*, 101, 131, 149, 216, 281 n.*471*, 300 n.*500*, 336 n.*555*, 356, 533, 562; **9:** 26 n.*37*, 49, 54, 120
  Walter, Mr. (1813-1887) – tutor, **7:** 151 n.*286*, 182, 222 n.*406*, 223, 288, 312, 348, 360, 392, 402 n.*682*, 406 n.*688*, 410, 419, 453, 469-471, 502, 503, 531; **8:** 184 n.*313*, 216, 262 n.*441*, 292 n.*488*, 293, 295, 303, 354, 356 n.*582*
Watson (of Guildford, Surrey):
  Charles Kaye (b. 1858), **8:** 500 n.*804*, 547
  George William, Rev. (1822-1863), **6:** 99 n.*155*, 231
  Georgina "Ina" Janet (b. 1862), **6:** 99 n.*155*, 101, 102, 107, 113, 138, 270, 271, 280; **7:** 28 n.*37*
  Harriet "Hartie" Selina (b. 1860) **6:** 99 n.*155*, 101, 102, 107, 113, 138, 270, 271, 280; **7:** 28 n.*37*; **8:** 500 n.*804*
  Mary Emma (1861?-1928), **6:** 99 n.*155*, 101, 102, 107, 113, 138, 270, 271, 280; **7:** 28 n.*37*; **8:** 500

Selina Georgiana née Dashwood (d. 1879), **6:** 99 n.*155*, 106, 138, 231, 270, 271, 280; **7:** 28 n.*37*
Watson, Hester (1809-1882) – Walter Watson's sister, **7:** 402 n.*682*, 406
Watson, Isy (b. 1884) – artists' model, **9:** 351, 352 n.*563*
Watson, Miss – friend of Miss Lloyd, **9:** 91 n.*165*
Watson, T. Malcolm (1854-1929) – dramatist, **9:** 88 n.*159*
Watts, Eliza (b. 1843) – Aunt Lucy's maid, **7:** 293, 294 n.*532*
Watts (of Little Holland House, Kensington, London):
Ellen Alice née Terry (1847-1928), see Terry
George Frederic (1817-1904) – artist, **4:** 36, 127 n.*100*, 301 n.*367*, 332, 334 n.*431*, 335 n.*432*, 336, 337, 359; **5:** 239 n.*387*; **8:** 556
Watts, Isaac (1674-1748) – writer, **1:** 76 n.*72*
Waynton, Miss – friend of the Barclays, **6:** 309 n.*511*
Wayte, Samuel William, Rev. (b. 1820), **5:** 228 n.*364*
Weak Woman (dr. Henry Byron), **6:** 398 n.*651*
Weatherley, Frederick Howard – dramatist, **9:** 162 n.*277*, 198 n.*325*
Weatherly, Frederick Edward – writer, **8:** 579 n.*925*
Webb, Charlotte (b. 1861) – teacher, **8:** 383 n.*629*, 403
Webb, Grace "Gracie" (b. 1890) – friend of the Earles, **9:** 140 n.*242*
Webb, Louey (b. 1869) – entertainer, **8:** 347, 348 n.*572*, 349, 361, 362
Webb, Mr. – secretary to Harry Furniss, **8:** 488 n.*791*
Webbe, Samuel (1740-1816) – composer, **2:** 87 n.*174*
Weber, Carl Maria von (1786-1826) – composer, **3:** 32 n.*47*, 70 n.*110*
Webling (of Paddington, London):
Ethel (b. 1860), **7:** 233 n.*430*, 234, 235
Josephine Emma (b. 1863), **7:** 233 n.*430*, 234
Louisa Betty (b. 1878), **7:** 233 n.*430*
Maria, Mrs. (b. 1831), **7:** 233 n.*430*, 234, 235
Peggy (b. 1871), **7:** 233 n.*430*, 234
Robert James, Mr. (b. 1829) – silversmith and jeweler, **7:** 233 n.*430*, 234
Rosalina (b. 1868), **7:** 233 n.*430*, 234
Ruth Ashford (b. 1866), **7:** 233 n.*430*, 234
Webster (of Crosthwaite, Cumberland):
Alexander Rhind, Rev. (1816-1890?), **1:** 55 n.*18*, 107; **2:** 89, 90 n.*181*, 91, 92; **3:** 9 n.*6*, 114, 116; **4:** 39; **7:** 226 n.*418*, 227
Charlotte Augusta (b. 1847), **2:** 90 n.*181*, 91, 94, 95; **3:** 115, 116 n.*162*, 117 n.*163*; **4:** 39
Harriet, Mrs. (b. 1816), **1:** 55 n.*18*, 72, 107; **3:** 115, 117 n.*163*
Mary Elizabeth (b. 1849), **2:** 90 n.*181*, 91, 94, 95; **3:** 115, 116 n.*162*, 117 n.*163*; **4:** 39
Webster, Benjamin Nottingham (1798-1882) – actor, **4:** 337 n.*436*; **5:** 69 n.*104*, 137 n.*220*
Webster (of Malvern, Worcestershire):
Miss, **4:** 118, 119
Mrs., **4:** 118, 119

Weddell (of Dorking, Surrey):
Ada Mabel (b. 1873), **8:** 416 n.*674*, 418, 421-423, 427, 429; **9:** 90
Alexander, Mr. (1824-1878), **8:** 416 n.*674*
Annie (b. 1863), **8:** 416 n.*674*, 421; **9:** 91
Ethel M. (b. 1870), **8:** 416 n.*674*, 417, 420, 424
Grace Bertha (b. 1868), **8:** 416 n.*674*, 417, 418, 423
Graham Chester "Cheddie" (b. 1877), **8:** 416 n.*674*, 421, 424; **9:** 90
Ida Georgina (1874-1960), **8:** 416 n.*674*, 421-425, 427, 429; **9:** 88 n.*160*
Lilian "Lily" G. (b. 1872), **8:** 416 n.*674*, 417, 421; **9:** 90
Mrs. (née Bokhia), **8:** 416 n.*674*, 417; **9:** 88 n.*160*
Wedding Breakfast (dr. John Orlando Parry), **5:** 157 n.*256*

Weddings:
Alexander, Evelyn Sophia née Dubourg, and Robert Gustavus, **8:** 165 n.*270*
Collingwood, Mary née Dodgson, and Charles, **6:** 82 n.*122*
Dodgson, Alice née Donkin, and Wilfred, **6:** 173 n.*270*
Dodgson, Isabel Mary née Cooper, and Skeffington Hume, **7:** 299 n.*541*
Duke of York and Princess May, **9:** 81 n.*147*
Fuller, Mary "Minnie" Frances née Drury, and Herbert Henry, **8:** 189
Hawke, Winifred née Stevens, and John Anthony, **9:** 158 n.*273*
Pollock, Amy Menella née Dodgson, and Sir Charles Edward, **5:** 123 n.*197*
Prince and Princess of Wales, **4:** 172 n.*168*
Skene, Lorina née Liddell, and William Baillie, **6:** 321 n.*534*
Southwell, Ethel Florence née Barclay, and Edmund Martin, **8:** 193
Wilcox, Fanny née Rooney, and William Edward, **4:** 200 n.*205*

"Weep no more, darling" (Charlotte "Claribel" Barnard) – song, **6:** 26 n.*29*
Weguelin, C. – actor, **4:** 225
Weguelin, John Reinhard (1849-1927) – artist, **7:** 538, 539 n.*871*
Weigall, Albert Bythesea (1840-1912) – teacher in Australia, **4:** 241 n.*269*
Weigall (of Frodingham, Lincolnshire):
Edward Mitford, Rev. (1833-1908), **4:** 241 n.*269*
Helen Sophia, Mrs., **4:** 241 n.*269*
Weigall (of Lambeth, Surrey):
Gilbert, Rev. (1857-1952), **9:** 63 n.*116*
Isabel Fortescue née Seymour (1856-1916), **7:** 80 n.*134*, 85; **8:** 60 n.*95*, 62, 306; **9:** 63 n.*116*
Weir, George R. (1853-1909) – actor, **8:** 423 n.*684*
Weiss (of London):
Georgina née Ansell, Madame (1826-1880) – singer, **3:** 32, 66
Willoughby Hunter (1820-1867) – singer and composer, **2:** 54 n.*106*
Welch, Elizabeth A. (b. 1863) – teacher, **7:** 361 n.*629*, 363
Welch, Mr. – teacher at St. Michael's College,Tenbury, **6:** 168 n.*262*

Welchman (of Blunham, Bedfordshire):
Constance (b. 1865), **6:** 297 n.*491*, 298, 299
Elizabeth, Mrs. (b. 1831), **6:** 297 n.*491*, 298, 299, 334
Maud (b. 1867?), **6:** 297 n.*491*, 298, 299, 334
William H., Mr. (b. 1822), **6:** 297 n.*491*, 334
Welchman (of Berkeley, Gloucestershire):
Emily Mary, Mrs. (b. 1833), **6:** 297 n.*491*, 298, 299
Thomas, Mr. (b. 1827) – timber merchant, **6:** 297 n.*491*
Weld (of London; and Norham Gardens, Oxford):
Agnes Grace (1849-1915), **3:** 87 n.*136*, 89 n.*138*, 93, 108 n.*156*, 140, 144, 148 n.*214*, 153, 172 n.*252*; **4:** 178, 283, 348; **7:** 99 n.*184*; **8:** 178 n.*293*, 272, 275, 332, 380, 594, 626; **9:** 181, 182 n.*302*, 194, 196, 306, 307 n.*486*
Anne née Sellwood (1814-1894), **3:** 87 n.*136*, 89, 93, 133, 140, 153; **4:** 283, 348; **7:** 99 n.*184*; **8:** 272, 275, 626
Charles Richard (1813-1869), **3:** 87 n.*136*, 88, 153; **4:** 348, 349, 353, 355
Welford, George, Dr. (1816-1904) – physician, **6:** 208 n.*326*
Wellington College, Sandhurst, Berkshire, **7:** 393
Wellington House, Bognor, Sussex, **6:** 228, 229
Wellington Square, Hastings, Sussex, **6:** 238, 270
Wellington visiting the plain of Waterloo (pic. Benjamin Haydon), **1:** 67
Wells (of Ryde's Hill, near Guildford, Surrey):
Emily A., Mrs. (b. 1857), **8:** 613 n.*972*
Frances M. (b. 1876), **8:** 613 n.*972*
John G., Capt. (b. 1834) – naval officer, **8:** 613 n.*972*
Wells Gardner, Darton, and Company – publishers, **8:** 452 n.*724*
Welton, James (1854-1942) – teacher and logician, **9:** 137 n.*239*
Wendlebury, Oxfordshire, **4:** 259; **5:** 24, 25 n.*23*, 26, 73
Wep-Ton-No-Mah (dr. Go-Won-Go-Mohawk), **9:** 277 n.*443*
Were (of Moscow, Russia):
Edward Ash, Rev. (1846-1915), **5:** 301 n.*470*, 307, 310, 313
Thomas Kennet (1838?-1916), **5:** 307 n.*475*, 313
Wesleyan School for Girls, Kensington, London, **4:** 325, 326 n.*413*
West, Ann – pupil at St. Aldates, **2:** 32
West (of Charlbury, Oxfordshire):
Charles Frederick Cumber, Rev. (b. 1836), **6:** 213 n.*331*
Eliza H., Mrs. (b. 1847), **6:** 212, 213
West, George – pupil at St. Aldates, **2:** 30
West, Samuel Hatch, Dr. (1848-1920) – physician, **7:** 500 n.*817*
West, William Edward Sackville, Lt. Col. (1830-1905) – army officer, **6:** 215 n.*334*
Westbourne Terrace, London, **5:** 34; **6:** 198
Westcott, Brooke Foss, Dr. (1825-1901) – professor of theology, **6:** 305 n.*506*
West Dean, Sussex, **7:** 470

Westham, Sussex, **9:** 216, 217
"Westhill, Edgar U. C." (pseudonym), **2:** 39
West Indies, **4:** 32
Westmacott (of Chelsham Road, Clapham, Surrey):
Alice Constance (b. 1859), **4:** 179, 285, 330 n.*422*; **6:** 251 n.*398*
Amy (b. 1856), **4:** 330 n.*422*; **6:** 251 n.*398*
Antoinette, **4:** 178, 285, 330 n.*422*; **6:** 14, 251 n.*398*
Emily Beatrice, **4:** 330 n.*422*; **6:** 14, 251 n.*398*
Florence, **6:** 14 n.*8*, 251 n.*398*
James Sherwood (1823-1900) – sculptor **4:** 36, 274 n.*320*, 283-285, 315, 330 n.*422*, 331 n.*425*; **6:** 14 n.*8*, 68, 86, 251
Sarah née Leslie (b. 1821), **4:** 283, 285, 315; **6:** 14, 86, 251
Violet O. (b. 1866), **6:** 251 n.*398*
Westminster, London, **4:** 226, 249, 253, 282
Westminster Abbey, **6:** 354; **7:** 24, 112, 236
Westminster Aquarium, **7:** 45
Westminster Deanery, **4:** 315, 333
Westminster Hospital, **6:** 467
Westminster Play, **3:** 140 n.*207*, 146
Westminster School, **1:** 101 n.*111*; **3:** 22 n.*27*, 29 n.*41*; **7:** 268, 319
Westmorland, **1:** 11
Westmorland, Lord, see Fane
Weston, Capt. – friend of the Pares, **6:** 171 n.*267*
Weston-super-mare, Somerset, **2:** 106
Westwood (of Walton Manor, Woodstock Road, Oxford):
Eliza née Richardson (1805-1882), **7:** 147 n.*277*
John Obadiah, Prof. (1805-1893) – scientist, **5:** 141 n.*225*; **7:** 147 n.*277*
Wethered, Edmund Peel, Rev. (b. 1863), **7:** 379 n.*654*, 380, 382, 384, 424
Wethered (of Hurley, Berkshire):
Esther Ellen Haworth née Peel (b. 1818), **5:** 58 n.*84*
Florence James, Rev. (1807-1867), **5:** 58 n.*83*, 58 n.*84*
Florence Thomas (b. 1840), **5:** 58 n.*84*
Wethered (of Measdie, Marlow, Buckinghamshire):
Evelyn A. (b. 1874), **8:** 202 n.*345*
Francis Owen (1864-1922), **8:** 202 n.*345*
Owen Peel, Lt. Col. (1837-1908) – army officer, **3:** 70 n.*109*
Wethered, Mrs. – cousin of Mrs. Ellison, **4:** 209 n.*218*
Wethered (of Seymour Court, Marlow, Buckinghamshire):
Owen Peel (1837-1908), see above
Thomas Owen (1832-1921), **3:** 70 n.*109*
Wetherell, Elizabeth, see Warner
Weybridge, Surrey, **6:** 227; **8:** 499
Weyden, Roger van der (1399-1464) – artist, **5:** 267 n.*434*
Whatford (of Seaside Road, Eastbourne, Sussex):
George L. (b. 1879), **7:** 359 n.*627*

Jack Henry, Dr. (b. 1855) – dentist, **7:** 358, 359 n.*627*, 454, 455, 460, 471; **8:** 41 n.*58*, 192, 345, 402, 476
Muriel (b. 1881), **7:** 359 n.*627*
Rose E., Mrs. (b. 1856), **7:** 359 n.*627*, 460, 471
Stuart L. (b. 1880), **7:** 359 n.*627*
What Will They Say in Brompton? (dr. Joseph Coyne), **3:** 133 n.*193*
Wheathampstead, Hertfordshire, **6:** 443
Wheeler, Thomas Littleton, Rev. (1834-1910), **4:** 121 n.*92*
Whelpton (of Spencer Road, Eastbourne, Sussex):
Catherine (b. 1865), **7:** 60 n.*96*
Catherine Anne née Urling (b. 1831), **7:** 60 n.*96*, 61
Eva H. (b. 1873), **7:** 60 n.*96*
Gertrude (b. 1867), **7:** 60 n.*96*
Henry (b. 1861), **7:** 60 n.*96*
Henry Robert, Rev. (1833-1902), **7:** 60 n.*96*, 61, 64, 67, 70 n.*113*, 462
Mary (b. 1870), **7:** 60 n.*96*
Maud E. (b. 1863), **7:** 60 n.*96*
Whicker (of Vassall Road, Lambeth, Surrey):
Ernest (b. 1859), **7:** 59 n.*94*
George (b. 1866), **7:** 59 n.*94*, 61
Harold (b. 1860), **7:** 59 n.*94*
Rose, Mrs. (b. 1828), **7:** 59 n.*94*, 61, 91, 129, 210
Rose "Rosie" (b. 1869), **7:** 59 n.*94*, 61, 74, 91, 129
William H., Mr. (b. 1829) – post office clerk, **7:** 59 n.*94*, 61, 91, 129, 210
While There's Life There's Hope (dr. Anon), **4:** 221 n.*242*
Whinlatter, Cumberland, **2:** 94
Whinyates, Edward Henry, Rev. (1836-1905), **6:** 87, 88 n.*131*, 89, 116
Whish (of Norfolk Square, Paddington, London):
Evelyn (b. 1872), **7:** 235 n.*434*
Frederika A., Mrs. (b. 1847), **7:** 235 n.*434*
George Clinton, Mr. (b. 1835) – government clerk, **7:** 235 n.*434*
Whitaker, Edward Wright, Rev. (1840-1881), **5:** 38 n.*47*, 43, 104 n.*162*; **6:** 438
Whitbourne, Worcestershire, **7:** 267
Whitburn, Durham, **1:** 67, 124 n.*154*, 125, 127, 129, 130, 132; **2:** 49 n.*98*, 86, 88, 89, 100, 101 n.*195*; **3:** 111 n.*159*, 164 n.*237*; **4:** 23, 24, 155, 157; **5:** 12, 15, 38, 174, 177, 377, 378 n.*560*; **6:** 41-43, 51, 106, 175, 208, 348, 462, 495
Whitburniana, **2:** 49 n.*98*
Whitby, Yorkshire, **1:** 48, 54 n.*13*, 59 n.*28*, 64 n.*41*, 95 n.*98*, 100; **2:** 15 n.*25*, 46, 47, 85, 88, 101-105; **3:** 51, 77, 81, 86, 93 n.*144*, 94; **4:** 36, 37, 66 n.*3*, 121, 233, 234, 241; **5:** 107, 108 n.*167*, 177, 269; **6:** 51, 110, 171, 175, 176; **7:** 65, 498; **8:** 30, 353
Whitby Gazette, The, **1:** 48, 54 n.*13*, 110 n.*128*, 116
Whitchurch, Oxfordshire, **7:** 427; **9:** 73

White, Arnold (b. 1849) – enthusiast in emigration, **8:** 327 n.*540*
White, Edward (b. 1820) – independent minister and writer, **8:** 455 n.*730*
White:
Florence "Florrie" Ada (b. 1880), alias Marjorie Chetwynd – actress, **9:** 164 n.*281*, 165-168, 170, 178
Mr. – actor, **9:** 165, 167, 168, 170
White, Henry (1812-1880) – historian and writer, **1:** 114 n.*137*
White, Jenny – actress, **4:** 221
White, Maria – niece of the porter at Lambeth Palace, **4:** 331 n.*424*
White, Miss – friend of the Bickersteths, **5:** 105 n.*163*
White, Mrs. née Bull, **4:** 67 n.*6*, 296 n.*356*
White, Mrs. née Lewis, **6:** 221; **7:** 186
Whitebait at Greenwich (dr. John Morton), **6:** 188 n.*292*
White Doe of Rylstone (bk. William Wordsworth), **3:** 155 n.*228*
Whiteford, Charles (b. 1808) – cashier, **6:** 122 n.*187*
Whitehall, London, **1:** 102
Whitehall Place, London, **4:** 271, 279; **5:** 59, 70, 222, 235; **6:** 112, 195
Whitehaven, Cumberland, **1:** 11
Whitehead, Henry (1863-1947) – lecturer, **7:** 491 n.*800*
White Lie, A (dr. Sydney Grundy), **9:** 54 n.*92*
Whitely Exerciser, **9:** 317 n.*507*, 321, 324
White, John Tahourdin (1809-1893) – writer on classical languages and grammar, **1:** 73 n.*66*
Whiteside (of India):
Daisy (b. 1860?), **6:** 402 n.*659*, 404 n.*664*, 405 n.*665*, 407
Maria C. E., Mrs. (b. 1838), **6:** 402 n.*659*, 404
William S., Mr. – merchant and farmer, **6:** 402 n.*659*
White Swans, The (bk. Hans Christian Andersen), **8:** 253 n.*425*
Whiting (of London):
Mr. – photographer, **4:** 249 n.*284*
Mrs., **4:** 249
Whiting, Mr. (brother of above), **5:** 136, 137 n.*219*
Whittington, Eliza (b. 1846) – friend of Elizabeth Dodgson, **8:** 240 n.*402*
Whittington and his Cat (dr. Anon), **5:** 41; **7:** 399, 400 n.*678*
Whittington and his Cat (dr. Abraham Henry), **7:** 504 n.*823*
Whitworth, Miss – nurse, **9:** 177 n.*297*, 214
Wicked World, The (dr. William S. Gilbert), **6:** 253 n.*401*
Wickham (of Twyford, Hampshire):
Charles Townshend (b. 1863), **7:** 271 n.*488*
Latham, Mr. (b. 1834) – headmaster, **1:** 87, 88 n.*91*, 91; **7:** 271 n.*488*
Wickham (of Twyford, Hampshire):
George Herbert (b. 1835), **1:** 87, 88 n.*91*
Latham (b. 1834), see above
Wide, Wide World, The (bk. Elizabeth Wetherell), **1:** 99 n.*108*
Wigan, Horace (1818-1885) – actor and dramatist, **2:** 82 n.*162*; **5:** 63 n.*93*,

85
Wig and Gown (dr. James Albery), **6:** 335 n.*555*
Wigmore Street, London, **2:** 126
Wilberforce (of York):
Edward (1834-1914), **3:** 53 n.*80*
Robert Isaac, Rev. (1803-1857) – archdeacon of York, **3:** 53 n.*80*
Wilberforce, Samuel, Dr. (1805-1873) – bishop of Oxford, **2:** 73 n.*147*; **3:** 37 n.*58*; **4:** 21, 34, 55, 57; **6:** 119 n.*182*, 120, 220, 284 n.*467*, 292 n.*482*
Wilbury House, Salisbury, **8:** 563

Wilcox:

Wilcox (of New Brighton, Cheshire):
Adelaide "Ada" Elizabeth Jane née Hart (d. 1880) – first wife, **7:** 78 n.*127*, 279, 280 n.*510*, 282
Ernest Shepley, Mr. (1854-1926), civil engineer – cousin, **1:** 124 n.*154*; **2:** 86 n.*172*; **4:** 188 n.*184*; **5:** 207; **6:** 333, 351, 352, 495; **7:** 78 n.*127*, 282
Frances Ada née Kipling (1851-1924) – second wife, **6:** 207 n.*323*; **7:** 124
Wilcox (of Leith, Scotland):
Anna "Annie" (b. 1831) – cousin, see Murdoch
Edward (1835-1872) – cousin, **1:** 124 n.*154*, 129, 133
Elizabeth "Bessie" Jane (b. 1828) – cousin, see Ferguson
George (1832-1869) – cousin, **6:** 103 n.*162*
George Hume, Mr. (1796-1853), HM customs officer – uncle, **1:** 122 n.*152*, 124 n.*154*, 133 n.*166*
Jane M. née Bentley (1810-1889) – aunt, **1:** 124 n.*154*; **7:** 448 n.*741*
Mary (b. 1834) – cousin, see Knight
Menella (1829-1886) – cousin, see Quin
Myers (1839-1874) – cousin, **1:** 133 n.*166*
Wilcox (of Ryton-on-Tyne, Durham):
Anne "Annie" née Patrick (b. 1846) – wife of cousin, **6:** 207 n.*323*, 495
Ethel Mary (b. 1870) – second cousin, **6:** 207 n.*323*
Herbert "Bertie" Metcalfe (b. 1868) – second cousin, **6:** 207 n.*323*; **8:** 612 n.*970*
Herbert Francis, Mr. (b. 1844), ship broker – cousin, **1:** 124 n.*154*; **4:** 86 n.*40*; **5:** 174 n.*289*, 377; **6:** 207 n.*323*, 333, 495; **7:** 171, 172 n.*320*, 173, 174, 178 n.*331*; **8:** 612 n.*970*
Wilcox (of Stokesley, Yorkshire):
Anne née Loy (1848-1902) – wife of cousin, **6:** 208 n.*327*
Frederick Hume, Mr. (1837-1880), solicitor – cousin, **1:** 124 n.*154*, 129; **4:** 86 n.*40*; **5:** 174 n.*289*, 377; **6:** 208 n.*327*, 333, 385; **7:** 40 n.*59*, 178 n.*330*, 279, 280 n.*510*, 290
Wilcox (of Whitburn, Durham):
Arthur Marwood (1840-1901) – cousin, see below

Charles "Charley or Charlie" Hassard (1852-1874) – cousin, **1:** 124 n.*154*; **2:** 86 n.*172*; **6:** 11 n.*1*, 208 n.*327*, 333, 344, 347, 350, 354, 358, 361, 362, 368 n.*603*
Clara Menella (1855-1896) – cousin, see Hitchcock
Elizabeth Georgina "Georgie" (1848-1934) – cousin, see Egerton Allen
Ernest Shepley (1854-1926) – cousin, see above
Frederick Hume (1837-1880) – cousin, see above
Henry "Harry" George (1839-1907) – cousin, see below
Herbert Francis (b. 1844) – cousin, see above
Isobella Lucy (1850-1936) – cousin, **1:** 124 n.*154*; **2:** 88 n.*178*; **5:** 174 n.*289*; **6:** 208 n.*327*, 344, 348; **7:** 84 n.*143*, 85, 134, 314, 437 n.*725*, 438; **8:** 257 n.*434*, 353, 458; **9:** 57 n.*103*
Katherine "Katie" Anna (1842-1868) – cousin, **1:** 124 n.*154*, 129; **2:** 88 n.*178*; **5:** 378 n.*560*; **6:** 30 n.*36*
Leonard James (1846-1876) – cousin, **1:** 124 n.*154*, 130; **5:** 174 n.*289*; **6:** 333, 353 n.*584*, 354, 443, 462
Margaret (1836-1887) – cousin, **1:** 124 n.*154*, 129; **4:** 98, 156; **5:** 41, 207; **6:** 160 n.*247*, 208 n.*327*, 348, 357, 361, 443, 477, 494; **7:** 40 n.*58*, 51, 124, 146, 279; **8:** 30 n.*36*, 32, 51, 54-57, 160, 329, 330 n.*542*, 353, 357
Mary Anne neé Marwood (1813-1870) – aunt, **1:** 10, 122 n.*152*, 124 n.*154*, 130, 133 n.*166*; **4:** 23; **5:** 179 n.*296*
Mary Dorothea "Dora" (1859-1935) – cousin, **1:** 124 n.*154*; **4:** 23, 155, 156 n.*143*; **5:** 12 n.*3*, 179 n.*296*; **6:** 208 n.*327*; **7:** 170 n.*318*, 182, 328, 346, 348; **8:** 30 n.*36*, 51-57, 353, 371, 455, 458; **9:** 73 n.*135*, 75, 203
William, Mr. (1801-1872), HM customs officer – uncle, **1:** 10, 122 n.*152*, 124 n.*154*, 130; **4:** 23; **5:** 174 n.*289*; **6:** 208 n.*327*, 216
William Edward (1835-1876) – cousin, see below
Wilcox (of Spelsbury, Oxfordshire):
Arthur Marwood, Rev. (1840-1901) – cousin, **1:** 124 n.*154*; **2:** 100; **4:** 156, 157, 176, 177, 182, 278; **5:** 95 n.*148*, 112, 113, 164, 207, 229 n.*366*; **6:** 208 n.*327*, 269, 291 n.*480*, 333, 383 n.*629*; **7:** 12 n.*4*, 51-53, 56, 61, 63, 109, 126, 227, 284, 289-291, 306, 354, 356, 357; **8:** 16 n.*10*, 22, 24, 124, 196, 203, 213, 218, 244, 253, 260, 261, 305, 329, 370, 404, 501, 545, 549, 551, 559, 564, 576, 581, 597; **9:** 12 n.*3*, 13, 69, 72, 196, 301
Mary "May" Anne née Allen (1848-1904) – wife of cousin, **6:** 208 n.*327*, 269, 466; **7:** 12 n.*4*, 51-53, 56, 61, 63, 109 n.*202*, 126, 227, 284, 289-291, 354, 356, 357, 359; **8:** 16 n.*10*, 22, 24, 102, 196, 214, 218, 244, 253, 260, 305, 329, 501, 514, 545, 551, 559, 564, 565, 576, 581, 597; **9:** 12 n.*3*, 13, 69, 72, 73, 202, 301
Wilcox (of Stoke, near Guildford, Surrey):
Edward George (1874-1905), **7:** 360
Elizabeth "Lizzie" née Pittar (b. 1848) – wife of cousin, **6:** 92 n.*143*, 160 n.*247*, 207, 208, 465; **7:** 11 n.*2*, 51, 91, 120, 178 n.*331*, 294, 328, 360, 393, 414, 419, 492

Henry "Harry" George, Capt. (1839-1907) – cousin, **1:** 124 n.*154*; **4:** 24, 324; **5:** 164 n.*270*, 377; **6:** 160 n.*247*, 333, 344, 408, 411, 465; **7:** 91, 120, 294, 360, 414, 415 n.*692*, 419, 492, 527; **8:** 141 n.*229*

Henry "Harry" Robert (1873-1949), **7:** 360

Hugh Hassard (1880-1925), **7:** 360

Louis Pittar (1876-1908), **7:** 360

Wilcox, Elizabeth "Bessie" (1794-1874) – distant cousin, **4:** 188 n.*183*; **6:** 83 n.*123*, 157, 198, 209, 219, 294, 333 n.*551*, 334

Wilcox, Elizabeth Deacon née Hume (1773-1847) – great-aunt, **1:** 10

Wilcox (of Scarborough, Yorkshire):

Frances "Fanny" Rodd née Rooney (1832-1919) – wife of cousin, **4:** 155 n.*142*, 200 n.*205*, 305; **5:** 12, 25, 38, 104, 109, 174 n.*289*, 378 n.*560*; **6:** 294, 457, 465, 467, 469, 470; **7:** 360, 489 n.*797*, 512, 513, 519; **8:** 30 n.*36*, 200, 290, 327, 371, 565, 566; **9:** 150, 298

Frances Menella "Nella" (1869-1932) – second cousin, **6:** 294, 456 n.*751*, 457, 465, 467, 469, 495; **7:** 360; **8:** 30 n.*36*, 32, 200, 290, 327; **9:** 150, 298

Theodore Robert (1868-1932) – second cousin, **5:** 378 n.*560*; **6:** 456 n.*751*, 495; **7:** 360; **8:** 30 n.*36*, 473, 474

William Edward, Mr. (1835-1876), HM customs officer – cousin, **1:** 124 n.*154*, 129, 133; **2:** 49 n.*98*, 85, 88 n.*178*, 89; **3:** 68 n.*105*; **4:** 15, 154, 155, 156, 200 n.*205*, 305; **5:** 12, 25, 38, 104, 150 n.*242*, 174 n.*289*, 175, 176, 377, 378 n.*560*; **6:** 11 n.*1*, 179 n.*278*, 181, 294, 333, 456, 457, 465, 467, 469, 470, 494 n.*817*

William Melville (1866-1958) – second cousin, **5:** 150 n.*242*; **6:** 11 n.*1*, 456, 495; **7:** 360; **8:** 30 n.*36*, 342 n.*563*, 353; **9:** 51 n.*88*

Wilkes, James, Mr. (b. 1812) – surgeon, **6:** 278, 346, 347; **7:** 256 n.*466*, 438; **8:** 48 n.*71*, 131, 408, 431

Wilkie, Miss – school mistress, **9:** 174 n.*291*

Wilkinson (of Gloucester Terrace, London):

Ellen "Nellie" G. (b. 1864), **6:** 351 n.*582*, 353

Ethel M. (b. 1863), **6:** 351 n.*582*, 353

Kathleen M. A. (b. 1871), **6:** 351 n.*582*, 353

Maria C., Mrs. (b. 1834), **6:** 351 n.*582*, 353

Maria "May" G. (b. 1867), **6:** 351 n.*582*, 353

Montague C., Mr. (b. 1829) – merchant, **6:** 351 n.*582*, 353

Montague G. (b. 1857), **6:** 351 n.*582*, 353

Wilkinson (of Beckenham, Kent):

Emma, Mrs. (b. 1846), **6:** 255 n.*405*

Richard H. W., Mr. (b. 1836), **6:** 254, 255 n.*405*

Wilkinson (of Glinton, Northamptonshire):

Florence Mary (1869-1953), **8:** 506 n.*815*, 515, 516

William Farley, Rev. (1838-1913), **8:** 506 n.*815*, 515, 516

Wilkinson, George Howard, Rev. (1833-1907), **6:** 198 n.*308*, 251, 257, 415;

8: 568 n.*905*
Wilkinson, James (b. 1846) – scout at Christ Church, **8:** 323 n.*534*, 326
Willard, E. S. (1853-1915) – actor and manager, **7:** 540 n.*873*; **8:** 168 n.*280*, 208, 486, 527; **9:** 215 n.*343*, 225, 226 n.*357*, 230
Willats, William Hale (b. 1837) – undergraduate at Christ Church, **1:** 87, 88 n.*91*, 89
Willatson, Ella – niece of Mrs. Rogers, **5:** 80 n.*125*
Willets, Miss – step-daughter of Prof. Legge, **7:** 162 n.*305*, 167
"Will he come?" (Adelaide Proctor and Arthur Sullivan) – song, **5:** 225, 226 n.*359*
Williams, A. May – logic pupil, **9:** 130 n.*227*, 265
Williams, Anna (1853-1924) – professor of singing, **8:** 444 n.*712*
Williams, Arthur (1845-1915) – actor, **8:** 524
Williams (of London; and the United States of America):
Barney (1823-1876) alias Bernard Flaherty – American actor, **3:** 80 n.*126*
Maria née Pray (b. 1828) – actress, **3:** 80 n.*126*
Williams, Isaac (1802-1865) – poet, **1:** 52 n.*9*, 98 n.*105*
Williams, Montague (1834-1892) – dramatist, **4:** 279 n.*328*; **5:** 93 n.*143*
Williams, Mr. – traveller, **6:** 247 n.*392*
Williams, Mr. – undergraduate at Merton, **8:** 552 n.*878*
Williams, Philip Seymour (b. 1843) – undergraduate at Christ Church, **4:** 197 n.*199*
Williams, Robert (1843-1886) – Aubrey Taylor's tutor, **4:** 348 n.*455*
Williams, see Monier-Williams
Williams, Thomas J. (1824-1874) – dramatist, **4:** 152 n.*137*, 273 n.*318*
Williamson (of Whitburn, Durham):
Ann Elizabeth née Liddell, Lady (1802-1878), **2:** 100 n.*193*; **4:** 42
Hedworth, Sir (1797-1861), **2:** 100 n.*193*; **3:** 164 n.*237*
Victor Alexander (1838-1924), **3:** 164 n.*237*
Williamson (of Stoke Newington, Middlesex):
Janie, **7:** 65 n.*104*, 75
Lottie, **7:** 65 n.*104*, 75
Mrs., **7:** 66
Nellie, **7:** 65 n.*104*, 75
Williamson (of Hurworth, Durham):
Mary (1828-1872), **5:** 172 n.*287*
Robert Hopper, Rev. (1813-1891), **5:** 151 n.*244*, 172 n.*287*
Willingdon, Sussex, **7:** 284
Willis' Rooms, London, **6:** 67
Williton, Somerset, **9:** 63
Willmore, Jenny (d. 1894) – actress, **4:** 315, 316 n.*396*
Wills, Freeman, Rev. (1842-1913) – dramatist, **9:** 162 n.*277*
Wills, William Gorman (1830-1891) – dramatist, **7:** 106 n.*197*, 114 n.*211*, 185 n.*347*; **8:** 81 n.*125*, 586 n.*936*; **9:** 78 n.*144*
Willshire:

Alice Mary, **4:** 292 n.*349*
Annette Laetitia née Maxwell (d. 1901), **4:** 292 n.*349*
Arthur Reginald Thomas (1850-1919), **4:** 292 n.*349*
Edith Annette, **4:** 292 n.*349*
Ernest Maxwell (1856-1900), **4:** 292 n.*349*
Mary Caroline (d. 1868), **4:** 292 n.*349*
Thomas (1789-1862), 1st Bart., **4:** 292 n.*349*
"Will you walk into my parlour?" (Mary Howitt) – poem, **2:** 17 n.*30*
Wilmington, Sussex, **7:** 458, 460
Wilmot, Robert Edward Eardley, Hon. (1830-1861), **4:** 32, 33
Wilna (Russia, now Lithuania), **5:** 349
Wilson (Felpham House, Sussex):
Alice Emily (b. 1861), **6:** 234 n.*369*
Amy L. (b. 1864), **6:** 234 n.*369*
Charles H. (b. 1855), **6:** 234 n.*369*
James, Mr. (b. 1824) – civil engineer, **6:** 234 n.*369*
Ralph F. (b. 1858), **6:** 234 n.*369*
Wilson:
Bertram – pupil at Richmond School, **1:** 21
Dick – pupil at Richmond School, **1:** 21
Harry – pupil at Richmond School, **1:** 21
Wilson, Blanche M. (b. 1862) – amateur actress, **7:** 511 n.*828*
Wilson, Edward "Teddy" (b. 1857) – nephew of William Holman Hunt, **4:** 245 n.*276*, 246
Wilson (of Ripon, Yorkshire):
Elizabeth, Mrs., **3:** 7 n.*2*
Thomas, Mr. (b. 1819) – Ripon Cathedral sexton, **3:** 7 n.*2*
Wilson, Eliza Jane Collingwood née Ribey (b. 1833), **8:** 404 n.*657*; **9:** 227 n.*361*
Wilson, Ida – subject of Munro sculpture, **4:** 21
Wilson (of Oxford):
James Humphrey Wilson, Dr. (b. 1856), **9:** 266 n.*421*, 270, 300
Katherine Campbell née MacMillan, **9:** 266 n.*421*, 270, 271, 278, 284, 300
Kathleen (b. 1891?), **9:** 266 n.*421*, 270
Wilson, James Maurice, Rev. (1836-1931) – mathematician, **6:** 134 n.*205*; **7:** 65 n.*103*, 72, 73, 83
Wilson, John Cook (1849-1915) – professor of logic, **8:** 169 n.*282*, 192, 306, 559; **9:** 51 n.*87*, 52, 124 n.*218*, 137 n.*239*, 295 n.*468*
Wilson, Kitty – friend of Isa Bowman, **8:** 526 n.*843*
Wilson, Margaret "Daisy" (b. 1877), **8:** 147 n.*237*
Wilson, Mary Agnes (1875-1927) – logic pupil, **9:** 143 n.*248*, 144, 150, 178, 183, 197, 204, 243, 251
Wilson, Miss – actress, **7:** 24 n.*26*
Wilson, Miss – studying at St. Hugh's Hall, Oxford, **9:** 251

Wilson, Mr. – civil service trainer, **6:** 41 n.*56*, 49, 58
Wilson, Robert James (1840-1897) – warden of Keble, **9:** 46 n.*81*, 47
Wilson Fox (of Hatfield, Hertfordshire):
Alice Theodora née Raikes (1862-1943) – distant cousin, **1:** 12; **6:** 159 n.*246*, 196, 251, 253, 269; **7:** 278 n.*507*, 328; **8:** 110 n.*180*, 114; **9:** 60 n.*111*
Dorothy Amabel (b. 1891), **9:** 60 n.*111*
William Arthur, Mr. (1861-1909) – barrister, **9:** 60 n.*111*
Wilson Todd (of Halnaby Hall, Darlington, Durham):
Aileen Frances Mary (1859?-1937), **4:** 178; **5:** 104 n.*161*
Elizabeth "Lizzie" Jane (1856-1931), **4:** 180; **5:** 104 n.*161*
Evelyn Frideswide (b. 1860), **4:** 179; **5:** 104 n.*161*
Jane Marian Rutherford née Todd (1832-1909), **5:** 103, 104 n.*161*
Margaret Annie (d. 1924), **5:** 104 n.*161*
William Henry, Capt. (1828-1910) – magistrate, **5:** 104 n.*161*
William Pierrepont (1857-1925), **5:** 104 n.*161*
Wilton, Marie, see Bancroft
Wimbledon, Surrey, **4:** 121, 342; **6:** 233, 328; **7:** 77; **8:** 617; **9:** 60
Wimpole Street, London, **2:** 20 n.*35*
Winchelsea, Sussex, **9:** 163, 333
Winchester, Hampshire, **3:** 174; **6:** 360, 411, 413, 415, 416, 438, 439, 478
Windermere, Westmorland, **2:** 96
Windlesham, Surrey, **6:** 192 n.*298*, 269, 353
Windsor, Berkshire, **4:** 184, 291, 315, 320; **5:** 82, 99; **6:** 123
Windsor Castle, **3:** 14 n.*13*; **4:** 57; **5:** 31
Windsor Castle (dr. Francis Burnand and Montague Williams), **5:** 92, 93 n.*143*
Windsor Coffee House, Euston, **4:** 226
Windsor Lodge, **4:** 324
Windsor Park, **4:** 291; **5:** 83 n.*130*
Wingfield, Charles Lee, Rev. (1833-1897), **6:** 67 n.*99*
Wingfield, Edward, Sir (1834-1910) – civil servant, **8:** 45 n.*67*
Wingham House, Reading, **7:** 166
Winkfield, Alfred, Mr. (b. 1838) – surgeon, **8:** 501 n.*805*
Winkfield, Berkshire, **4:** 291
Winter, Robert Reynolds (b. 1837) – pupil of Mr. Tristram, **3:** 49 n.*75*
Winter, William (1836-1917) – poet, **7:** 385 n.*665*
Winteringham, Lincolnshire, **4:** 234, 236, 240; **9:** 312 n.*496*
Winteringham, Mr. – proprietor of Croft Spa Hotel, **6:** 346 n.*575*
Winter Palace, St. Petersburg, Russia, **5:** 294, 295
Winterton (of Nottingham):
Emily "Emmie" (b. 1863), **6:** 412 n.*674*, 416-418, 420
Ernest, **6:** 418
Florence "Florrie" (b. 1864), **6:** 412 n.*674*, 416, 417, 420
Mary, Mrs. (b. 1840), **6:** 416, 420

Wise, Henry Edward (b. 1856) – undergraduate at Magdalen College, **7:** 244 n.*447*, 251 n.*457*
Wise (of Ripon, Yorkshire):
Lucy Ann (b. 1850), **9:** 227 n.*359*
Mary L. C. (b. 1856), **9:** 227 n.*359*
Samuel, Mr. (1812-1885) – solicitor, **9:** 227 n.*359*
Wither, Reginald Fitzhugh Bigg, Rev. (b. 1842), **6:** 295 n.*486*; **7:** 117 n.*219*
Witherby, Henry Forbes (1836-1907) – artist, **2:** 103 n.*198*, 104; **3:** 51 n.*77*, 77 n.*120*
Witherby, Robert Hale (1826-1914) – teacher, **3:** 95 n.*145*, 97
Witherby Typewriter Suppliers, **8:** 398
Without Love (dr. Augustus Dubourg & Edmund Yates), **6:** 255 n.*407*, 258
Witley, Surrey, **6:** 170, 227
Wittenham, Berkshire, **4:** 195
Wives as they were, and Maids as they are (dr. Elizabeth Inchbald), **2:** 123 n.*239*
Wix (of Great Dunmow, Essex):
Edwin W., Mr. (b. 1854) – solicitor, **7:** 301
Frances E., Mrs. (b. 1855), **7:** 301 n.*544*
Wodehouse (of Marylebone, London):
Henry J., Mr. (b. 1822) – barrister, **7:** 111 n.*205*
Rosanna née Lloyd (b. 1823), **7:** 110, 111 n.*205*
Woking, Surrey, **6:** 353, 472; **8:** 501
Woking Cemetery, **8:** 296
Wokingham, Berkshire, **6:** 89
Wolff, Henry Drummond Charles, Sir (1830-1908) – politician, **8:** 465 n.*750*
Wolmer, Viscount, see Palmer
Wolseley, Garnet Joseph, Sir (1833-1913), 1st Viscount – army officer, **6:** 340 n.*565*
Wolsey, Thomas (1471-1530) – cardinal, **6:** 364
Wolstenholme, Joseph (1829-1891) – mathematician, **7:** 487, 488 n.*793*
Wolston (of Croydon, Surrey):
Adela Maud (b. 1874), **8:** 36 n.*47*, 41, 42
Adela Sidney née Cayley (1850-1931) – second wife, **8:** 36 n.*47*, 42, 132
Alicia R. (b. 1862), **8:** 36 n.*47*
Christopher, Dr. (1834-1923) – physician, **8:** 36 n.*47*, 37, 39, 40, 42, 132
Evelyn (b. 1877), **8:** 36 n.*47*, 41, 42
Woman of the World, A (dr. Joseph Coyne), **6:** 27 n.*30*
Woman's Revenge, A (dr. Henry Pettitt), **9:** 213 n.*341*
Woman's Secret, A (dr. Anon), **5:** 313
Women's Branch of Oxford House in London, **9:** 349 n.*559*
"Wonder-Fountain," Dresden, Germany, **5:** 356
"Wonderful Ghost Story, A," in *All the Year Round* (Thomas Heaphy), **5:** 229 n.*366*

Wonderful Woman, A (dr. Charles Dance), **4:** 205 n.*214*; **5:** 42 n.*52*
"Wonderland" (Mary Manners) – poem, **8:** 252 n.*424*
Wonderland Quadrille, The (C. H. R. Marriott) – music, **6:** 189 n.*294*
Wood (of Hollin Hall, Ripon, Yorkshire):
Albert Charles (1841-1890), **2:** 13 n.*18*, 58 n.*117*
Charlotte Augusta, Mrs. (1821?-1861), **1:** 95, 96, 100; **2:** 13 n.*18*
Eliza Rose, see Fawcett
Frederick Henry, Mr. (1811-1886) – magistrate, **1:** 95, 96, 100; **2:** 13 n.*18*, 14 n.*23*, 15 n.*24*; **3:** 152 n.*221*
Henry Richard Hugh (1847-1883), **2:** 13 n.*18*
Wood (of Aukborough, Lincolnshire):
Amy M. (b. 1860), **4:** 240 n.*268*
Caroline N. (b. 1867), **4:** 240 n.*268*
Constance E. (b. 1862), **4:** 240 n.*268*
Ethel M. R. (b. 1872), **4:** 240 n.*268*
Harvey A. (b. 1870), **4:** 240 n.*268*
Henry, Rev. (1830-1912), **4:** 240 n.*268*
Isabella M., Mrs., **4:** 240 n.*268*
Wood, Arthur Augustus (1824-1907) – dramatist, **5:** 139 n.*22*
Wood (of West Grange, Ripon, Yorkshire):
Arthur John Harrison (b. 1847), **2:** 57 n.*113*
Caroline Martha née Harrison, **2:** 57 n.*113*
Thomas, Mr. (1821?-1896), **2:** 57 n.*1133*
Wood (of Erith, Kent):
Charles F. (b. 1868), **7:** 301 n.*546*
Charlotte Ernestina née Goschen (b. 1840), **7:** 301 n.*546*, 302, 303
Charlotte H. (b. 1877), **7:** 301 n.*546*
Dora E. W. (b. 1864), **7:** 301 n.*546*, 302, 303
Edith F. (b. 1865), **7:** 301 n.*546*
Fanny E. (b. 1870), **7:** 301 n.*546*, 302, 303, 305
Marion (b. 1875), **7:** 301 n.*546*
Percival W. (b. 1873), **7:** 301 n.*546*
Robert, Rev. (1837-1912), **7:** 301 n.*546*, 302, 303
Wood (of Litton's Hall, Oxford):
Charles James, Mr. (1832-1887), **4:** 260 n.*304*
Mrs., **4:** 260
Wood (of Skelton, Yorkshire):
Charlotte, Mrs., **2:** 14, 15 n.*24*; **3:** 150 n.*217*
Edward, Rev. (1796-1875), **2:** 14, 15 n.*24*; **3:** 150 n.*217*
Edward Malcolm (b. 1839), **3:** 150 n.*217*
Theresa "Lisa" Henrietta (b. 1844), see Currie
Wood (of Eastbourne, Sussex):
Constance "Connie" Esther (b. 1883), **9:** 178 n.*299*
George, Mr. (b. 1832) – railway porter, **9:** 178 n.*299*
Lillian "Lily" Maud (b. 1884), **9:** 178 n.*299*

Wood (of Ripon, Yorkshire):
Emma Juliana (1798-1885), **2:** 14 n.*23*, 16
Louisa Frances (1784-1868), **2:** 14 n.*23*, 16
Wood (of London):
Florence – actress, **8:** 419 n.*679*, 425
John, Mr. (d. 1863) – actor, **8:** 199 n.*339*
Mrs. (1832-1915) – actress, **6:** 314 n.*520*; **8:** 199 n.*339*, 419
Wood, George (b. 1850) – bursar of Pembroke, **9:** 233, 234 n.*369*
Wood (of Eastbourne, Sussex):
John J., Mr. (b. 1835), **7:** 301 n.*546*
Rebecca, Mrs. (b. 1841), **7:** 301 n.*546*
Wood, Mr. – manager of Avenue Theatre, **7:** 512
Wood, Samuel Theodore, Rev. (b. 1844), **7:** 139 n.*257*
Woodcock (of Wigan, Lancashire):
Agatha Maud (b. 1847), **5:** 58 n.*83*
Agnes (b. 1843), **5:** 58 n.*83*
Everilda Mary (b. 1845), **5:** 58 n.*83*
Lilias Frances Anne (b. 1849), **5:** 58 n.*83*
Lucy Jane (b. 1841), **5:** 58 n.*83*
Mabel Elizabeth (b. 1850), **5:** 58 n.*83*
Woodcock, Miss – possibly Lucy Jane, see above, **3:** 61
Woodcote House, Windlesham, **6:** 192 n.*298*
Wood Eaton, Oxfordshire, **9:** 67
Woodgate, Hamilton (b. 1835) – Fell scholar at Christ Church, **2:** 109 n.*213*, 110 n.*213*
Woodhouse (of Battersea Rise, Surrey):
Arthur Chorley, Rev. (1854-1944), **8:** 453 n.*727*
Margaret Helen née Morris, **8:** 453 n.*727*
Woodhouse, Charles Goddard (b. 1839?) – undergraduate at Christ Church, **2:** 68 n.*134*, 70-2, 85; **3:** 15, 16 n.*15*
Woodhouse (of Kingston upon Thames, Surrey):
Doris "Dolly" K. (b. 1879), **7:** 207 n.*384*, 527; **8:** 82 n.*129*, 328, 499
Effie L. (b. 1877), **7:** 207 n.*384*, 220, 221, 255, 289, 527; **8:** 328, 499
Henry M., Mr. (b. 1840) – broker, **7:** 207 n.*384*, 220, 255, 256, 269 n.*484*, 304, 314, 370; **8:** 82 n.*129*, 499
Mabel B. (b. 1870), **7:** 206, 207 n.*384*, 213, 220, 221, 255, 288, 304, 370, 527, 531; **8:** 38 n.*52*, 39, 328, 499
Mary L., Mrs. (b. 1849), **7:** 207 n.*384*, 220, 221, 255, 256, 269 n.*484*, 288, 289, 304, 314, 369, 370, 527; **8:** 82 n.*129*, 304, 328, 342, 499
Melville "Percy" (b. 1869), **7:** 207 n.*384*, 288, 527
Nora M. (b. 1868), **7:** 207 n.*384*, 213, 220, 221, 255, 288, 289, 304, 370, 527, 528, 531; **8:** 328, 329, 342, 499
Rowley (b. 1871), **7:** 207 n.*384*, 220, 221, 255, 288
Woodhouse (of Kensington, London):
Emily G. (b. 1831), **7:** 207 n.*386*; **8:** 82 n.*129*

Louisa T. (b. 1832), **7:** 207 n.*386*
Margaret R. (b. 1827), **7:** 207 n.*386*
Woodhouse (of East Budleigh, Devon):
Emmeline Dorothea "Dolly" (b. 1876), **9:** 145
Emmeline née Benson (1838-1921), **1:** 66 n.*48*; **7:** 32 n.*43*, 33; **8:** 153 n.*251*
George E. (b. 1867), **8:** 203 n.*347*
George Girdlestone, Rev. (1831-1897), **1:** 66 n.*48*; **2:** 64 n.*128*, 68 n.*134*, 71; **3:** 16 n.*15*; **7:** 32 n.*43*, 33, 207, 330; **8:** 153 n.*251*, 203, 277
Mary "Mamie" (b. 1859), see Crofts
Ruth Martin (1870?-1897), **8:** 277 n.*466*, 279-281, 306, 307, 318, 341; **9:** 70 n.*127*, 125, 127, 143, 144
Woodroffe (of Hastings, Sussex):
Alice Maud née Townshend (1847-1907), **7:** 54 n.*86*, 131, 134, 137, 140, 143, 144 n.*266*
Charles R. (b. 1879), **7:** 54 n.*86*
Clara Alice (b. 1868), **7:** 54 n.*86*, 132, 134, 137-139, 143, 144 n.*266*
Edmund G. D. (b. 1870), **7:** 54 n.*86*, 131
George William Plunkenett, Mr. (1842-1919) – Indian merchant, **7:** 54 n.*86*, 56, 131, 134, 135, 137, 140
Mabel (b. 1876), **7:** 54 n.*86*
Maud Violet (1873-1904), **7:** 54 n.*86*, 56, 72, 74, 139
William "Willie" Henry Plunkenett (1871-1953), **7:** 54 n.*86*, 56, 72, 131, 135, 136
Woodrooffe, Thomas, Rev. (1790-1878), **6:** 131 n.*202*
Woods, Constance Helen née Quin (1862-1893), **9:** 87 n.*157*
Woods, Margaret Louisa "Daisy" née Bradley (1855-1945) – poet and novelist, **8:** 69 n.*111*
Woods Sisters – child actresses, **7:** 510 n.*827*
Woodstock, Oxfordshire, **3:** 65; **6:** 490
Woodstock Election, **6:** 60 n.*92*
Woodstock Road, Oxford, **9:** 238, 269, 326
Woodward, Benjamin (1816-1861) – architect, **3:** 26 n.*37*; **4:** 35
Wooldridge, Harry Ellis (1845-1917) – artist, **7:** 34 n.*47*
Wooldridge, Martha (b. 1863) – actress, **6:** 457
Wooler (of Cleobury North, Shropshire):
Eleanor, Mrs. (b. 1844), **7:** 311 n.*555*, 312
William G., Rev. (b. 1836), **7:** 311 n.*555*, 312, 446
Wooler, John Pratt (1824-1868) – dramatist, **4:** 273 n.*318*, 309 n.*384*; **5:** 47 n.*62*
Woolgar, Sarah, see Mrs. Alfred Mellon
Woolland, Dorset, **7:** 151 n.*284*
Woolley, Amy P. (b. 1850) – logic pupil, **9:** 291 n.*457*, 293, 305, 306
Woolner (of Hendon, Middlesex):
Alice Gertrude née Waugh (1845-1912), **5:** 76 n.*115*

Thomas, Mr. (1825-1892) – sculptor, **4:** 35, 220, 221 n.*241*, 225; **5:** 76 n.*115*
Woolwich Royal Military Academy, Kent, **1:** 65, 66, 68; **2:** 19 n.*32*, 25 n.*47*, 33, 60
Wootton, Oxfordshire, **6:** 269
Worboys, William (fl. 1860-1868) – actor, **4:** 160
Worcester, **4:** 120; **6:** 239; **7:** 446; **9:** 32, 69
Worcester Cathedral School, **9:** 43
Worcester College, Oxford, **2:** 77; **4:** 13, 173, 203, 276; **6:** 132 n.*203*, 217; **7:** 24, 108, 269, 346, 453, 538; **8:** 11, 121, 196, 215, 335, 339, 399, 409, 517, 564; **9:** 47, 223
Worcester High School for Girls (later The Alice Ottley School), **2:** 86 n.*171*; **9:** 33 n.*56*, 42, 43 n.*73*
Wordsworth (of Dove Cottage, Grasmere, Westmorland):
Catherine (1808-1812), **2:** 91 n.*184*
Dora (1804-1847, **2:** 91 n.*184*
John (b. 1803), **2:** 91 n.*184*
Mary née Hutchinson, **2:** 91 n.*184*
Thomas (1806-1812), **2:** 91 n.*184*
William (b. 1810), **2:** 91 n.*184*
William, Mr. (1770-1850) – poet, **1:** 51 n.*5*, 73; **2:** 91 n.*184,* 99 n.*191*; **3:** 155 n.*228*; **8:** 535
Wordsworth, Christopher, Rev. Dr. (1807-1885), **3:** 167 n.*242*
Wordsworth, Elizabeth (1840-1932) – teacher, **7:** 273 n.*494*; **8:** 170, 171 n.*285*, 280, 502 n.*806*, 516; **9:** 349 n.*559*
Wordsworth (of Rochester, Kent):
John, Canon (1843-1911), **8:** 88 n.*142*
Susan Esther née Coxe (1843-1894), **8:** 88 n.*142*
Work (pic. Ford Madox Brown), **5:** 72 n.*109*
Works (bk. William Paley), **1:** 24; **2:** 10 n.*11*
Works (bk. David Ricardo), **3:** 158 n.*234*
World, The, **6:** 477; **8:** 150 n.*245*
Worplesdon Rectory, Surrey, **7:** 344
Worship, William Henry Edward, Rev. (b. 1860), **7:** 427 n.*713*
Worthing, Sussex, **6:** 236
Wounded Cavalier, A (pic. William Burton), **2:** 75 n.*151*
Wray (of Jersey):
Henry – governor of Jersey, **8:** 97 n.*159*
Mrs. née Drinkwater, **8:** 97 n.*159*
Wreck Ashore, The (dr. John Buckstone), **5:** 137 n.*220*
Wright (of Woking, Surrey):
Alfred Richard Henry, Mr. (d. 1930) – bank cashier and organist, **8:** 613 n.*973*
Isabel Ward née Powell (b. 1860?), **8:** 613 n.*973*
Leslie Isabel (b. 1883), **8:** 613 n.*973*

Wright, Edward Richard (1813-1859) – actor, **2:** 80 n.*158*, 128
Wright, Ethel E. (b. 1878), **9:** 242 n.*383*, 258, 259
Wright, Fanny – friend of Isa Bowman, **8:** 630 n.*997*
Wright, James Osborne – editor, **7:** 518
Writing to Papa (pic. Thomas Heaphy), **5:** 219 n.*350*
Wuthering Heights (bk. Emily Brontë), **2:** 74 n.*150*
Wyatt, Alice G. (b. 1860) – servant, **7:** 298 n.*540*
Wyatt, James (b. 1811) – print-seller and magistrate, **7:** 89 n.*158*
Wyburn, Cumberland, **2:** 95
Wych Street, London, **5:** 210
Wykeham House, Oxford, **6:** 394, 395 n.*646*; **7:** 100 n.*186*, 102, 109
Wykeham-Musgrave, Wenman Aubrey (1837-1915) – magistrate, **8:** 125 n.*202*
Wyld, Messrs., London – globe supplier, **5:** 232
Wyndham, Henry, Gen. Sir (1790-1860) – army officer, **3:** 149 n.*215*
Wynne (of Reading, Berkshire):
Capt. (d. 1880?), **7:** 166, 167 n.*314*
Lucy née Parish (b. 1852), **7:** 166, 167 n.*314*
Wynne, Edith (1842-1897) – singer, **4:** 281 n.*331*; **5:** 225
Wynne, Owen (b. 1843) – undergraduate at Christ Church, **4:** 79 n.*30*
Wynne-Finch (of Stokesley, Yorkshire):
Edward Heneage, Mr. (1842-1914), **7:** 182 n.*341*
Emily Caroline née Marwood (b. 1857), **7:** 182 n.*341*
Wynter, Miss – sister of Harriette Morrell, **6:** 304 n.*504*
Wynyates, see Whinyates
Wyper (of Govan, Lanarkshire):
Emily "Emma" Henrietta née Drury, **6:** 91 n.*140*, 94, 95 n.*148*, 122, 126, 159, 177, 196, 200, 259, 317, 339; **7:** 192, 193, 230, 236, 278, 315, 319, 350, 415, 453, 515; **8:** 58, 108, 110-112, 115, 126, 165, 171 n.*287*, 172, 189
James, Mr. (b. 1850) - stationer and publisher, **8:** 171 n.*287*, 172
Wytham, Berkshire, **4:** 76; **7:** 348

Yachting Cruise, A (dr. Francis Burnand), **5:** 157 n.*256*
Yarmouth, Isle of Wight, **4:** 346, 350
Yarnold – child actor, **5:** 193, 202
Yarnton, Oxfordshire, **9:** 64
Yates, Edmund Hodgson (1831-1894) – writer and editor, **1:** 112 n.*131*; **2:** 13 n.*16*, 14 n.*20*, 36, 37 n.*74*, 38, 39, 42, 44, 51, 52 n.*104*, 55, 61 n.*122*,
84, 88 n.*176*, 89, 99, 105, 107; **3:** 30, 31, 101 n.*149*, 102, 120 n.*170*, 126; **4:** 124, 139 n.*117*, 153, 338 n.*437*; **5:** 25, 125; **6:** 255 n.*407*
Yeatman, Huyshe Wolcott, Rt. Rev. (1845-1922) – bishop of Southwark, **9:** 317 n.*506*
Ye Fancy Fayre (dr. Richard Corney Grain), **7:** 354 n.*618*

Yeld & Charlton, Messrs., Sunderland – accountants, **7:** 172
Yeomen of the Guard, The (Gilbert and Sullivan) – operetta, **8:** 453 n.*725*
Yokohama conjurors, **8:** 364 n.*596*
Yonge (of Elderfield, Otterbourne, near Winchester, Hampshire):
  Charlotte Mary (1823-1901), **2:** 57 n.*115*; **4:** 47; **5:** 24, 147 n.*236*, 159; **7:** 100 n.*187*; **8:** 161, 326
  Frances Mary née Bargus, **5:** 147 n.*236*
York, **2:** 18, 55; **4:** 30, 133, 134; **5:** 189; **6:** 456, 494, 495
York Museum, **2:** 18
Yorke (of Bewerley Hall, near Pateley Bridge, Yorkshire):
  Alice née Simpson (b. 1837), **5:** 247 n.*401*
  John, Mr. (1827-1883) – magistrate, **5:** 247 n.*401*
Yorkshire, **1:** 9, 16; **2:** 61; **3:** 77; **5:** 82; **7:** 209
You Can't Marry Your Grandmother (dr. Thomas Bayly), **3:** 171 n.*250*
Young, Edward (1800-1890) – writer, **3:** 44 n.*70*, 45
Young, Henry Savill (1843-1906) – undergraduate at Brasenose College, **4:** 141 n.*120*, 204
Young, James – artist, **1:** 117 n.*143*, 134
Young, Sophie (b. c. 1840) – actress, **5:** 69 n.*104*
Young and Handsome (dr. James Planché), **3:** 12 n.*10*
Younge, Mabel (b. 1866) – actress, **9:** 15 n.*10*
Young Helpers' League (Barnardos), **9:** 109 n.*193*
Ysaÿe, Eugène (b. 1858) – violinist, **8:** 587 n.*937*

Zanzibar, East Africa, **7:** 164 n.*308*, 166, 438; **9:** 314 n.*501*
Zimmermann, Antoine – translator, **5:** 226, 227 n.*361*; **6:** 53 n.*74*, 78 n.*113*
Zohrab, Mr. – consul-general at Erzeroum, **7:** 89 n.*159*
Zoological Gardens, London, **3:** 133, 172
Zoological Gardens, Moscow, **5:** 323
Zulu-land, South Africa, **8:** 89

Further Errata and Information

Since the publication of all nine volumes of the surviving *Diaries*, further errors in transcription and footnotes have emerged. The following is a list of amendments since the publication of *Diary 9*. These changes have been taken into account in the Index given above.

Diary 1:
page

1855

65 Feb: 27. (Tu). footnote 44: Dodgson's expedition was, more likely, with Henry Martyn Collyns (b. 1833). He had just complete his BA degree at Christ Church, and probably stayed as a tutor, whereas his older brother, John Martyn Collyns (1827-1912), was already curate at Drayton, Oxfordshire.

67 Mar: 2. (F). The picture of "Wellington visiting the plain at Waterloo" was by Benjamin R. Haydon, and is now at the National Portrait Gallery.

71 Mar: 5. (M). footnote 60: Dodgson's copy of Walkingame was used at Richmond School, not Rugby as stated.

71 Mar: 6. (Tu). Liddon mentioned here is, more likely, John Liddon (b. 1835) who was studying mathematics at Christ Church. He took his degree in 1857. This applies to a number of entries when Dodgson used the name Liddon to represent either John, or his brother Henry Parry Liddon (1829-1890). I am grateful to Prof. Katsuko Kasai for alerting me to this point.

76 Mar: 16. (F). footnote 71. The lecture was probably given by Edward Hill Jekyll (1804-1876), late Captain in the Grenadier Guards. Although he studied at Christ Church, he did not take his degree, unlike his brother Joseph (1802-1841), BA 1824.

89 Ap: 27. (F). See above. This is probably John not Henry Liddon.

120 Aug: 20. (M). footnote 147. *Parish Musings: in verse* (1850) was written by John Samuel Bewley Monsell (1811-1875).

Diary 2:

1856

9 Jan: 5. (Sat). The actor Dodgson saw in *Henry VIII* was Drinkwater Meadows (1795-1869).

15 Jan: 11. (F). footnote 25: the cross reference should read "see n.*199* below."

25 Jan: 19. (Sat). Either John or Henry Liddon.

44 Feb: 25, (M). According to the Highgate School Register, Edmund H. Yates entered in August 1840, Robert Mayo entered in January 1844, and William H. Ranken entered in January 1847.

47 Mar: 1. (Sat). footnote 92: Quintin William Francis Twiss (1835-1900).

47 Mar: 4. (Tu). The book was probably *Household Surgery; or, hints on emergencies* by John Flint South (1797-1882), which was published in 1847 but reprinted many times.

63 Ap: 23. (W). footnote 127: William Ince (1825-1910).

73 May 20. (Tu). After Columbo there should be a comma.

78 June 5. (Th). In fact Dodgson's old school friend, Augustus Henry Mounsey (1834-1882), was with him at Rugby School, but he may have been with him at Richmond too.

81 June 12. (Th). footnote 160: the Lockhart family that Dodgson met on his stay at Putney were the children of Allan Eliott Lockhart (1803-1878), barrister, and his wife, Charlotte née Dundas. There were twelve children, but Dodgson only came into contact with the younger members of the family; Mary Dora (b. 1846), Jane Margaret (b. 1848), and Charles Walter (1850-1889). Miss Lockhart was one of the older daughters; Matilda Eliott (1832-1898) or Marianne Elizabeth (b. 1836).

84 June 26. (Th). footnotes 168 & 169: John W. Smith and his wife, Maria, had eight children. The two sons missing from the list are: William Grey (b. 1840, died young) and John William (b. 1841, died young). Mr. and Mrs. Brown could possibly be George Brown, rector of Redmarshall (a few miles from Dinsdale) and his wife, Ann née Webster. However Dodgson met them on 4 April 1856 (see n. *120*), but does not appear to have remembered them. And no family link with the Smiths has been found.

87 July 9. (W). footnote 175: The Robinson family descend from George Robinson (1757-1832) of Hendon Lodge, Sunderland.

91 Aug: 16. (Sat). Friar's Crag.

95 Aug: 26. (Tu). footnote 186: Henry Thomas Lutwidge (1786-1861).

97 Aug: 28. (Th). Rydal Falls.

100 Sep: 16. (Tu). Should say: "We had the music in *Macbeth*, 'Bonnie Prince Charlie' (Lady W.), 'The Chough & Crow,' 'Wanted a Governess' (one of Parry's songs) and as the encore to it 'The King of Otaheite,' 'My heart's in the Hielands' (Lady W.) and as its encore 'Merry Swiss boy,' 'March of the Cameron men,' etc." Footnote 194: "Bonnie Prince Charlie" is an anonymous song; "The Chough & Crow" is by the poet, Joanna Baillie (1762-1851); "Wanted a Governess" is a song (1840) by John Orlando Parry (1810-1879); "The King of Otaheite's Tea

Party" is a comic cannibalistic song (1856) by R. Topliff; "My heart's in the Hielands {Highlands}" is a song based on a poem (1789) by Robert Burns (1759-1796); "Merry Swiss Boy" is a traditional Tyrolese song, translated by William Ball and set to music (1827) by Ignaz Moscheles (1794-1870); and "March of the Cameron Men" is a song (1829) by Mary Maxwell Campbell (d. 1886).

103 Sep: 29. (M). footnote 199. The sister of Mary Agnes Bainbridge née Harvey (b. 1824) was Ann Adelaide Hippolyta Harvey (1811-1893) who married firstly Lt. George Hobson Bainbridge in 1839 (brother of Henry Bainbridge), and secondly Capt. George Percy Pickard (1801-1852) in 1845. Adelaide Loftus Joanna (1846-1898) was the only child from the second marriage.

110 Nov: 1. (Sat). footnote 214: the link between the Shuldham and Smedley families has now been made. The daughter, Sophia, of Bishop John Hume (1705-82), married Maj.-Gen. Shuldham, HEICS. John Hume's brother James (b. 1708) had a son, John (1742-1818), who became Dean of Derry. His daughter, Maria, married Rev. G. Hart. They had two sons, Thomas Barnard who married Elizabeth A. Smedley, and Edward who married Mary Smedley.

113 Nov: 12. (W). The man in for the Junior Scholarship was Henry Leland Harrison (b. 1837).

118 Nov: 19. (W). The Dean's father was Rev. Henry George Liddell (1787-1872).

121 Dec: 3. (W). footnote 235: Alfred Devaux arranged operas for the solo pianist.

122 Dec: 12. (F). Liddon is probably John, not Henry.

123 Dec: 13. (Sat). The extravaganza, *The Statue Bride, or the Elves*, was written by Charles Selby (1801-1863) with music composed by John Wade Thirlwall (1809-1875) and choreography by Madame Celine Celeste (1811-1882).

138 Index delete "Dolby, see Stainton-Dolby."

139 Index Girdlestone, Robert Baker (not Thomas).

142 Index Jefferson (not Jefferon).

145 Index Henry Thomas Lutwidge (great-uncle).

148 Index Pott, Alfred (not Potts).

Diary 3:

1857

12 Jan: 21. (W). The other actor was Henry Leslie (1830-1881).

25 Feb: 13. (F). Mrs. Ogilvie was Mary Ann Gurnell née Armstrong (d. 1875). Mrs. Lott was Elizabeth née Barnes (b.

1817) and her three children were Frederick Barnes (b. 1854), Mary Elizabeth (b. 1855), and Theophilus (b. 1856). A fourth child, Katherine P. (b. 1860), came later.

34 Mar: 7. (Sat). Again the link between the Shuldhams and Norrises is through the Humes (and hence also to Dodgson). Mrs. Norris was Caroline M. née Hume (b. 1812). Her father was James John Hume (1777-1816), Dodgson's great-uncle. In turn, the grandfather of James John was James Hume (b. 1708), see above.

34 Mar: 8. (Sun). James Norris's two eldest daughters were Caroline Lydia (b. 1847) and Charlotte (b. 1849).

49 Ap: 19. (Sun) Tristram's former pupil was probably Robert Reynolds Winter (b. 1837).

51 Ap: 22. (W). footnote 77: spelling of "Academy."

53 Ap: 30. (Th). footnote 80: Edward Wilberforce (1834-1914).

58 May 12. (Tu). Probably Elizabeth Anne Hart née Smedley (1822-1890?).

59 May 17. (Sun). Dodgson's cross reference "See June 27, 1863" is to a cut page from the *Diaries*.

61 May 20. (W). Mrs. Jacobson was Eleanor Jane née Turner (b. 1812).

61 May 21. (Th). Miss Woodcock was possibly Lucy Jane Woodcock (b. 1841).

62 May 26. (Tu). Dr. Acland's brother was probably John Barton Arundel Acland (1823-1904).

65 June 1. (M). The most likely Armitstead brother was Henry Sidney (1837-1912). He was still studying at Christ Church and took his degree in 1860.

68 June 9. (Tu). Cotton's brother is more likely to be Arthur Benjamin Cotton (b. 1832) who took his degree at Christ Church in 1854.

77 July 2. (Th). William Charles Thomas Dobson (not James).

82 July 3. (F). Miss Poole was Elizabeth (1820-1906).

97 Sep: 10. (Th). Salisbury Crays (not Crags).

103 Sep: 12. (Sat). The entertainment was by Mr. Howard Paul (1830-1905). Dodgson transposed the name.

104 Sep: 16. (W). Bowling (not Bowley).

121 Oct: 22. (Th). Mrs. Norris's step-sister was Catherine A. Adams née Hume (b. 1803).

124 Nov: 5. (Th). footnote 178: Francis Hayward Joyce (1829-1906).

130 Nov: 23. (M). John Liddon, not Henry.

141 Dec: 31. (Th). Miss Mulock (not Muloch).

1858

153 Jan: 22. (F). John Liddon, not Henry.
158 Feb: 23. (Tu). David Ricardo (1772-1823). *The Works of David Ricardo* was published in 1846.
176 Index Bayly, Thomas Haynes, 171 n.*250*
179 Index Craven, Henry Thornton
185 Index Liddon, John, 54 n.*83*, 61, 130, 153
186 Index Lutwidge, Henry Thomas (great-uncle), Mary née Taylor (great-aunt).

Diary 4:

1861

57 Reconstruction Shirley Hibberd (not Hibbard).

1862

77 June 10. (Tu). Warburton's brother was George Drought Warburton (1816-1857), writer, and his wife was Elizabeth Augusta née Bateman-Hanbury (b. 1832).
83 June 19. (Th). footnote 36: more likely to be Montague Bernard Baker (b. 1843), brother of Charles (b. 1833) and Henry (b. 1835), all sons of Rev. James Baker of Nuneham Courtney, Oxfordshire. Montague B. Baker matriculated at Pembroke College in 1860, and entered the Inner Temple in 1862. Thomas Kington Baker was not the brother of James Baker as listed.
84 June 21. (Sat). There were five (not three) Lowthorpe children. The missing two were Charlotte Lizzie (d. 1856) and William "Willie" Frederick Raikes (1857-1864).
97 July 6. (Sun) Mayow Wynell Mayow (b. 1811) was the incumbent of the church in Brompton.
98 July 8. (Tu) Minnie Fellowes is probably a mistake for Maudie Fellowes. She was Louisa Adela Maud "Maudie" Fellowes (b. 1857), daughter of Rev. Thomas Fellowes.
106 July 23. (W). footnote 74: the Rogers had six children, and the missing son was Leonard James (1862-1933).
123 Sep: 1. (M). footnote 96: the Henleys had eight children, and the missing daughter was Mabel Augusta (1871-1966). Frederick Currey (1819-1881), barrister, was married to Georgiana Innes née Pocock (1822-1867). They had six children: Frederick Innes (b. 1849), Menella "Minnie" (b. 1850), Florence (b. 1853), Isabel (b. 1855?), Hamilton (b. 1857), and Walter Francis (b. 1860).
128 Sep: 8. (M). The photograph entitled "the sleeping beauty" is a portrait of a daughter of either Uncle Skeffington Poole or Uncle Hassard Hume Dodgson. There is a copy in the Royal Photographic Society Archives at Bradford.

147 Nov: 25. (Tu). Eleanor Elizabeth Smith (1823-1896), known as "Miss Smith of Oxford," and her brother, Henry John Stephen Smith (1826-1883), Savilian professor of geometry at Oxford.

157 Jan: 2. (F). spelling of "preceded"

176 Mar: 22. (Sun). Not William Henry Charsley, but Robert Harvey Charsley (1826-1907), former curate of Iffley.

189 Ap: 8. (W). The two daughters of Horatio Tennyson were Cecilia (1859-1918) and Maud (b. 1860).

190 Ap: 9. (Th). Not "Nelly J" but "Nelly ditto" – i.e. Nelly Smedley. She was Winifred "Nellie" Smedley (b. 1847), as mentioned in n.*186*.

219 June 21. (Sun). footnote 219: Thomas Allen (1800?-1873) was the superintendent of the Warneford Hospital, Headington Lunatic Asylum, from 1853 until 1872. His wife, Charlotte L. (b. 1814), was matron at the Asylum. Mr. Allen was the brother of Mrs. Mary Anne Bayne née Allen (1805-1888). The Allens had three daughters: Mary (b. 1843), Charlotte (b. 1844), and Jane (b. 1846?).

223 July 20. (M). John, not Henry Liddon.

224 July 21. (Tu). footnote 248: probably Maj.-Gen. Arthur Le Pigou (b. 1826), and his wife, Jemima F. (b. 1826), and family: Frederica E. M. (b. 1857), Henrietta J. (b. 1859), Mary B. (b. 1860), and Elizabeth E. (b. 1863).

228 July 30. (Th). footnote 252: Dr. John Rutherfurd Russell (1816-1866).

237 Sep: 6. (Sun). footnote 265: Winteringham is in Lincolnshire (not Lancs.).

240 Sep: 7. (M). footnote 267: Madeline Catherine (1855-1925) – not Caroline.

244 Sep: 30. (W). footnote 274: *The Poetical Works of James Russell Lowell* (1853).

246 Oct: 1. (Th). footnote 279: Jane Elizabeth Senior née Hughes (1828-1877) was the wife of Nassau John Senior (1822-1891). The *DNB* described her as "a very graceful and accomplished woman…also generally loved for simplicity and sweetness of character."

251 Oct: 6. (Tu) Text should read "and a Mr. Le Gros {*sic*}, an artist."

1864

278 Mar: 22. (Tu). Catherine A. Ranken (b. 1843) was one of the two Miss Rankens. The other later married the artist Thomas B. Samon, but she died before 1881.

279 Ap: 1. (F). John, not Henry Liddon, who lived at 10 Whitehall Place, London. 19 Whitehall Place was the office of the Commissioners of Lunacy (Uncle Skeffington's office).

319 June 25. (Sat). The two Misses Richmond were Cecilia Sarah (b. 1847) and Edith (b. 1846).

331 July 10. (Sun) Dr. Edward Meyrick Goulburn (1818-1897) – not Soulburn, incumbent of St. John's, Paddington 1859-67.

338 July 16. (Sat). footnote 436: Charles H. Stephenson (1824-1905), major actor and dramatist.

339 July 18. (M). Henry Revell Reynolds (1800-1866), solicitor to the Treasury, and his second wife, Charlotte Ann née Bullock Webster (b. 1819). He had nine children. Those younger than Edith Mary (b. 1848) were Arthur Sutherland (b. 1851), Amy Beatrice (b. 1854), and Lily M. (b. 1863).

342 July 23. (Sat). footnote 444: Francis Richard Douglas (1818-1914), Lord Elcho, Earl of Wemyss.

344 July 27. (W). footnote 448: the two eldest children of George Bradley were Arthur Granville (1850-1943) and Margaret Louisa "Daisy" (b. 1855?).

355 Aug: 18. (Th). William T. Lambert (b. 1830) was the landlord of Plumbley's Hotel. His son was William T. (b. 1857), and he had three other children.

356 Aug: 18. (Th). footnote 466: Tennyson's headman was Charles Heard (b. 1828).

379 Index Liddell, not Liddells

380 Index insert Liddon, John, 223, 279

383 Index Nassau, Mrs. should be Senior, Mrs.

385 Index Parnell, Madeline Catherine

391 Index Combine Nelly J. and Winifred Smedley into Winifred "Nelly"; Sothern, Edward Askew (not David); and Soulburn should be Goulburn.

393 Index Taylor, John Wycliffe – not Wickliffe

Diary 5:

1864

13 Oct: 2. (Sun) footnote 3: cross reference should be "see n. *48* below" (not 51).

1865

42 Jan: 3. (Tu). Captain Horton Rhys (not Reece).

58 Mar: 25. (Sat). footnote 83: Faussett had seven brothers. The two missing step-brothers were Bryan (1811-1898) and Godfrey (1813-1887). His sisters from his father's first marriage to Marianne Elizabeth née Bridges (d. 1820?) were Susan (d. 1893) and Anne (d. 1868). One of his sister-in-laws was Lilias Frances Anne (not Lillias).

61 Ap: 6. (Th). footnote 89: Dinah Maria Mulock.

65 Ap: 9. (Sun). Dodgson has the name spelt incorrectly - Wycliffe, not Wicliffe.

70 Ap: 18. (Tu). John, not Henry Liddon.

90 July 9. (Sun). Sutton Courtney, not Courteney.

92 July 13. (Th). footnote 142: by this time the Terrys had moved to 24 Caversham Road, Kentish Town.

96 July 18. (Tu). Dodgson is incorrect – the play is called *The Toodles* and was by Richard John Raymond (1818?-1847?).

108 Sep: 14. (Th). footnote 169: Frances Dorothy (1828-1902) married in 1856, so she was not one of the Misses Jebb.

109 Sep: 18. (M). footnote 172: *The Lady of Lyons* was more likely the burlesque by Henry J. Byron, first performed in 1858.

112 Oct: 28. (Sat). Thorpe Mandeville, not Thorp. See above for sisters of William H. Ranken. His mother was Isabella K. Ranken (b. 1803).

116 Nov: 11. (Sat). footnote 181: The Butler of Christ Church was Henry Grant (1823-1876).

119 Dec: 5. (Tu). footnote 186: Henry Evans Gordon was treasurer from February to October 1865 (not 1965). One of the non-registered subscriptions came from Charles Leigh Adderley (not Lee).

120 Dec: 5. (Tu). footnote 187: Mrs. Mary Harington, not Harrington.

120 Dec: 15. (F). Thomas Allen's wife, as given above, was Charlotte L. (b. 1814), not Mary.

1866

127 Jan: 17. (W). footnote 203: Ellen Terry's estimate of the age of Percy Roselle (b. 1856) was incorrect; he was 10, not 18 or 19, which is closer to Dodgson's estimate of about 8.

148 May 8. (Tu). footnote 238: Frances Babington's niece, Emma Hume née Sykes (b. 1825), married Dodgson's distant cousin, Henry Hume (1816-1892).

150 May 23. (W). footnote 242: William Melville Wilcox (1866-1958) married Hilda May Catling (1904-1996) in 1935 when he was aged 70. They had one daughter, Valerie (b. 1936).

157 June 22. (F). footnote 255: Blanche Galton (1845-1936) was a soprano singer and actress.

159 June 25. (M). John, not Henry Liddon.

170 July 28. (Sat). Edith Mary (b. 1855), Julia Sant (b. 1856), and Ruth (b. 1858) were the three eldest daughters of William Alexander Cockburn (b. 1821), civil servant, and his wife, Julia Clementine née Sant.

1867

207 Mar: 30. (Sat). Loys Weedon (not Low).

209 Ap: 6. (Sat). footnote 333: Sant's portrait was probably of Julia Augusta Angerstein (b. 1851). Her sister, Frederica Caroline (b. 1855), was too young to be called Miss Angerstein.

211 Ap: 7. (Sun). footnote 337: Netty Smart was married to Greville Ewing Matheson (b. 1847?). His brother was Thomas Matheson (b. 1845).

212 Ap: 8. (M). John, not Henry Liddon.

212 Ap: 8. (M). footnote 340: Millais' brother was William Henry Millais (1828-1899).

220 Ap: 10. (W). John, not Henry Liddon.

226 Ap: 11. (Th). footnote 359: Louisa Pyne (1829-1904) sang "Home, Sweet Home" with music by Henry R. Bishop (1786-1855) and words by John Howard Payne (1791-1852). Other songs were sung by Helen Lemmens-Sherrington (1834-1906).

233 Ap: 29. (M). footnote 374: Walter Meysey Severne (1838-1878), MA Christ Church. No details of his wife have come to light.

244 May 21. (Tu). footnote 397: Annie Latham (b. 1830), wife of Henry Latham (1829-1871), London barrister, brought her daughter, Beatrice M. (b. 1861), to be photographed.

245 May 22. (W). footnote: Henry Bull (1787-1888) and his wife, Frances Sophia née Hughes (b. 1809), had four children: Caroline Frances Martha (b. 1842), Henry Edward (1843-1905), Cyril John Spier (1845-1888), and Florence S. (b. 1848).

253 June 26. (W). Bellini's opera is entitled *La Sonnambula* (not Somnambula).

315 Aug: 11. (Sun). footnote 487: Prince Nikolay Alexeyevich Orloff (1827-1885).

336 Aug: 19. (M). Richard Morris Hunt (1827-1895), American architect, and his wife, Catherine née Howland. Their son was Richard Howland (1862-1931), and they later had another son, Joseph Howland (1870-1924).

349 Aug: 26. (M). Dodgson was uncertain about the name "Golicen" – a name not listed in the Russian Royal Family. He probably meant Prince Constantine Galitzine (1832-1879), whose daughter was Olga (1861-1901).

385 Index Replace Brown, Susanna née Drewett with Isabella née Chaytor.

395 Index Harington, Mary (not Harrington).

400 Index Add Liddon, John, 70, 85, 159, 212, 220.

402 Index spelling of Millais; Minin (Bamina) Tower; and *Morning Kiss, The* (Bouguereau).

Diary 6:

1868

25 Ap: 10. (F). footnote 27: the children of Dean Saunders and his wife, Emma Frances née Walford (1815?-1882), were: Emma Isabella (b. 1841), Caroline Louisa (1843-1924), Oliver

Augustus (1844-1928), Mary Eliza (b. 1846), Margaret(ta) Annie (b. 1848), Agnes Harriet (b. 1850), Alfred Robert Henry (1853-1938), Florence Matilda (b. 1855), George Keble (1858-1861), and Ethel Gertrude (1859-1861). His orphaned niece, Wilhelmina Blanche (b. 1858), and nephew, Cecil Ernest Brassey Pigou (b. 1859), children of his late-brother James, also lived with the family.

29 May 11. (M). footnote 35: Col. Chambers is not identified, but his wife was Maria (b. 1827), widowed in 1881. They had two children, Katie and Rose.

34 June 10. (W). footnote 45: Frederick Symonds had a third daughter, Margaret (b. 1849), and a son, Horatio Percy (1851-1923). Miss Jeune was possibly Margaret "Meggie" Symons Jeune (b. 1840).

42 Aug: 9. (Sun). Lady Adelaide was probably Adelaide Frances Isabella Peel (1836-1917), third daughter of Baron Sudeley, and related by marriage to Sir Robert Peel.

47 Aug: 16. (Sun). footnote 66: Robert A. C. Austen and his wife, Maria Elizabeth née Godwin (d. 1904), had seventeen children, some already married at this time. The likely candidates for the two Misses Austen are: Sophia Harriet (b. 1833?), Victoria Augusta (b. 1840?), Beatrice (b. 1842), Caroline (1843-1905), Alice Mary (b. 1847), Elphrida (b. 1848), and Emily (b. 1850).

1869

61 Nov: 24. (Tu). pages 61 & 62 – date at foot should be 1868.

94 Sep: 4. (Sat). footnote 147: possibly Mrs. Georgiana Mangles (b. 1814).

98 Oct: 5. (Tu). footnote 153: Maj. Lewis Stafford Northcote (1831-1882), his wife, Isabella Jane née Weguelin (b. 1843), and his unmarried sister, Selina Helena Northcote (1844-1901).

103 Nov: 30. (Tu). Surprisingly there is no mention of the death of Dodgson's Aunt Margaret Anne Lutwidge at Hastings on this day.

1870

120 June 25. (Sat). Mrs. Leighton was Catherine (b. 1819), wife of Francis Knyvett Leighton (1806-1881), warden of All Souls.

1871

142 Mar: 24. (F). footnote 216: Miss S. Dodgson is certainly Sarah C. Dodgson (b. 1819) who was a trained nurse.

185 Sep: 22. (F). footnote 287: Jane Isabel Gathorne-Hardy (1842?-1862) was another daughter, and the dates for Margaret Evelyn should be (1858-1943).

1872

208 Ap: 5. (F). footnote 327: the sister of Mary "May" Anne Allen (1848-1904) was Beatrice (b. 1865). Their father was

Udney John Thomas Allen (b. 1824), vicar of Dalton-le-Dale, Sunderland.

209 Ap: 30. (Tu). The grandchildren of Prof. Bonamy Price were Beatrice (b. 1862) and Maud (b. 1864?). Their parents were Daniel Robert Fearon (1835-1919), barrister, and Margaret née Price (1838-1909).

226 July 27. (Sat). footnote 357: Emmeline F. Cave (b. 1846). Her niece was Olivia Beatrice Adelaide Miles (b. 1862), daughter of Edward Peach William Miles (1829-1889) and Olivia Caroline née Cave (d. 1870).

235 Oct: 3. (Th). footnote 373: John W. Richards (b. 1811), chaplain to St Michael's School at Bognor, and his wife, Frances A. A. (b. 1812). Their daughters are not identified.

236 Oct: 3. (Th). footnote 374: Stopford Augustus Brooke (1832-1916), and his wife, Emma Diana née Beaumont (d. 1874), see n.*368* above.

247 Dec: 31. (Tu). footnote 392: Mr. Pakenham Alderson was Edward Pakenham Alderson (1828?-1876) who married in 1868 Mildred Anne Cradock Hartopp (1829-1909), Lady Scott from her first marriage to Sir Francis Edward Scott (1824-1863), see n.*254* above. Also, Mr. Sandford was George Montagu Warren Sandford (1822-1879), MP for Malden, Essex.

248 Dec: 31. (Tu). footnote 393: the additional Campbell children were John Beresford (1866-1915), Mildred Louisa (1867-1951), and Cecil Arthur (1869-1932). They were the children of Hallyburton George Campbell (1829-1918), 3rd Baron Stratheden and Campbell, and his wife, Louisa Mary née Beresford (d. 1923).

1873

249 Jan: 2. (Th). footnote 395: Thomes Hughes' brother was William Hastings Hughes (1833-1909), sherry importer. His son and amateur actor was Henry "Harry" Hughes (1862-1896).

254 Jan: 11. (Sat). footnote 404: Miss Craik was Mr. Craik's cousin, Georgina Marion Craik (1831-1895), a writer of fiction.

255 Jan: 12. (Sun). footnote 405: probably Rev. Foster Stable Barry (1829-1908), headmaster of Mercer's School, London, and his family. His wife was Flaneisto (b. 1831), and the three children Dodgson saw were: {Edith} Alice (b. 1862), Mary Louisa (b. 1865), and Arthur L. (b. 1870).

268 Mar: 25. (Tu). Frederick Menzies (b. 1815), MA Brasenose, rector of Great Shefford, Berkshire 1866-87, and later canon of Christ Church.

1874

308 Jan: 1. (Th). footnote 509: Thomas Hill Green (1836-1882), professor of moral philosophy, and his wife, Charlotte B. (b. 1843).

314 Jan: 15. (Th). Probably Eustace Edward Fiennes (1864-1943), son of John Twisleton Wykeham Fiennes (1830-1907), 14th Baron Saye and Sele, a Christ Church man.

339 June 22. (M). footnote 562: Adelaide Catherine Hall née Elliot (1841-1926), wife of Basil Francis Hall (1832-1909), 7th Bart. Their daughter does not appear in any of the references and may have died young.

354 Aug: 26. (W). Alice B. George née Cole (b. 1845), wife of Hereford Brooke George (1838-1910), lecturer in modern history at New College. She was Bartholomew Price's sister-in-law.

364 Oct: 28. (W). Charles Edward Cutts Birch Appleton (1841-1879), BA St. John's College, Oxford, DCL 1871, man of letters, founded *The Academy* in 1869 and edited it until his death. He visited America in 1875 and took up the question of international copyright.

1875

378 Jan: 12. (Tu). footnote 620: the nephew and niece of Alexander Macmillan are now identified. His sister, Harriet Brimley Macmillan (b. 1830), married William Henry Farthing Johnson (1825-1901), a schoolmaster at Llandaff House, Regent Street, Cambridge. They had seven children: Harriet M. (b. 1855), George William (1857-1926), William Ernest (1858-1931), Alice (b. 1861), Augustine Henry (b. 1865), Reginald Brimley (b. 1867-1932), and another son whose name is not known. Dodgson probably met the two eldest children.

388 Ap: 17. (Sat). footnote 636: The Dodgson family home, "The Chestnuts," was leased (not rented).

415 Sep: 6. (M). spelling of *locum tenens*.

416 Sep: 12. (Sun). footnote 682: Rosalie Coster (b. 1865), daughter of Guillaume Coster (b. 1827) and his wife, Fanny (b. 1839), of Marylebone, London.

424 Oct: 8. (F). footnote 698: Minnie Gilby (b. 1868), daughter of Thomas Gilby (b. 1813), manufacturer, and his wife, Laura (b. 1834), of Essex House, Barnes, Surrey.

1876

444 Jan: 11. (Tu). footnote 726: Rev. Francis Slater (1837-1897), vicar of St. Giles, Cambridge.

451 Feb: 29. (Tu). footnote 741: Dr. James Sewell lived with his unmarried sisters, Emma (b. 1818) and Jane (b. 1820).

455 Mar: 29. (W). footnote 748: the parents of John Christian Fraser (1856-1899) were John Mattison Fraser (b. 1806), colonial broker, and Emilie (b. 1815).

463 May 25. (Th). The symbol used by Dodgson for "not equal to" was $\neq$.

479 Aug: 5. (Sat). footnote 792: Isabel M. {Mabel} Dallin (b. 1872), daughter of Thomas Francis Dallin (1841-1880), fellow of Queen's College 1864-71, lecturer and tutor 1866, public orator of the University 1877, and praelector of Greek and Latin. His wife was Edith Mary (b. 1851), and their other children were: Hetty J. (b. 1873), Francis T. (b. 1874), Mildred G. (b. 1876), and Edith W. (b. 1879).

482 Aug: 24. (Th). footnote 795: Florence Beaton's parents were Walter H. Beaton (b. 1842), timber merchant, and Caroline L. (b. 1849), of Holm Wood, Nightingale Lane, Battersea, Surrey. She had two brothers, Ernest (b. 1871) and Wilfred H. (b. 1874).

497 Index Allen, Charlotte L. replaces Mary, and Miss C. becomes Charlotte.

500 Index Bayne, Mary A. (not V.)

507 Index Conder (not Condor)

509 Index Davys: Blanche Helen is one entry (delete Helen).

512 Index Smith, Henry J. S. (not Stephen)

513 Index Smith, Henry J. S. (not Stephen)

515 Index Donkin, combine Eleanor and Mary "Polly."

516 Index Duckworth, combine Ada and Gertrude, and add William, Mr., 483 n.*796*, 484; Elliot (not Elliott); and Ellison, Constance Margaret, 389.

521 Index Hart: replace with Thomas Barnard, 459, and Elizabeth Anne née Smith, 459.

527 Index Knight: Mary "May," 333, and Mary née Wilcox, 333

533 Index Moseley, Maria Katherine née Anderson; Mosley, Mrs., 382.

535 Index Owen: combine Lucy O'Brien and "Tinie"; spelling of Palestine House.

539 Index Richards: Frances, 235 n.*373* and John W., 235 n.*373*.

542 Index Sewell: remove Elizabeth Missing, and add Emma and Jane, both 451.

550 Index Wilkes, James (doctor), 278, 346, 347.

Diary 7:

1877

32 Ap: 28. (Sat). footnote 43: Dodgson spelt the name incorrectly – he met William Carr Sidgwick (b. 1834), lecturer at Merton College, and his wife, Sarah J. (b. 1833).

51 July 31. (Tu). footnote 81: Mr. and Mrs. Dyer also had a daughter, Emma (b. 1873).

56 Aug: 11. (Sat). footnote 89: Gordon-Lennox, Charles Henry (1845-1928), Earl of March, Darnley and Kilrara, 2nd Duke of Gordon, and later 7th Duke of Richmond, was Captain of the Grenadier Guards. His wife was Amy Mary née Ricardo (d. 1879). They had six children: Emily (1869-1879?), Charles Henry (1870-1935), Evelyn Amy (1872-1922), Violet Mary (1874-1946), Esmé Charles (b. 1875), and Bernard Charles (b. 1878).

1878

100 Feb: 14. (Th). footnote 186: Possibly Frances Maria (1824-1888), daughter of George William Milman, or either Angelena Emily Maria (b. 1820) or her sister Jemima "Jeanie" Anna Maria (b. 1827), daughters of Francis Miles Milman. All were unmarried in 1878.

109 May 4. (Sat). footnote 201: Miss Milman must have been a cousin of Archibald Milman (his two sisters were aready dead) – see n.*186* above.

145 Nov: 20. (W). footnote 272: Jane A. de Brisay (b. 1829), wife of Rev. Henry de la Cour de Brisay (b. 1832), inspector of schools for Oxford.

1879

167 Mar: 21. (F). footnote 314: Lucy Wynne née Parish (b. 1852) was the wife of Captain Wynne (d. 1880?). Her unmarried sister, Florence Parish (b. 1856), was living with her in 1881. For details of her mother, see n.*300* above. Lucy's other sister was Alice (b. 1854).

1880

234 Jan: 9. (F). footnote 432: more likely to be Helen Plomer (b. 1839) living at 7 Chestfield Street, Hanover Square, London.

236 Jan: 10. (Sat). footnote 435: Dodgson spelt the name incorrectly – he was George Anderson Critchett (1845-1925), senior ophthalmic surgeon at St Mary's Hospital, London.

255 Ap: 1. (Th). footnote 465: the Richmond amateur photographer was Dr. Stacey Southerden Burn (b. 1852) – not Burne.

267 May 8. (Sat). footnote 479: Arthur Acland became MP for the Rotherham (not Rotheram) division of the SW Riding of Yorkshire.

280 July 15. (Th). footnote 511: the letter was to Gertrude E. Hunt (b. 1859), wife of Thomas Henry Carew Hunt (b. 1850), solicitor at Paddington, London.

312 Dec: 27. (M). footnote 557: Adelaide Margaret Slater (b. 1869), daughter of Rev. Francis Slater (1837-1897), vicar of St. Giles, Cambridge. Probably Violet Du Croz – see *Diary 6*, n. *616*.

1881

322 Feb: 20. (Sun). footnote 572: spelling of "manuscript."

378 Nov: 19. (Sat). footnote 652: Henry S. Holland's brother was Lawrence Gifford Holland (b. 1850).

1882

451 July 11. (Tu). footnote 747: sixth line down should read 19-250ths (not 19-25ths).

463 Aug: 22. (Tu). Dodgson's enquiry about the "blue china" children was to Alice Baker (b. 1846) – not Bluett.

503 Dec: 28. (Th). footnote 821: Dodgson's printer in St. Aldates was Elizabeth Baxter (b. 1828).

1883

508 Jan: 8. (M). footnote 825: Dodgson probably met James L. Johnson (b. 1801), brother of Henry W. R. L. Johnson of Trinity College.

527 Ap: 4. (W). footnote 852: Rev. Robert William Hippisley (b. 1818), son-in-law to Dodgson's Aunt Elizabeth, who married Grace Louisa Raikes (d. 1892) on 10 June 1841.

541 May 30. (W). Dodgson was uncertain of the name; it was Washington, not Hutchinson. Rev. Henry Washington (1856-1912) married Marie Jane Louise née Spearman in 1882. The school was run by Jessie Hunt (b. 1857).

544 June 12. (Tu). footnote 878: William Capes was rector of Bramshott (not Bramscott).

557 Index Collingwood: Ann Jane (not Amy).

572 Index Gregory, C. S. (Rev.), 520 n.*844*.

575 Index Herman, Henry (not Hermon); Higginson, Thomas Wentworth, 427 n.*712*.

581 Index Replace Livingston, Henry Beckham with Livingstone, Robert George.

582 Index Lytton, Edward Bulwer (not Bulwar).

584 Index Mayhew: Jane Innes née Griffin - not Jane Junes (Mrs.).

585 Index Milman: replace Margaret A. with Frances Maria.

590 Index Plomer: replace Elizabeth with Helen.

592 Index Rigaud: replace Gibbes with John.

597 Index Streatley, Berkshire (not Oxfordshire); Strong, Fanny Louisa née Erskine (not Ersking).

Diary 8:

1883

41 Oct: 10. (W) delete full-stop after "bed."

1884

102 Ap: 29. (Tu). footnote 168: May's father was Rev. Udney J. T. Allen (b. 1824) – see above.

135 Aug: 11. (M). footnote 221: spelling of "identified."

1885

171 Mar: 10. (Tu). spelling of Somerville Hall.

231 Aug: 13. (Th). footnote 390: Kathleen Duggan (b. 1877) and her *brother* Joseph (b. 1875), living with an aunt at Edinburgh in 1881.

238 Sep: 16. (W). footnote 400: Ferio (in the last sentence of this page) should be described as – In other words, No X is Y, Some Z is X, therefore Some Z is not Y.

1888

267 Ap: 2. (F). footnote 449: Alfred Clementson (1838-1927) matriculated at Emanuel College, Cambridge in 1856: BA 1860, MA 1863, ordained deacon 1862, priest 1863, curate of Brocklesby, Lincolnshire 1862-64, curate of Hanley Castle 1864-65, curate of Ashburton, Canterbury, New Zealand 1865-66, curate of Graveley, Hertfordshire 1867-68, Dixie Fellow of Emanuel College 1867-79, curate of Effingham 1869-74, curate of St. Paul's Cray 1874-76, curate of Fetcham, Surrey 1876-79, and vicar of Lechlade, Gloucestershire 1879-1901.

404 June 23. (Sat). footnote 657: Eliza Jane Collingwood Wilson née Ribey (b. 1833) was a cousin of Charles Collingwood, not his sister.

405 June 29. (F). footnote 658: Caroline M. N. Jeune (b. 1880) was the daughter of Evan "Evie" Browell Jeune (b. 1852).

1889

489 Nov: 7. (Th). footnote 792: William H. Gee b. 1838) was a bookseller at 28 Amsterdam Court, off High Street, Oxford.

1890

531 Sep: 20. (Sat). Rev. Frederic Horatio Fisher (1837-1915), vicar and rural dean of Fulham 1871-1890.

1891

547 Jan: 14. (W). footnote 872: Not Curteis, but Rev. Henry George Constable Curtis (b. 1866), curate of Holy Trinity, Guildford 1890-1893.

552 Feb: 25. (W). footnote 878: Roland E. L. V. Williams matriculated in October 1886, not 1866.

572 Aug: 15. (Sat). Devonshire Park Illuminated Fête.

636 Index Atkinson, insert Dorothy Home, 97 n.*158*; Baddeley, Blanche, 58 n.*90* – delete final comma.

639 Index Bourchier, not Bouchier.

659 Index Gillmore, Frank, 426 n.*688*.

665 Index Jebb: insert John, Mr., 165, 166 n.*274*, after Jebb, Isabel – and delete these entries from Jebb, Mr. on next line.

668 Index Lytton, Lord Edward Bulwer.
669 Index Change Madjeska to Modjeska, Helena née Opid.
675 Index Price: spelling of Bartholomew.
679 Index Somerville Hall, not Someville.

Diary 9:

1894

120 Jan: 9. (Tu). Dodgson incorrectly writes Thursden when the name is Fursdon.

160 Aug: 24. (F). footnote 275: Dodgson contributed "What the Tortoise Said to Achilles" to the April 1895 issue of *Mind*.

162 Aug: 31. (F). footnote 277: There were two versions of *Robert Macaire* but this was the French drama adapted by Charles Selby (1802?-1863). Dodgson saw the London production at the Lyceum on 3 July 1888.

167 Sep: 8. (Sat). footnote 284: Some of the actors are now identified; Lizzie Watkins (b. 1873), Katharine L. Clarke (b. 1871), and Annie Esmond (b. 1874).

174 Oct: 6. (Sat). footnote 292: Muriel Midwinter's father was, possibly, Rev. Henry Nathaniel Midwinter (b. 1848), chaplain at Ahmednagar, India.

182 Nov: 6. (Tu). footnote 302: the Misses Edwardes (not as Dodgson spelt the name) were Ela G. (b. 1876), Avice {not Alice} K. (b. 1880), Ethel (b. 1882?), and Sybil (b. 1883). They were the daughters of Rev. Stephen Edwardes (1826-1886), formerly vicar of Wolvercote, and his wife, Ellen (b. 1850), living at Surrey Lodge, 42 Banbury Road, Oxford.

183 Nov: 24. (Sat). footnote 304: Frederic Drew's wife was Sara Constance (b. 1847), and their remaining two children were: Mabel (b. 1877) and Frederic Henry (b. 1880).

186 Dec: 27. (Th). footnote 307: one of the other guests was Mrs. Helen D. Forbes (b. 1855).

1895

188 Jan: 23. (W). footnote 311: Lt.-Col. Robert Hamilton Simpson (b. 1829) and his wife, Eliza J. M. (b. 1845), from Stoke, near Guildford. Their son was Capt. Arthur C. P. W. Simpson (b. 1874) and his wife was Kathleen (b. 1872). The wife of Mr. Curtis was Laura M. (b. 1863).

227 Nov: 13. (W). footnote 360: Emily Eliza Harrison (b. 1825) of Mickley, near Ripon.

1896

266	July 7. (Tu).	footnote 419: possibly Mary C. Impey (b. 1867) or Isabella M. Impey (b. 1865), both from India, living at Holywell, Oxford.
	1897	
295	Feb: 12. (F).	footnote 467: Emilie Catherine Ginsburg (b. 1869) married Halford John Mackinder (1861-1947), barrister.
299	Mar: 20. (Sat).	footnote 475: possibly Catherine Barbara Osborn née Marriott (b. 1832) – see *Diary 6*, n.*173*.
300	Mar: 26. (F).	footnote 476: Eliza Castle (b. 1840) was the lodging-house keeper in Banbury Road.
403	Index	Delete references to Sister Margaret.
404	Index	Delete reference to Taylor, F. H.
405	Index	Replace Thursden by Fursdon.
407	Index	Watson, Isy (not Izy).
408	Index	Replace Wilson, Mrs. with Wilson, Eliza Jane Collingwood née Ribey.

*****

LEWIS CARROLL'S DIARIES

THE PRIVATE JOURNALS OF

CHARLES LUTWIDGE DODGSON

(LEWIS CARROLL)

A reconstruction of the missing volumes

with notes and annotations

BY

EDWARD WAKELING

VOLUME A

Containing Journal 1
January 1851 to December 1854
and Journal 3
September 1855 to December 1855

2007

Introduction

The first journal notebook of Dodgson's diary, probably covering the period from January 1851 to December 1854, is missing, presumed destroyed. These four years cover Dodgson's undergraduate years at Christ Church. According to Stuart Dodgson Collingwood, in *The Life and Letters of Lewis Carroll* (1898), Dodgson did not keep a diary during his years at Rugby School. There is a slight possibility that the journal may date from an earlier period, or from 1850 when he spent a year at home preparing for his university entrance.

The third journal notebook is also missing. This must have been a very small volume since it only covers three months. However, they were significant months in Dodgson's life because they mark the term just prior to beginning his career as lecturer in mathematics at Christ Church. He was appointed to this post in August 1855, but the Dean and Chapter gave him the duration of the Michaelmas Term 1855 to prepare for this key role. Dodgson continued to work as a tutor alongside other colleagues, but the time was also used to prepare lecture notes and devise an appropriate syllabus for the undergraduates. In this Dodgson, without doubt, consulted his mathematical mentor, Professor Bartholomew Price, Sedleian Professor of Natural Philosophy, who was an examiner and moderator in mathematics for the University. Collingwood tells us (p. 59) that his "college work, during 1855, was chiefly taking private pupils, but he had, in addition, about three and a half hours a day of lecturing during the last term of the year. He did not, however, work as one of the regular staff of lecturers until the next year."

In this reconstruction I used as much primary source material as is now available. I used surviving Dodgson family letters and the references made by Collingwood, including some extant diary entries which he included in *The Life and Letters of Lewis Carroll*. Other documentary evidence came from the Christ Church Archive and the Dodgson Family Collection. Some material is interpolated from the *Times* newspaper for the period, particularly the section entitled "University Intelligence." I have also tracked down books acquired by Dodgson during this time, and some books that he gave

away as gifts. He had written very little by this time; his first publications being in the *Whitby Gazette* during the summer of 1854. The family magazines, especially *Mischmasch*, add a little to his literary works in progress.

Some of the text is taken directly from Dodgson's surviving correspondence, but much of it is entirely my own invention. I have tried to emulate Dodgson's writing style and the kind of entries he made in the surviving journals. I have tried to include topics that would have interested him, but I must warn readers that a large part of this reconstruction is based on educated guesswork.

I used various databases of information to assist my research including the following:

Foster's Alumni Oxonienses, The Members of the University of Oxford, 1715-1886, Archive CD Books, 2001
The Dictionary of National Biography, Oxford University Press, CD-Rom, 1997.
Who's Who, 1897-1996, A. & C. Black, Oxford CD-Rom, 1996.
The *Times Newspaper Archive*, available on the internet.
The *Census* data for 1851, some available on the internet.

The most significant event during these four years was the sudden and early death of his mother at the age of 47 years. This traumatic event in his life would certainly have been noted, but his own personal pain and anguish at the loss of his mother was probably not expressed in detailed diary entries. His private journal was principally a way of noting events in his life, people he met, and places he visited; it was not a vehicle for expressing his inner-most thoughts and ideas. Surviving journals are, to a large extent, matter-of-fact and dispassionate; more of an *aide-memoire* for the future. Subsequent notes added to the pages of the journals indicate that he used them for reference and as a way of reminding himself what had happened in the past.

I have written in detail about the causes of the disappearance of the four missing journals. I am still of the opinion that they were suppressed by family members, but for reasons concerning internal family matters rather than any other perceived sensitivity. With the passing of time, such concerns would probably seem trivial today,

but his siblings, nephews and nieces, who were entrusted with his literary legacy, clearly felt that some matters were best kept to themselves, and they adopted the role of censor with a number of key primary sources such as the four missing volumes of the diary, his massive letter register, and his photographic register, among other documents and papers. Some may have been destroyed in haste when Dodgson's rooms at Christ Church were cleared for the new incumbent. Some may have been mislaid during movement to new residences by members of the Dodgson family. But letters written by the trustees of the C. L. Dodgson Estate over the years indicate that some material was deemed for their eyes only. This has, of course, been counter-productive in the longer term, and much wild speculation has arisen from the key missing items.

I have used the same editorial conventions as in the other published volumes of Dodgson's diaries, expanding abbreviations in letters and manuscripts for ease of the reader. For photographs taken by Dodgson, I have included the image numbers assigned by him, which I have indicated with the prefix "IN."

A number of people have helped me in this reconstruction by providing me with relevant information. I am particularly grateful to Judith Curthoys, archivist at Christ Church, Michael Vine (for translating and expanding Dodgson's "Collections" report at Christ Church), David Annal of the Family Records Centre for Census data, and staff at the National Library of Wales for providing me with access to the *Times Newspaper Archive*. Brian Partridge has again provided the cover illustration focusing on his undergraduate activity. My sincere thanks go to Selwyn Goodacre for proof-reading the draft text. I am especially grateful to the Trustees of the C. L. Dodgson Estate, Elizabeth Mead and Caroline Luke, for allowing me to publish this reconstruction, and for providing me with extremely valuable research information and background material from the family archive.

Edward Wakeling

Short Titles and Locations

Berg	Henry W. & Albert A. Berg Collection, New York Public Library
Berol	Alfred C. Berol Collection, New York University Library
Christ Church	Christ Church Library & Archive, Oxford
Collingwood	*The Life and Letters of Lewis Carroll* by Stuart Dodgson Collingwood (T. Fisher Unwin: 1898)
Diary 1	*Lewis Carroll's Diaries: Volume 1* edited by Edward Wakeling (Lewis Carroll Society: 1993)
Diary 2	*Lewis Carroll's Diaries: Volume 2* edited by Edward Wakeling (Lewis Carroll Society: 1994)
DNB	Dictionary of National Biography edited by Leslie Stephen (Smith, Elder, & Company: 1885-1900), and the CD-Rom version 1997
Dodgson Family	The main archive is at the Surrey History Centre, Woking, although some papers are still with individual members of the Family
Handbook	*The Lewis Carroll Handbook* edited by Williams, Madan, Green and Crutch (Dawson: 1979)
Harvard	Houghton Library, Harvard University
Letters	*The Letters of Lewis Carroll* edited by Morton N. Cohen with the assistance of Roger Lancelyn Green (Macmillan: 1979)
Lovett	*Lewis Carroll Among His Books*, by Charlie Lovett (McFarland: 2005)

Morgan	Pierpont Morgan Library, New York
Princeton	The Morris L. Parrish Collection, Princeton University Library, New Jersey
Thompson	*Henry George Liddell, A Memoir* by Henry Lewis Thompson (John Murray: 1899)
Venn	*Alumni Cantabrigienses* by John Archibald Venn (Cambridge University Press)

Otherwise, titles and authors of books used as references are given in full.

The Private Journal of Charles Lutwidge Dodgson

JOURNAL NUMBER 1

Diary for the year 1851
January to December

Jan: 1. (W). At Croft.[1]

Jan: 2. (Th). I take up my place at Christ Church later this month so I am busy preparing for my undergraduate studies.[2]

---

1 The Dodgson family moved to the Rectory, Croft-on-Tees, Yorkshire, in 1843, from Daresbury, Cheshire. Dodgson's father was appointed rector to this Crown living, following the death of the previous incumbent, James Dalton (1764-1843). Dalton matriculated at Clare College, Cambridge, in 1783: BA 1787, ordained priest 1788, MA 1790, rector of Copgrove, Yorkshire 1789-1813, vicar of Catterick 1791-1805, and rector of Croft, Yorkshire 1804-43. He married Maria née Gibson, and they had eight children: Cecil Wray (1806-1888), John (d. 1854), Charles James (1812-1880), and five daughters.

2 Dodgson matriculated at Christ Church on 23 May 1850, but was unable to take up a place as an undergraduate until January 1851. He probably spent much of 1850 at the family home, the Rectory, Croft-on-Tees, preparing for university life. In this, he was, most likely, assisted in his studies by his father, Archdeacon Dodgson. Charles Dodgson (1800-1868) matriculated at Christ Church in 1818: Student 1818-28, BA 1821, MA 1824, Perpetual Curate of Daresbury 1827-43, Examining chaplain to Charles Thomas Longley, Bishop of Ripon 1836-56, Rector of Croft 1843-68, Residentiary Canon of Ripon 1852-68, and Archdeacon of Richmond 1854-68.

Jan: 24. (F). Travelled from Croft to Oxford by train to take up residence at Christ Church. There is still no college room for me, so I am staying with Dr. Ley. He has kindly offered me a room.[3] I begin my studies on Monday.

Jan: 25. (Sat). I went to St. Mary's to hear Stanley preach. His sermon, which was well delivered, celebrated the festival of the conversion of St. Paul.[4]

---

3 Jacob Ley (1803-1881) matriculated at St. Alban Hall in 1822: migrated to Christ Church, BA 1826, MA 1828, ordained 1827, tutor, censor, catechist, librarian, proctor 1839, BD 1840, vicar of St. Mary Magdalen, Oxford 1845-58, and vicar of Staverton, Northamptonshire 1858-81. In his role as tutor, he had rooms at Christ Church in Tom Quad. As an undergraduate, he was probably tutored by Charles Dodgson senior. In any event, they knew each other sufficiently well for Ley to offer his spare room to the new undergraduate, Dodgson junior.

4 Arthur Penrhyn Stanley (1815-1881) matriculated at Balliol in 1833: scholar 1833-38, BA 1838, fellow of University College 1838-51, MA 1840, bursar 1843, tutor 1843-51, select preacher 1845 and 1872, dean 1848, canon of Canterbury 1851-58, chaplain to the Prince Consort 1854-61, Regius professor of ecclesiastical history and canon of Christ Church 1856-64, B & DD 1858, hon. fellow of University College 1864-81, and dean of Westminster 1864-81. Stanley made a name for himself preaching a number of radical sermons at Oxford in the late 1840s. He was closely associated with the forward-thinking group which also included Benjamin Jowett (see n. *181*) and Benjamin Brodie (see n. *35*), later to become the agitators for Oxford reform. He was appointed the secretary of the Royal Commission of Enquiry into the state of education at Oxford and Cambridge in 1851. Dodgson photographed him in July 1860 (IN597).

Jan: 26. (Sun). News from home that it pleased God to take to himself my dear Mother. I returned to Croft immediately to be with my family.[5]

Jan: 27. (M). My 19th birthday – one of the saddest I have ever experienced.

Jan: 28. (Tu). Cousin Menella Smedley arrived. She will help look after the family.[6]

---

5 Frances Jane Dodgson née Lutwidge (1803-1851), married Charles Dodgson, her first cousin, on 5 April 1827 at Christ Church, Hull. They had eleven children: Frances Jane (1828-1903), Elizabeth Lucy (1830-1916), Charles Lutwidge "Lewis Carroll" (1832-1898), Caroline Hume (1833-1904), Mary Charlotte (1835-1911), Skeffington Hume (1836-1919), Wilfred Longley (1838-1914), Louisa Fletcher (1840-1930), Margaret Anne Ashley (1841-1915), Henrietta Harington (1843-1922), and Edwin Heron (1846-1918). Her death, at the early age of 47 years, was recorded on the death certificate as "inflammation of the brain," a generalised statement leaving the actual medical cause uncertain. She was buried in Croft churchyard, near to the north wall of the church. The gravestone reads: "Sacred to the memory of Frances Jane the Beloved Wife of the Revd Charles Dodgson, rector of this Parish, who died January 26th, 1851. Aged 47." Dodgson's father received letters of condolence, including two from fellow graduates at Christ Church, Dr. Edward Bouverie Pusey (see n. *32*), dated 13 January 1851 (MS: Dodgson Family), and Charles Thomas Longley (1794-1868), Bishop of Ripon, dated 26 January 1851 (MS: Dodgson Family).

6 Menella Bute Smedley (1819-1877) was, in fact, the Archdeacon's cousin, daughter of his aunt Mary Smedley née Hume (1786-1868). On 13 February 1851, the Archdeacon received a letter from his Aunt Mary in which she wrote (MS: Dodgson Family):

Jan: 29. (W). The *Times* announces the death of our dear Mother.[7]

Feb: 2. (Sun). Aunt Lucy Lutwidge arrived. She, too, has offered to assist in looking after the family.[8]

What a crowning blessing to all your comforts is the recollection of the happy *happy* life of our sainted Fanny. I do not think I ever heard of anyone so highly favoured – as daughter – wife and mother – and few surely have ever passed into Glory knowing so little of earthly stain or sorrow. The last walk we took together she spoke to me of her rare and exceeding happiness. She told me that she was very happy at Daresbury but that while you took pupils there was always a drawback and she used to be continually picturing such a life as she led at Croft as the perfection of earthly happiness – and she said that sometimes when remembering this it was almost startling to find how exactly her wishes had been fulfilled and that for seven (I think) years she had been living precisely the life that she had most delighted to dwell upon in fancy, and then she spoke most touchingly and beautifully of the responsibility incurred by a lot of so much happiness – and that it really at times was "alarming" to look round her and feel that she had not a wish unfulfilled – I could have said "nor a duty also" but I felt that she was above my praise....

[7] The *Times* (29 January 1851), in the list of "Deaths" reported: " On the 26th inst., Frances Jane, the wife of the Rev. Charles Dodgson, rector of Croft, Yorkshire." The funeral probably took place a few days later. As was customary in these times, only the men attended the funeral; the women remained at home with the younger children.

[8] Frances Jane Dodgson's unmarried sister, Lucy Lutwidge (1805-1880) came to assist in looking after the family and the Dodgson household, devoting the rest of her life to the care of her nephews and nieces, and her brother-in-law.

Feb: 3. (M). My Father gave me my dear Mother's set of Lord Byron's works, in her memory.[9]

Feb: 10. (M). I return to Christ Church to begin my studies.[10]

Feb: 11. (Tu). Hall is divided up into "messes."[11] Among those in my mess are Cherry,[12] Hampden (was with me at Rugby),[13]

---

9 *The Works of Lord Byron*, in 6 volumes (1827), inscribed: "Presented to Charles Lutwidge Dodgson, in memory of his deceased Mother, to whom it had belonged, by his affectionate father, Charles Dodgson, Feb. 3, 1851."

10 Dodgson studied Classics (Latin and Greek Language and Literature), Theology, and Mathematics. For his finals, he took examinations in Classics (Summer 1854) and Mathematics (Autumn 1854).

11 According to Collingwood (p. 47) each mess consisted of about half a dozen men who had a table to themselves. The dishes and plates were of pewter, and the joint was passed round, each man cutting off what he wanted for himself.

12 Apsley Cherry (1832-1907) matriculated at Christ Church on 23 May 1850 (same day as Dodgson): BA 1854, commissioned in the 90th Regiment, Crimean War 1855, served in Indian Mutiny, campaign in Oudh 1857-59, South African War 1877-79, Kaffir campaign, Zulu campaign 1880, Maj.-Gen. 1887, JP for Hertfordshire and Berkshire, High Sheriff 1901. He assumed the additional name Garrard in 1892. He married Evelyn née Sharpin in 1885, and they lived at Lamer Park, Wheathampstead, Hertfordshire. They had one son and five daughters.

13 Charles John Hampden (1832-1888), son of the Bishop of Hereford, entered Rugby school in February 1846, the same term as

Pusey[14] and Woodhouse.[15] We dine at 5 each evening.

Dodgson. He matriculated at Christ Church on 23 May 1850 (same day as Dodgson): student 1850-69, BA 1855, MA 1858, barrister-at-law Lincoln's Inn 1863, and practised in the Oxford Circuit. However, all did not go well for Hampden at Christ Church. The Dean and Chapter Books (MS: Christ Church) for 20 October 1855 reported that: "Hampden, Student of this House, having on the 20 May 1853 having been summoned *punio vice* before the Dean and Chapter for gross misconduct when he did not appear as directed and having now absented himself from College from Saturday night last till Monday at noon without being able to give any satisfactory account of himself and having been convicted of divers low and irregular habits notwithstanding his express promise in a letter dated June 13. 1853 to conform for the future in all things to the 'rules of discipline and good conduct generally' is hereby admonished for a second time with a view to expulsion in case of a third offence – and also that he be rusticated for one year and that he be put off for his degree for one year and be deposed twelve places in the Student List." Despite his rustication, Hampden completed his degree in 1855, and maintained his studentship, which is unusual under the circumstances since "gross misconduct" normally meant that the studentship was forfeited. Possibly his parentage helped in his case.

[14] Philip Edward Pusey (1830-1880) matriculated at Christ Church in 1850: second class in mathematical moderations 1852, second class in mathematics finals, BA 1854, MA 1857. He was deaf and had other physical problems that prevented his ordination. He spent his life in theological study and assisting his father, Dr. Edward Bouverie Pusey. He joined Dodgson during the summer of 1854 in Professor Price's mathematical reading party at Whitby.

[15] George Girdlestone Woodhouse (1831-1897) matriculated at Christ Church in 1850: BA 1854, perpetual curate of Upper Gornal, Staffordshire 1861-67, and later a school proprietor in Devon. He married Emmeline née Benson (1838-1921), and they had five children: Mary "Mamie" (b. 1859), George E. (b. 1867),

Feb: 13. (Th). As Mr. Faussett is ill, his lectures have been postponed until his recovery.[16]

Feb: 14. (F). Colley came to tea.[17]

Ruth Martin (1870?-1897), Lawrence (b. 1874), and Emmeline Dorothea "Dolly" (b. 1876). Dodgson shared rooms with Woodhouse from April 1852 until December 1853, and composed "The Ligniad" for him in 1853 (see below). On 2 August 1897, Dodgson wrote to Woodhouse's widow: "Of all the friends I made at Christ Church, your husband was the very first who spoke to me – across the dinner-table in Hall" (see *Letters*, p. 1133).

[16] Dodgson's mathematical tutor and lecturer at Christ Church was Robert Godfrey Faussett (1827-1908). He matriculated at Christ Church in 1845: student 1845, BA 1849, MA 1852, mathematical lecturer 1850-55, ordained deacon 1858, priest 1859, curate of Halfway-street, Bexley 1858-62, mathematics moderator 1860-61, curate of Fretherne, Gloucestershire 1862-64, public examiner in mathematics 1864-65, steward 1865, curate of Begbroke, Oxfordshire 1867-69, treasurer of Christ Church, 1868-1886, and vicar of Cassington, Oxfordshire from 1875. After Dodgson's graduation, Faussett became his close friend and lifelong adviser. They met frequently and made joint excursions to London, enjoying a common interest in the theatre and other arts. Dodgson photographed Faussett in June 1857 (IN199). Faussett married Ellen Anne née Wethered (1847-1900) in 1869 and they had two children: Fermor (1870-1900) and Mary (b. 1873).

[17] Richard Henry Colley (1832-1902), of St. James' Priory, Bridgnorth, Shropshire, matriculated at Christ Church in December 1850: BA 1855, MA 1859. There is a possibility that Dodgson visited Colley at his family home in Shropshire. He noted that he went to Albrighton, Shropshire (about 10 miles from Bridgnorth) in a later diary entry (see *Diary 2*, p. 12). He wrote, commenting on the song "Call the Cattle Home," that "I remember hearing it sung at Albrighton." The visit to Albrighton (there are in fact two places with this name in Shropshire, the other just north of Shrewsbury)

Feb: 21. (F). Walked with Colley, followed by tea in my rooms.

Feb: 25. (Tu). Dr. Jacobson announced that he is giving lectures on the Book of Common Prayer. I think that it will be worthwhile my attending them.[18]

Feb: 28. (F). I record a very sad incident, namely my missing morning chapel. For some days now I have been in the habit of being called at ¼ past 6, and generally managing to be down soon after 7. In the present instance I had been up the night before till about ½ past 12, and consequently when I was called I fell asleep again, and was thunderstruck to find on waking that it was 10 minutes past 8. I have had no imposition, nor heard anything about it. It is rather vexatious to

---

must have taken place before 1855. Dodgson photographed Colley, probably in 1859, but no copy has survived. Dodgson's list of photographs (1860) included: "Colley, R. H., Esq., B.A., Ch. Ch."

[18] William Jacobson (1804-1884), matriculated at St. Edmund Hall in 1823: scholar Lincoln College 1825-27, BA 1827, fellow Exeter College 1829-36, MA 1829, librarian 1830, vice principal Magdalen Hall 1832-48, select preacher 1833, master of the schools 1834-35, perpetual curate Iffley 1839-40, public orator 1842-48, DD by decree 15 April 1848, canon of Christ Church 1848-65, Regius professor of divinity 1848-65, bishop of Chester 1865, hon. fellow Hertford College 1874-84, and hon. fellow Exeter 1882-84. Dodgson photographed him in June 1857 (IN239).

have happened so soon, as I had intended never to be late.[19]

Mar: 4. (Tu). I borrowed Coxe's *Christian Ballads*, thinking I might like to get a copy: however I found so many things in it I did not like, and so few I did, that I decided on not buying the book. As some of the ballads are sold separate I got the two I like best.[20]

Mar: 5. (W). Mr. Faussett being well again, lectures resumed.[21]

Mar: 6. (Th). A cold and wretched day. Colley and I went to the justice court, to hear the trials conducted, as the assizes began on

---

19 This entry is taken from Dodgson's letter to his sister, Mary, dated 6 March 1851 (see *Letters*, p. 13). Attendance at Chapel (in the Cathedral) was compulsory, and the most recently appointed Students checked off the names of the undergraduates from lists (see details of "prick bills" below). Impositions, such as writing out lines of Greek text, were given to offenders. The fact that Dodgson was a new undergraduate probably saved him; the Students did not recognise him, and they were probably unsure if he had attended.

20 *Christian Ballads, and Poems* (1840) by Arthur Cleveland Coxe (1818-1896), Bishop of Western New York, reprinted many times in both the United States and the United Kingdom. This diary entry is taken from Dodgson's letter to his sister, Mary, dated 6 March 1851 (see *Letters*, p. 12).

21 This diary entry is taken from Dodgson's letter to his sister, Mary, dated 6 March 1851 (see *Letters*, p. 14).

Monday, only to find that the assizes concluded yesterday, and the judges left Oxford last night. In afternoon, heard a sudden shrieking of dogs, as if fighting, but the fight, if any, was quickly over, having lasted for about the space of 3 seconds. Six dogs went headlong down the steps, which lead into the quad; six sticks came flying after them, and after that came their six masters, all running their hardest, and all in different directions. Eventually 3 dogs got away and ran straight home, 2 others were hunted up and down the quad by their masters, I suppose with the intention of beating them, but were never sufficiently caught for that purpose, and the sixth went home with its master.[22]

---

22 The undergraduates at Christ Church consisted of three distinct classes; the noblemen (who wore a gold tassle on their mortar-boards), the commoners (who wore a black tassle), and the servitors. For the noblemen, Christ Church was an extension of their comfortable life-styles at their country estates; riding, hunting, gaming, drinking, with a little study and much sport and entertainment. Some of the noblemen kept dogs. There is a sense that the Dean, Thomas Gaisford (1779-1855), turned a blind eye to the behaviour of the noblemen, accepting the lucrative payments for their residence at Christ Church. The academic set came from the gentlemen commoners; drawn from the church, army, and the medical and legal professions. Dodgson was a member of this group. The servitors were usually intelligent men from poorer backgrounds who were sponsored at attend university and often paid their way by working at menial tasks within Christ Church. The three classes of undergraduates rarely intermingled. Dogs had

Wrote to M.C.; it is her birthday on Monday.[23] She should get the letter tomorrow, and I hope she will keep it till Monday to open when her health is drunk.

I discovered a curious and far from satisfactory circumstance, namely that I have left all my silk neck handkerchiefs at home. The only things of the kind I possess here are the handkerchief I now have on, and a black satin tie for the evening. I have asked M.C. to hunt them up at Croft and send them.[24]

---

become a feature of Christ Church at this time. The Dean's verger, Keys, is remembered for his determination to keep the dogs out of morning chapel as they followed their masters. He stationed himself at the entrance to the choir and used a stout dog-whip to keep the dogs at bay (Thompson, p. 149). This diary entry is taken from Dodgson's letter to his sister, Mary, dated 6 March 1851 (see *Letters*, pp. 13-14).

[23] This was Dodgson's sister, Mary Charlotte Dodgson. She married Charles Edward Stuart Collingwood (1831-1898) on 13 April 1869 at Guildford. They had three children: Stuart Dodgson (1870-1937) teacher and Dodgson's first biographer, Bertram James (1871-1934) doctor, and Agnes Mary (b. 1875, died aged 7 weeks). Mary published a number of religious works during the last years of her life, including *Lord, I Believe, Simple Meditations on the Apostles Creed* (1899), *The Touch of Jesus* (1901), *"The Prince of Peace"* (1903), *Lift up your Hearts* (1910), and *Joy Bells For God's Children* (not dated).

[24] This diary entry is taken from Dodgson's letter to his sister, Mary, dated 6 March 1851 (see *Letters*, pp. 12-15).

Mar: 30 (Sun). Census Day.[25]

Ap: 11. (F). Collections. Faussett's account of my progress this term is encouraging.[26]

Ap: 12. (Sat). End of Lent Term. I went home directly by train instead of travelling viâ London to visit Uncle Skeffington as I had

---

[25] The 1851 Census of the United Kingdom was the first to include relationships and places of birth. Dodgson's name is spelt incorrectly (as "Dodson") in the Census returns. He is listed as an undergraduate of "Christ Church College" {*sic*}, unmarried, aged 19, and born at Daresbury, Cheshire.

[26] "Collections" were oral tests on books read during the term, and also included the end of term reports given by the tutors. A record of Dodgson's achievements during his undergraduate years (1851 to 1853, but not 1854, his final year) are in the Christ Church Archives. They indicated that, during his first term, his study of Sophocles' *Antigone* and *Trachiniæ* was graded *satis bene* (acceptably good); his work on Horace's *Epodes & Ars Poetica* was *bene* (good); his Greek or Latin prose composition and grammar was *satis* (acceptable); and his Mathematics was listed as *valde bene* (very good). The report also indicated a grade for "Tr," which probably stands for "translation," in which he was graded *satis*. The lesser known text, Sophocles' *Trachiniæ* (the women of Trachis), is mainly about the justification of divine retribution, Hercules being one of the principal figures in the tragedy. *Antigone* tells the story of the King of Thebes' daughter. Horace's *Epodes* consists of 17 poems on various subjects, some constitute invective, others are about love or politics. His *Ars Poetica* is actually one of Horace's *Epistles*, but seems to have been separated from the others. It concerns literary study and style. {I am grateful to Michael Vine for supplying these explanatory notes.}

initially planned.[27] The holidays are too short to spare much time for meandering. Instead, I took the train to Bletchley, and hence to Croft.[28]

Ap: 20. (Sun). Easter Sunday.

Ap: 29. (Tu). Returned to Oxford.

Ap: 30. (W). I begin the Easter and Act Term in new rooms. I have been allocated Room 8 on staircase 4 in Peckwater Quadrangle, overlooking the New Library. The room is small and is situated on the top floor.[29]

---

27 Robert Wilfred Skeffington Lutwidge (1802-1873), Dodgson's maternal Uncle Skeffington, matriculated at St. John's College, Cambridge in 1820: scholar 1820, barrister-at-law Lincoln's Inn 1822, BA (18th Wrangler) 1824, MA 1827, called to the Bar 1827, Commissioner in Lunacy 1842-5 and 1855-73, Secretary to the Lunacy Commissioners 1845, and Commissioner of Inquiry into the state of lunatic asylums in Ireland 1856.

28 This diary entry is taken from Dodgson's letter to his sister, Mary, dated 6 March 1851 (see *Letters*, p. 14). The Oxford and Bletchley Junction Railway had just been laid, and was not officially opened until 20 May 1851. However, Dodgson could have taken a train from Banbury Road (Oxford) to Bletchley since this was opened on 2 December 1850. This new branch railway-line linked Oxford with the London and North Western Railway (LNWR), taking passengers to Birmingham and hence to the North of England.

29 Most of the rooms in Peckwater Quad were occupied by noblemen, the walls lined with panelling to remind them of home. The top floor, known as the "garrets," were used by commoners.

My Father recommends getting a name-plate made by the Ch. Ch. carpenter. Now that I am unable to borrow Ley's copy of *Horatius Zeunii* I have purchased *Quintus Horatius Flaccus* for my studies in Greek History.[30]

May: 1. (Th). Submitted my name to the Junior Proctor for Responsions later this term.[31]

May 13. (Tu). Convocation. It was announced that a new museum of science is to be constructed possibly on a site in the Parks, near Wadham. A more central situation was felt to be too expensive and too extravagant.

---

[30] Johann Carl Zeune (1736-1788) was an editor of the works of Horace. Dodgson's library contained two copies of *Quintus Horatius Flaccus* (1820) in the *Pickering Diamond Classics* series; one copy is now in the Jon Lindseth Collection.

[31] Responsions were elementary examinations in Greek, Latin, Logic and Geometry which had to be passed by undergraduates before their degree, usually taken in the second year. Dodgson clearly took them sooner, and passed without much difficulty. In 1849 the rules for Responsions were revised and the standards raised. In 1850, a new examination called Moderations was introduced, to be taken between Responsions and Finals. Dodgson took his Moderations at the end of Michaelmas Term in 1852. He took his Finals in two parts; Classics at the end of Trinity Term in 1854, and Mathematics at the end of Michaelmas Term in 1854.

May 19: (M). Boat races commence, and continue until Friday 30 May.

June 16. (M). Responsions. I am fully occupied with work at the moment.[32]

June 19. (Th). A proposal to Convocation to build a new University Museum, and to put aside £30,000 for the site (not yet decided) and for the building, was defeated among much cheering. Dr. Pusey spoke against the scheme, urging that the money would be better spent on extending admission to the University to a larger class of students.[33]

---

[32] This diary entry is taken from Dodgson's letter to his sister, Louisa, dated 10 June 1851 (see *Letters*, p. 15).

[33] Edward Bouverie Pusey (1800-1882) matriculated at Christ Church in 1819: BA 1822, fellow at Oriel College 1823-29, MA 1825, canon of Christ Church and Regius professor of Hebrew 1828-82, BD 1832, DD 1836, and member of the council of Keble College 1871-80. He was a contemporary of Dodgson's father, and a close friend. He nominated Dodgson for a studentship at Christ Church in 1852 – see below. Pusey came into contact with Keble and Newman while a fellow at Oriel, from which grew a friendship and a religious movement aimed at stemming rationalism in the Church of England. His high Anglican views were not universally accepted, challenging others such as Maurice and Jowett who promoted a Broad Church. Pusey later sought union between the English and Roman churches. Dodgson's father supported Pusey's religious views, but Dodgson was more aligned to the Broad Church. Pusey married Maria Catherine née Raymond-Barker (d. 1839) in 1828. They had four children: a daughter (died aged 14),

June 30. (M). Collections. I have been studying hard for the past few weeks.[34]

July 2. (W). The *Times* announces the incident which happened at Christ Church recently, namely a drunken frolic by some members of the House in which one was shot and severely wounded. The Censors are investigating the matter.[35]

Philip Edward (see n. *14* above), Lucy (dates unknown), and Mary Amelia (1833-1910) who married James G. Brine in 1854.

34 Again, Dodgson did well in "Collections." His end of Trinity Term report (written by his Christ Church tutors) revealed continuing success. In his study of Æschylus' *Prometheus Vinctus*, *Supplices*, *Choephori*, and *Seven against Thebes* he was graded *haud male* (not at all bad); Juvenal *Satires, i-xi* he was *satis* (acceptable); Greek or Latin prose composition and grammar – *haud male*; translation – *bene* (good); and for Theology he scored *valde bene* (very good).

35 A letter to the *Times* dated 30 June 1851 gives details of the incident, stating: "a Gentleman Commoner of Christ Church, Oxford, was shot at and severely wounded whilst engaged with other members of the University in a drunken frolic, endeavouring to injure the property of an unoffending individual from not approving of the taste shown in the decoration of his house." The *Times* reported on 2 July that "We are glad to learn that Mr. Ross of Christ Church, who was wounded a few days ago…is going on favourably. It is understood that Sir. B. Brodie will pay him a visit tomorrow." The injured man was Alexander Henry Ross (b. 1830) who matriculated at Christ Church in 1847: BA 1851, MA 1865, barrister-at-law, Inner Temple 1854, and MP for Maidstone 1880.

July 3. (Th). Commemoration. The Sheldonian Theatre was full to capacity, with many ladies in the galleries. The men were very vociferous, cheering and hissing at every opportunity. The Bishop of Argyle, the Solicitor-General, and Sir Benjamin Brodie were among those receiving an honorary D.C.L.[36] In the afternoon, I left for London, staying at the Trafalgar Hotel, Spring Gardens.

July 4. (F). Went with Aunt Charlotte to the Exhibition. We were joined later by

---

[36] The events of the previous day were reported in the *Times* (4 July 1851):

> The commemoration of founders was holden today in the theatre in the usual manner. The demonstrations of applause and dissent were more than usually noisy and proved the interest taken in the proceedings by the undergraduates. The weather was propitious for the occasion, and the theatre seldom presented a more splendid array of beauty and fashion. Last year the honorary degrees were principally conferred on military heroes; this year, the recipients were bishops, missionaries, lawyers, and statesmen. The national anthem was received by a spontaneous burst of applause on the part of the undergraduates….

The honorary Doctors of Civil Law were the Right Rev. Alexander Ewing (1814-1873), DD, Bishop of Argyle and the Isles; Sir William Page Wood (1801-1881), FRS, Her Majesty's Solicitor-General, MP for the city of Oxford; Sir Benjamin Collins Brodie (1817-1880), FRS, eminent surgeon to Queen Victoria, and President of the Royal Society; Lieut.-Col. Francis Rawdon Chesney (1789-1872), Royal Artillery, surveyor of trade routes around the world; and the Ven. William Williams (1800-1879), BA Magdalen Hall, Archdeacon of Waiapu, New Zealand.

Aunts Henrietta and Margaret Lutwidge and Elizabeth Raikes. The building was within 10 minutes walk of Alfred Place, by means of some curious little short cuts through stable yards, etc.[37] On entering the exhibition building, the first impression is one of bewilderment – it looks like a sort of fairyland. As far as you can look in any direction, you see nothing but pillars hung about with shawls, carpets, etc., with long avenues of statues, fountains, canopies, etc., etc. The centre of the nave mostly consists of a long line of colossal statues, some most magnificent. A pair of statues of a dog and child struck me as being exceedingly good. There is an enormous one of Godfrey of Bouillon, with a horse a great deal larger than an elephant.[38]

Dined at the Stones. Then to a music party at the Watsons.[39]

---

[37] The Great Exhibition opened on 1 May 1851. Dodgson's Uncle Skeffington Lutwidge lived in Alfred Place, South Kensington. Dodgson's maternal Lutwidge aunts were Charlotte Menella (1807-1857), Margaret Anne (1809-1869), and Elizabeth Frances (1799-1883) who married Thomas Raikes (1790-1866) in 1825.

[38] Godfrey of Bouillon (c. 1060-1100), son of Count Eustace of Boulogne, a leader in the First Crusade and the first ruler in Jerusalem. He was known as a quiet, pious, hard-fighting knight.

[39] The Stones and the Watsons, probably friends of Uncle Skeffington, are not identified. This diary entry is taken from

July 5. (Sat). To the Royal Academy, and later to the Egyptian Hall with Aunt Charlotte to see "The Diorama of Jerusalem."[40]

July 7. (M). Went to a music party at the Campbells.[41]

July 8. (Tu). Spent day at Tunbridge Wells to visit Aunt Louisa at Shandon.[42]

Dodgson's letter to his sister, Elizabeth, dated 5 July 1851 (see *Letters*, pp. 17-19).

40 "The Diorama of the Holy Land" was a popular London attraction that conveyed the spectator through reconstructed scenes of Biblical places such as the route of the Israelites, the land of Goshen, Mount Sinai, the Dead Sea, and Jerusalem. This diary entry is taken from Dodgson's letter to his sister, Elizabeth, dated 5 July 1851 (see *Letters*, p. 19).

41 The Campbells are not identified. This diary entry is taken from Dodgson's letter to his sister, Elizabeth, dated 5 July 1851 (see *Letters*, p. 18).

42 Dodgson's uncle Charles Henry Lutwidge (1800-1843) died on 15 January 1843, aged 42, at Hastings. Anne Louisa née Raikes (1797-1877) was his widow living at Shandon, Tunbridge Wells. Charles H. Lutwidge matriculated at St. John's College, Oxford, in 1819: scholar 1820, curate of St. Mary-the-Less, Cambridge, vicar of Othery, Somerset 1824-31, curate of St. Paul's, Huddersfield 1831-33, vicar of Burton Agnes, York 1833-39, and rector of East Farleigh, Kent 1840-43. They had two children: Charles Robert Fletcher (1835-1907) known as Fletcher, and Caroline Louisa (1837-1877). This diary entry is taken from Dodgson's letter to his sister, Elizabeth, dated 5 July 1851 (see *Letters*, p. 18).

July 9. (F). Attended Mr. Brinley Richards' concert in the morning.[43] He is certainly a very able pianist.

July 10. (Th). Went on a visit to Gordon Square at the invitation of the Raikes. Saw Uncle Thomas and Aunt Elizabeth (I met them at the Exhibition last Friday) and a host of cousins.[44]

July 14. (M). Escorted cousin Lizzie Raikes by train to Hastings. We were both on a visit to our Aunts Henrietta and Margaret Lutwidge.

---

[43] Henry Brinley Richards (1819-1885), concert pianist, gave a performance of classical and modern music at the Queen Anne Street Rooms. He was a professor at the Royal Academy of Music and his most famous composition was "God Bless the Prince of Wales" (1862). This diary entry is taken from Dodgson's letter to his sister, Elizabeth, dated 5 July 1851 (see *Letters*, p. 18).

[44] Thomas Raikes had four children from his first marriage to Elizabeth née Armstrong (d. 1824): Robert (1818-1901) of Treberfydd, near Bwlch, Breconshire who married Frances née Taunton in 1841, Thomas (1823-1880) who was in the Indian Army, later Colonel in the Madras Fusiliers and Major-General, Grace Louisa (d. 1892) who married Rev. Robert Hippisley in 1841, and Anne (d. 1864) who married T. A. F. Reynolds. Thomas Raikes' marriage to Elizabeth Frances née Lutwidge produced three children: Charles (1828-1876) who married Mary Frances Bateman in 1868, Frederick (died young), and Elizabeth "Lizzie" Lucy (1832-1888) who married James Frederick Lowthorpe (b. 1829) in 1855. This diary entry is taken from Dodgson's letter to his sister, Elizabeth, dated 5 July 1851 (see *Letters*, p. 18).

They live at 2 Wellington Square where I remained for a few days.[45]

July 16. (W). Left Hastings for Croft.

Aug: 25. (M). There has not been much to report during the summer. My time has been spent mainly in reading and studying. For the entertainment of the family, I have devised more issues of *The Rectory Umbrella*, our seventh magazine.[46]

Oct: 9. (Th). Croft to Oxford.

Oct: 10. (F). Michaelmas Term begins.

---

[45] Henrietta Mary Lutwidge (1811-1872) was another maternal aunt. This diary entry is taken from Dodgson's letter to his sister, Elizabeth, dated 5 July 1851 (see *Letters*, p. 18).

[46] Dodgson's own account of the genesis of *The Rectory Umbrella* is given in the introduction to *Mischmasch*, where he gives a history of the various family magazines. He wrote: "This we started, we believe, in 1849 or 1850, in a ready-bound square volume. It was admired at the time, but wholly unsupported, and it took us a year or more to fill the volume by our own unaided efforts." Hence, we can assume that Dodgson was still contributing to this in 1851, and the summer holiday, away from the pressures of life at Christ Church, would have been more conducive to such creative activity. The manuscript comprised of six issues written and illustrated by Dodgson. He contemplated publishing it in facsimile in 1885, suggesting that he regarded it as having some literary merit. It was, however, first published by Cassell and Company Ltd., London, in 1932, edited by Florence Milner. The manuscript is in the Harcourt Amory Collection at Harvard.

Oct: 27. (M). M. Bué, Taylorian teacher of French, began his lectures for the term.[47]

Nov: 1. (Sat). The Dean and Chapter have awarded me the Boulter Scholarship.[48]

Nov: 5. (W). In the evening a large bonfire was lit in the middle of Peckwater Quad. I am

---

[47] Dodgson does not appear to have studied French before entering Christ Church. There is a strong possibility that he attended these lectures. Within a few years, he was sufficiently proficient in the language to be able to write in French, and to oversee the translation of *Alice's Adventures in Wonderland* which was published in 1869. He also conversed in French when he travelled to France in 1867. These lectures, open to all members of the University, were given by Jules Thomas Théodore Bué (b. 1817), Taylorian teacher of French from 1847. He was born at La Rochelle, of Huguenot stock, and was a teacher in the Bordeaux region before settling in England. He was attached to Magdalen College, and later created MA in November 1865. He married twice. The son of his first marriage, Georges Henri Bué (1843-1929), was commissioned by Dodgson to translate *Alice* into French. In fact both father and son worked on the translation (see Dodgson's letter to Macmillan dated 17 April 1867).

[48] Dodgson's good progress, indicated by his "Collections," was sufficient for the Dean and Canons to give him encouragement by awarding him the Boulter Scholarship worth £20 a year, held for two years. The scholarship, or exhibition as it was known, was founded by Hugh Boulter (1672-1742), Dean of Christ Church 1719-24, who left large sums to charity. Dodgson's award is not recorded in the Dean and Chapter books at Christ Church.

beginning to realise that my rooms here are not conducive to serious work.[49]

Nov: 22 (Sat). Read out the declamation in Hall. I chose as my theme *Formosa facies muta commendatio est.*[50]

Dec: 18. (F). Collections. At the end of my first undergraduate year at Ch. Ch., I have made some progress, but I must not be complacent, and should continue to study hard to maintain this position.[51]

---

49 The bonfire was on account of Guy Fawkes' Night, held annually on 5 November to celebrate the defeat of the gunpowder plot in 1605.

50 Each Saturday during term, a declamation in Latin or Greek was read out to the assembled body of the College. On this occasion, it was Dodgson's turn to read the paper he had written. The quotation he chose is attributed to Publilius Syrus and translates as "A beautiful face is a silent recommendation." Dodgson added at the end of his manuscript (MS: Morgan) "Read out in Hall, November 22, 1851." The full translation is reproduced in Morton Cohen's *Lewis Carroll, A Biography* (1995, pp. 535-536).

51 Dodgson's "Collections" report for the Michaelmas Term indicated that in Demosthenes' *De Corona* he was graded *satis bene* (acceptably good), in Lucretius' *De Rerum Natura, i-iii*, he was graded *bene* (good), in mathematics he scored *valde bene* (very good), in theology *bene*, in Latin translation *bene* +, and in Latin prose *bene*. *De Corona* (On the Crown) was Demosthenes' speech in defence of his actions during the conquest of Greece by Alexander the Great. Demosthenes helped Thebes revolt against Alexander in 335 BC, and looked possibly towards Persia to save Athens from Alexander, but after Gaugamela, Athens was isolated,

Dec: 19. (Sat). Term ends.

Dec: 21. (M). Oxford to Croft.

Dec: 25. (F). My Father gave me a copy of his Trinity Sunday Sermon, preached at Ripon, recently published at the request of the Bishop of Ripon, and of the clergy present.[52]

Dec: 31. (Th). At the end of the year of 1851, and at the end of my first year at Christ Church, I record some progress made, but I must maintain my efforts at all times if I want to be successful in my studies here, and match the success of my Father when he was at Christ Church.

---

and Demosthenes was attacked by rivals. *De Corona* is Demosthenes' masterpiece – he cleverly did not mention recent events, but his past glorious deeds for the benefit of the Athenians. Lucretius' *De Rerum Natura* is a poetic didactic treatise "On the Nature of the Universe" in which he expounds Epicurean atomic theory in order to dispel man's fears about death and the gods. {I am grateful to Michael Vine for providing these explanatory notes.}

[52] Dodgson's copy of *Do the First Works. A Sermon Addressed to the Newly-ordained Clergy at Ripon on Trinity Sunday 1851* by Charles Dodgson (London, Leeds, and Darlington, 1851), is inscribed "C. L. Dodgson with the author's most affectionate regards" (Berg). See Lovett, p. 105, for more details. Dodgson's father was examining chaplain to Bishop Longley at this time, and was responsible for the clergy newly ordained at Ripon.

Diary for the year 1852
January to December

Jan: 1. (F). The year begins at Croft. Fanny, Elizabeth and I gave Skeffington a new year gift.[53]

Jan: 19. (M). Croft to Oxford.

Jan: 21. (W). Lent Term commences.

Jan: 26. (M). Lectures begin again. In Classics we are studying the drama of *Oedipus* by Sophocles.

Jan: 30. (F). Heard Rev. E. A. Litton preach the University sermon at St. Mary's.[54]

---

[53] The gift was *The History of Napoleon Buonaparte* (Murray: 1830) in which was inscribed: "Skeffington Hume Dodgson, a New Year's gift from his affte. Sisters and Brother, Frances Jane, Elizabeth Lucy, Charles Lutwidge, 1852."

[54] Edward Arthur Litton (1813-1897), matriculated at Balliol in 1832: BA 1835, fellow of Oriel 1836-44, mathematical lecturer 1841, dean 1843, vice-principal of St. Edmund Hall 1851-54, Bampton lecturer 1856, rector of St. Clement's, Oxford 1858-60, and rector of Naunton, Gloucestershire from 1860. He was also the author of theological works. He married Anne (1821-1901) and they had two daughters: Edith Alice (1849-1919), and Adeline S. (b. 1857). Dodgson photographed Litton and his daughter Edith sometime between 1857 and 1859. According to the *Times*, this special sermon was preached on the anniversary of the martyrdom of King Charles I.

Feb: 5. (Th). Bode announced his withdrawal from the election of the new Professorship of Poetry.[55]

Feb: 18. (W). Convocation. Claughton was elected unopposed as the new Professor of Poetry.[56] The Vice Chancellor issued a warning against people attending a proposed steeple-chase near Oxford. This was not well received by some of the undergraduates who reside in Peckwater Quad, who clearly had intentions of attending.[57]

---

[55] John Ernest Bode (1816-1874), matriculated at Christ Church in 1833, BA 1837, MA 1840, student and tutor 1841-47, rector of Westwell, Oxfordshire 1847-60, rector of Castle Camps, Cambridgeshire 1860 until his death. He was a Bampton Lecturer and a minor poet. The *Times* (6 February 1852) reported that: "Bode withdraws from being a candidate for the Professorship of Poetry, the election for which takes place on the 18th. Mr. Claughton of Trinity, the only other candidate, is therefore sure to be elected." In a later contest for the Professorship of Poetry Bode was defeated by Matthew Arnold.

[56] Thomas Legh Claughton (1808-1892) matriculated at Trinity College in 1826: BA 1831, fellow 1832-42, MA 1833, ordained 1834, select preacher 1841, 1850, 1860 and 1868, vicar of Kidderminster 1841-67, professor of poetry 1852-57, DD 1867, bishop of Rochester 1867-77, and first Bishop of St. Albans 1877-90.

[57] The *Times* (19 February 1852) announced that: "The Vice Chancellor, Heads of Houses, and Proctors have issued an admonition warning all persons of the University against taking part in a steeple-chase advertised as about to take place in the

Ap: 8. (Th). Collections.[58]

Ap: 9. (F). To Croft.

Ap: 11. (Sun). Easter Day

Ap: 12. (M). I began reading *Bleak House* – Dickens' new novel. There are some excellent characters in the story, which promises to be well up to his usual high standard of writing.[59]

---

neighbourhood of Oxford." Such events had given rise to disturbances in the past between Town and Gown, and had encouraged gambling and bad behaviour, strongly disapproved of by the University.

58 Dodgson's written report for Hilary Term "Collections" indicated: Sophocles *Oedipus Tyrannus*, *Oedipus Coloneus haud male* (not at all bad), Cicero *In Verrem haud male*, Theology *bene* (good), Translation *satis* + (above acceptable), and Tr. Mathematics {probably trigonometry} *valde bene* (very good). Sophocles' Oedipus Trilogy (the Theban Plays) link the story of *Oedipus Tyrannus* with the continuing tragedy about the King of Thebes' daughter Antigone. In *Oedipus Coloneus* the action is set at Colonus near Athens where the blind king has fled in exile, accompanied by Antigone. Cicero's *In Verrem* is the published version of one of Cicero's few prosecution speeches given in 70 BC as part of the extortion charge he brought against Gaius Verres, the corrupt governor of Sicily. {I am grateful to Michael Vine for these explanatory notes}.

59 Charles Dickens' *Bleak House* was issued in monthly parts from March 1852 till September 1853. Dodgson probably bought these twenty parts (19 issues, the last two parts combined into one) and had them bound into one volume at a later date. His library

Ap: 19. (M). Back to Oxford. Easter and Act Term commences. I have moved to new rooms on the Cloister Staircase, room 4, which I share with Woodhouse.

Ap: 29. (Th). Convocation. Much confusion took place at the election of Rickards as the new Professor of Political Economy.[60]

May 18. (Tu). Boat races commence.

---

contained a first edition copy of *Bleak House* (1853) sold at the time of his death (see *Bibliophile*, p. 25, lot 501).

[60] George Kettilby Rickards (1812-1889) matriculated at Balliol in 1829: scholar Trinity College 1829-35, BA 1833, MA 1836, Michel fellow Queen's College 1836-43, barrister-at-law Inner Temple 1837, Drummond professor of political economy 1852-57, counsel to the Speaker of the House of Commons, and referee on private bills 1851-82, member of council of King's College, London 1871-73, and bencher 1873. In the election for Professor of Political Economy, Rickards defeated Neate of Oriel and Lowe of Magdalen. The *Times* reported (30 April 1852):

> We may venture to remark that the arrangements for voting on this occasion were such as would disgrace the commonest parochial election. The members of Convocation, instead of tendering their votes in a decent or orderly manner, rushed in a body to the table, and a scene of terrific scrambling and scuffling ensued; gowns were torn to tatters and caps crushed, and altogether there was ten times as much confusion in collecting some 500 votes as would arise from the polling as many thousands in any other place than Oxford. A great portion of the blame is no doubt to be attributed to the unseemly haste of the voters, but it is impossible wholly to acquit the authorities who presided over the election; and accordingly we advise them, unless they wish to see Convocation House converted into a bear garden, to manage matters more judiciously in future.

May 22. (Sat). Read the declamation in Hall. I took the title "*Nil prodest quod non laedere possit idem*" from Ovid's *Tristia.*[61]

May 28. (F). Bayne takes his BA degree.[62]

June 21. (M). Attended Corfe's exercise in the Sheldonian for his degree of Doctor of Music.[63]

---

61 The title translates as "Nothing aids which may not also injure us." The paper (MS: Morgan), written in Latin, ends with the statement "Read out in Hall. May 22, 1852." A full translation is reproduced in Morton Cohen's *Lewis Carroll, A Biography* (1995, pp. 536-537).

62 Thomas Vere Bayne (1829-1908) was a lifelong friend of Dodgson from childhood days at Daresbury. His father was headmaster of the nearby Warrington School. Bayne matriculated at Christ Church in 1848: student 1849-1908, BA 1852, MA 1855, tutor 1856-72, censor 1863-77, proctor 1867, member of the Hebdomadal council 1872-78, and keeper of the archives 1885. During his time as archivist, he collected many ephemeral works by Dodgson that survive to this day in his carefully arranged scrapbooks. He preceded Dodgson as curator of the Common Room.

63 These performances, albeit practical exercises as part of a degree, were open to the public. Charles William Corfe (1814-1883), matriculated at Christ Church in 1847 at the late age of 32: B.Mus. 1847, D.Mus. 1852, organist of Christ Church from his arrival (probably by appointment), praecentor or "coryphaeus" of music 1856-63, and "choragus" 1860. He was the composer of many anthems and songs. Dodgson photographed Corfe in 1859 or 1860. Dodgson's list of photographs (1860) stated: "Corfe, C. W., Esq., D. Mus., Organist of Ch. Ch. 1860." {The date given in this list may not be accurate.}

June 22. (Tu). Collections.[64]

June 23. (W). Commemoration. I took a long time getting into the Sheldonian Theatre: the heat and pressure were tremendous. I spent quarter of an hour wedged up in a passage, another quarter struggling violently up a narrow winding staircase. To make matters worse those above were continually trying to come down, and being told they couldn't: they in return told us we couldn't get up, but neither party believed the other. Lastly I spent another quarter with the heels of the boots hitched in among the railings on one side, and arching over men's heads against the railing on the other side, through which I got a view of the theatre; resting partly on the hands and partly on a pro-proctor under me, as the feet afforded rather a painful support than otherwise.

---

[64] Dodgson's "Collections" for the end of Trinity Term 1852 noted the following assessment of his achievements: Euripides *Hecuba, Orestes, Phoenissæ bene/satis bene* (between good and acceptably good), Virgil *Georgics haud male* (not at all bad), Theology *satis bene* (acceptably good), Political Rhetoric {?} *haud male* (not at all bad), Translation *satis bene*, and Tr. Mathematics {probably trigonometry} *valde bene* (very good). Euripides' *Hecuba* is the story of the Queen of Troy and her fate after the sack of Troy by the Greeks. The title of the play *Phoenissæ* is taken from the Phoenician women who constitute the chorus. The play is largely a mythological pageant. {I am grateful to Michael Vine for these explanatory notes}.

In the course of time however I reached the gallery for undergraduates and bachelors, under the ladies' gallery. The Bishop of Oxford and the Bishop of Exeter were there: both got loudly cheered. The English Verse recitation was loudly cheered: I liked some of it very much, the subject was "The Feast of Belshazzar." There were honorary degrees conferred on various people, one an Italian prince, another, I believe, the *Bishop of New York*, etc.[65]

---

[65] This entry comes from Dodgson's letter to his sister, Elizabeth, dated 24 June 1852 (see *Letters*, pp. 19-20). Samuel Wilberforce (1805-1873) was Bishop of Oxford, and Henry Phillpotts (1778-1869) was Bishop of Exeter. Edwin Arnold (1832-1904) won the Newdigate Prize for this poem given as the verse recitation. He matriculated at University College in 1850: BA 1854, MA 1856. The honorary degree of DCL (Doctor of Civil Law) was conferred on a number of worthy people during the Commemoration. They included: Don Domenico Lofaso di Pietra Santa, Duke of Serradifaleo and Prince of San Pietro (1773-1863); the Rt. Rev. Samuel Allen McCoskry (1804-1886), DD, Bishop of Michigan; the Rt. Rev. William Heathcote De Lancey (1797-1865), DD, Bishop of Western New York; the Hon. Sir John Taylor Coleridge (1790-1876), one of Her Majesty's Justices of the Court of Queen's Bench, late Fellow of Exeter; Sir John Gardner Wilkinson (1797-1875), FRS, MRSL, FRGS; the Rev. Jonathan Mayhew Wainwright (1793-1854), DD, Secretary of the House of Bishops in the United States; William Pulteney Alison (1790-1859), MD, Professor of Medicine in the University of Edinburgh, and one of the Physicians in Ordinary to Her Majesty in Scotland; and Richard Owen (1804-1892), Hunterian Professor of Comparative Anatomy and Physiology, and Conservator of the Museum of the Royal College of Surgeons.

I had a conversation with Mr. Gordon,[66] and one with Mr. Faussett on the work of the Long Vacation. I have much to do. For next term, I have bought Boeckh's *Public Economy of Athens*, which Mr. Gordon recommends me to read.[67]

Left Oxford for London in the evening, and after a perilous journey of an hour and a half, I arrived at 4 Alfred Place. Uncle Skeffington came about ½ an hour after my arrival, looking very well, and if anything, *rather* stouter than when I last saw him.[68]

---

66 Osborne Gordon (1813-1883) matriculated at Christ Church in 1832: student 1834-61, BA 1836, MA 1839, BD 1847, censor 1847, proctor 1846, Greek reader 1845, rhetoric reader 1846, catechist 1849, Wake librarian 1850, and rector of Easthampstead, Berkshire 1860-83. In his role as senior censor at Christ Church he was responsibility for the welfare of undergraduates. He was known as "a brilliant scholar and quaint humorist; a man of singular power and wide popularity. He had been in office for several years under Gaisford, and was not perhaps quite in sympathy with Liddell's views, though he always loyally supported his chief" (Thompson, p.168). Gordon was Dodgson's tutor in Classics.

67 This entry comes from Dodgson's letter to his sister, Elizabeth, dated 24 June 1852 (see *Letters*, p. 20). *The Public Economy of Athens* by August Boeckh (1785-1867), first published in 1828 in four volumes, translated from the German by George Cornewall Lewis (1806-1863). Dodgson's copy was probably the second revised edition (London: 1843).

68 Much of this diary entry comes from Dodgson's letter to his sister, Elizabeth, dated 24 June 1852 (see *Letters*, pp. 19-21).

June 24. (F). Uncle Skeffington has as usual got a great number of new oddities, including a lathe, telescope stand, crest stamp, a beautiful little pocket instrument for measuring distances on a map, refrigerator, etc., etc. We had an observation of the moon and Jupiter last night, and afterwards live animalcula in his large microscope: this is a most interesting sight, as the creatures are most conveniently transparent, and you see all kinds of organs jumping about like a complicated piece of machinery, and even the circulation of the blood. Everything goes on at railway speed, so I suppose they must be some of those insects that only live a day or two, and try to make the most of it.

Uncle Skeffington went to his office, where I joined him at 4. In the meantime, with time to spare, I visited the Royal Academy.[69]

June 25. (Sat). Fletcher arrived in the evening. He stays until Monday. Uncle Hassard and Aunt

[69] The *Imperial Dictionary* (1860), edited by John Ogilvie, defines “refrigerator” as “a vessel for cooling liquids, or condensing hot vapour into liquids, by the application of cold water.” It is not clear exactly what form of refrigerator Uncle Skeffington had acquired. The same dictionary defines “animalcula” as “little animals whose figure cannot be discerned without the aid of a magnifying glass.” This diary entry, and some subsequent entries for the next eight days, also comes from Dodgson’s letter to his sister, Elizabeth, dated 24 June 1852 (see *Letters*, pp. 19-21).

Caroline came to dinner, together with a number of cousins.[70]

June 27. (M). Aunt Louisa invited me over to Tunbridge Wells for a few days, but there is no time. I wrote saying that, regretfully, I was unable to come.

July 1. (F). Went, with Uncle Skeffington, to a dinner party given by one of his friends – a large gathering, mainly of ladies.

July 2. (Sat). To Croft. On arrival I found a number of the Smedleys visiting the Rectory.[71]

---

[70] Hassard Hume Dodgson (1803-1884) was Dodgson's paternal uncle. He attended Westminster School with his brother, Dodgson's father, becoming King's Scholar (Captain of the School). He matriculated at Christ Church in 1822: Student 1822-33, Ireland scholar 1826, BA 1826, MA 1829, entered Lincoln's Inn in 1827, migrated to the Inner Temple in 1844, practised as a special pleader 1829-71, a master of the Court of Common Pleas 1871-79, and of the Supreme Court of Judicature from 1879, being called to the Bar on 30 January 1872. He married Caroline (1809-1875), daughter of James Deacon Hume, on 27 August 1833 at Sevenoaks. They had ten children: Francis "Frank" Hume (1834-1917) who emigrated to Australia in 1865, Lucy Caroline (1836-1894), Percy (1838-1886) who also emigrated to Australia in 1865, Charlotte Mary (b. 1839), Louis Henri (1841-1849), Amy Menella (1842-1922) who married Charles Edward Pollock (1823-1897) on 23 December 1865, James Hume (1845-1912), Menella "Marla" Frances (1848-1917) who married Thomas William Bischoff (1845-1928) in 1879, Louis Henry "Hal" (b. 1850), and Laura Elizabeth (1853-1882).

[71] Most of these diary entries since 24 June are interpolated from Dodgson's letter to his sister, Elizabeth, dated 24 June 1852

Aug: 16. (Tu). I am spending part of the summer in Edinburgh. I travelled via Berwick a few days ago. Today, I visited Hamilton, the phrenologist, and he has written his account of my character. I return to Croft sometime next week.[72]

(see *Letters*, pp. 19-21). The Smedleys were related to Dodgson through Edward Smedley (1788-1836), his great-uncle, who matriculated at Trinity College, Cambridge in 1805: BA 1809, ordained deacon 1811, priest 1812, MA 1812, and fellow of Sidney Sussex College 1812-16. Lord Uxbridge granted him the living of Sherborne in December 1812. He was also curate of Meopham, Kent, preacher at St. James' Chapel, Tottenham Court Road, London, clerk in orders at St. James' Westminster 1815-19, and subsequently preacher and evening lecturer at St. Giles' Camberwell. He was prebendary of Lincoln in 1829, although he became totally deaf in 1828. He married Mary née Hume on 8 January 1816, and they had four children: Edward Hume (1817-1862), Menella Bute (1819-1877), Mary (b. 1821?) who married Edward Hart in 1840, and Elizabeth "Honie" (1822-1888) who married Thomas Barnard Hart in 1848. Mary Smedley née Hume's sister, Lucy (1775-1818), married Dodgson's grandfather.

[72] This trip is suggested by a document in the Dodgson Family Archive entitled "Character of C. L. Dodgson by Edd. Hamilton (of Edinr.) Phrenologist" dated 16th of an unknown month in 1852. Dodgson made a trip to Scotland in 1857, stopping off at Berwick for an overnight stay. It is possible that he travelled with a friend from Oxford, possibly Ranken or Barclay with whom he made similar expeditions. No other details of this excursion, if it took place, has come to light. Derek Hudson reproduced the account made by the Edinburgh phrenologist, Edward Hamilton, in his biography of *Lewis Carroll* (1954, p. 68), repeated in his *Lewis Carroll, An Illustrated Biography* (1976, p. 67). Having "felt Dodgson's bumps" his report began:

> This Gentleman has eight very prominent traits in his Character, namely, a strong love of children; a strong love of friends; much

Sep: 14. (W). This day, the Duke of Wellington, Chancellor of the University, died.[73]

Oct: 8. (Sat). Croft to Oxford.

Oct: 10. (M). Michaelmas Term begins.

Oct: 12. (W). The Queen came through Oxford on her way from Balmoral to Windsor. There was a large gathering at the railway station to see her go by.[74]

Oct: 13. (Th). Lord Derby has been elected as the new Chancellor of the University to replace the late Duke of Wellington.[75]

---

emulousness *and* amiability; much Circumspection; Lofty generous sentiments; much good taste for order & dress & elegance; Excellent analogical reason; & deep penetrating causality to trace the relation between cause & effect…."

73 Arthur Wellesley (1769-1852), Duke of Wellington, highly successful soldier and later politician, became Chancellor of Oxford University in 1834.

74 Queen Victoria travelled along the newly opened line of the Great Western Railway from Birmingham, through Oxford, to London.

75 The *Times* reported (13 October 1852) that Lord Derby was elected unopposed as the new Chancellor in a ceremony rushed through in thirty minutes, some people deeming it unseemly haste. Edward Geoffrey Smith Stanley (1809-1869), 14th Earl of Derby, matriculated at Christ Church in 1817 but took no degrees. He held the position of Chancellor until his death. He was Prime Minister in 1852, 1858-59, and 1866-68.

Oct: 24. (Sun). The University sermon was preached by Dr. Hawkins of Oriel.[76]

Oct: 25. (M). Gladstone came on a visit to Oxford.[77]

Oct: 30. (Sat). Gave my name to the Junior Proctor to enter the new system of Moderations recently introduced. The examinations take place later this term.[78]

---

76 Edward Hawkins (1789-1882) matriculated at St. John's College in 1807: BA 1811, tutor 1812, fellow Oriel College 1813-28, MA 1814, tutor 1819, dean 1826, BD and DD 1828, vicar of St. Mary the Virgin, Oxford 1823, select preacher seven times, Whitehall preacher 1827, Bampton lecturer 1840, Dean Ireland's professor of the Exegesis of Holy Scripture 1847-61, canon of Rochester, provost of Oriel College 1828, and rector of Purleigh from 1828 until his death.

77 William Ewart Gladstone (1809-1898) matriculated at Christ Church in 1828: BA 1832, MA 1834, DCL created 1849, MP for Oxford University from July 1847 until July 1865, and honorary Student in 1859. He was Chancellor of the Exchequer 1852-55, and Prime Minister 1868-74, 1880-85, 1886, and 1892-94. He spent a few days in Oxford, residing at Worcester College, thanking his constituents for their support.

78 The new system of Moderations was introduced in 1850 as a way of examining undergraduates prior to their Finals, usually during their second year of study. The University informed undergraduates that those intending to offer themselves for the public examination under Moderators in the current Term should present themselves to the Junior Proctor on certain days. They were required to show their matriculation paper, a certificate indicating that they had passed Responsions, and a list of the books and subjects in which they offered themselves to be examined, signed with their names. The Moderators for Classics, appointed by the

Nov: 5. (F). The University sermon was preached by Rev. Dr. Hook on the theme of the anniversary of the Gunpowder Plot.[79]

Nov: 25. (Th). Funeral of the Duke of Wellington in London, late Chancellor of the University. There were no lectures. Most of Oxford closed down for the day as a mark of respect; libraries, schools, and public buildings of the University were all closed.

Nov: 27. (Sat). Results of Moderations in Classics. I gained a Second Class. Woodhouse also gained a Second Class. The only Christ Church man to gain a First was Pember.[80]

University, were Osborne Gordon, George Rawlinson, Henry L. Mansel, and John Conington. The Moderators for Mathematics were Stephen Edwardes, Nicolas Pocock, and Barthomolew Price.

[79] Walter Farquhar Hook (1798-1875) matriculated at Christ Church in 1817: student 1817-27, BA 1821, MA 1824, B&DD 1837, student of Lincoln's Inn 1819, chaplain in ordinary to the King 1827, and Queen 1839-75, dean of Chichester 1859-75, vicar of Holy Trinity, Coventry 1828-37, prebendary of Lincoln 1831-59, vicar of Leeds 1837-59, and select preacher 1833-34 and 1858-59.

[80] Edward Henry Pember (1833-1911) matriculated at Christ Church in 1850: student 1854-61, BA 1854, MA 1857, barrister at Lincoln's Inn 1858, Queen's Council 1874, and bencher 1876. Dodgson photographed him in November 1878, but the photograph has not come to light.

Nov: 29. (M). The *Times* published the Moderations Class List in Classics for Michaelmas 1852.

Dec: 9. (W). Result of Moderations in Mathematics. I was one of five to gain a First Class, and the only Christ Church man to do so. Pusey gained a Second Class. Wrote to Elizabeth to give her news of my good fortune. Whether I shall add to this any honours at collections I cannot at present say, but I should think it very unlikely, as I have only today to get up the work in *The Acts of the Apostles,* 2 Greek Plays, and the *Satires* of Horace and I feel myself almost totally unable to read at all: I am beginning to suffer from the reaction of reading for Moderations.

Mr. Gordon has given me a copy of his Censor's speech (printed for private distribution): I think it beautiful Latin; it is mostly about the Duke of Wellington.

I vacate my Peckwater room this term. I have my eye on another set in Tom Quad for next term.[81]

Dec: 10. (Th). Collections.[82] The *Times* published the Moderations Class List in Mathematics.

---

[81] Most of this entry comes from Dodgson's letter to his sister, Elizabeth, dated 9 December 1852 (see *Letters*, p. 22). For the outcome of Dodgson's proposed change of rooms, see 14 January 1853 below.

Bell of Worcester,[83] Cookson of St. John's,[84] Fowler of Merton,[85] and Jones

---

[82] "Collections" at the end of Michaelmas Term 1852 brought Dodgson the following results: Euripides *Medea, Bacchæ bene* (good), Horace *Satires satis bene* (acceptably good), Mathematics *optime* (excellent), Theology *satis bene* (acceptably good), Translation *satis* + (above acceptable).

[83] George Charles Bell (1832-1913), matriculated at Lincoln College in 1851; scholar 1851-52, migrated to Worcester College, scholar 1852-57, BA 1855, fellow 1857-71, MA 1857, and tutor 1862-65. He won the junior mathematical scholarship in 1853 and the senior mathematical scholarship in 1857. He was appointed mathematical moderator in 1859-60 and examiner in 1863. He was assistant master at Dulwich College 1865-68, select preacher 1867 and 1885, headmaster of Christ's Hospital 1868, headmaster of Marlborough College 1876-1903, canon of Sarum 1886, chairman of the Teachers' Registration Council 1904, and principal of Queen's College, London 1904-10. He was rector of St Michael, Cornhill, St Peter le Poer, and St Benet Fink from 1906. He was made honorary fellow of Worcester College in 1896, almoner of Christ's Hospital from 1890, member of Council of Marlborough College 1903, governor of Dulwich College 1909, and of the Grey Coat Hospital 1910. Bell married Elizabeth Sophia née Milner (b. 1828), and they had four children: Helen Frances (1870-1946), George Milner (b. 1872), Olive Dade (b. 1875), and another daughter (listed but not named in *Who Was Who*).

[84] Christopher Cookson (1824-1874) matriculated at St. John's College in 1842: fellow 1842-60, BA 1846, MA 1850, BD 1855, and vicar of Dallington, Northamptonshire 1863-74.

[85] Thomas Fowler (1832-1904), matriculated at Merton College in 1850: second class in classics and first class in mathematics moderations 1852, first class in classics and mathematics finals, BA 1854, fellow of Lincoln College 1855-81, ordained deacon 1855, priest 1857, MA 1857, tutor 1855-73, sub-

of Worcester[86] were the other men who gained First Class.

Dec: 11. (F). Dr. Pusey sent me word that he has nominated me for a Studentship. I immediately wrote to my Father with the news.[87]

---

rector 1857-81, proctor 1863, president of Corpus Christi College 1881, and B & DD 1886. He was classics examiner at various times between 1864-79, Wykeham professor of logic 1873-89, select preacher 1873, and a member of the Hebdomadal council, delegate to the press, the museum, and of the University fund in 1869. He wrote several books on logic including *The Elements of Deductive Logic* (1867), and a history of Corpus Christi College (1893).

[86] George Meyrick Jones (1830-1922?) matriculated at Worcester College in 1848: BA 1852, MA 1855, ordained deacon 1854, priest 1855, curate of St. Paul's. Deptford 1854-56, vicar of Wellow, Hampshire 1883-91. At some stage, he changed his surname to Meyrick-Jones.

[87] Dodgson's father replied immediately; his letter (the full text is in Collingwood, pp. 53-55) began:

> My dearest Charles,
>
> The feelings of thankfulness and delight with which I have read your letter just received, I must leave to your conception; for they are, I assure you, beyond my expression; and your affectionate heart will derive no small addition of joy from thinking of the joy which you have occasioned to me, and to all the circle of your home. I say "you have occasioned," because, grateful as I am to my old friend Dr. Pusey for what he has done, I cannot desire stronger evidence than his own words of the fact that you have won, and well won, this honour for yourself, and that it is bestowed as a matter of justice to you, and not of kindness to me….

Oxford to London to stay with Uncle Skeffington for a few days.

Dec: 16. (W). From Uncle Skeffington, I migrated to Putney to stay with Uncle Hassard and family.

Dec: 23. (W). On this day, the Dean and Chapter made me a Student of Christ Church.[88] The

---

Dodgson's father wrote to Pusey in early 1849 when Dodgson was still at Rugby School, expressing his hope that a Studentship might be available when Dodgson went to Christ Church. Pusey replied on 13 January 1849 (MS: Dodgson Family):

> I thank you for the way in which you put the application to me. I have now, for nearly twenty years, not given a Studentship to any friend of my own, unless there was no very eligible person in the College. I have passed by or declined the sons of those to whom I was personally indebted for kindness. I can only say that I shall have very great pleasure if circumstances permit me to nominate your son.

Pusey wrote to Dodgson's father (MS: Dodgson Family) on 2 December 1852, indicating that he was going to nominate his son for a Studentship. He followed this up with another letter indicating that the nomination had been successful (Collingwood, p. 55):

> I have great pleasure in telling you that I have been enabled to recommend your son for a Studentship this Christmas. It must be so much more satisfactory to you that he should be nominated thus, in consequence of the recommendation of the College. One of the Censors brought me to-day five names; but in their minds it was plain that they thought your son on the whole the most eligible for the College. It has been very satisfactory to hear of your son's uniform steady and good conduct....

[88] The Chapter Books (MS: Christ Church) indicate that Dodgson was made "Scholares Junioces" on 23 December 1852,

conditions are that I remain unmarried and proceed to Holy Orders soon after I take my degree. From next term, I shall take my turn, with the other seven Students who were most recently nominated, to carry out the "prick bills" at morning and evening chapel.[89]

Dec: 27. (M). The *Times* announces that I have been elected a Student of Christ Church, together with Armitstead, Joyce, Fellows, Phillpotts and Jelf.[90]

---

making him 101st and last in the list of Students at Christ Church. Also elected Students were George Edward Jelf and Henry John Phillpotts. The entry was signed by the Dean and Subdean, and three of the canons, Dr. Jelf, Dr. Clerke and Dr. Jacobson.

89 The eight most recently appointed Students were expected to record the attendance of the undergraduates at Chapel each day. They were provided with a list, and as each person entered the Cathedral (used as the College Chapel), they used a pin to prick a mark against the name of that person, hence the term "prick bills."

90 The *Times* (27 December 1852) announced: "The following gentlemen have just been elected students of Christ Church: Armitstead, Joyce and Fellowes {*sic*}, from Westminster School; Philpots, Gelf, and Dodson {*sic*}." The Studentship came with conditions, mainly to ensure that tenure was for a short period, allowing a succession of future appointments. The first condition was for the holder of the Studentship to proceed to holy orders at a prescribed period after taking the BA and MA degrees (usually within four years), unless he was appointed to one of the Faculty Studentships. This is what happened in Dodgson's case – he was appointed Lecturer in Mathematics, and became a Faculty Student in 1858. This removed the necessity of proceeding to holy orders,

Dec: 31. (Th). To Ripon with the family. My Father gave me a copy of his most recently published sermon.[91]

---

although Dodgson prepared for ordination and became Deacon of the Church of England in December 1861. Students taking holy orders usually accepted a church living, and on taking up a parish they lost their Studentship. The other condition for all Students was to remain unmarried and not commit any grave breach of college discipline or public morality. Information regarding such breaches was discussed by the Dean and Chapter at their regular meetings (before the establishment of the Governing Body), and Studentships were immediately forfeited if these breaches were proven. There was a continuous need to appoint new Students, some allocated to undergraduates coming from Westminster School, and others at the discretion of the Dean and Chapter. On average, Studentships were held for between 10 and 15 years, and during that time, a small emolument was paid. The Faculty Studentships were held for much longer periods. Dodgson held his Studentship for the rest of his life. On this occasion, the other Studentships went to these members of Christ Church; William George Armitstead (1833-1907), Sidney Joyce (1834-1911), Walter Fellows (b. 1834), Henry John Phillpotts (b. 1834), and George Edward Jelf (1834-1908). The Dean and Chapter Book (MS: Christ Church) indicated on 25 June 1856 that "Fellows not having complied with the Order made December 22nd 1855 that he should proceed to the B. A. degree in his sixteenth Term and the Censor not having recommended an extension of time as allowed by the said Order his Student's place is now declared vacant." He eventually took his BA in 1858.

[91] *Ritual Worship. A Sermon preached at the consecration of the Church of St. Thomas in Leeds, on the feast of the purification of St. Mary* by Charles Dodgson (London, Leeds, and Oxford: 1852), inscribed: "C. L. D. With the Author's most affectionate regards" (Harvard). Together with the sermon is a printed letter entitled *A letter to the Lord Bishop of Ripon, on some objections taken to the Author's sermon, lately published under the title of "Ritual Worship"* by Charles Dodgson and inscribed "From the author."

At the close of the year, I give thanks for the honour and trust bestowed on me by the Dean and Chapter in granting me a Studentship of Christ Church. I do most sincerely pray that I may live up to this honour, and that I fulfil all my duties without any shortcomings. Most merciful Father, aid me in this new task, and bless the New Year about to commence, for thy dear Son, Jesus Christ's sake.[92]

Diary for the year 1853
January to December

Jan: 1. (F) The year begins at Ripon with Father's appointment as one of the new residentiary canons of the Cathedral. The whole family travelled to Ripon. We reside at the Canon's Residence, a large house near to the Cathedral. This will be our arrangement for future years, the

[92] Apart from studying mathematics and classics, Dodgson also took the opportunity to study theology in preparation for holy orders, one of the anticipated conditions of the Studentship. A book that he probably read around this time was *Aids to Reflection* by Samuel Taylor Coleridge (1772-1834). This was confirmed on 14 January 1855 when he recorded that "it is one of those books that improve on a second reading: I find very little in it even obscure now" (see *Diary 1*, p. 56).

family spending at least three months in Ripon before returning to Croft.[93]

Jan: 3. (M). The *Times* announced that Clerke has been appointed Sub-Dean of Christ Church, and also included Father's appointment as Canon of Ripon .[94]

Jan: 12. (W). Ripon to Oxford.

---

93 Rev. Charles Dodgson was collated and installed as one of the Canons of Ripon Cathedral in 1852, and took up the position for the first time at the beginning of 1853. His duties required residence at Ripon for the first 13 weeks of the year. The Dodgson household moved from Croft to Ripon each January for the next 16 years, returning in April. At this time, Charles T. Longley was Bishop, and Henry David Erskine (1786-1859) was Dean. The Old Residence (now called the Old Hall, which still exists) at High St. Agnesgate was rented to provide accommodation for the residentiary canons from 1841 until the end of 1858. Thereafter, a new residence for the Canons was built, and occupied by the Dodgsons in January 1859. This building has since been demolished. For more details, see *Lewis Carroll's Ripon* by Maurice Taylor (1998, reprinted 2002).

94 The *Times* (3 January 1853) under the heading of Christ Church, January 1, stated: "The Ven. Charles Carr Clerke, DD, Archdeacon of Oxford, chaplain to the Bishop of Oxford, has been appointed Sub-Dean of the Cathedral of Christ Church, on the resignation of Rev. Dr. Barnes. The Rev. Charles Dodgson, MA, of Christ Church, has been appointed Canon-Residentiary in the cathedral church of Ripon." Charles Carr Clerke (1799-1877) matriculated at Christ Church in 1814: student 1814-37, BA 1818, MA 1821, BD 1830, canon 1846-77, DD 1847, sub-dean 1852, archdeacon of Oxford 1830, rector of Milton, Berkshire 1836-75, and chaplain to the Bishop of Winchester 1869-73. He took over the role of sub-dean from Dr. Frederick Barnes (1771-1859).

Jan: 13. (Th). The University sermon was preached by Haddon of Trinity.[95]

Jan: 14. (F). Lent Term begins. I had hoped to move to new rooms in Tom Quad, but they were not available, so I remain here on the Cloister Staircase.

Jan: 26. (W). Gladstone dined at Christ Church with Dr. Jacobson, with whom he is staying for a few days.

Jan: 27. (Th). My 21st birthday. Aunt Lucy bought me *Introduction to the Literature of Europe* and *View of the State of Europe* both by Henry Hallam. My Father gave me *Milton's Poetical Works*.[96]

---

95 Arthur West Haddon (1816-1873) matriculated at Brasenose College in 1834 but migrated to Trinity: scholar of Trinity 1835-40, fellow 1840-58, dean and tutor 1841, public examiner in Classics 1844, vice-president 1848, junior bursar 1857, rector of Barton-on-the-Heath, Warwickshire 1857-1873, Bampton lecturer 1865, and hon. canon of Worcester 1870.

96 Dodgson's birthday gifts, *Introduction to the Literature of Europe* by Henry Hallam, Third Edition in 3 volumes, 1847, and *View of The State of Europe* by Henry Hallam, Tenth Edition in 3 volumes, 1853, are both inscribed: "Charles Lutwidge Dodgson. From his most affectionate Aunt Lucy Lutwidge. A Birthday Gift. January 27th 1853" (Private Collection). His father gave him two volumes of *Milton's Poetical Works, With Life, Critical Dissertation, and Explanatory Notes* by the Rev. George Gilfillan (Edinburgh and London, 1853), and the first volume is inscribed "Charles Lutwidge Dodgson. Given to him by his affectionate

Jan: 29. (Sat). I went to see Dr. Ogilvie to ask him if I may join his course of lectures in Theology.[97]

Feb: 3. (Th). The *Times* announced that the site of the proposed New Museum of Science is now agreed. It will be built in the Parks, adjacent to Wadham College.[98]

Mar: 22. (Tu). The Bodleian Library has a new heating system which is far superior to the previous system. It is said to run on steam from hot water and conveyed through cast

---

Father on his 21st Birthday, 1853." The second volume contains the signature "C. L. Dodgson" (Harvard).

[97] Charles Atmore Ogilvie (1793-1873) matriculated at Balliol College in 1811: BA 1815, fellow 1816-34, MA 1818, tutor 1819-30, bursar 1822, senior dean, B&DD 1842, Regius professor of pastoral theology 1842, and canon of Christ Church 1849. He was vicar of Ross-on-Wye, Herefordshire 1839-73. Dr. Ogilvie announced on 14 January that he proposed to begin a course of lectures, on Tuesday 1 February, intended for such members of the University as were qualified to become scholars in Theology. Dodgson was studying this subject together with classics and mathematics, and, with ordination in mind, he may have expressed a wish to join these lectures.

[98] This eventually became the University's Museum of Natural History, opened in 1860, and built near the Parks which are situated North of Oxford. The British Association for the Advancement of Science held their annual meeting there in June/July 1860, during which the much reported debate between Thomas Huxley and Samuel Wilberforce on the "Origin of Species" took place.

iron pipes carried round the reading room. Studying in the Library in winter has formerly been almost impossible as a result of the intense cold.

Mar: 25. (F). Collections.[99]

Mar: 27 (Sun). Easter Sunday

Ap: 6. (W). Easter and Act Term begins.

Ap: 16. (M). Mr. Price of Pembroke has been appointed the new Professor of Natural Philosophy.[100]

---

[99] Dodgson's "Collections" report for the Hilary Term indicated: Thucydides *History of the Peloponnesian War* i-ii *haud male* (not at all bad), History *satis* (acceptable), Quintilian *Institutiones Oratoriæ* i-vi *bene* (good), Pr. M. {Mathematical Probability?} *valde bene* (very good), Ethics i-iv {probably Aristotle's *Nicomachean Ethics*} *satis* + (above acceptable), Theology *bene* (good), and Translation prose accurate. Quintilian's *Institutio Oratoria*, probably published in 96 AD, is a treatise in twelve books of the training of an orator from babyhood to a grown man {notes supplied by Michael Vine}.

[100] The *Times* (18 April 1853) reported under the heading "Sedleian Professor of Natural Philosophy": "The Rev. Bartholomew Price, MA, FRS, Fellow and Tutor of Pembroke College, has been appointed to this position, vacant by the death of the Rev. G. L. Cooke. Mr. Price is the author of one of the best works on the *Differential Calculus*. The other candidate was Mr. Dale, of Balliol, also a distinguished mathematician." Bartholomew "Bat" Price (1818-1898) matriculated at Pembroke College in 1837: scholar 1837-44, BA 1840, MA 1843, fellow 1844, junior dean 1844, tutor and mathematics lecturer 1845, bursar 1851, vicegerent

Ap: 29. (F). At a meeting of Convocation, the estimated cost of the New Museum was announced; £48,000 for the building alone, and £57,500 for the building together with all fittings and heating. There is some opposition to this expenditure, with suggestions that the money could be better spent.

Ap: 30. (Sat). We have been fortunate enough to get a Classical First (Brown) in the Great-go schools: another man (Lord Lothian) who was expected to be a double First, took his name off; as it was said, because he was afraid of missing his First, and wanted to make sure next time.[101]

1864, public examiner 1847-48 and 1853-55, moderator from 1852, proctor 1858, Sedleian professor of natural philosophy 1853, hon. fellow of Queen's College, FRS, FRAS, visitor of Greenwich Observatory, Master of Pembroke 1892, and secretary to the Delegates of the Press. He published *A Treatise on the Differential Calculus* (1848) and *A Treatise on Infinitesimal Calculus* in 4 volumes (1852-60). He married Amy Eliza née Cole (1835-1909) in 1857, and they had seven children: Amy Maud (1858-1923), William Arthur (1860-1954), Mary Eliza Mabel (1862-1940), Alice Margaret (1863-1945), Rose Emelyn (1866-1894), Elinor "Nellie" Rokeby (1868-1956), and Bartholomew George (1870-1947). Dodgson frequently consulted Price about matters concerning his lectureship and mathematics in general. Price was instrumental in helping Dodgson publish his *Elementary Treatise on Determinants* (1867), and personally read Dodgson's paper on this subject to the Royal Society in 1866. Dodgson photographed Price in 1860.

[101] This comes from Dodgson's letter to his cousin, Francis Hume Dodgson, dated 4 May 1853 (see *Letters*, p. 23). Thomas

May 2. (M). Boat races begin and go on till the 13th. Christ Church is expected to do well in the races this term.[102]

May 3. (Tu). Went to Magdalen to hear Dr. Corfe's performance of Mendelssohn's *Antigone*, which was well attended.[103]

Edward Brown (1830-1897) gained a first class in Classics (announced in the *Times* on 30 April 1853), and a first class in Law and Modern History at the end of the year, becoming a Fellow of Oriel 1854-58, and master of Clifton College in 1864. William Schomberg Robert Kerr (1832-1870), 8th Marquis of Lothian, gained a First Class in Classics later in the year, and First Class in Law and Modern History in 1854.

102 In Dodgson's letter to Francis Hume Dodgson (4 May 1853) he indicated that "we have not made a bump yet, but have very fair hopes of doing so before they are over." Catching the boat in front, after a staggered start, and bumping it, improved the overall position of the Christ Church boat in the final list. The boat at the top of the list was declared "Head of the River."

103 The *Times* (4 May 1853) described the occasion: "Dr. Corfe brought forward Mendelssohn's *Antigone* in Magdalen Hall for the first time in Oxford. Messrs. Blagrave, Clementi, and many others from the bands of the Queen's and the Italian Opera, were engaged, together with Mr. Reinagle, of this city. The choruses were chiefly sung by the members of the University, and elicited great applause." Henry Gamble Blagrave (1811-1872), solo-violinist, played with the state band 1837-72; Clementi was probably a son of the composer, Muzio Clementi (1752-1832); Alexander Robert Reinagle (1799-1877) was the organist of St. Peter-in-the-East, Oxford, composer of the hymn tune "St. Peter" used for the hymn "How Sweet the Name of Jesus Sounds" (written by John Newton).

May 4. (W). The names of the Westminster candidates were read out in Hall: Frank Dodgson was among them. I wrote to congratulate him, asking him to let me know when he comes up to matriculate.[104]

May 5. (Th). Ascension Day. The University sermon was preached by Dr. Faussett, Canon of Christ Church.[105]

---

[104] Francis "Frank" Hume Dodgson (1834-1917), the eldest son of Uncle Hassard, matriculated at Christ Church on 18 May 1853 from Westminster School where he was Queen's Scholar. He was a student at Christ Church from 1853 until he transferred to the Woolwich Military Academy becoming lieutenant in the Royal Artillery on 6 March 1856 until 30 April 1856. He was commissioned again on 10 August 1856 but resigned on 9 December 1864, and then emigrated to Australia in 1865. He married Wilhelmina Ellen King (1857-1921) on 16 October 1882 in Queensland, and they had four children: Caroline Maud (1883-1962), Harriet Menella Lucy (1885-1979), Percy Hume (1887-1944), and Frances Charlotte (1891-1985). For Dodgson's letter to his cousin, Francis Hume Dodgson, see *Letters*, p. 23. The *Times* (7 May 1853) reported: "Oxford, Christ Church, May 6, Westminster School Election: The annual election of students to Christ Church took place on Wednesday, when Messrs. Oliver, Twiss, Williams, and Dodgson were elected. At the same time, Messrs. Gilbert, Madan, and Vincent (the latter the fourth son of Mr. Vincent, of this city) were elected scholars of Trinity College, Cambridge."

[105] Godfrey Faussett (1780-1853) matriculated at Corpus Christi College in 1797: scholar 1797, BA 1801, fellow of Magdalen 1802, MA 1804, BD 1822, DD 1827, Margaret professor of divinity 1827-53, prebendary of Worcester 1827, and canon of Christ Church 1840-53. He married, firstly, Marianne Elizabeth née Bridges, and they had four children: Bryan (1811-1898), Godfrey (1813-1887), Susan (d. 1893), and Anne (d. 1868). He married,

May 7. (Sat). Read the declamation in Hall for the third time. I chose the theme "*Contempta fama contemni virtutes*" from Tacitus's *Annals*.[106]

May 17. (Tu). Matriculation was held at Christ Church. Over 50 were admitted, including noblemen, gentleman commoners, and commoners, being a much larger number than usual. Frank Dodgson was with them.

May 18. (W). Trinity term begins. The University sermon was preached by the Rev. John Baker, Chaplain of Christ Church.[107]

---

secondly, Sarah née Wethered (1790-1875), and they had seven children: Henry Godfrey (1824-1878), William (1825-1913), Robert Godfrey (1827-1908), Thomas Godfrey (1829-1877), Sarah (1831-1928), Edward (1833-1841), and John Toke (1835-1893).

[106] The date is a guess. Dodgson was asked to read the declamation in Hall on four occasions during his undergraduate years. Of the four manuscripts, three are dated 22 November 1851, 22 May 1852, and 3 May 1854. It would seem likely that this paper was read sometime in 1853. The theme translates as "To despise fame is to despise merit." The paper (MS: Morgan) is written in Latin. A full translation is reproduced in Morton Cohen's *Lewis Carroll, A Biography* (1995, pp. 537-538).

[107] John Baker (1826-1860) matriculated at Christ Church in 1844: BA 1848, MA 1851, chaplain of Christ Church 1852. He died young and is buried in St Sepulchre's Cemetery, Oxford.

May 20. (F). There was a fatal accident on the river by Christ Church meadow – a rower was drowned.[108]

May 23. (M). Wrote out "The Ligniad, in two Books" for Woodhouse.[109]

May 24. (Tu). At Convocation, the cost of building the New Museum was submitted, but lost; placets 31, non-placets 35.

May 26. (Th). Called on Mr. Price at Pembroke. I enrolled in his proposed course of lectures on the principles and applications of Analytical Mechanics for next term. He explained the content of his course and the amount of preliminary mathematical knowledge which will be required for entering the course.

---

108 The *Times* (21 May 1853) recorded: "At Christ Church meadow, on the Isis, a young gentleman of the University, Mr. Edward Compton Dyson, scholar of Corpus Christi College, lost his life in consequence of the upsetting of a small and narrow boat or canoe, as it it termed, which he was paddling. This kind of boat is forbidden by the authorities. Another gentleman, in a similar boat, had a narrow escape at the same time."

109 Dodgson's autographed MS. of "The Ligniad" was a poem addressed to George Girdlestone Woodhouse, with whom Dodgson shared a room at Christ Church, which began "Of man in stature small." It was published in facsimile in *Lewis Carroll Observed* (1976, pp. 81-91).

June 6. (M). Arrival at Oxford of the new Chancellor of the University, Lord Derby, who will be installed tomorrow. During the evening there was a procession of boats on the river, in his honour.[110]

June 7. (Tu). A grand procession from Worcester to the Sheldonian Theatre with noblemen, college heads, doctors and proctors. The installation of Lord Derby took place at 11. A Horticultural Show took place in Worcester College Gardens in the afternoon, and in the evening there was a Grand Ball at the Town Hall.

June 8. (W). Dr. Goulburn, the current headmaster of Rugby School, gave a sermon at St. Mary's in aid of the Radcliffe Infirmary. The service included Beethoven's Grand Chant, an anthem and airs by Handel, and other musical performances. A concert was held in the Sheldonian Theatre at 3, and a banquet in the Hall of Christ Church. The celebrations continued with a Masonic Ball in the Town Hall in the evening.[111]

---

110 Lord Derby arrived in Oxford and resided with the Vice-Chancellor at Worcester in preparation for the formal ceremony on June 7, 1853. These events were reported in the *Times*.

111 Edward Meyrick Goulburn (1818-1897) matriculated at Balliol College in 1834: scholar 1834-41, BA 1839, fellow of Merton 1841-46, MA 1842, principal of postmasters, tutor and dean

June 9. (Th). The Installation Ode was given by the professors of poetry and music in the Theatre, and a large number of D.C.Ls were conferred by the new Chancellor, including Lord Redesdale, the Marquis of Blandford, and other noblemen, together with several members of Parliament and the Vice-Chancellor of Cambridge University.[112] Also gaining honorary degrees were the Bishops of Quebec, Ohio, and St. Andrew's, Sir Edward Bulwer Lytton, Sir Thomas Gladstone, and Sir Roderick Murchison.[113] Philip

---

1843-45, perpetual curate of Holywell, Oxford 1844-50, DCL 1850, headmaster of Rugby School 1850-58, DD 1856, minister of Quebec Chapel 1858-59, incumbent of St. John's, Paddington 1859-67, prebendary at St. Paul's, chaplain to the Queen, and dean of Norwich 1866. The events surrounding the installation of the new Chancellor of Oxford were reported in the *Times*, from where these entries are derived.

[112] Honorary DCLs went to John Thomas Freeman Mitford (1805-1886), 2nd Earl of Redesdale; John Winston Spencer-Churchill (1822-1883), Marquis of Blandford and later 7th Duke of Marlborough; and Thomas Charles Geldart (1797-1877), Vice-Chancellor of Cambridge University.

[113] Further honorary DCLs went to George Jehoshaphat Mountain (1789-1863), Bishop of Quebec; Charles Pettit McIlvaine (1799-1873), Bishop of Ohio; Charles Wordsworth (1806-1892), Bishop of St. Andrews; Edward Bulwer Lytton (1804-1873), 1st Baron Lytton and novelist; Thomas Gladstone (1804-1889), MP for Portarlington; and Roderick Impey Murchison (1792-1871), geologist, whom Dodgson photographed in 1860 (IN596). Details of

Pusey also received an honorary degree. A dinner for the Chancellor was held at Pembroke, and the final Installation Ball was held at the Town Hall.

June 17 (F). Collections.[114]

June 28. (Tu). Death of Dr. Faussett.

July 2. (Sat). The election of the new Margaret Professor of Divinity took place. The results were as follows:

Heurtley	53
Hansell	22
Woodgate	46
Foulkes	20

Dr. Heurtley also fills Dr. Faussett's place as canon of Christ Church.[115]

July 5. (Tu). Funeral of Dr. Faussett.[116]

---

the events surrounding the installation of the new Chancellor of Oxford University come from the pages of the *Times*.

[114] Dodgson's "Collections" report for the Trinity Term 1853 indicated: Thucydides *History of the Peloponnesian War* iii-iv *satis bene* (acceptably good), Virgil *Ænied* vii-xii *bene* (good), Ethics translation *satis* + (above acceptable), Theology *valde bene* (very good), and Pr. M. {? a branch of mathematics – probability?} *valde bene* (very good).

[115] The four candidates for the vacancy of Margaret professor of divinity were: Charles Abel Heurtley (1806-1895), Edward Halifax Hansell (1815-1884), Henry Arthur Woodgate (1801-1874), and Edmund Salisbury Ffoulkes (1819-1894).

July 8. (F). Oxford to Croft.

July 15. (F). Over the last few days I have been reading Henry Taylor's romance, *Philip van Artevelde.*[117]

July 25. (M) I have spent the last week writing a poem embodying Skeffington and Wilfred, which I have entitled *The Two Brothers*. These verses, I have decided, are of an insufficient high standard of merit, and too domestic, to submit to a contemporary magazine.[118]

---

116 The *Times* (11 July 1853) recorded: "The remains of the late Margaret Professor of Divinity were interred in one of the north chapels of the cathedral on Tuesday last. The service was read by Dr. Clerke, the Sub-Dean, and the pall was borne by Drs. Barnes, Pusey, Jelf, Jacobson, and Ogilvie, Mr. Ley, Mr. Chamberlain, and Mr. Benson."

117 Dodgson owned a copy of the Sixth Edition of Henry Taylor's *Philip van Artevelde*, dated 1852 but originally published in 1834, containing his monogram on the title-page (Harvard). Dodgson later met the author, Henry Taylor (1800-1886), in July 1862, and photographed him (IN881) and all of his children (see *Diary 4*, p. 92 & pp. 126-127).

118 Dodgson inserted "The Two Brothers," a poem of 156 lines, into *Mischmasch*. It begins "There were two brothers at Twyford school" and is dated 1853. Dodgson indicated that the purpose of *Mischmasch* was to provide an album of "articles of every kind, prose, verse, and pictures, provided they reach a sufficiently high standard of merit. The best of the contents will be offered at intervals to a contemporary magazine of a less domestic nature." This poem was not published in any magazine of the day.

Aug: 19. (F). Wrote a humorous paper which I have entitled "On the Population of the World."[119]

Oct: 8. (Sat). Returned to Oxford. The summer vacation has been a mixture of reading, studying, and writing for pleasure. I am contemplating a new domestic magazine which will probably be modelled on the "The Rectory Umbrella." I also consider writing for a wider audience, perhaps getting something into a local or national periodical.

Oct: 10. (M). Michaelmas term begins.

Oct: 15. (Sat). Found I had got the prickbills two hundred lines apiece, by not pricking in in the morning.[120]

---

119 Dodgson's spoof mathematical paper (MS. Princeton) with a proof for calculating the world's population is entitled "On the Population of the World" and is dated 19 August 1853. It has not been published. See also n. *119* below.

120 This actual entry in Dodgson's first journal was recorded by Collingwood. See above for a description of how the prick bills worked. Dodgson, at this time, was one of the eight most recently appointed Students of Christ Church who undertook this task. Failure to complete this daily chore resulted in an imposition, on this occasion writing out two hundred lines, probably in Latin or Greek.

Oct: 16. (Sun). University sermon. The Provost of Oriel preached in the morning, and Rev. F. Tate of University in the afternoon.[121]

Oct: 22. (Sat). Mr. Price's lectures on analytical mechanics commenced at 1 in the Clarendon.

Oct: 23. (Sun). Dr. Jacobson preached the University sermon at St. Mary's.

Nov: 5. (Sat). The Professor of Political Economy (Mr. Rickards) gave a lecture on Population, examining some of the leading theories, which was most interesting. It was held at the Clarendon, after Mr. Price's lecture.[122]

Nov: 6. (Sun). Dr. Pusey preached the University sermon in the morning, and Rev. R. Scott, of Balliol, in the afternoon.[123]

---

[121] The two preachers were Edward Hawkins, Provost of Oriel (see n. *73* above) and Rev. Francis Tate (1817-1867).

[122] For details of George Kettilby Rickards, see n. *58* above. Dodgson clearly had an interest in the population of the world (see 19 August 1853 above). The population of England in 1851 (from Census returns) was 16.9 million people. The population in Oxford for the same time was 27,843. In 1869, the estimated population of the world was 1,228 million.

[123] Robert Scott (1811-1887) matriculated at Christ Church in 1829: student 1830-35, BA 1833, fellow of Balliol 1835-40, MA 1836, B&DD 1854, master 1854-70, tutor and lecturer in mathematics 1837, junior dean 1838, lecturer in catechism and

Nov: 8. (W). I went, with friends, to a conjuring performance in Oxford last night. We understood that it was the great Mons. Robin, said by some to be the finest conjuror living, but I think, considering what a poor performance it turned out to be, this could hardly have been the truth. Large notices were stuck about in the town with a picture on the top representing the performer lifting off the table a sort of extinguisher or rather portable showerbath, under which are seen standing a young lady and gentleman, in graceful attitudes, and dressed in the height of fashion.

The audience, principally composed of University men, kept up a deafening noise most of the time, so that very few words, even of his opening speech, could be heard. After various tricks more or less good, but all old, he came to *the* trick of the extinguisher. The young lady was brought forward *first* (N.B. no young gentleman); she was mounted on the table; then came the showerbath, which was carefully put over

---

select preacher 1853-54, 1874-75, member of the Hebdomadal Council 1854-70, and delegate of the Press 1855-70. He was appointed Ireland professor of exegesis of scripture 1861-70, rector of Duloe, Cornwall 1840-50, prebendary of Exeter 1845-66, rector of South Luffenham 1850-54, and dean of Rochester 1870-87. He was joint author of the Greek/English Lexicon with Henry George Liddell, which was first published in 1843.

her: then followed, for the space of one minute, swellings and writhings in the sides of the said showerbath, as of someone getting down through a hole in the table, then the extinguisher was lifted off; and lo! she was gone![124]

A much more mysterious event than any of these happened to me this morning. Mr. Gordon sent for me to speak to him, and on my entering the room he said "Well, Mr. Dodgson, I have got an enormous sum to give you, twelve and threepence!" Of course I said "what for, sir?" and his reply may be fairly considered to have been a singular one, "Oh really I don't know, Mr. Dodgson, really I don't know – somebody gave it to me, somebody or other gave it to me," fidgetting about all the time as he counted out the money; this done, he hurried away to his breakfast. I mean to make some further enquiry about this, as on the whole I do not feel quite satisfied at present. Can it be a present from him? And if so, why such an odd sum, and such an odd way of giving it?

---

[124] This diary entry comes mainly from Dodgson's letter to his sister, Mary, dated 9 November 1853 (see *Letters*, pp. 24-25). The celebrated Victorian magician, Monsieur Henri Robin, a Dutchman despite his French pseudonym, made a number of visits to England, performing a range of popular tricks including the vanishing of his young assistants from beneath a large cone, and lifting a child in the air using just one strand of her hair.

The Dean has just shown his sincere regard for me by asking me to dinner tomorrow: I am not altogether overwhelmed with joy at the prospect.[125]

Nov: 9. (W). A notice was sent round reminding undergraduates that it is a requirement to dine within colleges. It went on: "The Heads of Houses and Proctors state that the practice of dining and supping at inns and confectioner's houses has much increased, to the detriment of the good order and discipline of the University, and the statutes of the University should be adhered to. Innkeepers are warned that people violating the statutes are liable to a fine for the first offence, and to be discommoned for the second." The notice appears to have been greeted with disdain by some members of the House, especially among the noblemen.

---

[125] This diary entry comes mainly from Dodgson's letter to his sister, Mary, dated 9 November 1853 (see *Letters*, pp. 24-25). Thomas Gaisford (1779-1855) matriculated at Christ Church in 1797: student 1800-16, BA 1801, MA 1804, classical scholar, Regius professor of Greek 1811-55, prebendary of Worcester 1825-28, prebendary of St. Paul's and of Llandaff 1833, rector of Westwell, Oxfordshire 1815-47, canon of Durham 1829-31, B&DD 1831, and dean of Christ Church 1831-55. His first wife, Helen née Douglas, produced three sons and two daughters. Although his published works were concerned with "classical or patristic literature, his own studies were by no means confined to these. He was well read in history, theology, and civil law, and was a good Shakespearean scholar" (*DNB*).

Nov: 13 (Sun).Dr. Bull gave the University sermon in the Cathedral.[126]

Dec: 4. (Sun). Again, the University sermon was held in the Cathedral, delivered by Archdeacon Clerke in the morning. Rev. C. P. Eden gave the afternoon sermon at St. Mary's.[127] There was a large congregation for Dr. Colenso, Bishop of Natal, who preached at St. Mary's in the evening.[128]

---

[126] John Bull (1790-1858) matriculated at Christ Church in 1808: BA 1812, MA 1814, tutor and censor, public examiner 1817-19, proctor 1820, BD 1821, curate of Binsey, rector of Sowton, Devon 1821, select preacher 1822, prebendary of Exeter 1823, DD 1825, archdeacon of Cornwall 1826, archdeacon of Barnstable 1826-1830, rector of Lezant, Cornwall 1826, prebendary of York 1826, canon of Christ Church 1830, and vicar of Staverton, Northamptonshire 1830-58.

[127] Charles Page Eden (1807-1885) matriculated at Oriel College in 1825: BA 1830, fellow 1832-51, MA 1833, junior treasurer 1836, dean 1838, examiner in Classics 1840-42, vicar of St. Mary the Virgin, Oxford 1843-50, select preacher 1838 and 1853, prebendary of York 1870, proctor in Convocation 1869, 1874, 1880, and vicar of Aberford 1850-85.

[128] John William Colenso (1814-1883) matriculated at St. John's College, Cambridge in 1832: Naden divinity student 1834, scholar 1835, BA (2nd Wrangler) 1836, fellow 1837-46, MA 1839, ordained 1839, tutor 1842-46, mathematical master at Harrow 1838-42, vicar of Forncett St Mary, Norfolk 1846-53, DD 1853, and Bishop of Natal 1853-83. He was created DCL at Oxford on 28 June 1854. He worked diligently to educate the Zulus, providing them with a written language, a Zulu grammar, dictionary, and translations from the Old and the New Testament. He aroused violent feeling and opposition by his Commentary to the Epistle to

Dec: 13. (Tu). Harington's father, the Principal of Brasenose, died today.[129]

Dec: 16. (F). Lord Palmerston revealed that University Reform will be debated in the next session of Parliament, and they will consider (i) the constitution of the University, (ii) the extension of admissions, (iii) the removal of restriction upon fellowships, and (iv) the application

---

the Romans, and his Critical Examination of the Pentateuch. He was formally deposed and excommunicated by Dr Gray, Metropolitan Bishop of Capetown, in 1863, but his position was confirmed by the Law Courts. He suffered greatly from misunderstanding and misrepresentation as a result of the invasion of Zululand in 1878. He denounced the Zulu war and exposed the corruption of some Colonial officials and their tyranny to natives {details from Venn}.

[129] Dr. Harington died suddenly and unexpectedly. The *Times* (14 December 1853) reported the circumstances, stating that Dr. Harington had driven out in his carriage on Friday with Mrs. Harington, and had caught a cold. He took a turn for the worse on Monday, and Dr. Jackson and Dr. Acland were called in. He died on Tuesday in the early hours of the morning, leaving a wife and four children, the eldest, a son, at Christ Church. Richard Harington (1800-1853) matriculated at Christ Church in 1818: BA 1821, fellow of Brasenose 1822-34, mathematical lecturer 1823, MA 1824, tutor 1825, junior dean 1827, Latin lecturer 1831, B&DD 1842, and principal 1842-53. He married, firstly, Cecilia née Smith (d. 1844), and they had two children: Richard (1835-1911) and Charles (1837-1868). He married, secondly, Mary née Paul (1815?-1886) on 2 July 1846, and they had three children: Robert "Bob" (1851-1855), Beatrice Cecilia (1852-1936), and Alice Margaret (1854-1901). After the death of Dr. Harington, Dodgson befriended Mrs. Harington and her three children, taking photographs of Beatrice (IN323, IN667, etc.) and Margaret (IN324, IN667, etc.).

of some parts of the endowments of colleges to the payment of professors and other persons. All this will have important consequences for Christ Church.[130]

Dec: 20. (Tu). Funeral of the Principal of Brasenose.

Dec: 21. (W). Collections.[131]

Dec: 22. (Th). Went down to London by train with Frank, and then to Putney. After dinner we went to the Westminster Play, *Adelphi* by Terence, performed in Latin. The acting was good, especially the two brothers, Ctesipho and Aeschinus.[132]

---

[130] Henry John Temple (1784-1865), 3rd Viscount Palmerston, matriculated at St. John's College, Cambridge, after gaining his first degree at Edinburgh University: MA 1806, Conservative MP for Newport, Isle of Wight 1807, lord of the Admiralty 1808, elected MP for Cambridge University 1811-31, held various government positions including foreign secretary in Lord Grey's administration, a position he held for eleven years. He became prime minister in 1855 and gained an increased majority at the general election in 1857, but resigned in 1858 after a defeat on the Conspiracy to Murder Bill. However, he became prime minister again in 1859. He was created hon. DCL at Oxford in 1862, and LL.D. at Cambridge in 1864.

[131] Dodgson's "Collections" report for Michaelmas Term 1853 stated: Herodotus' *History* i-ii *satis bene* (acceptably good), History *med* (moderate), Livy i-ii *bene* (good), History *satis* (acceptable), Translation *bene* (good).

[132] Dodgson's attendance at the Westminster Play was recorded on 21 December 1857 (see *Diary 3*, p. 140), in which he

Dec: 24. (Sat). Left Putney in the morning and went by train to Croft, arriving about 8 p.m.

The *Times* reports the appointment of Students at Christ Church. The Dean and Chapter have appointed Harington, Fisher, Longley, and Faussett. Also from Westminster School the following are given Studentships: Oliver, Twiss, Williams, and Frank Dodgson.[133]

---

states that he saw *Adelphi* four years ago and "I think the acting as a whole was inferior to the former one." In the play, Demea, a father of two sons, brings up one strictly, but entrusts the other to his brother, Micio, who is more easy-going. Both boys go astray, the eldest seducing Pamphila and then kidnapping a music-girl for his timid younger brother. Demea, disappointed in his method of bringing up his sons, learns to be more affable, thus courting popularity. The drama, by Terence (c.195 - 159 BC), is regarded as one of his finest plays.

[133] Henry Longley (1832-1899), Richard Harington, John Toke Faussett, and Wilfrid Fisher (b. 1833) were made Students from within the House, together with Frederick William Oliver (b. 1836), Quintin William Francis Twiss (1835-1900), Arthur Charles Vaughan Williams (1835-1875), and Dodgson's cousin, Francis Hume Dodgson, from Westminster School. As a result, Dodgson moved to 92nd position in the List of Students, moving him out of the last eight, thus removing his previous duties (being one of those responsible for the "prick bills"). Nominations for Students were in the hands of the Dean and Canons, usually exercising this role in rotation. But in 1854, this system changed. The Chapter Books (MS: Christ Church) indicate the change made on 22 February 1854, when it was reported: "Resolved. That upon the determination of the present Roll of Students, no new Roll shall be made, but that hereafter all Commoners of this House, having resided one year at the least therein and being of irreproachable moral conduct, as well as of competent learning (to be ascertained by the means of a good

Dec: 28. (W). The Rev. E. H. Cradock was appointed new Principal of Brasenose. The *Times* says the appointment was unanimous.[134]

Dec: 31. (Sat). The family migrated to Ripon.

Now at the close of the Old Year, I take counsel with myself for the future. My finals take place in 1854, and I must be more regular than ever, and change my bad habits of aversion to real hard labour. I must be resolved to devote time to work and study. I trust and pray that the most merciful God may aid me in this and all other good undertakings.

---

examination) shall be allowed to present themselves as Candidates for Studentship. The Dean and Canons in waiving the right of Nomination which they have enjoyed from time immemorial do not thereby admit that meritorious young Men have failed to obtain as opportunities offered, a place in the order of Students, but they are of opinion that the time has arrived for affording additional inducements to exertion amongst the younger Members of this Society and they hope that the step which they have now taken, will prove not only beneficial to individuals but conducive to the welfare of the foundation generally."

[134] Edward Hartopp Cradock (1810-1886), formerly Grove (assumed the surname Cradock by royal licence in 1849), matriculated at Balliol in 1827: BA 1831, MA (from Brasenose) 1834, rector of Tedstone, Delamere, Cheshire 1844-54, B&DD 1854, canon of Worcester 1848-54, and principal of Brasenose 1853-86. He married the Hon. Harriet Lister (b. 1810), maid of honour to Queen Victoria, and sister of Lord John Russell's first wife, in 1844.

Diary for the year 1854
January to December

Jan: 1. (Sun). The year begins at the Canons' Residence, Ripon.

Jan: 4. (W). We went, as a party, to spend the evening at the Deanery by invitation of Dr. Erskine. A Miss Anderson was present; by holding in her hand a folded paper containing some words written by a person unknown to her, she was able to describe his or her character. I was one of those chosen to try out her "powers" – the family pronounce the outcome as remarkable![135]

[135] The "clairvoyant" was, possibly, Maria "Minnie" Katherine Anderson (d. 1889). She was the youngest daughter of Rev. Richard Anderson (b. 1791) of The Grange, Bedale, Yorkshire, and in September 1864 she married Walter Moseley (1832-87), of Buildwas. Dodgson photographed Miss Anderson (IN1054) in August 1863. Collingwood reproduced her assessment of Dodgson's character (p. 56): "Very clever head; a great deal of number; a great deal of imitation; he would make a good actor; diffident; rather shy in general society; comes out in the home circle; rather obstinate; very clever; a great deal of concentration; very affectionate; a great deal of wit and humour; not much eventuality (or memory of events); fond of deep reading; imaginative, fond of reading poetry; *may* compose." The date of this character evaluation is uncertain. A document marked "C.L.D. per Miss Anderson" and an envelope addressed "C.L.D.'s character given by Minnie Anderson from holding (without seeing) a piece of his hand-writing not knowing it was his" survive in the Dodgson Family.

Jan: 14. (Sat). The Hilary Term commences, but Christ Church does not begin lectures for another week.

Jan: 16. (M). The *Times* announces that Sir R. H. Inglis is to retire from representing the University in Parliament due to ill health.[136]

Jan: 20. (F). Returned to Oxford. I have moved into the room next door: Cloister Staircase, room 5. This has a large sitting room and a smaller room where I shall sleep.[137]

Jan: 29. (Sun). Rev. E. Stokes preached the University sermon in the morning.[138]

---

[136] Sir Robert Harry Inglis (1786-1855) matriculated at Christ Church in 1803: BA 1806, MA 1809, barrister-at-law Lincoln's Inn 1818, became a Tory politician, MP Dundalk 1824-26, hon. DCL 1826, MP Ripon 1828-29, MP Oxford University 1829-1854 (11 Parliaments) during which he opposed parliamentary reform. He was president of the Literary Club and antiquary of the Royal Academy 1850, and was made Privy Councillor in 1854.

[137] The Cloister Staircase no longer exists at Christ Church. The rooms were decommissioned when the roof was raised on the East side of the Cloisters in the early 1860s. What remains of these rooms is now used as a store by the Cathedral choir – the ceiling being no more than four feet from the floor, making the space uninhabitable.

[138] Edward Stokes (1823-1863) matriculated at Christ Church in 1840: student 1842-60, BA 1844, MA 1846, tutor 1848-52, Greek reader 1852, proctor 1854, Whitehall preacher 1850-52, select

Jan: 31. (Tu). Mr. Price's lectures on analytical mechanics resumed today at the Clarendon.

Feb: 12 (Sun). The University service took place in the Cathedral this morning, Dr. Ogilvie preaching the sermon.

Feb: 28. (Tu). The death of the Rector of Exeter College was announced.[139]

Mar: 6. (M). The death of yet another head of college, the Master of Balliol, occurred today.[140]

Mar: 13. (M). The afternoon University sermon was preached by the Bishop of Oxford. St. Mary's was excessively crowded.

---

preacher 1852-54, and vicar of Staines, Middlesex, 1859-63. Dodgson photographed him in 1857 (IN217).

[139] Dr. Joseph Loscombe Richards (1797-1854) had been ill for some time, and was convalescing at Bonchurch, Isle of Wight when his death occurred. He died of consumption. His body was brought back to Oxford for burial in Exeter College Chapel where his wife's remains were interred in 1838, just one year after their marriage. The funeral was held on 7 March 1854.

[140] Dr. Richard Jenkyns (1782-1854) caught a violent cold at Convocation in the Sheldonian Theatre on Friday 24 February, which brought on the ailment that caused his demise (*Times*, 7 March 1854). He was attended by Dr. Acland and Dr. Latham from London, and nursed by his wife and his sister (Mrs. Gaisford). Death was brought about by "suffusion of water upon the lungs."

Mar: 14. (Tu). Funeral of Dr. Jenkyns – his body was taken for burial at Wells Cathedral.

Mar: 27. (M). Collections.[141]

Mar: 28. (Tu). The papers indicate that war has been declared against Russia.

Mar: 30. (Th). Convocation finally agreed to the outlay of between £30,000 and £40,000 for the new Museum. Placets 18, non-placets 4.

Ap: 4. (Tu). Rev. Robert Scott was appointed the new Master of Balliol.[142]

Ap: 16. (Sun). Easter Sunday

Ap: 26. (W). At Convocation, it was the turn of Christ Church to nominate one of the Proctors. Rev. E. Stokes was appointed Proctor together with Rev. R. Cholmeley of Magdalen.[143] Rev. T. J. Prout was

141 Dodgson was probably relieved that he did not need to take part in Collections during his final undergraduate year. He may have received an oral report from his tutors, but nothing was written on his Collections record.

142 The *Times* reported (6 April 1854): "His appointment will gratify a large circle of friends, and will, we believe, be received with great satisfaction generally."

143 Robert Cholmeley (1818-1880) matriculated at Wadham College in 1836: BA 1840 (from Corpus Christi), of Lincoln's Inn

appointed Pro-Proctor to act as Stokes' deputy. It was also announced that the Senior Proctor would receive names of candidates for public examination on Friday.[144]

Ap: 30. (Sun). University sermon given by Dr. Ogilvie.

May 3. (W). Read the declamation in Hall, taking a passage from Aristotle's *Ethics*.[145]

1840, MA 1843 (from Magdalen), fellow of Magdalen 1843-58, proctor 1854, B&DD 1858, and vicar of Findon, Sussex 1860-80.

144 Dodgson was required to submit to the Proctor his matriculation paper, a testamur of the Moderators or Examiners, a certificate from two professors, and a list, signed by the candidate, of the subjects and books in which he offered himself for examination. The Pro-Proctor was Thomas Jones Prout (1823-1909). He matriculated at Christ Church in 1842: BA 1846, MA 1848, tutor 1851-61, censor 1857-61, proctor 1859, vicar of Binsey, Oxfordshire 1857-91. He took an active role in the discussions to bring reforms to Christ Church, particularly in wresting power from the Dean and Chapter. This gave rise to his title, "The Man who Slew the Canons." However, his reputation for falling asleep during the long and sometimes tedious meetings held by the dons may have given rise to the model for the Dormouse in *Alice's Adventures in Wonderland* which is supported by the fact that the "treacle-well" is in the churchyard at Binsey, his "living." Dodgson photographed him in 1857 (IN238).

145 Dodgson's paper survives (MS: Berol) but is untitled. At the end, Dodgson wrote "Declamation read in Hall, May 3, 1854). The subject, written entirely in Latin and Greek, is from a sentence in Aristotle's *Ethics* which states "Every art and method aims at some good." A full translation is reproduced in Morton Cohen's *Lewis Carroll, A Biography* (1995, pp. 538-540).

May 4. (Th). Attended Schools for the Classics examination.[146] The room was full with several from Christ Church.

May 14 (Sun). University sermon given by Rev. E. Stokes of Christ Church.

May 25. (Th). Ascension Day. Rev. R. St. J. Tyrwhitt preached the sermon in the Cathedral.[147]

June 2. (F). I gained a Third Class in the Classics Finals. I put this down to a lack of work in preparing for the examinations. I mean

---

146 "Schools" was a separate building in which examinations for Oxford degrees took place, either written or oral examinations, organised by the Master of the Schools. Dodgson was later to parody the construction of the new Schools in his paper, *The Blank Cheque*, when he discovered that no budget had been allocated to the cost of erecting the new building. The number of candidates for examinations in the classical schools was 187 of whom 44 were taking honours.

147 Richard St. John Tyrwhitt (1827-1895) matriculated at Christ Church in 1845: student 1845-59, BA 1849, MA 1852, tutor 1852-56, rhetoric reader 1856, vicar of St. Mary Magdalen, Oxford 1858-72, and hon. fellow of King's College, London 1884. He married Eliza-Anne née Spencer-Stanhope (d. 1859) in 1858, and they had one son, Walter Spencer-Stanhope (1859-1934). His wife died soon after, and he then married Caroline née Yorke (d. 1883). They had six children: Cecil Robert (1862-1924), Alice Catherine "Kittie" (b. 1864?), Hugh St. John (b. 1865), twins Beauchamp Edward (b. 1867) and Mary Frances "Polly" (b. 1867), and Reginald Yorke (1870-1951). Tyrwhitt was a poet, writer, and art critic. He published *A Handbook of Pictorial Art* (1868), and *Hugh Heron Ch. Ch.* (1880), among many other works.

to do better when I take my Mathematics Finals at the end of the year. Mr. Price says that he is organising a reading party for undergraduates studying mathematics; I mean to join him, if my father will agree to my being away throughout the summer. The location for the reading party will be at Whitby, Yorkshire.[148]

June 7. (W). Beginning of the Act Term. All my efforts must now be focussed on getting a good result in the mathematics finals.

June 13. (Tu). Attended a large gathering in the Town Hall to hear the Bishop of Oxford and the Bishop of New Zealand report on the growing new diocese in the Antipodes.[149]

---

[148] The *Times* announced the results of the *Literae Humaniores* examinations (Classics) on 3 June 1854. Dodgson was one of 14 undergraduates in Class III. Many of his friends did better than he did; Thomas Fowler and Edward Pember both achieved a First Class, Samuel Bosanquet, William Ranken, and George Woodhouse both getting a Second Class.

[149] George Augustus Selwyn (1809-1878), first Bishop of New Zealand reported on the needs of his diocese, the development of this new colonial country, and the link with Oxford University. John Robert Godley (1814-1861), a graduate of Christ Church, was instrumental, with Edward Gibbon Wakefield, in establishing the Canterbury Association with the aim of setting up a colony in New Zealand. Sketched out by Wakefield in 1843, but developed with Godley's help in 1847, the "instant civilization" was planned to include endowed churches and schools, various trades, and a university based on Christ Church, Oxford. The new colony became

June 18. (Sat). The King of Portugal visited Oxford.[150]

June 26. (M). Commemoration. Celebrations were marred by the death of an undergraduate from St. John's who drowned while rowing on the river. The procession of boats in the evening was cancelled, but the concert, given by the Amateur Musical Society in the Town Hall, went ahead as planned.[151]

Christchurch, New Zealand, and the proposed college became the University of Canterbury. In May 1848, the Canterbury Association had 53 members including 30 Oxford graduates (17 Christ Church men) and 17 Cambridge graduates. Godley, and his Christ Church friends, were particularly influential on the management committee, which made important decisions about the new colony. The Association consulted Bishop Selwyn in whose diocese they proposed to establish the settlement, and he was supportive and offered practical advice. In May 1850, the Association published its scheme for the new college and schools, but lack of funds threatened to put an end to these plans. A public appeal revived the plans, and the first school was set up in March 1851. The university, however, did not materialise until 1872. Bishop Selwyn returned to New Zealand, and became much respected by the Maori people. On his return in 1868, he was made Bishop of Lichfield. After his death on 11 April 1878, a new college in Cambridge was named after him in recognition of his ministry both in this country and in New Zealand.

150 The *Times* (19 June 1854) reported the visit during which the King inspected "the chief public buildings and other places of interest." Peter V (1837-1861) came to the Portuguese throne in 1853.

151 "Gloom thrown on Commemoration proceedings" was the heading in the *Times* (27 June 1854), which reported: "Death by drowning of Mr. William Earle, commoner of St. John's College. In

June 27. (Tu). Horticultural Society Show in the gardens of New College, in spite of stormy weather. Sir William and Lady Heathcote were present.[152]

July 8. (Sat). Term ends.

July 20. (Th). Travelled to Whitby with Mr. Price for his Summer Mathematics Reading Party. I am to reside at 5 East View Terrace, with a magnificent view across this fishing town looking towards the ruined Abbey. The party consists of Almond (Balliol),[153] Bowden (University),[154]

---

the course of a skulling race among members of his college, his skiff was overturned. He was a fair swimmer, and struck off for the shore. Owing, perhaps, to the boisterous state of the weather, or to some other unexplained cause, he sank, before reaching it, in water about 7 feet deep. Three or four of his fellow collegians jumped in to render him assistance, and dived after him, but without success. He did not again rise to the surface, and his body was not recovered till he had been in the water a quarter of an hour."

152 Sir William Heathcote (1801-1881) had just become MP for Oxford University in February 1854, a position he held until 1868. He matriculated at Oriel College in 1817: BA 1821, student of the Inner Temple 1822, fellow of All Souls 1822-25, BCL 1824, MP for Hampshire 1826-31, DCL 1830, MP for North Hampshire 1837-49, MP for Oxford University February 1854-68, and hon. fellow of All Souls in 1858. He married, firstly, Caroline Frances (d. 1835), daughter of Charles George, 1st Lord Arden, on 8 November 1825, and, secondly, Selina née Shirley (d. 1901) on 18 May 1841.

153 Hely Hutchinson Almond (1832-1903) matriculated at Balliol in 1850: first class in classics and mathematics moderations

Fowler (Merton), Pusey (Ch. Ch.), Ranken (Corpus),[155] Short (New),[156]

1853, second class in classics and mathematics finals 1854. He rowed in the Balliol eight. He went on to become assistant master at Loretto School 1858, assistant master at Merchiston Castle School 1859-61, and headmaster of Loretto 1862-1903. He took his MA in 1862, and was awarded LLD (Glasgow). Among his publications were: *Edinburgh Health Lectures* (1884), "Football as a Moral Agent" in the *Nineteenth Century* (December 1893), *Christ the Protestant and other Sermons* (1899), "The Decline in Salmon and its Remedy" in the *Nineteenth Century* (June 1899), "The Breed of Man" in the *Nineteenth Century* (October 1900), and "Examinations for Woolwich and Sandhurst" in the *Fortnightly Review* (January 1899). He married Eleanora Frances née Tristram in 1876.

[154] James Bowden (b. 1835) matriculated at University College in 1852: first class in mathematics moderations 1854, second class in mathematics finals, BA 1856, MA 1858, ordained deacon 1858, priest 1859, curate of Crawley, Hampshire 1858-61, rector of Staunton, Worcestershire 1861-67, vicar of Oatlands, Surrey 1867-71, and rector of Ardingly, Sussex 1875-1911. He married but was a widower in 1881. He was still living in 1924, but disappears from *Crockford's Clerical Directory* soon after.

[155] William Henry Ranken (1832-1920) matriculated at Corpus Christi College in 1850: scholar 1850-62, first class in classics and second class in mathematics moderations 1852, second class in classics and first class in mathematics finals, BA 1854, ordained deacon 1856, priest 1858, MA 1857, fellow 1862-69, assistant master and fellow at Radley College 1855-60, curate of East Retford 1860-61, fellow Corpus Christi College 1862-69, junior bursar 1867, vicar of Sandford-on-Thames 1862-66, vicar of Radley, Berkshire 1865-67, vicar of West Houghton, Lancashire 1868, vicar of Marston Meysey 1873-82, simultaneously rector of Meysey Hampton, Gloucestershire 1869-84, and vicar of Christ Church, Surbiton 1884-1901, and rector of Byfield, Northamptonshire 1901-19. Dodgson composed "A Valentine" written in February 1860 to

Sidgwick (Corpus),[157] Wheeler (Worcester),[158] and Wingfield (New).[159]

Ranken when he was a master at Radley. Ranken's wife was Frances M. (b. 1845).

[156] Ambrose Short (b. 1833) matriculated at New College in 1851: second class mathematics moderations 1853, third class in mathematics finals, BA 1856, fellow 1851-64, ordained deacon 1858, priest 1859, MA 1858, headmaster of Oswestry Grammar School 1863-73, vicar of Bodicote, Oxon. 1873-92, rector of Saham-Toney, Norfolk 1892, and rural dean of Beccles and Thetford 1897-98.

[157] William Carr Sidgwick (b. 1834) matriculated at Corpus Christi College in 1852: exhibitioner 1852-57, first class in classics and second class in mathematics moderations 1854, first class in classics and fourth class in mathematics finals, BA 1856, fellow Merton College, 1857-73, MA 1859, tutor 1859-70, dean 1859, principal of postmasters and chaplain 1867-68, student of Lincoln's Inn 1869, and lecturer in logic and political economy Oriel College 1881-82.

[158] Thomas Littleton Wheeler (1834-1910) matriculated at Worcester College in 1852: first class mathematics moderations 1854, first class mathematics finals, BA 1856, ordained deacon 1857, priest 1858, MA 1859, curate of St. Michael's, Tenbury 1857-60, curate of St. Martin, Worcestershire 1860-65, perpetual curate Holy Trinity, Worcester 1865-71, and Hereford diocesan inspector of schools 1875-83.

[159] (Sir) Edward Wingfield (1834-1910) matriculated at New College in 1850: fellow 1850-72, first class in classics and second class in mathematics moderations 1853, SCL 1853, first class in classics and second class in mathematics finals, BA 1854, BCL 1857, MA 1859, barrister-at-law Lincoln's Inn 1859, assistant Under-Secretary of State for the Colonies 1878, permanent under-Secretary of State for the Colonies, 1897-1900, secretary for Orders

Mr. Price says that he will be helped by Prof. Donkin who will be staying at Whitby with his family.[160]

Aug: 19. (Sat). Trip to Goathland by rail to see "Mallyan's Spout." After leaving Goathland Station, the road down to the cascade consisted of mud and water, with a preponderance of the latter. I was rash enough to set the example of returning up the side of the cliff, instead of by the road. Only one of our men followed at first, and he did so, thinking the ascent would be easy. I reached a point where retreat was hopeless, and the only thing to do was to go on: the ascent took about ¼ of an hour: every here and there came a little platform where one could rest and consider the next thing to be done. Just at the top it was hardest of all; it was only to be done by crawling up through the mud, holding by 2 roots, without whose help it would have been impossible. My companion took about 5 minutes longer,

---

of St Michael and St George 1897-1900, and KCB 1899. He married Mary Georgina, daughter of the Ven. J. W. Sheringham, in 1872.

[160] William Fishburn Donkin (1814-1869), fellow of University College 1836-43, mathematical lecturer and examiner, and Savilian professor of astronomy 1842-69. He was one of the examiners for the Mathematics Finals at the end of 1854, together with Prof. Bartholomew Price, and Henry Pritchard (see n. *173* below).

and subsequently 4 other men reached the top, all covered with mud. Mr. Price and the remaining man more wisely went back as they came. We joined him again at the station, and boasted as much as possible of our feat, to prevent ridicule at our appearance. The Spout itself is a "poor little feeble, fluttering thing," scarcely worth so much trouble to see. However we had had a very pleasant expedition, and such a scramble as I have rarely engaged in.[161]

Aug: 22. (Tu). Day of the school-feast, held in the grounds near the Abbey. Mr. Price arranged for us to help in the proceedings. There was a large assemblage of inhabitants and visitors.[162] On our first reaching the ground the only sound audible was a unanimous chorus of screaming babies, but this was soon

---

[161] This diary entry comes from Dodgson's letter to his sister, Mary, dated 23 August 1854, written from Whitby (see *Letters*, pp. 26-29).

[162] One person Dodgson met at Whitby was Dr. John Dowson, possibly at this school-feast. He noted on 1 March 1856 (see *Diary 2*, p. 46) that, following a fit suffered by an undergraduate at Christ Church, a doctor in the Anatomy School "pronounced it to be epilepsy, and said he had better lie still some time and then be got to his rooms: he and Southey and I half led, half carried him to his rooms by the meadow gate, and there the Doctor (a Dr. Dowson, whom I remember to have met at Whitby) had to leave him."

drowned in the general noise. There were 6 long tables placed in a kind of hollow, which held about 300 children, who were rather oddly arranged, boys on one side of each table and girls on the other. The parents, babies, and other spectators assembled on the rising ground around them.

Mr. Keane mounted a bench in the middle, and rang a bell, in the fashion of town-criers.[163] He then said grace, after which the children sang a verse of the Old Hundredth.[164] Then came large baskets of currant-bread, and absurdly small jugs of tea, carried by ladies and teachers. Mr. Price and one of our men joined in carrying currant-bread.

---

163 William Keane (1818-1873) matriculated at Emmanuel College, Cambridge, in 1835: BA 1840, MA 1843, ordained deacon 1841, priest 1843, curate of Fenstanton, Cambridgeshire 1843-46, domestic chaplain to Marquis of Conyngham, canon St. Paul's Cathedral, Calcutta 1846-53, assistant secretary of the Missionary Society 1852, perpetual curate of Whitby St. Mary 1853-61, and rector there 1862-73. He married Elizabeth Fryer née Thomas (d. 1908) in 1853, and they had five children: John Thomas (b. 1854), Robert Keane Charles (b. 1856), Hilda Elizabeth (b. 1857), Jane "Janie" Maria Colpoys (b. 1858), and Marcus William Allatson (1861-1889). Dodgson photographed Rev. W. Keane in 1860 (IN624 & IN626), and later his wife, and youngest son Marcus (IN1067).

164 This is the hymn based on the 100th Psalm, "All people that on earth do dwell," written by William Kethe (d. 1608?) in 1561 and sung to the tune by L. Bourgeois.

In the middle of the feast down came the rain in torrents, and nothing was to be seen but flight, uproar, and confusion. All the visitors went home, I among others. Wheeler, who helped in the currant-bread, stayed through the shower, and related to us the rest of the proceedings. The feast went on when the sky cleared; I suppose they did not mind soaked bread and cold tea.

They had races and football afterwards: my friend Wheeler seems to have chiefly superintended affairs, as there seemed no one else to suggest any thing. He got up various races, giving a halfpenny as prize: ran as a hare, offering a halfpenny for whoever could touch him first: kept the footballs going, his chief task being to rescue the girls' football when it got among the boys, and, in a word, seems to have made himself generally useful. Mr. Keane chiefly devoted himself to scattering nuts to be scrambled for. The day seems to have ended with a speech from Mr. Keane.[165]

Aug: 23. (W). Today there is a strong wind blowing off shore, and threatening to carry Whitby and contents into the sea. There is sand

[165] This diary entry also comes from Dodgson's letter to his sister, Mary, dated 23 August 1854, written from Whitby (see *Letters*, pp. 26-29).

and sharp shingle flying in the air, that acts on the face like the smart cut of a whip. Wrote to Mary giving latest news of the Reading Party.

I have bought three other American poets in the cheap editions, Lowell, Willis, and Holmes. Lowell seems to be the only one at all worthy of the name.[166]

Aug: 26. (Sat). Sat on the beach and told stories to a group of children.[167]

---

166 This diary entry, too, comes from Dodgson's letter to his sister, Mary, dated 23 August 1854, written from Whitby (see *Letters*, pp. 26-29). The poets were James Russell Lowell (1819-1891), Nathaniel Parker Willis (1806-1867), and Oliver Wendell Holmes (1809-1894).

167 Thomas Fowler published his reminiscences of the Whitby reading party in the *St. James' Gazette* (11 March 1898) in which he wrote:

> Dodgson and I were both pupils of Professor Bartholomew Price (now Master of Pembroke) in a mathematical Reading Party at Whitby in the summer of 1854. It was there that *Alice* was incubated. Dodgson used to sit on a rock on the beach, telling stories to a circle of eager young listeners of both sexes. These stories were afterwards developed and consolidated into their present form.

Fowler means, of course, that some incidents emanating from this time were re-used by Dodgson when writing the *Alice* stories, the majority of which had their origins during the boat-trip to Godstow with the Liddell sisters on 4 July 1862. Derek Hudson lists a number of conjectures for scenes inspired by the Whitby visit – see *Lewis Carroll* (1954), pp. 74-76. Perhaps it is worth noting that no other

Aug: 31. (Th). My poem, which I have been composing over the last few days, was published in the *Supplement to the Whitby Gazette* today. It appears under my pen-name of "B. B."[168]

Sep: 7. (Th). The first chapter of my story, "Wilhelm Von Schmitz," was published in the *Whitby Gazette* today. Again, I used my pen-name "B. B."[169]

Sep: 14. (Th). The second chapter of "Wilhelm Von Schmitz" appeared.

Sep: 21. (Th). The *Whitby Gazette* published the third chapter of "Wilhelm Von Schmitz." I have left the fourth and final chapter with them: it will be published next week. The Reading Party came to an end. Working with Mr. Price has proved to be a most successful and worthwhile endeavour.

---

source supports the Whitby connections having any influence on the *Alice* stories.

168 This was "The Lady of the Ladle" published in the *Supplement to the Whitby Gazette*, issue number 9, dated Thursday, 31 August 1854. The poem recounts the tale of a young man who courts a local Whiby lass by the name of Matilda, but his over-fussy attention with his personal appearance delays his rendezvous with Hilda, and she gives up waiting for him.

169 The humorous story, in four chapters, is about a poet, William Smith, who tries to win the affections of a young girl named Sukie. But he is in competition with a waiter.

Sep: 22. (F). Returned to Croft. During the summer, I have contributed two poems to the *Oxonian Advertiser*, neither at all worth preservation.[170]

Oct: 10. (Tu). Term was due to commence today, but due to the cholera epidemic in Oxford, college will not meet until 21 October.[171]

Oct: 23. (M). Went to the Radcliffe Library to see the designs for the new University Museum. 33 submissions were on display showing plans and drawings of the proposed new building.[172]

---

170 The following poems were published in *Hall's Oxonian Advertiser* during the summer of 1854. All appeared under the heading "Poets' Corner" and were unsigned:

June 1854 (No. 18)
"The Past and the Future"
July 1854 (No. 19)
"There is a Tongue in Every Leaf"
August 1854 (No. 20)
"The Sailor's Evening Song"
September 1854 (No. 21)
"The Merry Heart."

None of these poems are clearly identified as being written by Dodgson. He did not reprint any in later publications of his verse.

171 The *Times* reported (13 October 1854) that "the epidemic in Oxford is rapidly declining; no cases of cholera have occurred for several days."

172 The *Times* reported (16 November 1854) that the Museum Delegates had selected six of the designs for the new Museum to be

Oct: 25. (W). Heard that Henry Pritchard of Corpus has been appointed one of the mathematical examiners this term.[173] Went to the Senior Proctor to put my name forward for the mathematical finals this term.

Oct: 28. (Sat). The Senior Proctor announced today that 88 have signed up for the mathematical finals.

Nov: 26 (Sun).Attended the University sermon in the Cathedral, preached by the Dean of Christ Church.

Nov: 28. (M). I am working thirteen hours a day to prepare for the Finals in Mathematics. I intend to work through the night before my *viva voce* examination.

Dec: 1. (F). First day of the Mathematical Finals.

Dec: 6. (W). Dr. Acland, together with graduates and undergraduates, are collecting old clothing for the use of our army in the East who, according to reports, are

---

submitted to the scrutiny of professional judges to ascertain the probable cost and soundness of construction. The rest were rejected.

173 Henry Pritchard (1820-1857) matriculated at Merton College in 1837: postmaster 1837-38, scholar Corpus Christi College 1838-47, BA 1841, MA 1844, fellow 1847-57, senior dean 1851, mathematical lecturer 1852, proctor 1852, BD 1853, and incumbent of Sheen, Staffordshire.

suffering from the severe weather conditions.[174]

Dec: 13. (W). I went to Mr. Price to see how I did in the Mathematics papers. The following were the sums total of the marks for each in the First Class, as nearly as I can remember:

Dodgson	.....	279
Bosanquet	.....	261
Cookson	.....	254
Fowler	.....	225
Ranken	.....	213

[174] Henry Wentworth Dyke Acland (1815-1900) matriculated at Christ Church in 1834: BA 1840, fellow of All Souls 1840-47, Lee's reader in anatomy 1845, BMed 1846, DMed 1848, Radcliffe Librarian 1851, natural science examiner 1857, Regius professor of medicine 1857-94, member of the Medical Council 1854-74 and president 1874-87, and a member of Sanitary Commission 1870-72. He was honorary physician to the Prince of Wales, and to Prince Leopold when he was at Oxford. He became Dean Liddell's doctor, and gave advice about the Dean's poor health, and even accompanied him on a trip to Madeira to be his personal physician. He was knighted in 1884. The *Times* announced (7 December 1854) that "Members of the University, anxious to testify their sympathy for the suffering of the wounded and sick of our army in the East have obtained permission to send loose articles of dress for their use; flannel clothing, boating jackets, cricket, boating or racket trousers, shooting jackets, overcoats of all kinds, dressing gowns, drawers, jerseys, slippers, handkerchiefs, woollen gloves and socks, cape, plaids and rugs." The Union Society acted as the centre for collecting these articles. England declared war against Russia on 27 March 1854. Peace was eventually declared in Paris on 31 March 1856.

Mr. Price also said he never remembered so good a set of men in. All this is very satisfactory.

I gave my Scout a bottle of wine to drink to my First. We shall be made Bachelors on Monday.[175]

Dec: 18. (M). Last day of term. Today, my BA degree was confirmed: First Class in Mathematics, Third Class in Classics.[176] I intend to read for the Senior Mathematical Scholarship next term: I hope that Mr. Price will provide me with some coaching. Mr. Gordon, Senior Censor, has also asked me to give some

---

[175] This diary entry comes from Dodgson's letter to his sister, Mary, dated 13 December 1854 (see *Letters*, pp. 26-29).

[176] An additional note (for Finals), which was added to Dodgson's "Collections" report for 1851-53 (no reports for 1854), indicated: achieved a III class in the study of Literae Humaniores (Classics), and achieved a I class in the discipline of Mathematics and Physics. In fact, Dodgson's First Class in Mathematics was announced in the *Times* on 14 December 1854:

The following class list has been issued by the Mathematical Examiners:

Classis 1.
Bosanquet, Samuel C., ex Æde Christi
Cookson, Montacutus H., e Coll. D. Jo. Bapt.
Dodgson, Carolus L., ex Æde Christi
Fowler, Thomas, e Coll. Mert.
Ranken, Gulielmus H., e C.C.C.

Dodgson's BA degree was announced in the *Times* on 19 December 1854 together with other degrees conferred by the University of Oxford which had taken place in a Congregation on 18 December.

tutoring to the undergraduates reading for mathematics next year.

I find I am the next First Class Mathematics Student to Faussett (with the exception of Kitchin, who has given up Mathematics) so that I stand next (as Bosanquet is going to leave) for the Lectureship.[177]

Dec: 26. (Tu). The *Times* announced that Ramsay, Rocke, and Cleaver are the new Students, and Lavie, Hewitt, and Edwards are the new Westminster Students.[178]

[177] George William Kitchin (1827-1912), matriculated at Christ Church in 1846: student 1846-63, BA 1850 (first class in classics and mathematics), tutor 1852, MA 1853, mathematical examiner 1854, and DD 1883. He was headmaster of the preparatory school at Twyford, Hampshire, until 1861, when he returned to Oxford to become censor of Christ Church. He was made proctor in 1863. He relinquished his position as censor in 1863 when he married Alice Maud Taylor (1844?-1930), but continued in Oxford, holding various posts including censor of unattached students 1868-83, lecturer in modern history 1871-82 and 1882-3, classical lecturer at Wadham College 1864-7, historical lecturer at Lincoln and Oriel 1874-81, lecturer at Queen's College 1875-9, until he became Dean of Winchester in 1883, and then Dean of Durham in 1894. He and his wife had five children: Alexandria "Xie" Rhoda (1864-1925), George Herbert "Ben" (b. 1865), Hugh Bridges (1867-1945), Brook Taylor (1869-1940), and Dorothy Maud Mary (1874-1953). Their daughter "Xie" was one of Dodgson's favourite photographic models. Dodgson photographed Kitchin when he was headmaster of Twyford School in 1858 (IN395), and again in 1863.

[178] James Henry Ramsay (1832-1925), Alfred Beale Rocke (1833-1887), and William Henry Cleaver (b. 1834), are listed in the

Dec: 31. (Sun) As the old year comes to an end, I pray for God's blessing in 1855.[179]

Chapter Books (MS. Christ Church) as the newly elected Students within Christ Church. The appointment of Germain Lavie (1836-1901), James Francis Katharinus Hewitt (1835-1908), and James George Edwards (1836-1903) as the three new Westminster Students moved Dodgson to 85th in the List of 101 Students.

179 At the end of the year, it was usual for Dodgson to list his achievements and failings, and his resolution to do better in the new year ahead. He ended his undergraduate years with a First Class BA degree in mathematics and a Third Class is Classics. He was also aware that he stood in line to be appointed mathematical lecturer at Christ Church, a career that he earnestly wished to pursue. Dodgson's disadvantage was that he would have to wait a couple of years before he could take his MA (in Oxford, that meant buying it, no examination was necessary). The lectureship would make him a senior member of the college, and a Faculty Student, but there was a prerequisite of the MA, which at this time he did not have. Events in 1855 changed the situation. The appointment of Henry George Liddell as the new Dean to replace Thomas Gaisford, who died on 2 June 1855 (see *Diary 1*, p. 100), gave an opportunity for the Chapter to promote Dodgson to "Master of the House," clearing the way for Dodgson's appointment as the new lecturer in mathematics at Christ Church. The Dean and Chapter Books (MS: Christ Church) for 30 June 1855 indicate that: "Dodgson and Rowley, Students of this House have respectively the former his Grace for the Degree of M.A. and the latter his Grace for the degree of B.A. by the appointment of Mr. Liddell on his Installation to the place of Dean according to custom." Dodgson recorded on 20 August 1855 (see *Diary 1*, p. 79) that he had learnt "the Dean's intention of making me Mathematical Lecturer next term...." Although the Dean and Chapter met on that day, there is no record of the appointment being made in the Books. It appears likely that Dodgson was given one term (Michaelmas) to prepare for this new role, taking up the position in January 1856. However, he continued with tutoring responsibilities through the rest of 1855.

The Private Journal of Charles Lutwidge Dodgson

JOURNAL NUMBER 3

Diary for the year 1855
September to December[180]

Sep: 28. (F). News came that Jowett, of Balliol, has been appointed the new Professor of Greek, filling the vacancy left by the death of our old Dean Gaisford.[181]

---

180 The last entry in Dodgson's second journal is dated 26 September and stated: "Heard from Kitchin: he seems to think I shall have the same work to do with Lloyd next term which I had with him last term." The third journal (now missing) covers just three months of Dodgson's life, and was, therefore, a small notebook covering the period during which he continued his work as a tutor in mathematics, and prepared for his new role as Lecturer in Mathematics. Charles Lloyd (1824-1862) matriculated at Christ Church in 1841: student 1841-62, BA 1845, MA 1847, mathematical tutor from 1855 sharing the role with Dodgson throughout the year. Although Lloyd was Dodgson's senior, his mathematical capability was inferior, which explains why he was not made mathematical lecturer.

181 The *Times* reported (29 September 1855): "Intelligence reached Oxford this morning that her Majesty has been pleased to confer the Regius Professorship of Greek, vacant by the death of the late Dean of Christ Church, on the Rev. Benjamin Jowett, M.A., Fellow and Tutor of Balliol College." Benjamin Jowett (1817-1893) matriculated at Balliol College in 1835: scholar 1835-39, fellow 1838-70, BA 1839, MA 1842, tutor 1842-1870, junior dean 1843, ordained priest 1845, senior dean 1845, junior bursar 1846, senior bursar 1848, public examiner 1849-51 and 1853, Regius professor of Greek 1855, Master of Balliol College 1870-93, lecturer in logic, and vice-chancellor 1882-86.

Oct: 8. (M). Returned to Oxford.

Oct: 9. (Tu). There is much change taking place at the Deanery. Dean Liddell is residing in Dr. Clerke's lodgings so that he can supervise the alterations personally.[182]

Oct: 10. (W). The first day of Michaelmas Term. At Congregation, the degrees of B.D. and D.D. were conferred on our new Dean.[183]

---

[182] Henry George Liddell (1811-1898) was appointed Dean of Christ Church on 7 June 1855, following the death of Thomas Gaisford. One of his first tasks was to make major improvements to the Deanery. Liddell's biographer, Henry Lewis Thompson, tells us (p. 147): "To his refined taste are due the panelling and decorations of drawing-room and hall, the opening out of the long gallery on the first floor as an additional reception-room, and the construction of the stately staircase, called the 'Lexicon' staircase, because its cost was defrayed from the profits on that book. Much delay took place before the Deanery was fit for occupation; a fire at Baker's factory in Lambeth destroyed all the new woodwork just as it was on the point of completion." Liddell's family were probably living with relatives. He spent his time overseeing the alterations, and coming to terms with a slightly resistant Chapter consisting of elderly canons. The Chapter was, to all intents and purposes, the governance of the college, and included the Sub-Dean Archdeacon Clerke, Dr. Barnes, Dr. Pusey (Regius Professor of Hebrew), Dr. Bull (Treasurer), Dr. Jelf (Principal of King's College, London), Dr. Jacobson (Regius Professor of Divinity), Dr. Ogilvie (Regius Professor of Pastoral Theology), and Dr. Heurtley (Margaret Professor of Divinity). Alterations at the Deanery were eventually completed by the beginning of 1856.

[183] Dean Liddell was made Bachelor and Doctor of Divinity at a Congregation of the University (meeting of the Heads of Colleges

Oct: 13. (Sat). My paper, "Hints on Etiquette: or Dining Out Made Easy," which I sent to Frank Smedley last month, is inserted in the 10th issue of *Comic Times*.[184]

Oct: 14. (Sun). Attended the University sermon preached at St. Mary's in the afternoon by Prof. Price.

Oct: 23. (Tu). Attended a meeting of Convocation at which an election was held to replace Prof. Donkin on the Hebdomadal Council, who had resigned on account of ill health. There were three candidates, and the results were as follows; Prof. Price 59, Dr. Macbride 50,[185] and Dr. Jacobson 34.

---

and the senior Members of the University), in recognition of his new role as Dean of Christ Church.

184 Dodgson had already published three items in the *Comic Times*, edited by Edmund Hodgson Yates (1831-1894); "Poetry for the Million" and "The Dear Gazelle" in issue no. 2 (18 August 1855), and "She's All My Fancy Painted Him" in issue no. 5 (8 September 1855). No copy of issue 10 appears to have survived; we know of this item from Dodgson's pasted clipping in the family magazine *Mischmasch*. Dodgson's distant cousin, Francis "Frank" Edward Smedley (1818-1864), was a writer, who, as an invalid, spent much of his life on a sofa. He was the grandson of Edward Smedley (1750-1825), Dodgson's great-great-uncle.

185 John David Macbride (1778-1868) matriculated at Exeter College in 1795: BA 1799, fellow 1800-05, MA 1802, BCL and DCL 1811, assessor of the Chancellor's Court 1812, lord almoner's

Oct: 26. (F). Another tragedy on the river.[186]

Oct: 30. (Tu). A Committee of Subscribers has been established to raise funds for a Greek Prize to be awarded in memory of our old Dean, to be called "the Gaisford Prize." Subscriptions are open until the 1st of December.[187]

Nov: 3. (Sat). The *Comic Times*, no. 13, contains my paper, "Photography Extraordinary."[188]

---

professor of Arabic 1813-68, principal of Magdalen Hall (later Hertford College) 1813-68. He had a particular interest in oriental literature.

[186] The tragedy was reported in the *Times* (27 October 1855): "We are sorry to report an accident on the river terminating in the death of a member of the University, Mr. Johns, of Pembroke College, whose body was not recovered till it had been in the water for above half an hour." John Tremenheere Johns (1837-1855) matriculated at Pembroke on 7 June 1855.

[187] By the end of the year, voluntary subscriptions had raised about £1,200 as a Foundation for two annual Prizes in memory of Thomas Gaisford, DD, Dean of Christ Church, and Professor of Greek, to be awarded for Composition in Greek Verse and Prose. The Prizes were open to all undergraduates and the judges were the Dean of Christ Church, the Regius Professor of Greek, and one other Member of Convocation nominated annually by the Vice-Chancellor. The first prize-men, awarded in 1857, were Joseph Henry Warner and Robert Dobie Wilson, both from Balliol College.

[188] Dodgson's humorous account entitled "Photography Extraordinary" shows the power of his imagination. He applies photography to the mind, thus enabling authors and writers to produce their works by a mechanical process not unlike developing

Dec. 5. (W). Went to the Sheldonian Theatre to hear a most interesting lecture given by Colonel Rawlinson on recent discoveries in Assyria and Babylonia. The Theatre was very full – at least 1,500 people attending. He showed how Persian tablets had been deciphered using an alphabet gained from certain proper names. He traced briefly the progress of cunieform discoveries from the beginning of the century to the present time. He called attention especially to the points where the deciphering of the tablets confirmed and elucidated Scripture. Colonel Rawlinson was loudly cheered at the end of his talk.[189]

Dec: 7. (F). At Congregation it was reported that a new Proctor cycle would come into effect in 1859, admitting Worcester and the

---

a photographic plate and print. We know of this piece only from his clipping in *Mischmasch*.

189 Col. (later Sir) Henry Creswicke Rawlinson (1810-1895) entered the East Indian Company's military service and acquired a good knowledge of Persian and Indian languages, becoming political agent at Kandahar in 1840. He distinguished himself in the Afghan war of 1842, became political agent in Turkish Arabia in 1843, and consul of Baghdad in 1844. He deciphered the celebrated cuneiform inscription of Darius Hystaspes at Behistun in 1846, He returned to England in 1855, MP for Reigate 1858-59, MP for Frome 1865-68, member of the Indian council 1868, president of the Royal Geographical Society 1871-72 and 1874-75, president of the Royal Asiatic Society 1878-81, and was knighted in 1891 (*DNB*).

Halls, based on the proportion of the Colleges on the number of their members, upon the books, estimated on the average of the last 10 years.[190]

Dec: 10. (M). There appears to be a controversy brewing concerning the new Regius Professor of Greek.[191]

---

[190] Dodgson's interest in the Proctor Cycle gained momentum in 1885 when he denounced a newly proposed Cycle as unfair and simplistic. The Cycle was devised to give the various Colleges of the University opportunity to nominate Proctors from among their number. He wrote three papers, including his own Cycle, that were circulated around the common-rooms to gain support for his own ideas (see *Handbook*, pp. 134-136).

[191] The *Times* reported (12 December 1855) that "Dr. Macbride, the Principal of Magdalen Hall, and the Rev. Mr. Golightly, M.A., of Oriel College, this day {10 December} called upon the Vice-Chancellor, and lodged with him a formal complaint against a work of the Professor of Greek, Mr. Jowett, as seeming to deny the doctrine of the Atonement." The complaint concerned Jowett's publication of *The Epistles of St. Paul to the Thessalonians, Galations, Romans, with Critical Notes and Dissertations* (1855). A further report followed (14 December 1855): "In consequence of the charge made against the Rev. B. Jowett, Regius Professor of Greek, by Dr. Macbride and Mr. Golightly, he was yesterday required by the Vice-Chancellor to renew his signature to the Thirty-nine Articles, as well as to the three articles in the 36th canon – a requirement with which he immediately complied." This charge of heresy resulted in a further difficulty when the salary of the Regius Professorship of Greek was reviewed in line with other Professorships, only to find that the authorities declined to increase his salary. Dodgson joined the controversy with his pamphlet, *Endowment of the Greek Professorship* (1861), and later with *The New Method of Evaluation, as applied to π* (1865), where "π" was

Dec: 12. (W). Frank Dodgson gained a Third Class in Moderations.[192]

Dec: 13. (Th). The *Times* contains a long letter from Prof. Price in reply to an undergraduate who has complained about this year's Mathematical Finals. Very few successful candidates were recorded (unlike the many successful candidates last year, of which I was one), with Prof. Price sympathizing with the disappointed candidate.[193]

Jowett's salary. Charles Portales Golightly (1808-1885) matriculated at Oriel in 1824: BA 1828, MA 1830.

[192] Francis Hume Dodgson gained a third class in Classics Moderations, but did not proceed to Finals. Instead, he was successful in the entrance examination for the Woolwich Royal Military Academy, and became a lieutenant in the Royal Artillery (see *Diary 2*, p. 19, n. *32*).

[193] The letter from Prof. Bartholomew Price (who was not one of the Examiners) was reprinted in full in the *Times* (13 December 1855). It began:

> My dear H----, The mathematical Class List which was issued last evening filled me with surprise and sorrow; with sorrow, I say, for yourself and the other candidates who are so much disappointed by it, and on account of the discouragement which it gives to mathematical studies at Oxford…."

He went on to state that all the candidates for honours had done well in Moderations, and his personal acquaintance with them showed that they were above the average of candidates for honours in this school. He then commented on the difficulty of the questions, but praised the character of the Examiners, leaving the matter open for the University authorities to investigate, should they be so inclined.

Dec: 31. (M). I am sitting alone in my bedroom this last night of the old year, waiting for midnight. It has been the most eventful year of my life: I began it a poor bachelor student, with no definite plans or expectations; I end it a master and tutor in Christ Church, with an income of more than £300 a year, and the course of mathematical tuition marked out by God's providence for at least some years to come. Great mercies, great failings, time lost, talents misapplied - such has been the past year.[194]

In the Mathematical Finals, no candidates achieved a First Class, only one achieved a Second Class, and five achieved a Third Class, including John Power Hicks (b. 1833) of Lincoln College, who may have been the anonymous complainer. In the previous year, five candidates achieved a First Class (including Dodgson), four achieved Second Class, and none achieved Third Class, with Price being one of the Examiners.

[194] This last entry is the only surviving entry from Dodgson's journal number 3, quoted by Collingwood.

Index

Page numbers are given, and if a reference is within a footnote, this is indicated in italics immediately after the page number.

Accidents on the river, 449 n.*108*, 471 n.*151*, 490 n.*186*
Acland, Henry Wentworth Dyke, 482, 483 n.*174*
Adelphi (Terence), 461 n.*132*
Æschylus, 411 n.*34*
Aids to Reflection (Coleridge), 440 n.*92*
Alfred Place, London, 413, 423
Alison, William Pulteney, 426 n.*65*
Almond, Hely Hutchinson, 472 n.*153*
Amateur Musical Society, 471
Anderson, Maria "Minnie" Katherine, 464 n.*135*
Animalcula, 428 n.*69*
Antigone (Mendelssohn), 446 n.*103*
Aristotle, 468 n.*145*
Armitstead, William George, 438 n.*90*
Arnold, Edwin, 426 n.*65*
Ascension Day, 447, 469
Assyria, 491 n.*189*

Babylonia, 491 n.*189*
Baker, John, 448 n.*107*
Balliol College, 455 n.*123*, 466 n.*140*, 467 n.*142*, 472 n.*153*, 487 n.*181*
Bayne, Thomas Vere, 424 n.*62*
Bell, George Charles, 435 n.*83*
Berwick, Northumberland, 430
Bishops of:
- Argyle (Alexander Ewing), 412 n.*36*
- Exeter (Henry Phillpotts), 426
- Michigan (Samuel Allen McCoskry), 426 n.*65*
- Natal (John William Colenso), 459 n.*128*
- New Zealand (George Augustus Selwyn), 470 n.*149*
- Ohio (Charles Pettit McIlvaine), 451 n.*113*
- Oxford (Samuel Wilberforce), 426, 466, 470
- Quebec (George Jehoshaphat Mountain), 451 n.*113*
- Ripon (Charles Thomas Longley), 419 n.*52*
- St. Andrews (Charles Wordsworth), 451 n.*113*
- Western New York (William Heathcote De Lancey), 426 n.*65*

Blagrave, Henry Gamble, 446 n.*103*
Blandford, Marquis, see Spencer-Churchill
Bleak House (Dickens), 422 n.*59*
Bletchley, Buckinghamshire, 408
Bode, John Ernest, 421 n.*55*
Boeckh, August, 427 n.*67*
Bosanquet, Samuel, 483, 485
Boulter, Hugh, 417 n.*48*
Bowden, James, 189, 473 n.*154*
Brasenose College, 460 n.*129*, 461, 463
Brodie, Benjamin Collins, 397 n.*4*, 411 n.*35*, 412 n.*36*
Brown, Thomas Edward, 445 n.*101*
Bué:
- George Henri, 417 n.*47*
- Jules Thomas Théodore, M., 407 n.*47*

Bull, John, 459 n.*126*

Campbell Family, 414 n.*41*
Census (1851), 407 n.*25*
Cherry, Apsley, 400 n.*12*
Chesney, Francis Rawdon, Lt.-Col., 412 n.*36*

Cholera in Oxford, 481 n.*171*
Cholmeley, Robert, 467 n.*143*

Christ Church:
Boulter Scholarship, 417 n.*48*
Cathedral, 459, 466, 469, 482
Censors, 411 n.*35*, 434, 484
Chapel, 403, 404 n.*19*, 438
Chaplain, 448 n.*107*
Chapter (Canons), 417 n.*48*, 437 n.*88*, 440, 447, 452, 462
Cloisters, 423, 442, 465 n.*137*
Collections, 407 n.*26*, 411 n.*34*, 417 n.*48*, 418 n.*51*, 422 n.*58*, 425, 434, 444 n.*99*, 452 n.*114*, 461 n.*131*, 467 n.*141*
College, 396, 397, 400
Commoners, 405 n.*22*, 448
Dean, 405 n.*22*, 417 n.*48*, 437, 440, 458, 462, 482
Deanery, 488 n.*182*
Declamation, 418 n.*50*, 424 n.*61*, 448 n.*106*, 468 n.*145*
Dogs, 405 n.*22*
Hall, 400 n.*11*, 418, 424, 447, 448, 450, 468
Mathematical Lectureship, 485, 486 n.*179*, 494
Matriculation, 396 n.*2*, 448
Meadow, 449
Noblemen, 405 n.*22*, 448, 458
Peckwater Quad, 417, 421, 434
Prick bills, 438 n.*89*, 454 n.*120*
Servitors, 405 n.*22*
Shooting, 411 n.*35*
Students, 436 n.*87*, 437, 438, 440, 462, 485
Sub-Dean, 441 n.*94*
Tom Quad, 434, 442
Westminster Scholars, 447,
Westminster Students, 462, 485

Christian Ballads (Coxe), 404 n.*20*
Cicero, 422 n.*58*
Clairvoyant, 464 n.*135*
Claughton, Thomas Legh, 421 n.*56*
Cleaver, William Henry, 485 n.*178*
Clementi, Mr., 446 n.*103*
Clerke, Charles Carr, 441 n.*94*, 459, 488
Colenso, John William, 459 n.*128*
Coleridge, John Taylor, 426 n.*65*
Coleridge, Samuel Taylor, 440 n.*92*
Colley, Richard Henry, 402 n.*17*, 403, 404
Comic Times, 489 n.*184*, 490 n.*188*
Cookson, Christopher, 435 n.*84*, 483
Corfe, Charles William, 424 n.*63*, 446 n.*103*
Corpus Christi College, 473 n.*155*, 474 n.*157*, 482 n.*173*
Coxe, Arthur Cleveland, 404 n.*20*
Cradock, Edward Hartopp, 463 n.*134*
Crest stamp, 428
Croft-on-Tees, Yorkshire, 396 n.*1*, 398, 408, 419, 420, 422, 429, 430, 441, 453, 462, 481

Dalton, James, Rev., 396 n.*1*
De Lancey, William Heathcote, 426 n.*65*
Demosthenes, 418 n.*51*
Derby, Lord, see Stanley
"Diorama of Jerusalem, The," 414 n.*40*

Dodgson:
Amy Menella (cousin), 429 n.*70*
Caroline Hume (sister), 398 n.*5*
Caroline née Hume (aunt), 428, 429 n.*70*
Charles (father), 396 n.*1*, 396 n.*2*, 400 n.*9*, 409, 419 n.*52*, 436 n.*87*, 439 n.*91*, 440, 441 n.*93*, 442 n.*96*, 470
Charlotte Mary (cousin), 429 n.*70*
Edwin Heron (brother), 398 n.*5*

Elizabeth Lucy (sister), 398 n.*5*, 413 n.*39*, 420 n.*53*, 434
Frances Jane (mother), 398 n.*5*, 399 n.*7*, 400 n.*9*
Frances Jane (sister), 398 n.*5*, 420 n.*53*
Francis "Frank" Hume (cousin), 429 n.*70*, 447 n.*104*, 448, 461, 462 n.*133*, 493 n.*192*
Hassard Hume (uncle), 428, 429 n.*70*, 437
Henrietta Harington (sister), 398 n.*5*
James Hume (cousin), 429 n.*70*
Laura Elizabeth (cousin), 429 n.*70*
Louisa Fletcher (sister), 398 n.*5*, 410 n.*32*
Louis Henri (cousin), 429 n.*70*
Louis Henry "Hal" (cousin), 429 n.*70*
Lucy Caroline (cousin), 429 n.*70*
Margaret Anne Ashley (sister), 398 n.*5*
Mary Charlotte (sister), 398 n.*5*, 406 n.*23*, 479
Menella "Marla" Frances (cousin), 429 n.*70*
Percy (cousin), 429 n.*70*
Skeffington Hume (brother), 398 n.*5*, 420 n.*53*, 453
Wilfred Longley (brother), 398 n.*5*, 453

Dodgson, Charles Lutwidge:
Bachelor's degree, 484 n.*176*
B. B. – pen-name, 480
Boulter Scholarship, 417 n.*48*
Celibacy, 438
Classics, 400 n.*10*, 407 n.*26*, 409 n.*30*, 411 n.*34*, 418 n.*51*, 420, 422 n.*58*, 425 n.*64*, 433, 434, 435 n.*82*, 444 n.*99*, 452 n.*114*, 461 n.*131*, 469, 484
Declamation read in Hall, 418 n.*50*, 424 n.*61*, 448 n.*106*, 468 n.*145*
French lessons, 417 n.*47*
Holy Orders, 438 n.*90*
Income, 494
Master of the House, 486 n.*179*
Mathematical Lecturer, 486 n.*179*, 494
Mathematics, 400 n.*10*, 407 n.*26*, 418 n.*51*, 422 n.*58*, 425 n.*64*, 434, 435 n.*82*, 444 n.*99*, 449, 452 n.*114*, 455, 466, 470, 482-484
Matriculation, 396 n.*2*
Moderations, 432 n.*78*, 433, 434
Music concerts, 414, 415
Photography, 397 n.*4*
Prayers, 440, 463, 486
Reading Party (Whitby), 472-480
Rectory Umbrella, The, 416 n.*46*
Rooms, 397 n.*3*, 408 n.*29*, 418, 423, 465
Scout, 484
Story-telling, 479 n.*167*
Studentship, 436 n.*87*, 438, 440
Theology, 403, 411 n.*34*, 418 n.*51*, 422 n.*58*, 425 n.*64*, 251, 435 n.*82*, 443 n.*97*, 444 n.*99*, 452 n.*114*
Tutoring, 485, 494

Domenico Lofaso di Pietra Santa, Prince of San Pietro, 426 n.*65*
Donkin, William Fishburn, 475 n.*160*, 489
Dowson, John, Dr., 476 n.*162*
Duke of Wellington, see Wellesley
Dyson, Edward Compton, 449 n.*108*

Earle, William, 471 n.*151*
Easter Day, 408, 422, 444, 467
East View Terrace, Whitby, 472
Eden, Charles Page, 459 n.*127*
Edinburgh, 430
Edwards, James George, 485 n.*178*
Egyptian Hall, London, 414 n.*40*
Erskine, Henry David, 441 n.*93*, 464

Euripides, 425 n.*64*, 435 n.*82*
Ewing, Alexander, Rt. Rev., 412 n.*36*
Exeter College, 466 n.*139*

Faussett:
Godfrey, Dr., 447 n.*105*, 452
John Toke, 462 n.*133*
Robert Godfrey, 402 n.*16*, 404, 407, 427, 485
"Feast of Belshazzar, The" (Arnold), 426 n.*65*
Fellows, Walter, 438 n.*90*
Ffoulkes, Edmund Salisbury, 452 n.*115*
Fisher, Wilfrid, 462 n.*133*
Fowler, Thomas, 435 n.*85*, 473, 483

Gaisford, Thomas, 405 n.*22*, 458 n.*125*, 486 n.*179*, 487, 490 n.*187*
Geldart, Thomas Charles, 451 n.*112*
Gladstone, Thomas, 451 n.*113*
Gladstone, William Ewart, 432 n.*77*, 442
Goathland, Yorkshire, 475
Godfrey of Bouillon, 413 n.*38*
Golightly, Charles Portales, 492 n.*191*
Gordon, Osborne, 427 n.*66*, 434, 457, 484
Gordon Square, London, 415
Goulburn, Edward Meyrick, 450 n.*111*
Grand Ball (Oxford Town Hall), 450
Grand Chant (Beethoven), 450
Great Exhibition (1851), 412, 413 n.*37*, 415
Guy Fawkes' Night (Gunpowder Plot), 418 n.*49*, 433 n.*79*

Haddon, Arthur West, 442 n.*95*
Hallam, Henry, 442 n.*96*
Hamilton, Edward, 430 n.*72*
Hampden, Charles John, 400 n.*13*
Handel, George Frederick, 450
Hansell, Edward Halifax, 452 n.*115*
Harington:
Richard, 462 n.*133*
Richard, Dr., 460 n.*129*, 461
Hastings, Sussex, 415, 416
Hawkins, Edward, 432 n.*76*, 455
Heathcote:
Selina née Shirley, Lady, 472 n.*152*
William, Sir, 472 n.*152*
Herodotus, 461 n.*131*
Heurtley, Charles Abel, 452 n.*115*
Hewitt, James Francis Katharinus, 485 n.*178*
Hicks, John Power, 493 n.*193*
"Hints on Etiquette: or Dining Out Made Easy," 489
Hippisley, Grace Louisa née Raikes, 415 n.*44*
Holmes, Oliver Wendell, 479 n.*166*
Hook, Walter Farquhar, 433 n.*79*
Horace, 407 n.*26*, 409 n.*30*, 434, 435 n.*82*
Horticultural Show (New College), 472
Horticultural Show (Worcester), 450

Inglis, Robert Harry, 465 n.*136*
Installation Ball (Oxford Town Hall), 452
Introduction to the Literature of Europe (Hallam), 442 n.*96*

Jacobson, William, 403 n.*18*, 442, 455, 489
Jelf, George Edward, 438 n.*90*
Jenkyns, Richard, 466 n.*140*, 467
Johns, John Tremenheere, 490 n.*186*
Jones, George Meyrick, 435, 436 n.*86*
Jowett, Benjamin, 397 n.*4*, 487 n.*181*, 492 n.*191*
Joyce, Sidney, 438 n.*90*
Jupiter, 428

Keane, William, 477 n.*163*, 478
Kerr, William Schomberg Robert, Lord Lothian, 445 n.*101*

Kitchin, George William, 485 n.*177*, 487

"Lady of the Ladle, The," 480 n.*168*
Lathe, 428
Lavie, Germain, 485 n.*178*

Letters:
Archdeacon Dodgson to CLD, 436 n.*87*
CLD to Elizabeth Dodgson, 413 n.*39*, 426 n.*65*, 434 n.*81*
CLD to Francis Hume Dodgson, 445 n.*101*
CLD to Louisa Dodgson, 410 n.*32*
CLD to Mary Dodgson, 404 n.*19*, 457 n.*124*, 476 n.*161*, 484 n.*175*
Edward Pusey to Archdeacon Dodgson, 436 n.*87*
Mary Smedley to Archdeacon Dodgson, 398 n.*6*

Ley, Jacob, 397 n.*3*, 409
Liddell, Henry George, 486 n.*179*, 488 n.*182*, 488 n.*183*
"Ligniad, The," 449 n.*109*
Litton, Edward Arthur, 420 n.*54*
Livy, 461 n.*131*
Lloyd, Charles, 487 n.*180*
Longley:
Charles Thomas, Rt. Rev., 396 n.*2*, 398 n.*5*, 419 n.*52*, 441 n.*93*
Henry, 462 n.*133*
Lothian, Lord, see Kerr
Lowell, James Russell, 479 n.*166*
Lucretius, 418 n.*51*
Lutwidge:
Anne Louisa née Raikes (aunt), 414 n.*42*, 429
Caroline Louisa (cousin), 414 n.*42*
Charles Henry (uncle), 414 n.*42*
Charles Robert Fletcher (cousin), 414 n.*42*, 428
Charlotte Menella (aunt), 412, 413 n.*37*, 414
Henrietta Mary (aunt), 415, 416 n.*45*
Lucy (aunt), 399 n.*8*, 442 n.*96*
Margaret Anne (aunt), 413 n.*37*, 415
Robert Wilfred Skeffington (uncle), 407, 408 n.*27*, 427-429, 437
Lytton, Edward Bulwer, 451 n.*113*

MacBride, John David, 489 n.*185*, 492 n.*191*
Magdalen College, 446, 467 n.*143*
Mallyan's Spout, Goathland, 475
Masonic Ball (Oxford Town Hall), 450
McCoskry, Samuel Allen, 426 n.*65*
McIlvaine, Charles Pettit, 451 n.*113*
Merton College, 435 n.*85*, 473
Milton's Poetical Works, 442 n.*96*
Mitford, John Thomas Freeman, Lord Redesdale, 451 n.*112*
Mountain, George Jehoshaphat, 451 n.*113*
Murchison, Roderick Impey, 451 n.*113*

New College, 472, 474 n.*156*, 474 n.*159*
New Zealand, 470 n.*149*

Oedipus (Sophocles), 420
Ogilvie, Charles Atmore, 443 n.*97*, 466, 468
"Old Hundredth," 477 n.*164*
Oliver, Frederick William, 462 n.*133*
"On the Population of the World," 454 n.*119*
Oriel College, 432 n.*76*, 455
Ovid, 424 n.*61*
Owen, Richard, 426 n.*65*

Oxford:
Assizes, 404
Parks, 409, 443 n.*98*
Town Hall, 450, 452, 470, 471

Oxford University:
Boat races, 410, 423, 446 n.*102*
Bodleian Library, 443
Chancellor, 431, 433, 450-452
Clarendon Building, 455, 466
Commemoration, 412 n.*36*, 425, 471
Committee of Subscribers, 490 n.*187*
Congregation, 491
Convocation, 409, 410 n.*33*, 421, 423, 445, 449, 467, 489
Finals, 409 n.*31*, 463, 469, 470, 482
Gaisford Prize, 490 n.*187*
Heads of Houses, 450, 458
Hebdomadal Council, 489
Member of Parliament, 465 n.*136*
Moderations, 409 n.*31*, 432 n.*78*, 434, 493
Museum, 409, 410 n.*33*, 443 n.*98*, 445, 449, 467, 481 n.*172*
Newdigate Prize, 426 n.*65*
Procession of boats, 450, 471
Proctor Cycle, 491, 492 n.*190*
Proctors, 409 n.*31*, 432, 450, 458, 467, 468, 482
Professor of divinity, 452 n.*115*
Professor of Greek, 487 n.*181*, 492 n.*191*
Professor of music, 451
Professor of natural philosophy, 444 n.*100*
Professor of poetry, 421, 451
Professor of political economy, 423, 455
Radcliffe Library, 481 n.*172*
Reform, 460, 461 n.*130*
Responsions, 409 n.*31*, 410
Schools, 469 n.*146*
Senior Mathematical Scholarship, 484
Sermons, 397, 420, 432, 433, 442, 447, 448, 455, 459, 465, 466, 468, 469, 482, 489
Sheldonian, 412, 424, 425, 450, 451, 491
Vice-Chancellor, 421, 492 n.*191*

Oxonian Advertiser, 481 n.*170*

Palmerston, Lord, see Temple
Pember, Edward Henry, 433 n.*80*
Pembroke College, 444 n.*100*, 449, 452, 490
Philip van Artvelde (Taylor), 453 n.*117*
Phillpotts, Henry, 426 n.*65*
Phillpotts, Henry John, 438 n.*90*
"Photography Extraordinary," 490 n.*188*
Phrenology, 430 n.*72*
Population of the World, 454 n.*119*, 455 n.*122*
Portugal, Peter V, King of, 471 n.*150*
Price, Bartholomew "Bat," 444 n.*100*, 449, 455, 466, 470, 472, 475-477, 480, 483, 484, 489, 493 n.*193*
Pritchard, Henry, 475 n.*160*, 482 n.*173*
Prout, Thomas Jones, 467, 468 n.*144*
Public Economy of Athens, The (Boeckh), 427 n.*67*
Pusey:
Edward Bouverie, Dr., 398 n.*5*, 410 n.*33*, 436 n.*87*, 455
Philip Edward, 401 n.*14*, 434, 452, 473
Putney, Surrey, 437, 461

Quintilian, 444 n.*99*
Quintus Horatius Flaccus (Zeune), 409 n.*30*

Radcliffe Infirmary, 450
Raikes:
Anne (cousin), see Reynolds
Charles (cousin), 415 n.*44*
Elizabeth Frances née Lutwidge (aunt), 413 n.*37*, 415
Elizabeth "Lizzie" Lucy (cousin), 415 n.*44*

Frederick (cousin), 415 n.*44*
Grace Louisa (cousin), see Hippisley
Robert (cousin), 415 n.*44*
Thomas (cousin), 415 n.*44*
Thomas, Mr. (uncle), 413 n.*37*, 415
Ramsey, James Henry, 485 n.*178*
Ranken, William Henry, 473 n.*155*, 483
Rawlinson, Henry Creswicke, Col., 491 n.*189*
Rectory Umbrella, The, 454
Redesdale, Lord, see Mitford
Refrigerator, 428 n.*69*
Reinagle, Alexander Robert, 446 n.*103*
Reynolds, Anne née Raikes, 415 n.*44*
Richards, Henry Brinley, 415 n.*43*
Richards, Joseph Loscombe, 466 n.*139*
Rickards, George Kettilby, 423 n.*60*, 455
Ripon, Yorkshire, 419 n.*52*, 439, 440, 463
Ripon Canon's Residence, 440, 464
Ripon Deanery, 464
Ritual Worship (Charles Dodgson), 439 n.*91*
Robin, Henri, Monsieur – conjuror, 456, 457 n.*124*
Rocke, Alfred Beale, 485 n.*178*
Ross, Alexander Henry, 411 n.*35*
Royal Academy, 414, 428
Rugby School, 400 n.*13*, 450 n.*111*
Russia, War with, 467, 483 n.*174*

St. John's College, 435 n.*84*, 471 n.*151*
St. Mary's (University Church), Oxford, 397, 420, 450, 455, 459, 489
Scott, Robert, 455 n.*123*, 467 n.*142*
Selwyn, George Augustus, 470 n.*149*
Short, Ambrose, 473, 474 n.*156*
Sidgwick, William Carr, 474 n.*157*
Smedley:
Edward (great-uncle), 429 n.*71*
Edward Hume (second cousin), 429 n.*71*
Elizabeth "Honie" (second cousin). 429 n.*71*
Francis "Frank" Edward (distant cousin), 489 n.*184*
Mary (second cousin), 429 n.*71*
Mary née Hume (great-aunt), 398 n.*6*, 429 n.*71*
Menella Bute (second cousin), 398 n.*6*, 429 n.*71*
Sophocles, 407 n.*26*
Solicitor-General (William Wood), 412 n.*36*
Spencer-Churchill, John Winston, 451 n.*112*
Stanley, Arthur Penrhyn, 397 n.*4*
Stanley, Edward Geoffrey Smith, Lord Derby, 431 n.*75*, 450 n.*110*
Steeple-chase, 421 n.*57*
Stokes, Edward, 465 n.*138*, 467-469
Stones Family, 413 n.*39*

Tacitus, 448 n.*106*
Tate, Francis, 455 n.*121*
Taylor, Henry, 453 n.*117*
Telescope stand, 428
Temple, Henry John, Lord Palmerston, 460, 461 n.*130*
Terence, 461 n.*132*
Thucydides, 444 n.*99*, 452 n.*114*
Times, 399 n.*7*, 411 n.*35*, 423 n.*60*, 434, 438 n.*90*, 441 n.*94*, 443, 444 n.*100*, 445 n.*101*, 446 n.*103*, 447 n.*104*, 449 n.*108*, 450 n.*110*, 450 n.*111*, 451 n.*113*, 452 n.*116*, 460 n.*129*, 462 n.*133*, 463 n.*134*, 465, 467 n.*142*, 470 n.*148*, 471 n.*150*, 471 n.*151*, 481 n.*171*, 481 n.*172*, 483 n.*174*, 484 n.*176*, 485 n.*178*, 490 n.*186*, 492 n.*191*, 493 n.*193*
Trafalgar Hotel, London, 412
Trinity College, 442 n.*95*
Tristia (Ovid), 424 n.*61*

Tunbridge Wells, Kent, 414, 429
Twiss, Quintin William Francis, 462 n.*133*
Two Brothers, The, 453 n.*118*
Tyrwhitt, Richard St. John, 469 n.*147*

University College, 455, 473 n.*154*

Vice-Chancellor of Cambridge University, 451 n.*112*
Victoria, Queen, 431 n.*74*
View of the State of Europe (Hallam), 442 n.*96*
Virgil, 425 n.*64*, 452 n.*114*

Wadham College, 409, 443
Wainwright, Jonathan Mayhew, 426 n.*65*
Watson Family, 413 n.*39*
Wellesley, Arthur, Duke of Wellington, 431 n.*73*, 433, 434
Wellington Square, Hastings, 416
Wells Cathedral, 467
Westminster Play, 461 n.*132*
Wheeler, Thomas Littleton, 474 n.*158*, 478
Whitby, Yorkshire, 470, 472-480
Whitby Abbey, 472, 476
Whitby Gazette (Supplement), 480
Wilberforce, Samuel, 426 n.*65*
"Wilhelm Von Schmitz," 480 n.*169*
Wilkinson, John Gardner, 426 n.*65*
Williams, Arthur Charles Vaughan, 462 n.*133*
Williams, William, Ven., 412 n.*36*
Willis, Nathaniel Parker, 479 n.*166*
Wingfield, Edward, 474 n.*159*
Wood, William Page, Sir, 412 n.*36*
Woodgate, Henry Arthur, 452 n.*115*
Woodhouse, George Girdlestone, 401 n.*15*, 423, 433, 449 n.*109*
Worcester College, 435 n.*83*, 436 n.*86*, 450, 474 n.*158*, 491
Wordsworth, Charles, 451 n.*113*
Works of Lord Byron, The, 400 n.*9*

Zeune, Johann Carl, 409 n.*30*